On Genesis

Augustinian Heritage Institute, Inc.

THE WORKS OF SAINT AUGUSTINE

A Translation for the 21st Century

Part I – Books

Volume 13:

On Genesis

THE WORKS OF SAINT AUGUSTINE
A Translation for the 21st Century

On Genesis:
On Genesis: A Refutation of the Manichees
Unfinished Literal Commentary on Genesis
The Literal Meaning of Genesis

I/13

introductions, translation and notes by
Edmund Hill, O.P.

editor
John E. Rotelle, O.S.A.

New City Press
Hyde Park, New York

Published in the United States by New City Press
202 Cardinal Rd., Hyde Park, New York 12538
©2002 Augustinian Heritage Institute

Library of Congress Cataloging-in-Publication Data:

Augustine, Saint, Bishop of Hippo.
    The works of Saint Augustine.
    "Augustinian Heritage Institute"
    Includes bibliographical references and indexes.
    Contents: — pt. 3, v .15. Expositions of the Psalms, 1-32
—pt. 3, v. 1. Sermons on the Old Testament, 1-19.
— pt. 3, v. 2. Sermons on the Old Testament, 20-50 — [et al.] — pt. 3,
v. 10 Sermons on various subjects, 341-400.
    1.   Theology — Early church, ca. 30-600.   I. Hill,
Edmund.   II. Rotelle, John E.   III. Augustinian
Heritage Institute.   IV. Title.
BR65.A5E53   1990   270.2   89-28878
ISBN 1-56548-055-4 (series)
ISBN 1-56548-175-5 (pt. 1, v. 13)

We are indebted to Brepols Publishers, Turnholt, Belgium,for their use of the Latin critical text
of *Enarrationes in Psalmos I-CL*, ed. D. Eligius Dekkers, O.S.B. et Johannes Fraipont,
Corpus Christianorum Latinorum XXXVIII-XL (Turnholt, 1946) 1-2196.

Nihil Obstat:John E. Rotelle, O.S.A., S.T.L., Censor Deputatus
Imprimatur: + Patrick Sheridan, D.D., Vicar General
                    Archdiocese of New York, July 22, 1999

Printed in the United States of America

Contents

On Genesis: A Refutation of the Manichees

Unfinished Literal Commentary on Genesis

The Literal Meaning of Genesis

repetition of the one day made by God really means—266; The ordinary days of the week are quite unlike the seven days of Genesis—267; Treating the light and day as spiritual realities is not a metaphorical interpretation—268; Day, evening, and morning in the knowledge of the angels—268; More about the order of day, evening, and morning in the angelic knowledge of things—269; Whether all things were created simultaneously, or one by one during the six days—271; All things both made simultaneously, and nonetheless also made in six days—273; Conclusion about the days of Genesis—275

The world really created on one day—276; Why the addition of "the greenery of the field"—277; The precise wording of the narrative gives us to understand that all things were created simultaneously—278; Why the hay is said to have been made before it sprang up—279; The nature of time in the six days of creation—282; Whether the verse "God had not rained" etc. supports the view of simultaneous creation—284; On the spring which watered the whole earth—285; The place of conjecture where scripture is silent—287; The particular instance of this spring—287; Reiterating the point that the creation of all creatures took place simultaneously, while their management and regulation is conducted over intervals and periods of time—289; Different ways of knowing things, following on these differences in God's working—290; God knows things before they exist—290; Parenthetical note on the proper phrasing of this sentence—291; What sort of life all things are in God—292; God is nearer to us than are many of the things he made—292; A brief recapitulation—293; How creation, much of it unknown to us, is known to God and to the "day," which is the spiritual, rational creation—294; The mystery of the kingdom revealed to the angels from the beginning—295; How God is still working—296; All things governed by divine providence—297; Further arguments in support of God's providential control of the world—298; An illustration of how even things we see developing and coming to be now were all created simultaneously at the beginning—299; Recapitulation of the "literal meaning" of Genesis 2:4-6—300

Two possible ways of reading this text; first the way of recapitulating the work of the sixth day—301; Difficulties about this way—302; The rest of the story evidently tells of events occurring in time—303; A warning not to take Augustine as saying things that in fact he is not saying—305; An untenable suggestion that it was only the human soul which was created on the sixth day—307; How could God address people on the sixth day who did not yet exist as such?—308; A question aired which the author thinks ought not to be pursued—309; Different levels of causality at which things pre-exist in their causes—310; How God made the man's body—312; The relationship between the primal formulae and what emerges from them in historical time—315; Whether the first man's body was formed embodying soul or spirit—318; Another twist to this question—319; The solution to the problem—321; A difficult question about the soul is deferred to the next book—323

On what can be meant by God puffing or blowing—324; Whether the soul was made out of nothing, or out of some already made spiritual material—326; Difficulties about the notion of spiritual material—328; Further remarks on the relationship between human and animal souls—330; The same continued, with an aside about the Manichees—331; If the human soul is not made out of non-rational soul, neither is it made out of any bodily element—332; A satisfactory compromise suggested by medical science—332; Conclusion to the findings of medical science; that the soul is not any kind of body—335; Further evidence that the soul is quite different from any of its bodily agents—336; The soul not made from some fifth element, nor from anything material at all—337; Difficulties about supposing that a causal formula of the soul was inscribed in the original six days of creation—339; The possibility considered of the human soul having been created in its full actuality at the original simultaneous creation of all things—341; A problem raised by this idea—341; A further question—342; The problem provisionally solved—342; To maintain that the soul was created only when it was breathed into the man already formed will not square with these texts of scripture—343; Conclusion: he hopes readers will at least have learned how to discuss hard questions without making rash assertions—345

Three ways of taking the account of Paradise: literally, figuratively, or both—346; What he said on this point in his two volumes on Genesis against the Manichees—348; What is said about Paradise is reconciled with what is written about the third and sixth days—350; How to explain the tree of life and the tree of knowledge of good and evil in an historical as well as an allegorical sense—351; The same continued, with a discussion of certain complicating factors—352; On the tree of knowledge of good and evil—354; On the rivers of Paradise—355; Question about the man being put in Paradise to work—356; The same continued, on a cosmic scale—357; Question about the man being put in Paradise to guard it—358; Why God is only called "the Lord God" from this point on—360; More about how God works and guards man—361; On the command given to Adam—363; Further reflections on the nature of good and evil; why Emmanuel did not have to experience the difference between them—364; More problems about the naming of the tree of knowledge of good and evil—365; Whether God gave the command to the man alone, or to the woman as well—367; In what way did God speak to Adam?—368; More about the twofold operation of divine providence—368; The point illustrated by a closer look at the way the soul moves the body—369; If this cannot be understood it must be believed, as also the truth about God's immovability which this about the soul is meant to illustrate—371; Returning to the twofold operation of God's providence, and the order established thereby—371; More on the interaction of creatures, especially of angels on lower orders of creation—372; A summing up of what has been said about God in relation to time and space, and about the twofold operation of his providence—373; Returning to the question of how God spoke to Adam—374

Book IX

Recapitulation about the making of the animals—376; Various ways in which God could have spoken—377; It was only for the procreation of children that the man needed the woman's help—378; Why they did not in fact couple in Paradise—380; Except for the purpose of procreation, another man would have been a more suitable companion for Adam—380; How one generation could have given way to the next had there been no sin—380; Why set aside the reason of having children? A comparison of the values of marriage and virginity—382; A bad reason for supposing that they would not have been allowed to mate in Paradise—383; Another misapprehension on the point—383; In Paradise they were not the slaves of carnal concupiscence—384; To doubt that the woman was made for the man to effect the peopling of the earth is to call in question everything we believe—386; It was for a prophetic or symbolic reason that the animals were brought to

Adam to be named, and that thus the need arose to make him a helper like him—387; The account of the making of the woman also clearly calls for a mystical or prophetic interpretation—389; Back to the "literal" explanation of Adam's encounter with the beasts and the birds—389; How the formation of the woman was actually done—391; Continuing the comparison between God's work and that of the angels—392; The different levels from which the causal ideas or formulae function—394; The same, continued, extending the point to the working of grace—395; Adam's prophetic utterance on waking from his ecstasy—396

The idea that the woman's soul was made out of the man's—398; Recapitulation of what has been said in the previous books on the origin of the soul—399; A choice to be made between three possibilities: a) that the formula of the soul was made in some primary creature; b) that only the first man's soul was made among those primary works, and from it all other human souls derive; c) that new souls are made subsequently, without any formula of them being made in the works of the first six days—400; Some things that definitely cannot be said about the nature of the soul—402; The idea of souls being created from some spiritual, angelic, matter aired and dismissed—403; The three positions to be tested against the evidence scattered through the scriptures—404; Testing these various opinions by the evidence of scriptural texts proves inconclusive—407; The bearing on the matter of a text to do with original sin, Romans 5:12, etc.—408; What is meant by flesh and spirit lusting against each other—409; Question of the involvement of infants in original sin—410; A possible response to this opinion—412; Wrestling with the problem of infants dying unbaptized—413; Back to a difficult text from the book of Wisdom—416; Seeing if the text can be applied to Christ—417; The bearing of Hebrews 7:4-10 on the question—419; The difference in the ways in which Levi and Christ were in the loins of Abraham and its bearing on the transmission of original sin—420; A text from the gospel: John 3:6—422; Summing up the debate—423; An admonition never to think of the soul as being a material body—424; Tertullian's belief that the soul is a body—425

The text of the chapter: the nakedness of the man and the woman—428; The serpent's cleverness; the relation of the serpent to the devil—430; Only with God's permission could the devil use the serpent in this way—431; Why God permitted the man to be tempted—431; The first sin, before the act of disobedience, was pride—432; More reflections on why God allows us to be tempted—433; The same, with the emphasis on the way in which bad people can be of service to the good—434; That the good can benefit from the punishment of the wicked is a matter of common experience—436; Why a serpent, particularly?—437; Of the nature of the devil himself, and of his sin—437; Intermezzo on pride and avarice—439; Back to the devil and his sin—440; About the blessed life, and its various degrees—441; Taking up the point of there being, perhaps, two kinds or categories of angels—442; The view that the devil was created in wickedness; a text of Job misapplied—443; Texts from Isaiah and Ezekiel, usually applied to the devil, more readily fit his "body"—446; Summing up what has been said about the devil's fall—448; The devil and the serpent—449; Back to the story of Genesis 3—451; Their eyes were opened, and they realized they were naked—452; About the "voice of the Lord"—454; The conversation between Adam and God—455; Excusing self, blaming others—456; The punishment of the serpent—457; The punishment of the woman—458; The man's punishment—459; The tunics of skin; God's anxiety—459; Adam cast out of Paradise—460; Some other

General Introduction

Augustine's personal interest in the subject of creation

The effort to think through the mystery of creation runs like a leitmotif through Augustine's work.[1] Ever since his first encounter with the Bible, a long time before his baptism, the creation story had occupied a central place in his thinking. When he became a Christian and a bishop, it continued to be a difficult text to deal with; he felt it to be an exegetical challenge that would demand the utmost effort of his intellectual powers.

Over a period of almost thirty years Augustine composed five commentaries on the biblical creation stories. As early as 388/389, when he returned to Africa, he produced his first effort at interpretation in the work *On Genesis: A Refutation of the the Manichees (De Genesis contra Manichaeos)*. Dissatisfied with the kind of exegesis practiced in that first work, he tried in the *Unfinished Literal Commentary on Genesis (De Genesis ad litteram liber unus imperfectus)* (393-395) to produce an interpretation according to the literal sense, but since he did not feel up to the task, he left it unfinished.

Thirdly, he deliberately ended his *Confessions* with an almost complete commentary on Genesis 1 that occupies the last three books (written 397-401).[2] After experiencing and confessing the creative presence of God in his own life

---

1. See D. Weber, *"In scripturis exponendis tirocinium meum succubuit*: Zu Augustins frühen Versuchen einer Genesis-Exegese," in *L'esegesi dei Padri latini dalle origini a Gregorio Magno* (Studia Ephemeridis Augustinianum 68; Rome, 2000) 225-232; C. Mayer, "Creatio, creator, creatura," in idem (ed.), *Augustinus-Lexikon* 2 (Basel, 1996) 56-116; L. Bescond, "Saint Augustin, lecteur et interprète de la Genèse," *Graphè* 4 (1995) 47-57; M.-A. Vannier, *"Creatio," "Conversio," "Formatio" chez S. Augustin* (Paradosis 31; Fribourg, 1991); eadem, "Le rôle de l'hexaéméron dans l'interprétation augustinienne de la création," *Studia Patristica* 22 (1987) 372-380; G. Pelland, *Cinq études d'Augustin sur le debut de la Genèse* (Montreal, 1972); idem, "Augustin rencontre le livre de la Genèse," in *De Genesi contra Manichaeos; De Genesi ad litteram liber imperfectus* (Lectio Augustini 8; Palermo, 1992) 15-53; K. Staritz, *Augustins Schöpfungsglaube dargestellt nach seinen Genesisauslegungen* (Breslau, 1931); R. Arteaga Natividad, *La creaciòn en los comentarios de San Agustín al Genesis* (Marcilla, 1992).
2. See J. C. Cooper, "Why Did Augustine Write Books XI-XIII of the *Confessions?" Augustinian Studies* 2 (1971) 37-46; N. Fischer and C. Mayer (eds.), *Die Confessiones des Augustinus von Hippo. Einführung und Interpretationen zu den dreizehn Büchern* (Freiburg, 1998) 489-652; K. Gritz, *Die Einheit der "Confessiones." Warum bringt Augustin zu den letzten Büchern seiner "Confessiones" eine Auslegung der Genesis?* (Dissertation; Tübingen, 1970).

(Books 1-9), he decided, in addition, to confess God as creator of the universe. The philosophical and spiritual depth of his reflections give this interpretation of Genesis its originality. Then, while finishing the *Confessions*, Augustine began his fourth commentary, on which he labored for about fifteen years (401-416). The title, *The Literal Meaning of Genesis (De Genesi ad litteram)*, shows his intention of explaining Genesis 1-3 literally and not allegorically. To these four treatments is to be added Book XI of *City of God*; here, around 416, the bishop of Hippo produced a more specialized commentary on the creation of the angels, since in his view the city of God originated in that creation.

Augustine also dealt with the subject of creation at the beginning of his *Answer to an Enemy of the Law and the Prophets (Contra Adversarium legis et prophetarum*, 419-420),[3] in his writings on the creed, that is, in *Faith and the Creed (De fide et symbolo)* and in *Faith, Hope, and Charity (De fide, spe et caritate)*,[4] in his anti-Pelagian works *Answer to Julian (Contra Iulianum)* and *Unfinished Work in Answer to Julian (Contra Iulianum opus imperfectum)*,[5] but also in his catechetical, liturgical, and pastoral instructions *(On the Creed, to Catechumens [De symbolo ad catechumenos]; Sermon 212; 214)*.[6]

Why did Augustine's mind thus constantly return to the subject of creation? First of all, his religious genius made the relationship between his self and God the focus of all his thinking. As the well-known words of the *Soliloquies* tell us, "I want to know God and the soul. Nothing else? Absolutely nothing else!"[7] Even in his prayer his desire found expression: "O God who are ever the same, I want to know myself, I want to know you."[8]

But there is an ontological basis for this religious relationship between man and God that Augustine experienced with such intensity and thought about so constantly. The reality of creation and the relationship between creature and creator underlie all religious acts. In the course of his conversion Augustine gained an existential awareness of the meaning of creation.[9] During his break with Manicheism, his assimilation of Neoplatonic ideas, and his final turn to the Church he realized ever more fully and deeply that he had been created by God and that he possessed his own being only within a relationship to the creator. Since God is Being itself, on which all being depends, it is possible for human

---

3. See R. J. Teske, "Problems with 'The Beginning' in Augustine's Sixth Commentary on Genesis," *The University of Dayton Review* 22 (1994) 55-67.
4. See C. Eichenseer, *Das Symbolum Apostolicum beim Heiligen Augustinus* (Kirchengeschichtliche Quellen und Studien 4; St. Ottilien, 1960) 163-195.
5. See E. TeSelle, "Nature and Grace in Augustine's Expositions of Genesis 1, 1-5," *Recherches Augustiniennes* 5 (1968) 95-137.
6. See H. Rondet, "La théologie de saint Augustin prédicateur," *Bulletin de littérature ecclésiastique* 72 (1971) 81-105, especially 85-78, 90-93.
7. *Soliloquies.* I, 2, 7 (CSEL 89, 11).
8. Ibid., II, 1, 1 (CSEL 89, 45).
9. See Vannier, *"Creatio"* (note 1, above), 20-66, 175-179.

beings to choose freely between turning to God *(conversio ad Deum)* and turning away from God *(aversio a Deo)* and so to determine their own self-fulfillment *(formatio)*. In Augustine's view, creation is destined to find its fulfillment through a return to God. The creator awaits the free response of his creature.

For Augustine, religion is simply the free and deliberate acknowledgment of human beings that as creatures they are ontologically dependent on God. It is not without good reason that his *Confessions* ends with an interpretation of the creation story, for it is here that *confessio*, the human being's praise of God, finds its real meaning: *confessio* becomes the acknowledgment, accompanied by praise, of the creative bond that constitutes the nature of the human person at its deepest level. It is in praise of God that the ontological bond *(ligamen)* is acknowledged and thereby becomes religion *(re-ligamen)*.[10]

The theological investigation of the mystery of creation

Augustine's thinking about creation was thus deeply rooted in his life story. As a theologian who regarded himself as obligated by the motto *Intellectum valde ama*,[11] he was inevitably very interested in thinking through what the Bible had to say about creation. Was not creation, after all, the reality that grounds and also necessitates the religious dimension of human existence? The fact of creation was, to his mind, beyond question: "Heaven and earth . . . cry out that they were made."[12] The question he asked himself was how concretely to understand this fact: "Let me listen, so that I may understand how you made heaven and earth in the beginning."[13] He wanted not only to hear but to understand the biblical message in Genesis. The creation of the world by God was a matter not only of faith but of reason.[14] Therefore, the understanding *(intellectus)* for which he strove had to do with creation not only as a truth of faith but also as something accessible to human reason.

It is characteristic of Augustine's conception of the *intellectus fidei* that the real object of this "understanding of the faith" was not the biblical text itself but the truth which the text expressed.[15] The text was only an authority that mediated

---

10. See A. Di Giovanni, "Significato ultimo delle *Confessioni* di S. Agostino," *Giornale di Metafisica* 20 (1965) 122-141; idem, "Sul fondamento teoretico della 'religione,'" *Filosofia e vita* 8 (1967) 46-50.
11. Letter 120, 3, 13 (CSEL 34, 716).
12. *Confessions* XI, 4, 6 (CCL 27, 197): *caelum et terra clamant, quod facta sunt* (trans. M. Boulding, *The Confessions* [Hyde Park, NY: New City Press, 1997] 288. Henceforth: Boulding with page number.).
13. Ibid., XI, 3, 5 (CCL 27, 196): *Audiam et intellegam, quomodo in principio fecisti caelum et terram* (Boulding, 287).
14. *The Literal Meaning of Genesis* 1, 14, 28: "At the same time Catholic faith prescribes and reason indubitably teaches [this]."
15. See *Confessions* XI, 3, 5; XII, 18, 27; XII, 24, 33 (CCL 27, 196, 229, 233).

between God as speaker and the human being as hearer. For this reason, the struggle to understand could not and ought not stop at an understanding of the text of Genesis but had to go beyond the text in order to grasp by reason the reality and truth of which the words of the Bible were speaking. This explains why Augustine's commentaries on Genesis not infrequently depart from the underlying text and discuss in detail problems that do not spring directly from the wording but from a speculative study of the truths implicit in the text.

Augustine's search for a deeper understanding of the mystery of creation was guided by two complementary principles. On the one hand, it had to respect the rule of faith or the authority of the text; on the other, it was necessary to respect the claims of reason.[16] But although these principles marked out the path to be followed in the search for knowledge of the truth, Augustine knew that his efforts at interpretation would always produce only an approximation to the truth and never a complete grasp of it: "The obscure mysteries of the natural order, which we perceive to have been made by God the almighty craftsman, should rather be discussed by asking questions than by making affirmations. This is supremely the case with the books which have been entrusted to us by divine authority, because the rash assertion of one's uncertain and dubious opinions in dealing with them can scarcely avoid the charge of sacrilege."[17]

Augustine's repeated efforts to interpret the account in Genesis tell us, on the one hand, how very aware this theologian was of the limits of his concrete results, and, on the other, how greatly his intellectual drive was inspired rather than discouraged by the difficulty of the material. Since in his understanding of it exegesis could not be reduced to a skill in interpreting texts but was, in the final analysis, one form of the search for God, no commentary on scripture could ever claim to be definitive. God allows himself to be found only inasmuch as he is sought constantly anew.[18] If Augustine's commentaries on Genesis left many questions open, if they could only discuss many problems but not give definitive answers to them, and if they intended only to offer solutions as hypotheses and not to demand their acceptance as categorically true, the deepest reason is to be found in his awareness that the questions which the sacred scriptures raised to the inquiring mind converged ultimately in the unfathomable mystery of God.

Augustine was neither the first nor the only early Christian thinker who devoted himself to the interpretation of the creation story. If, then, we are to appreciate properly his theological achievement in this area we must glance briefly at the history of the interpretation of these first chapters of the Bible.

---

16. See *The Literal Meaning of Genesis* XII, 14, 30: "the truth of the faith and sound understanding"; *ibid.*, VII, 24, 35: "if there is no scriptural authority or evident argument of reason against it."
17. *Unfinished Literal Commentary on Genesis* 1, 1; see *The Literal Meaning of Genesis* I, 18, 37; 1, 20, 40; IV, 28, 45; VII, 28, 42; IX, 1, 1.
18. See *The Trinity* XV, 2, 2 (CCL 50A, 460-62).

The tradition of interpretation of the Hexaemeron

The biblical story of the origin of the world and of the human race raised fundamental questions of a theological, cosmological, and anthropological kind. No wonder, then, that the reception and interpretation of the story in Genesis had an extensive and wide-ranging history.[19]

Even within the Old Testament those fundamental testimonies to the origin of the world were subjected to several rereadings. The intertestamental Jewish tradition of interpretation of the creation story is documented both by the Septuagint translation[20] and by the interpretation of the story in Philo of Alexandria.[21] The earliest Christian commentaries of the second and third centuries have not survived. Eusebius of Caesarea mentions interpretations of the Hexaemeron by a Rhodo, a Candidus, and an Apion,[22] but also by better known theologians Hippolytus and Origen.[23] But even in their other writings such authors as Justin, Theophilus, Irenaeus, Clement of Alexandria, and Origen raised problems of the interpretation of Genesis.[24] In ensuing centuries, too, renowned theologians such as Basil of Caesarea, John Chrysostom, Gregory of Nyssa, Ephrem the Syrian, Didymus of Alexandria, Lactantius, and Ambrose devoted works to the opening chapters of Genesis or to God's work in creation.[25]

The early Christian tradition of interpretation of Genesis took two directions: polemical, on the one hand, and catechetical and pastoral, on the other. First of all, philosophical views of Platonic, Aristotelean, and Stoic origin required Christians to state their own positions. In response to the idea of an eternal world or of a pre-existent matter which God shaped but did not create, theologians insisted that the world had a temporal beginning, that matter was created out of

---

19. See G. A. Robbins (ed.), *Genesis 1-3 in the History of Exegesis: Intrigue in the Garden* (Lewiston, 1988)l; A. S. Pease, "Caeli enarrant," *Harvard Theological Review* 34 (1941) 163-200; A. Hamman, "L'enseignement sur la création dans l'antiquité chrétienne," *Revue des sciences religieuses* 42 (1968) 1-23, 97-122; J.-P. Bouhout, "Pentateuque chez les Pères," *Dictionnaire de la Bible. Supplément* 7 (Paris, 1966) 687-708, especially 702-708.
20. See M. Alexandre, *Le commencement de livre Genèse I-V. La version grecque de la Septante et sa réception* (Paris, 1988); eadem, "Lire en grec le récit de la création: interprétation de la Genèse dans la littérature judéo-hellénistique," *M'yn, Sources* 2 (1981) 95-118.
21. R. Arnaldez, Introduction to *Philon d'Alexandrie, De opificio mundi* (Les oeuvres de Philon d'Alexandrie 1; Paris, 1961) 17-112.
22. Eusebius, *Ecclesiastical History* 5, 13, 8; 5, 27 (ed. minor E. Schwartz; Leipzig, 1932, 196, 214f.).
23. Ibid., 6, 22; 6, 24, 2 (Schwartz, 243).
24. See P. Nautin, "Genèse 1, 1-2, de Justin ô Origène," in *In principio. Interprétations des premiers versets de la Genèse* (Paris: études Augustiniennes, 1973) 61-94; G. T. Armstrong, *Die Genesis in der Alten Kirche* (Beiträge zur Geschichte der biblischen Hermeneutik 4; Tübingen, 1962).
25. See F. E. Robbins, *The Hexaemeral Literature, A Study of the Greek and Latin Commentaries on Genesis* (Chicago, 1912); Y. Congar, "Le thème de Dieu-Créateur et les explications de l'Hexaémeron dans la tradition chrétienne," in *L'homme devant Dieu. Mélanges De Lubac* 1 (Théologie 56; Paris, 1963) 189-222.

nothing, and that God created freely and not out of necessity. Since such opponents of Christians as Celsus, Porphyry, and Julian the Apostate not infrequently ridiculed elements of the creation story that seemed dubious to them, Christian apologists often had to take up questions in the interpretation of Genesis.[26] In addition, heretical currents stemming from gnosticism, Marcionism, Manicheism, and Priscillianism called for a theological explanation that would oppose any form of dualism and show evil to be not an independent substance but the result of human freedom and demonic activity.

Genesis also played an important role in the catechetical and pastoral instruction of the early Church. The reading and interpretation of this book of the Bible soon found a place in the first week of Lent, then in Holy Week, and then during the Easter Vigil.[27]

Augustine was thus in the line of a lengthy and comprehensive tradition of interpretation. He was familiar with important aspects of the early Christian interpretation of Genesis,[28] but the question of the concrete sources on which he drew can be answered with accuracy in only a few instances. At this period cosmological conceptions were generally part of the knowledge acquired by the educated class. It is possible indeed to find parallels in other authors for many of Augustine's concepts, ideas, and images, but it has not been possible to discover a common source text for them. Much in the Hexaemeron literature had made its way into the catechesis of the Church and was handed on orally, so that Augustine may have gotten to know it in these ways. In any case, he usually altered not only the language but also the content of his sources.

He may also have acquired an indirect knowledge of Greek sources through Latin translations. Nor can we exclude the possibility that he had available a kind of synopsis of various interpretations of the Hexaemeron.[29] Basic ideas in the cosmology of Philo of Alexandria may have reached him through the works of Origen, Basil, and Ambrose.[30] More important was the influence of Origen himself. Augustine knew his main work, *First Principles (De principiis)*, and the homilies on Genesis 1 and 2 through the Latin translations of Rufinus and Jerome; he may possibly have known Origen's commentary on Genesis, which

---

26. See S. Ackermann, *Christliche Apologetik und heidnische Philosophie im Streit um das Alte Testament* (Stuttgarter Biblische Beiträge 36; Stuttgart, 1997) 118-133; G. Rinaldi (ed.), *Biblia gentium* (Rome, 1989) 189-227.

27. See A. Ralphs, "Die alttestamentlichen Lektionen der Griechischen Kirche," *Nachrichten der königlichen Gesellschaft der Wissenschaften in Göttingen*. Phil.-hist. Klasse (1915) 26-136; B. Botte, "La choix des lectures de la veillée pascale," *Questions liturgiques et pastorales* (1952) 65-70.

28. See C. Bernardi, "*In principio fecit Deus caelum et terram*" in *San Agostino e le sue fonti* (Turin, 1960).

29. See Bouhout, "Pentateuque chez les Pères" (note 19, above), 708.

30. See Vannier, "*Creatio*" (note 1, above), 68.

exists today only in fragments.[31] So too it can be shown that he was acquainted with Basil of Caesarea's *Homilies on the Hexaemeron*, which Eustathius had translated into Latin, and which were frequently used by Ambrose.[32] Of Latin authors it was chiefly Ambrose who shaped Augustine's thinking on creation; Ambrose's allegorical interpretation of scripture made a new understanding of the Hexaemeron possible for Augustine and gave him extensive information on the subject from the most varied sources.[33]

As a result, the currents of tradition in both western and eastern theology flowed together in Augustine's several commentaries on Genesis and combined therein to form a new whole marked by a marvelous richness and intellectual depth. If, then, the literary genre of Hexaemeron interpretation reached its high point in Augustine, the reason was to be found not least in the fact that he was able skillfully to incorporate contemporary philosophy into his theological thinking.

The philosophical background of Augustine's interpretation of Genesis

Augustine's solid knowledge of the philosophy of his age enabled him to delve into the problems of the origin of the world and humanity in a speculative way, to translate his thoughts on heaven, the light, time, and eternity into formulas of almost scholastic precision, and to find theologically and metaphysically satisfying answers to problems in the face of which his predecessors could only retreat into allegorism.[34]

The theological reception of philosophical ideas was facilitated by the fact that the Neoplatonic conception of the universe, in particular, had a fundamentally religious cast. To the minds of the Neoplatonists the universe was not only good, it was holy. According to Plotinus the universe was one great sacrament.[35]

---

31. See B. Altaner, "Augustinus und Origenes," in idem, *Kleine patristische Schriften* (Texts und Untersuchungen zur Geschichte der altchristlichen Literatur 83; Berlin, 1967) 224-52, especially 229-236.
32. See B. Altaner, "Augustinus und Basilius der Grosse," ibid., 269-276, especially 270-272; idem, "Eustathius, der lateinische übersetzer der Hexaemeron-Homilien Basilius des Grossen," ibid., 437-447, especially 438-443; Vannier, *"Creatio"* (note 1, above) 71-73.
33. See Vannier, *"Creatio,"* 69-71.
34. See C. J. O'Toole, *The Philosophy of Creation in the Writings of St. Augustine* (Washington, DC, 1944); J. De Blic, "Platonisme et christianisme dans la conception augustinienne du dieu créateur," *Recherches de science religieuse* 30 (1940) 172-190; J. Wytzes, "Bemerkungen zu dem neuplatonischen Einfluss in Augustins *De Genesi ad litteram,*" *Zeitschrift für die neutestamentliche Wissenschaft* 39 (1940) 137-151; A. Pérez De Labordas, "El Mundo como creaciòn. Comentarios filosóficos sobre el pensamiento de san Agustín en el *De Genesi ad litteram,*" *Ciudad de Dios* 307 (1994) 365-417.
35. See A. H. Armstrong, *St. Augustine and Christian Platonism* (Villanova, 1967) 15.

But the reception was by no means uncritical or undiscriminating.[36] Augustine did indeed make use of many categories developed by Plotinus in order to supply Christian thought about God and creation with a conceptual basis and a philosophical structure. But that he did not take over the content of the Neoplatonic system can be seen in his rejection of the idea of emanation and his crucial holding to the idea of creation from nothing *(creatio ex nihilo)*.[37] Conversely, the incorporation of the Trinity into the process of creation shows the genuinely Christian orientation of Augustine's views.[38] The same is true of his thought on the world of the angels, which he saw hinted at in the creation of light and viewed as the archetype of every creaturely relationship to the creator.

On the other hand, we may not overlook the fact that Augustine's recourse to philosophy was at the cost of the biblical and salvation-historical conception of creation. The idea of a plan of salvation that began with the very act of creation made way for a metaphysical meditation on the being and order of creation. Because the Neoplatonic system was used as a help and a technique in gaining knowledge of the biblical message, the knowledge obtained was seen primarily in a metaphysical perspective.[39] The basic aim of Augustine's interpretation of the Hexaemeron was to grasp the being and structure of creation and not its role in the divine economy of salvation.[40]

Importance of Augustine's commentaries on Genesis

Augustine's explanations of the opening chapters of Genesis are doubtless overshadowed by his better known works, for example, the *Confessions*, *The Trinity*, and the *City of God*. Yet these exegetical works, and especially the great commentary on *The Literal Meaning of Genesis*, give a valuable insight into the method and self-understanding of his theological activity, but also into central aspects of his thought. The development of his method of interpretation from the

---

36. See W. A. Christian, "Augustine on the Creation of the World," *Harvard Theological Review* 46 (1953) 1-25; G. Madec, *Saint Augustin et la philosophie* (Collection des études Augustiniennes, Série Antiquité 149; Paris, 1996) 101-106.
37. See N. J. Torchia, *Creatio ex nihilo and the Theology of St. Augustine: The Anti-Manichaean Polemic and Beyond* (American University Series, Theology and Religion 205; New York, 1999); idem, "The Implications of the Doctrine of *Creatio ex nihilo* in St. Augustine's Theology," *Studia Patristica* 33 (1997) 266-273; Mayer, "Creatio, creator, creatura" (note 1, above), 78.
38. See *Unfinished Literal Commentary on Genesis* 1, 2: "Catholic teaching bids us believe that this Trinity is called one God, and that he made and created all the things that are, insofar as they are." See Mayer, "*Creatio, creator, creatura*," 71-74.
39. A. Solignac, "Exégèse et métaphysique: Genèse 1, 1-3 chez saint Augustin," in *In principio. Interprétations des premiers versets de la Genèse* (Paris: études Augustiniennnes, 1973) 153-171.
40. L. Scheffczyk, *Schöpfung und Vorsehung* (Handbuch der Dogmengeschichte, ed. M. Schmaus and A. Grillmeier; Freiburg, 1963) 62-65.

controlling allegorism of *On Genesis: A Refutation of the Manichees* to the literal exegesis of the monumental commentary on Genesis lets us see him maturing intellectually and shows the effort he made constantly to improve his exegetical tools.[41]

The methodological reflections that are woven into the exegesis at many points document in an impressive way Augustine's understanding of the responsibility of a theologian as a man who must constantly account to himself for the presentation of his results: "I have discussed the text and written down as best I could in eleven books what seemed certain to me, and have affirmed and defended it; and about its many uncertainties I have inquired, hesitated, balanced different opinions, not to prescribe to anyone what they should think about obscure points, but rather to show how we have been willing to be instructed whenever we have been in doubt about the meaning, and to discourage the reader from the making of rash assertions where we have been unable to establish solid grounds for a definite decision."[42]

Augustine's interpretations of Genesis were groundbreaking not only in their method but in their content as well. The relationship of time to eternity and of body to soul, the image of God in human beings, the fall, divine providence, and the origin of evil were not only given a thorough analysis in the various interpretations of the account of creation, but were thought through in a way that inspired the subsequent history of theology. Because Augustine the exegete did not stop at an interpretation of the text but, using the first chapters of the Bible, drafted a theology of the origins of the world and humanity, he succeeded in shedding light on the structure of being in general and formulating the fundamental coordinates of all creaturely existence.

Augustine's meditations and reflections on the biblical Hexaemeron had deep roots in his own life and specifically in his experience of conversion. Consequently, his primary objective was to bring out the existential aspect of the mystery of creation and to show, in keeping with his personal experience in the history of his own *conversio*, that creation by its very nature involved relations. Therefore the true greatness of human beings does not consist in the supposed autonomy of an individual who makes himself the ultimate norm. As an interpreter of Genesis, Augustine showed that human beings become greater the more they grow in their capacity to hear the deeper message of creation, the message of the creator himself. He was convinced that harmony with creation, the divine wisdom of which becomes our standard, does not mean a limitation of our freedom but is the expression of our understanding and our dignity. Only by

---

41. See *Revisions* I, 18 (CCL 57, 54). See Vannier, *"Creatio,"* 89-94; A. Penna, Introduction to *Sant' Agostino, La Genesi* 1 (Nuova Biblioteca Agostiniana 9/1; Rome, 1988) LXI-LXXX.
42. *The Literal Meaning of Genesis* XII, 1, 1.

turning to the creator, by contemplating God, by praising the light which God is, does the creature achieve its true form and become in fact that which it ought to be according to God's plan,[43] but which it can become only through a free choice. As the author of the *Confessions* puts it, the creature has but one choice: "of being converted to him who made it, so that it may live more and more fully on the fount of life, and in his light see light, and so be perfected, illumined, and beatified."[44]

---

43. See *ibid.*, IV, 22, 39.
44. *Confessions* XIII, 4, 5 (CCL 27, 244); Boulding, 345.

On Genesis: A Refutation of the Manichees

Introduction

Origin and intention

It is a known fact that in his search for truth and wisdom the nineteen-year-old Augustine took up the Bible but was soon disillusioned with it and laid it aside.[1] It may well have been the reading of Genesis that sapped the enthusiasm of the young student in the very first pages of the Old Testament. It is certain, in any case, that the attacks of the Manichees on the book of Genesis and especially on the story of creation were not the least of the reasons why he joined that sect around 373.[2]

The opening chapters of Genesis were the main focus of controversy between Manichees and Christians because faith in a single creator of the world was in direct opposition to the Manichean dualistic cosmogony. Manichean critics of Genesis 1, 1—2, 4 tried to prove that the biblical text was untenable. The anthropomorphic picture of God given there was absurd, and the question of the origin of evil was unanswerable on the assumption of a single, good creator God. The Manichees expressly rejected a figurative-allegorical interpretation of the Old Testament,[3] because only in light of this rejection did the strangeness and difficulty of the Old Testament text become really clear. The Manichees intended by their criticism to undermine the credibility of a Church that took this questionable text as a document of revelation, and thereby to dispose the faithful for an acceptance of the Manichean message. In the case of Augustine, this maneuver was completely successful in the beginning. As a young student he rejected both the text of the Old Testament and the authority of the Catholic Church.

At the same time, however, it was the Manichean cosmogony that caused Augustine to study more carefully the origin of the universe, for, as he wrote later on in the *Confessions*: "Their books are full of interminable myths concerning sky, stars, sun and moon."[4] On the basis of the demand for reason-

---

1. See *Confessions* III, 5, 9 (CCL 27, 30f.).
2. See E. Feldmann, *Der Einfluss des Hortensius and des Manichäismus auf das Denken des jungen Augustinus von 373* (Dissertation; Münster. 1975) 568-588.
3. See Evodius, *De fide contra Manichaeos* 38 (CSEL 25/2, 968). On Manichean criticism of the Bible see K. Pollmann, *Doctrina christiana. Untersuchungen zu den Anfängen der christlichen Hermeneutik unter besonderer Berücksichtigung von Augustinus, De doctrina christiana* (Paradosis 41; Fribourg, 1996) 11-21.
4. *Confessions* V, 7, 12 (CCL 27, 63); trans. M. Boulding, *The Confessions* (Hyde Park, NY, 1997) 121.

ableness that had first led him to the Manichees, he did not hesitate to give up this cosmogony, that is, this mythical representation of the origin of the world, in favor of a cosmology, that is, a philosophically acceptable explanation of the universe and its formation.[5]

A decisive help in overcoming his own reservations regarding the biblical account of creation and in recognizing the untenableness of Manichean criticism was the sermons of Ambrose on the Hexaemeron with their allegorism and Neoplatonic spirit; Augustine may have heard them in Milan during Holy Week of 386 when he was a candidate for baptism.[6] In these homilies Ambrose, too, came to grips with Manichean ideas. Augustine now realized that the Manichees wrongly appealed to Genesis 1:26 in order to criticize the anthropomorphic picture of God in the Old Testament. According to Ambrose, the image of God in the human being referred not to the body but to the spiritual soul.[7] Augustine also learned here, for the first time, that evil is not a material substance but a deficiency, namely, the lack of goodness. By way of such specific treatments the biblical preaching of the bishop of Milan led Augustine to the general insight that the Bible need not be interpreted exclusively according to the literal sense, as the Manichees demanded and followed in practice. Instead he became aware that the allegorical method of interpretation was also legitimate. Looking back, he wrote: "I then expended much mental effort on trying to discover if I could in any way convict the Manichees of falsehood by some definite proofs."[8]

A first written criticism followed in 387/388 in the work *The Catholic Way of Life and the Manichean Way of Life*, which was composed while Augustine was still in Rome. After returning to North Africa and his hometown, Thagaste, at the end of August, 388, Augustine found the necessary peace and leisure to compose his first commentary on Genesis within a year's time. With this he intended to counter the attacks of the Manichees: "The Manichees . . . do not just go wrong by taking these books of the Old Testament in a way that is not correct, but . . . blaspheme by rejecting them outright with detestation."[9]

As Augustine says when looking back later, within the little community in which he was living with like-minded fellows he was constantly being faced with questions that may have resulted from his comrades being unsettled by the attacks of the Manichees. It is a known fact that at that time Manichean propa-

---

5. See *Confessions* V, 14, 25 (CCL 27, 71f.). See M.-A. Vanier, "Manichéisme et pensée augustinienne de la création," in J. C. Schnaubelt and F. Van Fleteren (eds.), *Augustine: Second Founder of the Faith* (Collectanea Augustiniana; New York, 1990) 421-431.
6. See *Confessions* V, 14, 27 (CCL 27, 71); *The Advantage of Believing* 8, 20 (CSEL 25/1, 25). See P. Courcelle, *Recherches sur les Confessions de Saint Augustin* (Paris, 1968) 96-103. R.-J. Palanque, *Saint Ambroise et l'Empire Romain* (Paris, 1933) 519, argues for the year 387.
7. See *Confessions* VI, 3, 4 (CCL 27, 76).
8. *Confessions*, V, 14, 25 (Boulding, 132).
9. *The Literal Meaning of Genesis* VIII, 2, 5.

ganda was circulating in the Christian communities of Thagaste and of Madaura, which was the intellectual center of the region. Augustine collected his answers later on in *A Miscellany of Eighty Questions*.[10] Some of the problems dealt with in this work correspond exactly to the expositions in his work *On Genesis: A Refutation of the Manichees*: "Is God the originator of human misdeeds?" (Quest. 3); "Why are human beings evil?" (Quest. 4); "Evil" (Quest. 6); "Why did God will to create the world?" (Quest. 18).

Augustine thus recognized the serious danger with which the Manichean attack on the Old Testament account of creation threatened not a few Christians because of their lack of education.[11] For this reason he felt obliged, even while a layman and before having any ecclesiastical office, to defend the biblical book of Genesis, which was seriously challenged by the Manichean doctrine of the two eternal principles, Light and Darkness, as well as by the myth of a cosmic struggle between two kingdoms, in the course of which the world and humanity came into existence. In his *Revisions* Augustine wrote: "These two books . . . were published expressly against them [the Manichees] in defense of the old law, which they attack with all the zeal and fanaticism of their crazy delusion."[12] He realized that he must provide his fellow Christians, both lay and clerical, with arguments that could put a stop to the Manichees' destructive criticism of the Bible.

This goal was not to be reached solely through attacks on the Manichees.[13] The refutation of Manichean teaching on the origin of the world,[14] which claimed to be completely rational and internally consistent, had to be supplemented by a positive exposition of the Catholic views being attacked by the Manichees. Augustine described his purpose in this way: "What we have undertaken to do is to defend the things they find fault with in the Old Testament, insofar as the Lord is good enough to grant us the power to do so, and to demonstrate in those places that the blindness of human beings is no match at all for the truth of God."[15] At the same time, he had to show that the Church's teaching offered a plausible answer to the problems raised by the Manichean sect. Finally, since that group cleverly used some biblical passages to undermine the credi-

---

10. *Revisions* I, 26, 1 (CCL 57, 74).
11. See R. J. O'Connell, *St. Augustine's Early Theory of Man, A.D. 386-391* (Cambridge, Mass., 1968) 232-235.
12. *Revisions* I, 10, 1 (CCL 57, 30).
13. Later on (396), in his *Answer to the Letter of Mani Known as "The Foundation,"* Augustine refuted a Manichean "teaching manual" that had been circulated in North Africa.
14. In his *Answer to Felix, a Manichean* 1, 9 (CSEL 25/2, 811) Augustine says explicitly that the Manichees claimed to possess a teaching on this subject which Mani himself had received from the Holy Spirit. J. P. Maher, "Saint Augustine and Manichean Cosmogony," *Augustinian Studies* 10 (1979) 91-104, makes the point that Augustine had a reliable knowledge of this teaching.
15. *On Genesis: A Refutation of the Manichees* I, 4, 7.

bility of the sacred scriptures, Augustine intended to provide Christians with a way of reading that would yield a valid understanding of the Bible.

A commentary on the book of Genesis seemed a suitable way of achieving these several goals.[16] The work was indeed written against the Manichees *(contra Manichaeos)*,[17] but it was written primarily for Christians, whom Augustine wanted to enlighten regarding the basic question every religion seeks to answer: "How to think about God in a godly way *(quid de Deo pie sentiatur)*."[18]

In choosing to give an interpretation of Genesis 1-3, Augustine was able to make use of two fundamental areas of ancient philosophy: cosmology and anthropology (or ethics). In the early Christian tradition of interpretation Genesis 1—2:4 was regarded as an authoritative text on the origin of the world, and Genesis 2:4b—3:24 as an instruction on the nature of the human person (or instruction in ethics). Inasmuch as these passages also played an important part in the instruction of candidates for baptism,[19] Augustine's work *On Genesis against the Manichees* reflected the catechetical practice of his time.

Method of interpretation

At the beginning of his work Augustine tells his readers that some Christians with a literary education had read his earlier anti-Manichean writings and had been pleased with their elevated style. These same Christians had, however, asked him that in dealing with the Manichees he would keep the uneducated in mind and adapt his interpretation of the biblical story of creation to the intellectual level of persons incapable of following complex theological and philosophical arguments.[20]

It can be seen from the present work that Augustine did endeavor to respect "everyday usage" *(communis loquendi consuetudo)*. He cautiously introduces his principles of interpretation,[21] he repeats arguments and conclusions and supports individual theses with examples from everyday life[22] and from collo-

---

16. See the following introductions: R. J. Teske in his *Saint Augustine on Genesis. Two Books on Genesis against the Manichees, and The Literal Interpretation of Genesis: An Unfinished Book* (Fathers of the Church 84; Washington, DC, 1991) 3-43; D. Weber (ed.), *Augustinus, De Genesis contra Manichaeos* (CSEL 91; Vienna, 1998) 9-32; and L. Carrozzi, *Sant'Agostino, La Genesi difesa contro i Manichei* (Nuova Biblioteca Agostiniana 9/1; Rome, 1988) 3-46. See also J. P. Maher, *Saint Augustine's Defense of the Hexaemeron against the Manicheans* (Dissertation; Rome: Pontifical Gregorian University, 1947).
17. See *Revisions* I, 10, 1 (CCL 57, 29); *The Literal Meaning of Genesis* VIII, 2. See Letter 25, 2 (CSEL 34/1, 79), in which Paulinus of Nola describes Augustine's *On Genesis: A Refutation of the Manichees, The Catholic Way of Life and the Manichean Way of Life, On True Religion,* and *Free Will* as a "Pentateuch against the Manichees."
18. *On Genesis: A Refutation of the Manichees* II, 29, 43.
19. See Augustine, *The Instruction of Beginners* 17, 28—18, 30 (CCL 46, 152-155).
20. See *On Genesis: A Refutation of the Manichees* I, 1, 1.
21. For example, ibid., I, 22, 34.
22. For example, ibid., I, 6, 10.

quial speech.[23] There are striking stylistic differences from the early dialogues: there are hardly any complex periodic sentences and rhetorical figures, the language is seldom rhythmic, and the conversational tone prevails. But it is not in his language alone but also in the area of thought and argument that Augustine strives to adapt himself to the level of those simple faithful *(parvuli)*[24] whose anti-intellectualism he himself had brought with him from the Church to the Manichees fifteen years earlier.[25]

Looking back in his later work *The Literal Meaning of Genesis*, Augustine describes the intention and method of his first effort at interpretation: "My aim was to refute their ravings as quickly as possible, and also to prod them into looking for the Christian and evangelical faith in the writings which they hate. Now at that time it had not yet dawned on me how everything in them could be taken in its proper literal sense; it seemed to me rather that this was scarcely possible, if at all, and anyhow extremely difficult. So in order not to be held back, I explained with what brevity and clarity I could muster what those things, for which I was not able to find a suitable literal meaning, stood for in a figurative sense; I did not want them to be put off by being faced with reams of obscure discussion, and so be reluctant to take these volumes in their hands. Bearing in mind, however, what I wanted but could not manage, that everything should first of all be understood in its proper, not its figurative sense. . . ."[26]

The commentary itself, and not just this later statement, shows that at that earlier time Augustine saw figurative interpretation as the more suitable, because more flexible tool of thought than the often laborious search for the literal meaning. As his thoughts on interpretation at the beginning of the second book show, he gave priority to the literal interpretation.[27] But at the same time he was conscious of the great difficulties of practicing such an exegesis in consistent harmony with the truths of faith. He was aware of the limitations of his own theological, biblical, and philosophical competence in dealing with a text that raised many problems both of content and of linguistic expression.[28] He saw the danger that a literal understanding of the text could lead to a blasphemous idea of God, but when he chose the safer path of figurative interpretation,[29] he could

---

23. For example, ibid., I, 7, 11.
24. See ibid., I, 2, 2; I, 2, 5; I, 5 9; I, 17, 27.
25. See R. J. Teske, "A Decisive Admonition for St. Augustine?" *Augustinian Studies* 19 (1988) 85-92.
26. *The Literal Meaning of Genesis* VIII, 2, 5.
27. See *On Genesis: A Refutation of the Manichees* II, 2, 3; see *The Literal Meaning of Genesis* VIII, 1, 4; VIII, 2, 5. On the general question of biblical interpretation in *On Genesis: A Refutation of the Manichees* see C. Walter, *Der Ertrag der Auseinandersetzung mit den Manichäern für das hermeneutische Problem bei Augustin* (Dissertation; Munich, 1972).
28. See *Revisions* I, 18, 1 (CCL 57. 54).
29. See R. J. Teske, "Criteria for Figurative Interpretation in St. Augustine," in D. W. H. Arnold and P. Bright (eds.), *De Doctrina Christiana: A Classic of Western Culture* (Notre Dame,

appeal to the authority of the apostle Paul for taking this approach in his first attempt at exegesis of the Bible.[30] Moreover, allegorical interpretation was in the line of exegesis of Genesis that ran from Philo via Origen to Ambrose.

Not only did a figurative exegesis seem the safer method in comparison with a literal interpretation; it also enabled him, while drawing on his fund of metaphysical ideas, to find in Genesis all his own objections to the positions of the Manichees. In addition, a methodically figurative interpretation had the advantage of allowing him to communicate the truths of the faith in a vivid way by means of allegory and to impress them on his Christian readers.[31]

In characterizing this figurative meaning of scripture Augustine uses not only the words *figura* (see I, 13, 19) and *allegoria* (I, 22, 39), but also *aenigma* (II, 2, 3), *imago* (I, 17, 28), *similitudo* (I, 13, 19), *mysterium* (I, 3, 5), *sacramentum* (I, 22, 23), *signum* (I, 8, 14), and *velum* (I, 22, 33).

In Augustine's conception of things, however, the symbolic element of the creation story referred not only to spiritual and transcendent truths, these being understood by him wholly within the framework of his philosophical convictions. In this commentary on the scripture he drew a parallel, for the first time, between the six days of creation and the course of world history.[32] With a typological interpretation of the Hexaemeron as his starting point he worked out a doctrine on the ages of the world and a periodization of history. In later works he quite often repeats this division of history, but never again in the same detail and a comparable systematic form. To his mind, the biblical story of creation was not an historical account, but an advance notice of future events, in the guise of historical account: "There are no words therefore that can possibly describe how God made and established heaven and earth and every creature which he set in place there; but this commentary on the order of days, one by one, presents them as an account of things done, in such a way as to concentrate on them chiefly as predicting things to come in the future."[33] When interpreted typologically and understood as prophecy through history, the Hexaemeron makes known to human beings God's plan of salvation.

While the Manichees used the Bible as a treasury from which to draw citations in support of their theses, but citations torn from their contexts and no longer having any relation to the history of humankind, Augustine uses the Bible

---

1995) 109-122; idem, *St. Augustine on Genesis* (note 16, above) 21-24.

30. See *On Genesis against the Manichees* 2, 2, 3.

31. See J. Pépin, "Saint Augustin et la fonction protreptique de l'allégorie," *Recherches Augustiniennes* 1 (1958) 243-286.

32. See *On Genesis: A Refutation of the Manichees* I, 23,35-41. See P. Archambault, "The Ages of Man and the Ages of the World," *Revue des études augustiniennes* 12 (1966) 193-228; K.-H. Schwarte, *Die Vorgeschichte der augustinischen Weltalterlehre* (Antiquitas, Reihe 1; Abhandlungen zur Alten Geschichte; Bonn, 1966) 17-61; B. Kötting and W. Geerlings, "Aetas," in C. Mayer (ed.), *Augustinus-Lexikon* 1 (Basel, 1986-94) 150-158, especially 150.

33. *On Genesis: A Refutation of the Manichees* I, 23, 41.

in order to present this history as the continuous, purposeful saving activity of God on behalf of humanity. The "rest" of the creator on the seventh day is a symbol of the fact that after the ages of the world have run their course salvation history will end in a state of unalterable fulfillment.[34] Only then will God's activity as creator have reached its definitive conclusion. When thus interpreted, the biblical story of creation shows the world and history to be the two areas in which God's creative action embodies and manifests its power to create and determine history. The thoughts that Augustine will develop on a large scale later on in his *City of God* are thus already set forth, in a nutshell, in *On Genesis against the Manichees.*

Structure

The work does not have a homogeneous structure. It is true that it took modern biblical scholarship to recognize that the story of creation in Genesis 1-3 is made up of two different earlier narratives. But the early Christian interpreters were already aware that the account had two parts. In his first book, Augustine comments verse by verse on the first Genesis story (known today as the Priestly Document) and systematically discusses the objections of the Manichees. In the second book, however, he sets down the text of Genesis 2:4b—3:24 (known today as the Yahwist Document), and then explains some passages of it.

The result is the following structure.[35] After a Prologue (I, 1, 1-2) Book I first gives an historical commentary *(secundum historiam)* of the first story of creation (I, 2, 3—22, 34). The same text is then given a prophetic interpretation *(secundum prophetiam)*. At a first level of understanding, the seven days of creation point ahead to the seven ages of human history (I, 23, 35-41). In a second interpretive perspective they symbolize the seven stages in the lives of the faithful: from the first awakening of faith to rest in God after death (I, 23, 42—25, 43).

In Book II, before beginning his exegesis, Augustine explains the way his treatment will be structured: "So then, this whole text must first be discussed in terms of history, and then in terms of prophecy. In terms of history deeds and events are being related, in terms of prophecy future events are being foretold."[36] An historical commentary (II, 3, 4—23, 36) is followed by an interpretation on prophetic lines (II, 24, 37—27, 41), which again contains two parts. The biblical text is first related to the situation of a human group, insofar as the creation of Adam and Eve point ahead to Christ and the Church (II, 24, 37); then the text is

---

34. See ibid., I, 22, 34; I, 23, 41.
35. See D. Weber, "Communis loquendi consuetudo. Zur Struktur von Augustinus, *De Genesi contra Manichaeos*," *Studia Patristica* 33 (1996) 274-279.
36. *On Genesis: A Refutation of the Manichees* II, 2, 3.

related to the situation of the individual, insofar as the fall refers to the danger that individual orthodox Christians may be led astray by heretics (II, 25, 38—27, 41). After the completion of the exegesis an epilogue (II, 28, 42—29, 43) summarizes the most important Manichean criticisms of fundamental Catholic teachings about God, Adam, Eve, and Satan (II, 42). These objections, formulated mostly as questions, and the answer immediately given to each call to mind the method used in catechesis, while the brief summaries of the Manichean and the orthodox faiths (II, 43) call to mind the creed entrusted to each candidate before baptism.

The importance which Augustine attaches in this work not only to its antiheretical elements but also to its didactic intention can be seen in the fact that his interpretation of the biblical text is not limited to the passages criticized by the Manichees. Especially in Book I, he does usually present the relevant objections of his adversaries, but he also gives his interpretation even of passages not queried by the Manichees. This latter approach is especially to the fore in Book II, in which, apart from the concluding chapters, a reference to the Manichees is to be seen only occasionally.

Main contents

At first glance, Augustine's commentary resembles a series of answers to a series of very disparate questions. In fact, however, all the Manichean objections to the text of Genesis are reducible to this dilemma: one must accept the existence of an eternal principle that is parallel but opposed to God, or else one is caught up in a host of aporias and absurdities.

How did the Manichees argue? A day came, it is said (by Christians), when God created heaven and earth. But is it an acceptable hypothesis that a God exists who suddenly decided to create the world after not having done so previously through all eternity (I, 2, 3)? Why did he create at all (I, 2, 4)? According to Genesis, the earth was invisible and without any order. But it did already exist and must therefore have been previously created (I, 3, 5). Darkness covered the abyss. Therefore God himself was in darkness before he created light (I, 3, 6). Where did the darkness come from in which he existed at that point (I, 4, 7)? It, too, likewise existed by necessity!

This Manichean interpretation was internally coherent. The same postulate of a dualism found expression in the various questions. Behind the Manichean mythology, which was at first sight recondite, there was a logically structured dogmatic system as follows: In the primeval beginning, before any history, there existed originally a dualism formed of two natures, that is, Light and Darkness or Good and Evil or God and matter. Manicheism combined this doctrine of the two natures with a doctrine of three periods or times. The "time of the beginning" was the time in which the two unadulterated principles existed in opposition to one another. This first time was replaced by the "middle time" in which the attack of the world of darkness on the world of light led to a mingling of the two principles. The "third time" is the final state in which the dualism has been overcome. North African Manicheism identified the creator God of the Old Testament with the evil principle. In keeping with some earlier Christian traditions (Marcion) it therefore rejected the Old Testament and contrasted the good God of the New Testament with the evil God of the Old Testament. Because the created world is a mingling of light and darkness, it can only be the work of the evil God.

Augustine endeavored to refute this dualist system of thought on the basis of the Catholic creed and by way of Genesis itself. He discussed in detail the Manichean rejection of the Old Testament, the supposed pre-existence of matter, the conflict between light and darkness, the inadequate idea of God and of his freedom and immutability, the goodness of his activity, and finally the origin of evil. He set the one creator God over against the dualism of two principles, and over against the idea of an emanation he set the creative action of the all-powerful God who freely created the world out of nothing.[37] When Genesis spoke of darkness (Gn 1:2), it meant not an independent substance but the absence of light.[38] And when the biblical text used the phrase "in the beginning" (Gn 1:1), it did not provide any foothold for the existence of two equally eternal principles. The phrase did not imply any temporal reference but referred rather to Christ, since he was "the Word with the Father, through which and in which all things were made."[39] To the Manichean claim that evil was a substance Augustine opposed the dialectic of *conversio ad Deum* and *aversio a Deo*, in order to defend the freedom of the human will.[40]

The first book of *On Genesis: A Refutation of the Manichees* is given its structure by three main themes: creation; the human being as image of God; and the history of salvation. These three themes are directed against the central myth of Mani's teaching: its cosmogony, its anthropogony, and the doctrine of the three times.[41]

In Book II, apart from the epilogue, the dispute with the Manichees retreats into the background; only at isolated points does the exegesis show an unmistakable anti-Manichean thrust. The creation of man from the clay of the earth in

---

37. See ibid., I, 2, 4; I, 6, 10-7, 11.
38. See ibid., I, 4, 7.
39. Ibid., I, 2, 3.
40. See J. Ries, "La création, l'homme et l'histoire du salut dans le *De Genesi contra Manichaeos* de saint Augustin," in *De Genesi contra Manichaeos, De Genesi ad litteram liber imperfectus* (Lectio Augustini 8; Palermo, 1992) 65-97.
41. See *On Genesis: A Refutation of the Manichees* II, 7, 8-8, 11.

Genesis 2:7 greatly displeased the Manichees because they held the soul of Adam to be a particle of the divine nature. In contrast, Augustine explained in detail his understanding of the body-soul relationship before and after the fall.[42]

But Augustine had not only to come to grips with Manichean anthropogony; he also had to bring the materialistic and realistic portrayal in the biblical story into harmony with the spiritualizing movement of his own Neoplatonic philosophy. The complexity of this task led him to formulate his own anthropology in ways that did not always seem unambiguous. Did he hold the view that the first human beings were originally souls which then acquired a body only as a result of sin? Or did he believe that human beings had a bodily existence even before the fall, but that only after the fall did they receive bodies that were transitory and mortal? The interpretation of Augustine's views at that time has been the subject of intense discussion among scholars.[43]

There is also an anti-Manichean emphasis in the interpretation of the serpent in Paradise. Augustine does not let the opportunity slip of connecting the seductive words addressed to the first human couple (Gn 3:5) with the promise of a higher knowledge with which the Manichees had not only at one time drawn Augustine himself into fealty to them[44] but were still seeking missionary success among the faithful of the North African Church.[45]

Beyond a doubt, Augustine used various sources for this work, but a clear identification of them is possible in only a few instances. Chiefly deserving of consideration as concrete sources for Augustine's work are Ambrose *(On Paradise)*, Origen *(Homilies on Leviticus)*,[46] and Gregory of Elvira *(Homilies)*.[47]

Importance of the work

In this work that was composed before his ordination as a priest we can already see two literary genres in which Augustine would later distinguish himself as a theological writer: the exegetical commentary and the antiheretical treatise. Although in subsequent years he composed broader and deeper studies

---

42. See R. J. Teske, "St. Augustine's View of the Original Human Condition in *De Genesi contra Manichaeos*," *Augustinian Studies* 22 (1991) 141-154; R. J. O'Connell, book review of "R. J. Teske, *Saint Augustine on Genesis*," *Augustinian Studies* 22 (1991) 223-230; idem, "The *De Genesi contra Manichaeos* and the Origin of the Soul," *Revue des études augustiniennes* 39 (1993) 129-141.
43. See *The Advantage of Believing* 1, 9; 9, 21 (CSEL 15/1, 4 and 26).
44. See *On Genesis: A Refutation of the Manichees* II, 25, 38-26, 40.
45. See R. J. Teske, "Origen and St. Augustine's First Commentaries on Genesis," in R. J. Daly (ed.), *Origeniana Quinta* (Leuven, 1992) 179-185.
46. See Weber (ed.), *Augustinus: De Genesi contra Manichaeos* (note 16, above), 18-29; Carrozzi, *Sant'Agostino, Le Genesi difesa contro i Manichei* (note 16, above) 3-46.
47. See D. Weber, "Adam, Eva und die Schlange. überlegungen zu Augustins Interpretation des Sündenfalls in *De Genesis contra Manichaeos*," in *L'Etica cristiana nei secoli III e IV: Eredità e confronti* (Studia Ephemeridis Augustinianum 53; Rome, 1996) 401-407.

and interpretations of Genesis, his first work in this area is still not without its importance. The majority of the problems discussed in detail in the later works are already addressed in *On Genesis: A Refutation of the Manichees*. So, too, the answers later offered to these questions are given here in at least a basic way. The teaching on the city of God (I, 23, 38-41), the psychological analysis of the sinful act (II, 14, 21),[48] the essence of sin as pride, worship of the sinner's ego, and rebellion against God (II, 15, 42), the doctrine of the various senses of scripture (II, 2, 3), the theory of illumination (II, 16, 23-24), and, finally, the idea of the *rationes seminales* are but a few examples.

Anyone wishing to study the development of Augustine's theology, cosmology, anthropology, and conception of history will find in this work many anticipations of his later views. At the same time, the beginning stage represented by *On Genesis: A Refutation of the Manichees* makes it possible to measure the progress which Augustine made over the years in his exegetical method, theological terminology, and thinking about God, the world, and humanity. His first commentary gives evidence of the truth of the programmatic statement made at the beginning of this work. As he will later on in other controversies, Augustine here too appeals to the Pauline axiom in 1 Corinthians 9:11 in order to emphasize the deepening of the faith occasioned by the questioning of the heterodox. In not a few cases, it has been the stimulus of heretical views that has raised up theologians in the Church who have more deeply penetrated and better attested to the truth of the Christian creed.[49]

---

48. See *On Genesis: A Refutation of the Manichees* I, 2, 2. See *Expositions of the Psalms* 54, 22 (CCL 39, 672f.) 67, 39 (CCL 39, 896f.); *True Religion* 8, 15 (CCL 32, 197f.); *City of God* XVI, 2 (CCL 48, 499). See Y. Congar, "Die Wesenseigenschaften der Kirche," in J. Feiner and M. Löhrer (eds.), *Mysterium salutis* IV/1 (Einsiedeln, 1971), 357-599, especially 442-445; H. Grundmann, "*Oportet haereses esse*. Das Problem der Ketzerei im Spiegel der mittelaterlichen Bibelexegese," *Archiv für Kulturgeschichte* 45 (1963) 129-164, especially 148-152.

49. See *On Genesis: A Refutation of the Manichees* I, 2, 2. See *Expositions of the Psalms* 54, 22 (CCL 39, 672f.) 67, 39 (CCL 39, 896f.); *True Religion* 8, 15 (CCL 32, 197f.); *City of God* XVI, 2 (CCL 48, 499). See Y. Congar, "Die Wesenseigenschaften der Kirche," in J. Feiner and M. Löhrer (eds.), *Mysterium salutis* IV/1 (Einsiedeln, 1971), 357-599, espec. 442-45; H. Grundmann, "*Oportet haereses esse*. Das Problem der Ketzerei im Spiegel der mittelaterlichen Bibelexegese," *Archiv für Kulturgeschichte* 45 (1963) 129-164, especially 148-152.

Extract from *Revisions* (I, 10, 1-3)

1. Settled now back in Africa, I wrote the two books of *On Genesis: A Refutation of the Manichees*. It is true, of course, that I had had the Manichees in mind in those earlier books,[1] in whatever arguments I used in order to show that God is supremely good and unchangeable, and yet the creator of all changeable natures, and that no nature or substance is evil precisely as a nature or substance. These two books, however, were published expressly against them in defense of the old law, which they attack with all the zeal and fanaticism of their crazy delusion. The first book runs from where it says, *In the beginning God made heaven and earth* (Gn 1:1), as far as the completion of the seven days, where we read that God rested on the seventh day; while the second goes from where it says *This is the book of the creating of heaven and earth* (Gn 2:4) up to where Adam and his wife were sent away from paradise, and a guard was set over the tree of life. Finally at the end of that book I set the truth of the Catholic faith[2] over against the error of the Manichees, briefly and clearly intertwining what they say and what we in turn say in reply.

2. As for my saying: "That other light[3] however does not feed the eyes of birds, but the pure hearts of people who trust and believe God, and turn from a love of visible and time-bound things to the fulfillment of his commands, which is something all people can do, if they wish" (I,3,6): these new heretics, the Pelagians, must not think it is said in their way. It is, you see, absolutely true that all people can do this if they wish; but *the will is prepared by God* (Prv 8:35, LXX), and is so enlarged by the endowment of charity that they really can. The reason this was not added at this point is that it was not relevant to the question in hand there.

As for what you can read there (I,19,30), that we should take God's blessing them and saying *Increase and multiply* (Gn 1:28) to refer to their having children in the flesh after they sinned: if this cannot be taken in any other way but as

---

1. From the three books *Answer to the Academics* to the three *Free Will* written between his conversion in 387 in Milan and his return to Africa in 389.
2. He actually writes, with the curious idiom of what I call an inverted genitive, "the faith of Catholic truth." For the brief "intertwining" of what the Manichees say and what the Catholics say, see II,28,42—29,43.
3. The text used in the Italian edition omits the word "light," *lumen*; very possibly just a printer's error.

meaning that those two human beings would not have had human children unless they had sinned, I totally repudiate it.

Again, just because there are quadrupeds and winged creatures which seem to be solely carnivorous, it does not follow (I,20,31) that we can only take in an allegorical sense what the book of Genesis says about the green grass and fruit trees being given for food to wild animals of every kind and to all birds and all snakes. It could have happened, after all, that carnivores would have been fed by human beings on the fruits of the earth, had human beings, in return for the obedience with which they might have served God without any wrongdoing, earned the right to have all beasts and birds serving them in every conceivable way.

Again, you may well wonder how I could say about the people of Israel: "That people was still keeping the law with bodily circumcision and sacrifices in the middle of a kind of Gentile sea" (I,22,40), seeing that they were unable to offer sacrifices among the Gentiles, just as we see that they have continued to this day without sacrifices, unless their slaughter of a sheep at Passover may possibly be counted as a sacrifice.

3. In the second book there is also what I put about the word "fodder" very possibly signifying life (II,3,4); since the better translations have "hay" instead of "fodder," this does not seem after all to have been aptly said, seeing that the word "hay" is not as appropriate for signifying life as the word "fodder."

Again, I do not think I was right in ascribing the following words to a prophet: *What do earth and ashes have to be proud of?* (Sir 10:9), since they are not found in a book by an author we are absolutely certain should be called a prophet (II,5,6).

Nor did I understand the apostle in the way he himself meant it in quoting the text of Genesis, *The first man Adam was made into a living soul* (1 Cor 15:45), when I was myself explaining the text, *God breathed into his face the puff of life, and the man was made into a live soul*, or *into a living soul* (Gn 2:7). The apostle, you see, quoted this text to prove that there is an "ensouled" body,[4] while I on the other hand thought that what had to be demonstrated from this passage was that the whole man, not just the body of the man, was first made of a "soulish" or animal nature (II,8,10).

As for my saying, "Sins do no harm to any nature except its own" (II,29,43), the reason I said it is that the person who harms a just man does not do him any real harm, seeing that in fact he increases his heavenly reward, but really does harm himself by sinning, because on account of his will to do harm he will get

---

4. *Corpus animale, animale* being contrasted with *spiritale*, to make the contrast between our bodies in this life, animated simply by an *anima*, a soul (hence my neologisms "ensouled" and a little later "soulish") and our bodies in the resurrection which will be quickened by spirit, "enspirited." When we come to the passage itself in Book II, we may be able to see more clearly how Augustine's understanding of the verse differed from the apostle's.

back the very harm he has done. The Pelagians can certainly square this statement with their own doctrine, and say that that is precisely why the sins of others have never done babies any harm, because, as I said, "Sins do no harm to any nature except its own." What they fail to observe is that the reason original sin is contracted by babies, who of course pertain to human nature, is that in the first human beings it was human nature that sinned, and thus it is true that no sins did human nature any harm except its own.[5] It was indeed through one man, in whom all sinned, that sin entered the world;[6] I did not say, after all, that sins do no harm to any human being, but to any nature except its own.

Again, there is what I said a little later on in the same place: "There is no natural evil"; they could look for a similar escape route here, except for the fact that this refers to nature such as it was originally established without any flaw; that, after all, is what is really and properly said to be the nature of man. But we use the word in a transferred sense to call "nature" what a person is actually born with;[7] and it is that manner of talking the apostle was using when he said: *For we too were once by nature children of wrath, like the rest also* (Eph 2:3).

This work begins with the words: "If the Manichees were to choose the sort of people they meant to deceive."

---

5. This is a crucial, basic point about Augustine's doctrine of original sin, one stressed also by Aquinas, and an essential element in the Catholic doctrine: that original sin is *not* a personal sin, not an offense committed against God by any individual, not even by Adam and Eve, but is a "sin of nature." The expression "original sin," for which Augustine does bear much responsibility, is an unfortunate one, because "sin" does properly mean an act (or omission) committed by some person or persons; and human nature, not being an individual person or group of persons cannot commit any actual sin, or indeed perform any act—though it is true he says here, very carelessly, "In the first human beings it was human nature that sinned." But as human nature was at that point concentrated, so to say, in the first couple, it may be said to have sinned through being vitiated by that first sin actually committed by our first parents. So it suffers from an ingrained flaw or vice, and that is what is transmitted to children through their parents, from Adam and Eve on, together with the nature of which it is the flaw or vice. For Augustine this flaw or vice is *concupiscentia*, the lust inherent in the genital act; for Aquinas and a better, more developed theology, it is the lack of the grace of original justice, with which Adam and Eve were created, and which they forfeited by their actual sin.

6. See Rom 5:12.

7. The word *natura* in Latin being actually derived from *nascor*, "I am born."

Book I

Advised by friends to eschew elaborate rhetoric, he intends to help ordinary unlearned Catholics meet the attacks of the Manichees on the Old Testament

1, 1. If the Manichees were to choose the sort of people they meant to deceive, I too would also choose the appropriate words with which to answer them. But since they are hunting down both the well educated with their writings and the uneducated with their erroneous ways, and while promising them the truth are striving to turn them away from the truth, it is not with elegant and well-turned phrases that they are to be convicted of teaching nonsense, but with the evidence of reality. I fully agreed, in fact, with the opinion of some people who were genuine Christians and well versed in classical literature, who nonetheless saw clearly, on reading my other books[1] which I had published against the Manichees, that they would not be understood by the less well educated, or only with difficulty. They advised me out of the goodness of their hearts not to turn my back on the usual common way of talking, if I had it in mind to purge from the spirits of less educated people also such pernicious errors as these. The learned too, after all, can understand this ordinary and simple language, while the unlearned cannot understand that other sort.

2. So the Manichees then are in the habit of casting slurs on the scriptures of the Old Testament, which they have next to no knowledge of, and of mocking and deceiving with their gibes the weaker brethren and the little ones among us, who cannot then find any way of answering. There is no part of scripture, I mean to say, which it is not the easiest thing in the world to find fault with, to the dismay of those who do not understand it. But that is precisely why divine providence permits so many heretics to come along with various errors; it's so that when they taunt us and shower us with questions we do not know the answers to, we may at least in this way be shaken out of our mental sloth and start longing to become acquainted with the divine scriptures.

That is why the apostle too says: *There have to be many heresies, so that those who prove reliable may stand out among you* (1 Cor 11:19). Those who can

---

1. See note 1 above, on the extract from the *Revisions*. But the work he is more likely to have had in mind here is *The Catholic Way of Life and the Manichean Way of Life*, which he lists before this one on *Genesis* in *Revisions* I,7 as having been written in Rome while he was on his way back to Africa from Milan.

teach well are the ones who prove reliable in God's eyes. But they can only stand out among people when they teach; and they are unwilling to teach those who do not want to be taught. But many people are too lazy to want to be taught, unless they are sort of awakened from their slumbers by heretics making a nuisance of themselves with their taunts, so that then they start feeling ashamed of their ignorance, and begin to realize that they are being put in a dangerous position by this ignorance of theirs.

If they are people of sound faith, they do not give in to the heretics, but earnestly start inquiring what answer they can make to them. God, of course, does not abandon them; and so when they ask they receive, and when they seek they find, and when they knock the door is opened to them.[2] Those on the other hand who despair of being able to find what they seek in Catholic teaching are practically rubbed out by errors of all sorts; and if they still, nonetheless, go on persevering with their inquiries, they eventually return, tired out and thirsty after enormous toil, and almost dead, to the very springs from which they strayed away.

Answers to difficulties made by the Manichees about "In the beginning...,"
Genesis 1:1

2, 3. So then, this is how the Manichees are in the habit of finding fault with the book of the Old Testament which is called Genesis. On its first words, *In the beginning God made heaven and earth* (Gn 1:1), they ask, "In what beginning?" and go on to say: "If God made heaven and earth in some beginning of time, what was he doing before he made heaven and earth?[3] And why did it suddenly take his fancy to make what he had never made previously through eternal times?" Our reply to these questions is that God made heaven and earth in the beginning, not in the beginning of time but in Christ, since he was "the Word with the Father, through which and in which all things were made."[4] Our Lord Jesus Christ, you see, on being questioned by the Jews about who he really was, answered: *The beginning, as which I am also speaking to you* (Jn 8:25).

But even if we believe it was in the beginning of time that God made heaven and earth, we should of course understand that before the beginning of time there was no time. God, after all, also made times, and that is why there were no times before he made any. We cannot therefore say that there was any time when God had not yet made anything. How, I mean to say, could there be a time which God

---

2. See Lk 11:10.
3. Augustine says in *The Confessions* XI,12,14, that to this question "I will not respond with that joke someone is said to have made: 'He was getting hell ready for people who inquisitively peer into deep matters'; for this is to evade the force of the question." But no doubt he was tempted to do so on more than one occasion.
4. See Jn 1:1-3.

had not made, seeing that he is the one who forges all times? And if time began to be together with heaven and earth, no time can be found in which God had not yet made heaven and earth.

Why did it suddenly take his fancy? The question assumes that a lot of time had passed in which God had not constructed anything. But after all, no time, which God had not yet made, could have passed, since the constructor of times must be there before the times. Now the Manichees themselves certainly also read the apostle Paul, and praise him and hold him in honor; and by misinterpreting his letters they lead many people astray. So let them tell us why the apostle Paul said: ... *the recognition of the truth that accords with the loving kindness of God unto the hope of eternal life, which the non-lying God promised before eternal times* (Ti 1:1-2); what, I mean to say, could eternal times have had before them? This therefore is what they should be forced to explain, so that they may understand that they do not understand, when they thoughtlessly try to find fault with something about which they should instead have been making earnest inquiries.

4. If, however, they do not say, "Why did it suddenly take God's fancy to make heaven and earth?" but leave out the "suddenly," and just say, "Why did it take God's fancy to make heaven and earth?"[5]—you see, we do not say that this world is the same age as God, because the eternity of this world is not the same as the eternity of God. God, to be sure, made the world, and thus times began with the very creation that God made; and that's why times are called eternal.[6] All the same, times are not eternal in the same way as God is eternal, because God, being the constructor of times, is before all times. It's like all the things God made being *very good* (Gn 1:31); but they are not good in the same way as God is good, because he is the one who made, while they were what was made. Nor did he beget them from himself, to be what he is himself, but he made them out of nothing, so that they would not be equal either to him by whom they were made, or to his Son through whom they were made; and that is as it should be.[7]

So then, if these people ever say, "Why did it take God's fancy to make heaven and earth?" the answer to be given them is that those who desire to know God's will should first set about learning the force of the human will. You see,

---

5. He does not complete the sentence, but goes into a long digression about the difference between God's eternity and the eternity of time. But he repeats this "if" clause, and answers the question at the beginning of the next paragraph.

6. One will not find them, or the world or anything in it, called eternal in any modern English version of the bible; but where Augustine's bible used the word for anything created, we will sometimes find the word "everlasting" used; for instance, *of the everlasting mountains* (Ps 76:4), or phrases like "from age to age" or "for ever."

7. Literally, "for it is just"; *justum est enim.* It really looks as if a longer sentence has been cut off at this point, either in transmission, or else because Augustine was distracted by something while dictating, or because his mind suddenly went back to the question he started this section with, and to which he now returns.

they are seeking to know the causes of God's will, when God's will is itself the cause of everything there is. After all, if God's will has a cause, there is something that is there before God's will and takes precedence over it, which it is impious to believe. So then, anyone who says, "Why did God make heaven and earth?" is to be given this answer: "Because he wished to." It is God's will, you see, that is the cause of heaven and earth, and that is why God's will is greater than heaven and earth. Anyone though who goes on to say, "Why did he wish to make heaven and earth?" is looking for something greater than God's will is; but nothing greater can be found.

So let mere human beings put a curb on their brashness, and not go seeking what doesn't exist, in case they thereby fail to find what does. And if anyone desires to know God's will, they should first become friends with God, because anyone wishing to know a human person's will without being their friend would find everybody mocking their shameless folly. Nobody, however, becomes a friend of God except by total integrity of life and conduct, and by means of that end of the commandment of which the apostle says: *Now the end of the commandment is love coming from a pure heart and a good conscience and a faith unfeigned* (1 Tm 1:5).

God did not make heaven and earth out of any pre-existing material, and was not in darkness before he made the light

3, 5. As for what follows in the book of Genesis: *Now the earth was invisible and shapeless* (Gn 1:2), the Manichees find fault with it like this; they say: "How did God make heaven and earth in the beginning, if the earth was already there, invisible and shapeless?" So it is that by being keener on casting slurs on the divine scriptures than on getting to know them, they fail to understand even the most obvious things. What, I ask you, could be said more clearly than what we have here: *In the beginning God made heaven and earth; now the earth was invisible and shapeless?* This obviously means: In the beginning God made heaven and earth; now the very earth which God made was invisible and shapeless, before God distributed the forms of all things in their proper places and settings, with their duly arranged differences; before he said: *Let light be made*, and *Let a solid structure be made*, and *Let the waters be collected together*, and *Let the dry land appear* (Gn 1:3.6.9), and the rest of it which is set out in the same book in such a simple order that even little children can grasp it. Yet it all contains such great mysteries that those who have learned them either bewail the futile folly of all heretics, considering they are human, or find it a source of innocent merriment because they are so self-important.

6. It continues in the same book: *And there was darkness over the abyss* (Gn 1:2). The Manichees find fault with this by saying: "So was God in darkness

then, before he made light?" Indeed they themselves are in the darkness of ignorance, and that is why they do not understand the light God was in before he
made this light. These people, you see, know of no light except the kind they see
with the eyes of the flesh. And that is why they worship this sun which we share
the sight of, not only with the bigger animals, but also with flies and worms; and
they say that it is in a particle of the sun's light that God dwells.

But we for our part should understand that there is another light in which God
dwells, from which comes that light about which we read in the gospel: *That was
the true light, which enlightens every person who comes into this world* (Jn 1:9).
I mean, the light of this sun doesn't enlighten every person, but just the human
body and its mortal eyes; and here we are completely outclassed by the eyes of
eagles, which are said to be able to gaze at the sun much better than we can. That
other light, however, does not feed the eyes of birds, but the pure hearts of people
who trust and believe God and turn from a love of visible and time-bound things
to the fulfillment of his commands, which is something all people can do if they
wish,[8] because that light enlightens every person who comes into this world.
Darkness therefore was over the abyss before this visible light was made, about
which it goes on to speak next in this place.

Darkness is just the absence of light

4, 7. *And God said: Let light be made* (Gn 1:3), because where there is no light
there is darkness; not that darkness is actually something, but that the sheer
absence of light is called darkness. Just as silence is not an actual thing, but
where there is no sound it is called silence; and nakedness is not an actual thing,
but where a body is without clothes it is called nakedness; and emptiness is not
actually something, but a place in which there is no material body is said to be
empty. That's how darkness is not actually something, but where there is no
light, it is called darkness.

The reason I am saying this is that what they are in the habit of saying is:
"Where did the actual darkness over the abyss come from, before God made
light? Who had made or begotten it? Or if no one had made or begotten it, then
darkness was eternal"—as though darkness were an actual something. But, as I
have just said, it is the name given to the absence of light.

But they have been taken in by their own fables, and have come to believe that
there is a race of darkness, to which bodies belong, in their view, and the forms
and souls in those bodies; and that is why they think darkness is an actual something; and they fail to understand that darkness is only perceived when we
cannot see anything, just as silence is only perceived when we cannot hear

---

8. See the extract from *Revisions*, section 2, above.

anything. Now just as silence is nothing, so too darkness is nothing. But just as these people say that the race of darkness has been fighting against the light of God, so too any other simpleton can likewise say that the race of silence has been fighting against the voice of God.

However, we have not at present undertaken to refute and demolish these absurdities. What we have now undertaken to do is to defend the things they find fault with in the Old Testament, insofar as the Lord is good enough to grant us the power to do so, and to demonstrate in those places that the blindness of human beings is no match at all for the truth of God.

How the Spirit of God was borne over the water

5, 8. Coming now to the text: *The Spirit of God was being borne over the water* (Gn 1:2); this is how the Manichees usually find fault with it: "So the water," they say, "was where the Spirit of God lived, was it, and it contained in itself the Spirit of God?" They try with their twisted minds to twist everything, and are just blinded by their malice. After all, when we say, "The sun is being borne over the earth," we do not intend this to be understood, do we, as meaning that the sun lives in the earth, and that the earth contains the sun in itself?[9] And in any case the Spirit of God was not being borne over the water in the same way as the sun is borne over the earth, but in a different way which only few people understand. The Spirit, you see, was not being borne over the water through a certain distance of space, as the sun is borne over the earth, but through his own sublimely invisible power.

Let these people tell us, though, how the will of a craftsman is borne over the things that are to be crafted. But if they cannot grasp such human, everyday realities, let them fear God and seek in simplicity of heart what they do not understand, or else while they are bent on chopping up with their sacrilegious words the truth which they cannot see, the axe may slip and chop off their legs. I mean, the truth that abides unchangeable cannot be chopped up, but any blows that are aimed at it come boomeranging back, and strike much more severely those who have the nerve to take a swipe at what they must first believe if they are to earn the right to understand it.

9. Next they go on to ask, and question us in their insolent manner: "Where did the actual water come from, over which the Spirit of God was being borne? After all, it had not said earlier on, had it, that God had made the water?" If they

---

9. It is possible that an earlier generation of Manichees were more familiar with the Hebrew text here, and knew the verse as saying "the Spirit of God was hovering over the water"; in which case it would make slightly better sense to interpret it as meaning that the water was the place where the Spirit lived, like a water fowl. But the Manichees Augustine was dealing with were presumably using the same kind of Latin version of Genesis as he was, and so would just have been parroting what they had heard from their teachers from Syria and beyond.

were asking this question honestly and loyally, they would soon discover how the matter is to be understood. The water mentioned here, you see, does not mean the same as this water which we can see and touch, just as the earth which was called shapeless and invisible was not like this earth that can be seen and handled. But where it said *In the beginning God made heaven and earth*, by heaven and earth it meant the whole of creation which God made and set up.

The reason, though, that the names of visible things are given to these realities is out of consideration for the weakness of the little ones, who are less capable of understanding invisible things. So then the first thing to be made was basic material, unsorted and unformed, out of which all the things would be made which have been sorted out and formed; I think the Greeks call it *chaos*. This, you see, is what we read in another place, as said in praise of God: *You made the world from unformed material*, where some manuscripts have *from unseen material* (Wis 11:17).

Various names given to the basic material out of which God formed the cosmos; and this material he made from nothing

6, 10. And that is why we are dead right in believing that God made all things from nothing, because even though everything that has form was made from this material, this material itself all the same was made from absolutely nothing. We should not, you see, be like these people who do not believe that Almighty God could have made anything from nothing, when they observe that carpenters and craftsmen of any kind cannot make anything unless they have something to make it from, and that the carpenter is assisted by a supply of wooden planks and the silversmith by a supply of silver and the goldsmith by a supply of gold and the potter by a supply of clay, so that each can carry out his work. If they do not have the help, after all, of the kind of material they make things out of, they cannot make anything, since *they* are unable to make the material itself. I mean, the carpenter doesn't make wood, but makes something out of wood; and so with all other such craftsmen. But Almighty God did not need the help of any kind of thing at all which he himself had not made, in order to carry out what he wished. If, you see, for making the things he wished, he was being assisted by some actual thing which he had not made himself, then he was not almighty; and to think that is sacrilege.

7, 11. So then, that formless material which God made from nothing was first called "heaven and earth" where it said: *In the beginning God made heaven and earth* (Gn 1:1), not because that is what it already was, but because it was able to be that—the making of heaven, you see, is also described a little later on. It's as if, when we examine the seed of a tree, we were to say that the roots are there, and the trunk and the branches and the fruit and the leaves, not because they are in fact already there, but because they are going to come from there. That's how it says, *In the beginning God made heaven and earth,* as a kind of seed of heaven and earth, when the material of heaven and earth was still all unsorted; but because it was quite certain that heaven and earth were going to come from there, the material itself was also already called heaven and earth.

The Lord also talks in this way of speaking, when he says: *I will not call you slaves any longer, because the slave does not know what his master is doing; but I have called you friends, because I have made known to you everything that I have heard from my Father* (Jn 15:15)—not because this had already been done, but because it was most certainly going to be done. Shortly after that, you see, he says to them: *I still have many things to tell you, but you cannot take them now* (Jn 16:12). So why had he said, *I have made known to you everything that I have heard from my Father,* if not because he knew he was going to do this? So too the material could be called heaven and earth, from which heaven and earth had not yet been made, but nonetheless was not going to be made from anything else. Innumerable instances of such ways of speaking can be found in the divine scriptures, just as in our everyday talk, when we are absolutely certain that what we are expecting will happen, we say: "Take it as already done."

12. But he also wanted to call this still formless material invisible and shapeless earth, because among all the elements of the world, earth seems to have less specific form and appearance than the others. He called it invisible because of its darkness, and shapeless because of its formlessness. He also called the very same material water, over which the Spirit of God was borne as the will of the craftsman is borne over things to be crafted.[10] The reason though it is not absurd also to call this material "water," is that everything that is borne on the earth, whether animals or trees or grasses and anything else of that sort, starts off by being formed and nourished from moisture.

So all these names then, whether heaven and earth, or the earth invisible and shapeless and the abyss with its darkness, or the water over which the Spirit was being borne, are names for the formless basic material, so that an unknown thing may be introduced to the less educated in words they know; and not by one term only but by several, or else if only one were used people would think it was just that one thing they normally understood by that term. So then, it was called heaven and earth, because heaven and earth were going to come from it. It was called earth invisible and shapeless and darkness over the abyss, because it was formless without any appearance that could be perceived and handled, even if there had been any human being to perceive and handle it. It was called water, because it was there on God's work-bench, easy to work and malleable, for all

---

10. Even if there are few people who can get as far as understanding this, I am not sure all the same if it cannot be explained in human words, at least by a few people.

things to be formed from it. But under all these names there was the unseen and formless material out of which God set up the cosmos.

Quibbles about God seeing that the light was good

8, 13. *And God said, Let light be made; and light was made* (Gn 1:3). The Manichees are not in the habit of finding fault with this, but with what follows: *And God saw the light that it was good* (Gn 1:4). They say, you see: "So then, God did not know what light was before, or did not know what good was." Wretched creatures! That God was satisfied with his works causes them dissatisfaction, when they can see how a human craftsman, a carpenter for example, though in comparison with God's wisdom and power he is next to nothing, still takes such a long time over cutting and preparing his wood with axe and adze and plane, or turning it in a lathe and polishing it, until it measures up as far as it can to the standards of his craft and satisfies him as a craftsman. So then, because he is pleased with what he has made, does that mean that before he made it he did not know what good work was? Of course he knew in his mind, where the very knowledge of his craft is more beautiful than the things that are constructed by it. But what the craftsman sees inwardly in his knowledge of his craft he puts into effect outwardly in his work, and it is this, when perfectly finished, that satisfies him as a craftsman.

So then, *God saw the light that it was good*; these words indicate, not that some unfamiliar good suddenly dawned on God, but that something perfectly finished gave him satisfaction.

14. What if the text had said: "God observed with wonder that the light was good"?[11] What a hue and cry they would raise, what charges they would bring! For wonder or astonishment indeed does usually arise from unexpected things. And yet these people read in the gospel about our Lord Jesus Christ having wondered at, been astonished at, the faith of believers,[12] and they praise him for

---

11. What if the text had said, in the Latin: *Miratus est Deus lucem quia bona est*? The meaning of *miror* is, to be sure, "to be astonished, surprised, to wonder," in the sense of "marveling." And the problem is: why should Augustine have raised this curious possibility? And the thought occurred to me, as it has done on more than one occasion, that modern Spanish might give a clue to the change of meaning in Latin words in Augustine's Africa; and in Spanish *mirar* means to look, to gaze at. So perhaps *miror* in African Latin had come to mean, not just to be astonished, but also to see something with astonishment or wonder. I consulted my friend Dr. Duncan Cloud on the point, and he cited some evidence from the classical poets for the word's being used in the sense of *cum admiratione videre*, to see with astonishment or wonder; notably Virgil's *Aeneid*, V,35. Closer to Augustine, he referred me to Tertullian, *De Oratione* 22,9, addressing the Virgin: *Nemo miretur in tuam faciem*, "Let no one gaze on your face." So it seems there was already before Augustine's time a move of the word's meaning to what it came to have in Spanish. And again, perhaps some of those old Latin versions of Genesis circulating in North Africa did read here *Miratus est Deus*. But he does not suggest that here. I continue to find the section baffling.

12. See Mt 8:10.

it. Who though had made that faith in them if not the one who observed it with wonder? And even if someone else had made it, why should he who had fore-knowledge of things have observed it with wonder and surprise? If the Manichees can solve that problem, then they should note that the other one can be solved on the same lines. But if they can't solve it, what right have they to find fault with these texts which they won't allow are any concern of theirs, when they do not know the meaning of ones which they say do concern them?

You see, what is signified by our Lord being filled with wonder or astonishment at something is that we should be filled with wonder at it, because we still need to be moved or stirred in this way. So all such stirrings of his imperturbable spirit are signs, but signs of the master's teaching. And it is the same with the words of the Old Testament, which do not teach that God is weak, but which are used in order to flatter our weakness. Nothing, after all, can be said about God that is at all worthy of him. But so that we should be suitably brought up and helped to attain to those things that cannot be uttered by any human speech, things are said in scripture which we are able to grasp.

Why it does not say that God made the darkness

9, 15. *And God divided between the light and the darkness, and God called the light day, and the darkness he called night* (Gn 1:4-5). Here it does not say, "God made the darkness," because darkness as we have said above is just the absence of light. But still a distinction was made between the light and the darkness. Just as we make noise by shouting, while we make silence by not making a sound, because silence is when the noise stops, and yet we distinguish by some kind of sense between noise and silence, and call one thing noise and the other silence, so just as we are rightly said to make silence, in the same way God is rightly said in many places of the divine scriptures to make darkness, because he either does not give light to times and places or else withdraws it from them, just as he chooses.

This however is all said according to our way of understanding. In what language, after all, did God call the light day and the darkness night? Was it in Hebrew, or Greek, or Latin, or some other language? And so with all the other things he gave names to, you could ask what language he spoke. But with God there is just sheer understanding, without any utterance and diversity of tongues. But wherever it says "he called," it means "he caused to be called," because he so distinguished and arranged all things as to make it possible for them to be told apart and given names. Thus we, for example say: "That proprietor built this house," meaning he caused it to be built; and many such things are to be found throughout all the books of the divine scriptures. But later on we shall come back to the question of whether this is the right way of taking the expression, "God called," since the deeper we plunge into the scriptures and get used to them, the more familiar we become with their style and manner of speaking.[13]

Manichee slur on the order of evening and morning

10, 16. *And there was made evening and there was made morning, one day* (Gn 1:5). Here too the Manichees bring forward one of their slurs, thinking that this was said as though the day began from the evening.[14] They do not understand how the activity of making the light and dividing between the light and the darkness and calling the light day and the darkness night—so they do not understand how this whole activity belonged to the day; while it was after this activity, as at the close of the day, that evening was made. But because the night also belongs to its day, it doesn't say that one day has been completed until the night also has, when morning is made. Thus from then on the remaining days are reckoned from morning to morning. For now, when morning has been made and one day has been completed, the activity begins which follows from the morning which has already been made, and after that activity there is made evening, then morning, and another day passes; and in the same way the remaining days also pass from then on.

Difference between the water above and the water below the firmament

11, 17. *And God said, Let a solid structure be made in the midst of the water, and let it be a division between water and water; and thus it was made. And God made a solid structure, and divided between the water which is above the solid structure and between the water which is below the solid structure. And God called the solid structure heaven. And God saw that it was good* (Gn 1:6-8). I do not remember the Manichees finding any fault at all with this. However, that the waters were divided so that some would be above the solid structure, others below it, means in my opinion (since we have said that the basic material was given the name of water) that by the solid structure of heaven the basic bodily material of visible things was separated from the basic non-bodily material of things invisible. While the sky or heaven, I mean, is the most beautiful of all bodies, every invisible creature surpasses even the sky in beauty; and that perhaps is why the invisible waters are said to be above the sky, overtopping the heavens not by their local situation but by the greater worth of their nature—as a

---

13. I have switched around this sentence, beginning "But later on" and the one before it, beginning "Thus we for example." It seems clear to me that they have somehow or other ended up the wrong way around in the text.
14. As indeed it does in the Jewish way of reckoning!

few people are able to understand, though on this point one should beware of making any rash assertions, seeing how obscure it is and far removed from human perception. But however it may be, it must be believed before it can be understood.

And there was made evening and there was made morning, a second day (Gn 1:8). From now on all the phrases that are repeated are to be understood and explained as above.

The sea and dry land formed from the material earlier called invisible earth and then water

12, 18. *And God said, Let the water which is under the heavens be collected together into one collection, and let the dry land appear. And the water which was under the heavens was collected together into one collection, and the dry land appeared. And God called the dry land earth, and the collection of water he called sea. And God saw that it was good* (Gn 1:9-10). On this place the Manichees say: "If the whole world was full of water, how could the waters be collected together into one?" But it has already been said about the earlier verse that the name of waters was given to that basic material over which the Spirit of God was being borne, from which God was going to form everything. Now however, when it says, *Let the water which is under the heavens be collected together into one collection,* it means that that bodily material is being formed into the specific nature and appearance which these visible waters have. The very collecting together into one, you see, is the formation of these waters which we can see and touch. Every form, after all, is compressed into fitting the standard of unity.

And as for its saying, *Let the dry land appear,* what else is it to be understood as saying, but that that material is to receive the visible form which this earth has that we can see and touch? So that the earth was earlier on being called invisible and shapeless meant that the basic material was being named as unsorted and dark; and by the water over which the Spirit of God was being borne, another name was again being given to the same basic material. Now however, this water and earth are being formed from that material which was earlier on called by their names, before it received these forms which we can now see. We are told, by the way, that in Hebrew every collection of water, whether salt or fresh, is called a sea.[15]

---

15. The sea of Galilee, for example—the only example, perhaps.

Manichee quibble about the origin of poisonous, prickly plants, and trees that bear no fruit

13, 19. *And God said, Let the earth sprout grass for fodder-bearing seed according to its kind and likeness, and fruit trees making fruit, whose seed is in it acccording to its likeness. And thus it was made. And the earth thrust up grass for fodder and fruit trees making fruit whose seed is in it according to its likeness. And God saw that it was good. And there was made evening and there was made morning, a third day* (Gn 1:11-13). Here they are in the habit of saying: "If God gave orders for grass to spring from the earth for fodder, and also fruit trees, who gave orders for so many thorny and poisonous plants and grasses to spring up, and trees that bear no fruit?" In reply one must take care not to reveal any mysteries to the unworthy, nor to show them what things to come are being prefigured by the way things are said here.

So then what should be said is that it was through the man's sin that the earth was cursed, so as to bring forth thorns, not so that the earth itself should feel the punishment, since it lacks sensation, but that it might always be setting the criminal nature of human sin before people's very eyes, and thus admonishing them to turn away at some time or other from their sins and turn back to God's commandments. As for poisonous plants, they were created for punishing mortals or putting them through their paces, and all this on account of sin, because it was after sin that we became mortal. By unfruitful trees, however, human beings are being mocked and taunted, to make them understand how they should blush for shame at lacking the fruit of good works in the field of God, that is, in the Church, and to make them afraid, because they themselves neglect unfruitful trees in their fields and do nothing by way of cultivating them, of being neglected in their turn by God and left uncultivated.

So then, before the man's sin the text does not say that the earth produced anything but grass for fodder and fruit trees, while after his sin we see many prickly and unfruitful things springing up from the earth, for the reason, in my opinion, that we have just given. This, you see, is what the first man is told after he has sinned: *Accursed shall the earth be for you in all your works; in sadness and groaning shall you eat of it all the days of your life. Thorns and thistles shall it thrust up for you, and you shall eat the fodder of your field; in the sweat of your countenance shall you eat your bread, until you are turned back into the earth from which you were taken; for earth you are and into earth shall you go* (Gn 3:17-19).

Manichee slurs on the work of the fourth day

14, 20. *And God said: Let constellations be made in the solid structure of heaven, so as to shine upon the earth and to divide between day and night, and to be for signs and for times and for days and for years; and to be for brilliance in the solid structure of heaven, so as to shine upon the earth. And thus it was made. And God made the two lamps, the greater and the lesser; the greater lamp for the starting of the day, and the lesser lamp for the starting of the night, and the stars. And God placed them in the solid structure of heaven so as to shine upon the earth, and to preside over day and night, and to divide between day and night. And God saw that it was good. And there was made evening and there was made morning, a fourth day* (Gn 1:14-19).

Here the first question they ask is how it was on the fourth day that the constellations were made, that is, sun and moon and stars. How, after all, could the three previous days have been without the sun, since now we see that it takes the rising and the setting of the sun to complete a day, while the night is made for us by the absence of the sun, during its return from the other part of the world to the east? We answer them that it could have happened that the first three days were each reckoned according to the space of time it takes for the sun to go round, from the moment it comes out from the east until it returns again to the east. After all, human beings could be aware of this space and length of time even if they were living in caves, where they couldn't see the sun rising and setting. In this way it can be seen that such a space of time could have elapsed even without the sun, before the sun was made, and this space of time could have been divided up into those three days.

So this then is the answer we would give, were we not restrained by what it says there: *And there was made evening and there was made morning*, which we see cannot now be made without the sun's regular course. So then, it remains for us to understand that in that particular passage of time the actual changes from one work to the next were given these names: evening on account of the completion of the finished work and morning on account of the next work to come, from the similarity with human work, which for the most part begins in the morning and ends in the evening. The transference, you see, of words from human matters to express things divine is common form with the divine scriptures.

21. Next they want to know what it says about the constellations, *and let them be for signs and for times.* "Could those other three days, after all," they say, "have been lacking in times, or were not they included in periods of time?"

But in saying *for signs and times* it means so that times might be distinguished by means of these constellations, and told apart by human beings; because were time to run on without being distinguished by any precise moments, moments that are marked by the courses of the heavenly bodies, time could indeed run on and pass by, but it could not be grasped and articulated by human beings; like the hours which pass indeed on a cloudy day, and run through their proper time, but cannot be marked and distinguished by us.

22. As for its saying, *And God made the two lamps, the greater lamp for the starting of the day and the lesser lamp for the starting of the night*: it is really as if it said "for the empire of the day and for the empire of the night."[16] The sun, you see, does not just start the day, and then not also complete and finish it, while as for the moon, it sometimes comes out to us at midnight or at the end of the night. So if those nights on which it does this are not started by it, how was it made for the starting of the night? But if by "starting" you understand "being first," and by "being first" understand "being the emperor," then it is clear that the sun exercises imperial authority throughout the day, while the moon does so throughout the night, because even if the other constellations also appear then, she nonetheless surpasses them all with her brilliance, and therefore is very rightly said to be their empress.

23. As for its saying, *And let them divide between day and night*: here too they can cast a slur and say, "How had God already divided earlier on between day and night, if this is done by the heavenly bodies only now on the fourth day?" So therefore this is how it says here, *Let them divide between day and night*: it's as if it said, "Let them so divide day and night between themselves that the day is given to the sun, the night to the moon and the other constellations." These two periods had already been divided, but not yet between heavenly bodies. So from now on there would be certainty about the number of heavenly bodies, and about which would appear to human beings through the day and which through the night.

Quibbles about the work of the fifth day

15, 24. *And God said: Let the waters throw up reptiles of live souls and flying things flying over the earth under the solid structure of heaven. And thus it was made. And God made the great whales and every soul of animals and crawling things which the waters threw up, according to the kind of each, and every flying winged kind, according to the kind of each. And God saw that they were good; and God blessed them saying: Increase and multiply and fill the waters of the sea; and let flying things multiply upon the earth. And there was made evening and there was made morning, a fifth day* (Gn 1:20-23). The fault-finding they go

---

16. As Augustine will explain in his later and greater work, *The Literal Meaning of Genesis*, II,25,32, when dealing with the fourth day of creation, this curious problem arose from the translators of the old Latin versions being both excessively literal in their rendering of the Greek Septuagint and not too well versed in that language. The Greek word *arche* means both "beginning" and "rule"; so, as the versions we are familiar with put it, God made the sun to rule the day and the moon to rule the night. Where, the reader may ask, does "empire" come in? Well, the Latin word for "beginning" is *principium*, meaning "being first"; and from this comes the word *princeps* (English, "prince"), the number one person in the state; and this was the title of the post-Augustan Roman Emperors, who exercised a *principatus*, an imperial authority.

in for here is to ask—or rather to make a gibe—why it was not only the animals that live in the waters but also those that fly in the air and all with wings that the text says were born in the waters.

But everybody who is worried about this should know that this cloudy and moist air in which birds fly is usually classified with the waters by the most learned people who research these matters carefully. It is stiffened, you see, and made dense by exhalations and sort of steamy vapors from sea and land, and after a fashion grows fat enough on this moisture to be able to support birds in flight. That is why you get heavy dew on calm nights, and find the dew-drops on the grass in the morning.

In fact that mountain in Macedonia called Olympus is said to be so high that at its peak there is no wind to be felt and no clouds forming, because its height soars above this moist air in which birds fly around—and that is why, so the authorities insist, there are no birds flying up there. This information is said to come from people who were in the habit of climbing to the top of this mountain every year, to offer goodness knows what sacrifices. There they would scribble some signs in the dust, and find them unchanged the following year, which could not have happened if there had been any wind or rain in the place. Again, because the air up there was so thin that it couldn't fill their lungs, they would not have been able to last any time there unless they had held damp sponges to their noses, through which they could draw the denser sort of breath they were used to. So these people also testified that they had never seen any bird in that place.[17]

And so we have every justification for trusting scripture absolutely when it states that it was not only fish and other aquatic animals that were born of the waters, but also birds, because they fly around in this air, which rises up from the moist vapors of land and sea.

What was the point of God making so many different kinds of animal?

16, 25. *And God said: Let the earth throw up live soul according to every kind of quadrupeds and of snakes and of beasts of the earth. And thus it was made. And God made the beasts of the earth according to kind, and all crawling things of the earth according to kind. And God saw that they were good* (Gn 1:24-25). The Manichees are also in the habit of raising the following question and saying: "What need was there for God to make so many animals, whether in the waters or on earth, which are not necessary for human beings? Many of them are also pernicious and to be feared."

---

17. In *The Literal Meaning of Genesis*, III,2,2 where he also tells us about the meteorological peculiarities of Mount Olympus, Augustine quotes the poet Lucan as his authority; *Pharsalia* 2,271.

But when they say things like that, they are failing to understand how all these things are beautiful to their maker and craftsman, who has a use for them all in his management of the whole universe which is under the control of his sovereign law. After all, if a layman enters a mechanic's workshop, he will see many instruments there whose purpose he is ignorant of, and which, if he is more than usually silly, he thinks are superfluous. What's more, if he carelessly tumbles into the furnace, or cuts himself on a sharp steel implement when he handles it wrongly, then he reckons that there are many pernicious and harmful things there too. The mechanic, however, who knows the use of everything there, has a good laugh at his silliness, takes no notice of his inept remarks, and just presses on with the work in hand.

And yet people are so astonishingly foolish, that with a human craftsman they won't dream of objecting to things whose function they are ignorant of, but will assume when they notice them that they are necessary, and put there for various uses, and yet will have the audacity, looking round this world of which God is the acknowledged founder and administrator, to find fault with many things which they cannot see the point of, because they wish to appear knowledgeable about the works and the tools of the almighty craftsmen when in fact they know nothing about it at all.

26. I, however, must confess that I have not the slightest idea why mice and frogs were created, and flies and worms; yet I can still see that they are all beautiful in their own specific kind, although because of our sins many of them seem to be against our interests. There is not a single living creature, after all, in whose body I will not find, when I reflect upon it, that its measures and numbers and order[18] are geared to a harmonious unity. Where these should all come from I cannot conceive, unless it be from the supreme measure and number and order which are identical with the unchanging and eternal sublimity of God himself. If these insufferably talkative and wrongheaded people would just stop to think about this for a moment, they wouldn't go on boring us to death, but by reflecting themselves on all such beauties from the highest to the lowest would in all cases praise God the craftsman; and since none of these things is offensive to reason, then wherever our carnal senses are offended, they would put it down to what is due to our mortality, not to anything wrong with the things themselves.

Yes, of course all living creatures are either useful to us, or pernicious or superfluous. Against the useful ones they have nothing to say. Those that are pernicious are either to punish us or to put us through our paces or to frighten us, so that instead of loving and desiring this life, subject to so many dangers and trials, we should set our hearts on another better one, where there is total freedom

---

18. See Wis 11:20: *You have arranged all things in measure and number and weight*; here he substitutes "order" for "weight."

from all worries and anxieties, and get moving along the road to gaining it for ourselves by meritorious devotion.

As for the superfluous ones, what business is it of ours to call them in question? If you object to their not being of any use, be thankful they do no harm, because even if they are not needed for our homes, at any rate they contribute to the completion of this universe, which is not only much bigger than our homes, but much better as well; God manages it after all, much better than any of us can manage our homes. So then, make use of the useful ones, be careful with the pernicious ones, let the superfluous ones be. In all of them, though, when you observe their measures and numbers and order, look for the craftsman; and you won't find any other but the one with whom the supreme measure and supreme number and supreme order is to be found, and that is God, about whom it says what is so absolutely true, that he has *arranged all things in measure and number and weight* (Wis 11:20). In this way you will perhaps find more genuine satisfaction when you praise God in the tiny little ant down on the ground, than when you are crossing a river high up, let us say, on an elephant.[19]

Man made to God's image; Manichee gibes

17, 27. *And God said: Let us make man to our image and likeness; and let him have authority over the fishes of the sea and the flying things of heaven and all cattle and wild beasts, and all the earth, and all reptiles which crawl over the earth* (Gn 1:26). It is this question above all that the Manichees are in the habit of chattering on about, taunting us for believing that man was made to the image and likeness of God. What they have in mind, you see, is the shape of our bodies, and they are misguided enough to ask whether God has nostrils and teeth and a beard, and even internal organs and other things that are necessary for us. But of course it is ridiculous, not to say impious to believe there are such things in God, and that is why they deny that man was made to the image and likeness of God.

Our answer to them is that such bodily parts are indeed frequently mentioned in the scriptures when God is being proposed to hearers who are little ones,[20] and this not only in the books of the Old Testament, but also in those of the New. God's eyes are mentioned, and his ears, and lips, and feet,[21] and the Son is

---

19. Actually, he only says "high up on some beast of burden"; but an elephant makes his contrast better than any other such steed; so introducing it is, I suggest, absolutely true to his mind.

20. The Manichees were divided into two classes or groups, the Perfect, who were the leading lights and the aristocrats of the movement, and the Hearers, who were, so to say, its second class citizens, not committed to the rigorous discipline undertaken by the Perfect. Augustine himself had been a Hearer, and may well be reminding the Manichees here of the approach they too would have had to take in explaining deep matters to their "little ones," that is, the less well educated and the illiterate among their Hearers.

21. For example: ears in Jas 5:4, 1 Pt 3:12; eyes in Heb 4:13, 1 Pt 3:12; feet in Mt 5:35.

proclaimed in the gospel as being seated at the right hand of God the Father.[22] And the Lord himself says: *Do not swear by heaven, because it is the throne of God, nor by the earth, because it is the footstool for his feet* (Mt 5:34-35). Again, he says that it was by the finger of God that he was casting out demons.[23] But all those who have a spiritual understanding of the scriptures have learned to take these names as meaning, not parts of the body, but spiritual powers, as also such things as helmets and shield and sword[24] and many other such things. So then, the first thing to be said to these heretics is to ask them how they can have the impudence to aim gibes at the Old Testament for such ways of talking, when they can also see them used in the New—or perhaps they do not see them, but are struck blind when they start picking quarrels over them.

28. Nonetheless, they should know that in the Catholic school of doctrine the faithful who have a spiritual understanding do not believe that God is circumscribed in a bodily shape; and when man is said to have been made to the image of God, it is said with reference to the interior man, where reason is to be found and intelligence; and it is from this that he gets "authority over the fishes of the sea and the flying things of heaven, and all cattle and wild beasts, and the whole earth, and all the crawling things that crawl over the earth." After saying, you see, *Let us make man to our image and likeness,* he added straightaway, *and let him have authority over the fishes of the sea and the flying things of heaven,* etc. (Gn 1:26), precisely to make us understand that it was with reference, not to the body that man was made to God's image, but to the power by which he surpasses all cattle, all animals.

All the other animals, after all, are not subject to us on account of the body, but on account of the intelligence which we have and they do not—though as a matter of fact even our body is so constructed that it indicates how we are better than the beasts and therefore more like God. The bodies of all animals, you see, whether those that live in the water or those that live on land or those that fly around in the air, are bent forward to the earth, and do not have an upright posture like the human body. And this signifies that our spirit also ought to be held upright, turned to the things above it, that is to eternal, spiritual realities. In this way it can be understood, with the upright posture of the body there to remind us, that it is above all as regards the spirit that man was made to the image and likeness of God.

---

22. See Mk 16:19, Heb 1:3.
23. See Lk 11:20.
24. See Eph 6:16-17.

Authority over all animals given to humanity while still in its sinless state

18, 29. Sometimes they are also likely to say: "How did man receive authority over the fishes of the sea and the flying things of heaven and all cattle and wild beasts, when we see human beings getting killed by many wild beasts, and harm being done to us by many flying things which we would like either to avoid or to catch, and frequently aren't able to? So then, how can we be said to have received authority and power over these?"

Here the first thing to be said to them is that they go quite wrong in considering the man after sin, when he was condemned to the mortality of life as we know it, and lost that perfection which he had when made to God's image. But if his condemnation is of such a kind that he has so many animals under his command—I mean, although he can be killed by many wild beasts because his body is so fragile, he still cannot be tamed by any of them, while so many animals, indeed practically all of them, can be tamed by him—so then if this condemnation of man leaves him like that, what must we think about his final reign and dominion, which the divine voice promises him when he has been renewed and set free?

A spiritual interpretation of the blessing: Increase and multiply
and fill the earth

19, 30. As for the text, though, *Male and female he made them; and God blessed them, saying: Increase and multiply and reproduce, and fill the earth* (Gn 1:27-28), the question is indeed very properly asked how this coupling of male and female before sin is to be taken, and this blessing with the words, "Increase and multiply and reproduce and fill the earth." Is it to be taken according to the flesh or according to the spirit? It is quite legitimate, you see, for us to take it in a spiritual sense as well, and to believe that it was turned into a blessing of fertility in the flesh after sin.[25] Before that, you see, there was a chaste coupling of male and female, accommodated to his directing and her complying; and a spiritual brood of intellectual and immortal joys filling the earth; that is to say, giving life to the body and dominating it, that is, holding it in such subjection that the spirit suffered no opposition from it, no vexation.

A good reason for believing this is that they were not yet children of this age before they had sinned. For *the children of this age beget and are begotten* (Lk 20:34), as the Lord says, when he is pointing out that in comparison with the future life that is promised us this business of sexual reproduction is to be held in low esteem.

---

25. See his repudiation of this suggestion, or at least of its clear implication that without sin there would have been no sexual relations between Adam and Eve, in the extract from the *Revisions*, section 2, at the beginning of this volume.

A spiritual interpretation of the authority given them over all the animals

20, 31. And as regards their being told: *Have authority over the fishes of the sea and the flying things of heaven, and of all crawling things which crawl over the earth* (Gn 1:28): granted that it is by intelligence and reason that we clearly lord it over all these animals, this text can still also be properly understood in a spiritual sense, to mean that we should keep in subjection all the feelings and emotions of the spirit which we have in common with these animals, and should lord it over them by self-restraint and moderation. When these emotions, you see, are not strictly controlled, they break out and lead to the filthiest habits, and drag us off through a variety of pernicious pleasures, and make us like every kind of animal. When on the other hand they are controlled and brought into submission, they grow completely tame and live with us in a friendly association.

The emotions of the spirit, after all, are not something alien to us. They also browse together with us on the knowledge of the best ideas and moral principles and of eternal life, as it were on seed-bearing grasses and fruit trees and green plants.[26] And this is what gives us a happy and tranquil life, when all our emotions are in tune with reason and truth, and we call them joys and loves that are holy and chaste and good. If however they are out of tune, while nonetheless being heedlessly played on, they tear the spirit to pieces and scatter the fragments and make life utterly miserable; and then we call them disturbances, and lusts, and evil desires. About these we are now instructed to make every possible effort to crucify them in ourselves until *death is swallowed up in victory* (1 Cor 15:54). The apostle, you see, has this to say: *But those who belong to Jesus Christ have crucified their flesh, with its disturbances and desires* (Gal 5:24).

This at least, you see, ought to warn anybody off thinking that these words are to be understood in a purely literal, material sense: that green grass and fruit trees are given as food in Genesis to every kind of wild animal and to all flying things and all snakes, though we can see that lions and hawks and kites and eagles only feed on flesh, by preying on other animals; I believe the same is true of several kinds of snake which live in sandy deserts, where no trees or grass can grow.[27]

---

26. See Gn 1:29-30, where the first human beings are told that they will have the same vegetarian diet as all animals, the analogues of our emotions. Augustine, we must remember, is all the time talking, especially in an early work like this, in the Neoplatonic vein, in which the self, the "I" and "We," is just the human spirit or mind. But he is also stressing here, against the Manichees, that the body and its feelings and passions and emotions are not something totally alien to the real inner self, and hostile to it, an emphasis that will get more and more pronounced the older he gets and the more directly his pastoral responsibilities as a bishop put him in touch with the total, in-the-round humanity of his flock—and of himself.

27. See his comment on this in the passage from the *Revisions*, section 2, put at the beginning of this volume.

God saw that all things together were very good

21, 32. We must certainly not casually pass over the text: *And God saw all things whatsoever that he had made to be very good* (Gn 1:31). When it was dealing with them one by one, you see, it just said, "God saw that it was good"; but when it came to talking about them all, it was not enough to say "good" unless "very" was also added. God's individual works are found by sensible people who consider them to display, each in its own kind, admirable *measures and numbers and orders* (Wis 11:20); how much more must this be so with *all things together* (Sir 18:1), that is, with the universe itself, which is completed by all these individual things being brought together into one whole?

Every beauty, after all, that consists of parts is much more admirable in its totality than in any of its parts. Take the human body, for example; if we admire the eyes alone or the nose alone or the cheeks alone or the head alone, or the hands or the feet alone, and if we admire all the other parts one by one and alone, how much more the whole body on which all its parts, each beautiful by itself, confer their particular beauties? If by contrast a beautiful hand, which in the body was admired even on its own, is separated from the body, not only does the hand itself forfeit its own proper grace, but the other parts also are rendered unsightly without it. Such is the force and power of completeness and unity, that many things, all good in themselves, are only found satisfying when they come together and fit into one universal whole. The universal, the universe, of course takes its name from unity.

If the Manichees would only consider this truth, they would praise God the author and founder of the whole universe, and they would fit any particular part that distresses them because of our mortal condition into the beauty of the universal whole, and thus would see how God made all things not only good, but also very good. Thus if in some elaborate and well-turned speech we were to consider the single syllables, not to mention the single letters, which vanish the moment they are pronounced, we would find nothing in them to delight us and win our admiration. The whole speech, you see, gets its beauty, not from single syllables or letters, but from them taken all together.

Manichee mockery of the notion of God resting on the seventh day

22, 33. And now let us take a look at the text which they are in the habit of making fun of, with more impudence even than ignorance, where it says that God, on finishing heaven and earth and all that he had made, *rested on the seventh day from all his works, and blessed the seventh day and consecrated it, because he rested from all his works* (Gn 2:2-3). You see, what they say is: "What need did God have for resting? Was he perhaps worn out and tired by the works of the six days?" And they also point to the Lord's own evidence, where he says: *My Father is working up until now* (Jn 5:17), and on the strength of this they take in many unlearned people, whom they are trying to convince that the New Testament contradicts the Old.

But the people to whom the Lord says, *My Father is working up until now*, had over-literal ideas according to the flesh about God's resting, and by observing the sabbath in an over-literal way according to the flesh, they failed to see what was represented by the real meaning of that day. In the same way these people, though with a quite contrary intention, fail equally to understand the sacramental significance of the sabbath. Thus both have been ignorant of what the sabbath really is, the former by observing it over-literally according to the flesh, the latter by being over-literal in their detestation of it according to the flesh. So then, let each and every one of them cross over to Christ so that *the veil may be taken off* (2 Cor 3:16), as the apostle says. The veil is taken off, you see, when the covering of comparison and allegory is taken off, so that the naked truth can be seen.

34. So then, the first thing to be done is to notice and learn the rule for this manner of speaking in many places of God's scriptures. What else, after all, is signified when God is said to have rested from all his works, which he had made very good, but the rest which he is going to give us from all our works, if we too have done good works? It is in accordance with this figure of speech that the apostle also says: *For we do not know what we should pray for as we ought; but the Spirit himself pleads for us with inexpressible groans* (Rom 8:26). The Holy Spirit, after all, doesn't groan, as though he were in want or in sore straits, seeing that he intercedes for the saints at God's behest; but he is said to do so himself because he moves us to turn our groanings into prayers, which we only do as moved to it by him.

It is the same with that other text: *The Lord your God is testing you, in order to know if you love him* (Dt 13:3). It is not, you see, in order to know this himself, from whom nothing is hidden, but it's in order to make us know how much progress we have made in loving him that he permits us to be tried and tested. It is in accordance with the same manner of speaking that our Lord also says about the end of the world that he doesn't know the day and the hour.[28] Can there be anything, after all, that he is ignorant of? But because it was in the interests of his disciples to withhold this knowledge from them, he said that he didn't know, because by not telling them he caused them not to know.[29]

Those who are familiar with this figure of speech can invoke it to solve many apparent problems in the divine scriptures without any difficulty.

---

28. See Mt 24:36.
29. In accordance with the same style he also said that the Father alone knows the very day, because he made the Son know it.

Our ordinary way of talking is full of the same sort of thing; as when we talk about a cheerful day because it makes us cheerful and sluggish cold weather because it makes us sluggish, and a blind ditch because we do not see it, and a polished tongue because it produces polished words; and finally we talk about the times being at rest from all troubles, times in which it is we ourselves who are at rest from all troubles.[30]

But God was said to have rested from all his works, which he had made very good, because it is in him that we rest from all our works, if we have made our works good; because, too, our good works themselves are to be attributed to him who calls us, who instructs us, who shows us the way of truth, who entices us also to choose it for ourselves, and furnishes us with the strength to fulfill his commands.

The six days of creation represent the six ages of the world

23, 35. But I reckon that more thorough consideration is called for of why God's resting is assigned to the seventh day. For what I see throughout the whole tapestry of the divine scriptures is some six working ages, distinguished from each other by definite border posts, so to say, pointing in hope to rest on a seventh age; and I see these six ages as being like those six days in which the things were made which scripture describes God as making.

The first age

The very beginnings of the human race, you see, in which it began to enjoy this light, can be suitably compared to the first day, on which God made light. This age is to be counted as a sort of infancy of the total age of the world, which we ought to think of, in comparison with its vast extent, as one adult human being; every human being, after all, when first born and seeing the light of day, lives through the first age of infancy. This age stretches from Adam up to Noah in ten generations.[31] A kind of evening of this day is made by the flood, because our infancy too is sort of blotted out by a flood of oblivion.

The second age

36. And the morning of the second age starts from the days of Noah as a kind of childhood, and stretches up to Abraham in ten more generations.[32] And it can be suitably compared to the second day, on which the solid structure was made between water and water, because the ark which had Noah and his family in it

---

30. We do not say most of these things in English; but we can no doubt think of similar things we do say—for example, instead of blind ditches we talk of blind corners.
31. See Gn 5.
32. See Gn 11:10-27.

was a solid structure between the waters on which it was floating and the waters from above which were raining on it. This age is not blotted out by a flood, because our childhood is not wiped clean off the plates of memory by oblivion. We remember having been children, after all, but not having been babies. The evening of this age is marked by the confusion of tongues inflicted on the people who were building the tower,[33] and then morning comes with Abraham. But neither did this second age procreate the people of God, because childhood is not adapted to procreation any more than infancy.

The third age

37. So then morning is made from Abraham, and the third age follows, like adolescence. And it can be suitably compared with the third day, in which the earth was separated from the waters. All the nations, you see, are aptly signified by the name of sea, unstable in their errors and tossed about by the doctrinal futilities of idolatry as if by all the winds of heaven. So then from these futilities of the nations and the stormy waves of this world the people of God was separated through Abraham, like the earth when it appeared as dry land, thirsting, that is, for the heavenly showers of God's commandments. This people by worshiping one God, like earth watered to make it capable of producing beneficial crops, received the holy scriptures and prophecies. This age, you see, could already procreate a people for God, because the third age of life too, that is adolescence, is already capable of having children.

And that is why Abraham was told: *I have set you up as the father of many nations; and I will increase you exceedingly much, and I will set you up into nations, and kings shall come out from you. And I will set up my covenant between me and you, and between your seed after you in their generations for an eternal covenant, so that I may be God for you and for your seed after you; and I will give to you and to your seed after you the land in which you are dwelling, all the land of Canaan for an eternal possession, and I will be their God* (Gn 17:5-8). This age goes from Abraham to David in fourteen generations.[34] The evening of this age is in the sins of the people by which they transgressed the divine commandments, up until the malice of that worst of kings, Saul.

The fourth age

38. And from there morning is made with the reign of David. This age resembles youth; and in very truth, among all the ages of man youth reigns as king, and is the solid adornment of them all. And that is why it is suitably compared with the fourth day, on which the heavenly bodies were made in the solid structure of

33. See Gn 11:1-9.
34. See Mt 1:17.

heaven. What after all more manifestly signifies the splendors of kingship than the majesty of the sun? And the splendor of the moon indicates the people complying with the royal authority like the synagogue itself, and the stars represent its leaders, and all of them on the stable foundation of the kingdom, as in the solid structure of heaven. The kind of evening of this age occurs in the sins of the kings, for which that nation deserved to be taken into captivity and enslaved.

The fifth age

39. And the morning is made with the exile in Babylon, when by that captivity the people was gently set down to have a holiday abroad.[35] And this age reaches as far as the coming of our Lord Jesus Christ; being the fifth age, it marks the long slope down from youth to old age;[36] not yet old age, but no longer youth; the age of the older man, whom the Greeks call a *presbytes*; for an old man is called by them a *geron*, not a *presbytes*. And in very truth that is how this age sloped down in decline from the muscular vigor of the kingdom, and was enfeebled in the Jewish people, in the way a man grows older from his youth.

And it is suitably compared with that fifth day, on which the animals were made in the waters, and the flying things of heaven, after those people started to live among the Gentile nations as in the sea, and to have an unsettled and unstable residence, like flying birds. But clearly there were also great whales there, that is, those great men who were able to dominate the stormy waves of the world rather than submit to the slavery of that captivity. You see, they were not corrupted by any terror into worshiping idols. Here one should certainly notice that God blessed those animals, saying *Increase and multiply and fill the waters of the sea, and let the flying things multiply upon the earth* (Gn 1:22), because in fact the Jewish nation did multiply very much from the time when it was scattered among the nations. The kind of evening of this day, that is, of this age, comes with the multiplication of sins among the Jewish people, which so blinded them that they were even unable to recognize the Lord Jesus Christ.

The sixth age

40. Morning though is made from the preaching of the gospel by our Lord Jesus Christ, and thus the fifth day is brought to an end; now begins the sixth in which the age of the *old man* (Eph 4:22; Col 3:9) becomes evident. In this age, you see, that kingdom of the flesh has been thoroughly worn down, when not only was the temple demolished but the very sacrifices came to an end; and now that nation, as far as the authority of its kingdom goes, is dragging out as it were

---

35. Set down *in peregrino otio* in the Latin; literally "in foreign leisure"—which is what holidays abroad, so much the vogue nowadays, are presumably meant to be.
36. Latin had no word or phrase for "middle age," whereas Greek, it seems, was able to make that useful distinction between middle and old age.

the last shreds of life. In this age, however, as in the old age of a very old man, the *new man* (Eph 4:24; Col 3:10) is born, who is already living according to the spirit. For on the sixth day it was said: *Let the earth produce live soul* (Gn 1:24)—because what had been said on the fifth day was: *Let the waters produce*, not live soul, but *reptiles of live souls* (Gn 1:20), since reptiles are bodies, and that people was still enslaved to the law by bodily circumcision and sacrifices as though in the sea of the Gentile nations.[37] Here however he talks of "live soul," alive with the life in which a longing for eternal realities is beginning to show itself.

So then, the snakes and cattle which the earth produces signify the nations which are now steadily going to believe the gospel. About these it is said, in that receptacle which was shown to Peter in the Acts of the Apostles: *Kill and eat*; and when he called them unclean, he was given the answer: *What God has cleansed, do not you call unclean* (Acts 10:13.15).

Next the man[38] is made *to the image and likeness of God* (Gn 1:26.27), just as in this sixth age our Lord is born in the flesh, of whom it is said through the prophet: *And he is the man, and who will acknowledge him?*[39] And just as on that day *male and female* (Gn 1:27), so also in this age Christ and the Church. And the man is put in charge on that day of cattle and snakes and the flying things of heaven, just as in this age Christ rules the souls that defer to him, which have come to his Church partly from the Gentiles, partly from the people of the Jews. They have come so that people may be tamed and domesticated by him, whether they had been given over to fleshly concupiscence like cattle, or had been groping in the darkness and murk of curiosity as if they were snakes, or soaring up on the wings of pride as if they were birds.

And just as on that day the man and the animals with him feed on seed-bearing plants and the fruit of fruit trees and green plants, so too in this age any spiritual man who is a good minister of Christ and imitates him to the best of his ability feeds spiritually together with the people on the nourishment provided by the holy scriptures and the divine law. This is partly to make them

---

37. See the comment on this statement in the passage from the *Revisions*, section 2, at the beginning of this volume.
38. Augustine identifies the making of man in Genesis 1:27 with the making of the first man, Adam, from the mud of the earth in Genesis 2:7; so one has sometimes to translate him, as here, as saying "the man" (that is, the first man), while at others he is clearly talking about "man in general." Latin, having no definite or indefinite article, did not raise—or shall we say, it evaded—this particular little problem.
39. There is no such prophetic text. The old Maurist editors prudently give no reference; the text used by the Italian editors refers to Hebrews 2:6, whose author Augustine would certainly not have called a prophet. But there the author is quoting Psalm 8:4, "What is man that you should remember him?" etc. and indeed applying the whole psalm to Christ. I myself would suggest that since Augustine is here talking precisely of Christ's "birth in the flesh," the text he had in mind and was paraphrasing with excessive freedom, was Isaiah 53:8, "His begetting, who will declare?"

fertile with ideas and fluent speech, as by feeding on seed-bearing plants; partly to provide moral guidance for human life together, as by feeding on the fruit of fruit trees; partly to lend vigor to their faith, hope and charity right up to eternal life, as by feeding on green, that is to say evergreen, plants, which cannot be shriveled up by the summer heat of any tribulations. But spiritual people feed on these foodstuffs in such a way that they come to an understanding of many things, while those who are *of the flesh, that is, little ones in Christ* (1 Cor 3:1), like God's sheep, do so in such a way that they take many things on faith which they are unable as yet to understand; nonetheless all have the same food.

The seventh age

41. There is a sort of evening of this sixth day—and I hope to goodness it does not overtake us, provided that is it hasn't already begun, because it is the one about which the Lord says: *Do you suppose when the Son of Man comes he will find faith on the earth?* (Lk 18:8). After this evening there will be made morning when the Lord himself is going to come in glory. Then those who were told, *Be perfect, like your Father who is in heaven* (Mt 5:48), will take their rest with Christ from all their works. Such people, you see, do works that are "very good"; after such works indeed a rest is to be hoped for on the seventh day which has no evening.

There are no words, therefore, that can possibly describe how God made and established heaven and earth and every creature which he set in place there; but this commentary on the order of the days, one by one, presents them as the account of things done, in such a way as to concentrate on them chiefly as predicting things to come in the future.

24, 42. It may, however, worry some people that in these ages of the world we observed the first two being unfolded in ten generations each, while the three following ones are each woven out of fourteen generations,[40] and this sixth age is not defined by any particular number of generations at all. But then it can easily be seen in the case of any individual human being that the first two ages, infancy and childhood, cling to the senses of the body; of these there are five: sight, hearing, smell, taste and touch; double the number five, because of the two sexes, male and female, from which such generations arise, and you get ten.

But now from adolescence onward, when reason begins in human beings to get the upper hand, the five senses are joined by knowledge and activity, which guide and organize the life we lead. So now we start having the number seven. Double it in the same way because of the two sexes, and it clearly comes out to fourteen generations which the three following ages have, those of the adolescent, of the youth and of the older person. But just as old age in us is not defined

---

40. See Mt 1:17.

by any fixed number of years, but however long anybody lives after those five ages, it is counted as old age; so in the same way in this age of the world there is no evident number of generations, and this is to keep the last day under wraps, which has to be kept hidden for our own good, as the Lord pointed out.[41]

A more personal allegorical interpretation of the seven days

25, 43. We also, one and all, have those six days in our personal lives, distinguished from each other in good works and an upright way of life, after which we should be hoping to rest. On the first day we have the light of faith, when we begin by believing visible things,[42] and it is on account of this faith that the Lord was prepared to appear in visible form. On the second day we have a kind of solid structure in the discipline by which we distinguish between things of the flesh and things of the spirit, as between the nether and the upper waters. The third day is the one on which we separate our minds from the slippery slope and the stormy waves of fleshly temptations, like the dry land from the disturbances of the sea, to bear the fruits of good works, so that we can now say: *With the mind I serve the law of God, but with the flesh the law of sin* (Rom 7:25). On the fourth day, on which we have already been making and discerning spiritual perceptions in that solid structure of discipline, we see what unchangeable truth is, which shines in the soul like the sun; and we have the soul made a participant in this truth itself, and bestowing order and beauty upon the body, like the moon lighting up the night; and like all the stars, twinkling and shining in the night, we have those spiritual perceptions in the foggy darkness of this life.

Made stronger and braver by awareness of these things, we begin to produce results on the fifth day, acting in this most turbulent world, as in the waters of the sea, in the interests of brotherhood and good fellowship; we produce from bodily activities, which pertain to this sea, that is, to this present life, "reptiles of live souls," that is, works which benefit live souls; also "great whales," that is, the bravest kinds of action which contemptuously smash their way through the

---

41. See Acts 1:7; 1 Thess 5:1-2.
42. A strange description of faith, surely, as believing visible things! But it was basic to Augustine's Christian spirituality to accept, to trust, to believe the material world as telling us about its maker; and a basic affirmation against the Manichees, who had no trust or faith in the material world at all, but rejected it as evil. Augustine stayed with this idea and deepened it all his life. In *The Trinity*, XII and XIII, he will develop the idea of faith being an act of the feminine function of the mind, of knowledge as distinct from wisdom, and will conclude that the immediate object of Christian faith is the *incarnate* Word, precisely the flesh, the visible material humanity of Jesus Christ. There he has not been thinking any more of the Manichees, but rather of the Platonists. About them he had said in the *Confessions*, VII,9,13: "In their books I read (not that the same words were used, but precisely the same doctrine was taught...) that *in the beginning was the Word, and the Word was with God; he was God. He was with God in the beginning....*; but that *the Word was made flesh and dwelt among us*, I did not read there." So Christian faith begins with the man, Christ Jesus.

stormy waves of the world, and "the flying things of heaven," voices that is to say by which heavenly truths are proclaimed. On the sixth day, however, we produce "live soul from the earth"; that is, from the stronghold of our minds, where we already have the spiritual fruit of good thoughts and ideas, we direct all the movements of our spirit so that it may be "a live soul," one at the service, that is, of reason and justice, not of foolhardiness and sin. In this way too may the man be made to the image and likeness of God, male and female, which here means understanding and activity; and may these be mated to fill the earth with spiritual offspring, that is, to subdue the flesh and do all the other things which have been mentioned above as belonging to human perfection. In all these days of this sort evening consists in the completion or perfection of the various works, and morning in the start of the ones that follow.

After the works of this sort of six days, works that are very good, we should be hoping for everlasting rest, and should understand what it really means that *God rested on the seventh day from all his works* (Gn 2:2), because not only is he the one who works these good works in us, ordering us to work them, but it is also he that is rightly said to rest, because at the end of all these works he bestows himself on us as our rest. Just as a householder, you see, is rightly said to build a house, when he does it, not by the work of his own hands but of those whose services he commands, so too is he rightly said to rest from his works when the building is completed and he permits the men he was employing to have a holiday and to enjoy themselves in merrymaking.

Book II

A more detailed account of the creation of the man, to be taken figuratively, not literally

1, 1. The listing of the seven days and the presentation of their works is given a kind of conclusion, in which everything that has been said already is called *the book of the creating of heaven and earth* (Gn 2:4), even though it is only a small part of the book as a whole. But still it was entirely appropriate to give it this name, because these seven days furnish us with a miniature symbolic picture of the entire span of world history from start to finish. Then it goes on to tell the story of the man in more detail; and this whole account is to be analyzed in figurative, not literal terms, to put the minds of those who seek the truth through their paces, and lure them away from the business of the world and the flesh to the business of the spirit. This, you see, is how it goes:

This is the book of the creating of heaven and earth, when the day had been made on which God made heaven and earth, and all the greenery of the field before it was upon the earth, and all the fodder of the field before it sprouted. For God had not yet rained upon the earth, nor was there a man to work on it. But a spring was coming up from the earth, and was watering all the face of the earth. And then God fashioned the man from the mud of the earth and blew into his face the puff of life, and the man was made into a living soul. And then God planted Paradise[1] in Eden to the east, and put the man there whom he had fashioned. And God still produced from the earth every tree that had a beautiful look about it, and was good for eating; and he planted the tree of life in the middle of Paradise, and the tree of knowledge of good and evil.

Now a river was coming forth out of Eden, and was watering Paradise; from there it is divided into four parts. The name of one, Pishon; this is the one which goes round the whole land of Havilah; there is gold there, indeed the gold of that land is the best; there is carbuncle there and leek-green stone. And the name of the second river is Gihon; this goes round the whole land of Ethiopia. And the

---

1. Whenever Augustine is using "paradise" as a proper name for that original enchanted garden, as we also do in English, I give it a capital P. But whenever it has to be translated with an article, definite or indefinite, as in a phrase like "the paradise of pleasure," I give it a lower case p, because then it is being used in its original (Persian) sense of a park, nearly always a royal one.

third river is the Tigris; this is the one that streams down over against the Assyrians. And the fourth river is called the Euphrates.

And the Lord God took the man whom he had made and put him in Paradise to work there, and to guard it. And the Lord God commanded Adam, saying: From every tree that is in Paradise you shall eat for food; but of the tree of knowledge of good and evil you all shall not eat from it; for on the day you all eat from it, you all shall die the death.

And the Lord God said: It is not good for the man to be alone; let us make him a help like him. And whatever God had fashioned, from every kind of cattle and from every kind of beasts of the field, and from every kind of flying things flying under heaven, he brought them to Adam, for him to see what to call them;[2] *and what Adam called them all, live soul, that is its name. And after this Adam called out the names of all cattle and of all the birds of heaven and of all the beasts of the field; and according to what Adam called them, that is their name until the present day.*

But for Adam himself there was not yet any help like him. And God sent a slumber on Adam, and he fell asleep; and God took one of his ribs, and filled up its place with flesh, and God formed the rib which he had taken from Adam into a woman. And he brought her to Adam to see what he would call her. And Adam said: This now bone out of my bones and flesh from my flesh, this shall be called woman since she was taken from her man; and she shall be my help. For this reason a man shall leave father and mother and shall be joined to his wife; and they shall be two in one flesh. And they were both naked, Adam and his woman, and they were not embarrassed.

2. *Now the serpent was wiser than all the beasts which were upon the earth which the Lord God had made. And the serpent said to the woman: Why did God say that you are not to eat from every tree that is in Paradise? And the woman said to the serpent: From every tree that is in Paradise we do eat; but from the fruit of the tree which is in the middle of Paradise God said we are not to eat, not even to touch it, lest we die. And the serpent said to the woman: You will not die the death; for God knew that on the day you take a bite from it your eyes will be opened, and you will be as gods, knowing good and evil.*

And the woman saw that the tree was good for eating and that it was good for the eyes to see and to gain knowledge; and she took fruit from that tree and took a bite, and gave to her man; and Adam accepted it and took a bite; and their eyes were opened, and then they knew that they were naked; and they took fig-leaves for themselves and made themselves aprons. And when they heard the voice of the Lord strolling in Paradise at evening, Adam and his woman hid themselves

---

2. From 9,16 below it does seem as if this is how Augustine at this stage of his study of Genesis understood the phrase: that God brought the animals to Adam, not so that he, God, might see what Adam would call them, but so that Adam might see what he himself should call them.

from before the face of the Lord God at that tree which was in the middle of Para-dise.

And the Lord God called Adam and said to him: Adam, where are you? And he said to him: I heard your voice, Lord, in Paradise, and I was afraid, and I hid myself because I am naked. And the Lord God said: Who told you that you are naked—unless it's that you have taken a bite from that tree from which I had told you from it alone not to take a bite? And Adam said: The woman whom you gave me, she gave it me to eat, and I took a bite. And God said to the woman: Why did you do this? And the woman said: The serpent led me astray, and I took a bite.

And the Lord God said to the serpent: Accursed are you from all cattle and every kind of beasts. Upon your bosom and your belly shall you crawl, and earth shall you eat all the days of your life. And I will set enmity between you and the woman, and between your seed and between her seed. She will look out for your head, and you for her heel.

And to the woman he said: Multiplying I will multiply your pains and your sighs, and in pains shall you bring forth children, and your turning round shall be towards your man, and he shall lord it over you.

And then God said to Adam: Because you have listened to the voice of your woman, and have taken a bite from the tree about which I commanded you from it alone not to eat, accursed shall the earth be to you in all your works, and in your sadness and groaning shall you eat of it all the days of your life. Thorns and thistles shall it sprout for you, and you shall eat the fodder of your field. In the sweat of your countenance shall you eat your bread, until you turn back into the earth from which you were taken; because earth you are and into earth you shall go.

And then Adam laid upon his wife the name Life, because she is the mother of all the living. And then the Lord God made Adam and his woman tunics of skin and clothed them. And God said: Behold, Adam has become as if one of us for the knowledge of getting to know good and evil. And then lest Adam stretch out his hand to the tree of life and take from there for himself and eat and live forever, the Lord God sent him away from the paradise of delight, to work the earth from which he had been taken. And on being thrown out outside Paradise, he lingered over against the paradise of pleasure. And the Cherubim and that flaming sword which turns, these God set to guard the way to the tree of life (Gn 2:4—3:24).[3]

---

3. It is to be noted that this text of chapters 2 and 3 of Genesis differs in several particulars from the one Augustine comments on in his greater work, *The Literal Meaning of Genesis.* Sometimes this one looks like a closer translation, and sometimes it seems to incorporate little comments, or amplifications of the text.

Without prejudice to the study of the literal, historical sense, he is going to search out the figurative meaning of this story

2, 3. If the Manichees were willing to discuss the hidden meaning of these words in a spirit of reverent inquiry rather than of captious fault-finding, then they would of course not be Manichees, but as they asked it would be given them, and as they sought they would find, as they knocked it would be opened up to them.[4] The fact is, you see, people who have a genuine religious interest in learning put far more questions about this text than these irreligious wretches; but the difference between them is that the former seek in order to find, while the latter are at no pains at all to do anything except not to find what they are seeking.

So then, this whole text must first be discussed in terms of history, and then in terms of prophecy. In terms of history deeds and events are being related, in terms of prophecy future events are being foretold. One should not look with a jaundiced eye, to be sure, on anyone who wants to take everything that is said here absolutely literally, and who can avoid blasphemy in so doing, and present everything as in accordance with Catholic faith; on the contrary one should hold up such a person as an outstanding and wholly admirable understander of the text.

If, however, no other way is available of reaching an understanding of what is written that is religious and worthy of God, except by supposing that it has all been set before us in a figurative sense and in riddles, we have the authority of the apostles for doing this, seeing that they solved so many riddles in the books of the Old Testament in this manner.[5] Let us then stick to this way which we have in mind, assisted by the one who urges us to ask, to seek and to knock; let us in fact unravel all these figurative statements in accordance with Catholic faith, whether they are statements of history or of prophecy, without prejudice to any better and more diligent commentary, whether by ourselves or by any others to whom the Lord may be good enough to reveal the meaning of the text.

The greenery of the field and the fodder, Genesis 2:5, means the soul

3, 4. So then, *the day was made on which God made heaven and earth, and all the greenery of the field before it was upon the earth, and all the fodder of the field* (Gn 2:5). In the previous chapter seven days are counted; now it is said to be one day on which God made heaven and earth, and all the greenery of the field and all the fodder of the field. Under the name of this single day we can reason-

---

4. See Lk 11:9.
5. The only obvious example of such apostolic authority is Paul's treatment of the story of Sarah and Hagar and their children, Gal 4:21-31.

ably understand the whole of time to be signified. God, after all, made the whole of time simultaneously with the whole time-bound creation, the visible creation which is signified under the name of "heaven and earth." What should prompt our questioning, though, is that after naming the day which was made, and heaven and earth, he also added *all the greenery of the field and all the fodder.*

You see, when it said, *In the beginning God made heaven and earth* (Gn 1:1), it didn't also say that all the greenery of the field and all the fodder was made then; it's plainly there for us to read, after all, that all the greenery and fodder of the field was made on the third day, while the statement that *In the beginning God made heaven and earth* does not belong to any of those seven days. As yet, you see, he was calling the basic material out of which everything was made by the name of "heaven and earth," or else, more likely, he had first set before us the whole of creation under the name of heaven and earth when he said, *In the beginning God made heaven and earth*; and after that he expounded God's works one by one consecutively through the sequence of days, in a way required by their prophetic significance, as we explained in the first book.[6]

So what else can it mean, then, that after naming heaven and earth he now added the greenery of the field and the fodder, and kept quiet about all the rest, so much of it, which is to be found in heaven and on earth, or even in the sea, but that by the greenery of the field he wished the invisible creation to be understood, such as the soul? It is usual in the scriptures, you see, for the world to be called a field; I mean, the Lord himself said, *The field is this world* (Mt 13:38), when he was explaining that parable in which darnel was mixed in with the good seed. So then he calls the spiritual and invisible creation the greenery of the field because of its vigor and vitality, and we naturally give the same interpretation to the word "fodder" as sustaining life.[7]

4, 5. His adding next, *before it was upon the earth*, is to be understood as meaning before the soul sinned. When it has befouled itself with earthy lusts, after all, it is rightly said to have been born upon the earth, or to be upon the earth. And that is why he added: *For God had not yet rained upon the earth* (Gn 2:5)—because nowadays too God makes the greenery of the field, but by raining upon the earth. That is, he makes souls grow green again and flourish through his word; but he waters them from the clouds, that is, from the scriptures of the prophets and apostles. These are rightly called clouds because their words, which are over and done with as soon as uttered aloud over the air, become clouds of a sort when the obscurity of allegories is added to them like a kind of fog or mist; and then, when their meaning is squeezed out in commentaries and

---

6. The seven days of creation as representing the six ages of the world and the final, eternal day of the new heaven and the new earth, I,22,33—23,42.

7. See his comment on this interpretation of fodder in the extract from *Revisions* 3, placed at the beginning of this work.

bible studies, they pour down something like showers of truth on people of good understanding.

But this was not yet the case before the soul sinned, that is, before the greenery of the field was upon the earth. *For God had not yet rained upon the earth, nor was there a man to work on it* (Gn 2:5). A man working on the land, after all, needs the showers from the clouds, and about these enough has already been said. But after his sin the man began to work on the land, and to have those necessary clouds. Before he sinned, however, when God had made the greenery of the field and the fodder, which we have said mean the invisible creature, he was watering this creature from an inner spring, speaking directly to its understanding, so that it would not have to take in words from outside, like rain from the aforementioned clouds, but would be drenched from its own spring, that is, from the truth welling up from its innermost being.

The spring coming up from the earth, Genesis 2:6

5, 6. *For a spring*, he says, *was coming up from the earth and watering the whole face of the earth* (Gn 2:6)—from the earth, that is from the land about which it says: *It is you that are my hope, my portion in the land of the living* (Ps 142:5). When the soul was being watered by such a spring as that, it had not yet "cast out its innards" through pride. *The beginning*, you see, *of man's pride is to apostatize from God* (Sir 10:12); and since his swelling out through pride to exterior things has put a stop to his being watered from that interior spring, he is very properly jeered at by these words of the prophet, and told: *What has earth and ashes to be proud of, since in its lifetime it has cast out its innards?* (Sir 10:9).[8] What else is pride, after all, but leaving the inner sanctum of conscience and wishing to be seen outwardly as what in fact one isn't? And that is why, as the soul toils away now on the land, it stands in need of rain from the clouds, that is, of teaching by human words, so that even by such means, from being parched and withered like that, it may grow green and flourish again, and once more become the greenery of the field.

But if only it were willing and happy to catch the rain of truth, at least from these very clouds! It was on its account, after all, that our Lord agreed to assume our cloudy flesh and shed upon us that most abundant of all showers, the gospel itself, and then went on to promise that anyone who drank of its water would come back to that innermost spring and no longer need to look for rain from outside. He says, you see: *It will become in him a spring of water welling up into eternal life* (Jn 4:14). It was this spring, in my opinion, that before sin was coming up from the earth and watering all the face of the earth, because it was an

---

8. See the comment on thus treating the words of Sirach as those of a prophet, in the passage from *Revisions*, 3, placed at the beginning of this work.

interior source, and not desiring help from the clouds. *For God had not yet rained upon the earth, nor was there a man to work on it* (Gn 2:5). After saying, you see, *God had not yet rained upon the earth,* he also added the reason why he had not: because *there was not a man to work on it.*

The time, though, when the man started working on the land was when he had been sent away after his sin from the life of bliss he had enjoyed in Paradise. That, you see, is what is written: *And the Lord God sent him away from the paradise of delight, to work the earth from which he had been taken* (Gn 3:23); we shall look into this when we come to it in due course.[9] I have just mentioned it now so that we may realize that for humanity toiling away on the land, confined that is to say in the parched earth of its sins, divine teaching is essential from human words, like rain from the clouds. This sort of knowledge, however, *will be done away with* (1 Cor 13:8). *For we see now in a riddle,* as if seeking satisfying nourishment in the clouds; *but then it will be face to face* (1 Cor 13:12), when the whole face of our earth will be watered by an inner spring of gushing water. I mean to say, if we wanted to take it as meaning some spring of this visible water, when it says, *Now a spring was coming up from the earth, and was watering all the face of the earth*—well, it's hardly likely that, with so many perennial springs of streams and great rivers found throughout the earth, this one alone, which was watering all the face of the earth, should have dried up.

Summing up the exposition of Genesis 2:4-6

6, 7. In these few words, then, we have been presented with the whole of creation as it was before the sin of the soul. By the term "heaven and earth" the whole visible creation was signified; by the term "day" the whole of time; by the expression "the greenery and fodder of the field" the invisible creation; and by the spring coming up and watering all the face of the earth, the flood of truth drenching the soul before sin. Now this day, which we are saying signifies the whole of time, is suggesting to us that the invisible creation too, as well as the visible one, can experience time; as for the soul's being subject to alteration by time, this is indeed obvious to us from the great variety of its moods, and also from the fall itself by which it was made wretched, and again from its renewal, restoring it once more to happiness.

And that is why it did not just say, *When the day had been made, the day on which God made heaven and earth,* terms that refer to the visible creation, but also added *the greenery and the fodder of the field,* terms by which we have been saying that the invisible creature, such as the soul, is being signified, on account of its vigor and vitality. And accordingly it said: *When the day had been made,*

---

9. See below, 22,34.

the day on which God made heaven and earth, and all the greenery and fodder of the field (Gn 2:5), so that we might in this way realize that invisible as well as visible creatures belong to time, being subject to change because God alone is unchangeable, God who is before all times.

On the making of the man from the mud of the earth

7, 8. Now at long last, after being informed about the whole of creation, invisible as well as visible, and about the benefit conferred by the divine spring on the whole invisible creation, let us see what special information we are being given about the man, the matter that concerns us first and foremost. The first question, you see, that is usually raised by *God's fashioning the man from the mud of the earth* (Gn 2:7) is what sort of mud it was, or what material was being signified by the word "mud." These enemies, though, of the books of the Old Testament,[10] looking at everything in a fleshly, literal-minded way, and therefore always getting everything wrong, are in the habit of commenting sarcastically even on this point, that God fashioned the man from mud. What they say, you see, is: "Why did God make the man from mud? Did he not have anything better, celestial material for example, from which to make the man, so that he was reduced to making him, so fragile and mortal, from the muck of the earth?" What they fail to understand from the start is how many meanings both earth or water are given in the scriptures—mud, you see, being a mixture of water and earth.

What we are saying, you see, is that only after sin did the human body begin to be fragile and subject to decay and destined to die; the only thing in our bodies, after all, that horrifies these people is their mortality, to which we have been deservedly condemned. What in any case was so strange or difficult for God, even if he did make the man from the mud of this earth, about contriving a body for him that would not have been subject to decay, had the man kept God's commandment and not been willing to sin? After all, if we say that the beauty of the sky itself was made from nothing or from unformed material, because we believe its Craftsman to be all-powerful, what's so odd about the possibility of the body, which was made from any sort of mud you like, being made by the all-powerful Craftsman of such a kind that before the man's sin it would never cause him any trouble or excruciating pain or pester him with its defects, and would never be injured or go into a decline and fade away?

9. And so it is quite unnecessary to ask what God made the man's body from—if, that is, it is now just talking about the formation of the body. That, you see, is how I have heard that some of our people understand the text. They say that the reason it didn't add "to his image and likeness," after saying *God fash-*

---

10. He just says "of the old books."

ioned the man from the mud of the earth, is that now it is only talking about the formation of the body, while the moment when the interior man was being referred to was when it said: *God made the man to the image and likeness of God* (Gn 1:27).

But even if we understand that at this point too the man was made of body and soul, not in the sense that some altogether new work was being undertaken, but that what had been stated in summary form earlier on was here being unwrapped in a more detailed account; so if, as I am saying, we understand that in this place the man was made of body and soul, it was by no means absurd to give that mixture the name of mud. Just as water, you see, collects earth and sticks and holds it together when mud is made by mixing it in, so too the soul by animating the material of the body shapes it into a harmonious unity, and does not permit it to fall apart into its constituent elements.

On the blowing of the spirit of life into the man

8, 10. As for the way the text goes on: *And he blew into him the spirit of life, and the man was made into a living soul* (Gn 2:7); if he was still only a body, we must understand the soul being joined to the body in this place, whether it had already been made but was so to say in God's mouth, that is, in his Truth or Wisdom,[11] or whether it was made at the moment when God blew the spirit of life into that clay model; in this case God's so doing would signify his actual work of making the soul in the man by the spirit of his power. If on the other hand the man who had been made was already body and soul, God's breathing into him added sensation to the soul itself when the man was made into a living soul—not that God's breathing was turned into the living soul, but that it got to work on the living soul.

We ought not, all the same, to take the man who had been made into a living soul as being already spiritual or "enspirited," but still as merely animated, "ensouled."[12] The point, you see, at which he was "enspirited" or made spiritual was when he was placed in Paradise, that is, in the life of bliss and blessedness, and also received the command of perfection, so that he might be brought to finished completion by the word of God.[13] And so after he had sinned, turning his back on God's command, and had been sent away from Paradise, he

---

11. From which, however, it did not depart as though separated by space when it was blown into him, seeing that God is not contained in any place, but is present everywhere.
12. See note 4 on the extract from the *Revisions*, 3, put at the head of Book I of this work.
13. That is, I take it, first by his keeping the word of God, as uttered in the command not to eat of the tree of knowledge of good and evil; and finally through his being given by the eternal Word the knowledge he had refrained from grabbing. The manuscripts of the ancient world made no use of the distinction between upper case and lower case letters, to distinguish here between word and Word, as we do today; and neither, very properly, does the printed Latin text.

remained merely "ensouled" and "soulish." And that is why all of us who have been born of him after that sin first act out the "soulish" man, until we gain the spiritual, "enspirited" Adam, that is, our Lord Jesus Christ *who did not commit any sin* (1 Pt 2:22), and why on being created anew and brought to life by him we are restored to Paradise, where that thief earned the right to be with him, on the very day he finished this life.[14] This after all is what the apostle says: *But not first what is "enspirited" or spiritual, but what is "ensouled" or "soulish." For the first Adam was made into a living soul, the last Adam into a life-giving spirit* (1 Cor 15:46).

11. So that then is how we ought to understand this passage. We are certainly not to suppose that because it said, *He blew into him the spirit of life and the man was made into a living soul,* something like a part of God's nature was turned into the man's soul, and so be obliged to say that God's nature is subject to change—the error about which the truth presses hardest on these Manichees. Pride, you see, being the mother of all heretics, these have had the nerve to say that the soul is identical with God's nature. And on this point they are harried by us, when we say to them, "Therefore God's nature goes astray, and is wretched, and is riddled with vices, and commits sin, or even, as you yourselves say, is defiled by contamination with the filth of an opposing nature—and other such things, which it is impious to believe about the nature of God."

That the soul, you see, was made by the all-powerful God, and that accordingly it is not a part of God or identical with his nature, is stated quite plainly in another passage of scripture, where the prophet says: *And the one who fashioned the spirit for them all, he it is that knows all things* (Ps 33:15), and in another place: *who fashioned the spirit of man within him* (Zech 12:1). So then, that the spirit of the man was made is definitively proved by these texts. But the scriptures give the name of "the spirit of man" to the soul's power of reason, which distinguishes him from the animals and gives him mastery over them by natural law. It is about this spirit that the apostle says: *Nobody knows what a man has except the spirit of the man which is in him* (1 Cor 2:11).

I quote this in case there might still be people who say that while these texts prove that the soul was made, the spirit of the man was not made, and who insist that this spirit is identical with God's nature, and say that a part of God was turned into the man's spirit when God did that blowing. This also is utterly rejected by sound teaching, because the spirit of man too sometimes errs and sometimes has the right ideas, and so declares itself to be changeable, which in no way whatsoever is it lawful to suppose about the nature of God. Now there surely cannot be a surer sign of pride than for a human soul to claim to be what God is, when it is still groaning under such a huge pile of vices and miseries.

---

14. See Lk 23:43.

What is signified by the delights of Paradise

9, 12. Now at last let us take a look at the blissful state of the man, which is signified by the name of Paradise. Since people are accustomed, after all, to enjoy delicious rest in parks, and light dawns upon our bodily senses from the east, and the sky, a body high above our bodies and altogether more sublime, arches up from there: all that is the reason why the spiritual delights which go with the life of bliss are also being figuratively displayed by these words, and why Paradise is planted to the east. Let us take it then that our spiritual joys are signified by every tree that is beautiful to the gaze of the understanding, and good for eating, being the imperishable food on which blessed souls feed. The Lord too says, after all: *Work for the food which does not perish* (Jn 6:27), such as every idea which is food for the soul.

"To the east": to the light of wisdom in Eden, that is, in the immortal delights of the mind.[15] Delights, you see, or pleasure, or feasting is what this word is said to mean, if translated from Hebrew into English.[16] But it is left untranslated like this in order to give the impression of being a place, and to make the style of the whole passage more figurative. Every tree produced from the earth, then, we take as being every spiritual joy, the kind, that is, that overtops the earth, and is not wrapped up and overwhelmed in the entanglements of earthy lusts.

The tree of life, though, planted in the middle of Paradise signifies the wisdom by which the soul is made to understand that it has been set at a kind of mid-point in the whole order of things, so that although it has every material, bodily nature subject to it, it has to realize that the nature of God is still above itself. So it must not turn aside either to the right, by claiming to be what it is not, or to the left, by being slack and indifferent about living up to what it is.[17] That then is the tree of life, planted in the middle of Paradise.

As for the tree of knowledge of good and evil, again it is the halfway centrality of the soul, its integrity in the due order of things, that it signifies. This tree too, after all, was planted in the middle of Paradise; and the reason it is called the tree of distinguishing between good and evil is that if the soul[18] turns to itself with its back to God and wants to enjoy its own power without any reference to God, it swells up with pride, which is *the starting point of all sin* (Sir 10:13). And when the penalty follows upon this sin of the soul's, it learns by experience what

---

15. Literally, "in immortal and intelligible delights." Augustine is still, only a few years after his conversion, living and expressing himself in a platonic frame of thought, in which the truly real world is that of intelligible, unchanging ideas (*rationes* for Augustine; he has just used the word), as distinct from the only half-real, shadow world of appearances, which we observe with our senses.
16. Latin, of course, in the text.
17. See Is 30:21; Dt 5:32.
18. Which should be "stretching out to what lies ahead," that is, to God, "and forgetting what lies behind" (Phil 3:13).

the difference is between the good which it has turned its back on and the evil into which it has fallen. And this will be its tasting of the fruit of the tree of distinguishing between good and evil. So then, it is commanded to eat of every tree that is in Paradise, but not to eat of the tree in which good and evil are distinguished; that is, not to enjoy it in such a way as to violate and corrupt, as if by chewing it to pieces, the duly ordered integrity of its own nature.

What the rivers of Paradise indicate

10, 13. *Now a river was coming forth out of Eden* (Gn 2:10), that is from delights and pleasure and feasting, the river the prophet has in mind in the psalms, when he says: *You will give them to drink from the torrent of your pleasure* (Ps 36:8); Eden, you see, means "pleasure" in English. This river is divided into four parts and thus signifies the four virtues, prudence, fortitude, temperance and justice.[19] The Pishon, though, is said to be the Ganges, the Gihon the Nile, which can also be noticed in the prophet Jeremiah.[20] These two are now called by other names, like the river which is now called the Tiber, but was once called the Albula,[21] while the Tigris and Euphrates still have the same names.

By these names, however, as I was saying, spiritual virtues are signified, as even the translation of the names themselves will indicate, if you bear in mind the Hebrew or Syriac language, just as Jerusalem, while being a visible place on earth, still means spiritually "City of Peace," and Zion, while being a mountain on earth, nonetheless means "Contemplation." This name is often applied in scriptural allegories to the understanding of spiritual things. And that man who was going down from Jerusalem to Jericho, as the Lord says,[22] and was attacked on the road and wounded and left half dead by robbers, certainly obliges us to understand these places, although historically speaking they are to be found on earth, in a spiritual sense.

14. So then prudence, which stands for an actual contemplation of Truth that is totally foreign to any human lips, because it is inexpressible, so that if you wished to utter it you would be in labor with it rather than actually bringing it

---

19. The four cardinal, or hinge, virtues of ancient Greek ethics, duly incorporated into Christian moral theology. I give them their traditional names, in this following the *Encyclopedia Britannica* (article, "Cardinal Virtues"), though they cover a somewhat wider ground than these names now signify in contemporary English.
20. There is no mention of this river, or its identity with the Nile, anywhere in Jeremiah; but it is mentioned in Sirach 24:27, where after naming the other three rivers of paradise, the author says that instruction will come forth like Gihon at the time of vintage—a possible allusion to the flooding of the Nile. Augustine's memory, for once, is playing him tricks.
21. See Virgil's *Aeneid*, VIII,332. See also Augustine's greater work, *The Literal Meaning of Genesis*, VIII,7,13, and note 25 there.
22. See Lk 10:30.

forth;[23] so this prudence then goes round the land which has gold and carbuncle and leek-green stone, that is, a discipline of life that glistens brightly as if refined from all earthly dross, like the best gold; and truth which no falsehood can overcome, like the brilliance of the carbuncle which is not overcome by night; and eternal life, which is signified by the greenness of the leek-green stone, because of its vigor that never withers.

Next, that river which goes round the land of Ethiopia, very hot and steamy, signifies fortitude, stirred by the heat of action and never slackening. The third one, the Tigris, streams over against the Assyrians, and signifies temperance, which stands up to lust, the great adversary of prudent counsels; so the Assyrians are frequently mentioned in the scriptures as the arch-adversaries. Finally, of the fourth river nothing is said about what it streams over against, or what land it goes round; justice, you see, belongs to all parts of the soul, because it is the very order and balance of the soul, by which these three are bound together in concord—the first, prudence; the second, fortitude; the third, temperance; and in this total bonding and order, justice.

What the man did in Paradise, and his need for help

11, 15. As for the man being put in Paradise precisely to work there and guard it, that much more laudable kind of work was not in the least toilsome. Work in Paradise, I mean to say, is one thing, and work on the land, to which he was condemned after sinning, quite another. In fact what sort of work it was, is indicated by the addition of *and to guard it*. In the peaceful tranquillity, you see, of the life of bliss, where there is no death, work consists entirely in guarding what you hold.

He also received a commandment, which we have just dealt with above. Now the conclusion of the commandment clearly shows it was not addressed just to one person; what he says, you see, is this: *but on the day you all [24] take a bite from it, you all shall die the death* (Gn 2:17). He is already starting on the explanation of how the woman came to be made, and how she is said to have been made as a help for the man, so that by a spiritual coupling she might bring forth spiritual offspring, that is, the good works of divine praise; while he directs, she complies; he is directed by wisdom, she by the man, for *the head of the man is Christ, and the head of the woman the man* (1 Cor 11:3). And that is why it says: *It is not good for the man to be alone* (Gn 2:18). There still remained, after all, something for him to become, so that not only should the soul lord it over the body (the body's status being that of a slave), but that the manly reason should also have subject to itself its "animal" part, to be its help in ordering the body about.

---

23. Because the apostle too heard inexpressible words there "which it is not lawful for man to utter" (2 Cor 12:4).
24. This, I understand, is an idiom of the southern United States to indicate the second person plural, a most useful and necessary idiom in a case like this.

It was to provide an example of this that the woman was made, whom the natural order of things makes subject to the man. In this way what can be seen more clearly in two human beings, that is, in male and female, may be considered in a single person; that the interior mind, like the manly reason, should have as its subject the soul's appetite or desire, through which we put the limbs and parts of the body to work, and by a just law should keep its help within bounds—just as a man ought to govern his wife, and not let her lord it over her husband, because where this happens the result is a topsy turvy and miserable household indeed.

The stages by which God provided a help for Adam

16. So first of all, then, God demonstrated to the man how much better he was than cattle, and all brute animals; and this is the meaning of what it says next, that all the animals were brought to him, for him to see what to call them, and to label them with their names. This, you see, shows that man is better, in virtue of his rationality, than the beasts, because to distinguish them and differentiate between them by naming them is something only reason can do by making a judgment about them. This, however, is an easy step for reason to take; human beings soon realize, after all, that they are better than animals. The difficult step for reason is for us to realize that in ourselves the rational power which should govern is one thing, the "animal" power (appetite or desire) which should be governed by it, another.

The slumber of Adam from which Eve was made

12. And since it is by a more hidden kind of wisdom that we see this, the hidden sight of it is signified, in my opinion, by the slumber which God sent upon Adam, when the woman was made for him.

To see this, after all, we do not need these bodily eyes; but the more we withdraw our attention from these visible things to the inner world of the intelligence (and that is a kind of falling asleep), the better and more authentic is our sight of this. The very realization, you see, by which we come to understand that in us what exercises a rational mastery is one thing, what yields compliance to reason another, so this very realization then is a kind of producing of the woman from the man's rib, to signify their being joined together.

Next, so that each of us may exercise a proper lordship or mastery over this part of ourselves, and become a kind of wedded couple in the very self, with the flesh not warring against the spirit with its desires[25] but submitting to it, that is, the desire of the flesh not opposing reason but rather complying with it and thus

---

25. See Gal 5:17.

ceasing to be of the flesh—for all this we stand in need of perfect wisdom. The contemplation of this being more inward and hidden, and as far removed as can be from any of the bodily senses, this too can suitably be understood under the name of slumber. Then indeed, you see, is the man with the most complete propriety the head of the woman, when the head of the man is Christ,[26] who is *the Wisdom of God* (1 Cor 1:24).

17. It's true that he filled up the place of that rib with flesh, to suggest by this word the loving affection with which we should love our own souls, and not be harsh in blaming them for things, with which[27] we should love those we are in charge of. Flesh, you see, is not being mentioned in this place as signifying the desires of the flesh, but rather in the way the prophet talks about the people having the heart of stone taken away from them and being given instead a heart of flesh.[28] In the same way, after all, the apostle also says: *Not on tablets of stone, but on the fleshly tablets of the heart* (2 Cor 3:3). It is the difference in fact between a straightforward literal way of talking and a figurative one, such as the way we are dealing with here and now.

Accordingly, even if the real, visible woman was made, historically speaking, from the body of the first man by the Lord God, it was surely not without reason that she was made like that—it must have been to suggest some hidden truth. Was there any shortage of mud, after all, for the woman to be formed from, or couldn't the Lord, had he so wished, have painlessly removed the man's rib from him while he was still awake? So whether all this was said in a figurative way, or whether it was even done in a figurative way, it was certainly not pointlessly that it was said or done like this. No, it is all assuredly pointing to mysteries and sacraments,[29] whether in the way I with my slender capacities am attempting to explain it, or whether it is to be interpreted and understood in some other and better way, but still in accordance with sound faith.

The relationship between the man and the woman

13, 18. So then, the man said what his woman was to be called, as a boss might say of a minion, and said: *This now is bone out of my bones, and flesh from my flesh.* "Bone out my bones," possibly alluding to fortitude, and "flesh from my flesh," alluding to temperance. These two virtues, you see, are commonly held to

---

26. See 1 Cor 11:3.
27. Reading *quo* instead of the text's *quod*, which would give the sense, "because we should love those we are in charge of"; and also I suggest changing the mood of the verb from the indicative, *diligit*, to the subjunctive, *diligat*.
28. See Ez 11:19.
29. In the altogether wider meaning of the term current in Christian writings of Augustine's time, when it meant any sacred or hidden truth or reality signified by some other thing mentioned in scripture.

belong to the lower part of the spirit, which is governed by the prudence of reason. As for what it goes on to say: *this shall be called woman, since she was taken from her man* (Gn 2:23), this explanation of the origin of the name is not evident in the Latin language; no similarity, after all, is to be noted between the word *mulier* and the word *vir*. But in Hebrew it is said to sound as if we were to say in Latin, "This shall be called *virago*, because she was taken from her *vir*."[30] *Virago*, after all, or rather *virgo*, does have some resemblance to the word *vir* which *mulier* doesn't. But this, as I remarked, is the effect of diversity of language.

19. As for what it goes on to add: *A man shall leave father and mother and stick to his wife, and they shall be two in one flesh* (Gn 2:24), I can find no way of referring this to history, except that this is what usually happens with the human race. But in fact the whole thing is a prophecy, as the apostle reminds us, when he says: *For this reason a man shall leave father and mother and stick to his wife, and they shall be two in one flesh. This is a great sacrament; but I mean in Christ and in the Church* (Eph 5:31-32). If the Manichees, who use the apostle's letters to take many people in, were not blind when they read this, they would understand in what way the scriptures of the Old Testament are to be taken, and not have the effrontery to bring charges with their sacrilegious cries against something they know nothing about at all.

But that Adam and his wife were naked and not embarrassed signifies simplicity of soul and chastity. This you see is what the apostle too has to say: *I attached you to one man, to present you to Christ as a chaste virgin; but I am afraid that just as the serpent deceived Eve with his slyness, so your minds may be corrupted from the simplicity and chastity which is in Christ* (2 Cor 11:2-3).

The devil represented by the serpent

14, 20. Coming now to the serpent, it represents the devil, who certainly wasn't simple. That he was said, you see, to be wiser than all beasts is a figurative way of stating his slyness. It does not, however, say that the serpent was in paradise, but that the serpent was among the beasts which God had made. Paradise, after all, as I said above,[31] stands for the blessed life of bliss in which there was no longer a serpent, because it was already the devil; and he had fallen from his blessed state, because *he did not stand in the truth* (Jn 8:44). Nor is there anything strange about the way he could talk to the woman, though she was in

---

30. "She shall be called *ishshah*, because she was taken from her *ish*"; which we get very conveniently in English with "woman" and "man." Augustine cannot at the time of writing have been familiar with Jerome's Vulgate translation; but there it is in fact rendered, *haec vocabitur virago, quoniam de viro sumpta est*.
31. See 9,12 above.

Paradise and he was not; she was not in Paradise, you see, in a local sense, but rather as regards her blissful feeling of blessedness. Or even if there is such a place called Paradise, where Adam and the woman were actually living in the body, are we to understand the devil also making his approach there in the body? Not at all, but he made it as a spirit, as the apostle says: *According to the prince of the power of the air, the spirit who is now at work in the children of unbelief* (Eph 2:2).

So then, he doesn't appear visibly, does he, to those in whom he is at work, or approach them by a kind of bodily movement in material places? No, of course not, but in mysterious ways he suggests whatever he can to their thoughts. These suggestions are resisted by those who can truly say what again the apostle says: *We are not unaware of his wiles* (2 Cor 2:11). How, in any case, did he approach Judas, when he persuaded him to betray the Lord? Not by local movement, surely, not in a way to be seen by him with these eyes? But of course, as it says, he entered into his heart.[32]

The man will repel him, however, if he guards Paradise. God, you see, put the man in paradise *to work there and guard it* (Gn 2:15). In fact that is more or less what is said about the Church in the Song of Songs: *A garden enclosed, a fountain sealed* (4:12), into which that persuader of perversity naturally does not gain admittance. But all the same he did take in the woman, because our reason too can only be brought down to consenting to sin, when pleasurable anticipation is roused in that part of the spirit which ought to take its lead from the reason, as from its husband and guide.

21. Even now, when any of us slide down into sin, nothing else takes place but what then occurred with those three, the serpent, the woman and the man. First of all, you see, comes the suggestion, either in the thoughts, or through the body's senses, by seeing or touching or hearing or tasting or smelling something. If, when the suggestion has taken shape, our desire or greed is not roused to sin, the serpent's cunning will be blocked; if it is roused, though, it's as if the woman has already been persuaded. But sometimes the reason valiantly puts the brake on greed even when it has been roused, and brings it to a halt. When this happens, we don't slide into sin, but win the prize with a certain amount of struggle. If however the reason does consent and decide that what lust or greed is urging on it should be done, then the man is expelled from the entire life of bliss, as from paradise. Sin is already put down to his account, you see, even if the actual deed doesn't follow, since the conscience incurs guilt just by consent.

---

32. See Lk 22:3, Jn 13:2.

The value of noting how the serpent succeeded

15, 22. The way, though, in which the serpent succeeded in putting across the sin calls for careful consideration, as it directly concerns our salvation; the reason all this is written down, after all, is to put us on our guard against such things at the present time. So when the woman told him in answer to his question what command they had been given, he came back with: *You will not die the death; for God knew that on the day you take a bite from it your eyes will be opened, and you will be like gods, knowing good and evil* (Gn 3:4-5). In these words we can see it was through pride that the sin was put across—I mean, that's the catch in the words, *you will be like gods.* As also with the whole assertion, *for God knew that on the day you take a bite from it your eyes will be opened*; what else is to be understood but a suggestion that they should refuse to be under God any longer, but should be their own masters instead without the Lord, that they should not keep a rule apparently laid down by him out of a jealous refusal to let them be in control of their own lives, no longer needing inner enlightenment from him, but using their own wits, their own eyes so to say, to tell the difference between good and evil, which he had wanted to stop them doing?

So that then is how it was put across to them to be too fond of their own power, and by wishing to be God's equals, to make bad use of that halfway centrality, represented by the fruit of the tree set in the middle of paradise, by which they were subject to God, and had their own bodies subject to themselves; to act, that is, against God's law, and so forfeit what they had received, while they had wanted to grab what they had not received. Human nature, you see, did not receive the power to enjoy the state of bliss independently of God's control, because only God is able to enjoy blessedness and bliss by his own power independently of anyone else's control.

23. *And the woman saw*, he says, *that the tree was good for eating, and that it was good for the eyes to see and to gain knowledge* (Gn 3:6). How could she see, if their eyes were closed? But what we are meant to understand by these words is that after they had taken some of the fruit for themselves, those eyes were opened with which they saw that they were naked and were displeased at the sight; the eyes, that is, of cunning which are displeased at simplicity. When anybody falls away from that innermost, hidden light of truth, there is nothing that pride is ready to be pleased with except fraudulent pretenses. This is where hypocrisy too is born, which makes people think they are very clever, when they can deceive and take in anyone they want to.

The woman, you see, gave to her husband, and they both took a bite, and their eyes were opened, eyes we have just explained. And that is when they saw that they were naked, but with eyes asquint, to which the simplicity signified by nakedness seemed something to be ashamed of. And so, as they were no longer simple, they made themselves aprons from fig leaves, to cover their private parts, that is to conceal their simplicity, of which cunning pride was now ashamed. Fig leaves, though, signify a kind of itch (if the word can properly be applied in the incorporeal sphere) which the spirit in astonishing ways can be afflicted with, out of greed and a delight in telling lies. This is also why people who love playing the fool are said to be salty, *salsi* in Latin. Pretense, after all, is the principal element in tomfoolery.[33]

The meaning of their encounter with God in Paradise

16, 24. And so when God was strolling in Paradise at evening—that is, he was strolling in Paradise when he was already coming to pass judgment on them even before their punishment[34]—they heard his voice, and hid themselves from his sight. Who are the ones who hide themselves from the sight of God, but those who have turned their backs on him and are beginning to love what is their very own? You see, they already had a covering for their falsehood, and anyone who utters falsehood *is speaking from what is his own* (Jn 8:44). And that is why they are said to have hidden themselves at the tree which was in the middle of paradise, that is, at themselves, ranged as they were in the middle of things, below God and above bodies.

So then they hid themselves at themselves, in order to be troubled with miserable errors after forsaking the light of truth, which they themselves were definitely not. The human soul, after all, can participate in truth, but Truth itself is God, unchanging above the soul. So then, turn away if you will from this Truth and turn to yourself, and exult in your own seemingly free movements rather than in being directed and enlightened by God; but you will be plunged in the darkness of falsehood, since whoever speaks falsehood is speaking from what is his own. And so you will be troubled in that way, and illustrate the truth of the prophet's words: *My soul is troubled at myself* (Ps 42:6).

And so Adam is now questioned by God, not because God doesn't know where he is, but in order to oblige him to confess his sin.[35] And he answered that when he heard his voice he hid himself, since he was naked. His very answer was already an instance of a truly miserable error—as though his being naked, as God himself had made him, could displease God! But it is the very essence of error to assume that what is displeasing to oneself also displeases God. What the

---

33. And salt is used to conceal the unpleasant taste of food, to help the meat pretend it isn't bad—is that the idea behind this odd illustration of the point?

34. That is, the divine presence was in a kind of way being shaken about in them, when they themselves were not steady in keeping his commandment; and very properly at evening, that is, when the sun was already setting on them, that is, that inner light of truth was being taken away from them.

35. The Lord Jesus Christ, after all, asked any number of questions, but not because he didn't know the answers.

Lord said in reply, though, is to be seen as really sublime: *Who told you that you are naked—unless it's that you have taken a bite from the tree from which I had told you from it alone not to take a bite?* (Gn 3:11). He had been naked, you see, of pretense, but clothed with divine light. Having turned away from this and turned to himself, which is the meaning of taking a bite from that tree, he saw his own nakedness, and was displeased with himself as not having anything he could call his very own.

Putting the blame on others, in the last resort on God

17, 25. Next, as is the way with pride, he doesn't plead guilty to being the woman's accomplice, but instead puts all the blame for his own fault on the woman; and in this way, with a subtlety seeming to spring from the cunning the poor wretch had conceived, he wanted to lay his sinning at the door of God himself. He didn't just say, you see, "The woman gave it to me," but more fully: *The woman whom you gave me* (Gn 3:12). Indeed nothing is so characteristic of sinners as wishing to put whatever they are accused of down to God. This comes from that vein of pride by which the man sinned in wishing to be equal to God, free that is from his control just as God, being the Lord and master of all things, is free from any outside control. But because the man was simply unable to be God's equal in majesty and greatness, as he lay there in the sin he had fallen into, he attempted to make God his equal, or indeed his inferior, by showing that God had sinned while he himself was innocent.

And when the woman is questioned, she puts the blame on the serpent. So in each case it's as if the man had received a wife in order to comply with her directions instead of making her comply with his, or as if she had been unable to keep God's command instead of going along with the serpent's words.

The sentence passed on the serpent, representing the devil

26. The serpent for his part is not questioned, but immediately has sentence passed on him, because he is incapable of confessing to sin, and also has absolutely no possible excuse. It is not here, though, a matter of that condemnation of the devil which is being reserved for the last judgment, referred to by the Lord when he says: *Go into the eternal fire which has been prepared for the devil and his angels* (Mt 25:41); but it is the reason why he is to be shunned by us that is here said to be his punishment. His punishment consists, you see, in his having in his power those who ignore God's commandments. This is in fact clearly hinted at in the very words in which sentence is passed on him; and what makes the punishment all the greater is that he actually rejoices in this oh so unlucky power

of his, he who was accustomed before he fell to enjoy the sublime truth in which he did not stand.[36] And that is why even the cattle are ranked above him, not in power but in the way they keep to their nature. They didn't lose any heavenly bliss or blessedness, which they never had in the first place; but they pass their lives according to the nature which they did receive.

So then, this one is told: *Upon your bosom and your belly shall you crawl* (Gn 3:14), something indeed to be observed in snakes, which is now being taken from those visible animals and applied figuratively to this invisible enemy of ours. The word "bosom" signifies pride because that is where the driving force of the spirit resides, while by the word "belly" is signified fleshly desire, because this is perceived as the softer part of the body. And it is because he crawls by means of these vices toward those whom he wishes to deceive that it says: "Upon your bosom and your belly shall you crawl."

The meaning of Genesis 3:14

18, 27. *And earth*, he says, *shall you eat all the days of your life* (Gn 3:14), that is, all the days on which he exercises this power, before he receives that final punishment on the day of judgment; this, after all, appears to be the life he enjoys and boasts about. So then, there are two ways in which we can understand "earth shall you eat." Either it means that those you take in through earthy greed, that is sinners who are signified by the word "earth," will belong to you; or else, more likely, it is the third kind of temptation that is represented by these words, and that is curiosity.[37] One who eats earth, you see, penetrates deep and dark places, which are still for all that time-bound and earthly.

28. Enmity though will not be set between him and the man, but between him and the woman. This is surely not because he doesn't tempt men and take them in, is it? It's perfectly obvious that he does. Or is it because he didn't take Adam in but his wife? But that doesn't mean, does it, that he is not the enemy of the man, who was affected by that deceit through his wife—above all because it is here referring to the future: *I will set enmity between you and the woman* (Gn 3:15)? If however it's just that he didn't thereafter take Adam in, then he didn't thereafter take Eve in either.[38]

---

36. See Jn 8:44.
37. He means the curiosity that leads people to the practice of divination, and prying into the occult, something he is more inclined to accuse the Neoplatonists of than the Manichees. But the Manichees did, he also says, try to entice people to join them by promising them knowledge of the mysteries of the universe.
38. In this very dense paragraph he is arguing that it is difficult, to say the least, to make sense of any literal, "historical" interpretation of this point. But take it as having a figurative significance, and all becomes clear.

So why then is it stated like this, if not to show clearly that the only way we can be tempted by the devil is through that animal or "soulish" part which the author has shown to exist in every single human being, represented by the likeness or model of a woman, about which we have already had much to say? As for enmity, though, being set between the seed of the devil and the seed of the woman, the seed of the devil stands for his perverted suggestions, while the seed of the woman means the fruit of good works that resist these perverted suggestions. And that is why he looks out for the woman's heel, in order to catch her if unlawful pleasure creeps in; and she looks out for his head, in order to cut him off at the very beginning of his evil persuasive suggestions.

The penalty paid by the woman

19, 29. We come now to the woman's punishment, and find it raises no problem. The pains she has, after all, are manifestly multiplied, not to mention her sighs and tears over the disasters of this life. And while her bringing forth children in pain is something also undergone by the woman we can see, it still draws our attention back to that other one hidden inside each one of us. After all, female animals too bring forth their offspring in pain, and in them this is simply a consequence of their being mortal rather than a punishment for sin; so it can also be the case that in female human beings this is just a consequence of their bodies being mortal. But the severity of the punishment lies in this, that they come to this mortal condition of their bodies from that earlier state of immortality.

There is, all the same, a symbolic significance of great importance[39] in this sentence, and that is that restraining the will from any desire of the flesh is always painful to begin with, until it has been drilled into a better habit. When this has occurred, it is as if a child has been born, when, that is, the good habit has disposed one to good works. For this good habit to be born, the bad habit has to be fought against with pain. And then there is what is said after childbirth: *and your turning round shall be toward your man, and he shall lord it over you* (Gn 3:16). Do not most, if not almost all women give birth without their husbands being present, and so in fact they do not turn around toward them after delivery? As for those proud women who in fact lord it over their husbands, do they give up this vice after giving birth and allow their husbands to lord it over them? On the contrary, they assume that becoming mothers has given them a kind of added dignity and frequently become prouder than ever.

So then, what can be the meaning of its adding, after *in pain shall you bring forth children*, the words *and your turning round shall be toward your man, and he will lord it over you*? What else, but that when that part of the soul, which is

---

39. *Magnum sacramentum.*

taken up with the joys of the flesh, wishes to overcome some bad habit, it experiences difficulty and pain, and in this way brings forth a good habit; and that this now makes it all the more careful and eager to submit to the reason as to its husband; and that now, as though taught a lesson by the pains themselves, it turns around to the reason, and willingly follows its instructions, to avoid again trickling away into some destructive habit? So then, what seem to be curses here are in fact commandments, if we take care not to read what is spiritual in a carnal manner; for *the law*, you see, *is spiritual* (Rom 7:14).

The penalty paid by the man

20, 30. Then again, what are we to say about this sentence passed on the man himself? Are the wealthy by any chance, who get their living in the easiest way imaginable without ever working on the land, to be thought of as having escaped this punishment? This after all is how it is described: *Accursed shall the earth be to you in all your works, and in your sadness and groaning shall you eat of it all the days of your life. Thorns and thistles shall it sprout for you, and you shall eat the fodder of your field. In the sweat of your countenance shall you eat your bread, until you turn back into the earth from which you were taken, because earth you are and into earth you shall go* (Gn 3:17-19).

But if anything is certain, it is that nobody may escape this sentence. The very fact, after all, that everyone born in this life finds the search for truth impeded by the perishable body[40] is what is meant by the toil and grief which the man gets from the earth; and the thorns and thistles are the pricks and scratches of tortuous, intractable problems, or else the anxious thoughts about providing for this life, which frequently choke the word and stop it bearing any fruit in a man, unless they are uprooted and thrown out of God's field, as the Lord says in the gospel.[41]

And then it is through these eyes and these ears that we are instructed about the truth itself, and there is the difficulty of withstanding the fancies and notions which enter the soul through these same senses, although it is also through them that instruction about the truth enters in; so in this perplexity, whose countenance will not be sweating so that he may munch his bread?[42] All this we are going to suffer all the days of our life—of this life, that is, which is going to pass away. And what that man was told, who would soon be cultivating his own field, was that he was to endure all this until he turned back into the earth from which he was taken, that is, until he finished this life. Those of us, you see, who culti-

---

40. Solomon says, you see: "The body that is perishing weighs down the soul, and the dwelling made of earth oppresses the mind as it thinks about many things" (Wis 9:15).
41. See Mk 4:18-19.
42. That is, in figurative terms, feed upon the truth.

vate this interior field, and get our bread even though with much toil, can suffer such toil to the end of this life; but after this life there is no need to suffer it. Those however who perhaps fail to cultivate the field, and allow it to be overrun with thorns and thistles, have the curse of the earth on all their works in this life, and after this life will have to face either the fires of purgatory or eternal punishment. Thus nobody escapes this sentence; but one has to take steps to see that at least it is only sensed,[43] only experienced, in this life alone.

On Adam giving his wife the name of Life, and on God clothing them with tunics of skin

21, 31. Can anyone though help being puzzled when reading that after God had passed these judicial sentences, Adam calls his woman Life, *because she is the mother of all the living* (Gn 3:20), and this after she has earned death and is destined to bear mortal offspring? This surely can only be because Scripture is thinking of how, after she has given birth to her offspring in pain, her turning back to her husband will take place and he will lord it over her. About this offspring we have spoken above.[44] That, you see, is how there is life in her, and she is the mother of the living, because the life lived in sins is habitually called death in the scriptures, as when the apostle says that *the widow who lives for pleasure is dead* (1 Tm 5:6); and we also find sin itself signified by a dead man, where it says: *Whoever is baptized by a dead man and again touches him, what does he profit from his bath? So too the one who fasts over his sins, and walks away again doing the same things* (Sir 34:25-26). He put a dead man for sin, you see, while treating restraint and fasting from sin as a kind of baptism, that is, as purification from the dead man, and going back again to sinning as again touching the dead man.

So why then should that "soulish" part of us, which ought to submit to reason as to a husband, not be called Life, when through the reason itself it has conceived the burden of right living by the Word of life; and when, after the pains and groans of the labor of self-restraint with which it has withstood an evil habit, it has given birth to a good habit of acting rightly, why should it not be called the mother of the living, that is, of rightly performed actions, the opposite of which are the sins, which we have just maintained can be signified under the name of dead men?

32. This death, you see, which all of us who are born of Adam have owed to nature from the start, and with which God threatened Adam when he gave the command that the fruit of that tree was not to be eaten, so then this death is

---

43. Word play on *sententiam* and *sentiatur*. The whole sentence runs: *Ita nemo evadit istam sententiam; sed agendum est ut saltem in hac tantum vita sentiatur.*
44. See above, 19,29.

presented under the figure of the skin tunics. They themselves, you see, had made aprons out of fig-leaves for themselves, and God made them tunics of skin; that is, they set their hearts on the pleasures of lying after turning their backs on the face of Truth, and God changed their bodies into this mortal flesh, in which lying hearts are concealed.

It is not to be supposed, after all, that thoughts can remain hidden in celestial bodies in the same way as they do in these present bodies of ours; but just as some at least of our inner thoughts and feelings are revealed by the expression on our faces, and especially by our eyes, so I am convinced that in a similar way no feelings and thoughts of the spirit whatsoever are concealed in the transparent simplicity of heavenly bodies. And so such a dwelling place and such a change into angelic form will be earned by those people who even in this life, when it has been possible for them to conceal lies under tunics of skin, have still hated and avoided such falsehood out of a most ardent love of truth, and who only keep covered up what their listeners are unable to bear;[45] but lies they never tell at all. The time will come, you see, when nothing will be covered up; *for nothing is hidden which will not be made manifest* (Lk 12:2).

But these two continued to remain in Paradise, even though now under the sentence of God's condemnation, until it came to the tunics of skin, that is, to the mortal condition of this life. What more effective indication, after all, can be given of the death, which we are aware of in the body, than skins which are flayed as a rule from dead cattle? And so when the man went against the commandment and sought to be God, not by lawful imitation but by unlawful pride, he was cast down into the mortal condition of monstrous beasts.

Two ways of taking "Adam has become like one of us"

33. That is why the divine law mocks him from the mouth of God in the following way, mockery by which we in our turn are being advised as much as ever we can to beware of pride.

22. *Behold, Adam has become as if one of us for the knowledge of getting to know good and evil* (Gn 3:22). This ambiguous expression involves a figure of speech,[46] because "has become as if one of us" can be understood in two ways. In the first way, "one of us" as though he himself has also become God (and that is where the mockery comes in), as you can say "one of the senators," meaning of course "a senator." Or else it is because he would indeed have been a god, though

---

45. An allusion, it seems, to Jn 16:12: *I still have many things to say to you, but you cannot bear them now.*
46. The ambiguous expression is "as if one of us," and only ambiguous by stretching to the limits a point in the Latin, *tanquam unus ex nobis*, as I hope will become clear shortly. I think the figure of speech it involves *(facit figuram)* must be irony.

by his creator's generosity, not by nature, if he had been willing to remain under his authority, that it says "of us," *ex nobis,* in the way one calls someone an *ex*-magistrate or *ex*-governor who no longer is one.

But to what end has he become as if one of us? "For the knowledge of getting to know good and evil," so that this fellow might learn by experience what the difference is as he undergoes the evil, while God knows it by wisdom; and so that he might also learn by his punishment that there is no escaping the Almighty's authority, which he had refused to submit to by happily consenting to it.

34. *And then, lest Adam stretch out his hand to the tree of life, and live for ever, God sent him away from paradise* (Gn 3:22-23). Notice the nice choice of words, *he sent him away,* not "he shut him out," so that he could be seen to be as good as shoved out by the pressure of his own sins to the only place he was fit for. This is something a bad man often experiences when he begins to live among good people and refuses to change his ways for the better; it is by the pressure of his bad habits and associations that he is driven out of the company of these good people; they don't exclude him against his will, but he is only too glad to be sent on his way by them.

As for its saying, *lest Adam stretch out his hand to the tree of life,* here too we have an ambiguous expression.[47] This is how we speak, you see, when we say: "This is why I am admonishing you, lest you should do again what you have done," clearly wanting him not to do it; and again we can say: "This is why I am admonishing you, lest there be a chance of your being good"—that is, I am admonishing you because I don't despair of your being able to be good. That is how the apostle is speaking when he says: *Lest there be a chance of God giving them repentance so as to come to know the truth* (2 Tm 2:25).

So then it can appear that the reason the man was sent away to the wearisome labors of this life was in order that at some time or other he might indeed stretch out his hand to the tree of life and live for ever. The stretching out of the hand, surely, is an excellent symbol of the cross, through which eternal life is regained. Though even if we understand *lest he stretch out his hand and live for ever* in that other way, it was an entirely fair punishment that he should be barred from access to wisdom after his sin, until by God's mercy in the course of time the one who was dead might come to life again, and the one who was lost might be found.[48]

---

47. Again, the ambiguity lies in the Latin, in the negative conjunction *ne*; in English we don't really employ "lest" in the ambiguous way he goes on to illustrate. In the text he proceeds to quote from 2 Timothy the older versions, which stick close to the Greek and Latin, render the *nequando* of the Vulgate, Augustine's *ne forte,* by "if peradventure." Even more than in the previous case of "ambiguity" (previous section and note), we do seem to have the recently retired professor of rhetoric displaying a misplaced professional ingenuity in reading ambiguity into his text.

48. See Lk 15:32, the conclusion of the parable of the prodigal son.

So then, he was sent away from the paradise of delight to work the earth from which he had been taken, that is, to toil in this body and there if he could to save up merit and earn the right to return. He lingered, though, over against Paradise in misery, which is of course "over against" the blessed life of bliss. In my opinion, you see, the blessed life of bliss is signified by the word "paradise."

The Cherubim and the flaming sword

23, 35. *Now God set the Cherubim and the flaming sword which turns*, or, in one word, the flaming "whirling"[49] sword, *to guard the way to the tree of life* (Gn 3:24). According to those who have given us translations of the Hebrew words in the scriptures, "Cherubim" means "Fullness of knowledge."[50] By the flaming, whirling sword, on the other hand, are to be understood temporal punishments and pains, since time goes whirling and spinning along. The reason it is also said to be flaming is that all tribulation burns us up in one way or another. But being burned up to be got rid of is one thing, being burned up to be purified another. Even the apostle says, after all: *Who is being tripped up, and I am not being burned up?* (2 Cor 11:29). But this painful feeling was purifying rather than destroying him, because it was coming from charity. And the trials and tribulations which are suffered by the just belong to this flaming sword, *since gold and silver is tested by fire, and acceptable men in the furnace of humiliation* (Sir 2:5). And again: *The potter's vessels are tested by the kiln, and just men by the trial of tribulation* (Sir 27:5). So then, since *whom God loves he disciplines, and gives every son whom he receives a beating* (Heb 12:6), we know, as the apostle says, *that tribulation produces patience, patience through testing* (Rom 5:3-4). Thus we both read and hear, and must certainly believe, that the tree of life is being guarded by fullness of knowledge and the flaming sword. Nobody therefore can get to the tree of life except through these two, that is, through putting up with troubles and having the fullness of knowledge.

36. Yes, but putting up with troubles is something that practically everyone who is stretching out to the tree of life has to undergo in this life, while the fullness of knowledge seems to fall to the lot of far fewer people. So it's as if by no means all who reach the tree of life get there through fullness of knowledge, though all know what it is to put up with troubles, that is the flaming, whirling sword. But let us pay attention to what the apostle says: *But the fulness of the law*

---

49. *Versatilis*, which of course derives immediately from the verb in the phrase *quae versatur*, "which turns."
50. The same interpretation of the word is given by Augustine in his *Expositions of the Psalms*, on Ps 71(72), and on Ps 98(99); also in his *Questions on Exodus*, II, q.105. It would seem to have been a commonplace among his "learned" contemporaries. There is not the slightest warrant for it in the Hebrew word, on the origin and etymology of which the scholars are not agreed.

is charity (Rom 13:10), and let us see this same love contained in that twin commandment: *You shall love the Lord your God with your whole heart, and with your whole soul, and with your whole mind; and You shall love your neighbor as yourself; on these two commandments hangs the whole law, and the prophets* (Mt 22:37.39-40). Then we can take it without the slightest hesitation that one does not only come to the tree of life through the flaming, whirling sword, that is, through the endurance of temporal troubles, but also through the fullness of knowledge, that is, through charity; because *if I do not have charity,* he says, *I am nothing* (1 Cor 13:2).

The story is also prophetic of Christ and the Church

24, 37. But I promised[51] that in this book I would consider first the account of things that have happened, which I think has now been unfolded, and go on to consider next what they prophesy; and this still remains to be considered briefly. I don't reckon, you see, that this will take us very long once we have set up a kind of clear signpost which will direct us through everything else. The apostle, you see, says that there is a great sacrament in the text which says: *For this reason a man shall leave father and mother and stick to his wife; and they shall be two in one flesh* (Gn 2:24). He explains what he means by adding: *But I mean in Christ and in the Church* (Eph 5:31-32). So then, what as a matter of history was fulfilled in Adam, as a matter of prophecy signifies Christ, who left his Father when he said: *I came out from the Father and have come into this world* (Jn 16:28). He didn't leave the Father spatially, because God is not contained in a space, nor by turning away from him in sin, in the way apostates leave God; but by appearing among human beings as a man, when *the Word was made flesh and dwelt among us* (Jn 1:14). This again doesn't signify any change in the nature of God, but the taking on of the nature of a lower, that is, of a human, person. That is also the force of the statement, *he emptied himself* (Phil 2:7), because he did not show himself to us in the honor and rank he enjoys with the Father, but cosseted our weakness while we did not yet have hearts and minds clean enough to see the Word as God with God. So what else do we mean by saying he left the Father, but that he forbore to appear to us as he is with the Father?

Again, he also left his mother, that is, the Synagogue and her old literal observance of the law, his mother *from the seed of David according to the flesh* (Rom 1:3), and stuck to his wife, that is, to the Church, so that they might be two in one flesh. The apostle after all calls him the head of the Church, and the Church his body.[52] And so he too was put to sleep, falling asleep in death, in order that his

---

51. See II,2,3 above.
52. See Col 1:18.

consort the Church might be formed for him. Of this falling asleep the prophet sings as he says: *I fell asleep and took my rest* (Ps 3:5). So then the Church was formed for him as his consort from his side, that is, from faith in his death and in baptism, because his side was pierced with a lance and poured out blood and water.[53] He *was made*, however, as I have just remarked, *from the seed of David according to the flesh*, as the apostle says, that is, as though from the mud of the earth when there was no man to work on the earth, because no man "worked" on the Virgin of whom Christ was born. *But a spring was coming up from the earth, and was watering all the face of the earth* (Gn 2:6). It is entirely appropriate and right to take the face of the earth, that is, the dignity and worth of the earth, as being the Lord's mother the Virgin Mary, watered by the Holy Spirit, who is given the name of spring and water in the gospel;[54] so that from that kind of mud, as it were, that man might be made who was set up in paradise to work there and guard it—that is, set up in the will of his Father to fulfill it and keep it.

Heretics, especially Manichees, prophetically signified by the serpent

25, 38. The instruction which he received, after all, we too received in him, because every Christian not inappropriately represents the person and plays the part of Christ, seeing that the Lord says himself: *What you did to one of the least of mine you did to me* (Mt 25:40). And if only we did just enjoy, as he was told to, the fruit of every tree in Paradise, which all together signify spiritual delights: The fruit of the Spirit is love, joy, peace, patience, kindness, generosity, faithfulness, gentleness, and self-control, as the apostle says, and did not touch the tree of knowledge of good and evil planted in the middle of Paradise, did not want, that is, to be over-proud of our own nature, which as we have already remarked is just a mid-point in the scheme of things! If only, that is, we hadn't been led astray and so learned by bitter experience what the difference is between single-minded Catholic faith and the deceptions of heretics! That, you see, is how we came to distinguish between good and evil. *For there also have to be heresies*, he says, *so that those who are of approved worth among you may show up* (1 Cor 11:19).

For indeed in terms of prophecy that serpent signifies the various heretical poisons, and above all the one of these Manichees, and any others which are opposed to the Old Testament. I am convinced, you see, that nothing is more manifestly foreshadowed in that serpent than this crew—or rather that it is he

---

53. See Jn 19:34. The blood has traditionally been taken to represent the eucharist, and the water baptism, the two sacraments that as it were constitute the Church; but Augustine here seems to take them both as signifying baptism, no doubt having 1 John 5:6 in mind: *This is the one who came through water and blood, Jesus Christ, not in water only but in water and blood.*
54. See Jn 7:37-39; 4:14.

who is to be shunned in them. There are none, you see, who are more boastful and talkative than they are in promising knowledge of good and evil, and presumptuously assuming that they are going to demonstrate this distinction in the human person, as in the tree which was planted in the middle of paradise. And then as for the words, *You shall be like gods* (Gn 3:5), who else say it more often than these people, striving with their proud nonsense to lead others into the same kind of pride, and affirming that the soul is by nature what God is? And who more than these are responsible for the opening of the eyes of the flesh, forsaking as they do the inner light of wisdom, and imposing on their followers the worship of this sun which is reached by the eyes of the body? But as a matter of fact all heretics in general lead people astray with the promise of knowledge, and severely criticize those they find to be simple believers; and because the wares they are hawking are altogether the values of the world and the flesh, it's as if they are striving to bring people to the opening of the eyes of the flesh, in order to blind the inner eye of the heart.

26, But these people even find their own bodies displeasing, not because they bear the punishment of mortality which we earned by sinning, but to the extent of denying that God is the maker of bodies, as if finding their nakedness displeasing when their eyes of flesh were opened.

The Manichees tell lies about Christ and also declare that he told lies himself

39. But nothing more inexorably points to these people and picks them out than the serpent saying: *You will not die the death; for God knew that on the day you eat your eyes will be opened* (Gn 3:4-5). You see, what these people believe about this bit is that the serpent was Christ, and the story they stick to is that it was some god or other of a race of darkness (that's their expression) who gave that command, as though he begrudged human beings the knowledge of good and evil. This opinion, I imagine, gave birth also to the snake people, whatever they are,[55] who are said to worship the serpent as Christ, and who ignore what the apostle says: *I am afraid that just as the serpent led Eve astray by his cunning, so your good sense too may be corrupted* (2 Cor 11:3). So these then are the ones who, I reckon, were prefigured in this prophecy. Now what is led astray by the words of this serpent is our fleshly desire, and through it Adam is deceived, not Christ but the Christian.

You see, if he were willing to keep God's command, and persevered in living by faith[56] until he became capable of really understanding the truth, that is, if he

---

55. Ophites, a group of Gnostics who did identify Christ with the serpent of Genesis, and about whom Augustine would have learned, in all probability, from the handbook *Heresies* of the professional heresy detector of that age, Epiphanius, bishop of Salamis in Cyprus.
56. See Rom 1:17. The Christian he has in mind, evidently, is the one who is taken in by the Manichees and goes along with them, as he had done himself not so very long before.

worked in paradise and guarded what he had received, he wouldn't come to that deformed state of mind which would lead him, when displeased with the flesh as with his nakedness, to put together worldly, carnal coverings of lies, like fig-leaves with which to make himself an apron. That after all is what these people do when they tell lies about Christ and declare that he also told lies. And the way they hide themselves from the face of God is by turning away from his truth to their own lies. As the apostle says, *And they turn their ears indeed away from the truth, while they turn towards fables themselves* (2 Tm 4:4).

40. And indeed that serpent, to wit that error of the heretics which tempts the Church, against which that snake charmer, the apostle, sings his spell when he says: *I am afraid that just as the serpent led Eve astray by his cunning, so your good sense too may be corrupted* (2 Cor 11:3), so then that error crawls along on its bosom and belly, and eats earth. The only ones it takes in, you see, are either the proud, who arrogate to themselves a status that is not theirs, and readily come to believe that God most high and the human soul share one and the same nature, or else those tangled up in the desires of the flesh, who are only too happy to hear that whatever they do as they kick over the traces is not being done by themselves but by the race of darkness, or else finally the curious and inquisitive, who are worldly wise and enjoy the taste of earthly things, and go looking for the spiritual with a fleshly eye.[57]

There will be enmity though between this error and the woman, and between its seed and the woman's seed, if she gives birth to children, even though with pain, and turns toward her man, so that he may lord it over her. That, you see, is when the truth can begin to dawn on us that there is not one part of us belonging to God as its author, and another belonging to the race of darkness, as these people say, but rather that both that in us which has the right to govern and that lower element which has to be governed come from God, as the apostle says: *The man indeed ought not to veil his head, as he is the image and glory of God; but the woman is the glory of the man. For man is not from woman, but woman from man; in fact the man was not created for the woman's sake, but the woman for the man's. That is why the woman ought to have a veil over her head, for the sake of the angels. However, neither woman without man nor man without woman in the Lord; for just as the woman was from the man, so is the man through the woman, while all things are from God* (1 Cor 11:7-12).

---

57. See above, 17,26 for how the serpent's bosom represents the proud and its belly the lascivious; and xviii,27 and note 32 there, for the curious or inquisitive being signified by its eating earth.

Adam's fall and punishment interpreted allegorically

27, 41. Now let Adam get to work in his own field, and understand that the earth is yielding him thorns and thistles as a punishment, not as a mere fact of nature. And let him put this down to a divine judgment, not to heaven knows what race of darkness, because the golden rule of justice is to grant to each what is his own. Let him give the woman heavenly food, which he has received from his head, who is Christ; let him not receive forbidden fruit from her, the deceitful doctrine, that is, of the heretics with its great promise of knowledge, and the disclosure of some marvelous secrets or other, as a kind of seasoning to make the error more attractive—and effective. It is indeed the proud and prying greed of heretics which is crying out in the book of Proverbs under the figure of a woman, and saying: *Whoever is foolish, let him turn aside to me*; and inviting in those lacking in sense with the words: *Enjoy eating bread in secret, and find stolen water sweet to drink* (Prov 9:16-17).

And when anybody does, for all that, believe all this nonsense, brought to it by a lust for lying which lets him believe that Christ also told lies, it is absolutely unavoidable that by a divine judgment he should also receive a tunic of skin. What is prophetically signified by this, it seems to me, is not the mortality of the body, which is the historical signification we have already dealt with, but the fancies and imaginations drawn in from the senses of the flesh, which in consequence of his flesh-bound lies are imposed as a covering on the liar by a divine law. And in this garb he is sent away from Paradise, that is, from Catholic faith and truth, destined to live over against Paradise, that is to say, to work and speak against the same faith.

But should the time come that he turns back to God through the flaming sword, that is, through the troubles time brings, by acknowledging and grieving for his sins, and no longer blaming them on some extraneous nature (which doesn't exist) but on himself, in order to be worthy of pardon, and also through the fullness of knowledge, which is charity, by loving God who is supreme above all things and never changes, and by loving him with his whole heart and whole soul and whole mind, and by loving his neighbor as himself, then he will come through to the tree of life, and live for ever.

Conclusion; summary answers to Manichee objections

28, 42. So then, what do these people find to criticize in these passages of the Old Testament? Let them interrogate us in their usual manner, and let us give the answers the Lord may be pleased to grant us.

"Why did God make the man," they say, "knowing he was going to sin?"

Because even from a sinner he could produce many good results, allotting him his due place according to the standard of his justice, and because his sin didn't put any obstacle in God's way, seeing that if he didn't sin, there wouldn't be any death, and that because in fact he did sin, other mortals are set right as a result of his sin. Nothing, after all, is so effective in deterring people from sin as the thought of their imminent death.[58]

"He should have made him," they say, "in such a way that he wouldn't sin."

Well, but that's precisely what he did do; the man was so made, after all, that if he hadn't wanted to, he wouldn't sin.

"The devil," they say, "should not have been given access to the man's woman."

On the contrary, it's she who shouldn't have given the devil access to herself. She was so made, after all, that if she hadn't wanted to she wouldn't have done so.

"The woman," they say, "shouldn't have been made."

That amounts to saying that something good should not have been made, because she too of course is something good, and such a great good that the apostle says she is the glory of the man, and that all things come from God.

Again they say: "Who made the devil?"

He did himself; it is not, you see, by nature but by sinning that he became the devil.[59]

"Well at any rate," they say, "God should not have made him if he knew he was going to sin."

On the contrary, why should he not have made him, when through his justice and providence he uses the devil's malice to set many people right? Or perhaps you haven't heard the apostle Paul saying: *Whom I have handed over to Satan, that they may learn not to blaspheme* (1 Tm 1:20)? And about himself he says: *And lest my head should be swollen by the greatness of the revelations, there was given me a goad of the flesh, an angel of Satan to box my ears* (2 Cor 12:7).

"So then," they say, "the devil is good, because he is useful, eh?"

On the contrary, he is bad insofar as he is the devil. But God is good and almighty, able to bring about much goodness and justice from the devil's malice. The only thing, after all, that is credited to the devil is his own will by which he strives to work evil; God's providence, which makes good use of him, is not to his credit.

---

58. As Dr. Johnson, I believe, is supposed to have said: "Nothing so concentrates the mind as knowing that you are going to be hanged in the morning."
59. "Devil" from *diabolus*, of which the primary meaning in Greek is "accuser," "prosecutor," "adversary"; and it is an accurate translation of the Hebrew *satan*, as is evident from the first two chapters of the book of Job, where Satan really appears as the public prosecutor in the heavenly court, also combining with that role the work of *agent provocateur*, which makes him in due course the tempter.

The nature of God

29, 43. Finally, what is at issue between the Manichees and ourselves is a question of religion, and *the* religious question is how to think about God in a godly way. Now since we cannot deny that the human race is sunk in the sorry state of sin, *they* say that God's nature is sunk in a sorry state, while *we* deny that, and say that the nature which God made out of nothing is sunk in a sorry state, and has come to this pass, not by being forced into it but through its will to sin. *They* say that God's nature is forced by God himself to repent of sins; *we* deny this, but say instead that the nature which God made out of nothing is obliged after it has sinned to repent of its sins. *They* say that the nature of God receives pardon from God himself; *we* deny this, but say instead that the nature which God made out of nothing, if it turns back to its God from its sins, receives pardon for its sins. *They* say that God's nature is subject to the necessity of change; *we* deny this, but say that the nature which God made out of nothing is changed by its own will. *They* say that God's nature is injured by the sins of others; *we* deny this, but say instead that no nature is harmed by any sins except its own; and we say that God is so good, so just, so immune to harm, that he neither sins, nor does any harm to anyone who has refused to sin, and neither does anyone who has decided to sin do any harm to him.

They say that there is a nature of evil to which God was forced to hand over a part of his own nature to be tortured. *We* say that there is no natural evil, but that all natures are good, and God himself is the supreme nature and all other natures come from him; and all are good insofar as they exist, since God made all things *very good* (Gn 1:31), but ranged them in an order of graded distinctions, so that one is better than another; and in this way the whole universe is completed out of every kind of good thing, and with some of them being perfect, others imperfect, is itself a perfect whole, which God its founder and author does not for a moment cease to administer in a completely just regime. The one who chose to make all things good by his will is not subject to any necessity of evil, seeing that since his will presides over all things, he does not experience anything in any shape or form against his will.

So then, since *they* say all that, and *we* say all this, let everyone choose which side to support. I for my part have been speaking in good faith before God, and so without any love of confrontation, without any wavering over the truth, and without prejudice to any more careful and thorough treatment of the subject, I have set out what seemed to me to be right.

Unfinished Literal Commentary on Genesis

Introduction

Origin and intention

The Augustine who had been living a contemplative life in Thagaste had meanwhile become a priest in Hippo (391); there, together with some friends, he lived in a monastic community. Among his most important tasks during the ensuing period was the instruction of the faithful and the preaching of God's word to them. The Manichees were active in Hippo as elsewhere and, as Possidius tells us, not a few Christians were impressed by their propaganda.[1]

Given this situation, Augustine decided to compose another commentary on the book of Genesis.[2] In his *Revisions* he describes in detail the origin and fate of the work: "The two books on Genesis which I composed against the Manichees treated of the words of scripture according to the allegorical sense, because I did not dare expound in their literal meaning such great mysteries of the natural order; that is to say, how what is said there can be taken as strictly historical. So later on I wished to test what I was capable of in this most laborious and difficult work as well; but tyro that I was in the business of expounding scripture, I soon collapsed under the weight of such a burden. And without having completed one book, I laid aside a task I was unable to keep up.

"But when in this work I am engaged on here [that is, the *Revisions*] I was revising my minor works, this one, unfinished as it was, came into my hands. I had never published it and had decided to suppress it, since later on I wrote a work in twelve books, of which the title is *A Literal Commentary on Genesis*. In them indeed there seem to be many more questions asked than answers found, but still that earlier effort is in no way to be compared with them. However, I preferred to keep this one too after I had revised it, as a pointer that will not, I think, be without its use, to my first attempts at cracking open and exploring the divine writings; and I have decided its title is to be *Unfinished Literal Commentary on Genesis*."[3]

---

1. Possidius, *Life of Augustine* 6, 1.
2. On this work generally see L. Carrozzi, *Sant'Agostino, Libro incompiuto su la Genesi* (Nuova Biblioteca Agostiniana 9/1; Rome, 1988) 185-193; M. Marin, "Il *De Genesi ad litteram imperfectus liber*," in *De Genesi contra Manichaeos, De Genesi ad litteram liber imperfectus* (Lectio Augustini 8; Palermo, 1992) 117-151.
3. *Revisions* I, 18, 1 (CCL 57, 54). See D. Weber, "In scripturis exponendis tirocinium meum succubuit. Zu Augustins frühen Versuchen einer Genesis-Exegese," in *L'esegesi dei Padri*

The composition of the unfinished commentary can hardly have taken more than a year and must have been done between 393 and 395. When revising the work in 426, Augustine returned to the last verse he commented on (Gn 1:26a) and added a few sentences.[4] The addition consists of the final two paragraphs in modern editions. The commentary remained nonetheless incomplete. In the *Revisions*, departing from his practice in dealing with his other works, Augustine did not make any corrections of individual passages in this work; instead he referred to his comprehensive commentary in *The Literal Meaning of Genesis*. It is in the light of this last-named work, with which "that earlier one [the *Unfinished Literal Commentary on Genesis*] is in no way to be compared," that the reader is to judge the earlier work.

Intention and hermeneutics

Augustine introduced his commentary by setting down two important methodological principles.[5] Any appropriate exegesis presupposes, first, that a distinction is made between probability and certainty and, second, that the norm of faith is not forgotten. This briefly sketched hermeneutics relies, therefore, in equal measure on both *ratio* and *fides*. The significance of this position for exegetical practice is as follows: The interpreter of the sacred scriptures must not thoughtlessly propose uncertain and dubious theses in difficult questions about the world created by God and pass these off as definitively true. The only reasonable method is to advance "by asking questions [rather] than by making affirmations."

The uncertainty involved in asking questions should not, however, "exceed the bounds of the Catholic faith." Augustine then compares this approach to ecclesial exegesis with the way heretics interpret the scriptures. The latter subordinate the understanding of the Bible to their own subjective views. By way of contrast, Augustine prefixes to his commentary a short summary of the Catholic faith,[6] in order thereby to establish the framework within which he will investigate the biblical text in the manner already described.[7]

His own investiture with an ecclesial office was probably not the least of the reasons why Augustine here explicitly emphasizes the faith of the Church as a hermeneutical principle, in contrast to the approach in his earlier commentary on Genesis.[8] At around this same time (on October 8, 393), Augustine, a presbyter,

---

latini dalle origini a Gregorio Magno (Studia Ephemeris Augustinianum 68; Rome, 2000) 225-232.
4. See ibid.
5. See *Unfinished Literal Commentary on Genesis* 1, 1.
6. See ibid., 1, 2-4.
7. See ibid., 2, 5.
8. But see *On Genesis: A Refutation of the Manichees* II, 2, 3: "avoid blasphemy . . . and present everything as in accordance with Catholic faith."

had to give the opening sermon on the creed at the Council of Carthage (= *Faith and the Creed*). A few years later, in *Teaching Christianity*, his manual on interpretation, Augustine set down the principle that the *regula fidei* must provide the framework within which the interpreter of scripture takes his bearings.[9] Since, in Augustine's understanding of it, the rule of faith emerges from the interaction of clear passages of scripture and the Church's conscious faith, the norm of interpretation is not alien to and outside the scriptures. On the contrary, the rule of faith asserts the conviction that the scriptures, which had their origin within the Church, can be validly understood and interpreted only in and by the Church.

While Augustine does not mention the Manichees by name in his unfinished commentary on Genesis, certain of his assertions are clearly aimed at that sect.[10] Not only is the exegetical approach (a literal interpretation of Genesis) meant to show that the biblical account of creation was acceptable even when taken literally (the only sense which the Manichees regarded as legitimate) and could measure up to scientific and literary standards. In addition, the formulations of the rule of faith show that the confession of the creator God who created everything from nothing excludes a priori not only the philosophical idea of a demiurge but also and especially the dualism of the Manichean cosmogony.[11] The same is true of the assertion of the natural goodness of all things, by which Augustine clearly rejected the Manichean thesis of the substantiality of evil.[12] In his interpretation of the text Augustine repeatedly refers back to the faith of the Church as he has summarized it at the beginning; he does so in order to remind his readers of the unalterable basic facts that must give direction to any exegesis.[13]

The first principle which Augustine formulates in the opening chapter likewise comes repeatedly into play, namely, that definitive claims are not to be made as long as no irrefutable reason can be given for them or as long as other opinions seem no less plausible. Thus, for example, Augustine ends a series of hypotheses on Gen 1:1 with the observation: "It would have been impossible . . . to make any definitive assertions about these matters without incurring the charge of rashness *(nihil enim horum temere affirmare oportet)*."[14] In like manner, after allowing, in relation to Genesis 1:7, that "you may choose whichever [interpretation] you prefer," he qualifies this concession by saying: "only

---

9. See *Teaching Christianity* III, 2, 2: "You should refer . . . to the rule of faith, which you have received from the plainer passages of scripture and from the authority of the Church" (trans. Hill, 169). On the relationship between scripture and ecclesial tradition during the first centuries see J. N. D. Kelly, *Early Christian Doctrines* (London, 1993) 29-51.
10. See, for example, *Unfinished Literal Commentary on Genesis* 4, 11; 5, 23-24.
11. See ibid., 1, 2.
12. See ibid., 1, 3.
13. See ibid., 3, 6-10; 4, 13 and 18; 5, 19-20.
14. Ibid., 3, 10.

avoid asserting anything rashly, and something you don't know as if you did; and remember that you are just a human being investigating the works to the extent that you are permitted to do so."[15]

Both his realization of the inexhaustible depths of the divine words[16] and his awareness of his own limitations in the areas of exegesis, philology, physics, mathematics, astronomy, and so on allowed Augustine to propose numerous very divergent hypotheses, which he offered simply as possible interpretations of the biblical text. Indeed, it is not always clear which hypothesis he himself preferred.[17] On the other hand, it is clear in not a few passages which interpretative possibilities he favored or rejected.[18]

Exegesis

At the beginning of his commentary Augustine lists four ways of interpreting the Old Testament *(quattuor modi legis exponendae)*: "the way of history, the way of allegory, the way of analogy, the way of aetiology" *(secundum historiam, secundum allegoriam, secundum analogiam, secundum aetiologiam).*[19] As is shown by the appended definition of these exegetical terms and the application of each to the first verse of Genesis, Augustine seems to be thinking of four ways of reading Old Testament texts. An historical-literal reading (1) aims at an understanding of what has occurred and is being narrated. Aetiological (2) and analogical (3) readings likewise remain at the level of the literal meaning of the words, inquiring, on the one hand (2), into the reasons for a particular expression or a particular event and endeavoring, on the other hand (3), to show the compatibility and harmony with the gospel. An allegorical reading (4) looks beyond the literal sense for a higher, figurative sense. As Augustine explains in the *Revisions,*[20] he was attempting in this commentary a strictly historico-literal reading *(ad litteram/secundum historicam proprietatem)* of the text of Genesis.

---

15. Ibid., 9, 30; see 8, 29.
16. See *The Literal Meaning of Genesis* I, 21, 41; see *Teaching Christianity* III, 27,38 (CCL 32, 9f.); *Confessions* XII, 18, 27; XII, 32, 43 (CCL 27, 229 and 240). See Th. Finan, "St Augustine on the *mira profunditas* of Scripture. Texts and Contexts," in Th. Finan and V. Twomey (eds.), *Scriptural Intepretation in the Fathers: Letter and Spirit* (Patristic Hermeneutics. Proceedings of the Second Patristic Conference at Maynooth, 1993; Cambridge, 1995) 162-199.
17. See *Unfinished Literal Commentary on Genesis* 4, 18; 6, 27; 9, 30.
18. See ibid., 3, 10; 4, 13 and 17; 5, 19-20 and 25; 9, 31; 10, 32; 11, 34-35; 13, 40 and 42; 14, 46.
19. Ibid., 2, 5; *The Advantage of Believing* 3, 5 (CSEL 25/1, 7f.). On the subject see A. Penna, *Sant'Agostino, La Genesi* I (Nuova Biblioteca Agostiniana 9/1; Rome, 1988) LXI-LXV; Marin, "Il *De genesi* . . . ," (note 2, above) 123-127.
20. *Revisions* I, 18, 1 (CCL 57, 54).

His concrete understanding and practice of this exegetical undertaking can be seen in his interpretation of Genesis 1, 1, which begins his commentary after the conclusion of his programmatic explanations in the opening chapters. To inquire what the expression "in the beginning" *(in principio)* signifies when understood historically *(secundum historiam)* is to explain whether "in the beginning" means "in the beginning of time, or in the beginning, in the very Wisdom of God" *(in principio temporis; in principio, in ipsa sapientia)*.[21] The extensive weighing of the two hypotheses, as well as the demanding line of theological argument,[22] shows that in Augustine's thinking a commentary on the literal meaning of Genesis is not to be satisfied with a superficial understanding of the letter but must also grasp the metaphysical content of what the Bible is saying.

The story of creation does indeed use a language like that found in the historical books of the Bible. But what the language is describing is a metahistorical act that cannot be compared with the phenomenon of origin and development in the realm of human experience. As a result, the quest for the literal meaning of the divine creative act always requires that one move beyond the immediate reference of biblical statements to human experience and spatio-temporal categories.[23] Since sacred scripture adapts its manner of expression *(elocutio)* to the human capacity for understanding,[24] the exegete must be careful not to assign human concepts to God. Instead, the true literal meaning that is in keeping with the being of God must be found while respecting the *regula fidei*.[25]

In interpreting the literal meaning, Augustine, a former teacher of grammar and rhetoric, used the same methods employed in commenting on the ancient pagan authors.[26] This meant, on the one hand, a careful explanation of the words *(interpretatio verborum)* and, on the other, an explanation of the realities of which the text was speaking *(cognitio historiarum)*. Augustine is following this practice when he meticulously compares the sequence *(ordo)* of words in different verses of Genesis,[27] undertakes to give precise definitions of biblical terms *(principium, profunditas, tenebrae, nomen, dies, imago)*,[28] and analyzes

---

21. *Unfinished Literal Commentary on Genesis* 3, 6.
22. See ibid., 3, 6-8.
23. See Marin, "Il *De Genesi* . . . ," 127-130.
24. See *Unfinished Literal Commentary on Genesis* 13, 41: "the story is told in the only way it could be by human beings *(ita narratum est, ut hominibus potuit)*." See Marin, 135-138.
25. See *Unfinished Literal Commentary on Genesis* 5, 19.
26. See J. T. Lienhard, "Reading the Bible and Learning to Read. The Influence of Education on St. Augustine's Exegesis," *Augustinian Studies* 27 (1996) 7-25; F. Young, "The Rhetorical Schools and Their Influence on Patristic Exegesis," in *The Making of Orthodoxy* (Festschrift H. Chadwick; Cambridge, 1989) 182-99; Marin, "Il *De Genesi* . . . ," 130-143; idem, "*Nomen quasi notamen:* una nota su Aug. *Gen. litt. impf.* 6, 26," in G. A. Privitera (ed.), *Paideia Cristiana* (Studi in onore di M. Naldini; Rome, 1994) 227-234.
27. See *Unfinished Literal Commentary on Genesis* 9, 31; 10, 33; 13, 39 and 42; 15, 48.
28. See ibid., 3, 6; 4, 11-12; 6, 26; 7, 28; 16, 57.

repetitions, additions, omissions, and variations in the text.[29] In keeping with his programmatic statement at the beginning: *non affirmando, sed quaerendo tractandum est,*[30] he continually asks questions of the biblical text and subjects every nuance of what it says to a detailed analysis. The words *quaerere* or *quaestio* run like a refrain throughout Augustine's commentary on Genesis.[31]

In the practice of the ancient commentators the explanation of the words used was supplemented by an explanation of the realities mentioned in the text. Using various complementary sciences, a practice he later recommended in the second book of *Teaching Christianity*, Augustine, too, endeavored to explain problems of content in the biblical text. The fact that he acquired information about questions in physics, astronomy, and other natural sciences can be seen from places in the commentary on Genesis where he speaks about the cycle of the planets, the phases of the moon, and the origin of clouds, springs, and rivers.[32] Further references to the opinions of others (who are left anonymous) show that this exegete tried to acquaint himself with the "state of scholarship" in regard to Genesis.[33]

Importance of the work

Augustine's meticulous interpretation of the text of Genesis shows how the commentary respected the programmatic principles formulated at the beginning of the work. The many questions which the exegete puts to the biblical text and the abundance of his suggested answers attest that he was indeed determined to advance *non affirmando, sed quaerendo,*[34] that he distinguished carefully between opinions and certainties, and that he had equal respect for both reason and faith.

The reason why Augustine preserved and published this commentary despite its incompleteness may have been to leave behind him a document that would reveal an important phase of his theological and intellectual development.[35] As compared with his early work, *On Genesis against the Manichees*, the unfinished commentary on Genesis shows Augustine's effort to get beyond a primarily allegorical interpretation of the scriptures to an exegesis that was directed toward the literal meaning and made use both of the grammatical and

29. See ibid., 4, 12 and 13; 5, 25; 8, 30-9, 30; 10, 32; 11, 34 and 35; 13, 38-39 and 42; 14, 47; 15, 48-49 and 51-53; 16, 54.
30. Ibid., 1, 1.
31. See ibid., 2, 5; 3, 6-8 and 10; 5, 19, 21 and 24; 6, 26 and 27; 9, 30; 14, 44.
32. See ibid., 8, 29; 12, 37; 13, 38 and 40; 14, 44 and 47.
33. See ibid., 3, 7; 8, 29; 13, 40; 14, 46 and 47; 16, 62.
34. Ibid., 1, 1.
35. *Revisions* 1, 18, 1 (CCL 57, 54): "A pointer that will not, I think, be without its use, to my first attempts at cracking open and exploring the divine writings *(index . . . non inutilis rudimentorum meorum in enucleandis atque scrutandis divinis eloquiis)*."

rhetorical tools of textual explication and of the information supplied by the various auxiliary sciences. The results may clearly fall short of what is achieved in the later commentary on *The Literal Meaning of Genesis*, but the present work nonetheless does show Augustine's continual effort to achieve a perfection of his exegetical methods that would satisfy the demands of science and criticism.

Extract from *Revisions* (I, 18)

The two books on Genesis which I composed against the Manichees[1] treated of the words of scripture according to the allegorical sense, because I did not dare expound in their literal meaning such great mysteries of the natural order; that is to say, how what is said there can be taken as strictly historical. So later on I wished to test what I was capable of in this most laborious and difficult work as well; but tyro that I was in the business of expounding scripture, I soon collapsed under the weight of such a burden. And without having completed one book, I laid aside a task I was unable to keep up.

But when in this work I am engaged in here I was revising my minor works, this one, unfinished as it was, came into my hands. I had never published it and had decided to suppress it, since later on I wrote a work in twelve books, of which the title is *The Literal Meaning of Genesis*. In them indeed there seem to be many more questions asked than answers found, but still this one is in no way to be compared with them. However, I preferred to keep this one too after I had revised it, as a pointer that will not, I think, be without its use, to my first attempts at cracking open and exploring the divine writings; and I have decided its title is to be an *Unfinished Literal Commentary on Genesis*.

I found in fact that I had dictated it as far as these words: "Only the Father is Father, nor is the Son anything else but Son; because even while he is called the likeness of the Father, although this shows there is no unlikeness between them, still the Father is not alone if he has a likeness."[2] After that I repeated the words of scripture that needed to be considered and discussed over again, *And God said, Let us make man to our image and likeness* (Gn 1:26). Having dictated it all up to that point, I had left the book unfinished. What follows I decided to add when I was revising it, though even so I did not complete it by doing this, but even with this addition I have left it unfinished. If I had completed it, after all, I

---

1. Written between 388 and 390, while Augustine was still living as a layman in his community at his home town, Thagaste; O. Perler, *Les Voyages de Saint Augustin*, 433.
2. See 16, 60; and then, as he says, the opening words of section 61, repeating the scripture text. See notes 74 and 75 below. From what he says at the end of this paragraph, I think we may infer that he had intended this work to be a commentary just on the days of creation, Gn 1:1—2:4, whereas the 12 books of the later and major work go on to cover Gn 2 and 3, the stories of paradise and the fall.

would at least have discussed all the works and words of God that belong to the sixth day.

To make a note of the things I find unacceptable in this book, or to defend things that may be unacceptable to others when they are not well understood, seems to me to be unnecessary. I prefer in a word to advise people to read those twelve books which I composed long afterward as a bishop, and to pass judgment on this one in their light. This book begins with these words: "The obscure mysteries of the natural order, which we perceive to have been made by God the almighty craftsman, should rather be discussed by asking questions than by making affirmations."

Unfinished Literal Commentary on Genesis[1]

Introductory admonitions

1, 1. The obscure mysteries of the natural order, which we perceive to have been made by God the almighty craftsman, should rather be discussed by asking questions than by making affirmations. This is supremely the case with the books which have been entrusted to us by divine authority, because the rash assertion of one's uncertain and dubious opinions in dealing with them can scarcely avoid the charge of sacrilege. On the other hand the doubts and hesitations implied by asking questions must not exceed the bounds of Catholic faith. Many heretics, after all, have been in the habit of twisting their exposition of the divine scriptures to fit their way of thinking, which is quite at odds with the faith learned by Catholics. So before we undertake the study of this book of Genesis, we must briefly set out the Catholic faith.

2. Here then it is: that God the almighty Father made and established the whole of creation through his only-begotten Son, that is, through his wisdom and power[2] consubstantial and co-eternal with himself, in the unity of the Holy Spirit, who is also consubstantial and co-eternal. So Catholic teaching bids us believe that this Trinity is called one God, and that he made and created all things that are, insofar as they are, to the effect that all creatures, whether intellectual or corporeal,[3] or what more briefly according to the words of the divine scriptures can be called invisible or visible, are not born of God,[4] but made by God out of nothing, and that there is nothing among them which belongs to the Trinity,

---

1. Written shortly after Augustine was ordained priest in 393 or 394, according to the calculations of O. Perler, op. cit. 435.
2. See 1 Cor 1:24.
3. These are terms of the Neoplatonic philosophy which governed Augustine's thinking at this time—and which for most of his life he tended to equate too readily with Pauline and other biblical expressions. The "intellectual creation" was what Aristotle, developing Plato's ideas, would call separated substances, or subsistent intelligences (and which Christians would later equate with angels). These would also, however, for Augustine and the Neoplatonists, and indeed for Aristotle, include the human mind.
4. So one Vatican manuscript: *non de Deo nata*; others, followed by the Maurists, have *non de Dei natura*, "not of God's nature/substance."

except what the Trinity created—this nature was created.[5] For this reason it is not lawful to say or believe that the whole creation is consubstantial or co-eternal with God.

3. Again, that all things that God made, however, *are very good* (Gn 1:31), while evil things are not part of nature, but everything that is called evil is either sin or the punishment of sin, and sin is nothing but the twisted consent of the free will, when we stoop to things forbidden by justice which it is true freedom to abstain from. That is, sin consists not in the things themselves, but in the unlawful use of them. Now the use of things is lawful when the soul remains within the bounds of God's law and subject to the one God in unqualified love, and regulates other things that are subject to it without greed or lust, that is, in accordance with God's commandments. It is in this way, you see, that it will exercise control over them without any trouble or distress, and with the greatest ease and felicity.

The punishment though of sin is when the soul is tormented by created things themselves not being at its service, seeing that it declines to be itself at the service of God; this creation was once upon a time compliant to the soul, when the soul was compliant to God.[6] And so there is nothing evil about fire, since it is a creature of God; but all the same we in our frailty get burned by it as our sins justly deserve.

Again, that there are sins, however, which are said to be natural, because we cannot help committing them before God's mercy comes to the rescue, after we have fallen into this condition of life through the sin committed by free will.

4. Again, that humanity was made new once more through our Lord Jesus Christ, when God's inexpressible and unchangeable Wisdom herself deigned to take on full and complete humanity and to be born of the Holy Spirit and the virgin Mary, to be crucified, to be buried and rise again and ascend into heaven, which has all happened already; and to come to judge the living and the dead at the end of the age and the resurrection of the dead in the flesh, which is proclaimed as being yet to come; that the Holy Spirit has been given to those who believe in him, that mother Church has been established by him, which is called Catholic insofar as it has been in all respects perfected and is in no way defective and has spread through the whole wide world; that their previous sins have been

---

5. He must be referring, in a rather puzzling sentence, to the humanity of Christ; Christ as man is a creature, created by God the Trinity, and yet he "belongs" to the Trinity. At the back of Augustine's mind, I feel sure, is the text of Proverbs 8:22, divine Wisdom, identified with the eternal Logos or Word, saying *The Lord created me in the beginning of his work.* This was always something of a crux for the Fathers; it seemed to support the Arian error that the divine Word was created, the error against which the Nicene creed introduced the phrase "begotten, not made." The Latin word used here by Augustine, and in his Latin version of this text, is *condere,* not *creare.* Jerome got round the difficulty in his Latin Vulgate version by translating the Hebrew verb *qanani* "possessed me"; modern English versions, RSV and Jerusalem, disagree with him, and revert to "created me."

6. That is, before the fall.

forgiven to those who are repentant; and in eternal life and the promise of the kingdom of heaven.[7]

History, allegory, analogy, and aetiology

2, 5. We must now consider the things that can be asked about and discussed in this book, in accordance with this faith. *In the beginning God made heaven and earth* (Gn 1:1). Four ways of expounding the law have been laid down by some scripture commentators, which can be named in words derived from the Greek, while they need further definition and explanation in plain Latin; they are the way of history, the way of allegory, the way of analogy, the way of aetiology. History is when things done by God or man are recounted; allegory when they are understood as being said figuratively; analogy, when the harmony of the old and new covenants is being demonstrated; aetiology, when the causes of the things that have been said and done are presented.

Various historical ways of interpreting Gn 1:1

3, 6. So about these words, *In the beginning God made heaven and earth*, one may inquire whether they are only to be taken in an historical sense, or whether they also have some figurative meaning, and how they agree with the gospel, and what the cause is of this book's beginning in this way. As regards the historical sense, we ask what *in the beginning* means; that is, whether it is in the beginning of time, or in the beginning, in the very Wisdom of God, because the Son of God actually called himself the beginning when he was asked *Who are you, then?* and he said, *The beginning*,[8] *as which I am also speaking to you* (Jn 8:25). There is,

---

7. This exposition of the Catholic faith is presumably an amplified statement of the Apostles' Creed in its African form, that is, the baptismal creed of the African Church, with occasional reference, which the reader will recognize, to the Nicene Creed; but to this, however, in the form in which it left the Council of Nicea in 325, which ended with the words "and in the Holy Spirit." The rest of the creed as we recite it today, from "the Lord, the giver of life" to "the life of the world to come," was added at the Council of Constantinople in 381, and was not known in the Western, Latin-speaking Churches until very much later. That Council was assumed in the West to be a purely Eastern affair of the Greek-speaking Churches, as is clear from the distinctly hostile reaction to one of its decrees by Leo the Great after the Council of Chalcedon in 451; he would not accept its canon according the see of Constantinople the second place after the see of Rome, with precedence over Alexandria and Antioch.

8. The literal rendering by the Latin versions of a very peculiar Greek idiom, variously translated in modern versions. But R.H. Lightfoot in his commentary, published posthumously (Oxford, 1956), suggests that Jesus' answer should be construed as "From the beginning I am that which I am also telling you," and argues that this rendering recalls the basic teaching of this gospel that the speaker is the Word who "was in the beginning with God"; and this accords very well with the meaning of the Latin version Augustine had. Lightfoot rejects the Revised Version translation, and in effect all other contemporary translations, on the grounds that while they are possible translations of this Greek sentence, they do not really fit the whole context of this chapter—or of this gospel.

you see, a beginning without beginning, and there is a beginning with another beginning. The beginning without beginning only the Father is; and that is why we believe that all things come from one beginning. The Son however is the beginning in such a way that he is from the Father.

The supreme intellectual creature[9] can also be called the beginning of those things it is the head of, which God made. For since the beginning or origin of something is rightly called its head,[10] it was only the woman whom the apostle did not call the head of anything in that scale he set out;[11] because he called the man the head of the woman, and Christ the head of the man, and God the head of Christ; in this way is the creature linked up to the creator.

7. Or is the reason it says *In the beginning* that this was the first thing made? Or is it impossible for heaven and earth to have been the first thing to have been made in creation, if the angels and all the intellectual powers were made first, because we have to believe that the angels too are God's creation and were made by him? For the prophet had also mentioned angels in Psalm 148 when he said, *It was he that gave orders, and they were made, he that commanded, and they were created* (Ps 148:5.2).

But if the angels were the first thing to be made, one can ask whether they were made in time, or before all time, or at the actual start of time. If in time, time was already there before the angels were made; and since time also is itself something created, we are on the point of being obliged to accept that something was made before the angels. If however we say that they were made at the start of time, so that time began with them, then we have to rule out as false what some people maintain, that time began with heaven and earth.[12]

8. If, though, the angels were made before time, the question arises how it can be said in the following passage, *And God said, Let lights be made in the firmament of heaven, to shine upon the earth, and to divide between day and night; and let them be for signs and for times and for days and for years* (Gn 1:14). Here, after all, it may seem that that was when time began, when the heavens and the lights of heaven began to run their regular courses. But if that is the case, how could there be days before there was time, if time started with the courses of the lights of heaven, which are said to have been made on the fourth day? Or were these days arranged in this order as a help to human frailty, and to suggest sublime things to lowly people in a lowly manner by following the basic rule of

---

9. The phrase suggests the angelic creation; but in the context I think he must here be referring to the humanity of Christ, to the man Christ Jesus; thus giving a double justification to Jesus calling himself the beginning, both as the Word, the Wisdom of God, and as the man the Word became.

10. Not commonly in English; but the source of a river can also be called its head—Thames head, the source of the Thames.

11. See 1 Cor 11:3.

12. The opinion of most of Augustine's older contemporaries, such as Basil and Ambrose.

story-telling, which requires the story teller's tale to have a beginning, a middle and an end?

Or did it say there should be lights in *these* times, meaning the times which human beings measure by marking intervals of space in the movement of a body? There would be none of these times, you see, if there were no movement of bodies, and times so measured are the ones people are most immediately aware of. If we allow this, the question arises whether, apart from the movement of material bodies, there can be time in the movements of an immaterial creature such as the soul is, or the mind itself. This certainly experiences movement in its thoughts, and in this movement there is something that comes first, and something that comes next, and this cannot be understood without some interval of time. If we accept this, then it can be readily understood that there was time even before heaven and earth, if the angels were made before heaven and earth because that means there was already a creature which would move time along by immaterial movements, and so we rightly understand that time also existed with it, as it does in the soul, which has grown accustomed through the senses of the body to bodily movements. But perhaps it is not there in the supreme principalities and powers.

But however this may be—it is, after all, a most abstruse matter, quite impenetrable to human guesswork—this assuredly has to be accepted in faith, even if it exceeds our habits of thought, that everything created has a beginning and that time itself is something created, and thus itself also has a beginning, and is not co-eternal with the creator.

9. It can also be reasonably supposed that "heaven and earth" are put here for the whole of creation, so that both this visible firmament of ether[13] is called heaven, and so too is that invisible creation of the higher powers; and again that "earth" means the whole lower part of the universe, together with the animals that occupy it. Or else, is "heaven" what the whole sublime and invisible creation is called, while "earth" means the whole visible world, so that in this way too what is said here, *In the beginning God made heaven and earth*, can be understood to include the whole of creation? May one suggest, perhaps, that it is not inappropriate for everything visible to be called "earth" in comparison with the invisible creation, so that this alone is given the name of "heaven," since the soul too, which is invisible, was called earth when it started being swollen with love of visible things, and preening itself on their acquisition, as it is written, *What have earth and ashes to be proud of?* (Sir 10:9).

---

13. The Greek *aither*, originally just a poetic word for air, but later distinguished from the air of the lower atmosphere, and treated by Aristotle and others as a "fifth element" (a *quintessence*), of which the firmament and the heavenly bodies were made, it being assumed they could not be composed of any or all of the four terrestrial elements, earth, water, fire and air, because they do not appear to behave like any of these.

10. But the question also arises, whether it was all things already sorted out and put together that he called heaven and earth, or whether it was on the originally formless matter of the universe, which was distributed into all these formed and specific and beautiful[14] natures at God's wordless command, that he bestowed the name of heaven and earth. For although we have read the text, *You that made the world from formless matter* (Wis 11:17), still we cannot say that such matter itself, whatever sort of thing it may be, was not made by him, from whom we confess and believe that all things derive their being. So what we would have then, is that the ordering and arrangement of the things, all and sundry, which have been formed and sorted out is called "world," or "universe," while the basic material itself was named "heaven and earth," as being the seed, so to say, of heaven and earth, as being heaven and earth all mixed up and thrown in together by the craftsman, God, ready for receiving those forms.[15]

Up to this point we have been inquiring about the meaning of the text, *In the beginning God made heaven and earth*; it would have been impossible, after all, to make any definite assertions about these matters without incurring the charge of rashness.

Genesis 1:2; the earth invisible and shapeless; darkness over the abyss

4, 11. *Now the earth was invisible and shapeless, and there was darkness over the abyss; and the Spirit of God was being borne over the water* (Gn 1:2). The heretics who reject the Old Testament[16] are in the habit of pointing the finger at this passage, and saying, "How can God have made heaven and earth in the beginning, if the earth was already there?" They fail to understand that this verse was added to explain what the earth was like, about which it had already said, *God made heaven and earth*. So this is how we have to take it: *In the beginning God made heaven and earth*; but this earth, which God made, was invisible and shapeless, until it was sorted out by the same God and from its original mishmash established in a definite order of distinct things.

Or is it better to understand it like this, that in this execution of God's design the same material of the world was again being presented as had been first named heaven and earth, so that this would be the sense here: "In the beginning God made heaven and earth; but this that is called heaven and earth was the invisible and shapeless earth, with darkness over the abyss; that is, what was called heaven and earth was a kind of mixed-up material out of which the world

---

14. A double translation of the single word *speciosas*.
15. The image seems to be that of something like a foundry for making instruments of bronze or brass.
16. The Manichees; and earlier on in the second century Marcion and his followers.

(which consists of two chief parts, namely heaven and earth) would be fashioned by the sorting out of its elements and the bestowal on them of shape and form?" This mixed-up material could best be suggested to the comprehension of the common man if it was called earth that was invisible and shapeless, or unordered and unfurnished and darkness over the abyss, that is, over the vast deep; and this deep in turn was perhaps given this name because owing to its formlessness nobody's mind could fathom it.

12. *And there was darkness over the abyss.*[17] The question arises, whether the abyss was underneath and the darkness above, as though places had already been distinguished and defined. Or else, since the mishmash of material is still being explained, which is also called *chaos* in Greek, is the reason it says *there was darkness over the abyss* just because there was no light? If there had been, it would of course have been above, because it would have been lighting up from a higher point the things subjected to it—and indeed, if you consider carefully what darkness is, you will find it to be nothing but the absence of light. So this, therefore, is what it means by *there was darkness over the abyss*, as if it had said, "there was no light over the abyss." Hence this material, which is arranged and distinguished by God's subsequent activity into the forms of things, is called the invisible and shapeless earth, and the deep without light. In the preceding sentence it had been given the name of "heaven and earth" as being a kind of seed of heaven and earth, as I have already said, provided, that is, that God was not intending to point to the whole universe first by saying "heaven and earth," so that he could then go on to construct the parts of the world after suggesting the material it was to be made of.

Genesis 1:2; what may be meant by "water"

13. *And the Spirit of God was being borne over the water* (Gn 1:2). Nowhere had it said, "God made the water," and yet in no way may we believe that God did not make the water and that it already existed before he had constituted anything. He after all is the one *from whom are all things, through whom are all things, in whom are all things* (Rom 11:36), as the apostle says. Therefore God made the water too, and to believe otherwise is a serious error. So why does it not say that God made the water? Or again, did he also wish to call "water" the same material as he had already named either "heaven and earth," or "invisible and shapeless earth," or "abyss"? Why, after all, could it not be called water, if it could be called earth, since so far neither water nor earth nor anything else had been sorted out and formed?

---

17. I here follow the text of the Maurists; the CSEL text has here, what it has not had in the previous quotations, *over the face of the deep.* But that is the Vulgate reading, which scribes were always likely to introduce inadvertently; I do not think it probable that Augustine had two Latin versions before him, and first quoted one, then the other.

But perhaps it is not inappropriate that it was first called heaven and earth, secondly shapeless earth and abyss without light, thirdly water; so that first of all the material should be called by the name of the whole universe on account of which the material itself was made from absolutely nothing, that is, "heaven and earth"; secondly that its formlessness should be suggested by the name of "shapeless earth" and "abyss," because among all the elements earth is more formless and less shiny than the others; thirdly that the material as subject to the work of the craftsman should be signified by the name of "water." Water, after all, is more mobile than earth, and that is why, because it is easier to work and more readily moved about, the material as subject to the craftsman had to be called water rather than earth.

14. And air, to be sure, is more mobile than water, while it may without absurdity be supposed or understood that ether is more mobile even than air. But it would be much less appropriate to call the basic material by the name of "air" or "ether"; for these elements are thought rather to have an active force, while earth and water are more passive. If this is not very obvious, I think that at least it is apparent enough that the wind moves water and some things made of earth;[18] but wind is air that is moving with a kind of wave motion. So then, since air manifestly moves water, while what it is itself moved by to become wind is not apparent, who could doubt that the basic material is more suitably called by the name of water, which is moved, than of air, which does the moving? Now being moved is being passive, causing movement is being active.

To this we can add that the things the earth brings forth are irrigated with water in order to be produced and to grow, in such a way that it almost seems as if the water itself is being turned into this teeming vegetation. For this reason the basic material, when it was being presented as subject to the craftsman's working, would be more suitably indicated by the name of water because of its mobile plasticity and the way it itself turns into any living, growing body, than by the name of air, in which it is only mobility that can be observed, while it lacks the other qualities which would more accurately signify the basic material.

Thus the sense of the whole passage would be: *In the beginning God made heaven and earth*, that is the basic material which would be able to receive the form of heaven and earth. This material *was earth, invisible and shapeless*, that is, a formless depth also lacking light; which however, since it was subject to the craftsman moving and working it, was also named water precisely because it is so pliable in the hands of the one working it.

15. So in this whole presentation, then, of the basic material, it was first its end that was suggested, what it was made for, that is; secondly its formlessness, thirdly its subjection to the craftsman and its being entirely at his service. And so

---

18. Trees are the obvious instance. Ancient chemistry was very simple, with its four elements of fire, air, earth and water—and the fifth "celestial" element of ether.

first heaven and earth—that, after all, is what the basic material was made for; secondly earth invisible and shapeless and darkness over the abyss, that is, its very formlessness without light—which is why the earth was also called invisible; thirdly water subject to the spirit or wind[19] for receiving its appearance and forms. That is why the Spirit of God was being borne over the water, to give us to understand the Spirit as working, the water as what he was working on, that is, as workable material. For when we name one thing in three ways, as the material of the world, as formless material, and as workable material, heaven and earth are rightly linked to the first way; obscurity, confusion, depth to the second; a yielding plasticity to the third, and to work on this the Spirit of the craftsman is already being borne over it.

Genesis 1:2; the meaning of the spirit of God

16. *And the Spirit of God was being borne over the water* (Gn 1:2); not like oil over water or water over earth, that is, as though being borne up by it; but if we must take examples from visible things, as this light of the sun or the moon is borne over these bodies which it illuminates on the earth. This is not, you see, being borne up by them, but while being borne up together with the sky or heaven, it is being borne over these things.

Again we must beware of supposing that the Spirit of God was being borne over the basic material as though covering a spatial distance, but rather as exercising a skill in making and fashioning things, in the way that the intention of a craftsman is "borne over" the wood or whatever it is he is working on, or even over the parts of his body, which he applies to the work. And while this comparison is much better than one with any bodily thing, still it is scarcely worth anything at all for understanding how the Spirit of God is borne over the material of the world to work on it. But we cannot find any clearer comparison, or any that is closer to the matter we are talking about in things that people can grasp in any way at all. For this reason the best thing to do in this kind of reflection will be to hold on to the injunction, where it is written: *When you praise the Lord, exalt him as much as you can; he will still be beyond you* (Sir 43:30). This however is said if "the spirit of God" in this place is taken to be the Holy Spirit, whom we venerate in the inexpressible and unchangeable Trinity.

---

19. I have added "or wind," because I think he has in mind here what he said earlier on about wind moving water, and not yet immediately the Spirit of God, which he is going to mention in a moment. The word *spiritus* in Latin has a much more manifest connection with breath and wind than "spirit" does in English.

17. However, it can also be understood in another way; we could understand the spirit of God to be a created vitality by which this whole visible world and all bodily things are held together and activated, a vital force to which the almighty God has granted a kind of power to serve him by acting in the things that are being produced. Since such a spirit is better even than any ethereal body, because every invisible creature has precedence over every visible one, it is not inappropriately called the spirit of God. What, after all, of the things he has established, is not "of God," seeing that it is also said of the earth itself, *The Lord's is the earth and its fullness* (Ps 24:1); and there is the all-embracing text, *Since all things are yours, Lord, lover of souls* (Wis 11:26)?

This spirit, however, can only be understood in this way, if we take the text *In the beginning God made heaven and earth* to refer only to the visible creation, so that this invisible spirit would have been borne over the basic material of visible things at the start of their construction; still itself, of course, being something created, not God that is, but a nature made and set up by God.[20] But if we think that it is the basic material of the total creation, that is both of the intellectual and the animal and the bodily creation, that is signified by that word "water," then in no way at all can "the spirit of God" in this place mean anything but the unchanging and Holy Spirit, which was being borne over the basic material of all the things that God made and established.

18. There could be a third opinion about this spirit, and it could be assumed that by the word "spirit" the element air was designated, so that in this way the four elements from which this visible world makes its appearance would be put before us; to wit sky or heaven,[21] and earth and water and air; not that they were already distinguished from each other and furnished, but that in the as yet shapeless mishmash of that basic material they were still being marked out beforehand as due to originate from it; this shapeless mishmash being presented under the names of "darkness" and "abyss."

But whichever of these opinions is true, we are bound to believe that God is the author and founder of all things that have originated,[22] both those that are seen and those that are not seen[23] —not as regards their vices, which are contrary

---

20. This "created vitality," this "vital force," would seem to be almost equivalent to "nature," in the way we often talk about "what nature intends," or "the purposes of nature."
21. Augustine must have known that the first or highest of the four elements of ancient cosmology was fire, not sky. But of course the word "fire" has not yet occurred in the text, and he took it for granted that everyone knew that the sky or heaven was the "proper place" for fire, to which it tended by its very nature.
22. Here and in the preceding sentence he uses the verb *exorior*; it is a word he seems to derive from Plato's *Timaeus*, 29c, in Cicero's translation. He quotes the passage in *The Trinity*, IV, 24-25: "What eternity is to that which has originated, that truth is to faith." A more accurate translation direct from the Greek would be: "As being is to becoming, so is truth to faith (belief)."
23. See 2 Cor 4:18.

to nature, but as regards their actual natures—and that there is absolutely no created thing at all which does not derive from him the beginning and the completion of its kind and its substance.

Genesis 1:3: With what kind of voice did God speak?

5, 19. *And God said: Let light be made, and light was made* (Gn 1:3). We are bound to agree that it was not with a voice issuing from lungs and tongue and teeth that God said "Let light be made." Such ideas are literal-minded and of the flesh; and to think according to the flesh is death.[24] No, he said *Let light be made* in a way that defies expression. Whether, though, what was said here was said to the only-begotten Son, or whether what was said here is the only-begotten Son, and on being spoken is called *the Word of God through which all things were made* (Jn 1:1.3), is a question that can be properly asked, provided, however, that we set aside the impious assumption that the Word of God, the only-begotten Son, is like a sound uttered in the way that happens with us. The Word of God, on the contrary, through which all things were made, neither began to be nor will cease to be; but being born without any beginning, he is co-eternal with the Father.

That's why, if the saying of "Let light be made" both began and stopped, we must conclude that this word was said to the Son rather than being the Son. Even so, however, it was said in a manner that defies expression. So let no materialist, fleshly image creep into the soul and disturb the godly, spiritual understanding, because for anything to begin or cease in the nature of God, if taken literally, is a rash and headstrong opinion. Still, this way of thinking is to be permitted out of sheer humanity to the little ones and the fleshly minded, not though for them to remain stuck in it, but for them to rise up from it in due course. Whatever, you see, God is said to begin or to stop doing is in no way to be understood as happening in his own nature, but in his creation, which submits to him in all its wonderful ways.

What sort of light was made

20. *And God said: Let light be made.* Is that light meant which spreads itself out before these eyes of flesh, or some hidden kind which it is not given us to see by means of this body? And if a hidden sort, is it of a bodily nature, extending perhaps through the higher parts of the universe in outer space, or is it incorporeal, of the kind to be found in the soul, to which the senses of the body refer for a judgment on whether to shun things or seek them? This is a light that is not

---

24. See Rom 8:6.

lacking even in the souls of animals. Or is it that higher light which reveals itself in the power or reasoning, from which everything that has been created has its beginning?[25]

But whichever kind of light is being signified, we are still, surely, obliged to take it as something made and created, and not the light which shines in God's own Wisdom, which was born, not created—in case it should be assumed that God was without any light before he instituted this sort that we are now dealing with. Of this sort, after all, as the very words indicate clearly enough, it is stated that it was made. *And he said*, the text goes, *Let light be made, and light was made*. Light born of God is one thing, light which God made quite another. Light born of God is God's very own wisdom, while light that has been made is any kind that is subject to change, whether it be incorporeal or corporeal.

21. People often wonder, though, how there could be any corporeal light before the sky or the heavens existed, and the lamps in the sky, which are set out after this light here, as though the human mind could easily grasp, or grasp at all, whether there is any light in addition to the heavens, which nonetheless is distinguished and spread out through space and embraces the universe. But since we are permitted here to understand an incorporeal light, if we say that in this book it is not only the visible creation but the entire creation that is being set before us, what need is there to linger over this argument? And the question people ask, when were the angels made?—well perhaps they are being indicated here, very briefly indeed, but still most aptly and suitably.

Genesis 1:4: the goodness of the light

22. *And God saw the light, that it was good* (Gn 1:4). This statement should be understood as signifying, not joy at some unexpected good, but approval of the work done. What, after all, could be said more aptly about God, insofar as anything can be said about him among human beings, than to put "he said," "it was made," "he approved" in such a way that in "he said" his command is to be understood, in "it was made" his power, in "he approved" his benevolence? The inexpressible, after all, was rightly expressed to human beings through human agency in such a way as to profit them all.

Genesis 1:4: how light was divided from darkness

23. *And God divided between the light and the darkness* (Gn 1:4). From this it can be gathered with what ease the divine work produced these effects. There is

---

25. As the next sentence shows, he is clearly not here identifying the power of reason in us with God's uncreated wisdom, that is, with the Word. He must, I suppose, mean the angelic intelligences.

nobody, after all, who would suppose that the light was made in such a way that it was all mixed up with the darkness, and so needed to be separated from it later on;[26] but from the sheer fact of light being made there followed the division between light and darkness. *For what fellowship does light have with darkness?* (2 Cor 6:14). So God then divided between the light and the darkness simply by making the light, the absence of which is called darkness. And the difference between light and darkness is the same as the difference between being clothed and being naked, or between full and empty, and so forth.

The various meanings darkness can have

24. We have already said above in how many ways light can be understood; their contrary lacks can be given the name of darkness. Thus there is the light which can be seen by these bodily eyes and which is itself bodily or corporeal, such as the light of the sun and moon and stars and anything of that sort; its contrary is darkness, when some place lacks this light. Next there is the light that is the sentient life which is able to distinguish the things that are referred through the body to the soul for judgment, such as white from black, melodious from cacophonous, sweet-smelling from stinking, sweet from bitter, hot from cold, and so on and so forth. The light, after all, which is perceived by the eyes is one thing, that which enables it to be perceived through the eyes is another. The first, clearly, is in the body, while the second, though it gets from the body the things it perceives, is for all that in the soul. The darkness contrary to this is a kind of insensitivity, or perhaps it would be better to call it insensuality,[27] that is, an inability to perceive things, even though things are being presented that could be perceived if there were present in that life this light by which perception takes place.

And this is not the case when the services provided by the body are lacking, as in blind or deaf people, because this light we are now talking about is present in their minds, but the body's instruments are wanting. Nor is it like the way no voice is heard in the silence, when this light is there in the soul and the body's instruments are in order, but nothing is being brought in to be perceived. So you don't lack this light if you fail to perceive anything from these causes; but it is lacking when there is no such power in the soul, which is not then usually called

---

26. Augustine must have known perfectly well that this is precisely what the Manichees believed. One supposes that he is pretending they do not exist, just to show his contempt for them.

27. *Insensualitas.* What the distinction is which he is making is not at all clear. I suspect that he invented this word. The only reference for it given by Lewis & Short is to Augustine's work *Answer to Faustus, a Manichean*, which he wrote shortly after becoming a bishop, that is to say, some years after this book on Genesis. There he uses it to signify the non-sentient character of stones, as distinct, perhaps, from the insensibility of an unconscious person, or animal, or the specific insensibility of a person or animal that is blind.

soul, but simply life, such as is attributed to vines and trees and any kind of plant, unless of course some could in any way be persuaded that they do have such a thing, as some extraordinarily mistaken heretics are convinced that they not only sense things through the body, that is, that they see and hear and are aware of heat and fire, but that they also understand by reason and know our thoughts.[28] But that's a different question altogether. So insensitivity is the darkness corresponding to this light by which things are perceived; it's the darkness when any kind of life does not have the power of perception.

Now you will grant that this power is suitably called light if you grant that we rightly call light whatever makes things clear. When we say, "This is clearly tuneful, this is clearly sweet, this is clearly cold" (and anything else of this sort that we perceive through the body), this light that makes these things clear is of course inside in the soul, although the things that are so perceived are brought into it through the body. We can understand a third kind of light in creatures, the kind by which we calculate and reason. Its contrary darkness is non-rationality, such as qualifies the souls of brute animals.

25. So even if this opinion would have us understand that light, whether of the ethereal variety, or the sensual in which animals share, or the rational which both angels and men enjoy, was the first thing to be made by God among the realities of nature,[29] it must still be accepted that God divided between the light and the dark in the actual making of the light, because light is one thing, quite another those absences of light, which God arranged for in the opposite kinds of darkness. It does not say, you see, that God made the darkness, because it is real forms or species that God made, not absences and lacks, which come under the head of nothing. Thus it is that absolutely everything really was made by God the craftsman; but we must still understand that these absences and lacks were arranged for by him, when it says, *and God divided between the light and the darkness.*

Otherwise, I mean to say, even these very lacks and absences would not have their due place in the total pattern of things designed and controlled by God. As in singing, for example, the moments of silence introduced at definite, carefully chosen intervals, while being absences or privations of words and notes, are for all that well ordered and arranged by those who know how to sing, and they contribute to the overall sweetness of the whole song. Or in pictures, the shadows mark out the more striking features, and satisfy by the rightness not of form but of order and arrangement. Because our vices also do not have God for

---

28. He is presumably referring to the Manichees. I here follow an emendation suggested by the Maurists, and read, *sed etiam intellegere per rationem et cogitationes nostras nosse arbitrantur*; the CSEL text leaves out *per*, giving the odd meaning, "are considered also to understand reason and to know our thoughts."

29. Which opinion? I think we have to refer back to the beginning of 5, 20.

their author, but he is still in control as their regulator, when he sets sinners in that place, and compels them to suffer what they deserve; that's the point of the sheep being placed on the right hand, the goats on the left.[30]

So then, there are some things that God both makes and controls or regulates, while there are some that he only regulates. He both makes and regulates the just; but sinners, precisely as sinners, he does not make but only regulates, in that he sets those on his right, these on his left; and that he bids these go into eternal fire means they rightly get what they deserve. So it is that he both makes and regulates the forms and natures of different species, while as for the shortcomings of forms and the defects of natures, he does not make them but only regulates them. And so he said, *Let light be made, and light was made*; he did not say, "Let darkness be made, and darkness was made." Of these two, then, he made one, not the other, while all the same he regulated and arranged for each of them, when "God divided between the light and the darkness." Thus there is beauty in every single thing, with him making it, and with him arranging them in regular order there is beauty in all things together.

Genesis 1:5: whether "light" and "day," "darkness" and "night," are in each case just two names for the same thing

6, 26. *And God called the light day, and the darkness he called night* (Gn 1:5). Now "light" is the name of a particular thing, and so again is "day"; and "darkness" and "night" are also each a name. So the question arises whether names were being given to things in such a way that the thing which had a name given it could simply be indicated by another name,[31] so that it would have made no difference if the statement *God called the light day* had been reversed, and it could have run, "God called the day light and called the night darkness." What answer shall we give when we are asked, Was the name "day" given to the light, or the name "light" given to the day[32]? Both these words, of course, insofar as they are uttered to signify things, are names. The same question can be asked about the other pair: was the name of "night" given to the darkness, or the name of "darkness" given to the night? And yet in fact, as the text of scripture stands, it is quite clear that "day" is the name light was called by and "night" the name darkness was called by, because when it said "God made the light and divided between the light and the darkness," it was not yet dealing with words; the words "day" and "night" were brought in later—though the first pair, to be sure, "light"

---

30. See Mt 25:33, and the following verses. "That place" is presumably hell.
31. Here he adds a parenthesis, *non enim aliter poterat*, "for it could not have been otherwise," the meaning of which is totally obscure to me. I leave it to readers to make of it what they can. It is just conceivable that it was a stenographer's marginal comment.
32. The Latin as it stands, where the order of words does not carry the same weight as in English, could be construed both ways: *Vocavit Deus lucem diem et tenebras vocavit noctem.*

and "darkness," are undoubtedly words, which signify particular things, just as "day" and "night" are.

Is this then how the verse has to be taken, because a thing that has received a name cannot be stated otherwise than by some other name? Or is this calling of a name to be taken as constituting the actual distinction? Not every kind of light after all is day, or every kind of darkness night; but it is the light and the darkness that are distinguished by succeeding one another in a regular order that are called by the names of "night" and "day." (Every designation, indeed, has a distinguishing function, which is why a name, *nomen*, which has to note a thing distinctively, is really, so to say, a *notamen*; it must note a thing, that is, distinguish it, and thus help the expositor in the task of discernment.[33])

So perhaps the very division between the light and the darkness was the same as calling the light day and the darkness night, so that calling them that was to arrange them in their regular order. Or were these designations meant to indicate to us what kind of light and what kind of darkness he was talking about, as though he were to say, "God made the light and divided between the light and the darkness. The light I mean, though, is day and the darkness night; so you shouldn't understand any other kind of light which is not day, or any other kind of darkness which is not night." Because if every kind of light could be taken as being day, and every kind of darkness could be qualified with the name of night, there would have been no need, perhaps, to say, *And God called the light day, and the darkness he called night.*

How there could be night and day before the heavenly bodies were created

27. Again, the question can be asked what day he means and what night. If he wishes it to be taken as this day that starts with sunrise and closes at sunset, and this night which stretches from the setting of the sun to its rising, then I cannot work out how they could exist before the heavenly bodies were made which produce the light. Or could these sheer intervals of time, twelve hours on twelve off, as it were,[34] be so called, even without any distinction of light and shade? And how does this alternation, signified by the names "night" and "day," occur in that rational or sensual light, if that is what is meant in this passage? Or has this been put here with reference, not to what happens as a matter of course, but to

---

33. I place parentheses around this text because if Augustine had used footnotes in his time, this certainly would be one. One of its oddities is that it contains two words not to be found either in Lewis & Short, or the Oxford Latin Dictionary, or in Du Cange's Glossary of Late Latin; one of them, *notamen*, Augustine may well have invented for the occasion; the other, which I have translated as "the expositor," is *doctitantem*, presumably from a frequentative verb, *doctito*. The Maurists, and earlier editors, emend it to *doctitanter*, an equally unknown adverb from the same root, which could be rendered "instructively."

34. A very free paraphrase of *ipsa spatia horarum,* literally, "these spaces of hours."

what can happen, because it is possible for error to overtake reason and a kind of dullness to follow on sensation?

Genesis 1:5; God needs no period of time in which to effect his works

7, 28. *And there was made evening and there was made morning, one day* (Gn 1:5). The word "day" is not now being used in the same way as when it said *and God called the light day*, but in the same way as when we say, for example, there are thirty days in a month. Here, you see, we are including nights in the term "day," whereas in the previous verse day was being distinguished from night. And so after introducing God's work as achieved by the making of light, it goes on to say that there came about evening and there came about morning, one day, meaning one day from the start of day to the start of day, that is, from morning to morning, in the way we talk about days, as I said, to include nights.

But how was there made evening and morning? Or did God take as long to make the light and divide between the light and the darkness as it takes for a day of daylight to last, that is, excluding the night? What, in that case, of the text, *For the power to act is available to you whenever you will* (Wis 12:18)? Or were all things in fact completed by God as in a craftsman's thought-out design, not in a stretch of time, but in that very power which made to abide in a timeless state even those things that we perceive as not abiding, but passing away in time?[35] Even with our own speech, after all, when our words pass away to be succeeded by other words, it is not to be supposed that the same thing is happening with the thought that gives rise to the finished utterance. So then, although it is without any stretch of time being involved that God makes things, having "the power to act available to him whenever he will," all the same the time-bound natures made by him go through their temporal movements in time.

So then, perhaps it said *And there was made evening and there was made morning, one day* in the sort of way in which one foresees that something can or ought to be done, and not in the way in which it actually is done in a certain stretch of time. After all, it was in its essential nature that God's creative work[36] was observed in the Holy Spirit by the author who said, *The one who abides for*

---

35. He is here working, in a rather confused and confusing manner, toward an idea he will elaborate more fully in his final *The Literal Meaning of Genesis* II,8.19 and IV,22.39-23.40. It is, in brief, that God timelessly, abidingly, utters his creative designs in the Word; the things so designed come to be in themselves, in time; the angels observe them in their true essence by first seeing them in the Word, and then turn to look at them in their derived, time-bound being in themselves. That is the meaning of the repeated refrain, "It was morning , it was evening, the nth day;" morning when the angels turn to the Word, evening when they turn to look at things in themselves. I summarize his treatment in my translation of *The Trinity* II, note 17.

36. Reading with the Maurists, *Nam in ipsa ratione operationem* instead of *Nam non ipsam rationem operationum* of the CSEL text: "After all, it was not the very essence of the works..." There are several variations in the manuscripts; the passage seems rather corrupt.

ever created all things simultaneously (Sir 18:1). But in this book of Genesis the story of the things made by God most appropriately sets them out as it were through intervals of time; by this arrangement of the account in an orderly sequence, the divine plan itself, which cannot be directly and timelessly contemplated by our weaker intellects, is presented, so to say, as a spectacle for our very eyes to gaze on.

Genesis 1:6-7: The difference between the waters above and below the firmament

8, 29. *And God said: Let a solid structure be made in the midst of the water, and let it be dividing between water and water. And thus it was made. And God made a solid structure, and divided between the water which was below the solid structure and the water which was above the solid structure* (Gn 1:6-7). Were the waters the same above the structure as these visible ones below the structure? Or else, because it seems to be referring to that water over which the Spirit was being borne, and we were understanding that to be the basic material of the world, are we to suppose that this is also being distinguished in this place by the solid structure being placed in between, so that the lower water is the basic "body material," while the higher is the basic "soul material"? What is here talked of as a solid structure, you see, is in the next verse called "heaven." Now among bodies there is none better than a heavenly body. Heavenly bodies, that is to say, are one thing, earthly bodies another, and the heavenly ones are naturally the better; and I don't know how anything that surpasses their nature[37] can still be called a body. But perhaps there is a kind of force or energy subject to reason, the reason by which God and truth are known, and it is naturally formable by virtue and prudence; and as its fluctuating tendencies are checked and restrained by their action, it thereby takes on a kind of material appearance. So it is rightly called "water" by God, and is raised above the limits of the corporeal sky or heaven by virtue of its incorporeal nature, not in terms of spatial distance.

And since he has called the sky or heaven a solid structure, it is reasonable to take everything that is below the ethereal heaven, where everything is quietly steady and solid, as being more readily subject to change and dissolution. This kind of corporeal matter, before it received the forms of various distinct species, was called the water below the solid structure.[38]

---

37. As the waters above the firmament, I take it, surpass the firmament precisely by being above it. In the text I have avoided rendering the Latin *firmamentum* as "firmament," because the latter really only has one reference in English, the biblical one, whereas *firmamentum*, like the Greek *stereoma* which it faithfully translates, means generally a solid, supporting structure.
38. Here I have emended the CSEL text by simply reading the two words *a qua*, "from which," as one word, *aqua*, "water," and then punctuating with a full stop instead of a comma at the end of this sentence. The text, apparently supported by the manuscripts, and certainly that of the

There have been people who supposed that these visible and cold waters embraced the whole upper surface of the heavens. They have tried to bring forward a supporting argument from the slowness of one of the seven wandering stars[39] which is higher than the others and called Phaenon by the Greeks, and which takes thirty years to complete its significant orbit; what slows it up, so they suggest, is its proximity to those cold waters above the heavens. How this opinion may be defended by those who have inquired minutely into such matters I have no idea. None of these things, however, should be rashly asserted, but they should all be discussed tentatively and with moderation.

30. *And God said: Let a solid structure be made in the midst of the water, and let it be dividing between water and water. And thus it was made.* After saying *thus it was made*, what was the point of adding again, *And God made a solid structure, and divided between the water which was below the solid structure and the water which was above the solid structure*? Earlier on, you see, after saying, *God said: Let light be made; and light was made* (1:3), he did not go on to add, "and God made the light." Here on the other hand, after God said *Let it be made; and thus it was made*, there comes the addition, *and God made*.

Or does this just show that we should not understand that light as being of the bodily variety, and so the impression was to be avoided that God made it through the intermediary of some creature—by "God" here I mean the Trinity; whereas this solid structure of the sky, being corporeal, may be supposed to have received its specific form through some incorporeal creature? So that first the incorporeal nature would receive from the Truth the intelligible impression of what was to be physically impressed on the basic material, to make the solid structure of the sky; accordingly, where it stated, *and God said, Let it be made, and thus it was made*, it was first made perhaps in that rational nature, for the actual species to be impressed from that upon bodily material.[40]

Genesis 1:7-8

9. But when it adds, *And God made the solid structure and divided between the water which was below the solid structure and the water which was above the solid structure* (Gn 1:7), is the actual work in that basic material being signified, to make the bodily reality of the sky? Or is it possibly just for the sake of varying the expression, to save the text from boring repetition, that what was put

Maurists also, has one scarcely construable sentence from "This kind of corporeal matter" to "the upper surface of the heavens." I happily forgo the challenge of translating it here!

39. Only given the name "planets," *planetae*, in medieval Latin. The one which the Greeks call Phaenon we, and certainly the classical Latin authors before Augustine, call Saturn. Perhaps he was chary of bringing in the name of a pagan deity; "Phaenon" simply means "Shining one."

40. See above, footnote 34.

lower down had not been put in the previous verse, so that we do not have to poke and pry too scrupulously into every nook and cranny of the text? You may choose whichever you prefer; only avoid asserting[41] anything rashly, and something you don't know as if you did; and remember you are just a human being investigating the works of God to the extent you are permitted to do so.

31. *And God called the solid structure heaven* (Gn 1:8). Here too we can reflect on what was discussed above about naming things;[42] it is not every solid structure after all that is called heaven. *And God saw that it was good.* Here too you can look back to what was discussed about this above—the only difference being that I do not see the same order as there. Above, you see, *And God saw the light, that it was good*, and then it adds next, *God divided between the light and the darkness; and God called the light day, and the darkness he called night*; whereas here, after the work was described it went on to say that the work was done, and after the solid structure was called heaven it then says, *and God saw that it was good.*

If we are not to treat this variation simply as a way of avoiding boredom, then we are certainly obliged here to find confirmation of that text, *And God made all things simultaneously* (Sir 18:1). Why, I mean to say, did he there first see that it was good and next impose a name, while here he first imposed a name and next saw that it was good? Why indeed, if not that this indifference[43] indicates that there were no intervals of time in God's actual working, though they are to be found in the works it produced? An interval of time is involved when something is done first and something next, and without this there can be no telling of the story of things done, although God was able without this to effect these things.

And there was made evening and there was made morning, the second day (Gn 1:8). This has already been discussed above, and in my opinion the same considerations hold good here too.[44]

---

41. Reading *asserat* with the Maurists and all the manuscripts except one, instead of the CSEL text's *afferat*, "bringing forward." We must remember that in the older orthography the letter "s" in the middle of words was written very like the letter "f." In fact either reading is equally likely. Another possibility is that both words were in the original, and one omitted by scribal oversight, so that the text would have read: *tantum ne aliquid temere asserat atque incognitum pro cognito afferat.*

42. See above, 6, 26.

43. *Indifferentia*; in classical Latin this means lack of difference, similarity; and as what is being discussed here is precisely a difference between the order of things mentioned above and mentioned here, the Maurists followed those manuscripts which had *differentia*. Perhaps the use here of *indifferentia* (which no copyist would have preferred to *differentia*) indicates that by Augustine's time the word was acquiring the meaning it now has in English.

44. See above, 6, 26.

Genesis 1:9-10: By "waters" here the basic material of the world is meant

10, 32. And God said: Let the waters which are under the heavens be collected together into one collection, and let the dry land appear. And thus it was made (Gn 1:9). From this it can in all probability be inferred, I think, that the water mentioned earlier is the basic material of the world. I mean, if the universe had been filled to the brim with water, where could the water have been collected from or to? Whereas, you see, if he called a kind of basic material mishmash by the name of "water," this collecting together can be taken as its actual formation, to become the specific kind of water we now see. And the utterance *Let the dry land appear* can be understood as the formation of the land, for the land to have the actual appearance we can now see. After all, it had been called invisible and shapeless when the basic material still lacked this specific form.

So then God said *Let the water which is under the heavens be collected together*, that is, let the basic bodily material be put into shape or form, to be this water which we perceive; *into one collection*—the precise force of a shape or form is suggested by the word "one"; to be genuinely formed, you see, is to be brought into some kind of unity, since the source and origin of all form is supremely one. *And let the dry land appear*; that is, let it receive its visible appearance, distinct from the previous mishmash. And very properly is the water "collected together" to let the dry land appear; that is, the pervasive fluidity of the basic material is held in check, so that what is obscured may be illuminated.

And thus it was made. This too, perhaps, was first effected in the thoughts of the intelligent creation, so that what is said next, *And the water was collected together into one collection, and the dry land appeared,*[45] should not be regarded as a superfluous addition after it has already said "And thus it was made." But it means that after the rational and incorporeal activity, we should understand the corporeal, bodily activity as following.

33. *And God called the dry land earth, and the collection of water he called sea* (Gn 1:10). This matter of names is still with us; not every piece of water is sea, or everything dry is earth. So exactly what water and what dry land was meant had to be distinguished by names. But we can still not unreasonably take it that it was God's naming of them which distinguished and formed these elements. *And God saw that it was good.* Here too the same order is followed; so what was said above about it can also be applied to this passage.

---

45. Augustine's text, we must remember, followed the Greek Septuagint, which has a slightly more regular creation narrative than the Massoretic Hebrew text, which both the Latin Vulgate and all modern versions follow. So these words are still part of Gn 1:9 in his version.

Genesis 1:11: An additional work performed on the third day

11, 34. *And God said: Let the earth sprout grass for fodder-bearing seed according to its kind and likeness, and fruit trees making fruit, whose seed is in them according to their likeness* (Gn 1:11). After the earth and sea were made and named and approved of (which as I have said often enough is not to be taken as involving intervals of time, in case the inexpressible ease with which God works should be limited by some kind of slowness), it does not immediately add, as with the two preceding days, *there was made evening and there was made morning, a third day,* but instead another work is joined on, so that *the earth may sprout grass for fodder-bearing seed according to its kind and likeness, and fruit trees making fruit, whose seed is in them according to their likeness.*

This was not said about the light and the solid structure and the waters and the dry land; that light, after all, does not have any progeny to succeed it, nor is another heaven born out of heaven, nor does earth or sea give birth to other seas and other earths, which are to succeed them. So here it had to say, *bearing seed according to its kind and likeness, and whose seed is in it according to its likeness,* where the likeness of the ones that are born preserves the likeness of the one that is passing away.

35. But all these things are on the earth in such a way that they cling to the earth with their roots and are continuous with it, and again are somehow separate from it. That's why I think this account has preserved the special significance of this kind of nature by having them made on the same day as the earth appeared, and yet once more saying, "God said that the earth was to sprout," and once more concluding, *And thus it was made* (Gn 1:11).

Next, according to the rule established above, after saying *and thus it was made,* it subjoins the actual carrying out of the work: *And the earth produced grass for fodder-bearing seed according to its kind, and fruit trees making fruit whose seed is in it according to its likeness*; and again it says, *God saw that it was good* (Gn 1:12). And thus these works are both joined together in one day, and distinguished from each other by God's words being repeated. The reason I think this was not done with earth and sea is because there is a greater need to distinguish these other things,[46] which propagate themselves by their seed when they spring up and then fall away.

Or is it that earth and sea could be made simultaneously, not only in the thoughts of the spiritual creation, where all things were made simultaneously, but also in the successive moving around of bodies, whereas trees and every kind of plant could not come into being unless the earth were there first for them to germinate in; and for that reason God's command had to be repeated, both to

---

46. To distinguish them from the earth, presumably, in which they are rooted.

signify the making of things quite different from each other, and yet of things not to be made on another day, because they are fixed to the earth and continuous with it by their roots?

But one can also ask why God did not impose names on these things. Or was this left out because the great number of them hardly allowed for it? This question, though, is best left for consideration later on, when we observe other things that God did not call by their names, as he did with light and heaven and earth and sea. *And there was made evening and there was made morning, a third day* (Gn 1:13).

Genesis 1:14-15: Problem about heavenly bodies being "for days"

12, 36. *And God said: Let lamps be made in the solid structure of heaven, in order to shine upon the earth and to divide between day and night, and to be for signs and for times and for days and for years, and to be for brilliance in the solid structure of heaven, in order to shine upon the earth* (Gn 1:14-15). On the fourth day the lamps were made, about which it says, *and let them be for days*. So what about the three days that have passed without lamps? Or why will these lamps be "for days," if even without them there can have been days? Or is it because the march of time and its intervals can be more obviously distinguished by human beings in the motions of these lamps or luminaries?

Or is this counting of days and nights of value for distinguishing between that nature which was not made and those which have been made, so that morning was mentioned on account of the specific beauty of the things that were made, and evening on account of their deficiencies? Since as far as the one by whom they were made is concerned they are beautiful and shapely, whereas taken in themselves they can be defective, because they have been made from nothing; and insofar as they are not defective, this is no thanks to the stuff they are made of, which is from nothing, but thanks to him who supremely is, and who makes them to be in their proper kind and order.[47]

More questions about the lamps fixed in the firmament

37. And God said: *Let lamps be made in the solid structure of heaven, in order to shine*. Question: whether this was only said about the fixed stars, or also about the wandering ones? But the two lamps, the greater and the lesser, are counted

---

47. This paragraph seems entirely out of place here. It would have made better sense in 6, 28 above, where he discusses the morning and evening of the first day; or in 8, 43 below, where we come to the evening and morning of this fourth day. Did Augustine perhaps get the notes mixed up, from which he was dictating the work (the notes would have been on wax tablets), or was his amanuensis responsible for the confusion? Confusion, surely, there has been.

among the wandering stars; so how were they all made in the solid structure, when all the wanderers have each their own proper sphere or circle?[48] Or whether, since in the scriptures we read both of many heavens and of heaven,[49] it is to be understood that here the reference is to the whole ethereal machine which holds all the stars, under which a pure and tranquil atmosphere holds sway, under which again this lower atmosphere is agitated by turbulence and storms?

In order to shine upon the earth and to divide between day and night. Had God not already divided between the light and the darkness, and called the light day and called the darkness night? From this it is clear that he had divided between day and night. So what does it mean now, saying about the lamps, *and let them divide between day and night?* Or is the division now being made by the lamps in the sky in order for it also to be known to people who only make use of their eyes of flesh to contemplate these things,[50] whereas God actually made the division before he made the circuits of the heavenly bodies, as can only be seen now by very few people, with the aid of the Holy Spirit and calm unclouded reason?

Or did God divide between another day and another night, that is, between the specific form he was impressing on that basic formlessness, and the formlessness which still remained to be formed? Quite different though are this day and this night whose alternation is drawn to our attention by the turning of the heavens, something that can only be brought about by the rising and the setting of the sun.

Genesis 1:14: Times are a sign, or trace of eternity

13, 38. *And to be for signs and for times and for days and for years* (Gn 1:14). It seems to me that what he meant by *for signs* was clarified by his saying *for times,* so that we should not take "signs" as being something different from "times." He is referring now, you see, to these times which by their division into

---

48. According to the classical astronomy, given its final form by the second century astronomer Ptolemy, but deriving ultimately from Pythagoras and Aristotle, the planets, including sun and moon which also "wander," were embedded in concentric transparent crystalline spheres or globes or circles, which revolved round the earth at different rates; and the fixed stars were embedded in an outer sphere, which remained motionless; the whole thing involving many more "solid structures" than the single firmament of Gn 1.

49. With one manuscript, I here omit the next phrase, which runs in this text *sicuti in hoc loco cum dicitur caelum et firmamentum,* "as in this place when it talks of heaven and firmament," and in the Maurist edition *sicuti in hoc loco cum dicitur firmamentum caelum,* "as in this place when the firmament is called heaven;"—fairly clearly two variants of a not very helpful marginal comment. Many heavens are to be found all over the bible, most immediately in Gn 2:1; then in Dt 10:14, Job 15:15, Ps 18:1, to name only a few places; and Saint Paul, of course, was snatched up to the third heaven in 2 Cor 12:2. The seventh heaven appears to be a post-biblical elaboration.

50. Like mere astronomers?

periods signify that an unchanging eternity abides above them, so that time may be shown to be a sign, that is, a kind of trace, of eternity. Again, when he continues *and for days and for years*, he is showing what times he meant, so that days are made by the revolution of the fixed stars, while the obvious years are made when the sun goes through the whole sign-bearing circle,[51] but the less evident ones are made when each one of the wandering stars does the same in its own orbit. He did not say "for months," you see, because a month perhaps is the moon's year, so that in this way[52] twelve moon years make up one year of the star which the Greeks call Phaethon, and thirty sun years are one year of the star that is called Phaenon.[53] And perhaps in this way, when all the stars have returned to the same point, a "great year" is completed, about which many people have said many things.

Or does he say *for signs*, meaning those which assist navigators to direct their course aright, while by times he means like springtime and summer and fall and winter, because these too change in accordance with the circling round of the stars, and take their turns in due order, while *for days and for years* is to be taken in the way already explained?

39. *And let them be for brilliance in the solid structure of heaven, in order to shine upon the earth.* It had already been said above, *Let lamps be made in the solid structure of heaven, in order to shine upon the earth*; so why has it been repeated, do you suppose? Or could it be that just as it said about the plants that they should bear seed and that seed should be in them according to its kind and likeness, so here it is said about the luminaries with a contrary intention, *let them be made and let them be*; that is, let them be made and not produce, but just be themselves. *And thus it was made*; this order of phrases is being observed.

Question of what phase the moon was made in

40. *And God made the two lamps; the greater lamp the beginning of the day, and the lesser lamp the beginning of the night*[54] *and the stars* (Gn 1:16). What he means by the beginning of the day and the beginning of the night will soon become clear. As for his adding *and the stars* it is uncertain whether they belong to the beginning of the night or not. Some people, though, want it to mean here that the moon was first made at the full, because the full moon rises at the beginning of the night, that is, straight after sunset. But this is surely absurd, that we

---

51. Through all the signs of the zodiac.
52. I am here emending the text's *sicut*, "just as," to *ut sic*.
53. Phaethon, a poetic name for the sun; Phaenon, a name for the planet Saturn, which he is reluctant to call by its Latin name. See note 39 above.
54. "The beginning of the day, the beginning of the night": the African Latin text Augustine is following has mistranslated the Greek *eis archas*, which here means "for ruling." But the word *arche* does also have the meaning "beginning," as in Gn 1:1 or in Jn 1:1.

should take the starting point for our count from the sixteenth or fifteenth day, and not from the first.[55] Nor should the point influence you that the luminary that was made had to be made in its complete state. I mean to say, it is complete every day, but its completeness is not seen by us human beings except when it is opposite the sun. Since even when it is in conjunction with the sun, though it seems to be reduced to almost nothing, because it is under it, still even then it is full, because it is being illuminated on the other side, and this cannot be seen by those who are underneath, that is, by the inhabitants of the earth. It is not possible to demonstrate this in a few words, but it calls for subtle explanations, and needs to be illustrated by visible diagrams and models.

Making and placing the lamps are the same thing for God

41. And God placed them in the solid structure of heaven, in order to shine upon the earth (Gn 1:17). How is it that he said, *Let them be made in the solid structure*, and that he now says *God made lamps and placed them in the solid structure*, as though they had been made outside and then placed there later, when it had already been said that they should be made there? Or is this simply indicating yet again and again that God does not make in the way human beings do, but that the story is told in the only way it could be by human beings; that is to say, that with us "he made" is one thing and "he placed" another, but with God they are identical, because he places by making and makes by placing?

The explanation of "the beginning" of day, etc.

42. *And let them preside over day and night and divide between day and night* (Gn 1:18). This is what he had already said, *the beginning of day and the beginning of night*, which he here explains by saying *let them preside over day and night*. So we should understand that "beginning" as meaning "pre-eminence," because in the day there is nothing of all visible things more excellent than the sun, and nothing in the night more so than the moon and the stars. So now that other uncertainty need not worry us, and we can believe that the stars too were placed there to belong to the beginning, that is to the pre-eminence of the night.

---

55. Perhaps not so absurd as he thinks; Ps 81:3 reads in the RSV, taken from the Hebrew text like all modern translations: "Blow the trumpet at the new moon, at the full moon on our feast day." The Hebrew word for new moon is from the ordinary word meaning new, renew; but the word for full moon is of obscure origin according to Brown, Driver & Briggs, possibly a loan word from Assyrian. The point is, it is not obviously on the face of it just the opposite of "new"; and perhaps this verse of the psalm may indicate that at one time the Israelites had thought of the moon as new when it was full, shining brightly, and had reckoned their months from the day of the full moon, and not from what we now, and to be sure they in rabbinic times, called the new moon. Augustine's text of the psalms, following the Greek Septuagint, did not have the verse in that form, but "Blow the trumpet at the new moon, on the auspicious day of your feast."

And God saw that it was good. The same order is being observed. Let us bear in mind, though, that God did not call these things too by name, when it could have said, "And God called the lamps luminaries,"[56] because not every lamp is a luminary.

43. *And there was made evening and there was made morning, a fourth day* (Gn 1:19). If we think of these days which are marked by the rising and the setting of the sun, this was perhaps not the fourth but the first day, so that we may suppose the sun to have risen at the time it was made and to have set at the time the other luminaries were made. But those who understand that the sun is still shining somewhere else when it is night with us, and that it is night somewhere else when the sun is with us, will search out a more sublime manner of counting these days.

Genesis 1:20: Questions about fish and birds

14, 44. *And God said: Let the waters throw up reptiles of live souls and flying things flying over the earth under the solid structure of heaven. And thus it was made* (Gn 1:20). Are swimming animals called reptiles because they do not walk on feet, or because there are some which crawl on the earth under the water? After all, there are winged animals in the waters, like fish which have scales, or others which do not have them, but still make their way on wings.[57] Whether these should be counted among the flying things in this place may well be doubted, because it is a big question why he also allotted flying things at all to the waters and not to the air. We cannot, I mean, take it here as being just those birds which are at home on the water, like divers and ducks and any others of that sort, because if he had just said it about these, he would not have omitted to speak about other birds in another place—among which there are some which are so remote from anything to do with water that they do not even drink.[58]

Unless maybe he called this air that is contiguous to the land by the name of water, since it proves itself by dew-fall to be damp even on the finest nights, and

---

56. *Sidera*; another Latin word for stars, where we in English only have one. It can often be translated "constellations," but that would not do here. Substantively, it is tantalizing that Augustine does not explain this omission. It is probable that the author refrained from naming sun or moon, or particular planets and stars, because they were important deities, worshipped under those names in Babylon, where this creation narrative was in all probability being put into final shape, during the exile. We have seen grounds for supposing that Augustine himself felt a similar scruple at naming the planet Saturn, preferring the Greek "the Shining one"; notes 39 and 52 above.

57. Augustine had reason to be puzzled by the reptiles, which are introduced into the text by the Greek Septuagint. But it is hard to make sense of his further questions here. Did he mean fins by scales? Did he mean flying fish by those that do not have scales but make their way on wings? Who can say?

58. Another mystery of Augustinian natural history!

because it also condenses into clouds. Now clouds are water, as everybody can tell who has happened to be walking on mountains when the clouds come down, or even on the plains in fog or mist. It is in this air, of course, that birds are said to fly. They cannot do so in that higher and purer stratosphere which all the authorities call air in the strict sense, because it is too rarified to sustain their weight. There, they insist, there is neither any condensation of clouds nor any turbulence; indeed such is the absence of any wind up there, that on the top of Mount Olympus, which rises, we are told, above the level of this humid air, certain graffiti were regularly scrawled in the dust and found intact and unchanged a year later by those who used regularly to climb this mountain.[59]

The meaning of the solid structure extended in scripture to include the higher levels of pure air

45. For this reason it can be reckoned without absurdity that the divine scriptures call everything the solid structure of heaven right down to these spaces, so that consequently that most tranquil and genuine air may be held to belong to the solid structure. This notion of solidity, after all, can be applied to tranquillity itself and to many other such things. This is why I reckon we have that saying in several places in the psalms: *and your truth as far as the clouds* (Pss 36:5; 57:10). Nothing, after all, is more solid or serene than truth. But the clouds condense under this region of purest air. Yes, certainly the expression has to be taken metaphorically; but the metaphor is taken from realities which provide a certain similarity, so that the steadier and purer corporeal reality in creation, which extends from the summit of heaven down to the clouds, down that is to this foggy and stormy and humid air, is rightly seen as representing truth.

So then, the flying things that fly over the earth under the solid structure of heaven are suitably allotted to the waters, because this air is not unsuitably named water. By this we are also given to understand why nothing is said about air, about how or when it was made, because this air is included in the name of the waters, that other air in the name of the solid structure. And so in this way no single element has been overlooked.

This humid lower air made when God said: Let dry land appear

46. But someone may say, perhaps, "If we are to understand that it was at the words *Let the water be collected together* that water was made from that mishmash of basic material, and God called this collection sea, how can we under-

---

59. Augustine's authorities on Olympus must have known that it is regularly covered in snow during the winter; and he himself must have seen, or at least been aware of, the Alps during the time he had spent in and near Milan.

stand this lower air being made then, because it is not called sea, even if it can be called water?" For this reason it seems to me that it was at the words *Let the dry land appear* that not only the specific form of earth, but also of this grosser air was hinted at. It is through this, after all, that the earth is illuminated, to be clearly visible to us. In the single verb *let it appear* we are given an intimation of all the things without which it cannot become apparent, that is, its own specific form, and its being stripped of the waters, and the pouring round it of the air through which light is transmitted to it from the higher atmosphere.

Or rather, is the specific form of this air presented to us in the words *Let the water be collected together*, because when this air is condensed it seems to produce this water? And so perhaps he called its compression into density the collecting together of water, to become the sea, while that part of it that was not collected together, that is to say not thickened, is the water which is able to hold up the flying birds, and which is furnished with each name so that it can be called both more refined water and grosser air.

Or is it true perhaps, as some people would have it, that it is from the exhalations of sea and land that these airs are made sufficiently coarser than that higher and more limpid zone, to be suited to bearing up the wings of birds, but still sufficiently more rarified that these waters with which bodies are washed, to be perceived as dry and airy in comparison with them? And because it had already spoken about earth and sea, what need was there to say anything about their exhalations, that is about the waters for the birds, when you have realized that the purest and most tranquil kind of air has been allotted to the solid structure, the firmament?

The origin of springs and rivers

47. Neither has anything been said, after all, about how springs and rivers were made. Those, you see, who inquire more minutely into these matters and write articles about them, say that a sweet vapor is extracted from the sea by some influence coming down from the ether above,[60] that is to say, it is drawn upwards in a way entirely beyond our senses to perceive. From it, they say, are compressed the clouds, and thus, after moistening the earth, it is filtered down to drip into hidden caverns, from where as much of it as may be sweated out as may be pumped and channeled through various conduits to gush out in springs, whether small ones or ones sufficient to give birth to rivers. They would illustrate this by

---

60. *Aetherio superlapsu* is his phrase; "by an etherial superlapse." The second word is given in no dictionary that I have at hand. It looks like an Augustinian invention (or perhaps an invention of the authorities he refers to, whoever they were). I take it to be equivalent to *lapsu desuper*. Why neither they nor he thought of attributing the effect to the heat of the sun, given the illustration he goes on to provide from some kind of retort for distilling sea water, it is hard to understand.

pointing out what happens when sea water is boiled, and the steam led off through coils of pipes produces a liquid that is sweet to the taste. And it is plain to everybody how springs are reduced to a trickle when they experience the lack of rain.

The sacred history also testifies to this, when Elijah begged for rain in a time of drought. He ordered Elisha[61] to look out to sea while he himself prayed; when he saw a tiny little cloud rising out of it, he told the anxious king that rain was imminent, which soon drenched him thoroughly as he fled away. And David says, *Lord, who summon the water of the sea, and pour it out over the face of the earth* (Am 5:8; 9:6). For this reason it would have been superfluous for him, after mentioning the sea, to say anything about these other kinds of water, whether those dew-bearing ones which in their rarified state provide the birds with the airs they fly in, or these of springs and rivers, if the former issue from the sea's exhalations, and the latter from the showers that these return to the earth, to be absorbed by it.

More questions about birds and reptiles

15, 48. *Let the waters throw up reptiles of live souls* (Gn 1:20). Why did it add *live*? Could there be souls that were not alive? Or did he wish to point to this more evident kind of life which is to be found in sentient animals,[62] seeing that plants are without it? *And flying things flying over the earth under the solid structure of heaven.* If flying things do not fly in that purest kind of air, where no clouds arise, this makes it quite clear that this belongs to the solid structure, because it says here that it is under the solid structure of heaven that flying things fly over the earth. *And thus it was made.* That order is being observed again,[63] and that is why it is added here as in the other cases, except for the light which was made first.

Genesis 1:21

49. *And God made the great whales and every soul of crawling animals, which the waters threw up according to their kind, and every winged flying thing according to its kind* (Gn 1:21). We remember, of course that "according to its

---

61. It was not Elisha, but an unnamed predecessor as Elijah's servant. This episode takes place in 1 Kgs 18:41-46, while Elijah calls Elisha to follow him in 19:19-21, after he had run away from Jezebel to the mountain of God, Horeb, and heard the still, small voice.

62. The Latin word *animale*, animal, has an obvious connection with *anima*, soul, that is wanting in English.

63. By the Greek Septuagint text, which Augustine's version follows, and which "observes the order" much more regularly than the Hebrew Massoretic text and our modern versions which derive from that.

kind" was said of those creatures which renew themselves by seminal propagation; it has already been said, I mean, of grasses and trees. *And every winged flying thing.* Why did it add *winged?* Can there be a flying thing that does not have wings? But if there can be, did God not make this kind also, since there is no mention of when it was made? Or is it possible at all, in fact, for anything to fly without wings? Because even bats and locusts and flies and anything else of that sort which lacks feathers does not lack wings. But *winged* was added so that we should not only understand birds, since fishes too are winged and fly over the earth under the waters. That is why it did not say "birds" but "and every winged flying thing," meaning flying things generally. *And God saw that it was good.* This too is to be understood as in the other places.

Genesis 1:22

50. *And God blessed them, saying: Grow and multiply and fill the waters of the sea; and let flying things multiply upon the earth* (Gn 1:22). He wished the blessing to avail for fecundity, which shows itself in the succession of offspring, so that through this blessing, because[64] they were created weak and mortal, they might preserve their kind by giving birth. But since plants also keep the likeness of the species going by reproduction, why did he not bless them? Is it because they lack sensation, which is akin to reason? It is not without point, perhaps, that God uses the second person in blessing, in order after a fashion to constrain these animals, as though they could hear him saying *Grow and multiply and fill the waters of the sea.* And yet it does not continue in that person to the end of the blessing; it goes on, you see, *and let flying things multiply upon the earth*; he did not say, "Multiply upon the earth," unless maybe this is a way of signifying that the senses of animals are not sufficiently akin to reason for them to be able perfectly to grasp what he is constraining them to do, like things that have intelligence and can make use of reason.

Final proof that the days of creation are not days in the ordinary sense

51. *And thus it was made* (Gn 1:22). Here, surely, anyone slow on the uptake should finally wake up to understanding what sort of days are being counted here. God after all has given animals definite numbers for their seed, which maintain a wonderful consistency in their definite order, so that for a definite number of days those of each kind both carry their young in the womb and sit on their eggs to warm and hatch them; this natural regulation is maintained by God's wisdom, which *stretches from end to end mightily and disposes all things*

---

64. Reading *quia* with the Maurists, instead of the CSEL text's *qua*, "by which they were created weak and mortal"—nonsense!

sweetly (Wis 8:1). So how could they in one day both conceive and carry in the womb and hatch[65] what they have laid and rear them and fill the waters of the sea and multiply upon the earth? It does, after all, add *and thus it was made* before the evening comes.

But doubtless when it says, *there was made evening,* it is indicating unformed basic material, while when it says *there was made morning* it is the specific form, which has been impressed by the work in question on the material.[66] This, you see, is how he concludes the passage of the day, after the performance of the work. However, God did not say, "Let evening be made," or "Let morning be made"; there is just the briefest reminder of things done, with evening and morning signifying basic material and specific form, which of course God had already been said to have made; while as for any defect, on the other hand, that is to say a thing's tendency to slip back to basic material and nothingness—if we are right, that is, in supposing that this is hinted at by the name "night"—it did not say that it was made but only that it was set in order by God,[67] when it said above, *God divided between the light and the darkness* (Gn 1:4); so that the word "evening" would signify the unformed material, which although it was made from nothing still in fact is, and has the capacity to receive specific forms. It is also possible that nothingness in its very self was indicated by the name of darkness, which God did not make, and from which he made whatever he deigned to make in his inexpressible goodness, since he is almighty, who made so many things even from nothing.

Genesis 1:23

52. *And there was made evening and there was made morning, a fifth day* (Gn 1:23). Here, after he had said *And thus it was made*, he did not add his usual carrying out of the work, as if they were made all over again. This had already been said earlier on, you see;[68] nor was any new nature fashioned by that blessing, which was concerned with the begetting of offspring, but things that had already been made were being preserved thereby through successive generations. And that is why it did not even say *And God saw that it was good*; he had already approved, you see, of the thing itself, which now only had to be preserved in its young. And so here nothing has been repeated, except for its

---

65. He uses a rather singular word here: *vaporare*, to steam! It can be used in a more general sense of warming, but usually with a liquid object.
66. See above, the end of section 37, where he first broaches this idea—and expounds it clearly enough. His returning to it at this particular place, and at unnecessarily greater length is hard to explain. I suspect a certain confusion in the file of the author's notes, from which he was dictating the book.
67. See above, section 25.
68. In verse 21.

saying *And it was made thus*, and immediately adding about evening and morning. It was by naming them that the works performed over the basic material and the specific form imposed on it were signified—unless by any chance some better and more sublime explanation should occur to anyone engaged in this inquiry.

Genesis 1:24: The production of land animals

53. And God said: *Let the earth throw up live soul according to its kind; of quadrupeds and of serpents and of beasts of the earth according to kind and cattle according to kind. And it was made thus* (Gn 1:24). Why *live* is added when it says *soul*, and what *according to kind* may mean, and on the usual conclusion saying *and it was made thus*, the reader is referred to the discussion of these points above, and must be satisfied with that. But while the word "beast" in English signifies generally every kind of non-rational animal, here at least different species are to be distinguished, so that we take quadrupeds to be all beasts of burden, serpents to mean all reptiles, beasts, wild ones at least, to be all untamed quadrupeds, while cattle are quadrupeds which do not help us by working for us, but give their produce to those who stock them.

Genesis 1:25-26: The actual making of the land animals

16, 54. *And God made the beasts of the earth according to kind, and cattle according to kind, and all serpents of the earth according to kind* (Gn 1:25). This repetition, saying *and God made*, when it had already said, *and it was made thus*, should be treated according to the rule given above. Certainly here by the word "cattle" I think all those quadrupeds are signified which live under the care of human beings. *And God saw that it was good*—to be taken in the usual way.

The making of man; both connected with and distinguished from the making of other animals

55. *And God said: Let us make man to our image and likeness* (Gn 1:26). And here we must observe both a certain connection with and a distinction from the animals. On the one hand it says man was made on the same day as the beasts; they are all of them together land animals, after all. And yet on the other hand, because of the pre-eminence of reason, with respect to which man is made to the image of God and his likeness, it speaks separately about him, after concluding about the other land animals in the usual way by saying *And God saw that it was good*.

56. The point must also be considered that in the other cases God said *Let it be made, and it was made,* while here God said, *Let us make,* so that in this way too the Holy Spirit wished to suggest the superiority of human nature. To whom, though, does he now say *Let us make,* if not to the one to whom he said in the other cases "Let it be made." For *all things were made through him, and without him was made nothing* (Jn 1:3). But why do we suppose it was said in one way, *Let it be made,* if not to mean that he should make it at the Father's bidding; and in the other, *Let us make,* if not to mean that they should both make together?

Or else, everything the Father makes, he makes through the Son, and that is why it now says *Let us make,* so that we human beings, on whose account scripture itself was made, might have it demonstrated in our very selves that what the Son makes on the Father's instructions the Father himself also makes; so that what was said in the other cases, *Let it be made, and it was made* is here being explained as not meaning that the saying and the making happened separately, but as happening together simultaneously, since here it says, *Let us make.*

Why the terms "image" and "likeness" are both used

57. *And God said: Let us make man to our image and likeness* (Gn 1:26). Every image is like the thing it is the image of; and yet not everything that is like something else is also its image. Thus you can have images in a mirror and a picture that are also like each other; but still, if one is not derived from the other, neither of them can be called the image of the other. Only then, you see, is a thing an image of something else when it is, as it were, printed off from it. So why after saying *to the image* did it add *and likeness,* as though there could be an image that is unlike? So it would have been enough to say *to the image.* Or is there a difference between like and likeness, as there is between chaste and chastity, between brave and bravery, so that just as everything brave is brave with bravery, and everything chaste is chaste with chastity, so in the same way everything like is like with likeness?

Now our image is not in the most proper sense said to be our likeness, while it can still quite properly said to be like us: this because the likeness by which like things are like each other is right there where chastity is, by which any chaste things are chaste. Now chastity is chaste without being so by participation in something, while it is by participation in her that any chaste things are chaste. And she is in God, where also is that wisdom which is wise without participation, but by participation in which any soul is wise that is wise.[69] For this reason the likeness of God, through which all things were made,[70] is properly called

---

69. All this is in the language of what one might call Augustine's Christianized Platonism.
70. Here of course he is making "likeness," or rather "the likeness of God" into another name for the Son, the Word, who is much more commonly identified with the wisdom of God.

likeness, because it is not by participation in something else that she is like, but she is the primary likeness by participation in which all things God has made through her are like.

58. So perhaps the explanation of why it added *to the likeness* when it had already said *to the image* is that it was to show that what was called the image is not like God as though participating in any likeness, but is the very likeness in which all things participate which are said to be like. Just as that is where chastity is, in which souls participate to be chaste, and wisdom, in which souls participate to be wise, and beauty, in which whatever is beautiful participates in order to be beautiful. You see, if it had only said "likeness," it would not have signified that it is begotten of him, while if it had only said "image," it would indeed have signified being begotten of him, but would not have signified that it was like him in such a way as not only to be like but to be likeness itself. Now just as nothing is more chaste than chastity itself and nothing wiser than wisdom itself and nothing more beautiful than beauty itself, so nothing can be said or thought to be, or quite simply can be more like than likeness itself. From all this we are to understand that the Father's likeness is like him in such a way as most fully and perfectly to fulfill his nature.

The whole universe, in various ways, shares in the divine likeness

59. How far, though, the likeness of God, through whom all things were made, extends to the imposing of specific form on things, is indeed something that soars astronomically beyond human thought; all the same it is still permissible to opine, if we reflect on the matter, that every nature, whether it is perceived by merely sentient or fully rational observers, preserves, in its parts being like one another, the effigy of the whole universe. It is true that from the wisdom of God only rational souls can be called wise, and that this title is not extended beyond them; no cattle, after all, and much less trees or fire or air or water or earth can possibly be called wise by us, although it is through the very wisdom of God that all these things are insofar as they are. But on the other hand we do say that stones are like each other, and animals and men and angels.

But now in the case of individual instances, we have to say that earth could only be made so as to be earth, insofar as it has its parts and particles being like each other; and water in each of its particles is like the other particles, and could not otherwise be water; and any amount of air could in no way at all be air if it were unlike the rest of the air; and a particle of fire or light can only be made to be what it is insofar as it is not unlike other particles. So too, with any individual stone or tree or the body of any sort of animal, it can readily be perceived and understood that they would not be individually what they are if they did not have parts like each other in themselves, to say nothing of their being like others of their kind. And the more like each other the parts of which a body consists, the more beautiful that body is.[71] Coming now to souls, not only is their friendship with each other cemented by their having similar habits and morals, but also in each individual soul it is similar actions and virtues, without which there can be no constancy,[72] that indicate a happy or blessed life.

Now we can say that all these things are similar or like, but not that they are likeness or similarity itself. Therefore, if the universe consists of things that are like one another among themselves, in order that each may be whatever it is, and all of them together may complete the universe, which God both established and governs, it is assuredly through the over-arching and unchangeable and undefilable likeness of the one who created all things, that they were made such as to be beautiful with their mutually similar parts—not all of them, however, such as to be made to the likeness itself, but only those of a rational nature. Thus all things through the likeness, but not all to the likeness.

The divine likeness located in the human reason or mind

60. And so the rational nature was made both through the likeness and to it; there is no other nature, you see, placed between them, seeing that the human mind (and this is something it fails to perceive except when it is completely purified and blessed[73]) attaches itself to nothing but truth itself, which is also called the likeness and the image of the Father and his wisdom. We are quite right, therefore, to take the words, *Let us make man to our image and likeness* as referring to this, the innermost and principal element in humanity, that is, as referring to the mind. It is from this element, after all, which holds the leading place in human nature, which separates it from that of the brute beasts, that the worth of the whole human being is to be reckoned. The other things in us, though beautiful in their kind, are still common to us and animals, and therefore in us are to be priced cheaply.

Unless perhaps the fact that the human body is constructed to stand erect, for looking up at the sky avails to support the belief that the body itself was also made to the likeness of God, so that just as that likeness is not turned away from the Father, so the human body is not turned away from the sky as are the bodies of other animals, which are laid out prone on their bellies. But all the same this comparison is not to be taken as applying in every respect. Our bodies, after all, are very different from the sky, whereas in that likeness, which is the Son, there cannot be anything unlike the one he is like. Any other things that are like each

---

71. Not a widely accepted principle of aesthetics, I suspect.
72. By similar actions and virtues he evidently means consistency in behavior and virtues, their being the same, "like themselves," all through life.
73. In other words, when it is enjoying the beatific vision. See his work, *The Trinity* VIII, 2 for a fuller treatment, and qualification, of this idea that the mind knows things by attaching itself to the truth which is God.

other are also partly unlike each other; likeness itself, on the contrary, is not in any respect unlike. Yes, the Father all the same is the Father, nor is the Son anything else but the Son; because even while he is called the likeness of the Father, although this shows there is no unlikeness between them, still he is not the one and only Father, but has his likeness.[74]

Final section, added at time of revision; alternative interpretation of "Let us make man to our image and likeness"

61. *And God said: Let us make man to our image and likeness* (Gn 1:26). What has been said above is certainly a sufficient explanation of these words of scripture in which we read that God said *Let us make man to our image and likeness,* insofar as the likeness of God to which man was made can be taken to be the very Word of God, that is to say, the only-begotten Son; not of course that man himself is that same image and likeness, equal to the Father. Man too is for all that the image of God, as the apostle indicates by saying, *A man, certainly, ought not to cover his head, since he is the image and glory of God* (1 Cor 11:7). But this image made to the image of God is not equal and co-eternal with him whose image it is; nor would it be, even if it had never sinned.

However, there is a preferable choice of meaning in these divine words, of why we should understand that it was said in the plural and not in the singular, *Let us make man to our image and likeness;*[75] it is that man was made to the image, not of the Father alone or of the Son alone or of the Holy Spirit alone, but of the Trinity itself. This Trinity is a triad in such a way as to be one God, is one

---

74. This is where he left the work unfinished, only going on to the quotation at the beginning of the next section. See the passage at the beginning of this volume quoted from *Revisions* I,18, and note 3 there. The text here differs in a few, but crucial, respects from the text Augustine gives there. The CSEL editor has modified it here to agree with the text there; in particular he gives at the beginning of Augustine's quotation, *Pater tantum Pater est,* which is what I translated there. But he acknowledges that the CSEL text here has *Pater tamen Pater est nec Filius aliud,* etc., which is what I have translated here, and which in the context makes altogether better sense; Augustine is here meeting, not indeed very lucidly, an objection to what he has just said, that the likeness, which the Son is, is in no respect whatever unlike. Augustine then has to concede, to an imagined but unmentioned objector, that still the Father is the Father, and the Son is the Son and thus not the Father. But there would, no doubt, have been more than one draft of this unfinished work in Augustine's book cupboards. At the end of the quotation I read with some manuscripts *sed habet similitudinem* instead of what this edition and the *Revisions* text have, *si habet similitudinem.*

75. This explains why Augustine, when revising his works at the end of his life, decided to add this little section to this work of his comparative youth some thirty-six years previously. Having decided not to destroy it, and at the same time not to be bothered with completing it (because, quite rightly, he did not think it was worth it), he wished to let possible readers know that he had long since opted for this preferable interpretation of these words, that "to our image and likeness" meant to the image and likeness of the Trinity, Father, Son, and Holy Spirit, and not just to the image and likeness of the Son. This, of course is the master idea that he elaborates at great length in his masterpiece, *The Trinity.*

God in such a way as to be a triad. After all he did not say, as though speaking to the Son, Let us make man to your image—or to my image[76]—but he said in the plural, *to our image and likeness*; and who would dare to exclude the Holy Spirit from this plurality? Since this plurality is not three Gods but one God, one must realize that the reason why scripture later introduced the singular, and said, *And God made man to the image of God* (Gn 1:27), was to show that it should not be taken as though it were God the Father making to the image of God, that is, of his Son; otherwise how could what had been said be true, "to our image," if man had been made to the image of the Son alone? And thus, because what God said, "to our image," is true, that's why it went on to say *God made man to the image of God*, as though to say to his own image, and that is the Trinity itself.

62. There are some people, though, who think that the reason why "likeness" was not repeated and it did not say, "and God made man to the image and likeness of God," is because at that time he was only made to the image, while the likeness to him was being kept for later on in the resurrection of the dead, as though there could be any image in which likeness is not to be found! I mean to say, if it is totally not like, it is undoubtedly not image either. However, so that we may not appear to be answering them by reason alone, there is also the authority of the apostle James to be brought to bear, who says, when speaking of the human tongue: *With it we bless God and with it we curse men, who have been made to the likeness of God* (Jas 3:9).

---

76. Taking the Son as the image of the Father (according to the previous interpretation), we can imagine the Father saying to the Son "Let us make man to my image and likeness, which is what you are."

The Literal Meaning of Genesis

Introduction

Origin and intention

Augustine had not given up on his original plan of commenting on the literal meaning of Genesis. The new work, *The Literal Meaning of Genesis*, was meant to be a kind of Augustinian *summa* on the subject of creation.[1] Admittedly, as compared with the spiritually rich *Expositions of the Psalms* and the *Homilies on the Gospel of John*, the commentary may strike the reader as quite dull and at times even dry. But for this very reason the work allows us to get a better glimpse of Augustine the theologian at work as he studies the scripture and is absorbed by it and instructs his readers by letting them share in his own search for the meaning.

In the *Revisions* Augustine does not give any concrete occasion for this work, as he does for his other writings. He repeats what he says a number of times in the commentary: that he intended an exegesis that would be literal *(secundum rerum gestarum proprietatem)* and not allegorical *(secundum allegoricas significationes).*[2] His now deeper knowledge of the Bible, his previous attempts at interpretation, his study of other authors' exegesis of the Hexaemeron, and, finally, his religious and philosophical maturation—all these made it possible for him to achieve the several goals he sets for himself in this work.

Augustine's exegesis of Genesis undoubtedly had in good measure an apologetical aim, but his concern was no longer simply with the errors of the Manichees but rather with all false views of the text of Genesis. He refuted even errors that had only a broad connection with the idea of creation, for example, the pre-existence of souls as maintained by Origen,[3] and the Platonic doctrine of the transmigration of souls (metempsychosis) as modified by Porphyry.[4] Pagans confronted with the texts of the Bible felt the same difficulties Augustine himself had felt as a young man, and he wanted his exegesis to help them decode the true meaning of those texts. Nor does he fail to deal critically with the theses

---

1. See, for a general treatment, M. M. Gorman, *The Unknown Augustine: A Study of the Literal Interpretation of Genesis (De Genesi ad litteram)* (Dissertation; Toronto, 1975); P. Agaesse and A. Solignac, *La Genèse au sens littéral* I-VII (Bibliothèque Augustinienne 48; Paris, 1972) 11-79.
2. *Revisions* II, 24, 2 (CCL 57, 109); see *The Literal Meaning of Genesis* I, 1, 2; VIII, 2, 5.
3. See ibid., VI, 9, 15; VII, 9, 13.
4. See ibid., VII, 9, 13.

of other Christian exegetes such as Ambrose and Basil of Caesarea, though their names often go unspoken.[5]

It hardly needs saying that the exegesis of the bishop of Hippo always has a catechetical and pastoral character as well. Augustine wanted his commentary on Genesis to provide a solid biblical basis for the Church's preaching on God the creator and on the origin of humanity. His work thus looked to a broad and diversified circle of readers; Christians, heretics, and intellectual pagans were all to be addressed. Yet Augustine's primary reason for composing the commentary was scientific. He wanted to derive from the opening chapters of Genesis information on the origin of the world and humanity.

The relation between faith and science

It was a special concern of Augustine not to block the way of unbelievers to faith by presenting to them as binding matters of faith any interpretations of the Bible that contradicted the certain knowledge offered by the sciences. He expressly condemned the self-satisfied attitude of many Christians who appealed to the Bible in order to challenge truths that were attested as beyond doubt by both reason and experience. Such an attitude threatened to discredit the Bible in the eyes of pagans: "Whenever . . . they [non-Christians] catch out some members of the Christian community making mistakes on a subject which they know inside out, and defending their hollow opinions on the authority of our books, on what grounds are they going to trust those books on the resurrection of the dead and the hope of eternal life and the kingdom of heaven, when they suppose they include any number of mistakes and fallacies on matters which they themselves have been able to master either by experiment or by the surest of calculations?"[6]

Augustine showed a really modern awareness of problems when he rejected interpretations of the Bible that encroached on the realm of the sciences and tried to challenge that which was established by "experiment or the surest of calculations."[7] To his mind the Bible was not a manual on the natural sciences. He interpreted the account of creation in such a way that even when the biblical text raised questions proper to the natural sciences, he always focused his answers on theological aspects of the matter. For example, when the question arose of the shape and form of the heavens, he answered: "Many people . . . have many arguments about these points, which our authors with greater good sense passed over as not holding out the promise of any benefit to those wishing to learn about the

---

5. See ibid., II, 1, 2; II, 9, 20-22; VI, 12, 21. On the author's use of sources see A. Penna, *Sant'Agostino, La Genesi* I (Nuova Biblioteca Agostiniana 9/1; Rome, 1988) LVIII-LX.
6. *The Literal Meaning of Genesis* I, 19, 39; see II, 9, 20; V, 8, 23.
7. Ibid., I, 19, 39.

blessed life. . . . .The Spirit of God who was speaking through them [the scriptures] did not wish to teach people about such things that would contribute nothing to their salvation."[8]

In the course of his commentary Augustine repeatedly tells the reader his principles on the relationship between faith and science. Particularly programmatic are his statements in I, 21, 41, where he emphasizes two requirements. If there are scientific positions justified by sure arguments, the exegete has the task of showing that these positions do not in any way contradict the sacred scriptures. If, on the contrary, there are unambiguous truths of faith that contradict the theses of science, the exegete must, as far as he can, show the falsity of such theses or at least be convinced of their falsity. Unfortunately, Augustine's reflections are limited to cases in which there is clear certainty on the side of faith or on the side of science. The situation in which neither theologian nor scientist has clear certainty, but each has available only more or less plausible arguments, is unfortunately not considered. Augustine's position is nonetheless clear: there can be no opposition between two certainties; true science cannot be in conflict with a true interpretation of the scriptures. Even with regard to creation he was convinced that there was no contradiction between "the truth of faith and sound understanding *(veritas fidei et sanitas intelligentiae)*."[9] In these positions of principle Augustine distanced himself equally from both "the chatter of false philosophy" and "the superstitions of false religion."[10]

These reflections of the bishop of Hippo on the nature of knowledge were to be taken over in later centuries. To a large extent Thomas Aquinas made the Augustinian position his own in his *Summa contra gentiles* (1, 7). A year before Galileo was condemned by the Holy Office (1516), he cited key passages from *The Literal Meaning of Genesis* (especially I, 18, 36—19, 39) in a letter to Grand Duchess Christine of Lorraine.[11] In these passages Galileo found not only arguments in favor of his scientific theses, but at the same time a witness to the character of patristic exegesis, which, he emphasized, was unwilling to draw from the Bible any conclusions in the area of the natural sciences which might one day be refuted by experience or contrary proof.

Exegetical method

In the *Revisions* Augustine gives a pithy summary of the exegetical approach taken in his commentary: "The title of these books is *The Literal Meaning of Genesis*; that is, not the allegorical meanings of the text, but the proper assess-

8. Ibid., II, 9, 20.
9. Ibid., XII, 14, 30.
10. Ibid., I, 21, 41.
11. See Galileo Galilei, *Opera* I (Naples, 1970) 198-236.

ment of what actually happened."¹² At the very beginning of the commentary he distinguishes various genres and contents of the biblical books: "In all the holy books . . . one ought to note what eternal realities are there suggested, what deeds are recounted, what future events foretold, what actions commanded or advised. So then, in accounts of things done what one asks is whether they are all to be taken as only having a figurative meaning, or whether they are also to be asserted and defended as a faithful account of what actually happened."¹³ In the second of these two sentences, Augustine singles out the term "deeds" from the list of four, because Genesis is one of the biblical books that report deeds. Yet distinctions have to be made among such reports.

Yet, in addition to the literal sense they may also have a figurative meaning. Paul had already said of the history of Israel: "All these things, however, happened among them in figure" (1 Cor 10:11). But it is equally possible that an event reported in the Bible may have an exclusively figurative meaning: "Here the whole story is figurative, not a story of things actually done with a figurative significance."¹⁴ Augustine is here referring to the parables of the gospel, to stories that have a figurative meaning but do not report any real occurrences.

But the first three chapters of the book of Genesis raise a question: "Whether they are all to be taken as only having a figurative meaning, or whether they are also to be asserted and defended as a faithful account of what actually happened."¹⁵ Augustine mentions Christian commentators on Genesis who regard Paradise as purely a symbol of a spiritual reality and "suggest that history, that is, the account of events that actually happened, begins from the moment when Adam and Eve, turned out of Paradise, came together and had children."¹⁶ In fact, contrary to his original intention, his early *On Genesis against the Manichees* had drifted in that direction. For example, the spring rising up in paradise symbolized the spread of the truth that filled the soul before the fall; the trees of paradise were symbols of spiritual joys; the East was a symbol of the light of truth.¹⁷

In *The Literal Meaning of Genesis*, however, Augustine's position was unambiguous: "The narrative . . . in these books is not cast in the figurative kind of language you find in the Song of Songs, but quite simply tells of things that happened, as in the books of the Kingdoms and others like them."¹⁸ He admitted, indeed, that many details of the paradise story (for example, the tree of life and the making of the woman) were prophetic announcements of things future, but

12. *Revisions* II, 24, 1 (CCL 57, 109)
13. *The Literal Meaning of Genesis* I, 1, 1.
14. Ibid., VIII, 4, 8.
15. Ibid., I, 1, 1.
16. Ibid., VIII, 1, 2.
17. See *On Genesis: A Refutation of the Manichees* II, 6, 7; II, 9, 12.
18. *The Literal Meaning of Genesis* VIII, 1, 2.

he nevertheless maintained that these were also realities: "All these things stood for something other than what they were, but all the same they were themselves bodily entities. And when the narrator mentioned them he was not employing figurative language, but giving an explicit account of things which had a forward reference that was figurative."[19] Although in this commentary, too, Augustine interpreted figuratively many statements in the Genesis story, he did not dwell on this meaning but concentrated on the literal meaning.[20]

In view of Augustine's repeatedly announced intention of commenting in this work on the literal meaning of Genesis, modern readers are nonetheless disconcerted when they look a little more closely at the concrete interpretive procedure. That which the exegete offers as the literal meaning of the biblical text seems in fact to be often the result of an allegorical and figurative interpretation. Thus the days of creation are not temporal periods but categories in which for didactic purposes the biblical author summarizes creatures that were created simultaneously in time. The light is not the light perceptible by the senses; instead it signifies the enlightenment of intellectual creatures. Morning signifies the knowledge of creatures which the angels possess in the vision of God. Evening signifies the knowledge of creatures which the angels possess in virtue of their own created nature. In view of such examples the question arises: What did Augustine understand by "the literal meaning"?

As distinguished from the figurative sense, which looks at the Old Testament in the light of the New,[21] an exegesis of the literal sense means interpreting historical facts, not in their future dimension, but as they were.[22] There was no question in Augustine's mind but that on its first pages Genesis was reporting real events. This was true no less of the creation of the universe and human beings than of the fall. The act of creation was the "happening" par excellence, since the world came into being when called by God's word from nothingness into existence and since everything that exists, and even the whole history of humanity, is rooted in that original happening.

But the act of creation is a completely unique and incomparable event that does not take place within history but instead is the basis of time and history.[23] For this reason, the act of creation and the coming into existence of the universe can be described only inadequately in human language. Augustine stressed the metaphysical and analogical character of biblical language: "The transference . . . of words from human matters to express things divine is common form with

---

19. Ibid., VIII, 4, 8; see VIII, 5, 10; VIII, 7, 13; IX, 12 and 20-21; XI, 39, 52; XI, 40, 55.
20. See ibid., I, 17, 34; VIII, 7, 13; IX, 12, 22; IX, 14, 24; XI, 34, 45; XI, 36, 49; XI, 39, 52.
21. See ibid., IX, 13, 23; further examples in I, 1, 1.
22. Ibid., I, 17, 34: "According to their proper meaning of what actually happened, not according to their riddling, enigmatic reference to future events (*secundum proprietatem rerum gestarum, non secundum aenigmata futurarum*)."
23. See ibid., I, 2, 4; VIII, 1, 3.

the divine scriptures."[24] In order to express what took place outside of space and time God used language adapted to the capacity of the human understanding, and this necessarily meant using the categories of space and time.[25]

For exegesis this meant watching out for the anthropomorphic expressions which the biblical writers used in describing God's action.[26] A literal interpretation required, therefore, that the exegete not stop short at the surface, at the letter of what is said, but rather penetrate to the real intention of the biblical narrator, that is, God himself. The word by which God called things into existence, the repose he took after the act of creation, the temporal sequence of his actions, the change from morning to evening—all these must not be understood in the sense suggested by direct human experience. Instead, words and concepts must be so interpreted as to reflect the mystery of God and of his creative action. In keeping, then, with the doctrine formulated in *Teaching Christianity*, even in passages in which Augustine interpreted the scriptures in the literal sense, he also looked for the realities *(res)* to which words *(verba)* pointed as signs.[27] For example, when Genesis spoke of light, Augustine was convinced that the light perceptible by the senses was not the true light; rather, the light of the mind was the ultimate reality to which the biblical author, that is, God, intended to refer.[28]

There is, however, a difference to be noted in the interpretation of the first account of creation as compared with the second (Gn 1:1—2:4a and Gen 2:4b—3:24). Whereas Augustine gave a strictly figurative interpretation of the first account (while regarding this as the literal sense), his exegesis of the second account sticks very close to the meaning of the letter. The reason for the difference is that Augustine did not regard the two accounts as two narratives of the same event, but rather as two different narratives of two moments or aspects of creation. The first account tells of the first moment of creation, in which a single creative act of God called all things into existence in an inchoative state from which they were all to develop gradually. The second account, however, no longer describes an event on the threshold between time and eternity, but an event within time. This account deals with human beings, their life in paradise, and how by their free acts they refused to comply with God's plan.

Augustine holds fast to the literal meaning of this biblical story. For him, paradise was a real garden, the tree of life and the tree of knowledge were real trees, the rivers were real rivers. He thought that by maintaining the reality of the spatio-temporal framework of the paradise story he could best safeguard the truths of faith implied in the story. In his view, sticking to the literal meaning

---

24. *On Genesis: A Refutation of the Manichees* I, 14, 20.
25. See *The Literal Meaning of Genesis* V, 16, 34.
26. See, for example, ibid., VI, 12, 20.
27. See *Teaching Christianity* I, 2, 2 (CCL 32, 7).
28. See *The Literal Meaning of Genesis* IV, 28, 45.

even of external details also made other points certain: the state of spiritual and bodily integrity in which human beings were originally created; the reality of the first sin; finally, the punishment that followed the sin and that explains the present state of humanity. To relativize the historical character of the paradise story was, in his mind, to relativize also the truths of faith that were closely bound up with the account.

On the other hand, Augustine did not claim that in his exegesis he had always found the definitive solution of all the problems posed to the interpreter. Not infrequently he allows for the possibility of other, better explanations: "I myself may quite possibly come to a different interpretation that corresponds even better with the words of the holy scriptures. I am certainly not insisting on this one in such a way as to contend that nothing else preferable can be found."[29] As he looked back in his *Revisions* he says: "It is a work in which more questions were asked than answers found; and of those that were found only a few were assured, while the rest were so stated as still to require further investigation."[30] He expressly warned interpreters against letting themselves fail to wrestle seriously with the authentic meaning of the scripture simply because they want at any cost to cling to the explanations they have previously found: we should not cling to an opinion "in such a way that we want it to be that of the scriptures, when we should rather be wanting the cause of the scriptures to be our own."[31]

How then is the exegete to proceed when the obscurity of the scriptural text allows for several possible interpretations? Augustine lists three criteria of interpretation in such cases: the intention of the biblical writers, the context, and finally the rule of faith: "When we read in the divine books such a vast array of true meanings, which can be extracted from a few words, and which are backed by sound Catholic faith, we should pick above all the one which can certainly be shown to have been held by the author we are reading; while if this is hidden from us, then surely the one which the scriptural context does not rule out and which is agreeable to sound faith; but even if the scriptural context cannot be worked out and assessed, then at least only one which sound faith prescribes. It is one thing, after all, not to be able to work out what the writer is most likely to have meant, quite another to stray from the road sign-posted by godliness. Should each defect be avoided, the reader's work has won its complete reward, while if each cannot be avoided, even though the writer's intention should remain in doubt, it will not be without value to have extracted a sense that accords with sound faith."[32]

---

29. Ibid., IV, 28, 45; see I, 18, 37; IV, 28, 45; VII, 28, 42; IX, 1, 1; XII, 1, 1.
30. *Revisions* II, 24, 1 (CCL 57, 109).
31. *The Literal Meaning of Genesis* I, 18, 37.
32. Ibid. I, 21, 41. See Agaesse and Solignac, *La Genèse au sens littéral* I-VII, note complémentaire 1, 579.

In another passage Augustine emphasizes a further criterion of a valid exegesis: the "absolute certainty"[33] that is identical with the "scientific arguments" *(certissima ratio)* and experiments *(experientia)* of the scholar.[34] Augustine was thinking here of philosophical considerations and scientific observations. Where the unambiguous results of these cannot be harmonized with the view of exegetes, then the latter "is not what divine scripture contained, but what human ignorance had opined."[35] Augustine was convinced that in this case the exegete must include scientific results in his quest of an interpretation and respect them in the name of reason.

Structure

In his exegesis Augustine did follow the text of Genesis verse by verse, but his primary concern was to use the scriptures in his theological reflections on the basic truths of the faith *(intellectus fidei)*. Therefore he brought to the text his own questions and favorite problems (significance of the seven days; simultaneous or progressive creation; distinction between creation and providence; origin of evil; and so on). In addition, he had to take into account the concerns and difficulties of his readers, whether believing Christians, heretics, or pagans. As a result, he dwelt at length on subjects or biblical passages that were of special interest to him; he raised the most varied questions in connection with one and the same verse; and he looked for answers to these in numerous digressions and excursuses.

This approach, which combined detailed examination of each biblical verse with theological syntheses, meant that the space allotted in the commentary corresponded only partially to the character of the text. For example, books 6 and 7 comment on only a single verse of Genesis, while book 11 comments on twenty-five verses. Books XI and XII offer autonomous theological treatises on subjects that are only distantly connected with the texts of Genesis but were of special interest to Augustine or his readers. Thus the exegete interrupted his commentary in order to dwell in Book X on a question that occupied him throughout his life: the origin of the soul. At the beginning of Book XII he explicitly admits the excursive character of his reflections: "In this twelfth book . . . no longer engaged in the business of interpreting the sacred text which has claimed our attention hitherto, we will be freer to tackle in more detail the question of Paradise, because we do not wish to give the impression that we have shirked the problem raised by the apostle's apparently locating Paradise in the third heaven."[36] His reflections here are of fundamental importance for Augus-

33. Ibid., I, 19, 38.
34. See ibid., I, 19, 38-39.
35. Ibid., I, 19, 38.
36. Ibid., XII, 1, 1; see 2 Cor 12:2-4.

tine's theory of knowledge, his psychology, and his mysticism.[37] Thus it is, strictly speaking, Books I-IX and XI that comment on the text of the first three chapters of Genesis.

Augustine was thoroughly aware of the difference in character of the two accounts of creation in Genesis 1:1—2:4a and 2:4b—3:24, as well as of the problem of harmonizing them. If both stories came from the same author, as Augustine believed, why does Genesis 2:2 say that God completed his work and rested on the seventh day, even though the text then goes on to speak further of his creative work? Why does the second account say there were as yet no plants (Gn 2:5), whereas God had previously caused the earth to bring forth vegetation on the third day (Gn 1:12)? Why is it that God is said to have created human beings on the sixth day (see Gen 1:26), while this same creation is described again later on (see Gen 2:7)?

Augustine solved the problem by interpreting the twofold account of creation as describing two moments or aspects of God's creative action.[38] He took the position that God created all things simultaneously,[39] but that in this original creative act living beings had not yet been made independent substances but only existed potentially in the *causales* or *seminales rationes* which God had placed in the world.[40] From the outset, then, the created world was equipped, in the form of predispositions, with everything that belongs to it.[41] In accordance with the *rationes seminales* which at the very first moment had been placed in the world like seeds, the created world developed its potentialities at the proper times and in suitable places in accordance with the plan of divine providence.[42] Thus envisaged, the creation, which was accomplished perfectly once for all, was in one sense complete, in another incomplete. As a result, it could be said, on the one hand, that God rested on the seventh day inasmuch as he did not create any more kinds of creatures that were not contained actually or potentially in the original creative act. On the other hand, it was possible to speak of God's further action inasmuch as he governed the created world and intervened when and as he wished, as, for example, in the formation of Adam and Eve.

---

37. See M. E. Korger, "Grundprobleme der augustinischen Erkenntnislehre: Erläutert am Beispiel von *De Genesi ad litteram* XII," *Recherches Augustiniennes* 2 (1962) 33-57.
38. See *The Literal Meaning of Genesis* VI, 11, 18.
39. On the doctrine of simultaneous creation see C. Mayer, *"Creatio, creator, creatura,"* in *Augustinus-Lexikon* 1 (Basel, 1996) 76.
40. See M. J. McKeough, *The Meaning of the Rationes Seminales in St. Augustine* (Catholic University of America dissertation; Washington, DC, 1926); J. M. Brady, "St. Augustine's Theory of Seminal Reasons," *New Scholasticism* 38 (1964) 141-158; H. Woods, *Augustine and Evolution: A Study in the Saint's De Genesi ad litteram and De Trinitate* (New York, 1924); Mayer, *"Creatio . . . ,"* 86-91; P. Agaesse and A. Solignac, *La Genèse au sens littéral* VIII-XII (Bibliothèque Augustinienne 49; Paris, 1970), note complémentaire 21.
41. See *The Literal Meaning of Genesis* VI, 11, 19.
42. See ibid., IV, 33, 51; VI, 11, 18.

Corresponding to this distinction in the divine creative activity, the structure of Augustine's work is as follows:[43]

A. First account of creation (Books I-IV)
   1) Initial state of the world and the creations on the first day (Gn 1:1-5)
   2) Creations on the second, third, and fourth days (Gn 1:6-19)
   3) Creations on the fifth and sixth days (Gn 1:20-31)
   4) God's rest on the seventh day (Gn 2:1-3)
B. Transition (Book V)
   5) Meaning and differentiation of the two accounts of creation. Theory of the *rationes causales* (Gn 2:4-7)
C. Second account of creation (Books VI-XII)
   6) Creation of the human body (Gn 2:7a)
   7) Creation of the human soul (Gn 2:7b)
   8) Man in Paradise Excursus on God's government of the world (Gn 2:8-17)
   9) Naming of the animals and creation of woman (Gn 2:18-24)
   10) Treatise on the origin of human souls
   11) The first sin and its punishment (Gn 2:25—3:24)
   12) Treatise on the various kinds of visions

Date

To hardly any other of his works did Augustine devote such perseverance, such care and circumspection... As we know from his letters,[44] despite the urging and impatience of his friends, he kept the work to himself for a disproportionately long time in order that he might keep on shaping and improving it. Thus the composition of this great commentary on Genesis occupied more than about fifteen years. There is disagreement as to whether he began the work in 399 or 401 or 404.[45] It was published in 416.

Various indications point to composition in several stages. Books 1-9 were probably revised beginning in 410 or even shortly before. Augustine then ceased work on the commentary for a fairly long period, since not only was he in poor health, but the Donatist controversy, and especially the preparation for and subsequent assessment of the Conference of Carthage (411), made great demands upon him, the Pelagian controversy began, and the fall of Rome (410) called for a response from this theologian. He returned to the commentary in 412, but he

43. See Agaesse and Solignac, *La Genèse au sens littéral* I-VII, 22f.
44. Letter 159, 2 (CSEL 44, 499f.)
45. See A.-M. Vannier, *"Creatio," "conversio," "formatio" chez S. Augustin* (Paradosis 31; Fribourg, 1991) 88; Agaesse and Solignac, *La Genèse au sens littéral* I-VII, 25-31.

also introduced themes and reflections that occupied him to a great extent in 412-415 (origin of the soul, origin of evil, providence).

Importance of the work

Augustine's commentary on *The Literal Meaning of Genesis* represents an incomparably concentrated effort at presenting the mystery of the creation of the world in the light of all possible interpretations, from all possible angles, and by all the means available to the author in his time. Especially to be noted are his respect for the scientific theories of his age,[46] his questioning rather than assertive way of proceeding,[47] and finally the abundance of explanations of a philosophical kind.

It was clear to the author that his work could only be an attempt at an interpretation. Such a work, which includes numerous scientific and philosophical theories of the ancient world, undoubtedly contains not a few passages that are outdated and can only be of antiquarian interest. Yet this commentary on Genesis has an importance that transcends time, since it deals repeatedly with basic questions of philosophy and theology that are independent of the scientific standard of his age. The trinitarian dimension of the act of creation, the problem of simultaneous creation, the meaning of the days of creation, the didactic character of the creation story, the relationship of the first creation story to the second, the divine government of the world, the theory of *causae seminales*, the nature of the human body, the creation of the soul, the fall and its consequences: these are subjects to the discussion of which Augustine made contributions that are still of interest today.[48] In fact, the richest theological passages are those least concerned with exegesis, that is, those in which the writer moves beyond the immediate wording of the text and engages in penetrating reflections on the great subjects dealt with in the first pages of the Bible.

But Augustine's exegetical approach itself is also remarkable. In contrast to the established traditions of Hexaemeron exegesis, as seen, on the one hand, in the allegorism of Philo of Alexandria, Origen, Basil of Caesarea, and Ambrose and, on the other, in the pronounced literalism of an anti-Origenist such as Epiphanius of Salamis but also in John Chrysostom, an Antiochene, Augustine pursued an independent middle way that sought to avoid the defects and dangers of each opposed position.

---

46. See *The Literal Meaning of Genesis* I, 19, 39.
47. See *Revisions* 2, 24, 1 (CCL 57, 109).
48. See J. J. O'Meara, *The Creation of Man in St. Augustine's De Genesi ad litteram* (Villanova, PA, 1980); A. Di Giovanni, *Sant'Agostino, La Genesi* I (Nuova Biblioteca Agostiniana 9/1; Rome, 1988) XIX-XLIX.

A milestone was reached in the interpretation of Genesis when Augustine recognized that the spreading of God's work over six days was simply a literary garb and that the author did not intend to give a scientific description of the act of creation. Anyone who reads the interpretation of the creation story that is given in this work can only marvel at the strained exegeses that have been proposed right down into the twentieth century in the efforts at understanding the literary form of the six-day story of creation.

Despite his respect for the rights of human reason and for the results of objective science, the bishop of Hippo resolutely emphasized the primacy of the truths of revelation. He warned the faithful against letting themselves be blinded by the reputation of the secular sciences, against succumbing to a kind of faith in science, and against feeling a disinterest in or even a revulsion against the sacred scriptures: "Some of the weaker brothers and sisters . . . are in danger of going astray more seriously when they hear these godless people holding forth expertly and fluently on the 'music of the spheres,' or on any questions you care to mention about the elements of this cosmos. They wilt and lose heart, putting these pundits before themselves, and while regarding them as great authorities, they turn back with a weary distaste to the books of salutary godliness, and can scarcely bring themselves to touch the volumes they should be devouring with delight."[49]

The Literal Meaning of Genesis is an impressive testimony to the way in which Augustine lovingly immersed himself in the scriptures. For he was convinced that their very first pages had in store answers to humanity's great questions, answers which the most exact sciences and their methods could not give.

---

49. *The Literal Meaning of Genesis* I, 20, 40.

Extract from *Revisions* (II, 24)

During the same period[1] I wrote twelve books on Genesis, from the beginning until Adam was turned out of paradise and a flaming sword was put there, to guard the way to the tree of life.[2] But when eleven books were completed up to this point, I added the twelfth, in which paradise was more thoroughly discussed. The title of these books is *The Literal Meaning of Genesis*; that is, not the allegorical meanings of the text, but the proper assessment of what actually happened. It is a work in which more questions were asked than answers found; and of those that were found only a few were assured, while the rest were so stated as still to require further investigation. I began these books after those on the Trinity, but finished them sooner. So I have mentioned them here, in the order in which I began these works.

In the fifth book (19,38), and anywhere else in these books that I put about *the seed, to which the promises had been made, which was disposed through angels in the hand of the mediator* (Gal 3;19): that is not what the apostle has, nor the more reliable manuscripts which I examined later, especially the Greek ones. It was about the law, you see, that this was said, which many Latin manuscripts, in a mistaken translation, present as said about the seed. What I said in the sixth book (27,38; 28,39), that "Adam lost by sin the image of God according to which he was made," is not to be taken as meaning that no image at all remained in him, but that it was so misshapen as to stand in need of reshaping. In the twelfth (33,62-63), on the subject of hell, I think I should just have asserted that it is under the earth, rather than giving reasons why it should be believed or be said to be under the earth, as though it were not really so. This work begins, "All divine scripture is twofold."

---

1. As he wrote a small book *Holy Virginity*, which is to say about 400.
2. Thus on the first three chapters of Genesis.

Book I

Genesis 1:1-5: Creation of heaven and earth; the work of the first day

The multiple meanings of scripture

1, 1. All divine scripture is twofold, as the Lord points out when he says, *A scribe learned in the kingdom of heaven is like a householder bringing forth from his treasury new things and old* (Mt 13:52), which are also said to be the two testaments. In all the holy books, however, one ought to note what eternal realities are there suggested, what deeds are recounted, what future events foretold, what actions commanded or advised. So then, in accounts of things done, what one asks is whether they are all to be taken as only having a figurative meaning, or whether they are also to be asserted and defended as a faithful account of what actually happened. No Christian, I mean, will have the nerve to say that they should not be taken in a figurative sense, if he pays attention to what the apostle says: *All these things, however, happened among them in figure* (1 Cor 10:11), and to his commending what is written in Genesis, *And they shall be two in one flesh* (Gn 2:24), as *a great sacrament in Christ and in the Church* (Eph 5:32).[1]

Genesis 1:1-2: the state of the question

2. So if that text has to be treated in both ways, what is meant, apart from its allegorical significance, by *In the beginning God made heaven and earth* (Gn 1:1)? Does it mean in the beginning of time, or because it was the first of all things, or in the beginning, which is the Word of God, the only begotten Son? And how could it be shown that God produced changeable and time-bound works without any change in himself? And what may be meant by the name

---

1. The real twofold quality of scripture, he is saying, is not its obvious division into two testaments, but its all having both a figurative and a literal meaning. His giving priority to the figurative or spiritual meaning is in line with the practice of most of the Fathers, from Origen onward, but is the exact opposite, of course, of contemporary exegetical orthodoxy today—and indeed of the line Augustine is taking in this work.

168

heaven and earth? Was it the total spiritual and bodily creation that was termed heaven and earth, or only the bodily sort? In that case one would have to understand that in this book he kept quiet about the spiritual kind, and said *heaven and earth* in such a way as intending to signify the whole bodily creation, both the higher and the lower. Or was it the unformed basic material of both kinds that was called heaven and earth; namely, spiritual life as it can be in itself without having turned to the creator—it is by so turning, you see, that it is formed and perfected, while if it does not so turn it is formless, deformed; and bodily being, if it can be understood as lacking every kind of bodily quality, which is manifested in material that has been formed, when there are already various kinds of bodies, perceptible either by sight or by any of the body's senses?[2]

3. Or is "heaven" to be understood as meaning the spiritual creation, from the moment in which it was made, in all its perfection and everlasting blessedness, while "earth" means bodily material, still unfinished? Because *the earth*, he goes on, *was invisible and shapeless, and there was darkness over the abyss* (Gn 1:2), words in which he seems to indicate the unformed state of bodily being. Or is the unformed state of each kind of being indicated by these subsequent words—of the bodily sort where it says *the earth was invisible and shapeless*, of the spiritual where it says *and there was darkness over the abyss?* In this case we would interpret the dark abyss to mean the nature of life as being unformed unless it turns to the creator, which is the only way it can be formed so as not to be the abyss, and enlightened so as not to be dark. And in what sense does it say, *there was darkness over the abyss?* Is it just because there was no light? If there had been, it would of course have been over it and would as it were have poured over it; this is what happens with the spiritual creation when it turns to the unchangeable and incorporeal light, which God is.

In what way did God "say" things?

2, 4. And in what way did God say, *Let light be made* (Gn 1:3)? Was it in time, or in the eternity of the Word? And if it was in time, then of course it involved change. So how could God be understood to have said this except through some created being? He himself, clearly, is not subject to change. And if it was through a created being that God said *Let light be made*, how can light be the first thing created, if there already was a created being through which God said *Let light be made?* Or is light not the first thing created, because it has already said *In the beginning God made heaven and earth?* And could some voice have been produced in a temporal process involving change through some heavenly created being, to say, *Let light be made?* If that is the case, then it was this bodily

---

2. The Aristotelian concept of "prime matter."

light that we perceive with our bodily eyes which was made, when God said through a spiritual creature (which God had already made when he made heaven and earth in the beginning), *Let light be made*; said in a way in which through the interior and hidden motion of such a creature the words "Let light be made" could be said by divine inspiration.

5. Or did the voice of God, saying *Let light be made,* also make an audible sound, as did the voice of God when he said, *You are my Son, the beloved* (Mk 1:11); and this too through some bodily creature, which God had made when he made heaven and earth in the beginning, before light had been made, which was then made at the audible utterance of this voice? And if that is the case, what language was this voice speaking when God said *Let light be made,* since there was no diversity of languages yet, something that came about later on at the building of the tower after the flood?[3] What was the one and only language in which God spoke the words, "Let light be made"? And who was there, who needed to hear and understand, to whom this sort of utterance would be addressed? Or is this an altogether absurd and literal-minded, fleshly, train of thought and conjecture?

6. So what are we to say, then? Is the voice of God best understood as being the intelligible meaning of the audible utterance, *Let light be made,* and not the audible utterance itself? And the question then arises whether this does not belong to the very nature of his Word, about which it is said, *In the beginning was the Word, and the Word was with God, and it is God that the Word was* (Jn 1:1)? Seeing that it is said about him, *All things were made through him* (Jn 1:3), it is evident enough that light also was made through him, when God said, "Let light be made." If that is the case, then God's saying *Let light be made* is something eternal, because the Word of God, God with God, the only Son of God, is co-eternal with the Father, although when God said this in the eternal Word, a time-bound creature was made. While "when" and "some time" are time words, all the same the time when something should be made is eternal for the Word of God, and it is then made when it is in that Word that it should have been made, in the Word in which there is no "when" nor "some time," because that whole Word is eternal.

Is the light spiritual, corporeal, or both?

3, 7. And what is this light that was made? Something spiritual or something bodily? If something spiritual, you see, it could be the first thing created, which had first been called heaven, when it said, *In the beginning God made heaven and earth* (Gn 1:1), and was now perfected by this utterance; so that the text here,

---

3. See Gn 11:1-9.

God said, Let light be made; and light was made (Gn 1:3), should be understood as its being converted and enlightened, by its creator calling it back to himself.

8. And why is it put like this: *In the beginning God made heaven and earth*, and not like this: *In the beginning God said, Let heaven and earth be made; and heaven and earth were made*, in the same way as the account of light is given: *God said, Let light be made; and light was made?* Is it that first of all what God made had to be universally embraced and presented under the name of "heaven and earth," and then this had to be followed up piecemeal by how he made it, when it says of things one by one, *God said*; meaning that it was through his Word that he made whatever he did make?

Why God did not say "Let it be made" about the unformed basic material

4, 9. Or is it that when the unformed basic material, whether of spiritual or bodily being, was first being made, it was not appropriate to say *God said, Let it be made*, because it is by the Word, always adhering to the Father, that God eternally says everything, not with the sound of a voice nor with thoughts running through the time which sounds take, but with the light, co-eternal with himself, of the Wisdom he has begotten; and imperfection or incompleteness does not imitate the form of this Word, being unlike that which supremely and originally is, and tending by its very want of form toward nothing? Rather, it is when it turns, everything in the way suited to its kind, to that which truly and always is, to the creator that is to say of its own being, that it really imitates the form of the Word which always and unchangingly adheres to the Father, and receives its own form, and becomes a perfect, complete creature. Accordingly, where scripture states, *God said, Let it be made*, we should understand an incorporeal utterance of God in the substance of his co-eternal Word, calling back to himself the imperfection of the creation, so that it should not be formless, but should be formed, each element on the particular lines which follow in due order.

By so turning back and being formed creation imitates, every element in its own way, God the Word, that is the Son of God who always adheres to the Father in complete likeness and equality of being, by which he and the Father are one;[4] but it does not imitate this form of the Word if it turns away from the creator and remains formless and imperfect, incomplete. That is why allusion is made to the Son, not because he is the Word but only because he is the beginning, when it says, *In the beginning God made heaven and earth* (Gn 1:1); here he is being suggested as the source of creation still in its formless imperfection. But the Son is being alluded to as being also the Word where the text runs *God said, Let it be made*. Thus his being the beginning implies his being the source of creation as it

---

4. See Jn 10:30.

comes into being from him while still imperfect, while his being the Word implies his conferring perfection on creation by calling it back to himself, so that it may be given form by adhering to the creator, and by imitating in its own measure the form which adheres eternally and unchangingly to the Father, and which instantly gets from him to be the same thing as he is.[5]

What spiritual formlessness might be, and how it is formed

5, 10. The Son, after all, the Word, does not have an unformed life, seeing that for him not only is it the same thing to be as to live, but to live is for him the same as to live wisely and blessedly. A creature, on the other hand, even a spiritual and intelligent or rational one, which seems to be closer to that Word than others, can have an unformed life, because while for it also to be is the same as to live, to live is not the same as to live wisely and blessedly; if it turns away from the unchangeable Wisdom, after all, it lives foolishly and miserably. It is formed, however, by turning to the unchangeable light of Wisdom, the Word of God; it is to the one, you see, from whom it received existence, just to be and to live anyhow, that it turns in order to live wisely and blessedly. Eternal Wisdom, of course, is the origin or beginning of the intelligent creation; this beginning, while abiding unchangeably in itself, would certainly never cease to speak to the creature for which it is the beginning and summon it by some hidden inspiration it turn to that from which it derived its being, because in no other way could it possibly be formed and perfected. That is why, when he was asked who he was, he replied, *The beginning, because I am also speaking to you* (Jn 8:25).

11. Now what the Son speaks the Father speaks, because when the Father speaks, a Word is uttered which is the Son, with God uttering in an eternal manner, if "manner" it can be called, a co-eternal Word. For in God there is a supreme and holy and just courtesy and a kind of love in his activity which comes not from any need on his part but from generosity. That is why, before scripture came to the text, *God said, Let light be made* (Gn 1:3), it preceded it by saying, *And the Spirit of God was being borne over the water* (Gn 1:2). Now it may have wanted to call by the name of "water" the whole basic material of the bodily creation, to suggest in this way what all things which we can distinguish according to their kind were made and formed from, calling it water because we observe all things on earth to be formed and to grow in their various species from humid matter; or it may have wished to indicate a kind of spiritual life in a fluid, shifting state, as it were, before the form given it by its conversion. In either case, to be sure, the Spirit of God was being borne over it, because whichever it was that he had initiated, ready to be formed and perfected, it was subject to the good

---

5. The Word being eternally uttered by the Father is the same as the Son being eternally born of the Father, and so being God from God, Light from Light, true God from true God.

will of the creator. This means that when God said in his Word, *Let light be made*, and so on, what was made would abide in his good will, that is, would meet with his approval according to the measure of its kind. And thus it is right, because it met with God's approval, with scripture saying, *And light was made; and God saw the light that it was good* (Gn 1:3-4).

How the mystery of the Trinity is hinted at in these verses

6, 12. Just as at the very start of his beginning creation, which was mentioned under the name of "heaven and earth" on account of what was to be completed from it, the "threeness" of the creator is suggested, so too in creation's. Thus when scripture says: *In the beginning God made heaven and earth* (Gn 1:1), we understand the Father in the word "God" and the Son in the word "beginning"; the beginning, not for the Father but for the creation created at the start through himself, and chiefly for the spiritual, and consequently for the totality of creation; while with scripture saying: *And the Spirit of God was being borne over the water* (Gn 1:2), we recognize the complete indication of the Trinity being converted and perfected in order to be distributed into its various species, the same "threeness" should be suggested, of the Word of God, that is to say, and the Word's begetter, when it says *God said*; and of the holy goodness, by which God is pleased with whatever pleases him on its being perfected in its own small, natural way, when it says, *God saw that it was good*.

7, 13. But why did it first mention creation as incomplete and imperfect, and only mention the Spirit of God after that, with scripture saying: *Now the earth was invisible and shapeless, and there was darkness over the abyss*, and then continuing: *and the Spirit of God was being borne over the water* (Gn 1:2)? Was it because a love that is needy and in want loves in such a way that it is subjected to the things it loves; and so for that reason, when the Spirit of God was to be mentioned, in which his holy benevolence and love is understood, it is said to be borne *over* what he loves, in case it should be thought that it was out of the compulsion of his needs that God loved the things which were to be made, rather than out of the abundance of his generosity? With this very thing in mind, the apostle is going to say about charity that he will point out *an overwhelming way* (1 Cor 12:31), and in another place he says, *the charity of Christ that overwhelms knowledge* (Eph 3:19).

8, 14. Thus it was that when things also had been perfected and formed from that primal origin, *God saw that it was good*; it was out of the same genial courtesy, after all, that he took pleasure in what had been made, as that it had pleased him that it should be made. There are two things, in fact, on account of which God loves his creation: in order that it should be, and in order that it should abide. So in order that there should be something to abide, *the Spirit of God was being borne over the water*; while in order that it should abide, *God saw that it was good*. And what was said about light was said about everything else. Some things, you see, abide by soaring over all the whole rolling wheel of time in the widest range of holiness under God; while other things do so according to the limits of their time, and thus it is through things giving way to and taking the place of one another that the beautiful tapestry of the ages is woven.

The question of time; when did God say, Let light be made?

9, 15. So then, as for what God said: *Let light be made; and light was made* (Gn 1:3); did he say it on some day, or before any day? If, you see, he said it in the Word co-eternal with himself, he said it, clearly, in a timeless manner; but if he said it in a time-bound manner, he did not say it in the Word co-eternal with himself, but through some time-bound creation. And in this case light will not be the first thing created, because there was already another thing through which could be said, in time, *Let light be made*. Besides, what is understood to have been made before any day is that about which it says, *In the beginning God made heaven and earth* (Gn 1:1), where by the name of "heaven" is to be understood the spiritual creation already made and formed, as being the heaven of this heaven, which is the highest thing among bodies. Now it was on the second day that the solid structure was made, which again he called "heaven";[6] while by the name of earth, invisible and shapeless, and by the dark abyss[7] the incompleteness and lack of perfection of bodily reality was signified, out of which those time-bound things would be made, the first of them being light.

16. How, though, it was possible, through a creature which he made before time, for God to say in time *Let light be made*, it is rather difficult to work out. We do not, after all, accept that it was said with the utterance of a voice, because whatever such a thing as that is, it is certainly corporeal. Or did he make from that primal bodily substance in its incomplete state some corporeal voice with which to utter *Let light be made*? So then, some voice-producing body was created and formed before light. But if that is the case, there was already time for the voice to run through, and for the spaces occupied by the successive syllables to pass along. Now if time was already there before light was made, in what time would the voice have been made with which to utter *Let light be made*; to what day did that time belong? The count, after all, begins with the one day, and that the first, on which light was made.[8] Or does the whole space of time, on which both the voice-producing body was made through which to utter *Let light be*

---

6. See Gn 1:6-8. This is the "bodily heaven," not the spiritual heaven which is above it as its own heaven. For this idea of a "heaven of heaven" see note 19 below.
7. See Gn 1:2.
8. See Gn 1:5.

made, and on which the light itself was made, belong to that day? But every such voice is produced by the speaker on account of some listener's sense of hearing; this, I mean, has been so made as to perceive vibrations in the air. And so did that, whatever it was, invisible and shapeless matter have a sense of hearing, to which God could thus bellow and say, *Let light be made*? Well then, perish this absurdity from any thoughtful mind!

17. So was there some spiritual but still time-measured movement by which we are to understand that *Let light be made* was said, a movement produced by the eternal God through the co-eternal Word in the spiritual creation, which he had already made when, as it says, *In the beginning God made heaven and earth*; produced, that is, in that heaven of heaven? Or is this utterance too to be understood as not only made without any sound but also without any time-measured movement of the spiritual creation, while being somehow or other fixed and impressed on its mind and reason, by the Word, co-eternal with the Father, so that then, following this utterance, that lower, dark and unformed corporeal nature would be set in motion and turned toward the appropriate species, and light would be made?

But this really is problematic; here we have the spiritual creation which in its contemplation of Truth is beyond all time, and God giving an order outside time, and the spiritual creation hearing it outside time, but having these formulae[9] mentally impressed upon it from God's unchanging Wisdom like so many intelligible utterances, and then transmitting them to lower levels so that time-measured movements should be set up in time-measured things, whether for giving them specific form or for controlling them; how this could happen it is practically impossible to grasp. If, however, light, which was the first thing of which it was said that it should be made, and then it was made, is also to be taken as holding the first place in creation, then it is itself that intellectual, intelligent life, which would be in a formlessly fluid state unless it turned to the creator to be enlightened. But when it did turn to him and was enlightened, then that happened which was said in the Word of God: *Let light be made* (Gn 1:3).

How day number one was spent

10, 18. Nonetheless, if this was said timelessly, because time has no place in the Word, co-eternal with the Father, someone may perhaps wonder whether it also happened timelessly. But how can this be supposed, when after the light was made and divided from the darkness and they were labeled "day" and "night," scripture goes on to say: *And there was made evening, and there was made morning, one day* (Gn 1:5)? From this it appears that this work of God took up

---

9. *Rationes* in the Latin; a word that will almost dominate this whole treatise, and for which no single satisfactory translation can be provided.

the space of a day, and when this had been spent like that, evening came on, which is the beginning of the night. And then again when the space of a night had passed, the whole day was completed, so that morning could be made.

19. Indeed now, this really is astonishing: when God said, *Let light be made*, without any spacing of syllables, as an idea of his eternal Word, why it should take such a long time to make light, until the space of a whole day had passed, and evening could be made. Or was the light, perhaps, indeed made instantly, but the whole space of daytime could still be taken up in distinguishing it from the darkness, and giving each of them, once distinguished, their respective labels? It would be astonishing if this too could take God even as long to do as it takes us to say it. The distinction of light and darkness, surely, was *ipso facto* a consequence of the light being made; it could not, after all be light, unless it were distinguished from darkness.

20. As for *God calling the light day and the darkness night*, how long could this have taken, even if he had done it with the sound of a voice, syllable by syllable? No longer, surely, than it takes us to say "Let light be called day and darkness be called night." Unless of course anyone should be so crazy as to assume that because God is greater than everything else, even the fewest syllables uttered by the divine mouth could be spread over a whole day. What it comes to is this, that in fact it was by a word co-eternal with himself, that is with the inner and eternal ideas[10] of unchanging Wisdom, that *God called the light day and the darkness night*. Again, you see, it could be asked, if he did the calling with the words we use, what language he did it in, and what need there was for transient sounds where there was nobody's bodily sense of hearing, and no answer to the question could be found.

21. Or must it be said that as soon as this work of God had been performed, the light remained without night following it until a full day-time period had passed, and that the night which followed the day remained until a full night-time period had passed, and morning could be made of the next day with one day, and that the first, completed? But if I say that, I am afraid I will be laughed at by those who know for certain, and by those who can easily work out, that during the time when it is night with us the presence of light is illuminating those parts of the world past which the sun is returning from its setting to its rising, and that thus during the entire twenty-four hours, while it circles through its whole round, there is always day-time somewhere, night-time somewhere else.

So then, are we really going to station God in some part where evening can be made for him, while the light withdraws from that part to another? For it is also written in the book called Sirach as follows: *And the sun rises, and the sun sets, and leads on to its place*, that is to the place from which it rose. It continues, you

---

10. *Rationes* in the Latin.

see, and says, *Rising it proceeds thither to the south and circles round to the north* (Sir 1:5-6). So when the southern part of the sky has the sun it is day-time for us, but when in its circuit it reaches the northern part, it is night-time for us; yet that does not mean it is not day-time in the other part where the sun is present—unless maybe our hearts are inclined to accept the poetic fiction, so that we really believe the sun sinks into the sea and rises, well washed, on the other side.[11] Though if this were the case, the abyss itself would be lit up by the presence of the sun, and it would be day-time there. I mean, it would be able to illuminate even the waters, seeing that it could not be extinguished by them. But this is a monstrous supposition. Why? Because there was not yet even any sun.

22. Accordingly, if the light that was made on the first day was spiritual, surely it never set, did it, to be succeeded by night? While if it was corporeal, what then is that light which we can no longer see when the sun has set—because there was as yet no moon nor any stars? Or if it is always in the same part of the sky as the sun, not as the light of the sun, but as a kind of companion to it, always joined to it in such a way that it cannot be distinguished and identified apart from it, we come back to the same difficulty in solving this problem, because this light too as the sun's companion circles round in the same way as the sun from its setting to its rising, and is in the other part of the world during the time that this part in which we find ourselves darkens into night. This obliges us to believe—perish the thought!—that God was in one part, a part this light would desert so that evening might be made for him. Or had he, perhaps, made the light in that part of the world in which he was going to make man, and that is why, when the light had departed from that part, evening is said to have been made, even when that light which had left there was in the other part, ready to rise in the morning after completing its round?

The function of the sun on the fourth day

11, 23. So why was the sun made *with authority over the day* (Ps 136:8), *to give light upon the earth* (Gn 1:17), if that light which had also been called "day" had been sufficient for the making of the day? Or was that earlier light illuminating higher regions far from the earth, so that it could not be perceived on earth, and thus it was necessary for the sun to be made, and through its agency for day-time to be manifested to the lower parts of the cosmos? This can also be said, that the brilliance of the day was increased by the addition of the sun, so that a

---

11. Augustine probably had Ovid's *Metamorphoses*, Book 2 in mind, the beginning of which is devoted to myths about the sun. But in the classical myths of the sun that deity (or Titan) traveled in a chariot, drawn by the horses of the sun; and it is these horses that really needed washing in the ocean after their day's work, and received it, after being given an evening feed on some kind of ambrosian hay in the Hesperides, the western islands of the blessed.

day less brilliant than it is now may be supposed to have come into being through that light.

Then I know that this also has been said by someone: that first of all the essence of light was introduced in the work of the creator, by the words, *Let light be made; and light was made*; while later on when it talks of the luminous bodies, it relates what was made out of that light in the due order of days, in which it seemed good to the creator that all things should be made. But where this essence of light passed along to when evening was made, so that night in turn might run its course, this person did not say and neither do I think it can easily be ascertained.[12] It can scarcely be supposed, after all, that it was put out so that nocturnal darkness might follow, and then lit again so that morning might be made, before the sun took on this task, which as the same text testifies was made to begin on the fourth day.

How did evening and morning follow each other during the first three days?

12, 24. It is hard to work out and explain on what kind of circuit, before this happened, they could follow each other, those three days and nights of the light which was first made, while it retained its nature, if it is a bodily light that we must understand as being made then. Unless perhaps one were to say that some earthy and watery mass, before these elements were sorted out from each other, which the text tells us happened on the third day, was called darkness by God on account of its grosser thickness which light could not penetrate, or on account of the dense shadow which such a mass would necessarily cast if it was lighted up on the other side. The place, after all, which the mass of any body stops light reaching, is in shadow place lacking the light which would illuminate it unless an intervening body obstructed it; that is all that is meant by "shadow." If the mass of a body casts a shadow big enough to occupy as much space on the earth as daylight occupies on the other side, it is called night. Not any and every darkness, after all, is night; I mean in vast caves too, where light is prevented from breaking through by some obstructive mass of rock, it is certainly pitch dark, because there is no light there, and the whole of that space lacks light. Darkness of that sort, though, has never been called night, but only the sort which covers the part of the earth from which the day has been withdrawn. In the same way not every light is called day—after all, light comes from the moon and the stars and lamps and phosphorescence, and anything that glows—but only that light is called day which comes before night and is followed by it as it bows out itself.

25. But if that primordial light had been poured round the mass of the earth on all sides to cover it all, whether it was stationary or circling round, there would

---

12. Not only does Augustine not tell us who this person was, but neither do any of his learned editors, neither the Maurists nor their predecessors, nor the editors of the CSEL.

have been no part in which it could let night in to follow it, because it would not itself have withdrawn from anywhere to make room for it. Or was it just made on one side of the earth, so that as it circled round it would allow night from the other side to circle round too in its wake? Since water, you see, was still covering the whole earth, there was nothing to stop the mass of this watery globe from causing day on one side from the presence of light, and night on the other from the absence of light, which would follow round to the first side at the time of evening, while the light sank down to the other side.

As the water under heaven had first covered the whole earth, where did it recede to, for the dry land to appear?

26. So then, where were the waters collected together, if they had previously occupied the whole surface of the earth—those waters, that is to say, which were drawn aside so that the earth could be laid bare, what part were they collected into?[13] If there was already, you see, a piece of bare earth where they could be collected, the dry land had already appeared, and the abyss did not occupy the whole surface of the earth; but if it had occupied the whole surface, what was the place for the waters to be collected in for the earth to appear as dry? They were not, surely, collected into a pile, as happens on the threshing floor when the harvest that has been threshed is winnowed and then swept into a heap, and so lays bare the place it had been spread over and covered?

Who would ever say such a thing, when they can see the fields of the sea[14] spread out level on all sides, because even when waves raise up what seem like mountains of water, they are smoothed out again the moment the storm abates? And even if some shores are more extensively laid bare by the ebbing tide, it cannot be said that there are no other spaces of land where what has been drawn away from somewhere else can go to, and then return again to the place it had departed from.[15] But since it was quite simply the whole earth that was covered by the surges of the watery element, where would this retreat to in order to lay bare some parts? Or perhaps it was a more rarified water-like mist that was covering all the lands, and this was collected together by being condensed, so that out of many parts it could lay bare those in which the dry land might appear? Though again, the earth too, by subsiding and sinking far and wide, could have provided hollow places to receive the waters flowing together into them in

---

13. See Gn 1:9.
14. A poetic expression, not exactly quoted, but in all probability derived from Virgil's *Aeneid*, 10.214, which has *campos salis*. But it was a common kind of expression in classical poetic literature.
15. The only sea Augustine had experience of was the Mediterranean, which is almost tideless. But he will have known of course about Atlantic tides beyond the Pillars of Hercules—the straits of Gibraltar.

torrents, and in this way dry land could have appeared in those parts from which the wet had departed.

27. Basic material, however, in which even something as minimally specific as mist has appeared, is not absolutely shapeless and without form.

When had earth and water been created?

13. And therefore the question can still be asked: when did God create these visible species and qualities of the waters and the lands of the earth; I mean, there is no record of them in any of the six days. And so suppose that he did it before any day, according to what is written before these first days are mentioned: *In the beginning God made heaven and earth* (Gn 1:1). So we could understand by the word "earth" the earth species already formed and in essence visible, but with the waters manifestly covering all of it. Then we would not think of any form-lessness of basic material in the words of scripture which follow: *Now the earth was invisible and shapeless, and there was darkness over the abyss; and the Spirit of God was being borne over the water* (Gn 1:2), but of earth and water without light (which had not yet been made), but established with those qualities we are now so familiar with. So we could take it that the reason the earth was said to be invisible was that being covered with water it could not be seen, even if there had been anyone there to see it, while the reason it was called shapeless was that it had not yet been distinguished from the sea and girded with its shores and embellished with its fruits and animals.

So if that is the case, why were these particular species, which are unquestionably bodily, made before any day? Why does the text not run: "God said, Let the earth be made; and the earth was made," and again, "God said, Let the water be made; and the water was made"? Or both of them together, if they are both contained under what you could call the law of the lowest place: "God said, Let the earth and water[16] be made; and thus it was made"?

14. Why does it not say, when this had been done, "God saw that it was good"?

Why did God not "see that it was good" after creating formless matter, in verse 2?

28. It is, after all, obvious (that everything changeable is given form or shape out of something lacking form or shape) and at the same time Catholic faith prescribes and reason indubitably teaches that there could have been no basic material for any specific natures, unless it came from God the initiator and

---

16. The CSEL text omits "and water," which is there in the Maurist text—and required by the general sense of the passage. In neither edition is there any note in the apparatus, so I conclude that the CSEL omission is merely the result of a printer's oversight.

creator of all things, both formed and formable, about which one passage of scripture says to him: *You that made the world out of formless matter* (Wis 11:18). It is considerations of this sort, you see, that have convinced me that it was this basic material that was indicated by those words which spiritual foresight adapted even to less quick-witted readers or listeners, and which say before coming to any counting of days, *In the beginning God made heaven and earth,* and so on until it comes to *And God said,* so that from there on the order of things given form and shape might follow.

Formless matter prior as a source, but not prior in time, to the things formed out of it

15, 29. It is not because formless matter is prior in time to things formed from it, since they are both created simultaneously together, both the thing made and what it was made out of; but because that which something is made out of is still prior as its source, even if not in time, to what is made from it, that scripture could divide in the time it takes to state them what God did not divide in the time it took to make them. Just as a voice, after all, is the basic material for words, while words are what a voice is formed into, but the speaker does not first give vent to an unformed voice which he can later on gather up and form into words, so too God the creator did not first make formless material and later on form it, on second thoughts as it were, into every kind of nature; no, he created formed and fashioned material. If the question were asked, I mean, whether we make a voice from words or words from a voice, it would not be easy to find anyone so slow of wit as not to answer that it is rather words which are made from a voice. So too, although the speaker makes them both simultaneously, it is clear enough, on a moment's reflection, what he makes out of which.

For this reason, since God made them simultaneously, both the material which he formed and the things into which he formed it, and since both had to be mentioned by scripture and both could not be mentioned simultaneously, can anybody doubt that what something was made out of had rightly to be mentioned before what was made out of it? Because even when we just say "matter" and "form," we understand them as being together simultaneously, and we are unable to state them simultaneously. Now just as it happens in a very short space of time, when we utter these two words, that we utter them one before the other, so too in the longer form of a narrative, one thing had to be mentioned before the other, although God made each of them, as we have said, simultaneously. Thus what came first in the making solely as source comes first also in time in the telling. If two things of which neither is in any way prior to the other cannot be named simultaneously, how much less can their stories be told simultaneously! So then, there can be no doubt at all that this formless basic material, almost the same as nothingness though it be, was still made by none but God, and was simultaneously created with the things that were formed from it.

30. Let us take it as granted, then, that this formless basic material may be said to be signified by the words, *Now the earth was invisible and shapeless, and there was darkness over the abyss; and the Spirit of God was being borne over the water* (Gn 1:2), and that apart from what is put there about the Spirit of God, we are to understand the other words, while indeed being the names of visible things, as intended to suggest that formlessness as best it could be done to the less quick-witted, because these two elements, earth that is and water, are more manageable than the others in the hands of workmen for making things, and that is why this formlessness was the more suitably suggested by these names.

16 But if this is the most probable interpretation, there was no formed mass there which the light could illuminate on one side and on the other produce darkness, so that night could follow the departing day.

A suggestion that during the first three days night and day mean contraction and emission of light

31. We might, however, wish to understand the emission and contraction of that light as constituting day and night; but if so, we cannot see any reason why it should be done like that—there were no animals yet, after all, for whom this beneficial alternation could be arranged, and for whom, now that they have evolved, we see that it is arranged by the circling of the sun; nor does any example spring to mind which would enable us to accept as in the least likely such an emission and contraction of light for bringing about the alternation of night and day. Yes, the darting out of rays from our eyes is indeed the darting out of a kind of light, and it can be contracted when we fix our gaze on the air that is nearest to our eyes, and emitted when we turn our attention along the same line to things that are further away.[17] Nor does it cease, to be sure, to see things further away when it is contracted, but it certainly sees them more hazily than when the glance is emitted directly at them. But still, the light which is in the sense of the seeing subject is so slight, we are informed, that unless it was assisted by the light outside, we would be able to see nothing; and since it cannot be distinguished from that external light, it is hard, as I said, to find an example by which the emission of light into day and its contraction into night could be demonstrated.

---

17. The common theory of vision at the time—at least, the one Augustine took for granted—was that it is achieved by the eyes emitting rays which touch the objects seen and then transmit the impression back to the sense of sight; something like the antennae of certain insects—or the headlights of a motor car!

What can evening and morning, night and day, be for spiritual light?

17, 32. But if it was a spiritual light that was made when God said *Let light be made* (Gn 1:3), it is not that true light, co-eternal with the Father, that is to be understood, through which all things were made, and which enlightens every human being,[18] but that about which it could be said: *Before all things there was created wisdom* (Sir 1:4). When that eternal and unchangeable Wisdom, you see, which was begotten, not made, transfers itself into spiritual and rational creatures, as it does into holy souls, so that being thus enlightened they can themselves become sources of light, there is produced in them a kind of infection of shining, glowing intelligence; and this can be taken as made light, made when God said, *Let light be made*, provided there was already a spiritual creation, which was signified by the word "heaven," where it is written, *In the beginning God made heaven and earth*. This was not a corporeal heaven but the incorporeal heaven of the corporeal heaven,[19] set that is above every kind of body, not by degrees of space, but by the sublimity of its nature. How they could be made simultaneously, however, both what was being enlightened and its actual enlightenment, while being given different times in the narrative, we were explaining a short while ago when dealing with the basic material of things.

33. But on what terms are we to understand the night succeeding this kind of light, so that evening might be made? From what sort of darkness, for that matter, could this sort of light be divided, where scripture says: *And God divided between the light and the darkness* (Gn 1:4)? There were not any sinners and fools already, were there, falling away from the light of truth, between whom and those abiding in the same light God could divide, as between the light and the dark, and by calling the light day and the darkness night could show that he is not the operative cause of sins, but is still in control of them by the appropriate distribution of rewards and punishments? Or is "day" here the name for the whole of time, and is the roll of all the ages included in this word, and is that why it is not called the first day, but one day? *And there was made evening*, you see, it says, *and there was made morning, one day* (Gn 1:5). So if we take it like this, the making of evening would seem to signify the sin of rational creatures, while the making of morning would mean their restoration.

34. But this is an interpretation on the lines of prophetic allegory, which is not what we have undertaken in this work. We undertook, you see, to talk here about the scriptures according to their proper meaning of what actually happened, not according to their riddling, enigmatic reference to future events. So then, with

---

18. See Jn 1:3.9.
19. He is here echoing the biblical expression "the heaven of heaven" as in Ps 115:16, in the Latin Vulgate: *Caelum caeli Domino*; see also Dt 10:14. He has made the same allusion earlier on, in IX,15.17.

reference to the actual making and establishing of specific natures, how can we find any evening and morning in spiritual light?[20] Or is the division of the light from the darkness indeed the distinction of the formed from the formless thing, while the calling of them day and night suggests their ordered succession, to indicate that God leaves nothing unordered and unregulated, and that the very formlessness through which things change from species to species by a kind of transition is not something uncatered for, and that the retreats and advances registered in creation, by which time-bound things follow one another in turn, have their contribution to add to the splendor of the universe?[21] Night, after all, is regulated, ordered darkness.

35. This, though, is the reason why it said "God saw the light that it was good" immediately after the light had been made, when he could have said this after all the things mentioned on this day; that is, after setting out, one by one, *God said, Let light be made; and light was made; and God divided between the light and the darkness; and God called the light day and the darkness he called night,* he could then have said, *And God saw that it was good,* and then added, *And there was made evening, and there was made morning,* as he does in the other works to which he gives names. So the reason he did not do it like that here is that the point of that formlessness being distinguished from the formed reality was to show that this was not the end of its formation, but that there still remained some of it to be formed through the rest of creation, the bodily part now. And so, if it had said *God saw that it was good* after they had been distinguished from each other by that division and by those labels attached to them, we would have taken it to apply to these things done, to which in their own kind there was nothing now to be added. But because light was the only thing God had completely made in this way, *God saw the light,* he says, *that it was good,* and then distinguished it from the darkness by dividing and naming them.

Nor did it then say *God saw that it was good*; the reason, after all, why that formlessness had been separated was so that other things could still be formed from it. As for this sort of night that we are so familiar with—it's the sun's circuit, after all, that brings it on over all lands—it is when it is separated from the day by the distribution of the luminous bodies, it is after that division of day

---

20. We nowadays would regard such an expression as "spiritual light," and even a more usual expression like "the light of reason," as involving the figurative, or metaphorical (if not enigmatic) use of the word "light." But for Augustine it was within the word's proper range of meaning. If he was here extending that proper range, he was only anticipating, "prefiguring," what modern physicists do, so I was told in an argument I was having with a younger mathematician here. They extend the word "light," in technical use, to cover such phenomena as X-rays, Gamma rays—any rays you like to mention.
21. These meanings suggested for the calling of the light and the darkness day and night hardly seem to apply to the spiritual light which he is here preoccupied with. It is all questions, to be sure, not answers—but a certain mildly regrettable incoherence here in the questions! But perhaps he will go some way to meeting this criticism in the next section.

and night that the text says, *God saw that it was good*. This night, you see, is not some formless substance from which still other things might be formed, but a space full of air which lacks the light of day; and to this night, obviously, there was nothing of its own sort to be added to make it more specially beautiful or distinct. Evening, though, in the whole of those three days before the heavenly bodies were made, is not unreasonably, I think, to be understood as the end of a finished work; while morning on the other hand points to a work that is yet to come.

In what way God works

18, 36. But above all we have to remember, a point we have already made several times, that God does not work by time-measured movements, so to say, of soul or body, as do human beings and angels, but by the eternal and unchanging, stable formulae of his Word, co-eternal with himself, and by a kind of brooding, if I may so put it, of his equally co-eternal Holy Spirit. For what is said here in the Greek and Latin versions about the Spirit of God, that *it was being borne over the water*, according to the Syriac which is a language closely related to Hebrew (this is how a learned Christian Syrian[22] is said to have explained the word) is reported to mean not *was being borne over* but *was brooding over the water* in the way birds brood over their eggs,[23] where that warmth of the mother's body in some way also supports the forming of the chicks through a kind of influence of her own kind of love.

And so let us never think in a literal-minded, fleshly way of utterances in time throughout these days of divine works. The reason, I mean to say, why the very Wisdom of God took our weakness upon herself and came to gather the children of Jerusalem under her wings as a hen gathers her chicks was not that we should always remain little children, but that while being babies in malice we should cease to be childish in mind.[24]

37. And in discussing obscure matters that are far removed from our eyes and our experience, which are patient of various explanations that do not contradict the faith we are imbued with, let us never, if we read anything on them in the divine scriptures, throw ourselves head over heels into the headstrong assertion

---

22. This was very probably Saint Ephrem, a deacon of the Church of Edessa, who founded a school of theology there, and died in 373.
23. The words I have translated as "brooding" are first the noun *fotus*, and then the verb *fovebat*. These have a much wider range of meaning in Latin, to cover the whole notion of fostering or cherishing; and the primary meaning, indeed, of *fotus* is the application of a *fomentum* or poultice to sores and wounds. So Augustine here says a little more that I translate: "was fostering the water; not as swellings or wounds in the body are fostered by cold or suitably warmed compresses, but as eggs are fostered by birds . . ."
24. See Lk 13:34; 1 Cor 14:20.

of any one of them. Perhaps the truth, emerging from a more thorough discussion of the point, may definitively overturn that opinion, and then we will find ourselves overthrown, championing what is not the cause of the divine scriptures but our own, in such a way that we want it to be that of the scriptures, when we should rather be wanting the cause of the scriptures to be our own.

Augustine's method in this commentary

19, 38. Now with this text, *And God said, Let light be made; and light was made* (Gn 1:3): let us suppose that one person was of the opinion that it was bodily light that was made, and another that it was the spiritual sort. That there is a spiritual light in the spiritual creation is something our faith has no doubts about, but that there is a special celestial or cosmic light, or even one that is above the sky or was there before the sky, which could be followed by night—well, it is not against the faith for just as long as it is not proved with absolute certainty to be untrue. If this does happen, then this is not what divine scripture contained, but what human ignorance had opined.

Should reason, on the other hand, definitively demonstrate that this is true, it will still be uncertain whether it is what the writer wished to be understood by those words of the sacred books, or whether he had in mind something else that is no less true. While if the whole context of the passage proves that he did not have this in mind, that does not mean that what he did wish to be understood by them will be false; no, it will be both true and more worth knowing. If, however, the scriptural context does not tell against the writer having intended this meaning, it still remains to inquire whether he could not also have meant something else. And should we find that he could have done, then it will be uncertain which of them he actually did intend. And it can be held not unreasonably that he intended both meanings, if all the other details lend support to each of them.

39. There is knowledge to be had, after all, about the earth, about the sky, about the other elements of this world, about the movements and revolutions or even the magnitude and distances of the constellations, about the predictable eclipses of moon and sun, about the cycles of years and seasons, about the nature of animals, fruits, stones and everything else of this kind. And it frequently happens that even non-Christians will have knowledge of this sort in a way that they can substantiate with scientific arguments or experiments. Now it is quite disgraceful and disastrous, something to be on one's guard against at all costs, that they should ever hear Christians spouting what they claim our Christian literature has to say on these topics, and talking such nonsense that they can scarcely contain their laughter when they see them to be *toto caelo*, as the saying goes, wide of the mark. And what is so vexing is not that misguided people should be laughed at, as that our authors should be assumed by outsiders to have held such views and, to the great detriment of those about whose salvation we are

so concerned, should be written off and consigned to the waste paper basket as so many ignoramuses.

Whenever, you see, they catch out some members of the Christian community making mistakes on a subject which they know inside out, and defending their hollow opinions on the authority of our books, on what grounds are they going to trust those books on the resurrection of the dead and the hope of eternal life and the kingdom of heaven, when they suppose they include any number of mistakes and fallacies on matters which they themselves have been able to master either by experiment or by the surest of calculations? It is impossible to say what trouble and grief such rash, self-assured know-alls cause the more cautious and experienced brothers and sisters. Whenever they find themselves challenged and taken to task for some shaky and false theory of theirs by people who do not recognize the authority of our books, they try to defend what they have aired with the most frivolous temerity and patent falsehood by bringing forward these same sacred books to justify it. Or they even quote from memory many things said in them which they imagine will provide them with valid evidence, *not understanding either what they are saying, or the matters on which they are asserting themselves* (1 Tm 1:7).

Stating all possible meanings by way of questions

20, 40. It is in order to take account of this state of things that I have, to the best of my ability, winkled out and presented a great variety of possible meanings to the words of the book of Genesis which have been darkly expressed in order to put us through our paces. I have avoided affirming anything hastily in a way that would rule out any alternative explanation that may be a better one, so leaving everyone free to choose whichever they can grasp most readily in their turn, and when they cannot understand, let them give honor to God's scripture,[25] keeping fear for themselves. But since the words of scripture that we have been dealing with can be explained along so many lines, let those people now restrain themselves, who are so puffed up with their knowledge of secular literature, that they scornfully dismiss as something crude and unrefined these texts which are all expressed in a way designed to nourish devout hearts.[26] You could say they are crawling along the ground without wings, and poking fun at the nests of birds that are going to fly.

Some of the weaker brothers and sisters, however, are in danger of going astray more seriously when they hear these godless people holding forth

---

25. So the Maurists, with the support of most manuscripts, reading *ubi intelligere non potest, scripturae Dei det honorem.* The CSEL text reads . . . *non potest scripturam, Deo det honorem*—where they cannot understand the scripture, let them give honor to God.
26. The sort of person he had been himself before his conversion.

expertly and fluently on the "music of the spheres,"[27] or on any questions you care to mention about the elements of this cosmos. They wilt and lose heart, putting these pundits before themselves, and while regarding them as great authorities, they turn back with a weary distaste to the books of salutary godliness, and can scarcely bring themselves to touch the volumes they should be devouring with delight—shrinking from the roughness of the husks of the wheat and eagerly eyeing the flowers of the thistles. After all, they have no time to *be still* (Ps 46:11), and to *see how sweet is the Lord* (Ps 34:8), nor are they *hungry on the sabbath* (Mt 12:1); and that is why they are too lazy to use the authority they have received from the Lord to pluck the ears of wheat and go on rubbing them in their hands until they come to what they can eat.

What have we gotten from his "rubbing the grain in his hands" like this?

21, 41. Someone is going to say, "What about you, with all this rubbing of corn in this essay, how much grain have you extracted? What have you winnowed? Why is practically everything hidden still in a heap of questions? Affirm some of the many meanings you have argued can be understood."

To which I reply that I have happily reached this very food: namely that I have learned that we should not hesitate to give the answers that have to be given, in line with the faith, to people who make every effort to discredit the books our salvation depends on. So we should show that whatever they have been able to demonstrate from reliable sources about the world of nature is not contrary to our literature, while whatever they may have produced from any of their volumes that is contrary to this literature of ours, that is, to the Catholic faith, we must either show with some ease, or else believe without any hesitation, to be entirely false. And we should so hold onto our mediator, *in whom are stored up all the treasures of wisdom and of knowledge* (Col 2:3), that we are neither seduced by the chatter of false philosophy, nor frightened out of our wits by the superstitions of false religion.

And when we read in the divine books such a vast array of true meanings,[28] which can be extracted from a few words, and which are backed by sound Catholic faith, we should pick above all the one which can certainly be shown to have been held by the author we are reading; while if this is hidden from us, then surely one which the scriptural context does not rule out and which is agreeable to sound faith; but if even the scriptural context cannot be worked out and

---

27. Literally, "on the numbers of the heavenly bodies"; but I am sure he does not mean the count of heavenly bodies, how many there are—nothing so banal. He means the harmonies of their motions.

28. He actually writes, "when we read the divine books in such a vast array . . . "; I think I am justified in switching the preposition.

assessed, then at least only one which sound faith prescribes. It is one thing, after all, not to be able to work out what the writer is most likely to have meant, quite another to stray from the road sign-posted by godliness. Should each defect be avoided, the reader's work has won its complete reward, while if each cannot be avoided, even though the writer's intention should remain in doubt, it will not be without value to have extracted a sense that accords with sound faith.

Book II

Genesis 1:6-19: The second, third, and fourth days of creation

How there can be water above the solid structure of the sky

1, 1. *And God said: Let a solid structure be made in the midst of the waters, and let it be dividing between water and water. And thus it was made. And God made a solid structure, and divided between the water which was below the solid structure and the water which was above the solid structure. And God called the solid structure heaven. And God saw that it was good. And there was made evening and there was made morning, a second day* (Gn 1:6-8). About the word of God which God spoke, saying *Let a solid structure be made,* etc., and about the pleasure he took in it on seeing that it was good, and about evening and about morning, there is no need to go over the same discussion again; and so from now on, as often as these phrases are repeated, I give the reader notice that for the most part they are to be interpreted in accordance with our previous inquiry. Whether that is the heaven, however, being made now which soars above all the spaces of the air and all its height, where too the lamps and the stars are set on the fourth day, or whether the air itself is also being called the solid structure, is a question that can properly be asked.

2. Many people, you see, insist that these waters by their very nature cannot be above the heaven of the constellations, because their proper specific gravity dictates that they must either flow and float over the earth, or be carried up as vapor into the air that is nearest the earth. Nor should anybody try to refute them by appealing to the omnipotence of God, *for whom all things are possible* (Mk 10:27), and saying we just have to believe that he can cause even water, as heavy as what we know by our own experience, to spread over the substance of the heaven or sky in which the stars have their place. Our business now, after all, is to inquire how God's scriptures say he established things according to their proper natures, and not what he might wish to work in them or out of them as a miracle of his power.

Yes, to be sure, if God wished oil to remain sometimes under water, then it would; but that would not mean that we remained ignorant of the nature of oil, that it had been made such that if it were poured out underneath some water, it

190

would seek its proper place by breaking through to place itself above on the surface. So now therefore what we are inquiring into is whether the fashioner of things, who *arranged all things in measure and number and weight* (Wis 11:20), allotted not just one proper place to the weight of the waters round the earth, but also another on top of the heaven or sky which was solidified after being poured out round the outer limits of the air.[1]

3. Those who maintain that this is an impossible position to hold base their argument on the weights of the elements,[2] maintaining that the sky cannot possibly have been solidified up above into a kind of paved floor capable of sustaining the weight of the waters, because such solidity can only belong to things of earth, and anything of that sort is not sky or heaven, but earth, the elements being distinguished not only by their places but also by their qualities, so that it is in virtue of their specific qualities that they are allotted their specific places. Thus water's place is above earth, and even if it settles or sinks under the earth, as in caves and hidden potholes, it is still being held up by that part of the earth which it has underneath itself, not by that part which is above it. After all, if from the part of the earth above it any piece falls down, it does not remain on top of the water but breaks through its surface and sinks and goes down to the earth at the bottom; there it rests as in its own place, so that water remains on top, earth underneath. From this one concludes that even when it was above the water it was not being borne up by the water, but being held together by the compactness of the earth, as can be demonstrated from subterranean tomb chambers.

A problem raised by Psalm 136:6

4. Here it occurs to me to repeat the warning I gave in Book I about the mistake of relying on the evidence of a scriptural text against those who produce these subtle arguments about the weights of the elements,[3] and quoting perhaps what is written in the psalms: *who founded the earth on the water* (Ps 136:6), because such people do not acknowledge the authority of our literature and are ignorant of the way in which that was said, and so they are more likely to poke fun at the sacred books than to repudiate what they have come to hold by reasoned arguments or have proved by the clearest experiments.

One acceptable way of taking that verse of the psalm is to treat it as said figuratively; so since by the names of "heaven" and "earth" it is often the spiritual

---

1. This answers in some degree to the picture the authors of Genesis had of the firmament, as a kind of brazen dome over the world; in creating it, did not God, Augustine is wondering, act like a foundryman pouring molten brass into a mold to make bells. The Hebrew word, however, suggests a slightly different craft, that of a coppersmith beating out a sheet of metal into the appropriate shape.
2. The four elements of ancient chemistry: earth, water, air, and fire.
3. See Book I,19,39.

and the fleshly-minded members of the Church respectively that are signified, the psalmist would have been showing that the heavens refer to the serene understanding of the truth, where he says, *who made the heavens in understanding* (Ps 136:5), while earth refers to the simple faith of the little ones, a faith not built unreliably on fables and misguided speculations,[4] but most firmly on the teaching of the prophets and the proclamation of the gospel, and given solidity through baptism. And that is why he went on to add, *who founded the earth on the water.*

Or else, if someone obliges you to take the verse literally, it can be applied not unreasonably to the heights of the earth, whether on continents or islands, which soar up above the waters, or to the roofs of those caverns which overhang the waters with rock-like solidity. Accordingly, nobody may understand the literal sense of the words, "who founded the earth on the water" in such a way as to conclude that the weight of the waters was placed under the weight of the earth to support it as if that were the natural order of things.

Air by nature, being lighter than earth, lies above it

2, 5. Air, however, lies naturally above water (though it also spreads over the dry land because of its wider spaciousness); and this is proved by the fact that no bottle can be filled with water when pushed into it mouth downwards—a clear indication that air by its nature seeks the higher or upper place. The bottle, you see, seems to be empty, but is proved to be full of air when it is pushed mouth downwards into the water. Because the air can find no way of popping out through the uppermost part, and its nature will not allow it to go downwards under the water trying to rush in, it keeps the water at bay by its own filling presence, and refuses it entry.

When, though, the bottle is so put into the water that it does not have its mouth downwards, but is put in sideways, the water comes in at the lower edge while the air goes out by the upper one. Again, if the mouth of the bottle is open to the sky, when you pour in water the air goes out upwards by the parts where you are not pouring in and room is made underneath for the water to come in. But if the bottle is pushed down with greater force, so that water flows in suddenly from the side or from the top and covers the mouth of the bottle completely on every side, the air bursts through the water as it struggles upwards, to make room for the water at the bottom. And it is the air bursting through like this that makes

---

4. See 1 Tm 1:4; 4:7. His implicit identification here of the "carnal," the fleshly-minded, with the little ones is not entirely characteristic of him, I think. But underlying it is his assumption, almost certainly justified, that the uneducated are likely to be literal-minded in their understanding of what they read or hear.

bottles sob or gurgle, while the air escapes bit by bit, unable to do so all at once because the bottle's mouth is too narrow.

Thus if air is forced to get up on top of water, it thrusts aside even converging flows, when the water being driven in starts bubbling under the impetus of the air leaping out,[5] and lets it escape with exploding bubbles as it hurries to its own proper place and makes room for the water falling down to the bottom. But should you try to force it out of the bottle under the water, wanting it to give way so that the bottle can be filled when pushed mouth downwards right to the bottom, the bottle will be sooner covered with water on every side than a single tiny drop will gain entrance to it from the bottom.

Fire likewise lighter than air, and so lying above it

3, 6. Now that fire, as it leaps up to the heights, wishes to soar above even the nature of the very air we breathe, is something, surely, that everybody can perceive. I mean to say, if you hold a burning torch head downwards, its crown of flames will struggle up to the upper parts. But because the fire is then straight-away extinguished by the dominant pressure of the air all round and above it, and so being defeated by the excessive quantity of air is straightaway changed and converted into the same thing, it is unable to last out and leap up beyond the atmosphere's highest altitude.

And so the sky or heaven above the air is said to be pure fire, from which, so they suppose, the constellations and the great lamps are made, through the nature of that fiery light being squeezed and molded, that is to say, into those forms and shapes and patterns which we now observe in the sky. Now just as both air and water give way to the weight of particles of earth, so that they drop down to the earth, in the same manner air gives way to the weight of water, so that it drops down either to earth or to water. From this they want it to be understood that it is necessary in the same manner for air too, if anyone could release a particle of it in those loftiest regions of the sky, to fall by its own weight, until it reaches the airy regions underneath. From all this they conclude that much less is it possible for there to be any place for water above that fiery heaven, since air, though much lighter than water, cannot remain there either.

---

5. Reading *exilientis* with two manuscripts, thus qualifying the air. Both Maurists and the CSEL text read *exilientes*, making this word refer to the water (plural in the Latin). But the water is not getting out of the bottle, it is being pushed in. I suspect some copyists would have written this less likely variant thanks to an unconscious memory of Jn 4:14 or 7:37—of the sense of those passages, that is to say, not of the actual words.

Saint Basil's solution

4, 7. One person,[6] while accepting their arguments, made a praiseworthy attempt to demonstrate that there are waters above the heavens, in order to defend the reliability of scripture with reference to the manifestly visible phenomena. And first, which was only too easy, he showed that this air, or atmosphere, is also called heaven or sky; and not only in ordinary speech, as when we talk about a clear sky, or a cloudy sky, but also in the style of our scriptures themselves, where there is mention of *the birds of the sky* (Mt 6:26), though it is obvious that birds fly around in this air; and when the Lord was speaking about clouds, *You are able to judge*, he said, *by the face of the sky* (Mt 16:3). Now we can often observe clouds being condensed even in the air nearest to the earth, when they slide so low down the slopes of ridges that even the mountaintops rise up above them.

So then, after proving that this airy atmosphere too is called sky or heaven, he wished it to be accepted that the only reason for also calling it a solid structure or firmament was that its intermediate space divides between waters in the form of vapor and those waters which flow in a more tangible liquid form on the earth. And clouds to be sure, as anyone who has gone walking in mountains and hills can tell you, give precisely this impression of the assembly and condensation of the tiniest little drops; and if these thicken any further, so that several very small drops are joined into one big one, the air will no longer allow it to be held up there, but yields to the weight of it and lets it fall to the lowest level—and that is rain.

So this man then wished to show, that it is out of the air lying between the moist vapors from which clouds are condensed up above and the seas spread out down below, that the sky or heaven is constituted between water and water. So then, I judge this carefully thought out theory to be deserving of all praise. What he said, you see, is not against the faith, and can also be readily accepted when the grounds for it are set out.

8. It could appear, though, as if the specific weights of the elements need not prevent the waters from being able to lie above that lofty heaven in the form of those droplets in which they have been able to stay above this space of the air. While this is indeed heavier than the highest heaven and lies underneath it, it is undoubtedly lighter than water; and yet watery vapors, nonetheless, are not prevented by any weight from being above it. So then in the same way a lighter

---

6. The CSEL editors refer to Basil of Caesarea, in his *Hexaemeron* III,8. See also Saint Thomas Aquinas *Summa Theologiae*, I,68,1. Saint Thomas in this volume (questions 65 - 74 of the first part of his *Summa*) is contrasting throughout Saint Augustine's exegesis of Genesis 1 with that of Saint Basil, and other fathers like Saint Ambrose, who gave what we nowadays would call a more literal (quasi-fundamentalist) interpretation of the text—certainly a less sophisticated one!

exhalation of moisture in the form of still tinier droplets can be spread out even above that highest heaven, and not be compelled to fall down by its weight.

They themselves, as a matter of fact, put forward the most subtle arguments to show that there can be no material particle, however minute, which cannot be further divided, but that all bodies can be divided *ad infinitum*, because every part of a body is a body, and every single body necessarily has a half of its quantity.[7] For this reason, then, if water, as we observe, can be broken up into so many tiny drops that it can be carried up as vapor above this air which is by nature lighter than water, why could it not stay also above that still lighter heaven in the form of even tinier droplets and even lighter vapors?

The coldness of the planet Saturn

5, 9. Some of our people also set out to refute in another way those who assert that there can be no waters above the heaven of the constellations on account of the weights of the elements; they argue from the qualities of the constellations themselves and their courses. The same people,[8] you see, assert that the star which they call Saturn is the coldest of them all and takes thirty years to go through the circuit of the signs of the zodiac, just because it moves on a higher and therefore much more extensive orbit. The sun, after all, completes the same circuit in a year, and the moon in a month; the course being the shorter, so they say, the lower the orbit, so that the length of time taken corresponds to the space covered.

And so our people ask what it is that makes that star so cold, since it ought to be all the hotter, drawn along as it is through the loftier heaven. I mean, there can be no doubt that when a spherical mass is driven through a circular motion, its inner parts go more slowly, its outer ones faster, having to cover more ground while going through the same number of revolutions; and the faster they go, then of course the hotter they get. Accordingly, this aforementioned star should be hot rather than cold. For while by its own motive power it takes thirty years to travel through its whole circuit, the distance to be covered being so vast, nonetheless by the movement of the heaven in the opposite direction it is made to

---

7. Whoever these secular physicists were, they were not the heirs of Democritus, one of the early Greek natural philosophers, who put forward the earliest atomic theory, that the material world consists of indivisible particles or "atoms"; Aristotle accepted his theory. Just possibly it was rejected by the Academics, the degenerate heirs of Plato's Academy, whom the young Augustine had briefly gone along with after parting company with the Manichees. Saint Thomas, in his article on the work of the second day (*Summa*, I,68,2) following Aristotle, says that no natural or physical body is infinitely divisible, but only what he calls a mathematical body.

8. Ours, or their pagan opponents? Grammatically it could be either; but from what follows in the next few paragraphs it is clear that he means the latter.

rotate all the faster;[9] and because it has to experience this every day it is thus, so they tell us, that each single revolution of the heaven unrolls a single day, it ought to have generated greater heat from the more rapidly spinning heaven.

Indubitably, therefore, what makes it cold is the nearness of those waters set in place above the heavens, which these people refuse to believe who argue in the way I have summarized about the movement of the sky and the constellations. It is by drawing such inferences that some of our people meet those who refuse to believe there are any waters above the heavens and still insist on the coldness of that star whose circuit is nearest to the highest heaven, thereby forcing them to conclude that the substance of water is held up there not in the fine form of vapor, but in the solid form of ice. In whatever form, however, waters may be there, and of whatever kind, let us have no doubts at all that that is where they are; the authority of this text of scripture, surely, overrides anything that human ingenuity is capable of thinking up.

How the persons of the Trinity are indicated in the text

6, 10. But it has been remarked by some people—and it is a good point which I for my part do not think should be ignored—that after God had said, *Let a solid structure be made in the midst of the waters, and let it be a division between water and water*, it did not seem sufficient to continue, *And thus it was made*, without also adding, *And God made a solid structure; and God divided between the water which was above the solid structure, and between the water which was below the solid structure* (Gn 1:7). Now the way they understand it is to say that the person of the Father was indicated by the text, *And God said: Let a solid structure be made in the midst of the waters, and let it be a division between water and water; and thus it was made*; and then, so that the Son may be understood to have done what the Father said, so that it should actually be made, they reckon that it went on to say, *And God made a solid structure, and God divided*, etc.

11. But when we read first, *And thus it was made*,[10] by whom are we to understand that it was made? If by the Son, what need was there to go on to say, *And God made* and the rest? But if we are to understand the words *And thus it was*

---

9. Like a small cogwheel being spun round by a bigger one rotating in the opposite direction? Where Augustine and the pagan opponents he has in mind took their astronomy from is really rather obscure; it seems to bear little or no resemblance to the sophisticated Ptolemaic astronomy that was accepted by the learned ancient world up to the time of Copernicus.
10. Augustine's text, following the Greek Septuagint, puts the refrain "And thus it was made" ("And it was so" in the usual translation) before the longer statement, "And God made" etc. Throughout this creation narrative the Septuagint text is more uniformly consistent than the Hebrew text from which our modern versions (as also the Latin Vulgate of Saint Jerome) are taken.

made as meaning that it was made by the Father, it is not now the Father saying and the Son making, and it means that the Father can make something without the Son, so that the Son then makes, not this thing, but something like it, which is against the Catholic faith.

If however the thing about which it says *And thus it was made* is the same as what is being made when it goes on to say, *And God made*, what is to stop us understanding that the same one who said that it should be made is making what he said? Or is it even that they wish to pass over the text *And thus it was made*, and understand the persons of the Father and the Son only in the words, *And God said, Let it be made*, and then later in the words, *And God made*?

12. But we can still ask whether we ought to take it as the Father giving a kind of order to the Son in the text, *And God said, Let it be made*. But why did scripture not bother also to indicate the person of the Holy Spirit? Or is the Trinity to be understood like this: *And God said, Let it be made*; *And God made*; *And God saw that it was good*? But it is hardly consistent with the unity of the Trinity, that the Son should be understood to have made something as if under orders, while the Holy Spirit freely saw that what had been made was good, without anyone giving him orders.[11]

With what words, in any case, would the Son be given orders by the Father to make something, seeing that he is himself the Father's original Word, *through which all things were made* (Jn 1:3)? Or is it the case that as regards the text *Let a solid structure be made* (Gn 1:6) this very utterance is the Word of the Father, his only-begotten Son, in whom are all created things even before they are created? And anything that there is in him is life, because *whatever was made through him is in him life* (Jn 1:3-4[12]), and of course creative life, while under him life is a creature. So then, the things that have been made through him, because he governs them and holds them together, are in him in one way, while the things which he himself is are in him in another. He, after all, is life, which is in him in such a way that it is he himself, since he, the life, is the light of men.[13] So then, nothing could be created, whether before time (which does not mean co-eternal with the creator), or from the start of time, or in any particular time, of which the

---

11. It is surely the equality of the divine persons that this view would compromise, rather than their unity.
12. See Jn 1:3-4. Where most versions that most people are familiar with read these verses like this: "All things were made through him, and without him was not made anything that was made. In him was life" (so RSV), Augustine read them as follows: "All things were made through him, and without him was made nothing. What was made in him was life." The most modern editions of John's text follow this reading, as also the Jerusalem Bible.
13. See Jn 1:4. The thought here does seem very confused. There appears to have been no particular reason for him to bring in the reference to life here; it has nothing really to do with the main line of his thought, that all things made through the Word pre-exist in the Word in their *rationes*, their ideas. It was probably the case that as he was dictating, he got carried on to quote Jn 1:3-4; a little piece of "stream of consciousness" thinking.

creational formula—if it can rightly be called a formula[14]—was not alive with co-eternal life in the Word of God co-eternal with the Father; and that is why scripture, before introducing each element of creation in the order in which it says it was established, looks back to the Word of God, and first puts, "God said, Let that thing be made." It could not, you see, find any reason for creating a thing, about which it had not found in the Word of God that it ought to be created.

13. So then, God did not in fact say, "Let this or that creature be made" every single time that the phrase is repeated in this book, *And God said*. It was one Word, after all, that he begot, in which he said all things before they were made singly; but the scriptural style comes down to the level of the little ones and adjusts itself to their capacity by putting before them each single kind of creature one by one, and then looking back at the eternal formula of each kind in the Word of God. And it was not because that was being repeated that the author all the same repeated *And God said*.

Suppose, you see, he had wanted to put first, "A solid structure was made in the midst of the waters, to be a division between water and water"; then if someone had asked him how it had been made, he would rightly have answered, *God said, Let it be made*; that is, it was in the eternal Word of God that it should be made. It is from that point, therefore, that he begins the story of each thing made, which he would have had to mention in any case as he explained to a questioner how it was made even after telling the story of its making.

14. So then, when we hear, *And God said, Let it be made*, we understand that it was in the Word of God that it should be made. When on the other hand we hear, *And thus it was made*, we understand that the creature on being made did not overstep the limits of its kind prescribed for it in the Word of God. When finally we hear, *And God saw that it was good*, we understand, not that in the kindness and courtesy of his Spirit it pleased him as something known after it had been made, but rather that in that same goodness where it had pleased him that it should be made, it pleased him that it should remain made.

The meaning of "made"

7, 15. And that still leaves us with one more point to inquire about; why, after saying, *And thus it was made*, where the completion of the work is already indicated, he added, *And God made*. After all, simply by saying, *And God said, Let this or that be made; and thus it was made*, he has already given us to understand that God said it in his Word, and that it was made through his Word. And this was already enough to indicate not only the person of the Father but also that of the Son. I mean, if it was for the sake of showing the person of the Son that it repeats things, and says, *And God made*, can that therefore mean that it was not through

---

14. See Book I, note 12.

the Son that the water was collected together on the third day, because it does not say there *And God made the waters to be collected together*, or "God collected the water"? But even there, in fact, after saying, *And it was made thus*, he then repeated himself to say, *And the water was collected together which was under the heavens* (Gn 1:9).

Again, was the light also not made through the Son, where the writer made no repetitions at all? There too, you see, he could have said, "And God said, Let light be made; and thus it was made; and God made the light and he saw that it was good"—or at the very least, as in the collecting together of the waters, without saying, *And God made*, he could still have reiterated, "And God said, Let light be made; and thus it was made; and the light was made, and God saw the light that it was good." But without any kind of repetition at all, after stating, *And God said, Let light be made*, the only thing he added was, *And light was made* (Gn 1:3); and then he went on to tell about the light giving pleasure and being divided from the darkness and each of them being given their names, without any repetition.

The uncreated Wisdom of the Word impressed as a created light on the angelic intelligence

8, 16. So what then is the meaning of this repetition in the other cases? Is it a way of showing that on the first day, on which light was made, the setting up of the spiritual and intelligent creation is being announced under the name of light—the nature of this creation being understood to include all the angels and powers? And the reason he did not repeat the making, after saying, *And light was made*, is that the rational creation did not first come to a knowledge of its being conformed to the Word,[15] and then after that get formed, but in the very act of its conformation it came to knowledge of it, that is, in its being enlightened by the Truth, to which it turned to be formed. With the rest of creation however, which is lower in the scale, things are so created that first of all they are made in the knowledge of the rational creation, and then in their concrete specific kind.

For this reason light was first fashioned in the Word of God in terms of the formula by which it is fashioned, that is, in the Wisdom co-eternal with the Father, and next in the actual fashioning of light in terms of the nature which was fashioned. At the first stage it was not made but begotten; here in the second stage, however, it is made, because formed out of formlessness. And the reason *God said, Let light be made; and light was made* (Gn 1:3), was so that what was

---

15. I have added "to the Word," which is not in the Latin; but Augustine's shorthand would be puzzling in English. The reader is referred back to Book I for the background to what is being said here about the "forming" and "conforming" of the spiritual creation: 3,7; 5,10,11; 9,17.

there in the Word might be here in the actual work. The fashioning of heaven,[16] on the other hand, or the sky, was first in the Word of God in terms of begotten Wisdom, then it was made next in the spiritual creation, that is, in the knowledge of the angels, in terms of the wisdom created in them, and only next after that was the heaven made, so that the actual created heaven might be there in in its own specific kind. And the same applies to the separation, or the specific creations, of the waters and the lands, applies also to the nature of trees and herbs, applies to the lamps of heaven, applies to the animated beings sprung from the waters and the earth.

17. Angels, after all, do not see these sensible material things just by the senses of the body, as animals do; but even if they do make use of such senses,[17] it is rather a case of their recognizing such things, which they have a better knowledge of inwardly, in the very Word of God, by which they are enlightened in order to live wisely, since there is in them that light which was the first thing to be made, if we understand it as a spiritual light that was made on that day. So then, just as the formula or idea on which a creature is fashioned is there in the Word of God before it is realized in the fashioning of the creature, so also is knowledge of the same formula or idea first produced in the intelligent creation which has not been darkened by sin, and only then is it realized in the fashioning of the creature.

Angels, you see, did not progress like us to the gaining of wisdom, to *behold the invisible things of God by understanding them through the things that have been made* (Rom 1:20). No, from the moment they were created they have been enjoying the eternity of the Word in holy and devout contemplation; from there they look back—over their shoulders, as it were[18] —at these material things, and according to what they see within the Word they either approve good deeds or condemn sins.

18. Nor is it to be wondered at that God should first show his holy angels, formed in that primal fashioning of light, what he was going to create from then on. Nor, to be sure, would they have known the mind of God unless and to the extent that he himself had displayed it. *For who has known the mind of the Lord? Or who was ever his counselor? Or who first gave to him, and was repaid? Since from him and through him and in him are all things* (Rom 11:34-36). So then it was from him that the angels learned, when knowledge was produced in them of creatures to be made from then on, and after that these were made in their own specific kind.

---

16. That is, of the solid structure, called heaven, on the second day; he is not referring back to the first verse of Genesis.
17. Augustine, and most of his contemporaries, thought of angels—and demons—as having bodies of a sort, bodies even finer than air or fire; and if bodies, then bodily senses.
18. This is the translator's amplification of the text, to make the image more vivid.

19. So therefore, once light has been made, by which we understand the rational creation formed by the eternal light, whenever we hear in the creation of all the rest *And God said, Let it be made*, we should understand that scripture is turning its gaze back to the eternity of God's Word. When, though, we hear "And thus it was made," we are to understand that in the intelligent creation knowledge is being produced of the formula or idea, which is in the Word of God, of the creature to be fashioned; so this creature, in a certain manner, was first made in the kind of being which by a certain previous movement towards the very Word of God[19] first recognized it as due to be made. So finally, when we hear it repeated and said that "God made this and that," we are now to understand the actual creature being made in its own specific nature. Lastly, when we hear *And God saw that it was good*, we are to understand that God in his courtesy took pleasure in what had been made, so that it might remain in being in the manner proper to its kind, seeing that it had been his pleasure that it should be made, when *the Spirit of God was being borne over the water* (Gn 1:2).

On the shape of the sky

9, 20. The question is also commonly asked what we have to believe, according to our scriptures, is the shape and form of the sky. Many people, you see, have many arguments about these points, which our authors with greater good sense passed over as not holding out the promise of any benefit to those wishing to learn about the blessed life, and, what is worse, as taking up much precious time that should be spent on more salutary matters. What concern is it of mine, after all, whether the sky encloses the earth like a globe on every side, with the earth held level as the diameter of the total mass of the world, or whether it covers it on one side from above, like a lid? But because the trustworthiness of the scriptures is here in question, this, as I have reminded readers more than once, has to be defended from those who do not understand the style of the divine utterances, and who assume when they find anything on these matters in our books, or hear them read out from them, which seems to be contrary to explanations they have worked out, that they should not place any confidence in the scriptures, when they foretell or warn or tell them about other useful things.[20] It

---

19. I here emend *quodam motu in ipso Dei Verbo*, a certain movement in the very Word of God, to *quodam motu in ipsum Dei Verbum*. Augustine will in due course go on to describe the "movements" of the angelic mind first to the Word of God and then to creatures in themselves, which he will term respectively the angels' "morning knowledge" and "evening knowledge." He would never talk about movement *in* the Word of God. Assuming that he was dictating this work, or in any case that in the course of its transmission it was dictated to copyists, we must never forget that *ipso Verbo* and *ipsum Verbum* would have been pronounced in almost exactly the same way.
20. See note 3 above, and book I,19,39.

must be stated very briefly that our authors knew about the shape of the sky whatever may be the truth of the matter. But the Spirit of God who was speaking through them did not wish to teach people about such things which would contribute nothing to their salvation.

21. But, says somebody, how are these people, who attribute to the sky the shape of a sphere or globe, not contradicted by what is written in our literature: *who stretched out the sky like a skin* (Ps 104:2)? Certainly let it be contradicted by that, if what they say is false; this, after all, is true which has divine authority behind it, rather than that which is the guesswork of human weakness. But if it should happen that they can prove their case with evidence and arguments beyond any possibility of doubt, then it has to be demonstrated that what is said here among us about a skin is not contrary to those explanations of theirs. Otherwise, in any case (if you are going to be crassly literal-minded[21]) it will also be contrary to another place in these very scriptures of ours where the sky is said to be like a suspended dome.[22] What, I ask you, could be so different and opposed to each other as a skin stretched out flat, and the hollow curve of a dome? But if we are obliged, as indeed we are, to understand these two expressions in such a way that they are found to agree with each other and not to be in the least contradictory, then we are also and equally obliged to demonstrate that neither of them is opposed to those explanations, should they happen to be shown by rational arguments to be true, which inform us that the sky has the shape of a hollow globe all round us—provided, once again, it can be proved.

22. And even if that comparison on our side with a dome is taken literally, it will make no difficulty for those who say the sky is a globe; it is reasonable to assume that scripture wished to talk about the shape of the sky with reference to that part of it which is above us. So if the sky is not a globe, it is in one part—the part which covers the earth—a dome, while if it is a globe, then it is a dome all round. But as for the text about a skin, that is rather more serious, because it may seem to be be opposed, not to the globe, which may just be a human fabrication, but to our own dome. My treatment of this in terms of allegory may be found in the thirteenth book of my *Confessions*.[23] So whether the sky being stretched out like a skin is to be understood allegorically in the way I suggested there, or in some other way, still to satisfy the tiresome people who persist in demanding a literal explanation[24] I will say what in my opinion should be obvious to anyone

---

21. Translator's parentheses again.
22. See Is 40:22, according to the Greek Septuagint, which Augustine's Latin version followed. The Hebrew is less contrary to the "skin" of Ps 104, having "like a curtain," The word I have translated as "dome" is *camera*, which is just a slightly incorrect transliteration of the Greek.
23. Chapter 15, section 16. In the volume of the *Confessions* in this series the word I have translated "dome" is rendered by "vault," and there is no reference to the text from Isaiah.
24. But he is engaged in a Literal Commentary on Genesis! This remark here is very revealing about his real intentions, and his thoroughly "anti-fundamentalist" understanding of the literal sense. Both these comparisons of the sky, or the heavens, to a skin stretched out and to a dome

of sense. Each term, no doubt, that is both "skin" and "dome" can be understood figuratively; but what we have to see is how each can be explained literally. Well, if it is not only a curved but also a flat ceiling that can be called a dome,[25] then assuredly a skin for its part can be stretched out round a curve as well as on a flat plane. After all, both wine containers and footballs are skins.

Whether the heavens rotate or not

10, 23. Some brothers and sisters also raise the question of the movement of the sky, whether it stands still or rotates. Because if it rotates, they say, how can it be a solid structure? But if it stands still, how is it that the constellations, which are generally held to be fixed in it, go round from the east to the west, with the northern ones making shorter circuits round the pole, so that the sky would seem to be rotating like a sphere or globe, if there is another pole, hidden from us, at the other extremity, or like a discus if there is no other pole? My answer to them is that these matters require many subtle and laborious calculations for their investigation, if the truth is to be definitely established whether this or that is the case; and that I have no time now for going into them and discussing them, and nor should they have any either, these brothers and sisters whom I am keen to instruct in this work for their own salvation and the benefit needed by the Church.

This at least they should know, that on the one hand the name of "solid structure" does not oblige us to think of the sky as stationary—it is permissible, after all, to understand that it is called solid, not to indicate immobility, but purely and simply solidity, or its being the impassable boundary between the upper and lower waters. And on the other hand, if the truth convincingly shows that the sky is stationary, this does not rule out the circuit of the stars, or make it impossible for us to explain this. And in fact it has been established by those men who have indulged their idle curiosity by devoting their leisure to the study of these things, that even if the sky remained motionless and only the constellations moved, all the things that have been observed and recorded in their revolutions could still occur.

---

or vault are clearly poetic, metaphorical, not intended by the author to be taken as literal descriptions in the narrow sense. It is people who insist on ignoring metaphor that Augustine rightly regards as tiresome.

25. Which it scarcely can be in English; nor could it properly be the case with the Latin *camera*; but in works by Tacitus and Suetonius this had been transferred to signify flat-bottomed boats with a kind of domed or vaulted superstructure. However, what Augustine was more probably thinking of here was the extension of the word to mean any ordinary room or chamber—our English word that in fact is derived from *camera*.

When were earth and water created?

11, 24. *And God said, Let the water which is under the heavens be collected together into one collection, and let the dry land appear. And it was made thus. And the water which is under the heavens was collected together into its collection, and the dry land appeared. And God called the dry land earth, and the collection of water he called sea. And God saw that it was good* (Gn 1:9-10). We dealt sufficiently with this work of God in our previous volume, because it was involved with another matter that had to be investigated.[26] And so here let me briefly advise any who are not worried by the question of when the specific natures of the waters and the lands were created, simply to take it that the only thing done on this day was the separation of these two lowest elements.

Some people, however, are worried by the question why light and heaven or sky were made on particular days, while water and earth were made outside the count of days or before any days at all, and why those things were made at a word from God, with God saying, *Let it be made*, while these two were indeed separated at a word from God, but are not found to have been made at a word from God. Well, they do have a way of understanding it that accords with the faith, and here it is: what was said before any counting of days, that *the earth was invisible and shapeless*, here scripture was just setting out what kind of earth God had made, because it had just said, *In the beginning God made heaven and earth*, and only meant to suggest with these words the formlessness of bodily material. The author chose to give them more familiar names rather than obscure technical ones, afraid that if scripture were to distinguish basic material and specific form in so many words, the thought might creep into slower minds of attempting to separate them also in time, as though first came basic material and then later, after an interval of time, specific form was added to it. In fact, on the contrary, God created them together and established formed material, while scripture first stated its formlessness with the more familiar names, as I said, of earth or water. Earth and water, you see, even while presenting themselves to our sight as what they are with their specific qualities, are still closer to that formlessness, because of the ease with which they are broken down, than are the heavenly bodies.

But now with the numbering of the days all things formed out of the formless are being counted, and the author has already told of how the sky or heaven was made out of this bodily basic material. So because the sky's specific nature is so very different from that of earthly things, when he comes to what remained to be formed from the basic material in this lowest part of the cosmos, he was unwilling to insert it into the order of things created with the words, *Let it be made*, since this residual formlessness was not going to receive any such specific form as the sky had been given, but a much inferior and fainter one, closer to the

---

26. Book I,12,26 to 13,27.

original formlessness. So it was by the words *Let the waters be collected together* and *Let the dry land appear* that these two elements would receive their proper specific appearances, so well known to us, and manageable by us, water so unstable, earth so stable. And that's the reason the former is told to be *collected*, the latter to *appear*, because water is a slippery fluid, earth a stable solid.

Why the production of vegetation is included in the work of the third day

12, 25. *And God said, Let the earth sprout grass for fodder-bearing seed according to kind and according to likeness, and fruit trees making fruit, whose seed is in it after its likeness on the earth. And it was made thus. And the earth produced grass for fodder having seed according to its kind and according to likeness, and fruit trees making fruit, whose seed is in it according to kind on the earth. And God saw that it was good. And there was made evening and there was made morning, a third day* (Gn 1:11-13). Here we should note the skillful touch of the one who put the text into shape; because grasses and trees are sorts of creatures quite distinct from the specific form of the lands and the waters, and thus cannot be counted among the elements, they are spoken of separately as coming from the earth, and separately given the usual phrases, so that it says *And it was made thus*, and then what was made is repeated; it is also separately indicated that God saw that it was good. But all the same, because being fixed there by their roots they are continuous with the soil of the earth and entwined in it, he wished these things as well to belong to the same day.

How the first three days passed before the lamps in the heavens were made

13, 26. *And God said, Let lamps be made in the solid structure of heaven, in such a way that they may shine upon the earth and may divide between day and night, and may be for signs and for times and for days and for years; and may be for brilliance in the solid structure of heaven in such a way that they may shine upon the earth. And it was made thus. And God made the two great lamps, the greater lamp for the beginning of the day and the lesser lamp for the beginning of the night, and the stars. And God placed them in the solid structure of heaven in such a way that they might shine upon the earth, and might be for the beginning of the day and the night, and might divide between the light and the darkness. And God saw that it was good. And there was made evening and there was made morning, a fourth day* (Gn 1:14-19).

Coming now to this fourth day, what we have to ask is what the meaning might be of this arrangement, whereby water and earth were made or separated and earth sprouted plants before the heavenly bodies were made in the sky. And we cannot say, you see, that the better things were chosen to give a more orna-mental touch to the ends[27] and the middle of the series of days, the fourth of course being the middle one of the series of seven. It immediately occurs to us, I mean, that on the seventh day no creature was made. Or does the light of the first day, perhaps, correspond rather to the resting on the seventh, so that with the two ends of the series balancing in this way, the pattern could be perfected by weaving the outstanding lights into the middle?

But if the first day balances with the seventh, then the second in its turn should balance with the sixth. In what way, though, is the solid structure of heaven at all like man made to the image of God? Or could it be this, that as the heaven occupies the whole upper part of the cosmos, so to man has been granted the right to lord it over the whole of the lower part? But then what are we to make of the cattle and the wild beasts, which the earth produced in their various kinds on this same sixth day? What comparison can there be between them and the heavens?

27. Or since the first thing made under the name of light is understood to have been the formation of the spiritual creation, did it not rather then follow that the bodily creation too should be made, that is this visible cosmos, which was made in two days because of the two main parts of which the universe consists, namely heaven and earth? In terms of this comparison of ideas by which the total spiri-tual[28] and bodily creation is often named heaven and earth, so that this globe of more turbulent air is ascribed to the earthly part—it gets "bodified,"[29] after all, by damp exhalations, while if there is any stillness of air in which windy and stormy movements cannot arise, it belongs to the celestial part, it would follow that after the construction this total bodily universe, which is all in the one place in which the cosmos is located, it should be filled inside the whole with those parts that could be moved around from place to place with appropriate move-ments.

Now grasses and trees are not things of that kind. They are of course fixed to the earth by their roots, and although they have the movements involved in their growth, they still for all that do not move from their own places by their own efforts, but are nourished and grow wherever they have been planted. For this reason they belong more to the earth than to the kinds of things which move about in the water and on land. And so because two days were allotted to the establishment of the visible world, that is, of heaven and earth, it remains that for

---

27. Reading *fines* with two manuscripts, instead of the singular *finis* of the CSEL and the Maurist texts.
28. His line of reasoning is obscured, almost derailed in fact, by his bringing in the spiritual creation here: His concern is only at the moment with the material "heaven and earth."
29. *Corporascit*: a word very possibly coined by Augustine. Lewis & Short gives only one reference, to a work of Claudianus Mamertus from the end of the fifth century, two generations or so after Augustine.

these movable and visible parts which are being created within it, the remaining three days should be set aside.

As the sky or heaven was the first part to be made, so it is the first to be furnished;[30] so on the fourth day the heavenly bodies are made to illuminate with their shining the lower habitable level, and thus save its inhabitants from being introduced into a dark and gloomy habitat. And because the feeble bodies of the denizens of the lower habitat need to recoup themselves with rest and quiet after their constant moving around, that is why arrangements were made for them to be able to alternate sleeping and waking with the alternation of day and night as the sun goes round and round on its course. This night, however, was not to remain without its own *d'ecor*, but with the light of moon and stars was to give both comfort to those people who are often obliged to work at night, and sufficient time to meet the needs of some animals which cannot bear the light of the sun.

Problem of the luminaries being for signs and times

14, 28. As for the words, however, *And let them be for signs and for times and for days and for years*, who can fail to see how problematic is their implication that times began on the fourth day, as though the preceding three days could have passed without any time? What mind, therefore, is capable of penetrating the mystery of how those three days passed before times began, times which are said to have begun on the fourth day—or of whether indeed those days passed at all? Or is it with respect to the specific nature of the thing made[31] that day was named, and with respect to the absence of it, night, so that the basic material not yet formed by any specific nature, but from which all the other things were to be formed, was called night, just as the formlessness of matter can be understood, from their very liability to change, even in things that have been formed; it is not, after all, to be distinguished from their specific forms as being either remote from them in space or as being anterior to them in time. Or rather, was the

30. Reading *ornandum* with one manuscript and the Maurists instead of *ordinandum*, to be set in order, with the CSEL text. The consistent patristic tradition, set out clearly by Saint Thomas at the beginning of his treatment of the days of creation, *Summa Theologia*, Ia,65, divided the divine creative acts into three kinds: actual creation, Gn 1:1-2; distinction, Gn 1:3-10; adornment or furnishing, Gn 1:11-25; the creation of man falls outside this classification. So far in this work, however, Augustine has often spoken of order, and used the words *ordo* and *ordinare*, and not, so far, the word *ornare*. So some copyists, or even some of his stenographers, may quite easily, and subsconsciously, have heard *ordinandum* when *ornandum* was read out.
31. The specific nature (*species*) of the spiritual creation is what I think he must mean here; because "day" and "night" are only mentioned in the work of the first day, when God said, "Let light be made."

liability to change in the very thing made and formed, that is, its ability, if I may so put it, to fall apart, called night, because inherent in things that have been made is the capacity to change even if they do not do so?

While as for evening and morning, were they perhaps named, not as signifying the passing and the coming of a particular time, but as indicating a kind of boundary, by which can be understood how far the realm of one nature extends, and where the starting point of the next one begins? Or is some other explanation of these words to be looked for with greater diligence?

29. Who is there who could easily break open such a well-guarded secret? And what signs is he talking about, when he says of the heavenly bodies, *Let them be for signs*? He does not mean, after all, the kind that it is the sheerest folly to observe,[32] but the ones, naturally, that are useful and necessary for the purposes of this life, ones which sailors observe in navigation, or which we all look for in order to forecast the weather in summer and winter and in the changeable times of autumn and spring. And doubtless these are what he means by the "times" that are caused by the heavenly bodies: not just periods of time, but the changes in the moods of this sky above us.

I mean, if there was any movement, either bodily or spiritual, that preceded the fashioning of these lamps, of such a kind as to transfer something from what was being waited for in the future back to the past through the present,[33] this would not have been possible without time; and who would maintain that time only began with the fashioning of the heavenly bodies? But definite hours and days and years, which we are so familiar with, could only be produced by the movements of the heavenly bodies.

And so if this is how we are to understand "times, days and years," as various divisions which we measure with sun-dials and clocks, or which we are most familiar with in the sky, when the sun rises up from the east to its noonday height in the south and again sinks down from there to set in the west, so that the moon or some star can thereupon be observed rising in the east immediately after sunset, and when it in turn reaches its zenith in the south, that indicates midnight, and then it also sets with the sun coming back to usher in the morning. It is days

---

32. That is, the signs that astrologers claim to observe.
33. A kind of time machine which, I think he is suggesting, would be a necessary condition for the predictions of astrologers to have any validity. But the sequence of his thoughts in this whole passage is not in the least straightforward. In the next sentence he may be supposed to allow the possibility of such a time machine, by rejecting any suggestion that there was no time before the heavenly bodies were made—this on the authority of the text giving us three whole days before they were made. And then he goes on to talk about times in the sense of periods of time, days and years, being controlled by the heavenly bodies, though earlier he had seemed to confine the meaning of "times" to the seasons of the year. But all this only serves to remind us of how tentative his whole approach is to the interpretation of the text—little more than a tissue of questions. With such a procedure a straightforward sequence of thought is not to be expected.

that are measured by the whole[34] circuit of the sun from the east and back again to the east, while years, at least these familiar ones, are marked by the sun's shifts of orbit, not from east to west which happens every day, but when it goes round to the same places in the constellations of the zodiac, which it only does by completing three hundred and sixty-five days and six hours, which is a quarter of a whole day; it is this part multiplied by four that obliges us to add a whole day every leap year,[35] to keep the calendar straight. Such shifts of orbit also mark greater, less noticeable "years," which are said to be completed by the sun's passage through other constellations. So if that is the way we are to understand "times, days, years," nobody doubts their being produced by the constellations and the lamps. It is in fact put in such a way as to leave it uncertain whether the words, "Let them be for signs and for times and for days and for years," apply to all the heavenly bodies, or whether signs and times refer to the rest, while days and years are the business of the sun alone.

Question of the phase in which the moon was made

15, 30. Many people also inquire, with endless chatter, in what phase the moon was made—and if only they would chatter away in a merely inquisitive spirit, and not in an attempt, as in fact is the case, to teach others! They aver, you see, that the moon was made at the full on the grounds that it would not have been fitting for God to make anything imperfect among the heavenly bodies on that day on which it is written that these were made. Those who object to this, on the other hand, say, "So that should be called the first day of the month, not the fourteenth. Who, after all, ever begins to count like that?"[36] As for me, I stand in the middle between these two opinions, asserting neither of them, but definitely saying that whether God made the moon at its first phase or at the full, he made it perfect.

God, after all is the author and founder of things in their actual natures. Now whatever any single thing may in some way or other produce and unfold by its

---

34. Reading *totus* with one manuscript instead of the *totos* of the text, which would give, at the beginning of the sentence, "all days" instead of "the whole circuit." In rendering "from the east and back again to the east" I am following the Maurists, and what they claim are the better manuscripts, instead of the CSEL text which has "from the east as far as the west" with other manuscripts.
35. What he actually writes, translated literally, is: "which requires the insertion of a whole day which the Romans call the *bissextus*," literally "the twice sixth," the day they inserted after what we call 24 February, but they called the sixth day before the kalends of March.
36. Just possibly the ancient Hebrews! We have, after all, the words of Ps 81:3: *Blow the trumpet at the new moon, when the moon is full, on our feast*. This does at least suggest that at one time it was the moon at the full that was regarded as new, not what we now call the new moon. But of course that was not in the mind of the advocates of the moon being created at the full.

natural development through periods of time that are suited to it, it contained it beforehand as something hidden, if not in specific form and bodily mass, at least by the force and reckoning of nature,[37] unless of course a tree, void of fruit and stripped of its leaves throughout the winter, is then to be called imperfect, or unless again at its origins, when it had still not yet borne any fruit, its nature was also imperfect. It is not only about the tree, but about its seed also that this could not rightly be said; there everything that with the passage of time is somehow or other going to appear is already latent in invisible ways. Although, if God were to make anything imperfect, which he would then himself bring to perfection, what would be reprehensible about such an idea? But you would be quite within your rights to disapprove if what had been begun by him were said to be completed and perfected by any other.

31. These people do not complain about the earth, which God made when in the beginning he made heaven and earth, that it was invisible and shapeless, and is only later on the third day rendered visible and licked into shape. So why do they wrap themselves in the darkness of their questions about the moon? Or if they understand what was said about the earth, not as meaning any interval of time, since God created things simultaneously with their basic material, but as said to put it in the form of a story, why in this case, which is something that can be seen with the eyes, do they not notice that the moon has a complete body, perfect in all its roundness, even when its light is shaped like horns, as it begins or as it ceases to shine on the earth?

So then, if the light in it waxes and wanes, it is not the lamp itself but what is lit in it that varies; if, however, it is always shining out of one side of its globe, but seems to wax while it gradually turns that side toward the earth until it has turned it completely, which happens from the first to the fourteenth day, it is always full, but does not always appear so to the inhabitants of the earth.[38] The same is true even if it derives its light from the rays of the sun; you see, even in this case it cannot but appear with shining horns when it is next to the sun, because the other side, which is being lit up in its whole orb, is not turned towards the earth so that it can be seen. This only happens when it is opposite the sun, so that the whole side that is reflecting the sun's light is visible from the earth.

---

37. *Ratione naturae*; this difficult word *ratio* again, now, one may say, at the lowest end of its scale. At the highest the *rationes* of things are in the Word; at the middle level in the understanding of the spiritual creation, the angels; at the lowest in the nature of things, themselves.

38. This is on the theory that the moon has in itself its own source of light, that it is rather like a lighthouse with a revolving shutter, one half of its globe being blacked out, the other transparent. There can be little doubt, I think, that Augustine himself accepted what contemporary astronomers knew to be the case, that the moon's light is reflected from the sun, as he goes on to describe.

32. There are not wanting those, all the same, who say that they do reckon that the moon was first made by God halfway through the month, not because we have to believe it was made at the full, but because the words in God's own scriptures go like this: *the moon made for the beginning of the night* (Gn 1:16). But it is when the moon is full that it is seen at nightfall, while in its other phases it begins to be seen during the day before it comes to the full, and later and later in the night the more it is on the wane.

But if you understand that "the beginning of the night" in fact only means dominance over it, in fact the Greek word used here, where it has *archen*, suggests this more obviously, and then in the psalms it is written more plainly still, *The sun with authority over the day, the moon and the stars with authority over the night* (Ps 136:8.9), you are not obliged to count from the fourteenth of the month, and to believe that the moon when first made was not beginning its first phase.

On the relative brilliance of sun, moon and stars

16, 33. A question also commonly asked is whether these conspicuous lamps in the sky, that is, sun and moon and stars, are all equally brilliant, but because of their different distances from the earth appear to our eyes for that reason to vary in brightness. And about the moon those who take this line do not hesitate to say that its light is in itself less than that of the sun, by which they also maintain it is illuminated. Many of the stars, however, so they boldly assert, are equal to the sun, or even greater, but they seem small because they have been set further away. And for us, no doubt, it can be enough to know that whatever the truth may be in this matter, the stars were fashioned by God as their craftsman,[39] although we must hold to what was said with the apostle's authority: *One is the glory of the sun and another the glory of the moon and another the glory of the stars; for star differs from star in glory* (1 Cor 15:41).

But they can still say, even if they are not deliberately disagreeing with the apostle: "They do indeed differ in glory, but to the eyes of people on earth"; or else, because the apostle said this as a comparison with those who rise from the dead, who will not of course be one thing to the eyes of others and another in themselves: "The stars do indeed differ in glory in themselves as well; but all the same there are some which are even greater than the sun." So that being what they say, let them see for themselves how they can attribute such great primacy to the sun that they say it checks by its rays, or even turns back from their proper courses some of the stars, and those the principal ones, to which these people show the greater devo-

---

39. He doubtless had Ps 8:3 in mind: *When I see the heavens, the work of your fingers, the moon and the stars which you established.* The Hebrew text of the psalm seems to picture the heavens as a vast piece of embroidery into which God deftly sewed the moon and stars.

tion.[40] It does not, after all, make likely sense that the sun should be able by the violence of its rays to overcome greater stars, or even its equals.

Or if they assert that the higher stars at least of the northern zodiac signs are greater, those that undergo no such aggression from the sun, why do they pay more reverence to those that make a wider circuit through the signs? Why do they acclaim them as mistresses of the signs? Even if anyone, you see, were to maintain that these backward movements of the constellations, or should we say their slowing down, are not produced by the sun but by other obscurer causes, these people nevertheless in their extravagant absurdities, in which wandering far from the truth they suspect the hand of fate everywhere, still attribute the chief power and influence to the sun, as is certainly evident from their books.

34. But let them say what they like about the heavens, those who are strangers to the Father who is in heaven. As for us, though, it is not our business to inquire more precisely into the size and the spacing of the constellations, spending time on such things that is needed for more important and worthy matters. We even think it more worthwhile to attend to those lights that are greater than the rest, which scripture draws to our attention as follows: *And God made two great lights*, which for all that are not equal. It goes on to say, you see, after putting them ahead of the rest, that they differ from each other. It says, I mean: *the greater light for the starting of the day, and the lesser light for the starting of the night* (Gn 1:16). Let them at least grant this to our eyes, after all, that it is obvious that they shine more brightly than the rest upon the earth, and that it is only the light of the sun that makes the day bright, and that even with so many stars appearing, the night is never as light when there is no moon, as when it is being illuminated by its presence.

Against astrology and divination

17, 35. As for any of their clever talk whatsoever about fate, and the so-called proven results of their astrological calculations, which they call *apotelesmata*,[41] let us reject them as utterly injurious to the health of our faith. They even try, you see, to deprive us by their arguments of any reason for praying, and by an impious perversity, instead of the human criminal they put God, the author of the

---

40. It may seem strange to us that he here begins an attack on astrologers—and on Christians who consulted them—when he has been all the time discussing matters of astronomy. But we must remember that in the ancient world the distinction between these two approaches to the study of the heavens was by no means so definite as it is with us. My impression is that while Augustine admitted the validity of astronomy as a rational science, he did so halfheartedly, suspiciously, because it was nearly always teetering on the brink of astrology.

41. Literally, "completions"; the *apotelesma* of the month is the full moon. The astrologers used the word to signify the fulfillment, the verification of their predictions.

constellations, in the dock for evil deeds that are very properly condemned. But that our souls are not subject by nature to bodies, not even heavenly ones, they should learn from their own philosophers.

But that those heavenly bodies are not more potent than earthly bodies as regards the effects which these people themselves study, they should sooner or later come to realize at least from this; when many bodies of different species, either of animals or herbs or shrubs, are sown simultaneously at one point of time, and at one point of time a countless multitude of living forms springs up from them, then not only in different regions of the earth but in the same places there are so many variations in their development, in the things they do and the things they undergo, that these people, as the saying goes, may say goodbye to their star-gazing if they but turn their starry gaze on these facts.[42]

36. What though, I ask you, could be more senseless, more obtuse than to say, when these things have been conclusively demonstrated to them, that the fate-controlling secret of the stars is concerned only with subjecting human beings to their influence? Yet even here the case of twins proves them wrong, living different lives, differing in their good luck and their bad, dying different deaths, but still for the most part given the same constellations, because even if there was some interval between them as they emerged from the womb, still in some cases it is so small that it could not possibly affect these people's calculations.

The hand of Jacob, as he followed, when those twins were born, was found to be holding the foot of his brother going ahead of him.[43] They were indeed born in such a way that it would seem to have been one unusually long infant born double. The so-called constellations of these two could certainly not have differed in any way at all. So what could be more totally unlikely than that an astrologer, gazing at these constellations in the same horoscope, in the same moon, would say that one of them would be loved by his mother, the other not? I mean, if he said anything else, he would thereby be saying something false, while if he did say this it would indeed be true, but he would not be saying it on the basis of the silly little jingles of his books. And if they refuse to believe this story, because it is told in our books, can they eliminate as well the very nature of things? So then, when they claim that they are never wrong if they can ascertain the hour of conception, at least let them not be too proud, as men, to consider the conception of twins.

---

42. A feeble effort to echo, at least, the Latin pun or word play: *perdant sidera, si ista considerent*; literally, "they can lose the stars if they pay attention to these things." But the verb *considero* was possibly even coined as meaning primarily "put the stars, the *sidera*, together"; hence to observe, to pay attention to things.
43. See Gn 25:25-27.

37. And so it is that we have to admit, whenever anything true is said by these people, that it is said under some hidden prompting which human minds can experience while remaining entirely unaware of it. When this happens in order to ensnare people, it is the work of treacherously deceitful spirits, who are permitted to know some true things about temporal matters, being informed partly through the acuteness of their fine-spun senses, because they thrive in more fine-spun bodies; partly through the craftiness gained by experience, thanks to the enormous length of their lives; partly through holy angels revealing to them what they themselves learn from almighty God, and doing so at his command, as he distributes through his genuine but inscrutable justice to human beings whatever they deserve.

Sometimes, however, these same unspeakable spirits predict, as if by means of divination, what they themselves are going to do. For this reason, good Christian, you must be on your guard against astrologers and anyone impiously practicing divination, especially when they say things that are true, lest your soul should be ensnared by consorting with demons, and thus entangled in their nets by some deed of covenant and association.

Whether the luminaries of heaven are animated, living beings or not

18, 38. The question is also commonly asked whether these visible luminaries are solely and simply bodies, or whether they have their own kind of spirits to direct them; and if they do, whether they are also "enspirited" by them into living beings, as fleshly bodies are "ensouled" by the souls, the *animae*, of "animals," or without any such mixture are just directed on their courses by the presence of them alone. Although nothing can easily be grasped on this point, I am persuaded all the same that in the course of our study of the scriptures more suitable places may occur, where it will be permissible for us at least to form an opinion according to the rules of our sacred authority, even if we cannot demonstrate anything for certain.[44]

---

44. He does not return to this subject in this work, at any rate. Aquinas in his *Summa Theologiae*, Ia, q.70. a.3, lists the various opinions, both of the philosophers and the Christian fathers. Some, including Plato and the Platonists, followed among the fathers by Origen and Jerome, held that the heavenly bodies are living beings, animated or "enspirited" by intelligent spirits. Others, above all Aristotle among the philosophers, followed by Basil and John Damascene, held that they are directed or governed by intelligent beings (gods for the philosophers, angels for the Christians), and in this they were followed by Aquinas. He said that Augustine, and here he was almost certainly correct, continued more prudently to sit on the fence; and not only that particular fence, but also the one dividing both these ancient opinions from the more "materialist" one which we all take for granted today, and which had a few advocates even then, that the motions of the heavenly bodies can all be explained by purely physical causes, and do not indicate the presence of any intelligent "mover"—other than that of the creator himself.

For the present, however, we ought always to observe the moderation required of serious devotion to the truth and not commit ourselves rashly to any one opinion on such an obscure subject, in case perchance the truth may later on lay bare some other answer which can in no way be contrary to the sacred books either of the Old Testament or the New, but which we all the same detest out of love for our own error. Now it is time for us to move on to the third book of our work.

Book III

Genesis 1:20-31: The fifth and sixth days of creation

Why the living creatures of the waters and the air were produced before those of the dry land

1, 1. *And God said: Let the waters produce reptiles of live souls and flying things over the earth along the solid structure of heaven. And it was made thus. And God made the great whales and every animal of reptiles which the waters produced according to their kind, and every winged flying thing according to kind. And God blessed them, saying: Increase and multiply and fill the waters in the sea; and let flying things multiply over the earth. And there was made evening and there was made morning, a fifth day* (Gn 1:20-23).[1] It is now in the lower section of the cosmos that those things are being made which can move themselves with the spirit of life, and first the ones in the water, which is the element nearest in its quality to air. The fact is, the air borders so closely on that heaven in which the luminaries are placed that it too has received the name of "heaven"; I am not sure, though, whether it can also be called "the solid structure."

However, the plural, "heavens," is used with reference to one and the same thing as is called a single heaven. While this book, you see, mentions heaven, in the singular, as dividing between the waters which are above and those that are below, it says in that psalm, on the other hand, *And let the waters which are above the heavens praise the name of the Lord* (Ps 148:4-5). And if we are right in understanding the "heavens of the heavens" to mean the starry over the airy heavens, as the higher over the lower, and if we also find these in the same psalm, where it says, *Praise him, heavens of the heavens* (Ps 148:4), then it is clear enough that this air is not only called heaven, but also heavens.[2]

---

1. It is abundantly evident from this passage that Augustine was following a different text from the one he had used in his *Unfinished Commentary on Genesis*.
2. Here he adds, *sicut dicuntur et terrae, nec aliud significatur quam illa quae singulariter terra dicitur, quando dicimus orbem terrarum et orbem terrae*; which, as this literal translation will show, is a Latin idiom that has no corresponding usage in English: "as one can also talk about 'earths,' and nothing else is meant but what is called 'earth' in the singular, when we talk of the globe of the earths and the globe of the earth."

*That the heavens were destroyed in the flood means that the air was
transformed into the nature of water*

2, 2. That these airy heavens were also once destroyed by the flood is something we are told in one of those letters which are called canonical.[3] That wet
element, after all, which had increased in density and quantity to such an extent
that it topped the peaks of the highest mountains by fifteen cubits,[4] could not
reach as far as the stars. But because it had filled the whole or almost the whole
space of this more humid air in which the birds fly, it is written in that letter that
the heavens which had existed then were destroyed. I do not see how this can be
understood to have happened except by the quality of this denser air being turned
into the nature of water; otherwise, these heavens were not destroyed at that
time, but were pushed up higher, since water was occupying their place. And so
it is easier for us to believe on the authority of this letter that they were indeed
destroyed and others, as it says there, put in their place (this by means of extensive exhalations), than that they were pushed up higher in such a way that the
naturally loftier heaven had to give up its place to them.

3. No, to populate this lower section of the cosmos, which is often referred to
in its entirety by the name of "earth," it was right that animals should first be
produced from the waters and later on from the earth. For this it was necessary
that air should have such an affinity to water that it could be shown to be
condensed from its exhalations, and so could both effect *the spirit of the storm*
(Ps 107:25), that is, could assemble wind and clouds, and also sustain the flight
of birds. What one of the secular poets has said may of course be true: "Above
the clouds Olympus soars," and "The heights there know peace,"[5] because the

---

3. He is referring to 2 Pt 3:6, which actually says, *The world that then existed was destroyed by
being overwhelmed in the flood.* But he is interpreting it in the light of the next verse which
says, *But the heavens and the earth that now exist have been stored up for the fire.* He explains
this interpretation in detail in his *City of God* XX,18, which was of course written about twenty
years later. His calling this letter one of the canonical letters is rather odd; these non-Pauline
letters, of James, Peter, John, and Jude, are traditionally known as the Catholic epistles,
meaning that they were addressed to the universal Church, or the Church in general, not to any
particular local Churches.
4. See Gn 7:20. A cubit, the length of the forearm from the elbow to the tip of the middle finger, is
roughly 18 inches. It ought to be the same measure as the archaic English ell, also related to the
elbow. But the ell, at least the English ell so the dictionary informs us, is 45 inches; it probably
meant first of all the length of cloth that could be held in the crook of one's arm, which is *ulna* in
Latin; and this as a measure, being what could be grasped in the crook of both arms, was
according to Lewis & Short, quoting Pliny, a fathom, 6 feet.
5. Lucan, *Pharsalia*, 2,271.273; reading in the second part of the quotation *Pacem summa tenent*,
with the Maurists and the text of William Walker's *Corpus Poetarum Latinorum* (London,
1875), 611; instead of *Pacem magna tenent* with the CSEL and Weber's edition of Lucan's
work: "Great things know peace." But with the immediately preceding reference to Olympus,
"the heights" makes better sense—at least as far as Augustine was concerned, if not Lucan
himself, who does insert a sentence between the two phrases quoted which makes *magna*, in
contrast with *minima*, in that sentence slightly more probable than *summa*.

air at the summit of Olympus is said to be so rarified that it is never overcast with clouds, nor disturbed by winds, nor able to hold up birds in flight or support any human mountain climbers with the breath of this denser atmosphere which they have grown accustomed to at these lower levels. But for all that, it is air still, which means it has the same quality of diffusing itself as water does, and for this reason it too may be supposed to have turned into the humid nature of the latter at the time of the flood. It cannot, I mean, be supposed that it took over any of the space of the starry heaven, when the water had topped all the mountains, even the highest.

Various opinions about the changing of the elements into one another; the element, air, is not omitted in the creation narrative

3, 4. Yet as a matter of fact there is no little argument going on, among those who have solemnly wasted their leisure hours looking into these matters, about the conversion of the elements into one another. Some of these scientists say, you see, that they can all be changed and converted into each other, while others roundly assert that there is something altogether proper to each one of the elements which cannot in any way at all be converted into the quality of any other element. We shall discuss this point, maybe, if the Lord so wishes, more thoroughly in its proper place.[6] Meanwhile, as far as our present topic is concerned, I have thought it should just be mentioned, to help us understand how the order of things was preserved, by which it was right to tell of the aquatic animals being created before the terrestrial ones.

5. Nor must the idea be entertained for a moment that in this scriptural account any element of this world was overlooked, it being generally agreed that it consists of that well-known four, because it does seem as if sky and water and earth are mentioned in it, while it keeps silent about air.[7] But our scriptures in fact are in the habit of either referring to the cosmos by the name of heaven and earth, or of sometimes also adding sea. And so air is to be understood as belonging either to heaven, if there are any entirely calm and tranquil regions in its higher spheres, or to earth on account of this turbulent and murky level which is rendered more dense by the earth's damp exhalations—though it too is often enough referred to as heaven or sky. And that is why the text here does not run, "Let the waters produce reptiles of live souls, and let the air produce flying things flying over the earth," but states that each of these two kinds of animated beings is the product of the waters. So the waters in either form, whether as a

---

6. See below, 7,9 and 10, 15, where he does talk of one element changing into another. But he may have in mind here a place where he discusses the point more extensively.
7. Sky, of course, was never one of the four traditional elements; but it has already been established, in Book II,3,6, that the upper sky or heaven, where the sun and moon and stars were placed on the fourth day, consists of the fourth element, fire.

flowing and surging fluid allotted to reptiles of live souls, or as attenuated and held in suspension in the form of vapor and given over to flying things, are still assigned to the humid element.

The five senses in relation to the four elements

4, 6. And so it is that there are some people who make a very nicely thought-out distinction between the five manifest senses of the body with reference to the four familiar elements, as follows: they say that the eyes go along with fire and the ears with air, while they attribute the senses both of smell and of taste to the humid element. The sense of smell they ally to these humid exhalations that give density to this space in which the birds fly around, while they join taste to this element in its more substantial and liquid form. Everything, you see, that is tasted in the mouth is mixed with the fluid of the mouth in order to yield a taste, even if it seemed to be dry when it was taken. Fire, however, penetrates all things, to produce movement in them. Liquids, after all, congeal when deprived of heat, and furthermore, while the other elements can be heated to boiling point, fire cannot be cooled; indeed, it is more easily put out so as to stop being fire, than kept cold, or made cooler by contact with something cold. Touch, however, which is the fifth among the senses, is more closely allied to the element of earth; that is why you feel anything that touches any part of the body, which consists above all of earth.

They also say that nothing can be seen without fire or touched without earth, and thus every single one of the elements is in all the others,[8] but that each gets its name from what it has most of in it; while the reason sensation grows numb when the body, deprived of heat, gets too cold is that all movement, caused in the body by heat, slows down, the process being that fire works on air, and air on the liquids, and the liquids on everything earthy—the finer elements, that is, penetrating the grosser.[9]

---

8. *Ac per hoc elementa omnia in omnibus inesse.* This could also mean, "And thus it is that every single one of the elements is in all things." But particular things, like trees and stones and metals, can hardly be said to have been named after one or other of the elements. So I prefer to take him as in fact saying that you never find any of the four elements in a pure state, but always mixed up with the others. This will support the view of those ancient "scientists" who thought that it is possible to change the elements into one another, to effect transmutations, which was fairly evidently Augustine's own view. What they, however, were mostly interested in, one gathers, was changing anything else into gold.

9. The reasoning is almost as dense as the element earth; much more so than air made dense by humid exhalations! But it seems to go like this; the living body, consisting mainly of earth, is only capable of movement, and hence of sensation, because of the smaller amount of the fire element in it. But this vitalizing fire element only gets through to the dominant earth element by working on the air in the body, which works on the fluid or water element in it, which finally affects its earthy mass. So deprive the body of heat, and it will take a long time for it to warm up again and recover movement and sensation.

How the faculty of sensation is related differently to the four elements in each of the five senses

5, 7. Now the finer anything is in the realm of bodies, the closer it is to the spiritual realm, although differing widely in kind, seeing that the former is bodily, the latter not. And thus it is that, however acute the arguments may be about the senses of the body being arranged with reference to the various bodily elements, it is still not the body that is the subject of sensation, but the soul through the body; so this, being itself incorporeal, activates the power of sensation through the finer, the least coarse kind of body. In this way it starts movement in all the senses from the refined nature of fire, but it does not reach the same result in all of them. In the sense of sight, you see, it restrains the heat of fire, bringing only its light to bear, while in the sense of hearing the fire penetrates with its heat to the more fluid element of air. In the sense of smell, however, it goes through pure air and reaches the moist exhalation which gives this atmosphere of ours its coarser texture. In the sense of taste it also goes through this and reaches the humid element in its grosser liquid form; and having penetrated this as well and gone right through it, on reaching the heaviness of earth it activates the last of the senses, that of touch.

The element of air not overlooked by the author of Genesis

6, 8. So then, when the author came to the provision of the visible things that move naturally within the cosmos in the framework of its elements, he first gave an account of the heavenly lights, next of the aquatic animals and finally of the terrestrial ones. But this does not mean that he was ignorant of the distinct natures of the elements and their order in the cosmos, nor that he overlooked the element of air. But any regions there may be of the purest and most tranquil air, in which it is said that birds are unable to fly, are joined to the upper heaven; and under the name of "heaven" in the scriptures they are understood to belong to the upper part of the cosmos, while the whole of it may be generally signified by the name of "earth," from which the psalm verse begins, working down from the top: *Fire, hail, snow, ice, spirits of the tempest and all deeps* (Ps 148:8), until it comes to the dry land, which is properly called by the name of earth.[10]

And so that upper air, whether because it belongs to the heavenly part of the cosmos or because it has no visible inhabitants such as the narrator is concerned with at this point,[11] was neither overlooked, being included in the mention of heaven, nor counted in with the creation of animals. This lower air, on the other

---

10. He cheats a little, by moving "the deeps" from the end of verse 7, where they are preceded by "sea monsters," *dracones* in the Latin, to the end of verse 8 after "the spirit of the tempest" or stormy winds.

11. He is hinting that it does have invisible inhabitants, namely angels.

hand, which receives the humid exhalations of sea and earth and is somehow or other thickened up in order to be able to hold the birds up, only receives its animal inhabitants from the waters. It is its humidity, after all, that bears the bodies of winged fowl, which maneuver with their wings as they fly in much the same way as fish do with their equivalent of wings as they swim.

Flying creatures rightly said to have been created from the waters

7, 9. Accordingly it is almost like a scientist that the Spirit of God, who was assisting the writer, says flying things were produced from the waters. These waters, after all, obtained a twofold place: namely a lower one in the flowing billows and a higher one in the airy breezes, the former allotted to living things that swim, the latter to ones that fly. In the same way we see two senses corresponding to this element given to animals, the sense of smell for investigating vapors, that of taste for investigating liquids. That we also in fact feel water and wind with the sense of touch means that the solidity of earth is mixed into all the elements; but denser, coarser-grained objects, in addition to being felt, can also be handled by being touched.

That is why in the two main sections of the cosmos all these elements are embraced under the general name of "earth," as that psalm shows, listing all the higher beings under that first heading: *Praise the Lord from the heavens* (Ps 148:1); and all the lower ones under this other heading: *Praise the Lord from the earth* (Ps 148:7), where both the spirits of the tempest are named and all the deeps and the fire that burns you when you touch it, because it springs into being from earthy and humid movements in such a way that it is forthwith changed into another element. And although it indicates what its natural inclination is by thrusting upwards, it is for all that unable to escape into the calm of the higher heaven because it is overcome by so much air, turned into it and so extinguished. And thus it is that in this more perishable and sluggish section of creation fire is activated by turbulent movements in order to temper its severity and to render it both useful and terrifying to mortals.

10. So then, by the sense of touch, which properly belongs to the element earth, both the billowing flood and the sighing breeze can also be perceived; that explains why the bodies of aquatic animals too feed on earthy substances and, especially the birds, also take their rest on earth and raise their young there. Part of the moist element, after all, which is exhaled as vapor also extends over the dry land. And that is why, after scripture had said, *Let the waters produce reptiles of live souls and flying things* (it goes on) *over the earth*, it added with a sure touch, *along the solid structure of heaven* (Gn 1:20), which can clear up to some extent a point that previously seemed obscure. It does not say, you see, "*in* the solid structure of heaven," as it does with the luminaries, but *flying things*, it

goes, *over the earth along the solid structure of heaven*, that is to say, next to the solid structure of heaven, because to be sure this foggy and humid space, in which the birds fly around, borders on that space where they cannot fly, which thanks to its tranquillity and stillness now really does belong to the solid structure of heaven. So the birds then do fly around in heaven, or the sky, but in this one which that psalm also includes under the heading of "earth"; it is because of this heaven that they are called in many places "the birds of heaven"—not however in the solid structure, but along the solid structure.

Why fish are called reptiles of live souls

8, 11. Some people think that it was because of a certain dullness of sensation that the phrase *reptiles of live souls* is used, and not just "live soul." But if that were the case the birds would have been given the name of "live soul." So on the contrary, since they are called flying things—understand "of live souls"—in the same way as the others are called reptiles or crawling things, it has to be admitted, I suggest, that it is so phrased as if to say, "things among live souls that are crawling things or flying things," as one might say "low-born things of men," meaning "whoever among men are low-born." For although there are also land animals that crawl upon the earth, still the vast majority of them move about on feet, and reptiles that crawl on land are comparatively as few as creatures that walk are in the waters.

12. Some people, however, have expressed the opinion that the reason fishes are not called "live soul" but *reptiles of live souls* is that they lack any kind of memory or form of life even remotely approaching rationality. But this opinion comes simply from insufficient experience, because there are authors who have described many wonderful things that they have been able to observe in fish-ponds.[12] But even if their descriptions are untrue, it is still absolutely certain that fishes have memory. This is something I have myself experienced, and anyone who wants to can experience it too. There is, you see, a large fountain in the district of Bulla[13] that is chock-full of fish. People are habitually looking down into it and throwing in things which the fish will rush at together to grab first, or fight among themselves to tear them to bits. Being now used to this kind of feeding, whenever people stroll round the rim of the fountain, the fish too will

12. He no doubt had in mind, among other authorities, the ninth book of Pliny's *Natural History*, devoted to aquatic animals.
13. Bulla Regia was a small town on the inland route between Hippo Regius and Carthage, where Augustine preached Sermon 301A (Denis 17), and upbraided the citizens for still continuing to put on theatrical shows and spectacles, that made the place (in his view) what we would nowadays call "the porn capital of Africa"—which brought in, as it would today, considerable revenue from tourists; section 7 of that sermon. Perhaps here he is hoping this great fountain will be able to replace the equivalent of "blue movies" as the town's chief holiday attraction for the Carthaginian bourgeoisie.

swim back and forth with them in a shoal, waiting for those whose presence they are aware of to throw something in.

And so the point seems to me to be worth making that aquatic animals are here called reptiles or crawling things in exactly the same way as birds are called flying things. I mean if it were their lack of memory or dullness of sensation that deprived fishes of the title of "live souls," this would surely be granted to the birds, whose way of life we can observe with our own eyes to be both governed by memory and very talkative and to display great skill in the building of nests and the rearing of their chicks.

Refutation of those natural scientists who allotted each element its own animals

9, 13. I am also aware that some natural scientists[14] have classified animals in such a way as not only to call those ones terrestrial or earthy which crawl or walk on land, but to include birds in this class as well, because they too take their rest on land when they are tired out flying, while they say that the airy animals are demons, and the heavenly ones gods—our term for some of these is luminaries, for others angels. The same people, all the same, attribute to the waters the fishes and monsters *sui generis*, so that no element may be without its animals—as if, forsooth, there were no earth under the waters, or they could prove that fishes do not rest on it and thus restore their strength for swimming as the birds do for flying. Of course fishes, doubtless, do this less often than birds, because water is more effective than air at holding up bodies, so that it will also support land animals swimming, whether they have learned how to do this, like human beings, or do it naturally like quadrupeds or snakes.

Or if the reason they give for not accepting this argument is that fishes do not have feet, then it means that seals do not belong to the water, nor serpents and snails to the land or earth, seeing that the former have feet, while the latter, without any feet, I will not say rest on the earth, but hardly ever, if indeed ever, move away from it. As for dragons, which lack feet, they are said to take their rest in caves, and to soar up into the air. While these are not too easy to come across, this kind of animated creature is for all that definitely mentioned not only in our literature[15] but also in that of the Gentiles.

---

14. He says *philosophos*. But "philosophers" nowadays inhabit a rather different suburb of Academia, or rather a much narrower one. Aristotle, *the* philosopher of the ancient world for the scholastics, was also the leading natural scientist.

15. See, for example Psalms 74:14 and 104:26, where Augustine's text, following the Septuagint, has "dragon" instead of the "Leviathan" we may be more familiar with, and in the deutero-canonical literature the story of Bel and the Dragon (Daniel 14 in the Septuagint and Vulgate). He goes on to mention the literature of "the Gentiles," that is to say pagan Greek and Latin legends—Perseus, for example, rescuing Andromeda from the dragon—because the people he is criticizing would not accept the authority of "our literature."

Granted that demons may be called airy beings, scripture's account of the
production of birds from the water is still valid

10, 14. So then, let us grant that demons are airy animals, since it is in virtue of
their airy bodies that they have their power, and the reason they suffer no dissolution in death is that the element dominant in them is one that is more suited to
acting than to being acted upon or undergoing, with two others placed under it,
namely water and earth, and one placed above it, that is, the sidereal fire—there
being two elements, you see, assigned to undergoing or being acted upon,
humidity and humus,[16] while the other two are given over to acting—air and fire.
If this is the case, therefore, this distinction does not rule out what our scripture
points out, that it was not from air but from the waters that flying things were
produced, because it was still a place of humidity, even though indeed of a finer
quality, exhaled into the atmosphere and extended through it, that was allotted to
flying things.

Now air reaches from the boundary of the luminous heaven right down to the
level of the fluid waters and the bare earth. It is not, however, this whole space
that is made murky with humid exhalations, but only as far as that limit from
which the psalm begins to call everything earth, where it says, *Praise the Lord*
from the earth (Ps 148:7). The higher region of the air, on the other hand, on
account of its purity and tranquillity is joined in a shared peace to the heaven it
borders on, and shares in its name. If it was perhaps in this region that the transgressor angels were to be found before their transgression, together with their
prince, now the devil, then an archangel[17]—some of our people, you see, think
that they were not celestial or supercelestial angels—then it is hardly surprising
if after their sin they were thrust down into this foggy darkness, where it is still
air but now interwined with a fine humidity. This causes winds when stirred up,
and lightning and thunder when more vehemently roused; clouds when
contracted and rain when thickened even more; snow when the clouds freeze,
hail when the denser clouds freeze more turbulently; fair weather when it is
stretched out; and all this at the hidden orders and working of God controlling
from its heights to its depths the universe he created. So that psalm, after
mentioning *fire, hail, snow, ice, spirits of the tempest,* lest such things should be
thought to come about and run their course apart from divine providence, adds
straightaway, *that carry out his word* (Ps 148:8).

---

16. This is his play on words in the Latin, which I have kept in translation, even though we use
    "humus" to mean something slightly different. The Latin is simply an archaic word meaning
    earth or soil.
17. He discusses this opinion at slightly greater length in Book XI,16,22 below.

15. But if those transgressors wore celestial bodies[18] before they transgressed, it is also hardly surprising if these were turned as a punishment into something like air, so that they could now be acted upon and suffer pain from fire, that is, from the element higher up in the natural scale. Nor in any case were they allowed to occupy the loftier and purer regions of the air, but only these murky parts, which serve as a kind of prison for them until the time of judgment. And if there are further questions to be investigated more thoroughly about these transgressor angels, there will be some other place of scripture more suited to the matter. For the moment it is sufficient to make this point: if these turbulent and stormy regions of the air are able, on account of its nature where it reaches down to sea and land, to sustain airy bodies, they can also hold up those of birds, produced from the waters, on account of the tenuous exhalations from the waters. These, as we have seen, are inserted in the form of vapor into this same air where it is poured round the world next to the sea and land, and they interlace the breezes which distill the gentle dew when made heavier by the rigors of the night; while if the cold gets more severe they also lay on the ground the white mantle of hoar frost.

On the various kinds of animal created from the earth

11, 16. *And God said: Let the earth produce live soul according to kind; quadrupeds and reptiles and beasts of the earth according to kind, and cattle according to kind. And it was made thus. And God made the beasts of the earth according to kind and cattle according to kind and all reptiles of the earth according to kind. And God saw that they were good* (Gn 1:24-25). Now at last it was time to furnish with its animals the other part, the one that is properly called earth, of this lowest region with all its abysses and cloudy air, the whole of which is elsewhere in scripture embraced under the name of "earth." And the kinds of animal which the earth produced at a word from God are indeed plain enough. But all animals not endowed with reason are often in general usage lumped together under the name of "cattle" or the name of "beasts"; so it is worth inquiring what are here properly meant by "beasts" and what by "cattle." There is no doubt, of course, that by "reptiles" or crawling things he meant all serpents—though they too can also be called beasts, while the name of "cattle" is

---

18. That is, bodies of fire, that being the element proper to the celestial region. When talking of angels elsewhere, without particular reference also to demons, does Augustine assume that they too had airy bodies, being of the same created nature as demons? Aquinas thinks he does, and quotes him as the leading authority for the idea. But he only refers to this chapter, section 14, in his *Summa Theologiae* I, q.51, a.1, ad 1. Saint Thomas, however, clearly did not read on to this section 15, where Augustine is implying that they have bodies of fire, an idea he would have found supported by Ps 104:4, which he would have read as running: "who makes your angels spirits, and your ministers burning fire." See also the quotation of this verse in Heb 1:7.

not usually applied to serpents.[19] Again, the word "beasts" is commonly applied to lions and panthers and tigers and wolves and foxes, to dogs too and even monkeys and others of that sort, while the name "cattle" is more usually and suitably attributed to those animals which human beings have turned to their own use, whether for helping them with work, like oxen and horses and any other such, or with wool and food. like sheep and pigs.

17. So what then are the quadrupeds? Because although all these animals, apart from some serpents, walk on four feet, unless for all that he had wanted some to be signified properly by this name, he would surely not have also mentioned quadrupeds here—though he does leave the word out in his repetition. Or are deer perhaps and antelopes and wild asses and boars properly called quadrupeds here, because neither can they be included among beasts, where there are lions, nor have they been domesticated by human beings, though they are like those other cattle—as if these animals were left over, and this general name, common to them and many others because of the number of their feet, was applied to them nonetheless with a special significance?

Or because he said *according to kind* three times, is he inviting us to consider three kinds? First *according to kind* quadrupeds and reptiles, where I reckon he indicates what kind of quadrupeds he means, namely those that are in the class of reptiles, like lizards and geckos and anything else of that sort. And the reason, perhaps, he did not repeat the word "quadrupeds" in the repetition is that they were already included under the word "reptiles." So he did not simply say "reptiles" there, but he added, *all reptiles of the earth; of the earth*, because there are also the ones of the water, and *all*, so as to understand here those that also move on four feet, which had properly been signified above by the name of "quadrupeds."

Secondly beasts, about which he says again *according to kind*—any animal, apart from serpents, that savages its prey with claws and teeth. While as for cattle, about which for the third time he says *according to kind*, they are those that do not tear others with either kind of brute force, but either with horns, or not even this.

I said earlier on, you see, that one can easily tell how widely the name "quadrupeds" ranges by counting the feet, while the name "cattle" or "beasts" can

---

19. When it comes to the cursing of the serpent in Gn 3:14, almost all English versions, from the Authorized Version on, have it cursed "beyond all cattle." In this they follow not only the Hebrew, but also the Greek Septuagint, which has the word *ktena*. Now while the Latin Vulgate studiously avoids the word "cattle" here, and has "among all animals," *animantia*, the text Augustine was using had *ab omnibus pecoribus* (Book XI,1,1 below); but when he comes to discuss this part of the passage in detail, 36, 49 of the same book, he says nothing about the use of this word, and simply refers the reader for his discussion of the serpent's punishment to the two books he wrote on Genesis against the Manichees, in which he says nothing on this particular point either. I think it probable that he understood the words to mean "by all cattle" rather than "from" in the sense of "beyond all cattle."

sometimes cover every non-rational animal. But there is also the word *ferae*, which usually has the same value in the Latin language as "beasts";[20] however, that was no reason for neglecting a consideration of how these names, which are not put here in this passage of scripture for nothing, can be specifically distinguished from each other, something that can easily be noted in everyday speech.

The special point of the phrase "according to kind"

12, 18. The reader may also wonder, and not without justification, whether the phrase *according to kind* comes up again and again just by chance, as it were, or whether there is some meaning in it, as though they were already in existence beforehand, though the account of their creation is only now being given. Or can it be that "their kind" is to be understood as being in the higher, that is of course the spiritual, ideas according to which they are created lower down the scale? But if that were the case, this would also have been said about light, about heaven, about the waters and the lands, about the lamps of heaven. Which of these is there that does not have its eternal and unchanging idea powerfully present in the very Wisdom of God, who *reaches mightily from end to end, and disposes all things sweetly* (Wis 8:1)? In fact, though, this expression begins to be used about the grasses and the trees, and so on until we get to these terrestrial animals, because although it is not used about those that were created from the water at their first mention, it is there all the same at the repetition, where it says: *And God made the great whales and every soul of crawling animals, which the waters produced according to their kind, and every winged flying thing according to kind* (Gn 1:21).

19. Or is it because these things sprang into being in such a way that others would be born of them and in succeeding to them would preserve the shape and form of their origin? Is that why they are said to be *according to kind*, on account of their propagating offspring, with whose continued existence in mind they were being created? But why does it say about the grasses and trees, not only "according to kind," but also *according to likeness*, since animals too, whether aquatic or terrestrial, reproduce according to their likeness? Or is it that, since likeness follows on kind or genus, he did not want to repeat it every time? After all, neither is mention of seed repeated every time, though it is present in animals, even if not in all of them, as well as in grasses and trees. It has been observed, you see, that some animals are born of water or of earth without having any distinction of sex; and thus their seed is not in them, but in the elements from which they arise by spontaneous generation.

---

20. In the English language we have no distinct name that I can think of as an equivalent to "beasts"; *fera* can only be translated as "wild beast."

This then is the significance of *according to kind*, where we are to understand both the efficacious force in the seed and the likeness of succeeding generations to their predecessors, because none of them was created just to exist once and for all by itself, whether to continue for ever, or to pass away with none to succeed it.

20. So why did it not also say about man, "Let us make man to our image and likeness according to kind," since human reproduction is an obvious fact? Was it because God did not make the man such that he would die, had he been willing to keep the commandment, and for that reason there was no need for any to succeed him on his decease; but it was only after his sin that he was *compared to irrational cattle and became like them* (Ps 49:12.20), so that from now on *the sons of this age* (Lk 20:34) would beget and be begotten, to make possible the continued existence of the race of mortals? But then what is the significance of that blessing given after the making of man: *Increase and multiply and fill the earth* (Gn 1:28), which could only happen, of course, by reproduction?

Or should nothing be said about this in passing, until we come to that place in scripture where these things will have to be more thoroughly investigated and discussed? Perhaps, you see, it is sufficient to say now that the reason *according to kind* was not said about man is that only one individual was made, from whom even the woman was also made. There are not, after all, many kinds and species of human being as there are of herbs, trees, fish, flying things, serpents, cattle, beasts; consequently we should take "according to kind" as in fact meaning according to their species, to distinguish from everything else things that derive their likeness to each other from one original seed.

Why a blessing like that given to humanity was only given to aquatic animals

13, 21. Another question that is asked is what merit distinguished the aquatic animals in the eyes of the creator, so that they alone should be blessed like human beings. God, you see, blessed them too, saying: *Increase and multiply and fill the waters of the sea; and let flying things multiply upon the earth* (Gn 1:22). Was it enough for it to be said for one kind of creature, so that it could be understood to apply in consequence to the rest which increase by reproduction? In that case it should have been said for the first thing of that sort to be created, namely for grasses and trees. Or perhaps, since these would have no affection for the offspring to be propagated and would reproduce without any sensation, did he judge them to be unsuitable recipients of a blessing with these words, *Increase and multiply;* but first he said it where such affection was to be found, so that it could be understood as also having an unspoken reference to terrestrial animals? It was, however, necessary to repeat it for man, in case anybody should say that there is any sin in the business of procreating children, as there is in the lust involved in fornication or in the immoderate use, or rather misuse, of marriage.

On the creation of insects

14, 22. There is also a real question about the creation of the minutest animals, whether they were created in the original establishment of things, or from the putrefaction consequent upon material things being perishable. Most of them, you see, are either bred from the sores of living bodies, or from garbage and effluents, or from the rotting of corpses; some also from rotten wood and grass, some from rotten fruit; and we cannot possibly say that there are any of them of which God is not the creator. All things, after all, have in them a certain worth or grace of nature, each of its own kind, so that in these minute creatures there is even more for us to wonder at as we observe them, and so to praise the almighty craftsman for them more rapturously than ever. Indeed he made all things in the Wisdom who *reaches from end to end and sweetly disposes all things* (Wis 8:1), and who does not leave even the very last and least of things without due shape or form, things that disintegrate in accordance with their natural properties, and whose disintegration fills us with horror, punished as we are by our own mortality. No, she creates animals whose bodies are as tiny as can be, but whose senses are so sharp that if we pay close attention we are more amazed at the agile flight of a fly than at the stamina of a sturdy mule on the march; and the cooperative labors of tiny ants strike us as far more wonderful than the colossal loads that can be carried by camels.

23. But as I said, the question is whether we are to believe that these smallest of creatures were also introduced in the original establishment of things, whose creation is recounted in this series of six days, or later on from the consequent disintegration of perishable bodies. And it can indeed be said that the tiniest things which spring from the waters or the earth were created then; among them one may include without absurdity those that are born of the vegetation which appeared when the earth blossomed. Now this preceded the making of the luminaries as well as of the animals, and furthermore its roots make it a kind of extension of the earth. So these creatures, coming into being on the day when the dry land appeared, should be understood as supplementing the furnishing of the habitation rather than as belonging to the number of its inhabitants.

But as for the rest which are generated from the bodies of animals, especially dead ones, it would be quite ridiculous to say that they were created at the same time as the animals themselves were, unless possibly there was some natural tendency in all animated bodies, so that they already had seeded and threaded into them beforehand, as it were, the first beginnings of the future animalcules, which were going to arise, by an inexpressible arrangement, in their various

230 The Literal Meaning of Genesis

kinds from the decay of such bodies, all things being put in motion without any change in him by the creator.

The creation of poisonous animals

15, 24. The question is also commonly asked about various poisonous and dangerous animals: whether they were created after the sin of man as a punishment, or rather had already been created as harmless, and only began after that to do sinners harm. Nor should we be surprised at the idea, considering what happens occasionally even in the times of this difficult and woeful life in which there are none so just that they could boldly call themselves perfect. We have the apostle bearing honest witness to this when he says, *Not that I have already received this or am already perfect* (Phil 3:12). Then again, bodily trials and troubles are still necessary for training and perfecting us in virtue, weak as we are; and once more we have the apostle illustrating this in his own case, when he says that to stop him getting swollen-headed at the greatness of the revelations shown him, he was given *a thorn in the flesh, an angel of Satan to buffet him*, and that when he had asked the Lord three times to relieve him of it, he answered him: *My grace is enough for you, since virtue is perfected in weakness* (2 Cor 12:7-9). Holy Daniel too was certainly not lying to God when he not only prayed for the sins of his people but also confessed his own.[21]

And yet Daniel survived safe and sound and fearless among the lions,[22] while the apostle had a deadly viper clinging to his arm and doing him no harm.[23] So it would have been quite possible for these creatures to do no harm when they were created, if no occasion had arisen for punishing vices and frightening people off them, or for testing virtue and making people perfect, when it is a matter both of giving examples of patience to help others make progress and of people growing in self-knowledge through their trials. And it is only just that the eternal salvation which had been disgracefully lost through wilfulness, should be courageously won back again through pain.

Why beasts were created that harm each other

16, 25. Someone is going to say: "Then why do beasts injure one another, though they neither have any sins, so that this kind of thing could be called punishment, nor by such trials do they gain at all in virtue?"

---

21. See Dn 9:4-19.
22. See Dn 6:22.
23. See Acts 28:3-5. I have the viper on Paul's arm rather than on his hand, in an attempt to reproduce Augustine's jingle: *in ipsius apostoli manu mortifera vipera inhaesit nec laesit*. He, to be sure, manages two jingles: *mortifera vipera* as well as *inhaesit nec laesit*.

For the simple reason, of course, that some are the proper diet of others. Nor can we have any right to say, "There shouldn't be some on which others feed." All things, you see, as long as they continue to be, have their own proper measures, numbers and destinies.[24] So all things, properly considered, are worthy of acclaim; nor is it without some contribution in its own way to the temporal beauty of the world that they undergo change by passing from one thing into another.[25] This may escape fools; those making progress have some glimmering of it; to the perfect it is as clear as daylight.

And certainly all such goings-on in the animal world provide us human beings with plenty of salutary admonitions; thus we should observe what trouble we ought to take over our spiritual, everlasting health and welfare by which we so surpass all non-rational animals, when we see them, from the biggest elephants down to the smallest little worms, doing whatever they are capable of, whether by resisting or by taking precautions, to safeguard their bodily, time-bound health and welfare, such as has been allotted to them according to their place on the lower scale of creation. None of this would be evident unless there were some beasts that prey on the bodies of others for the sustenance of their own bodies, while the others look after themselves either by their ability to fight back or by their speed in taking flight, or by taking refuge in their hiding holes.

And after all, even bodily pain in any animate creature is itself a great and wonderful power of the soul, which is quickening the entire organism and holding it together by being mixed in with it in a manner beyond words, and giving it a certain unity in its own small measure; the pain it feels means, if I may so put it, that it is not indifferent to the organism being spoiled or broken up, but reacts to this with indignation.

A worry about the bodies of the dead that have been eaten by wild animals

17, 26. Granted that dangerous animals injure living human beings either as a punishment or to provide them with salutary and useful tests and trials or to cure their ignorance of themselves, this other point may doubtless still worry some people: why they also tear to pieces for their food the bodies of dead human

---

24. He is alluding to Wis 11:20: *You have arranged all things in measure, number and weight.* Here, instead of "weights" as the last of the trio, Augustine has *ordines*. He discusses this text at considerable length later on in this work, Book IV,3,7 to 5,12; or rather he uses it in his discussion of why there were six days of creation; and he uses the verb *ordino* in connection with "weight." He extends the notion of weight to cover the natural tendency of everything towards its own proper place, to cover what the scholastics will call the natural appetite in things, which in human beings is the will and its love. Thus by their "weight" things are pointed towards their proper end, ordained to their proper destiny. So here, after some hesitation, I have decided on "destinies" as the best word to render *ordines*.
25. By, for example, being eaten by another! This is surely what he must mean in the context.

beings—as though, indeed, it made any difference to our ultimate good through what channels this now lifeless flesh passes in the secluded depths of nature, from which it is in due course to be extracted and refashioned by the marvelous omnipotence of the creator! Here too, in fact, the wise can learn a lesson—so wholeheartedly to trust themselves to the faithful creator, who governs all things, the greatest and the least, at his secret pleasure, and for whom our very hairs are numbered,[26] that they do not let vain anxieties about the disposal of their lifeless corpses fill them with dread of any kind of death, but instead have no hesitation in bracing themselves with devout courage to be ready for it in whatever shape it comes.

Why and when thorns and thistles and trees that bear no fruit were created

18, 27. The same kind of problem commonly arises over thorns and thistles and some kinds of tree that bear no fruit: why or when they were created, seeing that God said: *Let the earth produce grass for fodder seeding seed, and fruit trees making fruit* (Gn 1:11). But people who are worried by this are unaware, it would seem, of common formulae in human law, which talk about "usufruct"; what is referred to, after all, in the word "fruit," is the thing's uses for those who enjoy it.[27] And how many uses there are of all the things the earth brings forth and nourishes through their roots, well the obvious ones these people can observe for themselves, the more special less known ones they can learn about from the experts.

28. About thorns and thistles, indeed, a more unconditional answer can be given, because after his sin the man was told about the earth: *thorns and thistles shall it bring forth to you* (Gn 3:18). Still, that does not mean one can simply say that that was when these things began to spring up from the earth. It is possible, after all, that many uses can be found for seeds of this kind too, and so they could have had their place without any penal inconvenience to the man. But that these too should be produced in the fields in which he was now condemned to toil away, this served, we can suppose, to pile on the punishment, since they could have come up elsewhere as food for birds and cattle, or for some human uses or other.

Though as a matter of fact the following way of taking these words does no violence to them either; *thorns and thistles shall it bring forth to you* can be understood to mean that while the earth did bring them forth previously, it did not do so to add to the man's labor, but to provide food for animals of whatever sort—there are some, you see, which find these kinds of plant, both with softer and harder leaves, appropriate and pleasant to eat; but it was when the man

---

26. See Lk 12:7.
27. *Fructus* derived from *fruor*, I enjoy.

started to toil away at the earth after sinning that it started to bring these things forth *to him*, to make his work all the more difficult. So it would not have to mean that these things sprang up previously in other places, and later on in the fields which the man was cultivating to get crops from, but in the same places both before and after; before, though, not to the man; after, however, to the man. That would be what was signified by adding *to you*, because it did not say, "thorns and thistles shall it bring forth," but *shall it bring forth to you*; that is, "These things shall begin to make extra hard work for you, which previously were being produced purely as food for other animals."

Why it is only in the creation of man that God says "Let us make, etc."

19, 29. *And God said, Let us make man to our image and likeness; and let him lord it over the fishes of the sea and the flying things of heaven and all cattle and all the earth and all reptiles crawling over the earth. And God made man to the image of God; he made him male and female, he made them and blessed them,*[28] *saying: Increase and multiply and fill the earth and lord it over it, and prince it*[29] *over the fishes of the sea and the flying things of heaven and all cattle and all the earth and all reptiles crawling over the earth. And God said: Behold, I have given you every seed-bearing fodder seeding seed, which is on all the earth, and every tree which has in it fruit of seed-bearing seed—it shall be for you as food and for all beasts of the earth and all flying things of heaven and every reptile crawling on the earth, which has in it the breath of life—and every green fodder as food. And it was made thus. And God saw all the things that he had made, and behold they were very good. And there was made evening and there was made morning, the sixth day* (Gn 1:26-31).

---

28. Both the Maurists and the CSEL text punctuate this passage in the usual way. But this was not Augustine's way, as can be seen most clearly in *The Trinity* XII,6.8. There he formally explains his preference for his own idiosyncratic punctuation—he no doubt did not regard it as idiosyncratic himself! And a few pages later on here in this work, 22,34, near the end, we will find him saying: "On account of their being joined in one, *God made*, it says, *man to the image of God*. And in case anyone should think that it was only the spirit of man that was made, although it was only as regards the spirit that he was made to the image of God, *he made him*, it says, *male and female*, to give us to understand that the body was also being made now." Back here in the long passage being quoted, one manuscript omits *Deus* after *benedixit*, in this also being true to Augustine's reading of the text, and so I follow this manuscript, as against the Maurists and CSEL.
29. *Principamini*; a word not given in any Latin dictionary; my guess is that the translators of the version Augustine was using had invented it, because they had just used the good Latin word *dominamini*, "lord it," for another word introduced by the Greek Septuagint with reference to the earth. A common, in some ways the most authentic, title for the Roman Emperors was *princeps*, "prince." Albert Blaise, *Dictionnaire Latin-Français des Auteurs Chrétiens* (Strasbourg, 1954), gives many references to the fathers for this deponent verb *principor*, the oldest being to the Latin text of Irenaeus' *Against Heresies* 3,34,4.

The Literal Meaning of Genesis

There will be more fruitful passages time and again later on for a more thorough reflection on the nature of man. Now however, to conclude our examination and discussion of the works of the six days, I must briefly insist in the first place that the following point is not to be passed over lightly: that while with the other works it says, *God said: Let it be made*, here on the other hand we have, *God said: Let us make man to our image and likeness*, to insinuate, that is, a plurality of persons, if I may so put it,[30] on account of Father and Son and Holy Spirit. He immediately advises us, however, of the unity to be understood in the godhead by saying, *and God made man to the image of God*; not as though the Father made to the image of the Son, or the Son to the image of the Father—otherwise it would not be true to say "to our image," if man were made to the image of the Father alone or of the Son alone—but it is put like this: "God made to the image of God," as much as to say, "God made to his image."

When it now says *to the image of God*, after saying above *to our image*, it is giving a clear signal that that plurality of persons is not leading us to say or to believe or to understand gods in the plural, but to take Father and Son and Holy Spirit—the trinity on whose account it says *to our image*—as being one God, on whose account it says, *to the image of God*.

In what respect man was made to the image of God; and why it does not say after the creation of man, "And thus it was made"

20, 30. Here we must not neglect that other point either, that after saying, *to our image*, he immediately added, *and let him have authority over the fishes of the sea and the flying things of heaven* and of the other animals which lack reason, giving us to understand, evidently, that it was in the very factor in which he surpasses non-rational animate beings that man was made to God's image. That, of course, is reason itself, or mind or intelligence or whatever other word it may more suitably be named by. That is why the apostle too says: *Be renewed in the spirit of your minds and put on the new man, who is being renewed for the recognition of God according to the image of him who created him* (Eph 4:23-24; Col 3:10), where he makes it plain enough just in what part man was created to God's image—that it was not in the features of the body but in a certain form of the illuminated mind.

31. Now with that light of the first day, if by that name is rightly to be understood the created intellectual light which shares in the eternal and unchangeable Wisdom of God, it did not say, "and thus it was made" and then repeat with *and*

---

30. I think he is excusing his use of the word *pluralitatem*; not indeed his own invention, as it had already been employed by Ambrose, according to Lewis & Short. But no doubt it would have struck Augustine, the professional rhetorician, as a neologism, at least in its theological use. Apart from that it seems to have been just a grammatical term for "the plural."

God made, because as I have already argued to the best of my ability there was not being made in that first of creatures some knowledge of the Word of God, so that after that knowledge something lower down the scale would be made which was already being created in that Word; but that very light was being made first, in which knowledge would be made of the Word of God by whom it was being created; and this knowledge would itself be the light's conversion from its formlessness to the God forming it, would be its being created and formed. Later on, however, with the rest of creation it says *and thus it was made*, which signifies knowledge of the Word first being made in that light, that is, in the intellectual creature; and next, when it says, *and God made*, it indicates the actual making of that kind of creature, of which it had been said in and by the Word of God that it should be made.[31]

Well, it is this principle that is being kept to in the making of man. God, you see, has just said, *Let us make man to our image and likeness* etc.; and then it does not say, *and thus it was made*, but leads straight into, *and God made man to the image of God*, precisely because human nature too is intellectual like that light, and that is why being made is the same thing for it as recognizing the Word of God by whom it is being made.

32. I mean, if it said, *and thus it was made*, and after that led into *and God made*, it would be understood as being first made in the knowledge of the rational creation, and then being made in some actual creature which was not rational. But because here too we have a rational creature, it too was perfected by the same recognition. Just as after man's fall into sin *he is being renewed in the recognition of God according to the image of him who created him* (Col 3:10), so too it was in that recognition that he was created, before he grew old in crime, so that he might again be renewed, rejuvenated, in the same recognition.

As for things however that were not created in that knowledge, because they were being created either as bodies or as non-rational souls, knowledge of them was first of all made in the intellectual creation by the Word, by whom it was said that they should be made, and on account of that knowledge it said, *and thus it was made*, to indicate that the knowledge of them was now made in that nature which was able to know this in the Word of God beforehand; and then the actual bodies and non-rational creatures were made, on account of which it next added, *and God made*.

---

31. He is here condensing what he had set out at somewhat greater length in Book II,8,16; and there he had been leading up to this central idea of his, which governs his whole interpretation of the creation narrative, practically from the beginning of Book II. So readers are advised to refresh their memories from there.

Difficulty about the food provided for man, in connection with his conditional immortality

21, 33. How, though, the man was made immortal, and at the same time received for his food with the other animals "grasses for fodder-bearing seed and fruit-bearing trees and green herbs," it is difficult to say. If, after all, it was through sin that he was rendered mortal, then surely before sin he would not have needed such nourishment. Nor, what is more, could that body have faded away out of hunger.

As regards what they are told, *Increase and multiply and fill the earth,* although it hardly seems that this could have been done without the intercourse of male and female—and here too we have a clear indication that our bodies are mortal—still it can be said that with immortal bodies there could have been another way, so that children would be born solely through family affection without any disfigurement of lust; born neither to take the place of deceased parents nor to die themselves, until the earth was filled with immortal human beings; and that with a just and holy people being thus set in place, such as we believe will exist after the resurrection, a final limit would also be put to the whole business of birth. Yes, this can indeed be said, and how it may be said is matter for further consideration.[32] But surely nobody will have the face to say this too, that any but mortal bodies could be in want of nourishment to keep them going.

---

32. What he is suggesting by this qualification, I think, is that he would not agree that sexual intercourse would be unnecessary in a "non-lapsarian society" and that all births would be virginal, brought about purely by "family affection," *pietatis affectu.* For him this *pietatis affectus* would take the place of the "disfigurement of lust," *corruptionis concupiscentia,* in the generative sexual act. The whole passage is based on the assumption, common to all Augustine's contemporary exegetes, that Genesis 1 and 2 formed a single narrative; also that our first parents, before their sin, were superhuman human beings, both in mind and in body. No modern exegetes would take such a line; but the point is worth making that it is a necessary Christian belief (that is, a necessary pre-supposition to more central Christian beliefs) that if there had been no sin, human beings would not have died; that *it was through the envy of the devil that death entered the world* (Wis 2:24). Without it, we cannot do justice to the central Christian notion of life, and of eternal life, the fullness of life, consisting in communion with God, being that for which God created mankind in the beginning. As it says in the same book (Wis 1:13), *God did not make death, and he does not delight in the death of the living.* Yes, death is a natural event, and is frequently so treated in scripture; but to see it as purely and simply such would be to devaluate the redemptive death of Christ, whose death gave death an expiatory value, precisely because it also has a dimension as the punishment of sin, as the self-inflicted punishment of sin, death as the inner consequence, almost the inner meaning of sin, seeing that sin is essentially a deliberate turning away from the living God, the God of life. May I refer the reader to a book of mine; *Being Human: a Biblical Perspective* (Geoffrey Chapman, London 1984; see in particular chapters 5A and 12A).

*The opinion that Genesis 1:27 refers to the creation of the human spirit,
2:7 to the creation of the body*

22, 34. There are some people, however, who have even put forward this conjecture: that at this time it was the interior man who was made, while the body of the man was made later on, when scripture says, *And God fashioned the man from the slime of the earth* (Gn 2:7); so that the word used here, *made*, applies to the spirit, the word *fashioned* to the body. They have disregarded the fact that man can only have been made male and female with respect to the body. There may be the most subtle arguments, to be sure, about the actual mind of man, in which he was made to the image of God, that its activity as a kind of rational life is divided between the contemplation of eternal truth and the management of temporal affairs; and that in this way it was made, as it were, male and female, with the former function directing, the latter conforming.[33] With this division of roles however, that part alone is rightly said to be the image of God which clings in contemplation to the unchangeable Truth. It was as symbolically representing this that the apostle Paul says the man alone *is the image and glory of God, while the woman*, he goes on, *is the glory of the man* (1 Cor 11:7).

And so, although this external diversity of sex in the bodies of two human beings symbolizes what is to be understood internally in the one mind of a single human being, still the female too, because it is simply in the body that she is female, is also being renewed in the spirit of her mind in the recognition of God according to the image of him who created that in which there is no male and female.[34] Now just as women are not cut off from this grace of the renewal and reshaping of the image of God, although their bodily sex has a different symbolic signification, according to which the man alone is called "the image and glory of God;" by the same token too in that original creation of man in terms of which "man" included woman as well, the woman of course also had her

---

33. He himself propounds such subtle arguments in *The Trinity* XII,1,1-4 (Volume III/1 in this series) and indeed practically constructs the rest of that book on the idea. Our passage here rather implies that he got the idea from some other author or authors. He returns to the point later on in Book VI,7,12, and in note 6 on that passage I suggest that the author he was indebted to may well have been the Donatist scholar Tychonius.

34. See Col 3:10, Eph 4:23, Gal 3:28. See note 27 on Book XII of *The Trinity* in this series, for a defense of Augustine against his feminist critics, some of whom insist on maintaining that this theory of his shows he denied that women are also made to the image of God. Here in our text he will in a moment or two go on to repudiate this charge quite expressly. What he is in fact doing is defending the apostle from such a charge because of his words in 1 Cor 11:7. There Augustine is at pains precisely to interpret the apostle figuratively and not literally. Origen was the most notable Christian exegete to maintain that Gen 1:26-28 tells of the creation of the human spirit or soul, while 2:7 tells of the fashioning of the body. He maintained this in the extreme form of presenting the creation of the body as a punishment for some primal sin of the human soul, the body being provided for it as a penal prison.

mind, a mind endowed with reason, with respect to which she too was made to the image of God.

But on account of their being joined in one, *God made*, it says, *man to the image of God*. And in case anyone should think it was only the spirit of man that was made, although it was only in the spirit that he was made to the image of God, *he made him*, it says, *male and female* (Gn 1:27), to give us to understand that the body was also being made now. Again, in case anyone should suppose that it was made in such a way as to represent each sex in a single person, like those called hermaphrodites who are born occasionally, he shows that he put it in the singular on account of their being joined in one, and because the woman was made from the man, as will become clear later on when he begins to unfold more thoroughly what is said here in a nutshell; and that too is why he immediately continues in the plural, saying *he made them and blessed them* (Gn 1:27-28). But as I have already said, we shall be inquiring more thoroughly about the creation of man in the passage of scripture that follows on this.

What "And thus it was made" refers to here

22, 35. Now we have to note the fact that after saying, *And thus it was made*, he added straightaway, *And God saw all the things that he had made, and behold they were very good*. What is meant here is the actual right and provision given to the human species to take for food the fodder of the field and the fruits of trees.[35] He referred *and thus it was made*, you see, to what started from the place where he says, *and God said: Behold, I have given you seed-bearing fodder* etc. The fact is, if we refer his saying *and thus it was made* to everything that has been said earlier, the consequence will be that we will have to admit that they had already increased and multiplied and filled the earth on the sixth day, though we find scripture itself testifying that this only happened after many years.[36]

For this reason, after the man had been given this right to eat, and had come to know it when God told him, it says *and thus it was made*—in the very fact, of

---

35. This is meant by the words *and thus it was made*, not by the words that were added straightaway after that. There are two points being argued simultaneously here, in a typically complex and allusive way. The first proceeds from the fact that whereas on previous days the words *and thus it was made* are followed in one form or another by a repetition of what God has said should be made—either by *and God made*, or by *and the waters produced*, and so on; and only then did we hear that God saw that it was good; here the intermediate "repetition" is omitted, that is, because the man being an intelligent creature belonging with the angels to the intelligent creation, immediately knew what God had said through an impression of the divine idea in the divine Wisdom. That is why he stresses that God's seeing the goodness of everything is mentioned straightaway after *and thus it was made*. The second point being argued is that these words refer only to the right to eat, not to the actual eating; and certainly not to everything else mentioned in these verses, especially not to the blessing given, *Increase and multiply and fill the earth*.
36. See Genesis 5; and then for the process to be resumed after the flood, 10 and 11.

course, that the man came to know it when God told him. I mean, if he had already done it then, that is, had taken the things that had been given him for food and eaten them, scripture would have followed its established pattern, and after saying *and thus it was made,* which serves to express prior knowledge, would next have introduced the activity itself as well, and said, *and they took and ate.* It could have been said like that, you see, even if God were not mentioned, as in the passage where it says: *Let the water which is under the heavens be collected together into one collection, and let the dry land appear;* it then adds, *and thus it was made,* and does not say next, *and God made,* but still makes the usual repetition like this: *and the water was collected together into its collection,* etc.

Why it does not say individually about the human creature "And God saw that it was good"

24, 36. Now he did not say individually about the human creature, as in the other cases, *And God saw that it was good,* but after the man was made and given rights, whether to rule or to eat, he concluded about them all: *And God saw all the things that he had made, and behold they were very good.* This is certainly a point that deserves investigation. The man could, after all, have been paid individually the same respect as had been paid individually to the other things that had been made before, and then finally it could have been said of all the things God made, *behold they were very good.* Perhaps because all the works were completed on the sixth day, is that the reason why it had to be said about them all, *And God saw all the things that he had made, and behold they were very good*? But then why was it said about the cattle and the beasts and the reptiles of the earth, which also belong to the same sixth day? Unless, of course, they were entitled to be called good both individually in their own kind and generally with all the other things, while the man, made to the image of God, was only entitled to be called this generally with the rest! Or was it because he was not yet completed, because not yet established in paradise—as if this that was left out here was said later on after he had been put there!

37. So what are we to say then? Was it that God foreknew the man was going to sin, and not to remain in the perfection of his image, and so did not wish to call him good individually, but only together with the rest, as though hinting at what was going to happen? Because when the things that have been made remain as what they were made, to the extent they received it, like those things that have not sinned or those that cannot sin, they are both good individually, and in the totality they are all very good. It was not for nothing, you see, that "very" was added, because the parts of the body too, if they are beautiful even by themselves, are all still much more beautiful in the total structure of the body. Thus the eye, for example causes pleasure and admiration; but still, if we saw one

separate from the body, we would not call it as beautiful as we do when we observe it fitted into its proper place, in relation with the other parts, in the whole body.

Those things, however, which lose their proper comeliness by sinning, do not in the least for all that bring it about that they too are not good when rightly coordinated with the whole, with the universe. The man therefore before sin and in his own kind was of course good; but scripture forbore to say this, in order to say instead something that would foreshadow something yet to come. What was said about him, you see, was not untrue, because while someone who is good as an individual is clearly better when taken together with all the others, it does not follow that when he is good taken together with all the others he must also be good as an individual. And so it was arranged that something should be said which would be both true in the present and would signify foreknowledge of the future. God, after all, while being the best creator of natural things, is also the most just co-ordinator of sinners; so that even if things individually become deformed by transgressing, nonetheless the totality together with them in it remains beautiful. But now let us leave what follows to be dealt with in the next volume.

Book IV

Genesis 2:1-3: The completion of creation; the seventh day

How the six days of creation are to be understood

1, 1. *And heaven and earth and all their furniture*[1] were finished. And God finished on the sixth day his works which he had made; and God rested on the seventh day from all his works, which he had made. And God blessed the seventh day and sanctified it, because on it he rested from all his works, which God had begun to do (Gn 2:1-3). It is indeed an arduous and extremely difficult task for us to get through to what the writer meant with these six days, however concentrated our attention and lively our minds. The question is: Did those days pass, and now with the seventh added do they find themselves repeated, not of course in reality but in name, as times unroll? In time as a whole, after all, many days come which are like the ones that have passed, but none returns as the same identical day.

So then, did those days just pass? Or else, while these which are known by their names and number run on day by day in the course of time, do those days of creation abide in the current state of things? On this interpretation it would not only be in those three days before the luminaries were made, but again and again in every recurring series of three days that we would understand the name "day" to signify the actual specific nature of a thing that has been created, and its "night" to consist in its deprivation or defect, or any other better word there may be to signify the loss of its specific nature by some change in its proper form and by its verging on deformity and slipping into it. Such change is built into every created thing, whether as a mere possibility, though absent in actual fact, as in the higher heavenly beings,[2] or as a reality in the lowest things, to fulfill in them the time-bound beauty of things changing in an ordered way and yielding to and succeeding one another, as clearly happens with earthly and mortal things. Then "evening" would be for all things, as it were, the *terminus ad quem* of their complete and perfect establishment, while "morning" would represent their starting line.[3]

---

1. *Ornatus*. For this word and its rendering as "furniture" see note 30 on Book II.
2. A possibility that was realized in actual fact by the sin of Lucifer and his rebel angels.
3. Not Augustine's image; he uses the word *exordium*, which is a metaphor (I suspect a rather hackneyed one) from the business of weaving cloth on a loom.

To work out the answer to all this is certainly difficult. It may be the one or the other; or even a third more likely solution may be found, which will unfold, maybe, as discussion of the matter proceeds, to the question of how in those three days we are to understand the meaning of "night" and "evening" and "morning." But in any case it will not be beside the point for us to consider the perfection of the number six in the inner nature of numbers itself. This is something we behold with the mind, in the light of which we also number or count things that impinge on the senses of the body, and arrange them in a harmonious, numerical order.[4]

The perfection of the number six

2, 2. So then we find the number six to be the first perfect number for the reason that it is completed by its parts.[5] There are, you see, also other numbers that are perfect for other reasons and causes. Well then, we have called six a perfect number in that it is completed by its parts, those parts at least of which the number whose parts they are is a multiple; of such a part, you see, you can ask how many times. The number three can of course be called a part not only of six, of which it is a half, but of all the others that are more than three. I mean, three is also the greater part of four and five; four after all can be divided into three and one, and five into three and two. And of seven and eight and nine and any number beyond them three is not the greater or half but a smaller part. Thus seven can be divided into three and four, and eight into three and five, and nine into three and six. But with none of these can it be said of three how many times it goes into them, except with nine, of which it is a third, as it is a half of six. And so of all these that I have mentioned none is completed by x times three except six and nine.

3. So the number six, as I started to say, is itself completed by its parts being counted together and added up. There are other numbers, you see, whose parts added up make a smaller sum, others a bigger one. But as for those which are completed by their parts, which neither exceed them nor fall short of them when

---

4. Arrange them *numerose*. We are back with his beloved text, Wis 11:20, *You have arranged all things in measure and number and weight*. Number meant so much more than mere arithmetic for Augustine, and indeed for his contemporaries in general. To begin with it also meant music; and then following on this there was a whole mystique of number, the study and practice of which constituted the art or science (both, indeed) of what we may term numerology or—a less hybrid term—arithmology. A book that teems with this is the Apocalypse, the book of Revelation; and the author there is only developing material he has to hand in the books of the Old Testament. It is this art/science that will be governing the next long chapter on the number six.

5. In modern, more technical but also more lucid terms, it is the sum of its divisors; that is, $6 = 1 + 2 + 3$. The next such, my mathematical adviser informs me, is 28; $28 = 1 + 2 + 4 + 7 + 14$. For the next few in the series see note 8 below.

added, but come to the exact sum of the number itself, they are much fewer, and only found at ever-increasing intervals.[6] Of these the first is six. The number one, you see, has no parts; I mean, we use the word "one" as a number in counting in such a way that it has no half or any other part, but is really and truly and simply one. Two has one as its part, its half part, and no other. Three has two parts; one part, about which it can be said how many times, and that is the number one, which is a third of it; and another bigger part about which it cannot be said how many times, and that is the number two. So neither of this number three can the parts in the sense we now mean, about which you can say how many times, be added up. Going on to four, it has two such parts, because one is a quarter and two is a half of it; but add them up, that is one and two together, and they make three, not four. So its parts do not complete or perfect it, because added together they come to less. Five only has one such part, that is the number one, which is a fifth of it, because neither of two nor three, its lesser and larger parts, can it be said how many times. Six, on the other hand has three such parts; a sixth, a third, and a half; a sixth of it being one, a third two, and a half three. Now add these parts together, that is one and two and three, and together they complete and perfect six.

4. Coming now to the number seven, the only such part it has is a seventh, which is one; eight has three, an eighth, a quarter and a half, that is one, two and four. But these likewise added up make seven, stopping below the number they are parts of; so they do not complete the number eight. The number nine has two such parts, a ninth, which is one, and a third, which is three; together these only come to four, a long way short of nine. The number ten has three such parts; one as its tenth, two its fifth, five its half; add them up, they reach eight, not ten. Eleven has only an eleventh, as seven only has a seventh, five only a fifth, three only a third, and two only a half; in all cases the number one.

Twelve, however, when its parts of this sort are added up, is not completed but exceeded; they make in fact a greater number than twelve, reaching as far as sixteen. It has, you see, five such parts; a twelfth, a sixth, a quarter, a third, a half. I mean, its twelfth part is one, its sixth two, its quarter three, its third four, its half six; but one and two and three and four and six added up to a total make sixteen.

5. And not to waste time, in the infinite series of numbers a great many are found which only have one such part, like the numbers three and five, and the rest of that sort; or else they have several such parts which added up together either fall short of their total, like eight and nine and a great many others, or

---

6. This last phrase is not a translation, but only a rather desperate attempt to say roughly what he means by *certis intervallorum rationibus pauciores*; "fewer by definite reasons of intervals." The Latin *certus* means "certain" in English only in the sense of definite, sure, never in the vague sense of "there are certain things you must not do in polite society," or "it was with a certain sense of relief that we saw the last of him." The Latin here would be *quidam*.

exceed it, like twelve and eighteen, and many more such. So more numbers are to be found of any of these sorts, than of those which are called perfect in that they are completed by their parts of this kind being added up together. I mean, after six the next one we find is twenty-eight, which likewise consists of the total of its parts. Of these, you see, it has five; a twenty-eighth, a fourteenth, a seventh, a quarter, a half; that is, one and two and four and seven and fourteen, which added up together complete twenty-eight.[7] And the further the series of numbers proceeds, the longer, proportionately, are the intervals at which these numbers are found, which equal the sum of their parts in this manner, and which are called perfect. Those numbers, you see, whose parts do not add up to the whole are called imperfect, while those whose parts exceed the whole are called pluperfect.[8]

6. So it was in a perfect number of days, that is, six, that God perfected his works, which he had made. That, you see, is what is written: *And God finished on the sixth day*[9] *his works which he had made* (Gn 2:2). But I become even more addicted to this number when I also consider the order of the works themselves. For just as this number rises step by step in its parts into a triangle,[10] for one, you

---

7. I here omit a tautological phrase: "for they become twenty-eight." It is not quite so tautological in the Latin, because where he has been mostly using the ordinal numbers and talking, literally, of "the sixth number, the seventh, eighth, etc." until here we have just had "these added up complete the twenty-eighth," I have nearly always rendered with the cardinal, "number six, seven, etc." So here, after saying that these parts complete the twenty-eighth number he adds, indeed somewhat superfluously, "for they become twenty-eight." The whole exercise of these last few sections illustrates well enough what a fearfully cumbersome business arithmetic must have been in the ancient Roman world, before they were introduced to Arabic numerals. See note 5 above, where it is all put in a nutshell.

8. Latin appears not to have invented this useful grammatical term, which I here apply to mathematics to translate Augustine's *plus quam perfecti*. Curiosity led me to look for a list of perfect numbers; the *British Encyclopedia* was totally uninformative; but the *Oxford English Dictionary* quoted V. Mandey's *Syst. Math. Arith. 5* (1709-1728) as follows: "There are found but few Perfect Numbers: to wit from 1 to 40,000,000 only these: 6; 28; 496; 8128; 130,816; 2,096,128; 33,950,336." I note an interesting feature: that the final digit of all these numbers is alternately 6 and 8.

9. Augustine follows the Greek Septuagint in reading "the sixth day." Other ancient versions have the same, and are followed by some modern commentators, for example Bruce Vawter, *A Path through Genesis* (Sheed & Ward, London, 1957), p.46; the Catholic Biblical Association of America, *The Book of Genesis* (Confraternity of Christian Doctrine, Patterson NJ, 1948), p.4. Claus Westermann, however, *Genesis 1-11; a Commentary* (English translation, SPCK, London 1984) 78, and note 2a.80, keeps to the Massoretic Hebrew text, which has "the seventh day," and says in his note, a little dogmatically one may think: "[Ancient versions] read 'the 6th day'; even though this reading makes more sense, the Massoretic Text should not be altered." In this learned obscurantism he is followed by all current English versions, including the Jerusalem Bible and its French original—all except the gallant American Confraternity Version.

10. A triangle standing on its apex. The easiest way for ancients to work with numbers was to imagine them as dots arranged in geometrical patterns; we inherit this manner when we talk about the square of numbers. For them, at least for Augustine, keen on the mystical symbolism of numbers, the triangle of numbers was quite as important as the square or the cube. The

see, is followed by two and three in such a way that no other number can be inserted between them, and they are each and every one of them the parts of six that it consists of: one a sixth, two a third, three a half, so light was made on one day, the fabric of this universe on the two that followed, the upper part, that is the solid structure, on one, the lower part, that is sea and earth, on the next. He did not fill the upper part with any kind of bodily provender, because he was not going to place there any bodies needing sustenance of that sort; but the lower part, which he was going to furnish with animals suited to it, he enriched beforehand with the foods that would be necessary to supply their wants. So on the remaining three days were created those things which would visibly move around, powered by themselves and appropriate forces; first the lamps in the solid structure, because the solid structure had been made first, and next animals in the lower part, as due order required, those from the waters on one day, those from the land on the other.

And there can be none so out of their minds that they would have the face to say that God was unable to make all things in one day if he so wished, or if he so wished in two;[11] on one day the spiritual creation and on the other day the bodily, or on one day heaven and all its appurtenances, and on the other the earth with all the things that are on it; and in a word, when he wished and as long as he wished and in the way he wished—who would ever say that anything would have been able to resist his will?

All things in measure and number and weight

3, 7. For this reason, when we read that he perfected all things in six days, and find that six, when we take a look at it, is a perfect number, and that the order of creation runs its course in such a way as to show up even the graded distinction, so to say, of the parts by which this number is perfected, let us call to mind what is said to him in another place in scripture: *You have arranged all things in*

---

arithmetical triangle that gave him most pleasure was that of 17, which comes to 153, and so was used again and again in his sermons to interpret the great catch of 153 fish in Jn 21:11; see in this series, Vol.III,6, Sermon 229M, note 13; also Vol.III,7, Sermons 248,5; 249,3; 250,3; 251,5; 252A,6. The number 6, which is our concern here, is the sum of the triangle of 3—three dots on the base line, two on the next line, one at the apex. His most complex reflection on the mystical value of 6 is to be found in *The Trinity* IV,7-11, where he relates it to the number 46, Jn 2:20: *It has taken forty-six years to build this temple, and will you raise it up in three days? But he was speaking of the temple of his body.*

11. He is here anticipating what was in fact his preferred view, that God created all things on one day, and that the six days of Genesis 1 represent the serial playing over of the ideas of what he created, their *rationes* in the Word, to the spiritual or angelic intelligence, which we have already been observing. He finds support for this view in Sir 18:1: "He who lives forever created all things simultaneously"—*creavit omnia simul.*

measure and number and weight (Wis 11:20). And then, after calling upon God
to help by his inspiration and encouragement, let the soul which can do so think
about whether these three, measure, number, weight, in which, as it is written,
God has arranged all things, were somewhere or other before the whole natural
cosmos was created, or whether they too were created; and if they existed
beforehand, where were they? After all, before creation there was nothing
except the creator. Therefore they were in him. But how? I mean, we read that
these other things that have been created are also in him;[12] so are these three identical with him, while the others are in him by whom they are governed and
directed?

And how are these identical with him? God, after all, is neither measure nor
number nor weight, nor all of them together. Or rather, as we ordinarily understand measure in the things we measure, and number in the things we number or
count, and weight in the things we weigh, no, God is not these things; but insofar
as measure sets a limit to everything, and number gives everything its specific
form, and weight draws everything to rest and stability, he is the original, true
and unique measure which defines for all things their bounds, the number which
forms all things, the weight which guides all things; so are we to understand that
by the words *You have arranged all things in measure and number and weight*
nothing else was being said but "You have arranged all things in yourself"?

Measure is in God without measure, number without number, weight
without weight

8. It is a great thing, a concession granted to few, to soar beyond everything
that can be measured and see measure without measure, to soar beyond everything that can be numbered and see number without number, to soar beyond
everything that can be weighed and see weight without weight.

4. In fact, you see, measure and number and weight can be noticed and
thought about in other things besides stones and planks and similar masses of
material, and any other material objects, whether on earth or in the sky. There is
also a measured way of doing things, to avoid going too far by exceeding all
bounds and doing what cannot be undone; and there is a numbering of the spirit's
passions and powers, by which it is helped to pull itself together, pulling away
from the deformity of folly, and towards the form of wisdom; and there is a
weighing for the will and for love, which shows what should be weighed and for

---

12. For example, in Rom 11:36, in the Latin: *quoniam ex ipso et per ipsum et in ipso sunt omnia*;
"since from him and through him and in him are all things." For the last phrase the Greek has
"to him." But see also Col 1:16: "because in him were created all things in the heavens and on
the earth."

how much[13] in seeking or avoiding it, preferring or disregarding it. But this measure of spirits and minds is kept in bounds by another measure, this number formed by another number, and this weight drawn by the gravitational pull of another weight.

But the measure without measure is the standard for what derives from it, while it does not itself derive from anything else; the number without number, by which all things are formed, is not formed itself; the weight without weight to which are drawn, in order to rest there, those whose rest is pure joy is not itself drawn to anything else beyond it.

9. But if you only know the words "measure" and "number" and "weight" with reference to visible objects, you have a slave's knowledge of them.[14] So you should rise above everything you know in that way, or if you are not yet able to do so, at least do not cling to words which you can only think about in a mean and abject manner. These words, you see, will have all the richer a flavor for you as referring to higher things, the less you are mere flesh with reference to lower things.[15] But there are perhaps people who are trying to achieve serenity of mind and spirit by gazing on those sublime realities, and do not like applying to them words which they have learned to use in connection with feeble and worthless things; well, they are certainly not to be coerced into doing this. Provided, after all, that they understand what has to be understood, there is no need to worry very much about what it is called. It is, however, important to know what kind of likeness these lower things have to those higher realities. There is, you see, no other route along which reason can rightly direct its course and its efforts to move from here to there.[16]

---

13. Weighing in the ancient world also connoted pricing or valuing things. In this section he is co-ordinating the trio measure, number and weight, with another trio, whose translation is not always a simple matter: *modus, species, ordo.* He will be doing it again and again in this particular book of *The Literal Meaning of Genesis.* I usually translate them by "limit" or "bound," "form" or "specific form," and "order," for this latter sometimes substituting "direction," "guidance," and on one occasion "destiny." His most sustained discussion and explanation of this trio is in his little work, *On the Nature of the Good.* The most accessible modern discussion of them is to be found in Jim O'Donnell's Commentary on the *Confessions,* volume 2, 46 and the following, on *Confessions* I,1,12. Precisely what he meant a little earlier by "there is a numbering of the spirit's passions and powers" (*et est numerus et affectionum animi et virtutum*), I am rather at a loss to say.
14. You know them *serviliter,* in a servile fashion. He is making in effect a distinction like the conventional one he also often makes between servile fear and filial fear, the latter being precisely, in Latin, the fear of *liberi,* free-born children, for their father. He also doubtless had at the back of his mind Jesus' argument with "the Jews" in Jn 8:31-36, where he tells them that the truth will set them free, and they reply that they are the seed of Abraham and have never been slaves to anyone.
15. An untranslatable play on words: "these words will be all the more *cara* to you as referring to higher things, the less you are *caro* with reference to lower things."
16. Here in fact, while not coercing these very "spiritual" people, he is hinting broadly enough that their imageless spirituality is totally misconceived.

10. But now if anyone wishes to say that the measure and number and weight, in which according to the evidence of scripture God has arranged all things, have been created, then if he arranged all things in them, what did he arrange these three things in? If in some other things, then how did he arrange all things in them, when he arranged them in other things? So then there can be no doubt that these three in which all things were arranged were not themselves among the things that were arranged.

The idea of measure and number and weight, with reference to which all things were arranged, is there in God himself

5, 11. Or shall we perhaps assume that it says, *You arranged all things in measure and number and weight* (Wis 11:20), with the meaning of "You so arranged all things that they would have measure and number and weight"? Because if it said, "You have arranged bodies in colors," it would not also follow from this that the very Wisdom of God, *through whom all things were made* (Jn 1:3), was to be understood as having first had in herself the colors in which she would make bodies. No, this is how it would be taken: "You have arranged all bodies in colors," as much as to say, "You have so arranged all bodies that they would have colors"—as if, I ask you, all bodies could be understood to have been arranged by God the creator in colors, that is, so arranged that they should be colored, in any other way than by there being some idea in the very Wisdom of the one so arranging them of the colors to be distributed to every single kind of body, even if this idea was not there called color. That, you see, is what I was saying, that provided the reality is granted, there is no need to sweat about words.

12. So then, let us suppose for the sake of argument that it said, *You have arranged all things in measure and number and weight*, as though it meant that they were so arranged that they would have their own proper measures and their own proper numbers and their own proper weight, which would change in them in keeping with the character of each kind of thing, by growing and shrinking, increasing and diminishing in number, becoming lighter and heavier, in accordance with God's arrangements; does that mean that as these things change, we have to say God's plan is changeable in which he arranges them? May he himself ward off such madness!

6. So then,[17] since these things were so arranged that they would all have their own measures and numbers and weights, where did the one who was arranging them perceive them himself? Not outside himself, to be sure, as we perceive bodies with our eyes, since clearly they were not even there yet, when they were

---

17. This chapter heading in the Maurist edition seems totally superfluous; I keep it purely for reference—as indeed I infer the Maurists did themselves, after finding it in earlier editions. They put it in the middle of section 12, giving no number to the paragraph that follows.

being arranged for the making. Nor did he perceive them inside himself in the way that we perceive in our thoughts the appearances of bodies which are not there before our eyes, but which we form in our imaginations from what we see or have seen. So in what way did he perceive these things, so as to arrange them like that? In what way indeed, but that in which he alone is able to?

How we perceive the perfection of the number six

13. And yet we mortals and sinners, whose *souls are weighed down by perishable bodies, and whose thoughts, thinking of many things, are pressed down by this earthly dwelling* (Wis 9:15), though even if we had hearts of the purest and the most straightforward of minds, and were already *the equals of the holy angels* (Lk 20:36), we would not of course know the very substance of God in the way he knows it himself.

7. We too for our part do not perceive this perfection of the number six outside ourselves, as we do bodies with our eyes, nor inside ourselves either as we do the appearances of bodies and the images of visible things, but in an altogether different way. For although something like little material objects may thrust themselves before the eyes of the mind when the composition or the arrangement or the division of the number six is being thought about, still reason, prevailing over them more effectively from above, does not assent to them, and instead surveys a number's essential virtue from within. This survey enables it to say with absolute assurance that what is called "one" in the series of numbers cannot be divided into any parts, while there are no material bodies that cannot be divided into innumerable parts, and that it would be easier for heaven and earth to pass away,[18] constructed though they were in accordance with the number six, than to bring it about that the number six is not completed by its parts. And so the human spirit should always be giving thanks to its creator, by whom it was so created that it could see this which no soul of birds, no soul of beasts can see, though together with us nonetheless they see heaven and earth and the lamps of heaven and the sea and the dry land and all the things that are in them.

14. That is why we cannot say that the reason the number six is perfect is that God perfected all his works in six days, but rather that the reason God perfected his works in six days is that six is a perfect number. And so, even if none of these existed, it would still be perfect, while unless it were perfect these would not have been completed and perfected in accordance with it.

---

18. See Mt 5:18; Mk 13:31.

How God's resting on the seventh day is to be understood

8, 15. So now then we come to what is written about God resting on the seventh day from all his works which he had made, and his blessing and sanctifying this day precisely because he rested on it from all his works. But before we attempt as best we can, and to the extent that we are assisted by him, to reach that far with our understanding, we must first purge from our minds the materialistic ideas about this that people sometimes express. Is it right and lawful, I mean, to say or to think that God found his work hard going when he created the things that have been described above, when *he spoke and they were made* (Ps 148:5)? In that way, surely, not even human beings would find it hard going, if something were made the moment they said it was to be made. Yes, it is true that human words are uttered aloud by sounds in such a way that a long speech will tire one; still, when the words spoken are as few as we read, where it is written that God said "Let light be made, let a solid structure be made," and all the rest until the end of his works, which he finished on the sixth day, it would be the height of absurdity, utter nonsense, to think that this was hard, laborious toil even for a human being, let alone for God.

In what sense God is said to rest

16. Or would someone, perhaps, want to say that for God to say that things should be made, which then were made forthwith, was not hard, laborious toil for him, but possibly thinking about what ought to be made was, and it was on his mind being set at rest with the complete perfecting of things that God rested, and on that score that he blessed and sanctified the day on which his emotional tensions over this business were first relieved? But it is of course the height of folly to entertain such an idea,[19] seeing that God's faculties are as incomparably and inexpressibly sufficient for the creation of things as are his facilities.

9. So all that remains for us to understand, perhaps, is that he granted rest in himself to the rational creation in which he also created the man, after perfecting him through the gift of the Holy Spirit, *through which charity is poured out in our hearts* (Rom 5:5), so that we should be borne along by the impetus of desire to the place where we shall rest, the place, that is, where we shall look for nothing further, when we reach it. After all, just as God is rightly said to do whatever we do by his working in us, so God is rightly said to rest, when we rest thanks to his munificence.

---

19. Again an untranslatable play on words: *Quodsi haec sapere multum desipere est.* If we were discussing matters of taste, we could translate, "to show taste like that is to be utterly tasteless"; but when *sapere* and its opposite are referred, as they usually are, to ideas we cannot find suitable English equivalents.

17. We are indeed quite right to understand it in this way, because for one thing it is true, and for another it does not call for great perspicacity to see that God is said to rest when he makes us rest, just as he is said to come to know when he ensures that we come to know something. God, after all, does not come to know in time something he did not know previously, and yet he says to Abraham: *Now I have come to know that you fear God* (Gn 22:12), where we cannot take it to mean anything else, can we, but "Now I have made you come to know"? It is by these manners of speech, when we speak of things that do not happen to God as though they did, that we acknowledge it is he who makes them happen to us, those things at least that are praiseworthy, and these only to the extent that scriptural usage allows it. I mean, we certainly ought not to say anything of the sort about God, which we do not read in his scriptures.[20]

18. The apostle, I consider, was employing this manner of speech when he said: *Do not grieve the Holy Spirit of God, in whom you were sealed on the day of redemption* (Eph 4:30). It is impossible, after all, for the very substance of the Holy Spirit, by which he is whatever he is, to be grieved, since he is in possession of eternal and unalterable bliss, or rather is itself eternal and unalterable bliss. But because he dwells in the saints in such a way as to fill them with charity, by which as human beings they cannot but rejoice in time at the progress made by the faithful and at their good works, and by the same token cannot but be grieved at the lapsing and the sins of those over whose faith and piety they were rejoicing (such grief is praiseworthy, because it comes from the love which the Holy Spirit pours into them[21]), for this reason the Spirit himself is said to be grieved by those who act in such a way that the saints are grieved by their behavior, and this purely and simply because they have the Holy Spirit. It is his gift which makes them so good that the wicked sadden them, especially those whom they either knew or believed to be good. Not only is no fault to be found with such sadness, it is on the contrary to be most highly praised and commended.

19. The same apostle again made admirable use of this way of speaking, where he said: *But now, having come to know God, or rather being known by God* (Gal 4:9). It was not only then, after all, that God had come to know them, *foreknown* as they were *before the foundation of the world* (1 Pt 1:20); but it was only then that they had come to know him by his munificence, not by their own merits or abilities. He therefore preferred to use a figure of speech, and to say that they would then be known by God when he granted them the benefit of his coming to be known by them, and apparently to correct himself, as though what

---

20. See *The Trinity*, I,11,23, where he also reverses the principle, so to say, and uses it to explain that difficult text of Mk 13:32, where Jesus says that not even the Son knows the hour and the day; this means that he "makes others not know; that he did not know this in such a way as to disclose it to the disciples." Also see *The Trinity* III,11,25, in particular Augustine's own footnote there, where he enlarges a little on the point.

21. See Rom 5:5.

he had said quite strictly had not been said correctly—he preferred to do this rather than to allow them to claim that they had been able all by themselves to do what God had enabled them to do.

Whether God himself could properly be said to rest

10, 20. So then, this understanding of the matter may possibly satisfy some people—that what is put in the text here about God resting from all the works he had made, which were very good, means that he makes us rest when we have done good works. I for my part, however, having undertaken a thorough study of this passage of the scriptures, am constrained to inquire in what kind of way God too was able to rest, though certainly by mentioning his rest to us he was advising us to hope to find our final rest in him.

Now we have seen that he made heaven and earth and the things in them and that he finished them all on the sixth day. But it cannot be said that we created any of these things, with him giving us the ability to do so, and thus that the reason it said *God finished on the sixth day all his works which he had made* was that he authorized us to finish them. So too with what is said here: *God rested on the seventh day from all his works, which he had made*; it is not surely our rest, which we are going to enjoy when he grants it to us, but *his* rest that we ought first of all to understand here, *his* resting on the seventh day after finishing his works. What first has to be demonstrated about all the things that are written here is that they actually happened and were actually done, and only after that, if need be, should any lessons be drawn about their further significance.

It is certainly quite right to say that just as God rested after his good works, so we too are going to rest after our good works. But this is yet another reason why it is right to demand that just as we have discussed the works of God, which clearly enough were his works, so too we should reflect upon God's rest which is shown to be properly his.

How to reconcile God's resting on the seventh day with his "working until now," John 5:17

11, 21. So it is that we are forced by the most compelling of reasons to work out, if we are able to, and to state how each can be true: both what is written here that God rested on the seventh day from all his works which he had made, and what he himself through whom they were made says in the gospel: *My Father is working until now, and I myself am working* (Jn 5:17). That, you see, is the answer he gave to those who were complaining that he failed to observe the sabbath which had been enjoined on them of old on account of God's rest, on the authority of this text of scripture. And indeed it can credibly be said that the Jews were commanded to observe the sabbath as a shadow of what was to come,[22] to prefigure the spiritual rest which God was promising in a kind of secret code, on this model of his own rest, to the faithful doing their own good works. And the Lord Jesus Christ, who suffered only at the precise time he willed, also underlined the mystery of this rest by his burial. It was of course on the day of the sabbath that he rested in the tomb, and he had the whole of that day as a kind of holy vacation, after he had finished all his works on the sixth day, that is, Preparation Day,[23] which they call the sixth of the sabbath, when what had been written about him was fulfilled on the very gibbet of the cross. This in fact was the actual word he used when he said: *It is finished; and bowing his head he surrendered his spirit* (Jn 19:30).

So why should we be surprised if God wished to point forward to this day on which Christ would rest in the grave, and to this end rested from his works on one day, before proceeding from then on to work the unfolding of the ages, in order to verify these other words too: *My Father is working until now*?

Another way of reconciling God's resting with his continuous working

12, 22. God can also be understood to have rested from establishing different kinds of creatures, because he did not now establish any new kinds any more. But he rested like this in such a way as to continue from then on and up till now to operate the management of the things that were then set in place, not as though at least on that seventh day his power was withheld from the government of heaven and earth and of all the things he had established; if that had been done, they would forthwith have collapsed into nothingness. It is the creator's power, after all, and the virtuosity, the skill and tenacity of the almighty, that causes every created thing to subsist. If this tenacious virtuosity ceased for one moment to rule and direct the things that have been created, their various species would at once cease to exist, and every nature would collapse into nothingness. It is not, you see, like a mason building houses; when he has finished he goes away, and his work goes on standing when he has stopped working on it and gone away. No, the world will not be able to go on standing for a single moment, if God withdraws from it his controlling hand.

23. Indeed, the very expression employed by the Lord, *My Father is working until now*, points to the continuousness of his work, by which he holds together and manages the whole of creation. It could, you see, have been understood

---

22. See Heb 10:1.
23. He uses the word used in the Greek text, which was simply transliterated in the Latin versions, *parasceve*. My guess is that it was the usual word in Christian circles for what we call Good Friday. I was in fact tempted to translate "on the sixth day, that is, Good Friday." The key word to this passage is "finished"; God finished, *consummavit*, his works on the sixth day; Christ said on the cross, as he died on the sixth day of the week, "It is finished," *consummatum est*.

differently if he had said, "and is now working," where we would not have to take the work as being continuous. But by saying *until now,* he forces us to understand it in the other sense as meaning, that is, from the time when he had worked at the original establishment of all things. And then there is what is written about his Wisdom: *She reaches from end to end mightily, and arranges all things sweetly* (Wis 8:1), about whom it is also written that her movement is swifter and more nimble than all movements;[24] from this it is clear enough to those who look into the matter rightly that she bestows this incomparable and inexpressible and this—if you can grasp it—this motionless movement of hers upon things by disposing them sweetly, so that undoubtedly if this is withdrawn, and she abstains from this activity, they will perish forthwith.

And then there is what the apostle said when he was proclaiming God to the Athenians, that *in him we live and move and are* (Acts 17:28); interpreted straightforwardly, to the extent of the human mind's capacity, it will support this conviction which makes us believe and say that God is ceaselessly at work in these things which he has created. We are not in him, I mean to say, like his substance, in the way it is said that *he has life in himself* (Jn 5:26); but evidently, since we are something different from him, we are only in him because he is working at this, and this is his work by which he holds all things together, and by which his Wisdom *reaches from end to end mightily and arranges all things sweetly,* and it is by this arrangement that "in him we live and move and are." From this the conclusion follows that if he withdraws this work from things, we will neither live nor move nor be.

It is clear therefore that not for one single day did God cease from the work of controlling the things he had created, in case they should thereupon be deprived of the natural movements by which they are kept alive and active and so remain what they are, each in its own proper nature; they would indeed stop being anything at all, were that movement withdrawn from them of God's Wisdom, by which *she arranges all things sweetly.* For this reason we take it that God so rested from all his works which he had made that from now on he set up no new kind of nature any more, not so that he stopped holding together and directing the ones which he had already set in place. Thus both statements are true: that *God rested on the seventh day* (Gn 2:2), and that *he is working until now* (Jn 5:17).

On the observance of the sabbath, and the Christian sabbath

13, 24. And indeed we can already see his good works; it is only after our good works, however, that we shall see his rest. It was in order to represent and point to this rest that he commanded the Hebrew people to observe one day[25]—which

24. See Wis 7:24.
25. See Ex 20:8.

they did in so literal-minded, materialistic a way[26] that this was the day on which they found fault with the Lord our savior on seeing him working, and on which he gave them this splendid answer about the work of the Father, with whom he too was working equally, not only at the government of the whole created universe, but also at our salvation. Now however, in the time after the full revelation of grace, that observance of the sabbath, in the shape of leaving one day vacant or free from work, has been eliminated from the observances of the faithful.

What they do in fact observe in this present time of grace, those who work whatever good they work in the hope of a future rest and who do not boast about these good works of theirs as though they had any good which they had not received,[27] is a perpetual sabbath. They accept, you see, and understand the sacrament of baptism as if it were the day of the sabbath, the day, that is, of the Lord's inactivity in the tomb, and so they rest from their former works, and *walking now in newness of life* (Rom 6:4), they acknowledge that God is at work in them, who both works and rests simultaneously, both bestowing on his creation the management it requires and enjoying in himself an eternal tranquillity.

The question raised: why God only sanctified the day of his rest

14, 25. Finally, he himself neither grew tired when he created things, nor found it a relief when he stopped; but he wished through his scripture to urge upon us a desire for rest by intimating to us that he had sanctified the day on which he himself rested from all his works. At no time, I mean, during the six days in which all things were created is he said to have sanctified anything; nor before the six days themselves, where it is written, *In the beginning God made heaven and earth*, did it add, *and sanctified them*; but he wished to sanctify this day, on which he rested from all his works that he had made, as though with him also, who experiences not the slightest toil or trouble in his work, rest and quiet is worth more than any activity. The gospel indeed makes the same point for us in the case of human beings, where our savior says that because Mary, seated at his feet, was resting quietly in his word, hers was the better part rather than Martha's, although she out of the loyal devotion with which she was attending to his needs was busy with many things, and working what was indeed a good work.[28]

But how this may be even understood in God it is difficult to say in words, even if in thought one may be able to capture a faint idea of why God should have

---

26. In the Latin, simply *tam carnaliter*; in such a fleshly way.
27. See 1 Cor 4:7. What he means here by "a perpetual sabbath" is of course not that which is celebrated by the saints in the heavenly Jerusalem, as in Peter Abelard's splendid hymn, *O quanta qualia sunt illa sabbata*, but the Christian's everyday life lived in the innocence of baptismal grace.
28. See Lk:11:38-42.

sanctified the day of his rest, though he had not sanctified any day of his work, not even the sixth on which he both made the man and completed and perfected all the works together. And first of all what human mind is sharp enough to grasp what God's actual resting might consist in? But yet, unless it really did consist in something, scripture would certainly not have put this down here. Let me say plainly what my position is, with the preliminary assertion of these two indubitable truths: that God did not delight in some kind of temporal period of rest after hard toil and the much desired end of his business; and that it was not falsely or vainly that these scriptures, so deservedly surpassing all others in their authority, said that God rested on the seventh day from all the works which he had made, and for that reason sanctified this same day.

An answer proposed to the question just raised

15, 26. Now it is a vice and weakness of the soul to take delight in its works in such a way that it finds rest in them rather than in itself from them, though there can be no doubt that something in the soul by which they have been made[29] is better than the actual things that have been made. So it is evident then that God is being presented to us as a model by this scripture, which says that he rested from all his works which he had made, not taking delight in any of them in such a way as to suggest that he really needed to make it, and would either be somehow diminished if he had not made it, or be more blessed when he had. Anything, you see, that comes from him does so in such a way that it owes its being what it is to him, while he himself owes his being blessed to nothing that comes from him. For this reason he showed that in loving himself he preferred himself to the things he had made, by sanctifying, not the day on which he began to make them, nor the one on which he completed and perfected them, in case his joy should seem to have been increased by them whether in the making or the completion of them but the day on which he rested from them in himself.

And he himself, indeed, has never been without this rest, but he pointed it out to us through the seventh day; and by not deputing any day to represent his rest but the one which followed upon the completing and perfecting of all things, he also signified that this rest of his can only be attained by those who have been made perfect. In this way the one who is always quietly at rest actually took his rest in our eyes at the time when he showed us that he took it.[30]

---

29. The idea of them in the soul's intellect, the intention and decision to make them in its will.
30. Augustine discusses the meaning of the sabbath and God's resting on the seventh day in several of his sermons, usually in the context of the ten commandments; the commandment about keeping the sabbath holy was for him and his contemporaries the third, not the fourth commandment, and so he delights in associating it with the Holy Spirit, the Sanctifier. See Sermons 8,17 and 9,6 (III,1 in this series); 33,3 (III,2); and 270,5 (III,7). In none of these, however, does he voice the interesting idea of Jesus keeping the sabbath rest as he lay in the tomb, after "finishing his work" on the cross.

God's resting on the seventh day means he stands in need of no other good

16, 27. This point too is to be noted, that God's resting by finding bliss in himself ought to suggest to us the right way to understand how he is also said to find rest in us; he is only said to do so when he bestows on us rest in himself. God's rest therefore, to those who understand it correctly, means his being in need of no one else's good; and for this reason his resting in us is certainly in himself, because we too find bliss in the good which he is, not he in the good which we are. To be sure, we too are something good, deriving our being so from him who made all things very good, ourselves included. Accordingly, besides him there is no other thing that is good which he himself did not make; and thus he stands in need of no other good besides himself, seeing that he does not need the good which he made. This is his resting from all his works, which he made.

But what good things could he thus creditably not have needed, if he had not made any? Because in this way too, you see, he could be said not to be in need of any good things, not just by resting in himself from what had been made, but quite simply by not making any. But if he was unable to make good things, it would be a failure of power, while if he was able to and yet did not, it would be a serious case of envy. So then, because he is both omnipotent and good, he made all things very good, while because he finds perfect bliss in the good which he is himself, he rested in himself from all that he had made—with the rest, of course, which he had never ceased to enjoy. But were he actually said to have rested from making things, this would inevitably be understood to mean that he did not make any, while unless he were said to have rested from what had been made, he would not be so clearly shown to be in no need of the things he made.

28. And so on what better day than the seventh could this properly have been brought to our attention? If you understand the perfection of the number six, about which we have spoken above, you will recollect that it was suitably applied to the perfecting of creation. Now if creation was to be perfected in the number six, as in fact it was, and that resting of God was to be brought to our attention as demonstrating that he did not need even perfect creatures to make him blessed, then obviously the day to be sanctified by making this point was the one that follows the sixth, the one on which we were to be aroused to long for this rest, so that we too might find rest in it.

Our rest is to be found in God

17, 29. Nor would we be making a just and loyal comparison, if we wished to be like God in such a way, that exactly as he rested from his works in himself, so we too should rest from our works in ourselves. What we are meant to rest in, surely, is a certain unchangeable good, which is what the one who made us is for us. This therefore will be our supreme rest, wholly without pride and truly religious, that just as he rested from all his works, because he himself, not his works, is the good in which he finds bliss, so we too should be spurred on by the hope of resting one day in that same good, not only from our works but also from his, and should desire to reach it after our good works, which we acknowledge to be his in us rather than our very own. In this way he again will be resting after his good works, when he grants us rest in himself after the good works which we have done, thanks to our having been justified by him.[31] While it is indeed a great thing for us to have derived our very being from him, it will, you see, be an even greater thing for us to have attained our rest in him, just as the reason he himself is in bliss is not because he made all these things, but because being in no need of them even when made, he found rest in himself rather than in them. So that is why he sanctified the day not of work but of rest, intimating in this way that it was not in his making but in his not needing the things he had made that his blessedness and bliss consisted.

30. So what, then, is such a lowly and easy statement to make, and what such an exalted and arduous truth to reflect upon, as God resting from all his works which he had made? And resting where, if not in himself, because only in himself does he find blessedness and bliss? When, if not always? While among the days during which the finished consummation of the things he established is recounted and the special status of God's rest is distinguished from them, on which if not on the seventh day which follows on the completion and perfecting of them all? It is from perfect things, you see, that he rests, needing not even perfected products to make him more blessed and blissful than he is.

Why the seventh day had a morning but no evening

18, 31. And with him indeed his rest has neither morning nor evening, because it does not open with a beginning nor close with an end; but with the perfecting of his works it has a morning and does not have an evening.[32] This means that the perfected creation has in fact a kind of start to its turning towards the quiet rest of its creator, while this has no end as a kind of term to its being perfect, like the things that have been made. And thus God's rest begins, not for God himself, but for the perfect completion of the things he has fashioned, so that what is being perfected by him may begin to rest in him, and therein have its morning—in its own specific nature, you see, it was given its finishing touches as if in the

---

31. See Rom 8:30.
32. He does not say precisely what has a morning and no evening. The whole sentence (which I have divided into two sentences) is rather incoherently written. This illustrates very well what he said at the beginning of section 30 about how arduous it is to reflect on this whole matter. He was dictating as he was thinking the matter out, groping in his mind for what he wished to say, feeling his way toward it.

evening—but in God it cannot now have any evening, because there will not be anything more perfect than that perfection.

32. In those days, you will remember, on which all things were being created, we took evening to represent the finishing post for the creature that had been fashioned, and morning the starting post for the one to be fashioned next. And thus the evening of the fifth day is the finishing post for the creature fashioned on the fifth day, while the morning which was made after that evening is the starting post for the creature to be fashioned on the sixth day; and when that had been fashioned there was made evening as its finishing post. And because nothing else remained to be fashioned, there was made morning after that evening in such a way that it would not be the starting post for fashioning another creature, but the start of quiet rest for the universal creation in the quiet rest of the creator.

Not even heaven and earth, you see, and all that is in them, not even, that is, the totality of the spiritual and bodily creation abides in itself, but clearly in him of whom it is said, *In him we live and move and are* (Acts 17:28), because even if each part can be in the whole it is a part of, the whole itself, all the same, is in him by whom it was fashioned. And for that reason it is to be understood that on the completion of the sixth day there was no absurdity in morning being made after its evening, not to indicate the start of the fashioning of another creature as on the other days, but to indicate, for the whole of what had been fashioned, the start of its abiding and resting in the quiet rest of the one who fashioned it. This is a quiet rest which for God has neither start nor finish, while for creation it has a starting point but no finishing point. And that is why the seventh day begins for this creation with a morning, but does not terminate in any evening.

33. Now if evening and morning on the other days signify alternations of times such as now occur in the period of every day, I cannot see what should have stopped an evening closing the seventh day and a morning ending its night, so that it would have said, "And there was made evening and there was made morning, a seventh day." After all it too is one of the days which make up the seven, by whose regular repetition the months and years and ages run their course. So the morning which would be placed there after the evening of the seventh day would be the start of the eighth. About this from now on it had to keep quiet, because it is the same as the first, to which we all come back, and in this way the weekly series continues to unroll.

So it is altogether more probable that these seven-day periods follow one another under the names and number of those first seven, and thus unfurl their sails to run before the wind of time,[33] while those first six days were unfolded, in a manner quite beyond what we are used to in our experience, with the original

---

33. Again, the translator's metaphor, enlarging on Augustine's paler (perhaps more sober and restrained), *sibimet succedentes currendo temporalia peragere spatia*; "following one another lay out by running the spaces of time."

fashioning of things, so that in them neither evening nor morning, neither light itself nor darkness, presented the same alternations as they do in these days through the circling round of the sun. This is something we are obliged to admit at least for those three days which were mentioned and counted before the fashioning of the lamps in the sky.

34. And thus, whatever kind of evening and morning there may have been in those six days, in no way at least can the opinion be upheld that on the morning which was made after the evening of the sixth day God's rest was started off—we would be rashly and in fact nonsensically supposing in that case that some temporal good could accrue to that eternity, that unchangeable simplicity. No indeed, but on the contrary that quiet rest of God, by which he finds rest in himself and bliss in the good which he is for himself, neither starts for him nor terminates, while for the creation that has been finished and completed the same quiet rest of God does have a starting point. This is because the perfection of every single thing is established, according to the limited measure appropriate to it, not so much in the whole of which it is a part as in him from whom it derives, like the whole itself, its very being; and only there may it finally come to rest, may it attain, that is, the goal of its own momentum.

And thus the whole universe of creation, which was finished in six days, has one terminus in its own nature, another in the goal which it has in God; this, not like God himself, but still in such a way that it can come to no stable and properly established rest, except in the quiet rest of the one who does not have to make any effort to get anything beyond himself in order to find rest in it. And for this reason, while God abides in himself, he swings everything whatever that comes from him back to himself, like a boomerang,[34] so that every creature might find in him the final terminus and goal for its nature, not to be what he is, but to find in him the place of rest in which to preserve what by nature it is in itself. I know that I have not used the word "place" properly, its proper use being to refer to spaces occupied by bodies. But such bodies too only remain in a place when they reach it by the effort, as it were, of their own weight, in order to rest there once they have gained it; and for this reason we can not unsuitably transfer the word from bodily to spiritual matters, and talk about "place" there also, though the reality itself is totally different.

35. So then, what that morning that was made after the evening of the sixth day represents is, in my judgment, the start of creation's sharing in the quiet rest of the creator; after all it could not rest in him unless it had been perfected. Accordingly, when all things had been finished on the sixth day and evening had been made, there was also made the morning on which the finished creation would begin to rest in him by whom it had been made. At this start it found him resting in himself, the very place where it too could find rest, and stay in it all the

---

34. A comparison not actually found in the original Latin.

more immovably and securely, the more it needed him, not he it, to ensure its quiet repose. But since what the whole created universe is going to be, whatever mutations it has gone through, will certainly not be nothing, the whole created universe will, for that reason, always abide in its creator; and thus after that morning there was not next any evening.

36. I have said all this to show why the seventh day, on which God rested from all his works, had a morning after the evening of the sixth day, but had no evening itself.

Another explanation of why the seventh day had a morning without an evening

19. There is another thing which by my reckoning can be better and more appropriately understood about this point, but which is rather more difficult to explain; and that is that it was not only for creation but for God himself that his resting on the seventh day had a morning without an evening, that is, a start without a finish. If it had said, you see, "God rested on the seventh day" without adding "from all his works which he had made," it would be pointless for us to be looking for a start to this rest, seeing that God, whose quiet rest is eternal, without start, without finish, does not begin to rest. But since it was in not needing them that he rested from all his works which he had made, one does indeed understand God's rest as neither begun nor terminated; but his rest "from all his works which he had made" began from the moment in which he perfected and completed them. Before his works existed, after all, he would not have rested by not needing what he did not need even when they were perfected. And because there has been absolutely no time when he ever did need them, this blessedness and bliss by which he does not need them will not be brought to perfection by making progress, and that is why no evening was attached to the seventh day.

Whether the seventh day was created

20, 37. But the question can certainly be asked, and it calls for proper consideration, how God may be understood to have rested in himself from all his works which he had made, seeing that the text says, *And God rested in the seventh day* (Gn 2:2); it did not say, you see, "in himself," but *in the seventh day*. So what, then, is the seventh day? Is it some kind of creature, or just a period of time? But even periods of time were "co-created"[35] together with time-bound creatures,

---

35. From a verb, *concreo*, which may have been coined by Augustine; the earliest references given by Albert Blaise, *Dictionnaire Latin-Français des Auteurs Chrétiens* (Strasbourg, 1954), are all to works of Augustine. Here we have the past participle, *concreatum*—"periods of time" are in the singular in the Latin.

and thus they too are undoubtedly creatures; nor in fact are there any times, nor could there have been nor can there be, of which God is not the creator. And thus this seventh day also, if it is a time—who can have created it but the creator of all times? But as for those six other days, the previous text of holy scripture indicates with which or in which creatures they were created. For this reason, of these seven days which we are familiar with, which indeed pass away but somehow hand on their names to the ones that follow them, for the naming of six we know when the first six were created; as regards the seventh day, however, which is known by the name of the sabbath, we do not see when God created it. He did not make anything, I mean to say, on that day; on the contrary, on this seventh day he rested from what he had made in six days. So how then did he rest on a day which he had not created? Or how did he create it immediately after the six days, seeing that he finished on the sixth day all the things he had created, and did not create anything on the seventh day, but rather rested on it from all the things he had created?

Or did God perhaps create only one day, the repetition of which would cause many so-called days to pass and to run across the screen,[36] so that there was no need to create the seventh day, because it was made, naturally, by the seventh repetition of this one day? The light, in fact, about which it is written, *And God said: Let light be made, and light was made* (Gn 1:3), he distinguished from the darkness and called it day, and the darkness he called night. And so that was when God made the day, whose repetition scripture calls the second day, and then the third and so on up to the sixth, on which God finished his works; and consequently the seventh repetition of that originally created day received the name of the seventh day, on which God rested. And thus the seventh day is not a creature on its own, but the same one coming round seven times, the one which was fashioned when God called the light day and the darkness night.

On the light that preceded the lamps in the sky, and on the alternation of day and night

21, 38. Once again, therefore, we find ourselves slipping back into the same problem, from which we seemed to have extricated ourselves in the first book,[37]

---

36. Augustine of course says nothing about a screen, being unfamiliar at that time with either cinema or television or computer. But all the same, the image is extremely apt for his thought, because as we have seen already, and will shortly find repeated in some detail, it was indeed his view that God created everything in one day—indeed instantaneously—and that the narrative of the six days of creation (and the seventh day of rest) tells of a kind of serial projection of the basic elements of the divine work onto the screen of the intelligence of the spiritual creation; in more traditional terms, tells of the serial impression upon that spiritual intelligence of the eternal ideas of his works contained in his eternal Word.

37. See I,4,9—5,11; 10,19-22; 14,28-30; 17,32-35.

and having to ask again how light could circulate to produce the alternations of day and night, not only before the lamps of heaven but even before heaven itself, called the solid structure, was made; before finally there was any specific form of earth or sea, round which the light would circulate, with night following when it had passed along. Driven on by the difficulty of this problem, we ventured to decide at the end of our discussion that we should say the light created originally is the forming and shaping of the spiritual creation, while the night is the material of things still to be formed and shaped in the remaining works, material that had been laid down when in the beginning God made heaven and earth, before he made the day by a word.

But now at this stage we have been forcibly reminded by our reflection on the seventh day that the easy and sensible thing to do is to admit our ignorance about what is so remote from any experience of ours, and say that we simply do not know how that light which was called day, if it means bodily light, affected the alternations of night and day whether by its circulation or by contraction and emission; or how, if it is spiritual, it was made present to the fashioning of all creatures, and by its presence made day, by its absence night, evening at the start of its absence, morning at the start of its presence. Much rather this, than that we should pit our strength in a matter that is plain as daylight against the words of divine scripture, and say that the seventh day is something different from the seventh repetition of that day which God made. If that is the case, you see, either God did not create the seventh day, or else he created something after those six days, that is, the seventh day itself; and so what is written will be untrue, that on the sixth day he finished all his works and on the seventh rested from all his works. But of course this cannot be untrue; and so it remains that the presence of that light, the day which God made, was repeated through all his works, as often as a day was mentioned, and again on the seventh day on which he rested from his works.

How spiritual light may be understood to have manifested the alternation of day and night

22, 39. But we did not find out by what kind of circulation, or advance and retreat, bodily light could display the changes of night and day before the heaven was made which is called the solid structure, in which the lamps in the sky were also made; so we ought not to leave this question without some statement of our own considered judgment, that that light which was first created is a spiritual, not a bodily light, and that just as it was made after darkness,[38] by which one understands that it turned from its own formlessness towards the creator and thus was formed, so too, after evening, morning was made, meaning that after

---

38. The darkness that was over the abyss. Gn 1:2.

acknowledgment of its own proper nature, of its not being what God is, it goes back to praising the light which God himself is, and by which it is formed as it gazes upon it. And because the other creatures which are made below it are not made without its knowledge, that surely is why the same day is repeated every time, so that by its repetition as many days may be made as there are distinct kinds of things created, to be brought to an end with the perfection of the number six.

Thus the evening of the first day is also its self-knowledge, that it is not what God is; while the morning after that evening, which marks the conclusion of the one day and the beginning of the second, means its turning to refer what it was created as to the praise of the creator, and to receive from the Word of God knowledge of the creature which is made after itself, that is, of the solid structure. This happens first in its knowledge, when the text says, *And thus it was made* (Gn 1:6); and then in the actual solid structure itself, when after "and thus it was made," the text goes on to add, *And God made a solid structure* (Gn 1:7). Then comes the evening of that light, when it knows the solid structure, not in the Word of God as before, but in its own nature; this being a lesser degree of knowledge, it is rightly known by the name of "evening."

After this there is made morning, which concludes the second day and starts off the third; this morning again marks the conversion of this light in the same way, that is, the turning of this day to the praise of God for his work of making the solid structure, and to its reception from his Word of knowledge of the creature to be fashioned after the solid structure. And thus when God says, *Let the water which is under the heavens be collected together into one collection, and let the dry land appear* (Gn 1:9), that light knows this in the Word of God, by which the utterance is made; and that is why it continues, *And thus it was made*, that is, in its own knowledge derived from the Word of God; next, when it adds, *and the water was collected together, etc.*, after already saying *and thus it was made*, the creature itself is made in its own specific kind; and when it is again known in its own specific kind by that light, which had already known in the Word of God that it was to be made, there is made evening for the third time; and in this manner from then on until the morning after the evening of the sixth day.

Angelic knowledge of things in the Word of God, and in the things themselves

23, 40. There is, of course, a very great difference between knowledge of a thing, whatever it may be, in the Word of God and knowledge of it in its own specific nature. The former rightly belongs to the day, the latter to the evening, since in comparison with that light that is to be contemplated in the Word of God, all knowledge by which we know any creature at all in itself can be called, not in the least improperly, night. This in its turn differs so much from the error or ignorance of those who do not even know the creature in itself, that in comparison with that it can be called, not unsuitably, day.

It is like the life the faithful lead in this flesh and this world; in comparison with the life of unbelievers and godless people it is not unreasonably classified as light and day, with the apostle saying: *You were once darkness, but now light in the Lord* (Eph 5:8); and again: *Let us cast away the works of darkness, and clothe ourselves in the armor of light; let us walk honorably, as in the day* (Rom 13:12-13). On the other hand, unless this day, again in comparison with that day in which after being made *equal to the angels* (Lk 20:36) we shall see God as he is, were itself also night, we would not need here the lamp of prophecy, about which the apostle Peter says: *We have the more certain prophetic word, to which you do well to pay attention, as to a lamp shining in a dark place, until the day dawns, and the morning star rises in your hearts* (2 Pt 1:19).

The knowledge of the angels

24, 41. For this reason, since the holy angels with whom we shall be equated after the resurrection, if we keep to the way (which Christ has become for us, right to the end), always see the face of God, and enjoy the Word of God, his only-begotten Son in his equality with the Father, and since in them wisdom was created as the first of all things,[39] there can be no doubt that they have first come to know the universal creation, in which they themselves were the first to be established, in the Word of God himself, in whom are the eternal ideas[40] even of things which were made in time, as in the one *through whom all things were made* (Jn 1:3). Only after that do they know creation in itself, by glancing down below, as it were, and then referring it to the praise of the one in whose unchangeable Truth they originally see the ideas according to which it was made.

So then they see it there as it were in daylight, which is why their wonderfully harmonious unity by sharing in that truth is the day that was originally created, while here they see it as if in the evening twilight; but then straightaway morning is made (this can be observed in all six days) because angelic knowledge does not linger in what has been created without straightaway referring it to the praise and love of the one in whom it is known, not as already made but as due to be made; by staying in this Truth it is day. I mean, if the angelic nature were to turn

---

39. An allusion to Prv 8:22, which in Augustine's version, taken from the Greek Septuagint, has Wisdom saying, *The Lord created me in the beginning of his ways.* This was a real crux for the Church Fathers, who in accordance with the constant tradition, derived from the scriptures, identified Wisdom with the Son, the Word; so how could she say she was created? Here Augustine is implicitly solving the problem by saying she is "created" in the created impression she stamps on the angelic intellect.
40. *Rationes* in the Latin.

to itself, and to take greater pleasure in itself than in the one it is made blessed by sharing in, it would swell with pride and fall, as the devil did—about whom we must talk in his proper place, when a discussion of the serpent leading the man astray will be required of us.

Why night is not mentioned again during each of the six days

25, 42. So then, the angels know the creature in itself in such a way that by free and love-inspired choice[41] they prefer to that knowledge their knowing the creature in the truth through which all things were made, in which they have been given a share. And that is why night is not mentioned throughout all the six days; but we have "after evening and morning one day," likewise "after evening and morning the second day," next "after evening and morning the third day," and so on right up to the morning of the sixth day in which the seventh day of God's rest begins. The days do include their nights, but still it is the days not the nights that we are told about. For then it is, you see, that night belongs to day, not day to night, when the sublime and holy angels refer their knowledge of the creature in itself to the honor and love of him in whom they contemplate the eternal ideas according to which things were created, and in that wonderfully harmonious contemplation are themselves the one *day which the Lord has made*; to this may the Church be joined once it has been delivered from "its sojourn in this vale of tears,"[42] so that we too may *exult and be merry in it* (Ps 118:24).

Repeated explanation of what the repetition of the one day made by God really means

26, 43. So then, by the sixth repetition of this day, the evening and morning of which can be understood on the lines set out above, the whole created universe was completed and finished, and there was made the morning on which the sixth day would end, and from which the seventh would begin which was not going to have an evening, because God's rest is not a part of creation. When this was being fashioned in the course of the other days, in itself as already made it was known differently from the way it was known in him in whose Truth it was seen as due to be made; and it was this knowledge of it in itself, like the sight of things drained of color, that made the evening.

And so in this account of the creation of things the day is not to be understood as the form of the actual work, nor the evening as its termination and the morning

---

41. A more telling expression in the Latin: *electione ac dilectione*.
42. The Latin just has "from this sojourn," *ex hac peregrinatione*; but this, I think, requires the slight expansion I give it, echoing a phrase from the well-known hymn to Our Lady, "Hail Queen of heav'n, the ocean star," to mean anything to English readers.

as the start of another work, or we would be compelled to say against scripture either that the seventh day was fashioned as a creature outside the six days, or else that the seventh day was not itself something created. Instead, that "day which God has made" is itself repeated through his works, not in a bodily circular motion but in spiritual knowledge, when that blessed company of angels before anything else contemplates in the Word of God that about which God says *Let it be made*; and in consequence this is first made in their own angelic knowledge when the text says, *And thus it was made*, and only after that do they know the actual thing made in itself, which is signified by the making of evening. They then refer this knowledge of the thing made to the praise of that Truth where they had seen the idea of making it, and this is signified by the making of morning.

And thus throughout all those days there is just the one day, which is not to be understood after the manner of these days that we see measured and counted by the circuit of the sun, but in a different kind of mode which has to allow for those three days that were mentioned before the fashioning of these lamps in the sky. This mode, you see, does not just operate as far as the fourth day, so that from then on we should be thinking of these usual ones, but right up to the sixth and seventh. Hence the night and day, between which two *God divided* (Gn 1:4), are to be taken in quite a different sense from this night and day, between which he said that the lamps he created were to divide, when he said, *And let them divide between day and night* (Gn 1:14). That, you see, was when he established this kind of day, when he fashioned the sun, which brings on this day by its presence, while that day which was fashioned originally had already gone through three days when these lamps were created on that day's fourth repetition.

The ordinary days of the week are quite unlike the seven days of Genesis

27, 44. Now clearly, in this earth-bound condition of ours we mortals can have no experiential perception of that day, or those days which were named and numbered by the repetition of it; and if we are able to struggle towards some understanding of them, we certainly ought not to rush into the assertion of any ill-considered theory about them, as if none more apt or likely could be mooted. So for the sake of argument, let us suppose that these seven days, which in their stead constitute the week that whirls times and seasons along by its constant recurrence, in which one day is the whole circuit of the sun from sunrise to sunrise—that these seven represent those first seven in some fashion, though we must be in no doubt that they are not at all like them, but very, very dissimilar.

Treating the light and day as spiritual realities is not a metaphorical interpretation

28, 45. And please let nobody assume that what I have said about spiritual light and about the day being constituted in the spiritual and angelic creation, and about what it contemplates in the Word of God, and about the knowledge by which the creature is known in itself and its being referred to the praise of unchangeable Truth, where first the idea was seen of the thing to be made, which once made was known in itself: that none of this can be said strictly and properly, but that it all belongs to a kind of figurative and allegorical understanding of day and evening and morning. Certainly it is different from our usual way of talking about this bodily light of every day, but that does not mean that here we have the strict and proper, there just a metaphorical, use of these terms.

After all, where you have a better and surer light, there you also have a truer day; so why not both a truer evening and a truer morning? In these familiar days the light knows a kind of decline towards sunset, to which we give the name of evening, and again a return towards sunrise, which we call morning; so why should we not call it evening there, when there is a turning from the contemplation of the creator to look down at the creature, and morning when there is a looking up again from knowledge of the creature to the praise of the creator? Not even Christ, you see, is called light in the same way as he is called a stone;[43] no, he is called the first properly and strictly, the second of course metaphorically.

So then, if anybody is not satisfied with the line which I have been able in my small measure to explore or to trace, but requires another theory about the numbering of those days, by which they may be better understood, not as prophetic types and figures, but as a strict and proper account of the way the foundations of this creation were laid, then by all means let him look for one and with God's help find one. I am certainly not insisting on this one in such a way as to contend that nothing else preferable can be found, while I do insist that holy scripture did not intend to suggest to us that God rested as if he were tired out, or racked with anxiety and worry.

Day, evening, and morning in the knowledge of the angels

29, 46. Accordingly, someone may perhaps wish to take me up and argue that the angels of the loftiest heavens do not successively gaze, first upon the ideas of creatures which are there unchanging in the unchangeable truth of the Word of God, and next upon the creatures themselves, and thirdly refer their own knowledge of them to the praise of the creator, but that their minds have the marvelous

---

43. For "light" see Jn 1:4.8; 8:12; 9:5; 12:46; Mt 4:16; Lk 2:32; for "stone" see Mt 21:42; Acts 4:11; 1 Pt 2:4-8.

facility of being able to do all three things at once. All the same, they will surely not say—or if anyone does, we should certainly not pay any attention—that those thousands of angel citizens of the heavenly city[44] either do not contemplate the eternity of the creator, or are unaware of the mutability of creatures, or are not prompted also by that lower kind of knowledge of theirs to praise the creator. Granted, they may be able to do all this simultaneously; let them do it all simultaneously. Then they can and they do; so then they simultaneously have day and evening and morning in themselves all together.

30, 47. Nor, I presume, is it to be feared that anyone already capable of reflecting on these matters should think this cannot happen in that sphere, on the grounds that it cannot happen with these days which are produced by the circuit of the sun. True, this cannot happen in one and the same part of the earth; but anyone surely can see, if they stop and think for a moment, that the world as a whole simultaneously has day where the sun is, and night where it is not, and evening where it is sinking, and morning where it is rising. We of course in our various countries cannot have all of them simultaneously; but that is no reason why we should equate this state of things on earth and the circling around of bodily light in time and space with that spiritual home country, where it is always day in the contemplation of unchangeable Truth, and always evening in the knowledge of creatures in themselves, always morning in praising the creator for this knowledge too.

That kind of evening, after all, is not caused by the withdrawal of light from up above but by the differentiation of knowledge acquired down below; nor does that kind of morning mean early knowledge dawning after a night of ignorance, but the raising up of evening knowledge also to the glory of the creator. Finally, without even naming night, the psalmist says, *At evening and morning and noon I will declare and proclaim; and you will hear my voice* (Ps 55:17), meaning maybe through successive times here, but still signifying, as I see it, what would be done without any succession of times in the home country, for which he was yearning and sighing in his exile.

More about the order of day, evening, and morning in the angelic knowledge of things

31, 48. But granted that this angelic company, this unity of the one day which God originally fashioned, performs all these intellectual acts simultaneously now, did it also do this simultaneously then, at the time it was all being created? Surely throughout those six days, when the things which it pleased God to fashion in them one by one were being fashioned, this spiritual day first received

---

44. See Heb 12:22.

them in the Word of God, so that they would be made first in its own knowledge where scripture says, *And thus it was made*; next, after they had been made in their own proper nature to be what they are, and had pleased God because they are good, it got to know them once more with another, lower kind of knowledge, which is signified by the name of "evening;" and then "there was made evening and morning," when God would be praised for his work, and knowledge of another creature, which was to be made next, was received from the Word of God before it actually was made. So they were not then all simultaneous, day and evening and morning, but one after the other, in the order mentioned by scripture.

32, 49. Or were they all happening simultaneously even then, since there was no question of intervals of time such as these days mark, when the sun rises and sets and goes back to its place to rise again, but it was a matter of the spiritual power of the angelic mind, comprehending all that it wished in a simultaneous knowledge with the utmost facility—even so, not thereby without any orderly linking of preceding and following causes? Knowledge, after all, cannot arise unless it is preceded by objects to be known; and these again are first in *the Word through which all things were made* (Jn 1:3), before they are in all the things that have been made.

And so the human mind first experiences through the senses of the body the things that have been made, and from there gains such knowledge of them as its human weakness allows; and next it looks for their causes, if by any manner of means it may attain them where they abide primordially and unchangingly in the Word of God, and may thus come to *an understanding of his invisible things through those that have been made* (Rom 1:20). Is anyone unaware of how slow and dull the mind is at doing this, how difficult it finds it, and what a long time it takes, on account of *the perishable body which weighs down the soul* (Wis 9:15)—this, even when it is being hurried along by its fervent and eager desire to persevere in pressing on to this goal?

The angelic mind, on the other hand, adhered in unalloyed charity to the Word of God, after being created in due order before all the rest, and so it first saw in the Word of God the things to be made before they were made; and thus before being made in their own proper nature, they were first made in the knowledge of that mind, when God said, "Let them be made." Once they were made like that, it also came to know them in themselves, with an inferior kind of knowledge of course, which was called evening. This knowledge was naturally preceded by the things that were made, because whatever can be known is there before knowledge of it; unless what is to be known is there first, after all, it cannot be known.

After that, if the angelic mind were to be pleased with its own knowledge in such a way that it took more delight in itself than in its creator, no morning would be made—that is, it would not rise up from its knowledge to the praise of the creator. When, however, this was done, there was something else to be made and known, with God saying, *Let it be made*, so that once again it would be made in the knowledge of the angelic mind, and again scripture could say, *And thus it was made*; then after that in its own proper nature, in which it would be known with the evening that followed.

50. And so it is, that even if here we do not have things happening at intervals, one at a time, nonetheless the idea of a creature to be fashioned came first in the Word of God, when he said, *Let light be made*; and then light itself followed, in which the angelic mind was formed, and made in its own nature. But it did not follow in such a way as to be made somewhere else; and that is why scripture did not first say, *And thus it was made*, and then go on to say, "And God made the light." But the light was made immediately after the divine utterance, and the created light adhered to the creating light, seeing itself in it, that is, seeing the idea according to which it was made. But it also saw itself in itself, that is, as being quite different, because made, from the one who made it. And that is why, after God had seen what had been made and been pleased with it because it was good, and light had been divided from darkness and light had been called day and darkness night, then evening also was made. This, because such knowledge too was necessary, to distinguish from the creator the creature known differently in itself from the way it was known in him; and then morning and something else to be foreknown, which was to be made by the Word of God, first in the knowledge of the angelic mind, next in the actual nature of the solid structure.

And that is why scripture has, *God said: Let a solid structure be made*, and then goes on, *And thus it was made*, in the knowledge of the spiritual creation foreknowing it before it was made in itself. Next *God made a solid structure*, now of course the solid structure in its own nature, of which there would be a lesser, as it were evening, knowledge. And so on, right up to the end of all the works and up to God's resting, which has no evening because it was not made like a creature, with the possibility of knowledge of it being reduplicated, the first and major kind in the Word of God as in the day, the subsequent and minor kind in itself as in the evening.

Whether all things were created simultaneously, or one by one during the six days

33, 51. But if the angelic mind is able to grasp all the things simultaneously, which the text puts one after the other in an ordered chain of causes, does that mean that the things which were being made were all made simultaneously, like the solid structure, like the collection of waters and the appearance of bare lands, like the shooting up of shrubs and trees, the arranging of the great lights and stars, the aquatic and terrestrial animals, and not rather made one after the other at intervals according to the predetermined days? Or perhaps we ought not to think that when they were originally set up they were governed by the same natural motions as we now observe, but rather were fashioned according to the wonderful and inexpressible virtuosity of the Wisdom of God, *who reaches from end to end mightily, and disposes all things sweetly* (Wis 8:1). She, after all, does not reach there by steps, or arrive as if by pacing out the distance.

Accordingly, God fashioned all things with the same ease as she moves with so effectively, because it was through her that they were fashioned, so that the time-measured movements with which we now see them act and acted upon, each according to its own specific nature, come to them from those implanted formulae or ideas[45] which God so to say scattered like seed in the very moment of fashioning them, when *he spoke and they were made; gave orders, and they were created* (Ps 33:9).

52. And so things that move slowly were not set up slowly in order to be slow moving, nor did the fashioning of the ages take the time that they themselves do to run their course. Times, you see, and seasons dance to the measures[46] which they received, but not in a time-measured way, when they were created. Otherwise, if it is the natural motions of things and the usual periods of these days with which we are familiar that we think of when these things were made originally by a word from God, they would all have needed not just one day but several more. Thus vegetation that pullulates from roots and dresses the earth with its finery would first have to germinate underneath in the soil, then break out into the open air after a definite number of days, every kind according to its own species, even if up to this point everything happened as scripture tells it about the nature of things created on the third day.

Then again, how many days would have been needed for birds to start flying, if from their very origins they had to reach the stage of feathers and wings through the number of days proper to their nature? Or perhaps only eggs were created, is that it, when it says on the fifth day that the waters were to throw up every winged flying thing according to its kind? Or granted for the sake of argument, that the reason this could have been said quite rightly is that the eggs contained in liquid form everything that would coalesce through a definite number of days and then somehow or other break out of the shells; and this

---

45. *Rationes.*
46. The Latin says, literally, "carry through those numbers," *hos numeros peragunt.* Augustine clearly has in mind Wisdom 11:20: *You have arranged all things in measure and number and weight;* so I am taking what is perhaps an undue liberty in substituting here "measure" for "number." But I think in fact that it conveys his meaning better in English, as also does my introducing the figure of dancing; for I am pretty sure he was thinking here in a musical metaphor, in terms, no doubt, of a choir or orchestra. But whereas for him, of these two words it was "number" that found expression in musical rhythm, for us it is more usually "measure;" and this in turn we refer to dancing more than to singing or playing musical instruments.

because the very formulae[47] of their measures and numbers were already present, being woven incorporeally into the texture of corporeal things: why could not this have been rightly said even before the egg stage, when in the liquid element itself the very same formulae were being made, according to which the fowls of the air would be able to arise and reach full growth and perfection through the periods of time proper to each kind? The creator, after all, about whom scripture told this story of how he completed and finished his works in six days, is the same as the one about whom it is written elsewhere, and assuredly without there being any contradiction, that *he created all things simultaneously together* (Sir 18:1).

And consequently, the one who made all things simultaneously together also made simultaneously these six or seven days, or rather this one day six or seven times repeated. So then, what need was there for the six days to be recounted so distinctly and methodically? It was for the sake of those who cannot arrive at an understanding of the text, "he created all things together simultaneously," unless scripture accompanies them more slowly, step by step, to the goal to which it is leading them.

All things both made simultaneously, and nonetheless also made in six days

34, 53. So then, how can we say that the presence of that light in the angelic knowledge from evening to morning was repeated seven times, when it would have been sufficient for these three, that is both day and evening and morning, to be grasped by it simultaneously just once? Just as the whole created universe, after all, was all made simultaneously, so the angelic light could simultaneously both account for day by contemplating it all in the original and unchangeable ideas according to which it was fashioned, and account for evening by knowing it all in its own proper nature, and account for morning by rising to praise the creator from that inferior knowledge too.

Or how could morning come first, for the light to know in the Word what was there for God to make next, with evening then following for the light to know this in itself, if nothing was made before and after, because all things were made together simultaneously? Indeed, though, both statements are true: both that the things mentioned were made "before and after" in the course of the six days, and that they were all made simultaneously, because each passage of scripture, both the one telling the story of God's works through these days, and the one saying

---

47. *Rationes* again. These formulae or ideas are not to be identified with those contemplated by the angels in the Word of God, because these cannot be said to have been made or created. Rather they are the created manifestations of the uncreated ideas, and are elsewhere called by Augustine *rationes seminales*, seminal formulae planted like seeds, programmed into the whole created universe which was all made simultaneously, instantaneously, on the one day of creation.

that he made all things simultaneously, are speaking the truth. And they are both true with one truth, because they were both written under the inspiration of the one *Spirit of truth* (Jn 16:13).

54. But in matters where what comes before or after is not indicated by intervals of time, while one can indeed talk about "simultaneous" as well as about "before and after," it is still easier to understand what is said to be simultaneous than what is before and after. For example, when we look at the sun rising, it is obvious enough that our glance could not reach it before it had first crossed the whole space of air and sky between; and who could even begin to guess what a long distance that is? Clearly this glance of ours, or this ray from our eyes,[48] could not get as far as crossing the air which is above the sea before it had first crossed the air above the land, whatever Mediterranean region we may be in, from the place we are in as far as the seashore. If there are still more lands after the sea along the line of our vision, our glance cannot cross the air above them before it has first negotiated the space above the sea, and after that extended itself from there. Let us suppose that after those lands across the Mediterranean only Ocean remains;[49] can our glance also cross the air that spreads over Ocean before first crossing whatever air there is over the land this side of Ocean? Now Ocean is generally held to extend incomparably far. But however vast it is, the rays from our eyes will first have to cross the air above it, and after that whatever lies beyond, before they are able to reach the sun, which we are observing.

Now because we said "before" and "after" so often here, does that therefore mean that our glance does not cross all these spaces instantaneously, that is, simultaneously, in one single blink? If when about to observe the sun we turn our faces towards it with our eyes shut, won't we rather think, as soon as we open them, that we found our glance already there, than that we dispatched it there, and will it not seem that our eyes were not even opened before our glance reached its destination? And undoubtedly this is a ray of bodily light, darting out of our eyes and touching things set so far away with a speed beyond comparison or calculation. Accordingly it is quite certain on the one hand that this ray passes through all those immense spaces simultaneously in one blink, and no less clear on the other what is crossed by it before and after.

---

48. For the curious theory that we see things by emitting rays from our eyes, which put us in "sight touch" with the object like the antennae of certain insects, see Book I,16,31, and note 20 on that text.

49. Ocean was a proper name for the ancients, and there was only one ocean, thought of as a gigantic river encircling the earth. So Augustine's glance, sent on such a painstaking journey toward the rising sun, would cross the same ocean as the one he was more familiar with to the West of him, beyond the Pillars of Hercules, the straits of Gibraltar. This picture of ocean really only fits a view of the earth as flat, a view entertained by no educated person in Augustine's day; certainly not by him, as what he said above, 30,47, about day and night, morning and evening, all happening simultaneously, but of course in different parts of the world, makes clear.

55. When the apostle wished to express the speed of our resurrection, he rightly said that it would happen *in the blink of an eye* (1 Cor 15:52). Nothing more rapid, after all, can be found in the movements or pulses of corporeal things. Now if the glance of eyes of flesh is capable of such swiftness, what must the glance of even the human mind be capable of? How much more that of the angelic mind? What now must be said of the swiftness of that supreme Wisdom of God, who *reaches everywhere on account of her purity, and nothing defiled affects her* (Wis 7:24.25)? So then, in these things that were made all together simultaneously, nobody can see what should be made before or after which, except in that Wisdom through whom they were made simultaneously, and in order.

Conclusion about the days of Genesis

35, 56. So then, this day which God made in the first place—if it is the spiritual and rational creation, that is, the supercelestial angels and powers—was presented with all the works of God in a sequence or order which is the order of knowledge. Thus it would foreknow in the Word of God the things that were to be made, and then know them as creatures already made; this, however, would not be at distinct moments of time, but would be a knowledge of before and after in the sequence of creatures, of all at once simultaneously in the effective work of the creator. For he did indeed make things that were going to be in the future; but he made time-bound things in a timeless manner, to let times made by him run their proper course.

Now these ordinary seven days, which are unfolded and folded up again by the rotation of light from the heavenly bodies, bear a kind of shadowy resemblance to those primordial days; and accordingly they serve to remind us to investigate those days in which the created spiritual light was presented with all the works of God through the perfection of the number six, and was then able to have a morning, but not an evening, on the seventh day of God's rest. This was because God did not rest on the seventh day as though he needed the seventh day to have a rest in, but in the sight of his angels he rested from all his works which he had made—rested in himself, of course, who was not made. In this way his angelic creation, which like a day with its evening had been presented with the knowledge of all his works both in God himself and in the works themselves, would recognize that after all his very good works there remained nothing better than God himself resting from all of them in himself, and needing none of them to increase his blessedness and bliss.[50]

---

50. The Latin of this last chapter of Book IV bears all the marks of having been dictated in haste and not corrected; it is exceedingly dense and sometimes really defies grammatical analysis. So the translation is admittedly at times just a paraphrase.

Book V

Genesis 2:4-6: How these verses, with their problems,
confirm the opinion that creation was the work of one day

The world really created on one day

1, 1. *This is the book of the creating of heaven and earth when the day was
made God made heaven and earth,*[1] *and all the greenery of the field before it was
upon the earth, and all the hay of the field before it sprang up. For God had not
rained upon the earth, and there was no man to till the land. But a spring was
coming up from the earth and was watering all the face of the earth* (Gn 2:4-6).
Now indeed that theory gets more definite confirmation, according to which
God is understood to have made one day, from which those six or seven could be
counted off just by repeating this one, seeing that holy scripture now says it quite
openly, and sums up in a certain manner everything said from the beginning up
to this point by concluding: *This is the book of the creating*, or making, *of heaven
and earth, when the day was made*. Nor is anybody going to say, you see, that
heaven and earth are here mentioned in the same way as where it said, before the
fashioning of the day was introduced: *In the beginning God made heaven and
earth* (Gn 1:1). How that could be taken in the sense of God making something
apart from day, before he made the day, I explained in its own place, saying what
I thought, without denying anybody the right to put forward a better explanation.
Now, however, *This*, he says, *is the book of the creating of heaven and earth,
when the day was made*, and thereby he shows clearly enough, in my opinion,
that he is not here mentioning heaven and earth in the same way as in the beginning before day was made, *when there was darkness over the abyss* (Gn 1:2), but
in the way that heaven and earth were made when the day was made, that is,
when the various parts and kinds of things which the total creation is composed
of, to present us with this phenomenon we call the cosmos, were formed and
distinguished from one another.

---

1. I leave this curious sentence unpunctuated, because Augustine wishes to construe the central
clause, "when the day was made," both with the words that go before it and with those that
come after it. It is perhaps worth bearing in mind that manuscripts in those days, such as the one
he had before him, had no punctuation, as we know it, at all.

2. So then, the heaven being mentioned here is the one which God called the solid structure when he had created it, together with all the bodies in it; and the earth is the one which with all the things in it was allotted the place at the bottom with the abyss. He goes on, you see, to add, *God made heaven and earth*, so that both by putting the name of heaven and earth first, before mentioning the making of the day, and by repeating it again when he had mentioned it, he is not allowing us to assume that he has now named heaven and earth in the same way as in the beginning, before the day had been created. This, after all, is how he wove his words together: *This is the book of the creating of heaven and earth when the day was made God made heaven and earth*; so should anybody wish to understand what is placed first, *the book of the creating of heaven and earth*, in the same way as it said *In the beginning God made heaven and earth* (Gn 1:1) before he fashioned the day, just because here too heaven and earth are first mentioned and next the day is made, they would be put right by the words that follow, because the name of heaven and earth is also added again after the mention of the making of the day.

3. Though as a matter of fact, the use of the conjunction *when* here in the inserted clause *when the day was made*, should extort the admission from anyone inclined to be argumentative that no other understanding of the text is possible. Had it been inserted, you see, so as to read, "This is the book of the creating of heaven and earth; the day was made; God made heaven and earth;" then you could perhaps maintain that "the book of the creating of heaven and earth" is being said in the same way as *In the beginning God made heaven and earth* before the day was fashioned; and that then *the day was made* is added just as there it went on to tell of how God made the day; and that finally it immediately goes on to say *God made heaven and earth*, as though now it is just like all these things being made in the earlier account after the fashioning of the day.

But in fact it is inserted as a temporal clause, to read *when the day was made*, whether you connect it with the previous words to make one sentence: *This is the book of the creating of heaven and earth, when the day was made*; or with those that come next, again to make a complete sentence: *When the day was made, God made heaven and earth*. In this way he is obliging us beyond a shadow of doubt to understand that he has mentioned how heaven and earth were made when the day was made. Next, after saying *God made heaven and earth*, it adds, *and all the greenery of the field*, which was manifestly made on the third day. This makes it more limpidly clear than ever that this is the one and only day that God made, and that it was by the repetition of it that the second and the third and the rest were made, up to the seventh day.

Why the addition of "the greenery of the field"

2, 4. Now by the expression "heaven and earth" the author, according to the normal style of the scriptures, clearly wishes the whole of creation to be understood here; so one may well ask why he added *and all the greenery of the field* (Gn 2:5). The reason it was put in, so it seems to me, was to drive home the point of precisely what sort of day he was drawing our attention to, when he said *when the day was made*. One could readily jump to the conclusion, after all, that this day of bodily light was meant, which goes round and round to provide us with the alternations of day-time and night-time. But then we recall the order in which things were fashioned, and find that all the greenery of the field was created on the third day, before the sun was made on the fourth day, the sun which regulates by its presence this everyday normal day we are used to. So when we hear the words, *When the day was made, God made heaven and earth and all the greenery of the field*, we are being admonished to turn our thoughts to that special day we should be striving to track down with our minds, which even if it is a physical day of goodness knows what kind of light quite beyond our ken, or (as we have been arguing) a spiritual day in the harmonious unity of the angels' mutual companionship, is certainly not such as the one we are familiar with here.

The precise wording of the narrative gives us to understand that all things were created simultaneously

3, 5. We would also be keeping strictly to our point if we took a glance at what he could have said, compared with what he actually did say. He could have said, after all, *This is the book of the creating of heaven and earth, when God made heaven and earth*, where by "heaven and earth" we would also understand everything in them in the way divine scripture is in the habit of speaking. By "heaven and earth," sometimes adding "and sea," it indicates time and again the whole of creation, occasionally also adding *and everything in them*. So whichever of these he said, we would understand the day to be included, whether the one which he originally fashioned, or this one made by the presence of the sun. But that is not what he did say; no, he inserted the day separately, saying: *when the day was made* (Gn 2:4).

Nor did he speak like this, and say, "This is the book of the creating of the day and of heaven and earth," as in the order in which we were told things were made;[2] nor like this: "This is the book of the creating of heaven and earth, when the day was made and heaven and earth, when God made heaven and earth and all the greenery of the field"; nor like this: "This is the book of the creating of heaven and earth, when God made the day and heaven and earth and all the greenery of the field"; nor like this: "This is the book of the creating of heaven and earth; God made the day and heaven and earth and all the greenery of the field." While the ordinary way of speaking, after all, would have required some such turns of phrase

---

2. In the six-day account of creation, day (light) first, then heaven (the firmament or solid structure), then earth and sea; Gn 1:3-10.

as these, what he actually did say was: *This is the book of the creating of heaven and earth when the day was made God made heaven and earth and all the greenery of the field* (Gn 2:4-5), as though to suggest that when the day was made, then it was that God made heaven and earth and all the greenery of the field.

6. Again, the earlier account indicates the day made originally, and labels it *one day* (Gn 1:5); after which it goes on to count the second on which the solid structure was made, and the third on which the specific forms of land and sea were distinguished from each other, and the land produced trees and grass. Or is this perhaps what we were struggling to prove in the previous book, that God made all things together simultaneously, seeing that where that arrangement of the story had all things created and completely finished in due order in six days, now all things are being concentrated in one day—with the addition also of some kind of shrubs, for the reason no doubt which I gave above, that if readers should happen to understand here one of our ordinary kind of days, they would be corrected when they recalled that God said the earth should produce the greenery of the field before this ordinary solar day?[3] So now we get evidence in support, not from another book of holy scripture[4] that God created all things simultaneously, but from next door neighbor's testimony on the page following this whole matter, which gives us a hint with the words, *when the day was made God made heaven and earth and all the greenery of the field.*

So now you should understand that this day was repeated seven times for the seven days to be made, and also grasp if you can, when you hear that all things were made when the day was made, that this sixfold or sevenfold repetition happened without any intervals or periods of time. And if you are not yet able to grasp this, leave the contemplation of it to those who have the capacity, while you yourself go on making progress by walking more slowly with scripture at your side, where she does not desert your weakness but matches her steps to yours in motherly fashion. For she speaks, you see, in such a way that she mocks the proud by her sublimity, fills the attentive with awe at her profundity, feeds the mature with her truthfulness, fosters the little ones with her kindliness.

Why the hay is said to have been made before it sprang up

4, 7. So what is the meaning, then, of what follows? This, you see, is how the text is stitched together: *When the day was made God made heaven and earth,*

---

3. See Gn 1:11. I have changed the punctuation somewhat drastically here, to make a rather longer sentence, a longer question than we have in the Latin. The editors end the question at "some kind of shrubs," thus rather obscuring the reference of what follows to precisely this little addition. It must be admitted that Augustine's whole sentence here is something of a syntactical mess; an indication of rather hasty composition.
4. The allusion is to Sir 18:1, which states, in the Latin text, that "he who lives for ever created all things *simul.*"

and all the greenery of the field before it was upon the earth, and all the hay of the field before it sprang up (Gn 2:4-5). What do we have here? The question must surely be asked, must it not, where he made these things before they were on the earth and before they sprang up? Is there any of us who would not be more inclined to believe that the time God made them was when they sprang up, not before they did so, unless we were assured by this divine utterance that God made these things before they sprang up? So even if you are unable to work out where they were made, you will at least take it on faith that they were made before they sprang up, if you believe this text of scripture, being the God-fearing sort of person you are. The godless, of course, do not believe it.

8. So what are we to say? What several people have thought, that what is meant is that all things were made in the very Word of God before they sprang up on the earth? But if that is how they were made, it was not when the day was made, but before it was made that they were made. Scripture, however, says quite openly, *When the day was made God made heaven and earth, and all the greenery of the field before it was upon the earth, and all the hay of the field before it sprang up.* So if it was when the day was made, it was certainly not before the day was made, accordingly not in the Word, which is co-eternal with the Father, before the day, before absolutely anything was made, but when the day was made. Whatever is in the Word, after all, before every creature, was assuredly not made; but these things were made, when the day was made, as the words of scripture make very clear, but nonetheless before they were upon the earth and before they sprang up. That is what is said of the greenery and the hay of the field.

9. So then, where? Was it in the earth itself, in their causal formulae,[5] in the way they are all there already in their seeds, before they evolve somehow or other and unfold their growths and their various manifestations in their proper time? But these seeds that we can observe are already upon the earth, they have already sprung up. Or is it that they were not upon the earth but below the surface of the earth, and the reason they were made before they sprang up is that the time they sprang up was precisely when the seeds sprouted and broke out with their first growths into the open air, which we now see happening through the periods of time accorded to each kind of plant? So is it seeds that were then made "when the day was made," and was it in them that all the greenery of the field and all the hay was to be found, and not yet in that form and appearance in which they have now sprung up over the earth, but in the energy of the formulae with which the seeds are programmed? So were seeds the first thing that the earth produced?

But that is not how scripture was talking when it said, *And the earth produced grass for fodder,* or grass for hay, *sowing seed according to kind and according to likeness, and fruit trees making fruit, of which its seed is in it according to kind*

---

5. *Causaliter et rationaliter;* in what he will elsewhere call their seminal or ingrafted formulae; *seminales, insitae rationes.*

upon the earth (Gn 1:12). From these words, I mean, it appears rather that seeds sprang from grass and trees, while these came not from seeds but from the earth, particularly as God's very own words also say the same thing. He did not say, you see, "Let seeds in the earth sprout grass for hay and fruit trees," but what he said was, *Let the earth sprout grass for hay sowing seed*, to suggest seed coming from grass, not grass from seed; *and thus it was made, and the earth produced* (Gn 1:11-12). That is, first it was made thus in the knowledge of that day,[6] and the earth now produced, so that this might also be made in the actual creature which was then fashioned.

10. So then in what way, before they were upon the earth and before they sprang up? As though it was one thing for them to be made together with heaven and earth, when that day was made, of which we have no knowledge or experience, which God made first; another for them to spring up now upon the earth, through the intervals of time suited to each kind of plant, which can only happen in the course of these days that are made by the sun circling round in its course—is that it? But if that is indeed the case, and that day is the harmonious fellowship and unity of the supercelestial angels and powers, there is certainly no doubt that God's creation is known to the angels in a way very, very different from the way it is known to us. Quite apart from their knowing it in the Word of God *through which all things were made* (Jn 1:3), what I am saying is that even in itself it is known to them very differently from the way it is known to us. It is known to them, if I may so put it, primordially or in its origins, as God originally fashioned it, resting from his works by not fashioning anything more after setting it up. To us, on the other hand, it is known according to the way things previously fashioned are managed and regulated in the orderly course of time, according, that is, to the way in which God is working until now in those things that were completed and finished in the perfect number of six days.

11. So the earth is said to have produced grass and trees then in their causes, that is, to have received the power to produce them. It was in the earth, that is to say, that things which were going to be realized in the course of time had already been made, if I may so put it, in the roots of time. Later on, after all, God certainly *planted Paradise along the east, and drew out from the earth there every tree that had a lovely look about it and was good for eating* (Gn 2:8.9). It cannot, however, be said that he then added something to creation which he had not made before, something as it were to be added later to the perfection of all the very good things he finished and completed on the sixth day. No, all the natures of shrubs and trees had already been made in the first setting up of creation, and from this work of setting things up God rested. But from then on he managed and shifted about through their times and courses those very things he had set up in

---

6. The angelic intelligence.

the work from which he had then rested; and in so doing he not only planted Paradise at that time, but also goes on planting now all the things that are coming to be. Who else, after all, even now creates these things if not the one who *is working until now* (Jn 5:17)? But he creates these things now from those that are already there, while then things were created by him when they had been absolutely non-existent, when that day was made which had also itself been absolutely non-existent, namely the spiritual and intellectual creation.

The nature of time in the six days of creation

5, 12. And so creatures once made began to run with their movements along the tracks of time, which means it is pointless to look for times before any creature, as though times could be found before times. If there were no movement, after all, of either the spiritual or bodily creation, by which things to come in the future would succeed things in the past through the present, there would be absolutely no time at all. But no creature could move, of course, if it did not exist. So it is time that begins from the creation rather than the creation from time, while both are from God; *from him*, after all, *and through him and in him are all things* (Rom 11:36). Nor should the statement that time begins from the creation be taken to imply that time is not a creature, since in fact it is the movement of creatures from one state to another, with things following each other as regulated by God managing everything he has created.

Accordingly, when we reflect upon the first establishment of creatures in the works of God from which he rested on the seventh day, we should not think either of those days as being like these ones governed by the sun, nor of that working as resembling the way God now works in time; but we should reflect rather upon the work from which times began, the work of making all things at once, simultaneously, and also endowing them with an order that is not set by intervals of time but by the linking of causes, so that the things that were made simultaneously might also be brought to perfection by the sixfold representation of that day.

13. And so it was in the order of causes, not of time, that the first thing to be made was formless and formable material, both spiritual and corporeal, from which would be made whatever had to be made, since this too would not have existed before it was set in place; nor was it set in place by any other than by the supreme and true God from whom are all things. Whether this basic material was signified by the name of heaven and earth, which God made in the beginning before he fashioned that one day, and was already called that because it was from it that heaven and earth were made, or whether it was suggested by the earth being invisible and shapeless and by the darkness of the abyss has already been discussed in the first book.

14. The things, however, that were formed out of that formlessness are more evidently and naturally said to have been created or made or fashioned; and the

first to be made was the day. It was only right, after all, that the first place in creation should be held by that nature which was able to come to knowledge of the creature through the creator, not of the creator through the creature. Secondly the solid structure, from which the corporeal world starts; thirdly the specific appearance of sea and land, and potentially, if I may so put it,[7] in the earth on land the nature of grasses and trees. This, you see, was how the earth produced them at the word of God before they had sprung up, by receiving in itself all their numbers,[8] which it would extrude through the periods of time proper to each kind of plant.

Next, after this dwelling place, so to say, for things had been fashioned, the lamps and constellations were created, so that the higher part of the cosmos might be furnished with visible things that move about within the cosmos. On the fifth day the element of water, being adjacent to heaven and the air, produced at God's word its indigenous inhabitants, all things to wit that swim and fly; and these too potentially in their numbers, which were to be extruded through suitably timed movements. On the sixth day land animals likewise, as the last things from the last of the elements of the cosmos,[9] but still nonetheless potentially, for their numbers to be visibly unfolded by time later on.

15. All this order of duly ordered creation was known to that day;[10] and through this knowledge it presented itself somehow or other six times as six days, and while it is in fact just one day, it thus exhibited the things that have been made, coming to know them first in the creator and subsequently in themselves. It did not linger in them, however, but referred this subsequent knowledge of them to the love of God, thus providing evening and morning and noon in all cases, not as periods of time but as marking the order of the things fashioned. Finally it presented its knowledge of the quiet rest of its creator, with which he rested in it from all his works, knowledge in which it has no evening, and for this reason it was found worthy to be blessed and sanctified. That is why the number seven is somehow dedicated to the Holy Spirit, and is commended to us as such by scripture and the common teaching of the Church.[11]

---

7. He excuses his use of this word, because in classical Latin *potentialiter* and the adjective *potentialis* meant "powerfully" and "powerful." Perhaps Augustine was the first writer to use them in the sense they normally have in English, which derives from their use in scholastic Latin; but again they had possibly already been used in this sense in translations of Aristotle.

8. I presume *numeri* here, taken from that favorite text, Wis 11:20, *You have disposed all things in measure, number and weight,* means the same as what he elsewhere calls *rationes seminales* seminal formulae.

9. Earth, coming after the element of water, which came below air and fire (here represented by "heaven").

10. That is, known to the angelic intelligence. If this equivalence of "that day" is not borne in mind, this paragraph will prove very baffling.

11. The reference is primarily to the seven gifts of the Holy Spirit, Is 11:2, and then to such texts as Zec 3:9, 4:10, and Rv 1:4, 3:1, 4:5, which are all ultimately based on the passage in Isaiah.

16. So this then is the book of the creating of heaven and earth, because *in the beginning God made heaven and earth* (Gn 1:1) as a kind of formability, if I may so express it,[12] of material which was subsequently to be formed by his word, and which preceded its own formation, not in time but in origin, because assuredly when it was to be formed, the day was first made: *When the day was made God made heaven and earth and all the greenery of the field before it was upon the earth, and all the hay of the field before it sprang up* (Gn 2:4-5)—the point we have been discussing, though something clearer and more in harmony with the text, you may well think, could have been observed and stated, or may be so in the future.

Whether the verse "God had not rained" etc. supports the view of simultaneous creation

6, 17. As for what comes next: *For God had not rained upon the earth, and there was no man to till the land* (Gn 2:5), it is difficult to work out where it fits in and what it is suggesting to us. Is it as if the reason God made the hay of the field before it sprang up was that he had not yet rained upon the earth, since if he had made the hay after the rain, it would seem that its springing up was due more to the rain than to its being made by him? So what, then? Is what springs up after rain made by any other agent than by the same God?

Why, though, was there no man to till the land? Had God not already made the man on the sixth day, and on the seventh rested from all his works? Or is he reminding us by way of recapitulation that when God made all the greenery of the field and all the hay, he had not yet rained upon the earth and there was as yet no man, seeing that he made these things on the third day, man only on the sixth? But when God made all the greenery and all the hay of the field before it sprang up on the earth, not only was there no man to till the land, but there was not even any hay either on the earth, which he says, of course, was made before it sprang up. Or is the reason God made these things on the third day precisely that there was no man as yet to make them by cultivating the earth? As if, forsooth, there were not so many trees and so many kinds of grasses that are born of the earth without any human cultivation!

18. Or is the reason that each statement is made, both that he had not yet rained upon the earth, and that there was as yet no man to till the land, something like this? Where there is no human cultivation, you see, these things do grow as a result of rain; but there are some things that even rain will not make to grow without the aid of human labor. That is why now both kinds of assistance are needed for all species of plants to grow; but then each kind was lacking. That is

12. A word undoubtedly of Augustine's own coining.

why it was by the power of his word that God made these things, without rain and without human labor. Even now, after all, he is the one that makes them, but now by means of rain and of human hands—though *neither the one who plants is anything, nor the one who waters, but the one who gives the growth, God* (1 Cor 3:7).

On the spring which watered the whole earth

19. So what is the meaning then of what he adds next: *But a spring was coming up from the earth, and was watering all the face of the earth* (Gn 2:6)? That spring, surely, flowing as abundantly as the Nile does for Egypt, could easily serve the whole earth for rain. So why is it put to us as something remarkable that God made those growing things before it had rained, when the spring watering the earth could give quite as much assistance as rain? Or if not quite so much, then perhaps only smaller plants would start growing, but still some, for all that.

Or is scripture here again talking, as its habit is, in a weak and simple style to the weak and simple, and yet all the same suggesting something more profound for those to grasp who have the capacity? We have seen, after all, how by mentioning that day, just a few moments ago, he signified that one day was made by God, and that it was when the day was made that God then made heaven and earth, so that we should ponder as best we could God making all things simultaneously at once, even though the count of six days earlier on seemed to show intervals of time between his works. Thus, when he had said that with heaven and earth God made all the greenery of the field before it was upon the earth, and all the hay of the field before it had sprung up, he added, *for God had not yet rained upon the earth, and there was as yet no man to till the land*; as though to say that God did not make those things in the same way as he makes such things now, when it rains and men work. These things, after all, now happen over periods of time, of which there were none then, when he made all things simultaneously in the moment from which times too began.

7, 20. So as for what follows, then: *But a spring was coming up from the earth, and was watering all the face of the earth* (Gn 2:6); from here on, in my judgment, we are being informed what things were being made over intervals of time, after that first establishment of creatures in which all things were made simultaneously. And he was quite right to begin from that element from which all species, whether of animals or grasses or trees, take their rise, to run through their time-governed measures and numbers, as allotted to their particular natures. All the primordial seeds, I mean to say, from which every kind of flesh or fruit is born, are moist and grow and develop out of moisture. But they have within them the most efficacious numbers, which bring along with them potentialities consequent upon those perfect works of God, from which he rested on the seventh day.

21. A very proper question, however, is what this spring might be that was capable of watering the face of the whole earth. If it existed at that time, after all, and has since been blocked up or has dried up, we have to look for the reason. Now, I mean, we see that there is no such spring by which the whole face of the earth is watered. So perhaps the sinfulness of mankind also earned this punishment, to have the vast and lavish flow of that spring cut off and the lands deprived of such ready-made fertility, thus adding to the hard labor of their inhabitants.

Human guesswork could certainly assert this (though it is not recounted by any text of scripture) were it not tripped up by the fact that the sin of mankind, which was punished by the imposition of hard labor, occurred after the delights of Paradise. Now Paradise had its own outsize spring—which we will have to talk about in greater detail at its own place[13]—from whose single head, the story tells us, four great rivers flowed, well known to the nations. So where was that spring or those rivers when this one spring, greatest of them all, was coming up from the earth and watering all the face of the earth? It is certain, you see, that Gihon, one of those four which is said to be the Nile, was not at that time watering Egypt, when a spring was coming up from the earth and saturating not only Egypt but all the face of the earth.

22. Or must we suppose that God wished to water the whole earth from one gigantic spring, so that the things he had originally planted in it could from now on start growing with the help of this moisture, each through the number of days proper to the various species, and that later on, having planted Paradise, he cut off the flow of that spring, and filled the earth with many springs, as we now see it, while he divided the flow from the one spring of Paradise into four huge rivers? In this way the rest of the earth, full of various kinds of its creatures[14] working their way through the appropriate numbers of their growing times, would also have its springs and rivers, and Paradise, planted in the choicest place, would send out those rivers from the head of its own spring.

Or did he first of all irrigate the whole earth from that one spring of Paradise, flowing much more abundantly to begin with, and in this way fertilize it all to bring forth through the numbers of their growing times those species which he had created in it without any intervals of time? And then later on did he cut off that vast spouting gush of waters in that place, in order that from then on they

---

13. Gn 2:10-14. See below, Book VIII, 7, 13-14. I treat Paradise as a proper name, because it is most likely that Augustine and his contemporaries also thought of it like that. It is in origin a Persian word meaning a park, introduced into the Genesis story by the Greek translators, where the Hebrew just has the ordinary word for "garden."

14. The earth can claim plants as in a special way "its" creatures, since their whole existence, from beginning to end, is derived from it so totally.

might flow from various river heads and springs through the whole earth? And next after that, in the region of that spring, which was no longer irrigating the whole earth, but only issuing in those four memorable rivers, did he then plant Paradise as a place in which to put the man he had made?

The place of conjecture where scripture is silent

8, 23. Now not everything is written in scripture about how the ages ran their course after that first establishment of things, and how various stages followed one another in the management of creatures made at the beginning and finished on that sixth day, but only as much as the Spirit who was inspiring the author judged would be enough, not only to provide knowledge of things that had happened, but also to foreshadow things that were to come. So we in our ignorance have to fill in by conjecture the gaps which he by no means out of ignorance left in the picture. In this we have to strive in our own small way, to the extent that he assists us, to ensure that no absurdity or contradiction is attributed to the holy scriptures, which would offend the good sense of readers and lead them to conclude that things which could not have happened are mentioned by scripture as having happened, and so to decide either to give up the faith, or to have nothing to do with it in the first place.

The particular instance of this spring

9, 24. Accordingly, we have to ask about this spring, how what is said about it, that *it was coming up from the earth and watering the whole face of the earth*, should not seem to be impossible. If what we have already said about it should seem to people to be impossible, let them look for another explanation themselves, but still one which will demonstrate the truthfulness of this statement of scripture—which certainly is truthful, beyond any shadow of doubt, even if it were not demonstrated. Should they wish by their arguments, I mean, to convict it of being false, then either what they are going to say about the setting up and management of creatures will have not a word of truth in it, or else if it is true, then the reason they think what scripture says is false will be because they do not understand it.

Thus they might contend that it is quite impossible for the whole face of the earth to have been irrigated from one spring, however vast, because if it was not irrigating the mountains then it was not irrigating the whole face of the earth, while if it was also irrigating the mountains, then this was not now the bestowal of fatness but the inundation of a flood, and if the earth was then like that, everything was all sea, and the dry land had not yet been separated from it.

10, 25. We can answer them by saying that this could have happened at successive times, just as at a definite time the Nile floods all the flat lands of

Egypt and then at another time returns to its bed. Or if this stream is thought to collect its annual flood waters from the rains and winter snows of heaven knows what unknown and distant part of the world, what can be said about the alternating tides of Ocean, what about some shores which are laid bare for a great distance at the ebb, and covered again by the waves at the flood? To say nothing of what we are told about the wonderful variations in the flow of some springs, which every few years at a fixed time overflow and water the whole countryside, for which at other times they scarcely provide enough drinking water from deep wells. So why should it be incredible, if from one outlet of the abyss, alternately pouring out and sucking back its waters, the entire earth was then irrigated?

But scripture may well have wished to call the whole "vasty deep"[15] of the abyss itself a spring, not springs, because of its nature as a single entity (in that part of it alone, to be sure, which the earth confines in subterranean caverns, from which all springs and streams distribute themselves through a variety of arteries and channels and burst forth, each in its own place; thus not including that other part called the sea, which spreads far and wide for all to observe, encircling all lands with its bitter, salt waves,); and to talk of it coming up from the earth through innumerable crannies and underground streams, and on all sides watering the whole face of the earth, as if with its hair blowing and streaming in the wind; so not with a continuous flat surface as of the sea or a marsh, but as we observe water flowing along river beds and between winding banks and then overflowing and flooding neighboring fields when they rise. Who, I ask you, would decline to accept such an explanation, but people laboring under a spirit of contentious obstinacy?

You could also understand its talking of the whole face of the earth being watered, in the same way as one can talk of the whole of a garment[16] being colored, even if it is only made so by patchwork, not uniformly; especially since at that time, when the earth was so young, one may believe that most if not all of it was flat plains, over which streams bubbling up could be dispersed and extended far and wide.[17]

26. To sum up about this spring: did it in fact gush forth from one particular place somewhere or other, or was it called one spring as being a kind of single reservoir in the bowels of the earth for all the water of all springs, great and small, to spread over the earth, and was it coming up from the earth in this way

---

15. While Augustine was probably not familiar with Shakespeare's *Tempest*, his translator, happily, is.
16. He says, literally, "the whole face of a garment," to draw the parallel with the disputed phrase in the scriptural text. But one cannot really say that in English, and to substitute another word like "area" would not be any better at drawing this parallel.
17. Does this suggest that Augustine, and some of his learned contemporaries, had a sound geological instinct that mountains are of comparatively recent geophysical formation? Hardly, you may well say; but the modernity of what he implies is rather striking.

through all its outlets and so watering the whole face of the earth? Or else—and this is rather easier to believe—seeing that he did not say, "One spring was coming up from the earth," but simply, *A spring was coming up from the earth*, he just put the singular for the plural, as a kind of collective noun, so that in this way we can understand it as meaning many springs over the whole earth watering their different places and regions. Thus we talk about "the soldiery," meaning soldiers in general, or about "the locust plague"[18] or "the frog plague" with which the Egyptians were afflicted, when there was a countless number of locusts and frogs. In any case let us take up no more time wearing ourselves out over how big it was or how many.

Reiterating the point that the creation of all creatures took place
simultaneously, while their management and regulation is conducted
over intervals and periods of time

11, 27. But let us come back yet again to that question, whether our considered opinion can stand up in all cases, whereby we were saying that God worked in one way with all creatures at their first establishment, works from which he rested on the seventh day, and in another at their management and regulation, at which *he is working until now* (Jn 5:17); that is, that he then worked at making all things simultaneously, without any intervals or periods of time between, while now he works through periods of time. Thus we see the constellations being moved through such intervals from their rising to their setting, the sky being changed from summer to winter, plants budding after so many days, growing bigger, turning green, withering; animals also at definite turning points in the course of time being conceived and fully formed and born, and running their course through every age until old age and death; and all other such temporal processes. Who but God, after all, works these things, even without any such movement on his part? Time, I mean, does not happen to him.

So then between those works of God from which he rested on the seventh day, and these which he is working on until now, scripture inserted a kind of joint in her narrative, advising us that she had finished unrolling those and was beginning now to weave these on the loom. The notice that she had finished unrolling those was put like this: *This is the book of the creating of heaven and earth when the day was made God made heaven and earth and all the greenery of the field before it was upon the earth, and all the hay of the field before it sprang up; for God had not rained upon the earth, and there was no man to till the earth* (Gn 2:4-5), while the weaving of these other works began like this: *But a spring was*

---

18. Ps 105:34 reads in the Latin Vulgate, *He spoke, and the locust came, and the young locust without number.* In verse 30 it has "frogs" in the plural; but Augustine's version may well have had "the frog" also in the singular here.

coming up from the earth, and was watering all the face of the earth (Gn 2:6). From this mention of this spring onwards, whatever the narrative tells of was henceforth done through periods of time, not "all things simultaneously."

Different ways of knowing things, following on these differences in God's working

12, 28. So then, the unchangeable formulae for all creatures in the Word of God are one thing, another those works of his from which he rested on the seventh day, yet another these which carrying on from those he is working on until now; and of these three it is the one I put last that is known to us somehow or other through the senses of the body and our familiarity with this life. As for the other two, however, they are so far removed from our senses and from what ordinary human thought is used to, that we have first of all to believe them on divine authority, and then to come to some kind of knowledge of them from the things we already know, in the greater or lesser degree of which we are capable with divine assistance.

God knows things before they exist

13, 29. So then, as regards those unchangeable and eternal divine formulae, this is how scripture gives us the evidence that the very Wisdom of God knew before they were made all the things that were made through her: *In the beginning was the Word and the Word was with God and God is what the Word was. This was in the beginning with God. All things were made through him, and without him was made nothing* (Jn 1:1-3). So then, could any of us be so out of our minds as to say that God did not make the things which he had known about?[19] Accordingly, if he knew about them, where did he come to do so if not with himself, with whom the Word was through whom all things were made? I mean, if he knew about them outside himself, who had taught him? *For who has known the mind of the Lord, or who has been his counselor? Or who has first given to him and will be given something back? Since from him and through him and in him are all things* (Rom 11:34-36).

---

19. The reasoning here is almost totally opaque. How are the opening verses of John evidence that God's Wisdom knew all things before they were made? And how does this rhetorical question, winding up the argument, really fit it? This is really a veiled statement that God made things which he knew beforehand; but what seems to be required is a statement that he knew beforehand the things he then made. Perhaps, however, with a little of the mental and verbal gymnastics which Augustine so often requires of his readers, it can be turned into such a statement; it is saying, in effect, that if God made things, then he knew beforehand what he was doing. As for the first problem, the solution hinges, I would say, on the identity of God's Wisdom with his Word. Wisdom (which embraces knowledge) almost by definition knew what God was going to make; that she in fact took part in making them is then proved by the text that says of God's Word (= his Wisdom) that all things were made through him.

30. Though as a matter of fact, what comes next in the gospel gives sufficient support to this judgment. The evangelist, you see, goes on to say: *What was made in him is life, and the life was the light of humanity* (Jn 1:3-4); because rational minds, that is to say, which is the genus in which the man was made to the image of God, do not have any other true light of their own except the very Word of God, through whom all things were made, and it is only by sharing in him that they will be able to be purified from all iniquity and error.

Parenthetical note on the proper phrasing of this sentence

14, 31. This sentence then should not be spoken like this: *What was made in him, is life,* so that we first pause after *what was made in him,* and then add *is life.* Is there anything, after all, that was not made in him, seeing that it says in the psalm, after mentioning many creatures, even earthly ones, *In wisdom you have made them all* (Ps 104:24); and the apostle says, *since in him were fashioned all things in heaven and on earth, visible and invisible* (Col 1:16). So the consequence, if we phrase the sentence like that, will be that even the earth and whatever is in it is life; and if it is absurd to say that all this is alive, how much more so to say that it is life?[20] Especially as he distinguishes what sort of life he is talking about, when he adds, *and the life was the light of humanity.*

So this is how we must phrase it: after saying, *what was made,* we must then go on to say *in him is life*; not in itself, that is to say, not in its own nature in which it was made in order to be a work and a creature, but in him it is life, because he knew all things that were made through him before they were made; and thus they were in him, not as the creature which he made, but as life and the light of mankind, which is Wisdom herself and the Word himself, the only-begotten Son of God. So then, what was made is life in him in the same way as it says: *Just as the Father has life in himself, so he has given the Son to have life in himself* (Jn 5:26).

32. Nor should we overlook what some of the better corrected manuscripts have: *What was made, in him was life,* so that we should understand "was life" in the same way as *In the beginning was the Word, and the Word was with God, and God is what the Word was.* So then, *what was made,* already *was life in him,* and not any kind of life—after all, cattle too are said to be alive, which are incapable of the joy of sharing in Wisdom—but "the life was the light of humanity."

---

20. With the strong sense that Augustine gives throughout to *factum est* and to *fieri* as the passive of *facere,* "to make," we may concede that it is absurd. But taking them in the weaker sense the Greek word John uses really has, of "coming to be," then the phrasing he rejects makes very good sense: "All things came to be through him, and without him nothing came to be. What came to be in him, was life"; for what came to be in the Word was that the Word became flesh, and it was this, the incarnate Word, Jesus Christ, that was life, the life which was the light of humanity.

Rational minds, for their part, once purified by his grace, are able to attain to that sort of vision, which nothing can surpass in excellence or bliss.

What sort of life all things are in God

15, 33. But even if we accept this reading as saying *What was made, in him was life*, the statement still remains that that which was made through him is to be understood as being life in him; life in which he saw all things when he made them, and indeed "as he saw them. so he made them," not seeing them outside himself, but in himself he so "numbered off"[21] all the things which he made. Nor is his vision different from the Father's, but they are one and the same, just as the two are one substance. In the book of Job also, you see, Wisdom herself, through whom all things were made, is thus presented: *Wisdom though*, he says, *where was she found? Or what is the place of knowledge? Mortals do not know her way, nor will she be found among men* (Jb 28:12-13). And a little further on: *We have heard*, he says, *of her glory; the Lord has commended her way and he himself knows her place. For he perceives everything that is under heaven, and knows all the things in the earth which he has made; when he made the balances of the winds, the measures of the water, as he saw them so he numbered them off* (Jb 28:23-25).

This and similar evidence proves that all these were in the knowledge of the maker before they were made, and of course were better there, where they were truer, where they are eternal and unchangeable. All this should be enough for anyone to know, or at least to believe unshakably, that God made all these things; and I do not imagine anyone could be so witless as to suppose that God made anything he did not know. Accordingly, if he knew them before he made them, it follows that before they were made they were known "with him" in such a way as to be eternally and unchangeably alive and to be life, while once made they existed in the way all creatures do, each according to its kind.

God is nearer to us than are many of the things he made

16, 34. So then, that eternal and unchangeable nature, which God is, has it in itself to be, as Moses was told: *I am who I am* (Ex 3:14); thus the manner in which it is differs totally from that in which these things are that have been made. Only that, you see, really and truly and primordially is, which always is in the same

---

21. He is alluding in advance to the text from Job he is about to quote. The verb rendered "numbered off" is *enumeravit*, which usually means simply to count up, to tote up. But for Augustine it is clearly associated with those "numbers" which are almost the equivalent of his "seminal ideas/formulae"; so one has to keep "number" as a verb in the English also. See above, 5,14, and note 8 there.

way, and not only never changes but is absolutely incapable of changing. So without bringing into existence[22] yet any of the things which he made, he has all things primordially in himself in the same manner as he is. After all, he would not make them unless he knew them before he made them; nor would he know them unless he saw them; nor would he see them unless he had them with him; and he would not have with him things that had not yet been made except in the manner in which he himself is not made.

So what I am saying is that although that substance is inexpressible and can only be presented by one human being to another in words taken over from space and time, though it is before all times and all places, still for all that the one who made is nearer to us than the many things which he made. *For in him we live and move and are* (Acts 17:28), while most of these things are remote from the human mind on account of their dissimilarity in kind, being corporeal. Nor is our human mind capable of seeing them where they are with God, in the formulae according to which they were made, so that in this way we might know how many, how great and of what sort they are, even though we do not see them with the senses of the body. The fact is they are remote from our bodily senses, being so far away, or cut off from our observation and activity by the interposition of other bodies.

The result is that it is much harder work to find out about them than about the one by whom they were made, and furthermore it is incomparably more satisfying and worthwhile for the devout mind to come into the slightest contact with him, than for it to comprehend the whole universe. So how right the book of Wisdom is to find fault with the investigators of this world and age! *For if they were capable*, it says, *of so much that they could appraise and weigh up the world, how is it that they did not all the more easily find its Lord?* (Wis 13:9). The foundations of the earth, after all, are inaccessible to our eyes, and the one who laid the earth's foundations draws near to our minds.

A brief recapitulation

17, 35. Now for the time being let us consider those things that God made "all simultaneously," from which he rested on the seventh day after finishing and

---

22. Translating *nihil horum . . . existens*. While this verb, *existere*, ninety-nine times out of a hundred means "to exist," on the hundredth occasion, exclusive apparently to Augustine, it does have the transitive sense of bringing into existence. He is quoted for this usage both by Lewis & Short and by Albert Blaise, *Dictionnaire Latin-Français des Auteurs Chrétiens*, each referring to the same text in *The City of God* XIV, 13. Perhaps future lexicographers would care to add this reference to V,16,34 of this other, earlier work of his. One could alternatively make the following emendation: the text runs— *. . . existens et omnia primitus habens . . .* ; by emending *existens et* to *existente*, one would be making an ablative absolute of the first clause, and relieving God of being the subject of *existens* as well as of *habens*. So the sense would be: "with none of the things he had made yet existing, he has all things primordially in himself."

completing them on the sixth; later on we will go on to consider the works on which he is working up until now. He himself, you see, is before all ages, while things like the world itself, which have existed from when the age began, we say are "from the age"; and others, like those that come to birth within the world, we say are "in the age."[23] So then, after saying, *All things were made through him, and without him was made nothing,* scripture said a little later: *He was in this world, and the world was made through him* (Jn 1:10). About this work of God it is written in another place, *You who made the world from formless matter* (Wis 11:17). This world is frequently called by the name of "heaven and earth," as we have already mentioned several times, and scripture says God made it *when the day was made* (Gn 2:4). We have already discussed these words as much as seemed necessary, to work out how both assertions could apply to the establishment of this world: both that it was finished in six days with all the things that are in it; and that it was then made when the day was made; and also how that other text too could apply, that *he created all things simultaneously* (Sir 18:1).

How creation, much of it unknown to us, is known to God and to the "day,"
which is the spiritual, rational creation

18, 36. There are many things in this universe of God's creation which we do not know, whether things higher up in the heavens than our sense perception can reach, or things in regions of the earth that are maybe uninhabitable, or things hidden down below, either in the depths of the abyss, or in secret gulfs and cavities of the earth. Before these things were made, therefore, they naturally did not exist. So how were they known to God, seeing they did not exist? And again, how would he make things which were not known to him? After all, he cannot be said to have made anything without knowing what it was. So then it is things he knew that he made, not things he made that he knew. Accordingly, before they were made, they both existed and did not exist; they existed in God's knowledge, they did not exist in their own nature.

And thus it is that that day was made, to which things would become known in each way, both in God and in themselves; in the first way as with a morning or daytime knowledge, in the second as with an evening knowledge. To God himself, however, since he had made them, I dare not say they became known in any other way than that by which he had known them in order to make them, he *with whom there is no change or shadow of oscillation* (Jas 1:17).

---

23. This odd little aside about the ages and the age (*saecula, saeculum*) rather interrupts the flow of thought here, and anticipates what he is going to say about it below in 19,38, where the subject is introduced by a quotation from Eph 3:9.

The mystery of the kingdom revealed to the angels from the beginning

19, 37. He certainly does not need reporters to inform him about things lower down the scale, as if to keep him abreast of current affairs; but in that simple and wonderful way he has a steady and unchanging knowledge of all things. He does have reporters, however, both for our sake and for their own, because for them to wait upon God obediently in that manner, ready to consult him about these lower matters and to comply with his behests and commands from above, is good for them in accordance with their proper nature and mode of being. Now reporters are called *angeloi*, angels, in Greek; and this is the general name given to that heavenly city above in its entirety, which we consider to have been the first day that was fashioned.

38. The fact is, they were not even kept in the dark about that mystery of the kingdom of heaven, which was revealed at the appropriate time for our salvation, so that once delivered from this exile we might be welcomed into their company. They would scarcely be ignorant of this, after all, seeing that the seed which came at the appropriate time was disposed through them in the hand of the mediator,[24] that is, by the authority of him who is their Lord, both in the form of God and in the form of a servant.[25] Again, the apostle says: *To me the least of all the saints has been given this grace, to proclaim among the nations the unsearchable riches of Christ, and to shed light on what the disposition of the sacrament might be, which was hidden from the ages in God who created the universe, so that there might be made known to the principalities and powers in the heavenly places through the Church the manifold wisdom of God, according to the plan of the ages which he made in Christ Jesus our Lord* (Eph 3:8-11).

So then, this was hidden from the ages in God, but in such a way nonetheless that the manifold wisdom of God would be made known to the principalities and powers in the heavenly places through the Church, because that is where the original Church is, into which this Church too is to be gathered after the resurrection, so that we may be equal to the angels of God.[26] So it was made known to them from the ages, because the total creation is not before the ages, but from the ages. It is from the creation, after all, that the ages arose, and it is from the ages, since its beginning is the beginning of the ages. But the Only-begotten Son,

---

24. See Gal 3:19. In the *Revisions* II,2,24 he corrects this mistaken understanding of Saint Paul's words; it was the law, not the seed, that was mediated through angels, and not in the hand of *the* mediator, Christ, but of *a* mediator, Moses. See the extract from the *Revisions* printed before the beginning of Book I of this work.

25. See Phil 2:6.7.

26. See Lk 20:36. Augustine has also misinterpreted this passage from Ephesians; Paul is definitely saying that the mystery hidden from the ages in God is only made known to the principalities and powers in the heavenly places through the Church here below, when God's plan in Christ has been carried out.

through whom the ages were made,[27] is before the ages; and that is why, speaking in the person of Wisdom, he says, *Before the ages he founded me* (Prv 8:23), so that the one to whom it was said, *You have made all things in Wisdom* (Ps 104:24), might indeed make all things in her.

39. But that what was hidden is not only made known in God to the angels, but is also apparent to them here when it is published and put into effect, is something to which the same apostle bears witness as well: *And without a doubt,* he says, *great is the sacrament of piety, which was manifested in the flesh, was justified in the spirit, appeared to the angels, was preached among the nations, was believed in the world, was taken up in glory* (1 Tm 3:16). And it would be surprising, unless I am very much mistaken, if God is ever said to know anything at a particular moment in time, without its really meaning that he causes it to be known, whether by angels or by human beings.[28] This manner of speaking, when what is brought about is signified by what brings it about, is frequent enough in the holy scriptures, especially when something is being said about God, which Truth itself, presiding over our minds, cries out cannot apply to him if taken literally.

How God is still working

20, 40. So now let us come at last to the distinction between the works of God which he is working on up till now, and those works from which he rested on the seventh day. There are people, you see, who reckon that it was only the world itself that was made by God, while everything else is now being made by this very world, as God indeed arranged and commanded, but that he himself does not work at anything.[29] Against them we bring that statement of the Lord's: *My Father is working until now* (Jn 5:17); and in case anyone should suppose he is working on something alone with himself, and not in this world, *The Father abiding in me,* he says, *performs his works; and as the Father raises the dead and brings them to life, so too the Son brings to life whom he will* (Jn 5:21.[30])

Next, to show that it is not only such great and outstanding deeds that God works at, but also these earthly and minor matters, we have the apostle saying: *Fool, what you sow is not brought to life unless it dies; and as for what you sow, you are not sowing the body that is going to be, but the bare grain of, well, wheat or one of the others; but God gives it a body as he has decided, and every kind of seed its own proper body* (1 Cor 15:36-38). So then, let us believe, or if we are

---

27. See Heb 1:2. For this concern to distinguish "before the ages," "from the ages," "in the ages," see 17, 35 above, and note 23.
28. See Book IV,9,17 above, note 20.
29. Was this, perhaps, a naive Christian variation on the Stoic idea of a "world soul"?
30. With an intrusion from some other similar, half remembered text, like Jn 14:10.11.

able to, let us even understand that God is working until now in such a way that if his working were to be withheld from the things he has set up, they would simply collapse.

41. But clearly, if we suppose that he now sets any creature in place in such a way that he did not insert the kind of thing it is into that first construction of his, we are openly contradicting what scripture says, that he finished and completed all his works on the sixth day. Yes, within the categories of the various kinds of thing which he set up at first, he manifestly makes many new things which he did not make then. But he cannot rightly be thought to set up any new kind, since he did then complete them all.

And so by his hidden power he sets the whole of his creation in motion, and while it is whirled around with that movement, while angels carry out his orders, while the constellations circle round their courses, while the winds change, while the abyss of waters is stirred by tides and agitated by cyclones and water-spouts even through the air, while green things pullulate and evolve their own seeds, while animals are produced and lead their various lives, each kind according to its bent, while the wicked are permitted to vex the just, he unwinds the ages which he had as it were folded into the universe when it was first set up. These, however, would not go on being unwound along their tracks, if the one who set them going stopped moving them on by his provident regulation.

All things governed by divine providence

21, 42. Indeed it is incumbent upon us to take a lesson from these things that are being formed and born in time on how we ought to regard such matters. It is not, after all, for nothing that it is written about Wisdom that to her lovers *she shows herself merrily on their paths, and goes to meet them with all providence* (Wis 6:16). Absolutely no attention is to be paid to those who would have us believe that only the loftier parts of the cosmos, that is, those that extend upward from the upper limits of this grosser atmosphere, are governed by divine providence, while this lowest part, consisting of the earthy and moist element and of this air that is nearest to us which grows damp from the misty exhalations of land and water, and in which winds and clouds spring up together, is the play-thing rather of chance and fortuitous upheavals. Against such people, you see, we have the words of the psalm, after which conducting the praise of the deni-zens of heaven, turns also to these lower beings and says: *Praise the Lord from the earth, dragons and all deeps of the abyss; fire, hail, snow, ice, spirits of the tempest, which carry out his word* (Ps 148:7).

Nothing, I agree, appears to be so rolled around by chance as all these storms, this frequent turbulence that affects the constantly changing face of the sky—which too is not improperly classified under the heading of "earth." But when the psalm adds *which carry out his word*, it shows clearly enough that the subjection of these things as well to the regulation of the divine command, while it does indeed escape our notice, is not absent from the nature of the universe.

But why turn to the psalm? We have it from the mouth of the Savior himself that not a single sparrow falls to the ground without the will of God, and that he is the one who clothes the grass of the field, so soon to be thrown onto the bonfire.[31] Does this not confirm our confidence that it is not just the whole of this part of the cosmos allotted to things mortal and perishable, but even the most insignificant and disregarded particles of it, that are governed by divine Providence?

Further arguments in support of God's providential control of the world

22, 43. Now these people who deny this and do not agree with holy words of such weighty authority, but assume that this part of the cosmos is just tossed about by fortuitous upheavals rather than being regulated by the Wisdom of the divine Majesty, set about "proving" their point by a double argument: the one I have just mentioned about the unpredictable irregularity of storms; and another from the good and bad fortunes of human beings, which happen to them in total disregard of their deserts. But if they would only observe in this same part of the cosmos the marvelous ordering of the bodily organs of any living creature you like, which is apparent to any person of average intelligence and sense, not just to members of the medical profession who have dissected and examined them sedulously in performance of their art, then surely they would exclaim, would they not, that not for a single moment of time does this same part of the world cease to be governed by God, from whom comes every standard of measures, every balance of numbers, every system of weights.[32]

So can there be any idea, then, more absurd, more insipidly irrational than to assert that this whole part of the cosmos is void of the beck and call of Providence, when you can see how the least, the meanest things in it are formed with such regular precision, that if you reflect upon them a little more attentively, the inexpressible wonder of it will almost make your hair stand on end? And since the nature of the soul excels the nature of the body, what could be more mindless than to suppose that there is no judgment of providence upon the morals of human beings, when so many indications of its ingenuity can be brilliantly demonstrated in their flesh? But because these trifles are readily available to our senses, and we can easily investigate them, the ordered regularity of things is limpidly evident in them, while matters in which the order is not apparent to us are reckoned to lack any order by people who assume that anything they cannot see does not exist, or else if they allow its existence assume that it is just like whatever they are used to seeing.

31. See Lk 12:28.6.
32. See Wis 11:20.

An illustration of how even things we see developing and coming to be now were all created simultaneously at the beginning

23, 44. We, however, whose steps are being directed through holy scripture by the same divine Providence, lest they should stray into that kind of perversity, must now make every effort to track down with God's help, from the clues also supplied by his very works, where and how he created simultaneously, when he rested from his completed works, these things we see around us, on whose forms and appearance he is still working right up till now through the succession of times and seasons.

So let us consider then the beauty of any kind of tree you like, in its trunk, its branches, its leaves, its fruits. This admirable sight did not of course suddenly spring into being in its full stature and glory, but in the order with which we are also familiar. Thus it rose up from its roots, which the first sprig had fixed in the earth, and from there grew all these parts in their distinct forms and shapes. That sprig, furthermore, came from a seed; so it was in the seed that all the rest was originally to be found, not in the mass of full material growth, but in the potentiality of its causative virtue. That full growth, you see, was built up from a supply of earth and moisture.[33] But much more wonderful and remarkable is that virtue in a tiny grain which enabled the surrounding moisture mixed with earth to be turned as the basic material into the specific wood of that tree, into the spread of the branches, into the green and the shape of the leaves, into the succulent form of the fruit and the wonderfully disposed order of all these. Does anything, after all, sprout or hang from that tree which has not been extracted and brought out from the hidden treasure of that seed?

But that seed came from a tree (not the same one, it is true, but another) and that tree again from another seed; sometimes, though, a tree also comes direct from a tree, when a cutting is taken and planted. So then, both seed from tree and tree from seed and tree from tree; but never seed from seed unless tree first between, while tree from tree, even if no seed between. Each therefore follows the other alternately, but both come from the earth, not the earth from them. So their first parent is the earth.[34] The same too with animals, though there could be a doubt whether their seed first came from them, or they from their seed; still, whichever of these came first, it is utterly certain that it came from the earth.

45. Now just as all these elements, which in the course of time and in due order would constitute a tree, were all invisibly and simultaneously present in that grain, so too that is how, when God created all things simultaneously, the

---

33. Two of the elements of ancient chemistry—and biochemistry.
34. His thoughts now go back, without his actually telling us so, perhaps even without his noticing it himself, to the original production of trees from the earth on the third day of creation; it is fairly evident that he has the sixth day of creation in mind when he goes on to say that "it is the same with animals."

actual cosmos is to be thought of as having had simultaneously all the things that were made in it and with it *when the day was made* (Gen 2:4). This does not only mean the sky with the sun and the moon and the stars, the cycle of whose movements gives the appearance of such regularity, and the earth and the deeps of the abyss, which experience, so to say, unpredictably variable movements, and which together contribute to the cosmos its lower part; it also includes those things that water and earth produced potentially in their causes, before they could evolve through intervals of time, as they are now known to us in the works on which God is continuing to *work until now* (Jn 5:17).

Recapitulation of the "literal meaning" of Genesis 2:4-6

46. All this being so, *This is the book of the creating of heaven and earth when the day was made God made heaven and earth and all the greenery of the field before it was upon the earth, and all the hay of the field before it sprang up* (Gn 2:4-5)—but not in the way in which he makes them by the work he works at until now, by means of rain and human agriculture; that, you see, is why he added: *For God had not rained upon the earth, and there was no man to till the land* (Gn 2:5). No, he made them then in the way in which he created all things simultaneously, and finished them on day number six, when he presented the day he made six times with the things he made, not as a series one after another in time, but as a series to be known in due order in their causes. From these works he rested on the seventh day, and was happy also to offer his quiet rest to the awareness and joy of the same single day. And that is why he blessed and sanctified the day, not in any of his works but in his resting.

Thus it is that without setting up any further creature, but steering and guiding by his regulatory action all the things he made simultaneously, he continues to work without ceasing, simultaneously both resting and working, in the way the matter has already been studied and discussed. As for those works of his on which he is continuing to work right up till now, and which have to be unrolled as the times themselves unwind, Scripture makes a start at telling the story of them when it says: *But a spring was coming up from the earth, and was watering all the face of the earth* (Gn 2:6). As we have said about this spring all that we thought had to be said, let us make a fresh start at reflecting on what follows.

Book VI

Genesis 2:7: The creation of the man from the dust of the earth

Two possible ways of reading this text; first the way of recapitulating the work of the sixth day

1, 1. *And God fashioned the man, dust from the earth, and blew into his face the puff of life. And the man was made into a living soul* (Gn 2:7). Here the first thing to be looked into is whether this is recapitulating what we read about the making of the man on the sixth day, so that now we are being told how he was made; or whether on the day when God made all things simultaneously, he also made the man among them, like the hay of the earth before it had sprung up. In this case the man too, after being already made in some secret workshop of nature in another manner, like all the things which God created simultaneously "when the day was made," would with the onset of time also be made in this manner in which he now passes his life in this visible form, whether well or badly, just as the hay, which was made before it had sprung up on the earth, now sprang up with the onset of time and the irrigation provided by that spring, so that it might be upon the earth.[1]

2. So first of all then, let us try taking it as going back and recapitulating the sixth day. Perhaps, that is to say, the man may have been made on the sixth day just as the day itself was originally made, as the solid structure, as the earth and the sea. We should not say of these, after all, that after being already made in some kind of starting process they were stored away and only later, with the onset of time, burgeoned clearly into this visible appearance which the finished

---

1. He does not make himself very clear about the difference between the two ways he proposes of reading this verse. At first it looks as if one way is to read it as the amplification of what God did on the sixth day, while the other is to read it as saying that the man was also included in all the things that God made simultaneously on the one and only day of creation, "when the day was made" (Gn 2:4). But Augustine is not in fact retreating from the position he established in Book V that God indeed created all things simultaneously on that one day, and that the six days of Gn 1 are so many "repetitions" of this one and only day of creation. So the alternative to reading the verse as recapitulating what is said about creating the man on the sixth repetition of the one day is to read it as stating something that God did after setting time in motion, after "the onset of time," which in Book V,7,20 Augustine considered to have started with the spring coming up from the earth (Gn 2:6).

universe presents, but rather that from the starting point of the ages, "when the day was made," the whole universe was established, and that simultaneously among its component elements were established those things that would start burgeoning with the onset of time, whether vegetation or animals, all of them according to their kind.

It is not to be thought of, surely, that the very constellations, after being originally made, were stored away among the elements of the universe, and emerged later on with the onset of time, to blaze forth into the forms which now shine in the sky, but rather that they were all created simultaneously in the sequence of that perfect number six, "when the day was made." So the question is whether the man too was already made like that in the actual form in which he lives his natural life and spends it either well or badly, or whether he also was made in some secret workshop, like the hay of the field before it sprang up, so that his being made from the dust would be for him to burgeon later on with the onset of time.

Difficulties about this way

2, 3. Let us try taking it then as meaning that he was molded from mud on that actual sixth day in this familiar visible shape, but that this was not mentioned then, and is now being put to us by way of recapitulation, and let us see whether scripture itself agrees with us. This certainly is what was written, when the story of the sixth day's works was still being told: *And God said: Let us make man to our image and likeness; and let him have authority over the fishes of the sea and the flying things of heaven and all cattle and all the earth and all crawling things which crawl over the earth. And God made the man, to the image of God he made him; male and female he made them, and God blessed them saying: Increase and multiply and fill the earth and lord it over it, and have authority over the fishes of the sea and the flying things of heaven and all cattle and all the earth and all reptiles crawling over the earth* (Gn 1:26-28).[2] So then, he had already been formed from mud, already put to sleep for the woman to be made from his side; but this had not been mentioned, and was mentioned at this point by way of recapitulation.

Well, but on the sixth day it was not that the male was made, and the woman made later on with the onset of time; but, *He made him*, it says; *male and female he made them and blessed them.* So how then, with the man already placed in Paradise, was the woman made for him? Or had this also been left out, for scripture to recall at this point? In that case, Paradise was also planted on the sixth day

---

2. It looks as if Augustine was here using a different manuscript or codex of Genesis from the one he used when he first transcribed this passage, Bk III,19,29 above. The differences in this translation follow differences in the Latin text.

and the man placed there and put to sleep for Eve to be formed; and when she had been, he woke up and gave her a name. But none of this could have been done except over intervals of time. And so it follows that none of it was done in the way that all things were created simultaneously.

The rest of the story evidently tells of events occurring in time

3, 4. However easy, after all, a human being may think it is for God to have done all this simultaneously with the rest, we know with absolute certainty that the words of a human being can only be uttered aloud over intervals of time. When we hear the man's words, therefore, when he was giving names either to the animals or to the woman, or when he also went on to say, *For this reason a man shall leave his father and mother and be joined to his wife; and they shall be two in one flesh* (Gn 2:24), whatever the syllables this was uttered with, not even any two of them could have been spoken simultaneously; how much less, then, could all of this have happened all together with all the things that were created simultaneously! And this would mean that those "all things" were not after all created simultaneously at the absolute starting point of the ages, but that they were made over successive intervals of time, and that that day originally established was of a material, not a spiritual nature, and was making morning and evening by heaven knows what kind of circling round of light, or by its emission and contraction.

But taking into consideration everything that has been discussed above in the preceding books, we have concluded more probably and reasonably that it was a spiritual day which was sublimely instituted at the beginning, and that the day was called a kind of wise light, whose presence was vouchsafed to the simultaneous creation through six stages of knowledge arranged in due order; and that this opinion chimes in with the words of scripture, because it says later on, *When the day was made God made heaven and earth, and all the greenery of the field before it was upon the earth, and all the hay of the field before it sprang up* (Gn 2:4-5); and is also supported by what is written elsewhere: *The one who lives for ever created all things simultaneously* (Sir 18:1). So there can be no doubt that this account of the man being molded from the mud of the earth, and a wife being formed for him from his side, does not belong to the creating of all things simultaneously and God resting when they were complete, but to that divine work which is continuing now through the ages as they unroll, at which *he is working until now* (Jn 5:17).

5. What it comes to is that the very words in which the story is told how God planted Paradise, and placed in it the man he had made and brought the animals to him for him to give them names, and how, since no helper like him was found among them, he then formed the woman for him from the rib he had removed

from him, are enough to indicate to us that none of this belongs to that work of God from which he rested on the seventh day, but rather to this at which he goes on working through the march of time until now. When Paradise, you see, was being planted, this is how he tells the story: *And God planted Paradise in Eden to the East, and put the man there whom he had molded. And God still cast up from the earth every tree that had a beautiful look about it and was good for eating* (Gn 2:8-9).

4. So when he says, *he still cast up from the earth every tree that had a beautiful look about it,* he makes it perfectly clear that he was now casting up trees from the earth quite differently from the way the earth then on the third day produced grass for fodder, seeding seed according to its kind, and fruit trees according to their kind. This surely is the force of *he still cast up*: over and above, that is to say, what he had already cast up. Then, of course, it was done potentially, causally, in the work involved in creating all things together simultaneously, from which he rested on the seventh day when they were completed; whereas now it was being done visibly in the work belonging to the march of time.

6. Unless maybe someone wants to say that not every kind of tree was created on the third day, but that some kinds were put aside to be created on the sixth, when the man was made and established in Paradise. But scripture states in the clearest terms what things were created on the sixth day, namely "live soul" exemplified in every kind of quadruped and crawling thing and beast, and man himself to the image of God, male and female. Now it could indeed pass over how the man was made, while telling us all the same that he was made on that day, in order to take up the story later on of exactly how he had been made—that is, from the dust of the earth, and the woman for him from his side. But it could not possibly pass over any specific kind of creature, either when God said *Let it be made* or *Let us make*, or when it says *Thus it was made*, or *God made*. Otherwise it would have been pointless to distinguish things so carefully for every single day, if we could be left with any suspicion of the days being mixed up, so that while grass and trees were allotted to the third day, we were to believe that some trees were also created on the sixth day, which scripture kept quiet about on the sixth day itself.

5, 7. Finally, what answer shall we give about the beasts of the field and the flying things of heaven, which God brought to Adam, to see what he would call them? Here is what the text says: *And the Lord God said: It is not good for the man to be alone; let us make for him a help suited to him. And God still fashioned from the earth all the beasts of the field and all the flying things of heaven, and he brought them to Adam to see what he would call them; and everything that Adam called a live soul, that is its name. And Adam gave names to all cattle and to all the flying things of heaven and to all the beasts of the field. For Adam, however, there was not found a helper like him. And God cast alienation of mind over Adam, and he fell asleep. And he took one of his ribs and filled up its place with flesh. And the Lord God built the rib which he had taken from Adam into a woman* (Gn 2:18-22).

So if, when a help like the man was not to be found among cattle and the beasts of the field and the flying things of heaven, God went on to make him a help like him out of a rib from his side, and this was done after he had still molded these same beasts of the field and flying things of heaven from the earth, and brought them to him, how can we understand this to have been done on the sixth day, seeing that on that day the earth produced live soul in accordance with God's word, while it was on the fifth day that the waters produced flying things, likewise in accordance with God's word? So then, it would not say here, *And God still molded from the earth all the beasts of the field and all the flying things of heaven*, when the earth had already produced all the beasts of the field on the sixth day, and the water all the flying things on the fifth, unless it had been done in another way then, that is potentially and causally, as befitted that work by which all things were created together simultaneously, from which he rested on the seventh day, and in another way now, as we see the things which he creates over intervals of time in the way he is working until now.

And thus it was in the course of these most familiar days of material light, which are made by the sun going round and round, that Eve was made from the side of her man. That is when it was, after all, that God still molded beasts and flying things from the earth, among which a help like Adam himself was not to be found, and she was formed. So it was in the same sort of days that God also molded him from mud.

8. Nor can it be said that the male indeed was made on the sixth day, the female some days later, since on the sixth day itself it says as clearly as anything, *Male and female he made them and blessed them* etc., all of which is said about them both and to them both. So then, in one way both of them then, and in another way both of them now; then, that is to say, in terms of a potentiality inserted as it were seminally into the universe through the Word of God, when he created all things simultaneously, resting from them on the seventh day, from these, all things would be made and happen, each in its own time, through the ordered course of the ages; now, on the other hand, in terms of the work to be bestowed on the march of time, at which "he is working until now"; and it was right and proper for Adam to be made now in his own time from the mud of the earth, and his woman out of the man's side.

A warning not to take Augustine as saying things that in fact he is not saying

6, 9. Let us take it then as established that in allotting some of the works of God to those invisible days in which he created all things simultaneously, some to these visible ones in which he is working every day at whatever is being as it were unwrapped in time from those primordial wrappings, we have been following the words of scripture, and been led by them to make the distinction in a way that is not absurdly wrongheaded. The point is admittedly somewhat difficult to grasp, and those who are rather slow on the uptake may find it hard to make head or tail of it. So what we now have to beware of is being thought to hold and express opinions which we know perfectly well that we do not hold or express.

For although, you see, I have been directing the reader's steps as carefully as I could, I imagine all the same that several people are groping in the dark in these places and are thinking that the man was first made in that work of God in which he created all things simultaneously, in such a way as to be actually living some sort of life and thus to hear, believe, and understand the words of God addressed to him, when God said, *Behold, I have given you every seed-bearing fodder* (Gn 1:29). So please, would anyone who thinks this be assured that I have neither held nor expressed this opinion.

10. And again, if I say that in that first establishment of things, in which God created all things simultaneously together, man was not to be found as he is now, not only as an adult but not even as an infant, not only as an infant, but not even as a fetus in his mother's womb, not only this, but not even as the visible seed of a human being; such people will suppose that he was not to be found there at all. So then, let them go back to scripture, and they will find there that on the sixth day man was made to the image of God, made, indeed, male and female.[3] Next let them inquire when the woman was made, and they will find it was outside those six days; the time she was made, after all, was when God was still molding from the earth beasts of the field and flying things of heaven,[4] not when the waters produced flying things and the earth produced living soul, which also includes beasts.[5]

So both then and later on; not either then and not later on, or later on and not then; and not different ones later on, but the very same ones in a different way then, in a different way later on. They will ask me: "In what way later on?" I will answer: "Visibly, with the appearance of the human constitution as we know it—not however born of parents, but he from mud, she from his rib." They will ask: "In what way then, the first time?" I will answer: "Invisibly, potentially, in their causes, in the way things to come are made when they have not yet been made in actual fact."

11. Here, very likely, they will be at a loss to understand. Everything they are familiar with, after all, down to the bodily materiality of seeds, is being eliminated.

---

3. See Gn 1:27.
4. See Gn 2:19-22.
5. See Gn 1:20.24.

The man, you see, was not even anything like that when he was made in that first setting out of six days. Seeds do indeed provide some sort of comparison with this, on account of the growths to come that are bound in with them; before all seeds, nonetheless, are those causes. But this such people do not understand.

So what am I to do but advise them, as best I can, to trust God's scriptures, and to believe that the man was made both then, when "God made heaven and earth when the day was made," about which scripture says elsewhere, *The one who lives for ever created all things simultaneously* (Sir 18:1); and also then, when no longer creating things simultaneously but each in its own time, he molded him from the mud of the earth and the woman from one of his bones? Scripture, in fact, does not allow us either to understand them as being made like that on the sixth day, or for all that as not being made at all on the sixth day.

An untenable suggestion that it was only the human soul which was created on the sixth day

7, 12. So then, perhaps what was made on the sixth day was their souls, where the image of God is rightly to be understood, in the spiritual reality of their minds, so that their bodies might be formed later on? But this too is something we are not permitted by the same text of scripture to believe; first, because of that completion of God's works, I do not see how these could be understood to be complete if anything was not there established in its causes which would later on be realized visibly; secondly, because the difference of sex between male and female can only be verified in bodies. But if anyone should suggest that each sex is, so to say, represented in every single soul with reference to its intellectual understanding and its rational activity,[6] what will he make of the fruits which God gave them on that very day for food, which of course would only be suitable

---

6. A suggestion that Augustine takes up and works out at considerable length in *The Trinity* XII,1,1-4 and 14,22—15,25, equating intellectual understanding with the "word of wisdom" and rational activity with the "word of knowledge" (1 Cor 12:8). But the way he mentions the point here rather suggests that this was not an original idea of his own, but one derived from someone else, which he then, many years later, developed himself. He has already in fact noted the point in passing earlier on in this work, III,22,34; see note 33 on that passage. Now one of the works on which he was engaged about the same time as this *Literal Meaning of Genesis*, at which time he was also beginning *The Trinity*, was *Teaching Christianity*, vol I/11 in this series. And in this, at the end of the third book, he sets out some rules for interpreting scripture drawn up by a Donatist scholar, Tychonius, for whom Augustine clearly had some respect. His seventh rule is called "recapitulation," a term we have found Augustine using here in this volume of *The Literal Meaning of Genesis*. It is true that when referring to it in *Teaching Christianity*, Augustine does not illustrate it by mentioning this suggestion; but that may well have been because Tychonius did link it to the idea of only the human soul having been created on the sixth day, which Augustine, as we see, could not accept. So I am tempted to infer that it was from Tychonius that Augustine in fact derived the idea of the two mental functions of intellectual understanding and rational activity being analogues in the soul to the distinction of male and female in the body.

for human beings with bodies? Because if anybody should wish to take this food also in a figurative sense, they would be departing from the proper literal meaning of what actually happened, which in narratives of this kind is the first thing that has to be established with every possible care.

How could God address people on the sixth day who did not yet exist as such?

8, 13. "So how," you may say, "was he talking to beings who could not yet either hear or understand, because they were not even there in a form capable of catching his words?" I could reply that God addressed them in the same way as Christ addressed us when we were not yet born and only due to to arrive on the scene so long in the future—and not only us but also all those who are going to be born after us. It was to all, I mean, whom he knew would be his in the future that he said: *Behold, I am with you up to the very end of time* (Mt 28:20). In the way the prophet was known to God, who said to him: *Before I formed you in the womb I knew you* (Jer 1:5), in the way Levi was tithed while he was in the loins of Abraham,[7] so why not Abraham himself too like that in Adam, and Adam himself in the first works of the universe when God created all things simultaneously?

But the words of the Lord, spoken by his actual mouth, and God's words, spoken through the mouths of prophets, are time-bound, bodily utterances, and with all their syllables take up and use up corresponding intervals of time. The case was very different, though, when God said: *Let us make man to our image and likeness; and let him have authority over the fishes of the sea and the flying things of heaven and all cattle and all the earth and all crawling things which crawl over the earth*; and: *Increase and multiply and fill the earth and lord it over it, and have authority over the fishes of the sea and the flying things of heaven and all cattle and all the earth and all crawling things which crawl over the earth*; and: *Behold, I have given you every seed-bearing fodder seeding seed which is over all the earth, and every fruit tree which has in it fruit of seed-bearing seed, which shall be for you for food* (Gn 1:26.28-29). These words of his were uttered before any sound waves in the air, before any voices from lips or clouds,[8] uttered in that supreme Wisdom of his, through whom all things were made, uttered, not as if to be dinned into human ears, but to insert in things already made the causes of things still to be made.

With them he was making by his almighty power things still in the future, and was establishing as it were in the seed or root of all times the man still to be

---

7. See Heb 7:9-10.
8. The allusion here is to God's words heard at the giving of the law on Mount Sinai (Ex 20), or at the baptism of Jesus (Mk 1:11), at his transfiguration (Mk 9:7), and when he was answered by his Father with a voice from heaven (Jn 12:28).

formed in his own due time. This was when he was establishing the point from which the ages, established by him who is before all ages, were to begin. Some created things, you see, precede others in time, while some precede others in their causes; he though precedes all the things he has made, not only in his pre-eminence as the cause of all causes, but also in his eternity. But this is something we may, I hope, discuss later on at more appropriate places in the scriptures.

A question aired which the author thinks ought not to be pursued

9, 14. Now we must bring to a close what we have begun discussing about man, and show that restraint which requires us, faced with the profundities of scripture, to be painstaking in our researches rather than cavalier in our assertions. I mean, that God knew Jeremiah before he formed him in the womb we are not permitted to doubt, seeing that he says in the clearest terms, *Before I formed you in the womb, I knew you* (Jer 1:5). But where he knew him before he thus formed him, whether in his proximate causes, as Levi was tithed in the loins of Abraham, or in Adam himself, in whom the human race was set up as in its root; and in him, whether as he had already been formed out of mud, or only made causally among those works which God created all simultaneously; or whether it was not rather before any creation, in the way he chose and predestined his holy ones *before the foundation of the world* (Eph 1:4); or in fact in all his preceding causes, both ones I have mentioned and ones I have not, before he was formed in the womb—I really do not think we ought to inquire too minutely, as in any case it would be almost, if not totally, beyond our feeble powers to discover.

What has to be agreed is that Jeremiah, from the moment he was born of his parents and saw the light of day, lived his own life, growing up to be capable of living it well or badly; but that in no way at all was he so capable before that, not only before he was formed in the womb, but not even once he had been, and before he was born. There is, after all, not the slightest hesitation in that judgment of the apostle's about the twins in Rebecca's womb not yet doing anything either good or bad.[9]

15. Nonetheless it is not for nothing that it is written that not even an infant, *whose life on earth has lasted but a day, is pure of sin* (Job 14:5, LXX), and in that verse in the psalm that: *I in iniquities was conceived, and in sins did my mother nourish me in the womb* (Ps 51:5), and that in Adam all die, *in whom all sinned* (Rom 5:12). For the moment, however, let us hold with complete certainty that, whatever parental merits, whatever divine grace may be passed on to children before they are born, whoever God may sanctify before birth, there is on the one hand no unfairness with God, and nobody on the other does anything as a personal

---

9. See Rom 9:11; Gn 25:22-25.

act, either good or bad, before birth. Let us be equally certain that the opinion some people hold, according to which souls sinned, some more some less, and were thrust down into different kinds of body, depending on the different degrees of their guilt,[10] is not compatible with the apostle's assertion in the plainest terms that those who have not yet been born have done nothing either good or bad.

16. And this raises another question, to be dealt with in its proper place: what the whole batch or lump[11] of the human race contracted from the sin of our first parents, who were just the two of them, all by themselves; that the man, though, could have earned nothing of the kind for us before he was molded from the dust of the earth, before he lived in his own time, there is no question whatever. We could not say, after all, that Esau and Jacob, who did nothing either good or bad, so the apostle has told us, before they were born, derived any liability from their parents if their parents themselves had done nothing good or bad either. Nor could we say that the human race sinned in Adam if Adam himself had not sinned; and Adam would not have sinned unless he had been alive at his own time, able to live either well or badly. So it is pointless looking for any sin or good deed of his, while he was only set up in his causes among all the things created simultaneously, and not yet living his own proper life, or even existing there in his parents living theirs. In that original establishment of the world, you see, when God *created all things simultaneously* (Sir 18:1), the man was made in order to come into being in the future—there was the idea or formula of one to be created, not any action of one already created.

Different levels of causality at which things pre-exist in their causes

10, 17. But all this is different in the very Word of God, where these things were not made but are eternal; different in the constituent elements of the universe, where all things to come in the future were made simultaneously; different again in things that are being created, not now simultaneously but each in its own time, in accordance with its simultaneously created causes, like Adam already formed out of mud and "ensouled" by the breath of God, like the hay that sprang up; different in seeds, in which it is as if the primordial causes are being repeated again, derived from things which came into being in accordance with the cause which he first established, like grass from the earth, seed from grass.

In all these cases things already made received the characteristic activities of their own proper time, which came forth in manifest forms and natures from the secret formulae that are causally latent in creation; things like the grass which sprang up over the earth, and the man made into a living soul, and other things of

---

10. An opinion favored by the great biblical scholar and theologian of Alexandria, Origen (died 254), which was condemned as heretical long after his death.

11. The metaphor is taken from the bakery, the human race being regarded as an enormous batch of dough, infected by Adam's sin with "the leaven of malice and wickedness" (1 Cor 5:8).

this sort, whether shrubs or animals, which belong to that work of God at which he is working until now. But these things too carry within them a repetition, so to say, of their very selves, invisible in some hidden power of reproduction, derived from those primordial causes of theirs, in which they were inserted into the world that was created "when the day was made," before they ever burgeoned into the visible manifestations of their specific natures.

11, 18. If those first works of God, you see, when he created all things simultaneously, had not been complete in their own fashion, there can be no doubt that what was needed for their completion would have been added later on, to put together a kind of completeness of the universe from all the particular elements of its two halves, so to say, as if they were parts of a whole which would be completed by joining them together. Again, if those works had been completed in the way they are now completed when they burgeon into manifest forms and activities each in its own time, then clearly either nothing would be made from them after those times, or else that would be made which God is not ceasing to work at producing from these things that are continuing to spring up, each in its own time.[12]

Now, however, the truth is that those things which were due to be "unwrapped from their wrappings" in the course of subsequent ages, and which God created simultaneously with all things when he made the world, were both completely finished then in a certain way and also started off in a certain way; completely finished indeed, because they have nothing in their natural manner of running their course in time which was not made causally in that primordial creation; started off, however, since they were seeds in a sense of future realities, destined to germinate in suitable places from hidden obscurity into the manifest light of day through the course of the ages.

To give us sufficient proof of this the words of scripture itself are quite remarkably apt, if you keep wide enough awake in reading them. It says, you see, both that the works were finished and that they were started; if they had not been finished, after all, it would not say, *And heaven and earth and all their arrangement were finished. And God finished on the sixth day his works which he made; and God rested on the seventh day from all his works which he had made.*[13] *And*

---

12. A formidably impenetrable statement! But I fear that all he is doing is obscuring, by scrupulous qualifications, his desire to say that if the original simultaneous creation of the universe in its causes had not been complete in its own way, then God would have completed it by doing those things that he went on to do when the "march of time began," like making the man from the dust of the earth.

13. This sentence, from "and God rested," is not found in any of the manuscripts, but is added by the Maurists and earlier editors—rightly in my opinion. It is unlikely that Augustine would have gone straight from the finishing of the works on the sixth day to the blessing of the seventh without first even mentioning what God did on the seventh. But it would have been the easiest thing in the world for either stenographers taking his dictation, or the first copyists making fair copy from the stenographers' tablets, to jump from one sentence beginning "And God" to the next one beginning in the same way.

God blessed the seventh day and consecrated it; and again, unless they had been started then, the text would not continue *because on that day God rested from all his works which God started to do* (Gn 2:1-3).

19. Here therefore, if anyone should ask how he finished and how he started—he did not, you see, finish some works and start others, but finished and started the very same ones, certainly, from which he rested on the seventh day—the answer is clear from what we have said above. That is to say, we understand God to have finished these works when he created all things simultaneously so completely, that there was nothing for him still to create in the series of times which had not already been created by him here in the series of causes, while we take him to have started in that he here fixed the causes which he would put into effect later on.

Accordingly, *God formed the man dust of the earth*, or mud of the earth—that is, from dust or from mud of the earth—*and breathed*, or puffed, *into his face the breath of life, and man was made into a live soul* (Gn 2:7). He was not then predestined, because that was done before all ages in the foreknowledge of the creator; nor then causally either started in his finished completeness or finished completely at the starting stage, because that was done at the start of the ages in the primordial ideas when all things were created simultaneously; but he was then created in his own time, visibly in the body, invisibly in the soul, consisting as he does of soul and body.

How God made the man's body

12, 20. So now, then, it is time for us to see how God made him, first his body from the earth; later on we shall also see about his soul, if we find we are up to it. But that God molded the man from mud with actual material hands is an excessively childish notion, so that if scripture had actually said this, we ought rather to believe that the author was employing the word metaphorically than that God is furnished with such limbs as we see in our own bodies. It says, after all: *Your hand scattered the nations* (Ps 44:2), and: *You led out your people with mighty hand and and upraised arm* (Ps 136:12); and is there anybody so witless as not to understand that the name of this limb is being used to stand for God's authority and power?

21. Nor is any attention to be paid to what some people think, that what makes the man God's chief work is that with all the other things *he spoke and they were made* (Ps 148:5), while this one he actually made himself; no, it is rather that this one he made to his own image. The reason it says there that "he spoke and they were made" is that they were made by his Word, like a man telling other men to do things with words expressing out loud thoughts conceived in time.[14] That, however, is not how God speaks, except when he speaks through a bodily crea-

---

14. This is a paraphrase for a clause that I confess baffles me: *sicut per hominem hominibus dici potuit verbis, quae temporaliter cogitantur et voce proferuntur*; "as could have been said through a man to men with words that are thought in time and uttered out loud."

ture, as he did to Abraham, to Moses, to his Son through the cloud.[15] But before there was any creation, in order that there might be a creation, it was spoken with that Word which was in the beginning, *God with God*; and because *all things were made through him, and without him was made nothing* (Jn 1:1.3), then of course the man too was made through him.

It is certain, after all, that heaven was made with a word, because "he spoke and it was made"; and yet it is written: *And the heavens are the work of your hands* (Ps 102:25). And about what you could call this lowest basement level of the universe it is written: *Since his is the sea and he made it, and the dry land his hands molded* (Ps 95:5). This should not, therefore, be seen as the man's special privilege, that for the rest of creation "God spoke and they were made," while this one he made himself; or that he made the rest with a word, this one with his own hands. No, what gives the man his pre-eminence is that God made man to his image, in this respect that he gave him an intelligent mind, which puts him ahead of animals, something we have already discussed earlier on.[16] If, thus given the place of honor, he fails to understand so as to use it well, he will be compared to the beasts he has been put in charge of; that, you see, is what is written: *The man, established in honor, did not understand; he was matched with the senseless cattle and became like them* (Ps 49:12), because God also made the beasts, but not to his image.

22. Nor can it be said: "He himself made the man, while as for the beasts he gave the order and they were made"; he made both the man and them, after all, through his Word, through which all things were made. But because this same Word is both *his wisdom and his strength* (1 Cor 1:24), his hand is spoken of as meaning, not a visible limb, but his effective power. This same text, you see, which says that God molded the man from the mud of the earth, also says that he molded the beasts of the field as well from the earth, when he led them to Adam, together with the flying things of heaven, to see what he would call them. That, you see, is what is written: *And God still molded from the earth all the beasts* (Gn 2:19). So if he himself formed both the man from the earth and the beasts from the earth, what pre-eminence does the man enjoy in this respect, other than that he was created to the image of God? This, however, not as regards the body, but as regards the intelligence of the mind, which we will talk about later on.

In his body too, though, he has a characteristic which would be an indication of this, the fact that he was made upright in posture, by which to remind himself that he should not aim at earthly goals, like animals which get all their pleasure from the earth, which is why they all move about belly down, leaning forward horizontally. Thus his body too is adapted to his rational soul, not as regards the lineaments and

---

15. See, for example, Gn 18; Ex 3:2; Lk 9:35; Jn 12:28.
16. See Bk III, 19,29—21,33. But there he keeps on referring the reader to what he is going to say when he discusses the making of the man, here in this book.

shapes of his limbs, but rather with respect to his standing up vertically, his head towards the sky, in order to gaze at those things that are sublime in the body of the universe itself, just as the rational soul ought to straighten itself up to look at what is most excellent in the spiritual realm, in order to *savor the things that are above, not the things that are on the earth* (Col 3:2).

13, 23. But in what manner did God make him from the mud of the earth? Was it straightaway as an adult, that is, as a young man in the prime of life? Or was it as he forms human beings from then until now in their mothers' wombs? There is no one else, after all, who does this but the one who said, *Before I formed you in the womb, I knew you* (Jer 1:5), so that the only thing proper to Adam was that he was not born of parents but made from earth; so was this done in such a way that by growing up through "the ages of man," he would complete the number of years which we see that nature has allotted to the human race? Or is this a matter, rather, which it is not our business to inquire about? Whichever of these he did, after all, he did what was in the power of a God both omnipotent and wise, and what befitted him to do.

While he set the proper times, I mean, for different kinds and qualities of things to develop from a latent to a manifest state of being, he in no way abdicated the supremacy over everything of his will. That is, he gave creation its numerical rhythms by his power; he did not bind his power to these same numerical rhythms. His Spirit, you see, was so borne over the world in the making,[17] that it continued also to be borne over it once made, in terms not of place or space but of supereminent authority.

24. Is anybody unaware, I mean, that when water mixed with earth comes to the roots of a vine, it is led up into the vine-stock as rich nourishment, and there takes on the quality with which it goes on into the budding bunch of grapes, and becomes wine as this grows, and sweetens the wine as it matures, which still has to ferment when it is pressed out, and left to settle and age until it is fit to drink with real profit and pleasure? Does that mean that the Lord had to go looking for a vine or earth or these set intervals of time, when with a wonderful conciseness he turned water into wine, and such wine as even a tipsy table guest could praise?[18] Did the one who instituted time need the help of time?

Is not a definite number of days, appropriate to each species, required for every kind of snake to be conceived, formed, hatched, reach full growth? Were these days looked for to turn the rod in the hand of Moses and Aaron into a serpent?[19] And when these things happen they are not happening against nature except from our point of view, to which the course of nature appears from a

---

17. See Gn 1:2.
18. See Jn 2:7-10.
19. See Ex 4:3; 7:10.

different angle, but not from God's point of view, since nature for him is simply what he has made.

The relationship between the primal formulae and what emerges from them in historical time

14, 25. What it is our business, though, to inquire about is how those causal formulae were set, with which he primed the universe when he first created all things simultaneously. Was it so that all things that come to birth in the way we see, whether shrubs or animals, would go through the different intervals of time appropriate to each species in its taking shape and its growth; or so that they would be fully formed forthwith, in the way it is believed that Adam was made without any growing pains in adult manhood? But why should we not believe that those formulae contained each potentiality, so that anything would be actualized from them that pleased the one who would make them?

If we limit them, you see, to the first mode, it begins to look as if not only was that turning of water into wine a deed done in defiance of them, but so also are all miracles which are performed in defiance of the usual course of nature. If, on the other hand, we limit them to the second mode, there will be the much more absurd consequence that these everyday forms and appearances of nature run through their various spans of time in defiance of those primary causal formulae of everything that comes to birth. It remains, therefore, that they were created with an aptitude for each mode, whether for this one by which temporal events most commonly transpire, or for that one by which rare and miraculous things are done, as it may please God to do whatever is appropriate to the time.

15, 26. In any case, the man was made, in accordance with primary causes, in such a way as to be the first man. So he did not have to be born of parents, who were not there before him anyway, but to be formed from mud in accordance with the causal formula in which he was originally made; because if he had been made otherwise, God would not have made him among the works of those six days. When he is said to have been made among them, it was, surely, the actual cause that God made, by which the man was to come to be in his own time, and in accordance with which he was to be made by the one who both finished what he had started on account of the perfect completeness of the causal formulae, and started what was to be finished on account of the ordered march of time.

So then, if in those first causes of things which the creator originally inserted into the world he not only put that he was going to form the man from mud, but also in what manner he was going to form him; whether as in the womb of a mother, or in the form of a young man, there can be not the slightest doubt that he did it as he had prescribed it there; he would not, I mean, go against his own program in making him. If, however, he only put there the virtual possibility of the man being made, in whatever manner he was made, so that it could be done both this way and that, that is, that whatever it was it would be there, because it was able to be there both this way and that, while he reserved to his own will the one way in which he was actually going to make him and did not weave it into the constitution of the world, it is clear that in this case the man was not made in a way contrary to how he was in that primordial establishment of causes, because there too it was prescribed that he could be made in this way, though it was not there prescribed that he necessarily would be made in this way. This, you see, was not written into the establishment of creation, but left to the good pleasure of the creator, whose will is what imposes necessity on things.

16, 27. We too, after all, with our rather feeble human capacity, can know, here and now about things that have come to be in time, what is due to the nature of each, which we will have gathered by experience; but about whether it will actually happen so in any particular case, we are entirely ignorant. It is the due of this young man's nature, for example, that he should grow old; but whether this is also God's will for him, we do not know. But it would not even be the due of his nature unless this had first been so in the will of God, who established all things. And of course the hidden formula of old age is there in the youthful body, as that of youth is in the child's body; nor can it be perceived with the eyes, as can childhood in a child, as youth in a young man; but by another kind of awareness it is inferred that there is present in nature something latent whereby these hidden rhythms[20] are brought out into the light of day, whether of youth emerging from childhood, or of old age emerging from youth. So then the formula which prescribes that this is a real possibility is hidden, but from the eyes, not from the mind. Whether on the other hand it is also something necessary, of that we are altogether ignorant. We know indeed that what prescribes it as a possibility is there in the nature of the body itself, while manifestly not there is any formula prescribing that it is necessary.

17, 28. But perhaps the necessity of this man actually growing old is written into the world, while if it is not in the world, it is in God. For it is what he wills that will of necessity be in the future, and it is those things that he has foreknown which will really be in the future. Many things, you see, will be in the future as determined by lower, secondary causes, while if they are also in God's fore-knowledge like that, they really will be in the future. But if they are there in a different manner, they will rather be in the future as they are there, where the one who foreknows them cannot be mistaken. Thus old age, we say, lies in the future for this young man; but for all that it is not in the future if he dies before reaching it, while this will happen as determined by other causes, whether ones woven into the world or ones reserved to the foreknowledge of God.

---

20. *Numeri*; literally "numbers." See one of his favorite quotations, Wis 11:20: "You have arranged all things in measure, and number and weight."

Thus with reference to some causes of things in the future, Hezekiah was going to die; but God added fifteen years to his life,[21] thereby doing something, of course, which he had foreknown *before the foundation of the world* (Eph 1:4) that he was going to do, and which he had reserved to his own will. So he did not do something that was not going to be in the future; on the contrary, this rather was what was going to be in the future, which he had foreknown he was going to do. And yet those years would not rightly be said to have been added, unless they were added to something which with reference to other causes would have been different. With reference, therefore, to lower, secondary causes, he had already reached the end of his life; while with reference to those which lie in the will and foreknowledge of God, who had known in eternity what he was going to do at that time—and this really was what would be in the future—he was going to reach the end of his life when he actually did reach it; because even though this was granted to his prayers, the fact that he was going to pray a prayer that deserved to be heard was also something, surely, foreknown by the one whose foreknowledge cannot be mistaken. And that is why what he foreknew would of necessity come to pass in the future.

18, 29. Hence, if the causes of all that was to be in the future were sown in the world when "that day was made" on which God created all things simultaneously, Adam was not made otherwise when he was formed from mud already in adult manhood, in the more credible view, than he was in those causes when God made the man in the works of the six days. He was there, in this case, not only as a possibility of being made like that, but also as of necessity having to be made like that. God, after all, no more made him[22] contrary to the cause which he deliberately predetermined, than he makes anything contrary to his own will.

If, however, he did not stick all causes into creation as originally established, but reserved some to his own will, these which he reserved to his own will are not indeed dependent on the necessity of those which he created; nonetheless these which he reserved to his own will cannot be contrary to those which he set up in creation by his will, because God's will cannot be contrary to itself. So he set them up in such a way that what they are the causes of has the possibility of issuing from them, but does not do so of necessity; while the other causes he so concealed that from them issues of necessity what he put as a possibility in the created causes.

---

21. See 2 Kgs 20:1-7.
22. Reading *fecit* with the Maurists and most of the manuscripts, instead of CSEL's *facit*, "makes things"—a general statement, rather than a particular one with reference to Adam, which I am sure Augustine was more likely to have made.

Whether the first man's body was formed embodying soul or spirit

19, 30. Again, a question often raised is whether it was an embodiment of soul[23] that was first formed for the man out of mud, such as we now have, or an embodiment of spirit, such as we shall have when we rise again. For although this sort of body will be changed into that—*it is sown, you see, embodying the soul, it rises embodying the spirit* (1 Cor 15:44)—still the reason there is some debate about what sort was first made for the man is that if it was an embodiment of soul that was made, we will not receive again[24] what we lost in him, but something altogether better to the extent that spirit surpasses soul, when we shall be *equal to the angels of God* (Lk 20:36). But while the angels can indeed surpass other human beings, in their justice as well as their nature, can they also surpass the Lord? And yet it says about him: *You have made him a little less than the angels* (Ps 8:5; Heb 2:7); in what respect, if not because of the weakness of the flesh which he took from the virgin, *accepting the form of a slave* (Phil 2:7), in which he died to redeem us from slavery?

But why should we spend any more time discussing the point? After all, there is not a shadow of doubt about the apostle's judgment on this matter. When he wished to present evidence to prove that there is a body embodying soul,[25] he did not point to his own or anyone else's body which could be seen then and there, but rather turned to this very place in scripture, and presented it with the words: *If there is an embodiment of soul, so also is there of spirit. That too is how it is written: The first man, Adam, was made into a living soul, the last Adam into a life-giving spirit. But not first the one with the spirit, but the one with the soul; later the one with the spirit. The first man from the earth, earthy; the second man from heaven, heavenly. As the earthy one, such are those who are earthy; and as the heavenly one, such are those who are heavenly. And just as we have put on the image of the earthy one, so let us also put on the image of him who is from heaven* (1 Cor 15:44-49). What answer can be made to that? So then, we now bear the image of the heavenly man by faith, due to have in the resurrection what

---

23. *Animale corpus*, contrasted with *corpus spiritale*. *Animale* does not mean "animal," but literally "soulish," that which has, is quickened by, an *anima;* and to translate *spiritale* as "spiritual" conveys entirely the wrong impression in current English, suggesting to most people an immaterial body, which amounts to a bodiless body. In contrast to *animale* it means being quickened by spirit, no longer by soul. "Soul" and "spirit" are by no means synonymous in scripture, whether in the Hebrew of the Old Testament or the Greek of the New; on the contrary, they are nearly always in mutual opposition, so that in Saint Paul, who is here just following Old Testament usage, *psychikos*, having a psyche or soul, is mostly synonymous with *sarkikos*, being carnal or fleshly.

24. In the resurrection of the dead.

25. In fact, Saint Paul was wishing to prove that real, material bodies will rise again in the resurrection of the dead, but that then they will be embodiments of spirit, not of soul. It is Augustine who is wishing to prove, from Saint Paul, that Adam's body was an embodiment of soul—which indeed he does quite legitimately.

we now believe. But we have worn the image of the earthy man from the very starting point of the human race.

Another twist to this question

20, 31. Here another question confronts us; how are we renewed, if we are not brought back through Christ to what we first were in Adam? For although many things, when renewed, are brought to a better, not to their original condition, they are still being renewed from a condition that is inferior to the one they have just been in before. So how is it that that son was dead and came to life again, had been lost and was found, how is it that the first robe is brought out to him, if he is not getting back the immortality which Adam lost?[26] How, though, did he lose immortality if he had a body that was merely "ensouled"? It will not, you see, be an "ensouled" but an "enspirited"[27] body when *this perishable thing puts on imperishability and this mortal thing puts on immortality* (1 Cor 15:53).

So we are caught on the horns of a dilemma; on the one hand the judgment must stand, which we have just quoted, giving as an example of the "ensouled" body the text, "the first man, Adam, was made into a living soul"[28]; on the other this renewal and retrieval of immortality may not unreasonably be thought of as being a future return to the original condition—precisely, that is, to what Adam lost. To solve the problem some people have supposed that at first indeed the man had an "ensouled" body, but that while he was settled in Paradise he was changed, as we also shall be in the resurrection. The book of Genesis does not in fact mention this; but to reconcile the two testimonies of the scriptures, the one that talks of an "ensouled" body, and the many which are found in the sacred writings about our renewal, they were convinced that this was the necessary solution.

21, 32. But if this is so, then our efforts to take those trees and their fruits in their proper historical meaning, besides any figurative signification they have, will be in vain. Who, I mean to say, would ever suppose that food of that sort

---

26. See the parable of the prodigal son, Lk 15:11-32, in particular verses 32 and 22. It was a conventional patristic exegesis to see the first robe which the father ordered to be brought out for the returning prodigal as representing what was lost for humanity by Adam's sin. As we shall see, Augustine will argue that this was primeval innocence or grace, not specifically immortality. But evidently many people thought that what "the first robe" stood for was immortality.

27. The Latin words I am rendering "ensouled" and "enspirited" are *animalis* and *spiritalis*. They would normally be translated "animated" and "spiritual." But he is, in line with his quotation from 1 Cor 15, making a contrast between having a soul, our present "mortal" condition, and having a spirit—in fact a share in God's Spirit. So I felt constrained to invent these two terms. See note 23 above.

28. Here the Maurists complete the quotation from 1 Cor 15:53 and add "the last Adam into a life-giving spirit;" CSEL prints it, but in brackets, and indicates that it is absent from all the manuscripts. It is not in fact germane to the problem he is dealing with.

from fruit trees could have been necessary for immortal and "enspirited" bodies? However, if no other solution can be found it is better that we should opt for understanding Paradise in a spiritual sense, than that we should either think that man is not renewed, when scripture mentions this so often, or reckon that he has something restored to him which there is no indication that he ever lost. Add to this, that the very death of the man, which so much scriptural evidence agrees that he earned by his sin, indicates that he would have gone without dying if he had not sinned. So then, how was he mortal, if he was not going to die? Or how was he not mortal, if he only had an "ensouled" body?

22, 33. For this reason some people consider that it was not the death of the body which he earned by sin, but the death of the soul, which iniquity brings about.[29] They believe, you see, that because of his "ensouled" body, he would have departed this body, to the rest, that is, which is enjoyed by the saints who have already fallen asleep, and at the end of the world would receive back the same organism in immortal form. What this means is that the death of the body would have occurred, apparently, from natural causes as with other animals, not from sin. But the apostle again opposes these people, and says: *The body indeed is dead because of sin, while the spirit is life because of justice. But if the Spirit of him who raised up Christ from the dead dwells in you, the one who raised up Christ from the dead will also raise up your mortal bodies through his Spirit dwelling in you* (Rom 8:10-11). And thus the death of the body too comes from sin. So then, if Adam had not sinned he would not have died in the body either, and accordingly he would have had an immortal body too. So the question remains, in what way immortal, if merely "ensouled"?

23, 34. But again, those who think that his body was changed in Paradise, to become "enspirited" from being merely "ensouled," fail to see that if he had not sinned, there was nothing to prevent him after life in Paradise, which he would have lived obediently and justly, from receiving this very same change of body for eternal life, where he would no longer be needing bodily, material food. So why should we be necessarily obliged, just for this reason, to understand Paradise in a figurative and not a proper historical sense, because the body would not be able to die, except for sin? It is indeed true that he would not have died even in the body, unless he had sinned; the apostle in fact says in so many words: *the body is dead because of sin* (1 Cor 15:45). All the same, it could still be merely "ensouled" before his sin, and after a life lived justly be "enspirited" when God willed.

---

29. Reading *facit* with one manuscript, instead of *fecit*, "brought about," which is the reading of the Maurists, of CSEL, and presumably the other manuscripts. But here I think Augustine is making, or quoting "some people" as making, the general statement applying to all iniquity, rather than a particular one which only applies to Adam's sin; they are fitting that sin into a general category. The change from one to the other, by copyists or stenographers, could have come about as easily in either direction.

The solution to the problem

24, 35. "So how," they ask, "are we said to be renewed if we don't get back what was lost by the first man, *in whom all sinned*"(Rom 5:12)? Clearly, there is a way in which we get this back, and there is a way in which we do not get this back. And so it is not the immortality of an "enspirited" body that we get back, which the man did not yet have; but what we get back is the justice[30] from which the man fell through sin. So we shall be renewed from the staleness of sin, not to the original "ensouled" body which Adam had, but to something better, that is, to an "enspirited" body, when we are made *equal to the angels of God* (Lk 20:36), fit for heavenly mansions, where we will not need any food that decays. So then, we shall *be renewed in the spirit of our minds* (Eph 4:23), *according to the image of him who created us* (Col 3:10), which Adam lost by sinning. We shall also be renewed in the flesh, though, *When this perishable thing puts on imperishability* (1 Cor 15:54) so that it may be an "enspirited" body, into which Adam had not yet been changed, but into which he was to have been changed if he had not earned the death of his "ensouled" body by sinning.

36. Finally, the apostle did not say, "the body indeed is mortal because of sin," but: *the body is dead because of sin* (Rom 8:10).

25. Before sin, in fact, the body could have been said to be both mortal for one reason and immortal for another; mortal, that is, because it was able to die, and immortal because it was able not to die. It is one thing, after all, not to be able to die, like natures which God created immortal,[31] while it is quite another to be able not to die; and this is the way the first man was created immortal, something to be granted him by means of the tree of life, not by his natural constitution. From this tree of life he was cut off when he had sinned, so that he could die,[32] while if he had not sinned he would have been able not to die.

So then, he was mortal in virtue of the make of his "ensouled" body, immortal in virtue of his maker's favor. If the body, you see, was simply "ensouled," then it was certainly mortal, because it was able to die, though it was also immortal for the reason that it was also able not to die. Nor will it enjoy the immortality of not

---

30. The more usual word for rendering *justitia* in biblical and theological contexts is "righteousness"; the word "justice" is avoided because it is considered to have too limited a connotation of law and order, and judges and law courts. But while this is true, I still think it is the best word in the scriptural and theological context, first because "righteousness" has become such a "churchy" word, and secondly because "justice" is so easy to link with the concept of "justification." What is meant by this is our being justified by God, that is our being treated as not guilty, our being declared innocent by him, and thus in truth having innocence restored to us. Adam enjoyed this innocence before he sinned, but as a gift of God's grace. After the development of the doctrine of original sin, this state of pre-lapsarian innocence came to be known as "original justice."

31. The spiritual creation, angels (and the ones which fell, demons); and according to some thinkers of that time, the heavenly bodies also.

32. See Gn 3:22-24.

being able to die at all unless it is "enspirited," which is something we are promised will be ours in the resurrection. Accordingly, that "ensouled" and thereby mortal body, which would be "enspirited" and thereby altogether immortal on account of justice, became on account of sin, not mortal, which it had been before, but dead, which it need not have become, if the man had not sinned.

26, 37. How, after all, could the apostle call this body of ours dead, when he was talking about people who were still alive, if not because the very condition of dying, as a result of the sin of our first parents, stuck fast to their descendants? This body too, you see, is merely "ensouled," as was also that of the first man. But this one, while in the same class as an embodiment of soul, is much worse off, because it is under the necessity of dying, which that one was not. For although it still remained for it to be changed and "enspirited" and so receive full immortality, where it would not need perishable food, still if the man lived justly his body would be changed into an "enspirited" state; he would not go down to death.

With us, however, even if we live justly, the body is going to die; and it is because of this necesity, coming down from the sin of that first man, that the apostle called our body dead, since *in Adam we all die* (1 Cor 15:22). Again, he says: *As the truth is in Jesus, you are to put off, in line with your previous habits, the old man, the one who is being corrupted on the lines of deceitful desires*, that is, who has become Adam through sin. But see what follows: *But be renewed in the spirit of your minds, and put on the new man, the one who in line with God was created in justice and true holiness* (Eph 4:21-24). There you are; that is what Adam lost through sin. So it is in this that we are being renewed as regards what Adam lost, that is, as regards the spirit of our minds; but as regards the body, which is sown embodying soul and will rise embodying spirit,[33] we shall be renewed with a better one, which Adam did not yet have.

27, 38. Then again, the apostle says: *Stripping off the old man with his deeds, put on the new, who is being renewed for recognition of God according to the image of the one who created him* (Col 3:9-10). This is the image stamped on the spirit of his mind which Adam lost through sin;[34] and this is what we get back through the grace of justification, not an "enspirited" and immortal body which he did not yet have, and which all the saints rising again from the dead will have; this after all is the reward of the merit which he lost. Accordingly, that *first robe* (Lk 15:22) is either the actual justice from which he fell or else, if it does signify the putting on of bodily immortality, then he also lost this in the sense that because of his sin he was unable to attain it. Someone, after all, who did not

---

33. See 1 Cor 15:44.
34. See *Revisions* II,24,2. There he writes: "In the sixth book I said that Adam lost by sin the image of God according to which he was made. This is not to be taken as meaning that nothing of it remained in him, but that it was so disfigured as to need reworking."

receive the wife he hoped for, having offended the man he hoped to get her from, is said to have lost his wife as well as his honor.[35]

28, 39. According to this opinion then, Adam had an "ensouled" body, not only before Paradise, but when he was already established there, although in the inner man he was "enspirited" according to the image of the one who created him. This he lost by sinning,[36] also earning the death of his body, which by not sinning he would have deserved to have changed into an "enspirited" body. I mean, if his inner life was also just something "ensouled," we cannot be said to be renewed to this feature of his. Those, after all, who are being told, "Be renewed in the spirit of your minds," are being told precisely to become "enspirited"; but if he was not that even in his mind, how are we being renewed to what the man never was?

Now the apostles and all the just certainly still had merely "ensouled" bodies; but all the same they were living an "enspirited" inner life, being renewed, that is to say, "for recognition of God according to the image of the one who created them." This does not mean, however, that they would no longer be able to sin, were they to consent to iniquity; that spiritual people too can fall when tempted to sin is shown by the apostle, where he says: *Brothers and sisters, even if a person is caught in some offense, all you who are spiritual correct such a one in a spirit of gentleness, taking a look at yourself, in case you too should be tempted* (Gal 6:1). He said this in case anyone should deem it impossible for Adam to sin if he was "enspirited" in mind, though only "ensouled" in body.

All this being so, we are still in no inordinate hurry to affirm anything for sure, but instead we are waiting to see whether the rest of scripture does not block this understanding of things.

A difficult question about the soul is deferred to the next book

29, 40. There follows, you see, a question about the soul of extreme difficulty, which many people have wrestled with, and left to us to wrestle with too. It may be because I have not been able to read everything written by all who have dealt with it in accordance with the truth of our scriptures, and who have been able to reach an answer that clears up all doubts; or it may be because it is such a vast question, that even if they have found a genuine solution, they are not easy for such as I am to understand; whatever the reason, I must confess that nobody has yet managed to persuade me I can ever have such a grasp of the soul, that I may assume there is no further question to be asked. Whether I am now going to find and define anything certain, I do not know. But what I can do in this line, I will undertake, if the Lord assists my efforts, to set out in the next volume.

---

35. I suspect there is a reference here to some current piece of scandal in high circles, perhaps even in the imperial court.
36. See note 34 above.

Book VII

Genesis 2:7, continued: On the creation of the soul

On what can be meant by God puffing or blowing

1, 1. *And God fashioned the man with dust from the earth, and puffed into his face the puff of life, and the man was made into a living soul* (Gn 2:7). We also set ourselves the task of considering these words of scripture at the beginning of the previous volume, and discussed what seemed to be the intention of scripture about the man thus made, and particularly about his body, as much as we thought sufficient. But because there is a problem, and no small one either, about the human soul, I reckoned that that should be deferred to this volume, not knowing how much the Lord was going to help me, eager as I am to speak correctly; but at least I knew this, that I was not going to speak correctly unless, and to the extent that, he did help me. "Correctly," though, means truly and relevantly, without either brashly refuting or brazenly asserting anything while there is still any doubt over its being true or false, whether in the light of Christian faith or of Christian learning; but unhesitatingly affirming whatever can be taught on the clear evidence of facts and by the light of reason, or on the unambiguous authority of the scriptures.

2. First, then, let us take a look at what is written here: God *puffed*, or blew, *into his face the puff of life*. Several codices, you see, have *breathed* or *exhaled*[1] *into his face*. But since the Greek codices have *enephusesen*,[2] there is no doubt that *puffed* or *blew* is what is to be said. Now we were inquiring in the previous volume about the hands of God, where the man was being thought of as having

---

1. *Inspiravit* in the Latin, being given as an alternative to *spiravit*. But we do not have a word "inbreathed" in English, and "inspired" would clearly not do; nor for a rather different reason would "inhaled."

2. From *emphusao*, which in classical Greek certainly had the stronger sense that Augustine and his Latin versions give it here. It is the same word as we find in Jn 20:22, where the risen Christ breathed on the disciples and said "Receive the Holy Spirit." Augustine and his versions, however—and also the Vulgate, which in Gn 2:7 has *inspiravit*—there read *insufflavit*, and so are still thinking of something stronger than just breathing; perhaps the evangelist too wanted to give the impression of Jesus *blowing* the Holy Spirit into the apostles.

been shaped or formed out of mud; so what is to be said now on the words written here, "God puffed," if not that just as he did not form or shape with bodily hands, so neither did he puff with gullet or lips? However, it is precisely by this word that scripture in my opinion has come most effectively to our aid over a most difficult question.

2, 3. Some people, you see, have supposed on the strength of this word that the soul is something from the very substance of God, meaning that it is of the same nature as he is; and the reason they think so is that when human beings puff they expel something from themselves in the puff.[3] But we should really be advised by this very word to repudiate such an idea as dead against Catholic faith. We, after all, believe that the nature and substance of God, which is believed by many, understood by few, to consist in the Trinity of persons, is altogether unchangeable, while as for the nature of the soul, who can doubt that it can change, whether for better or for worse? And accordingly the opinion that the soul and God are of one substance is simply sacrilegious; for what else does it mean but that he too is assumed to be changeable? So then it is to be believed and understood, and to be doubted in no way whatsoever, that the soul, as the right faith holds, comes from God as a thing which he has made, not as being of the same nature as he is, whether as something he has begotten or in any way at all produced from himself.

3, 4. "And how," they ask, "is it written: *He puffed into his face, and the man was made into a live soul*, if the soul is not a part of God or quite simply the substance of God?"

But in fact it is the use of this very word that makes it quite clear that this is not so. When human beings puff, after all, the soul itself certainly moves the nature of the body which is subject to it, and it is from that, not from itself, that it makes the puff—unless of course these people are so crass, they do not know that it is from our alternately inhaling and exhaling, as we breathe in from the air around us and breathe out again, that the puff is made which we produce when we puff deliberately. If on the other hand it is not from the surrounding atmosphere, breathed in and out, but from the very nature which our bodies consist of that we expel something by puffing, the nature of the body is not the same as that of the soul—a point on which these people too, of course, agree with us.[4] Accordingly even in this case the substance of the soul, which governs and moves the body, is one thing, and quite another is the puff which it makes, not from itself, but from the body subject to it as to its governor and mover.

---

3. He is almost certainly referring to the Manichees, to whom he will return explicitly in 11,17 below.
4. The whole drift of the Manichee religion was to release spirit from the grip of matter, hence souls from bodies.

And so we have—in incomparably different ways indeed, but still we have the soul ruling its subject the body and God ruling his subject the creation; why then should God not rather be understood to have made the soul from creation his subject when he is said to have puffed, seeing that the soul itself, though not master of its body in the same way as God is of the universe, still makes a puff by moving the body, and not out of its own substance?

5. We could indeed say that it is not even God's puff that is the man's soul, but that God by puffing made the soul in the man. But then it could possibly be thought that the things he made with a word are better than what he made with a puff, because with us too a word is better than a puff; so for the moment there is no reason, in terms of the aforesaid argument, why we should hesitate to say that God's puff is the soul itself, provided it is understood that it is not God's nature or substance, but that for him to puff is the same as to make a puff, while to make a puff is the same as to make the soul.

This opinion is supported by what God says through Isaiah: *For breath will proceed from me. and I have made every puff*; what follows, you see, teaches us that he does not mean any kind of bodily puff; because after saying *I have made every puff, and on account of sin,* he goes on, *I have saddened him a little and have struck him* (Is 57:16-17). So what can he be calling a puff but the soul, which has been struck and saddened on account of sin? What therefore is *I have made every puff* but "I have made every soul"?

4, 6. And so if we were to say that God is something like the soul of this bodily, material universe, the universe itself being for him like the body of a single animating principle, we would be right in saying that by puffing he only made a bodily material soul for the man out of his own body, from the air at his disposal; but we would be wrong to think that what he gave by puffing he had given from his very self. No, it would be from the air of his own body, entirely at his disposal, as the same sort of thing all round it is at the soul's disposal, something bodily to make a puff out of, not out of its very self. Now however, because in fact we say that it is not only the bodily part of the universe that is subject to God, but that he is above everything created, whether bodily or spiritual, we are to believe firmly that by puffing he made the soul neither from his very self nor from bodily material elements.

Whether the soul was made out of nothing, or out of some already made spiritual material

5, 7. Whether he made it, though, out of that which quite simply was not, that is out of nothing, or out of some sort of thing which had already been made by him in the spiritual order, but was not yet soul, is a question that can properly be asked. If, you see, we do not believe that God still goes on creating anything out of nothing after that creation of all things simultaneously, and do believe that his resting from all the finished works which he had started to make means that whatever he made from then on would be made out of these, then I do not see how we can understand him to go on making souls out of nothing. Or should we say that in those works of the first six days he did indeed make that hidden day as (if this is what we should rather believe) the common spiritual and intelligent nature of the angels, and the visible universe of heaven and earth, and that in these now already existing natures he created the ideas or formulae of other natures yet to come in the future, not these actual natures themselves? Otherwise, if they had already been created as they were to be in the future, they would not any longer be things to come in the future. In that case there was not yet any nature of the human soul among the things actually established, and it then began to be when God made it by puffing and introduced it into the man.

8. But that is not the end of the question, which still has to be asked, whether God created out of nothing the nature which is called soul and which did not previously exist; this would mean that his actual puff was not made from any substance at his disposal, as we were saying about the puff the soul makes out of its body, but was quite simply made out of nothing at the moment God chose to puff, and was made as the soul of the man. Or was there, on the other hand, something spiritual already there, although whatever this was it was not yet the nature of soul, and was it from this that God's puff was made in order to be the nature of soul? In the same way there was not yet any nature of the human body before God had formed it from the mud, or dust, of the earth; dust or mud, after all, was not human flesh, but still it was something from which that, not yet in existence, would be made.

6, 9. So then, can one really believe that in those works of the six days God established not only the causal formula of the future human body but also the material it would be made from, earth that is to say, from the mud or dust of which it would be molded, while for the soul he only established there the formula to which it would be made, without any appropriate material of its own kind which it would be made from? If the soul, you see, were something unchangeable, we ought not to be inquiring in any way at all about its quasi-material; but as it is, its changeableness is obvious enough through its sometimes being rendered misshapen by vices and errors, sometimes being put into proper shape by virtues and the teaching of truth, but all within the nature it has of being soul. In the same way flesh, in its own nature which it has of being flesh, is both embellished with health and disfigured by diseases and wounds.

But just as this, apart from being already flesh and in that nature ranking high as being beautiful or low as being misshapen, also had some material, that is to say earth, from which to be made in order to be entirely flesh; in the same way soul too, possibly, before being made in the actual nature which is called soul, whose beauty and misshapenness consist respectively in virtue and vice, could have had some appropriate spiritual material which was not yet soul, just as earth, from which flesh was made, was already something, though it was not flesh.

Difficulties about the notion of spiritual material

10. But then earth was filling the lowest part of the universe before ever the man's body was made from it, and thus contributing to the totality of the universe, so that even were no flesh to be made from it of any animated being, it would still with its own specific nature complete the mass and fabric of the universe, which thereby gets its name of heaven and earth.

7. As for that spiritual material, however, if there was any from which the soul would be made, or if there is any from which souls are still being made, what precisely was it? What name, what specific nature, what function does it hold among created things? Is it alive, or not? If it is, how does it act? What does it contribute to the effectiveness of the whole? Does it live a happy, blessed life, or a miserable one, or neither? Does it quicken anything? Or is it unoccupied with any of this, and resting idly in some hidden place of the universe without conscious sensation or vital movement?

If, you see, it was not yet any sort of life at all, how could it be the material, neither bodily nor alive, for life yet to be in the future? So this is plainly untrue, or excessively obscure. If on the other hand it was already living a life neither blessed nor miserable, how could it be rational? But if that material became rational at the moment when the nature of the human soul was made from it, then non-rational life was the material of the rational, that is of the human, soul. So what was the difference, then, between that and merely animal soul? Or was it already potentially rational, not yet actively so? After all, we see how the infant soul, already of course the soul of a human being, has not yet begun to use reason, and yet we already call it a rational soul; so why should we not suppose that in that material from which it was made even sentient activity was stilled, just as in this infant soul, which is certainly that of a human being already, rational activity is stilled for the time being?

8, 11. But now suppose it was a blessed life from which the man's soul has been made; this means that it has become something worse, and consequently that it is not now the soul's material, but that the soul is just a kind of flux or discharge from it, because when any material is formed or shaped, especially by God, it is without a doubt shaped into something better. Though even if the human soul could be thought of as being a discharge from some kind of life made by God in a certain state of blessedness, not even in that case can it be supposed to have deserved to begin to be so from some act of its own, except from the moment it began to live its own proper life after being made into a soul animating flesh, and using the senses of the flesh as its messengers, and being aware in itself of living with its own will, intelligence, and memory. You see, if there is something, and that something blessed, there for God to breathe this discharge from it into the flesh he has formed, thus making the soul as if by puffing, this something is in no way changed or altered, nor does it lose anything when this flux from which the soul is made is discharged from it.

9. It is not, after all, a body, to be diminished by any sort of exhalation.

12. If, however, non-rational soul is somehow or other the material from which the rational, that is the human, soul is made, again the question has to be asked what was this non-rational sort made from, because it too has no other maker but the creator of all natures. Was it made from bodily material? So why not this rational sort too? Unless of course anyone chooses to deny that God could make all at once what can also be made, so to say, in stages. Accordingly, whatever stages may be introduced, if body is the material of non-rational soul and non-rational soul is the material of the rational, it is undoubtedly the case that body is the material of the rational soul—something that no one, as far as I know, has been brazen enough to assert, except for those who classify soul itself as some kind of body.

13. And then care has to be taken lest it should be supposed that there can be a transference of soul from brute beast to human being (which is clean contrary to the truth and to Catholic faith), if we concede that non-rational soul is like the underlying material from which the rational soul may be made. In this case, you see, it will come about that if it becomes the soul of a human being when changed for the better, when changed for the worse it will become a brute beast's—an absurdity of which even the successors of some of those philosophers[5] were ashamed, and so they said that they had not actually thought that, but had been misunderstood.

And I think it is rather the same as if someone were also to come to this conclusion from our scriptures, where it says: *Man established in honor did not understand; he was matched with senseless cattle and became like them* (Ps

---

5. Which philosophers? He has not named any so far in this Book VII, unless he is referring to those whom he has just dismissed rather contemptuously as having thought that soul—and for that matter, God—is to be classified as some sort of body. In this event he may have had Aristotle in mind, who was indeed commonly misunderstood at that time to have taught that the soul is made from a "fifth element," a *quintessence*, the stuff from which he in fact supposed the heavens and the heavenly bodies to be made. But then in the next paragraph Augustine mentions, as a kind of afterthought, the idea of the transmigration of souls entertained by some philosophers, possibly even by Plato. Now he certainly has not yet discussed that idea in this work. But he does discuss it in *The Trinity* XII,15,24; and there he uses the same phrase, which I translate "successive states of soul," *revolutiones animarum*, as we find here. This discussion does indeed come at the end of Book XII, which was probably written several years after he finished this work on Genesis. But he began work on *The Trinity* at roughly the same time as *The Literal Meaning of Genesis*. So just possibly he was dictating the two works concurrently, and got his wires mixed up, and here thought he had already mentioned the Platonic theory of reminiscence, and the very similar one of transmigration.

49:13); or again that other text: *Do not hand over the soul that acknowledges you to the beasts* (Ps 74:19). There are no heretics, after all, who do not read the Catholic scriptures, and the only thing that makes them heretics is that they do not understand these well, and then obstinately insist on their own false interpretations against the true meaning of them. But however it may or may not be with the opinion of the philosophers about the successive states of souls, it is at any rate entirely inconsistent with Catholic faith to believe that there can be a transmigration of the souls of animals into human beings, or of human souls into animals.

Further remarks on the relationship between human and animal souls

10, 14. That human beings certainly become like brute beasts by the kind of lives they lead is something both screamed at us by the newspaper headlines,[6] and attested by scripture. That's the sense of what I have just quoted: *Man established in honor did not understand; he was matched with senseless cattle and became like them,* but in this life, of course, not after death. It was into the power of such beasts, accordingly, that the person did not want his soul to be surrendered, who said: *Do not hand over the soul that acknowledges you to the beasts*—the sort the Lord warns us to beware of where he says that *they are wearing sheep's clothing, but inwardly are ravening wolves* (Mt 7:15); or else he means the devil and his angels, because he too is called both a lion and a dragon.[7]

15. With what kind of argument, after all, do those philosophers support their case, who think that after death the souls of human beings can be transferred into beasts, or those of beasts into human beings? This one certainly, that similarity of behavior draws them to this; for example misers into termites,[8] the greedy and grasping into hawks, fierce and proud people into lions, those bent on unclean pleasure into pigs and other things like that. That is the line they take, and they fail to notice that in no way at all on these grounds can it happen that the soul of an animal is transferred after death into a human being. I mean to say, in no way at all will a pig resemble a human being more closely than another pig; and when lions grow gentle they become more like dogs or even sheep than like men. Since, therefore, animals do not depart from the behavior of animals, and even those which do become a little different from the rest are still much closer in

---

6. Yes, an anachronism; but I think it gets exactly the tone of his phrase *ipsae res humanae clamant*: "human affairs themselves scream."
7. See Ps 91:13; Lk 10:19; 1 Pt 5:8; Rv 12:3, etc.
8. *Formicas,* which are of course just ants. But ants are not, for most of us, really repellent enough insects. I was tempted to use the obsolete word "pismires," which means ants; clearly repulsive creatures. But I properly restrained myself, and have compromised with "termites"—ants on a larger and less innocuous scale.

resemblance to their own than to humankind, and differ from human beings far more widely than from other animals, these souls will never belong to human beings, if like really does attract like.

But if this argument is false, how can that opinion be true, seeing that they offer no other reason to show that it is even likely, let alone true? So I myself am more inclined to believe what their later followers also say, that those men who originally proposed these ideas in their books intended it rather to be understood that people become like brute beasts in this life by any kind of perverse and shameful behavior, and thus are changed after a fashion into brute beasts; and that they hoped by thrusting the disgrace of it in this way under their very noses to recall them from the depravity of their lusts and ambitions.

The same continued, with an aside about the Manichees

11, 16. Things, after all, that are said to have happened, like some people remembering in which animal bodies they had been, are either just stories that have been made up, or else were produced in their minds by demons playing jokes on them. I mean, if it can happen in dreams that people recall by a false memory having been what in fact they never were, or having done what they never did, why should we be surprised if by a just and undeclared judgment of God demons are conceded the power of producing something similar in the minds of people who are awake?

17. Much worse, however, and more detestable than those heathen philosophers, or any others hooked on this futile theory of the transmigration or successive states of souls, are the Manichees, who think of themselves or like to be thought of as Christians. The others at least distinguish between the nature of the soul and the nature of God, whereas these people, who say that the soul is the very substance of God and quite simply the same as what God is, have no hesitation in saying that it is changeable to such a loathsome extent, that there is no kind of grass or grub, according to their quite astonishingly crazy ideas, with which it has not been mixed up and into which it cannot be recycled.

Let them only, however, clear their minds of questions about the obscurest of matters, which inevitably land them, as they mull over them in their crude, literal-minded way, head over heels in such false, noxious and monstrous opinions; let them only get a firm grip on what has been naturally and truly grafted into every rational soul without the slightest possibility of doubt, that God is altogether unchangeable and imperishable; and their whole thousand-sided fable will immediately collapse—that mythical picture they have painted in their sacrilegious mumbo-jumbo of God being subject to change in the most loathsome ways.

*If the human soul is not made out of non-rational soul, neither is it made
out of any bodily element*

18. The material, therefore, for the human soul is not any non-rational soul
either.[9]

12. What then is it from which the soul was made by the puff of God? Was it
some kind of body that was both earthy and moist? In no way; that rather is what
flesh was made from, after all. What else, I mean, is mud but moist earth? Nor
can it be supposed that the soul was made of moisture alone, as though the flesh
was from earth, the soul from water. It is surely too absurd to think that the soul
of the man was made from the same material as the flesh of a fish and a bird.[10]

19. So then from air, perhaps? A puff, you see, accords with this element; yes,
but our puff, not God's. That is why we said above[11] that this idea could be suitably entertained if we supposed God to be the soul of the universe as of one
gigantic animated being, so that in this case he would puff the man's soul from
the air of his body, just as ours puffs from the air of its own. Since, however, it is
common ground that God is far and away above the whole body of the universe
and the whole spiritual realm which he created, how can this seriously be maintained? Or could it be that the more present God is by his unique omnipotence to
his universal creation, the more it was within his power to make a puff out of air,
to be the man's soul?

But the soul is not corporeal, while anything made out of the corporeal
elements of the universe must necessarily be corporeal, and this air too is
counted among the elements of the universe. Even were the soul said to be made
from the pure element of that heavenly fire, it would be wrong to believe this.
There have indeed been those who maintained that every kind of body can be
changed into every other kind of body; but that any kind of body, whether earthly
or heavenly, is ever converted into soul and becomes an incorporeal
substance—well, I know of nobody who has ever held this, and faith has no
room for it.

A satisfactory compromise suggested by medical science

13, 20. Finally[12]—if we are not to dismiss what the medical men not only say,
but insist that they can prove to be true—although every sort of flesh manifestly

---

9. He had already ruled out, in sections 10 and 11 above, the possibility of the human soul's
material being some kind of spiritual matter. The non-rational soul he has just also dismissed is
a kind of half-way stage between spiritual matter and normal bodily or material matter, which
he is now going on to discuss, and eliminate.
10. Made on the fifth day, when the waters produced fishes and birds.
11. Chapter 4, section 6.
12. Reading *Denique* with the Maurists, instead of *Deinde* with the CSEL text; this carries a
connotation of "consequently" which does not really fit the context.

displays the solidity of earth, it still has in it too a certain amount of air, which is contained in the lungs and also distributed from the heart through the veins which they call arteries; and of fire it not only has the quality of heat, centered on the liver, but also that of brightness, which on their showing is strained or clarified, as it were, and whisked up to the highest area of the brain, as though to the heaven of our body. From here the eyes flash their rays,[13] and from the brain's mid-point, from a kind of North Pole,[14] other fine tubes lead not only to the eyes but also to the other senses: to ears, to nostrils, to palate for hearing, smelling and tasting. And these people show that the sense of touch, which is spread through the whole body, is likewise governed by the same section of the brain through the marrow of the neck and that contained in the little bones out of which the backbone is stitched together, so that from there tiny rivulets of the finest sort, which activate the sense of touch, may spread out through all the limbs of the body.[15]

14. The soul therefore receives from these quasi-messengers information about any bodily things that are not hidden from it. So much, however, is it something entirely different itself, that when it wishes to understand either divine things, or God himself, or even quite simply to consider itself and its own powers and to come by something that is certainly true, it turns away from this light of the eyes, finding it to be not only no help but even something of a hindrance for this task. How then can it be in the same genus, of which the highest species is the light which darts out of the eyes, which only helps it to perceive bodily shapes and colors, while the soul itself has countless other things to turn to, totally unlike any kind of body, things it can only observe by intelligence and reason, to which none of the senses of the flesh aspires?

15, 21. Accordingly the nature of the human soul is not of earth nor of water nor of air nor of any kind of fire; but all the same it administers the coarser material of its body, namely a kind of moist earth which has been given the quality of flesh, by means of the finer kinds of body, that is by means of light and air; without these two, you see, there is neither any sensation in the body, nor any deliberate movement of the body by the soul. Now just as one has first to know

---

13. For this preferred theory of vision in Augustine's time—at least the theory preferred by him—see Book I,16,31, note 20. The sense of sight was clearly thought of as functioning by a kind of radar, the rays transmitted from the eyes being as it were sensitized by the object seen, and thus activating the sense.

14. *De cujus medio velut centro quodam.* Here *centrum* has its original Greek meaning of a thorn or prickle, the kind which it was hard for Saul to kick against (Acts 26:14); in this context more precisely the prick of the compass needle providing the center from which the circle is described. But as Augustine has just called the top of the brain the "heaven" of the human body, the North Pole, indicated by the Pole Star, very nicely conveys his meaning.

15. These "rivulets" are the nerves; while here he, and doubtless the medical science of his time, talks of them conveying light round the body, elsewhere he will talk of them being filled with "spirits," in roughly the same sense as we call certain alcoholic beverages "spirits."

what a thing is before knowing what to do with it so sensation comes before movement. The soul therefore, being something non-bodily, first activates the kind of body which is nearest to being non-bodily, like fire (or rather light) and air; and then through these the other coarser elements of the body, like moisture and earth, which constitute the solid mass of the flesh, and which are more subject to being acted on than equipped to act.

16, 22. So then it seems to me that all that was meant where it said: *the man was made into a live soul* (Gn 2:7), is that he began to have sensation in the body, which is in fact the surest indication of flesh being animated and alive, because even bushes are moved not only by some external force acting on them, as when they are being shaken by winds, but also by that inner motion which drives whatever belongs to the growth and beauty of a tree, by which sap is drawn into the root, and there turned into all that constitutes the nature of the herb or tree. None of this happens, after all, without internal movement. But this movement is not deliberate, like the one which couples the control of the body to sensation, as in every kind of animal which scripture calls "live soul."[16] Unless we too, of course, had that other kind of motion within us, our bodies would neither grow nor produce nails and hair. But if that were the only sort of movement in us, without sensation and the power of deliberate movement, the man would not have been said to have been made into a live soul.

17, 23. Accordingly, since the front part of the brain, from which all the senses are distributed, is situated at the forehead, and it is in the face that are to be found the instruments, so to say, of sensation, except for the sense of touch, which is spread through the whole body, this too, however, is shown to have its source in the front part of the brain, from which connections are led back through the crown and the neck to the marrow of the spine, of which we were speaking a moment or two ago; from there the face too of course has its sense of touch, like the whole body—apart from the senses of seeing, hearing, smelling and tasting which are located in the face alone. That in my opinion is why it is written that *God blew into the man's face the puff of life, when he was made into a live soul* (Gn 2:7). The front part naturally and rightly takes precedence over the back part, both because it leads while the other follows, and also because from it comes sensation while from the other comes movement—thus deliberation preceding action.

18, 24. And since bodily movement, which follows upon sensation, always involves intervals of time, and since we cannot perform deliberate movements over intervals of time without the aid of memory, that is why the brain is shown to have three ventricles;[17] one in front, at the face, from which all sensation is

---

16. See Gn 1:20-24.
17. The Latin *ventriculum* means literally "little belly"; so he actually says "the brain is shown to have, as it were, three little bellies" (three ventricles).

controlled; a second behind at the neck, from which all movement comes; the third between the two, in which they demonstrate that memory is active; otherwise, since movement follows upon sensation, you may fail to link to your perceptions what has to be done, if you have forgotten what you have done on previous occasions.

These medical men say there are sure and certain indications to prove all this, as when these parts, affected by some disease or defect, have each made clear enough what they are for by failure in the functions of sense perception, or of movement of limbs, or of remembering how to move the body, and when the appropriate cure has been applied to them after examination has established what will be most effective for putting right what was wrong.[18] But the soul is acting in these parts as in, or on, its instruments; it is not itself any of these, but it is quickening, animating and controlling them all, and through them looking after the interests of the body and of this life, in which "the man was made into a live soul."

Conclusion to the findings of medical science; that the soul is not any kind of body

19, 25. While therefore we are inquiring where it comes from itself, that is from what material, so to say, God made this puff which is called the soul, we ought not to think of any kind of body. Just as God, after all, surpasses every kind of creature, so the soul by the very worth of its nature surpasses every bodily creature. Nonetheless it administers the body through light and air, as being the kinds of body with the closest resemblance to spirit; in the world at large too, after all, they are the most excellent of the elements, better suited to acting than moisture and earth, whose mass makes them more liable to be acted upon. So then, bodily light conveys some message; but that to which it conveys the message is not what the light is; and that to which it conveys the message is the soul, not identical with the messenger.

And when the soul feels and is vexed by the body's afflictions, it is offended at the activity with which it governs and cares for the body being thwarted

---

18. In this last part of the sentence, from "and when the appropriate cure," I am paraphrasing, I trust correctly, what seems to me to be a sentence of totally uncoordinated syntax. It runs: . . . *eisque adhibita curatio cui rei reparandae profecerit exploratum est.* This is the reading both of the Maurist and the CSEL text, and there is no help in the apparatus criticus. The Latin of my translation would be: . . . *eisque adhibita curatio postquam quid cuique rei reparandae profecerit exploratum est.* I am suggesting that this must have been roughly what Augustine intended to dictate, but that being distracted by something, he dictated what the actual text has; or else that he did dictate something like what I have translated, but too quickly for his stenographers to keep up with him, so that they produced the text, surely defective, which we have. But if I could be shown how the text we have is in fact syntactically coherent, I would be delighted.

through the disturbance of the body's constitution—and this offense is called pain. And the air which is diffused through the nerves obeys the will to move the limbs, but is not itself the will. And that middle part of the brain passes on the message of the movement of the limbs to be held by the memory, but is not itself the memory.

Finally, when these services, so to call them, fail totally through some major defect or disorder, with the messengers of sensation and the ministers of movement giving up altogether, the soul itself takes its departure, as having no reason why it should linger. If however they do not fail as totally as usually happens in death, the soul's intentions are upset, as of one struggling to restore what is falling to bits and lacking the strength to do so; and from the area in which it is being upset it knows which section of its services is involved, so that if at all possible it may come to the rescue with some remedy.

Further evidence that the soul is quite different from any of its bodily agents

20, 26. For indeed that the soul is one thing, another these its bodily services, or instruments, or tools (or whatever else they may more suitably be called) becomes crystal clear from this further evidence; it is frequently so utterly wrapped up in its thoughts that its attention is completely withdrawn from everything else, and it is unaware of the many things there before its wide open and perfectly healthy eyes; and if the person is even more deeply absorbed in his thoughts, while walking along he may suddenly stop—withdrawing, you see, the well's commanding nod from the movement service by which the feet were being set in motion. If his concentration, however, is not quite intense enough to stop him in his tracks, but is still such that it is not free to nudge that middle part of the brain which records the body's movements, he sometimes forgets both where he is coming from and where he is going, and without noticing it passes the homestead he was making for—nothing wrong with the nature of his body, but his soul has been called away to some other matter.

So we have then these bodily particles of the bodily heaven, particles that is of light and air, which are the first to be at the beck and call of the animating soul, in that they are closer to its incorporeal nature than are moisture and earth, so that the whole mass of the body is administered through their immediate instrumentality. But whether God took them from the surrounding and over-arching atmosphere and mixed them in or joined them to the body of the living man or whether like flesh he made them too from mud, is a question of no relevance to the matter in hand. It is quite credible that every kind of body can be changed into every other kind of body; but to suppose that any kind of body can be changed into soul is ridiculous.

The soul not made from some fifth element, nor from anything material at all

21, 27. Accordingly, we should pay no attention either to the idea some people have entertained, that there is a sort of fifth bodily element from which souls may be made, which is neither earth nor water nor air nor fire, whether this more tempestuous kind on earth, or that pure and bright fire of heaven[19] but heaven knows what different kind of thing, which lacks any familiar name, but is still some kind of body. If those who hold this opinion mean by "body" the same as we do, which is anything that has length, breadth and height so as to occupy some local space, then this is not soul nor may we suppose that soul is made from it. Whatever it is, after all, it can, to put the matter briefly, be divided or circumscribed in any of its parts by lines, whereas if the soul could thus be treated, in no way would it be able to know about lines which are not capable of being cut down the middle lengthwise, such as it nonetheless knows cannot be found in actual bodily form.[20]

28. Nor does the soul strike itself as being any such thing—since it is unable to be ignorant of itself—even when it is seeking to know itself. When it is seeking itself, after all, it knows that it is seeking itself, which it could not know if it did not know itself. Nor does it seek, or go looking for itself from anywhere else than from itself. So then since it knows itself looking for itself it obviously knows itself; and the whole of it knows everything it knows. And so since it knows itself looking, the whole of it knows itself; therefore it also knows the whole of itself; nor is it knowing anything else, but all of it knows itself. So why then does it still go on seeking itself, if it knows itself seeking? I mean, if it were ignorant of itself, it could not possibly know itself seeking itself.

But this is all in the present, while what it is seeking about itself is what it was before or what it is going to be. So let it stop now suspecting that it may be some sort of body, because if it were such it would know itself to be such, seeing that it knows itself more surely than it knows heaven and earth, which it knows through the eyes of its body.[21]

---

19. But for Aristotle at least, with whom the idea seems to have originated, the fifth element or quintessence was precisely the "fire" of which the celestial spheres and bodies are composed, a distinct element from our familiar fire, because it manifestly has a distinct kind of natural motion. Just another little indication of how Aristotle was misinterpreted in this thoroughly neo-Platonic age of late antiquity.

20. Pure mathematics, a purely intellectual form of knowledge, further proof of the immateriality of the soul—that is, of the mind.

21. A much more coherent and satisfactory account of what it means for the mind to seek to know itself is to be found in *The Trinity* X,3,5—xi,16. There he is commenting at length on the Delphic command, *Know thyself,* and says that it means, essentially, "Think about yourself." It is to be noted that in *The Trinity*, a work of much more mature and profound reflection, he identifies the self with the mind, *mens*, while here in *The Literal Meaning of Genesis* he identifies it with the soul, *anima*.

29. I forbear to say that that thing of the soul's which even cattle are understood to possess—or the birds of the sky, since they revisit their dwellings or nests—by which the images of all bodily things are retained, is in no way like any sort of body; and of course this, in which the bodily likenesses of things are contained, ought if anything to be like a body. But if this is not any kind of body, seeing that it is certain that bodily likenesses are not only retained there as remembered but are also imagined and made up in countless ways at will, how much less can the soul be like a body in any other of its powers at all!

30. But if they are using "body" in some other way to mean everything that is, every nature and substance that is to say, it is not indeed a manner of speech that is admissible, else we would not find in speaking any way of distinguishing bodies from things that are not bodies; still, we should not trouble ourselves too much over the word.[22] What we are saying is that whatever the soul is, it is neither one of these four well-known elements, which are manifestly bodies, nor is it what God is. But you cannot state better what it is than by saying that it is the soul or spirit of life. The reason for adding "of life," you see, is that this air too is often called spirit. Though as a matter of fact they have also called the same air the soul, so that now one cannot find a name properly to distinguish this reality, which is neither body nor God, nor insensate life which can be assumed for trees, nor life without rational mind, such as is to be found in cattle, but life which is now less than that of the angels and is going to be what that of the angels is, if it has lived here by the instructions of its creator.

31. Even if there are doubts and questions, however, about where it comes from, that is about what material, so to say, it has been made from, or what perfect and blessed nature it has issued from as a kind of flux or discharge, or whether it has quite simply been made from nothing, about this at least there must be no doubt at all; that if it was anything before, what it was was made by God, and it has now been made by God to be itself a live soul; after all, it was either nothing, or at least it was not what it now is. But that part of our inquiry in which we were seeking the quasi-material from which it may have been made has now engaged our attention long enough.

---

22. This use of the word "body" was to be found rather disconcertingly in Augustine's African predecessor, Tertullian, who quite happily calls God a body. He does in fact use the word to distinguish concrete realities from abstractions; concrete from abstract nouns. When we say that "God" is a concrete noun, we are not afraid of being taken to mean that God is a solid substance like concrete. Augustine returns to the subject in Book X, and there offers a detailed criticism of Tertullian's views at the end of that book, 25,41—26,45.

Difficulties about supposing that a causal formula of the soul was inscribed in the original six days of creation

22, 32. But now, if it was quite simply nothing, the question has to be faced how we can understand its causal formula being said to have been there in the first works of God during the six days, when God made man to his image, which can only be rightly understood with reference to the soul. It is to be feared that when we say that God did not create the actual natures or substances which were going to exist in the future while he was creating all things simultaneously, but some sort of causal formulae of those future realities, we may be thought to be saying something quite meaningless. What, after all, are these causal formulae to which God could be said to have made the man to his image, when he had not yet molded his body from mud, not yet made him a soul by puffing? And even if there was some hidden formula of the human body, to which it could be formed in the future, at least there was also some actual material from which it could be formed, namely earth, in which that formula could be latent as in a seed. But as for making the soul, that is, for making the puff which would be the man's soul, what causal formula could then have been set up when God said, *Let us make the man to our image and likeness* (Gn 1:26)—which can only be rightly understood with reference to the soul—if there was no actual nature there in which to set it?

33. If this formula, you see, was in God, not in creation, then it had not yet been set up; so how then could it be said, *God made the man to the image of God* (Gn 1:27)? But if it was already in creation, that is, in the things which God made simultaneously, in what sort of creature was it? In a spiritual or a corporeal one? If in a spiritual one, was it activating anything in the bodily mass of the universe, whether in the heavens or on earth? Or was this formula just dormant in a spiritual creature[23] before the man was set up in his proper nature, just as in human beings already leading a human life the generative formula is present in a latent and dormant way, only functioning through copulation and conception? Or was that spiritual creature, in which this formula was latent, also not doing any of its proper work? Then what had it been created for? Was it just to contain the formula of the human soul to come, or of souls to come in the future, as if they could not exist by themselves but only in some creature already living its proper life, as the generative formula can only be found in some definite nature or other, already in complete existence?

So then some kind of spiritual creature has been put in place as a parent of the soul, to have in itself the formula of the future soul, which does not actually emerge from it except when God makes it to be breathed into the man. From a

---

23. Reading with the Maurists *an in ea erat haec vacans* instead of the CSEL text's *et in ea erat hoc vacans*. Augustine's whole drift is still clearly interrogative here, and he is still asking about *haec ratio*, this formula.

human being too, after all, it is none but God who creates the offspring, whether in the seed or in the already formed fetus, through *Wisdom reaching everywhere because of her purity, such that nothing defiled may gain entry into her* (Wis 7:24-25), *while she stretches mightily from end to end, and disposes all things sweetly* (Wis 8:1).

But I really do not know how one can understand heaven knows what sort of spiritual creature to have been created, which is not mentioned among those works of God made during those six days, in which God is said to have made the man on the sixth day, the man he had not yet made in his proper nature, but still only by a causal formula in that creature which has not been mentioned. It ought particularly to have been mentioned, after all, as something that had been finished in such a way that it was not itself still due to be made according to its own preceding causal formula.[24]

23, 34. Or when God made the man on the sixth day to his image, did he perhaps insert this causal formula for making the soul in the nature of that day which he established at the beginning, if that day is rightly taken as being intelligent spirit, thus fixing in advance the cause and formula on which he would make him after those seven days? On this showing he may be supposed to have created the causal formula of the man's body in the nature of earth, that of his soul in the nature of that first day. But when you say this, what else are you saying but that angelic spirit is the quasi-parent of the human soul, if the pre-established formula for creating the human soul is in it, just as that of future offspring is in a human being? The result of this will be that while human beings are indeed the parents of human bodies, angels are the parents of human souls. God of course will be the creator of both bodies and souls, but of bodies out of human beings, of souls out of angels; or of the first body out of earth and the first soul out of the angelic nature, where he had fixed their causal formulae in advance when he originally made the man among the things which he created all together simultaneously; but from then on he is creating human beings now from human beings, body from body, soul from soul.

If you find it hard to swallow this idea of calling the soul the daughter of an angel, or of angels, that of its springing from the bodily heaven will be much harder; so how much more so from sea and earth![25] Much less therefore was the causal formula of the soul pre-established in any bodily creature when God made the man to his image, before he animated him with a puff, after forming

---

24. Reading *secundum suae causae praecedentem rationem facienda* with the Maurists. The CSEL text omits *causae*; but I think this must be only a printer's error, as there is no reference to the point in the apparatus criticus.
25. An oblique allusion here, I suppose, to the second, third, fourth, and fifth days of creation; and perhaps a side swipe at various pagan myths about the origin of the soul.

him in his proper time from mud, if it is absurd to suppose that the soul was causally established in the angelic nature.

*The possibility considered of the human soul having been created in its full
actuality at the original simultaneous creation of all things*

24, 35. So let us see then whether this could possibly be true (it certainly seems
to me that ordinary human opinion will find it more tolerable), that among those
first works in which God created all things simultaneously he also created the
human soul, which in its own time he would breathe into the limbs of the body
formed out of mud, while of this body he causally created, among those things
simultaneously set up at the beginning, the formula to which the human body
would be made when it was due to be made. You see, we can only correctly
understand the words *to his image* with reference to the soul, and the words *male
and female* (Gn 1:27) as having reference to the body.

So let it be supposed then, if there is no scriptural authority or evident argument of reason against it, that the man was made on the sixth day in such wise
that while the causal formula of the human body was created in the elements of
the world, the soul was itself created just as the original day was established, and
once created was stored away among the works of God until in due time he chose
to insert it by puffing, that is by breathing it into the body formed out of mud.

A problem raised by this idea

25, 36. But here again a problem arises that cannot just be shrugged off. If, you
see, the soul had already been made and was being stored away, where could it
possibly be better off than there? So what cause was there for the soul, living
there in all innocence, to be inserted into the life of this flesh, in which it would
offend by sinning against the one who created it, and as a result be deservedly
overtaken by misery and toil and the torment of damnation? Or must it be said
that it had a natural inclination of its own will to administer the body; and since
life in the body can be lived both justly and iniquitously, it would have there
whatever it chose, either reward for justice or punishment for iniquity? In this
way one would avoid going against the apostle's judgment in which he says that
those not yet born have done nothing either good or bad (Rom 9:11). That inclination of the will toward the body, to be sure, is not yet an act of either justice or
iniquity for which account has to be rendered at the judgment of God, at which
all are going to receive *according to what they have carried out in the body,
whether good or evil* (2 Cor 5:10).

So why then may we not now also suppose that the soul at a signal from God
came to the body where, if it was willing to act in accordance with his command,
it would receive the reward of eternal life and the companionship of angels,

while if it ignored this command it would pay the perfectly just penalty, whether of daily toil and trouble or of eternal fire? Or does this very fact that compliance with God's will is of course a good action rule this idea out of court, because against it will be the fact that "those not yet born have done nothing either good or bad"?

A further question

26, 37. All this being so, we will also have to admit that the soul was not created in that original set of things in such a state as to have foreknowledge of its future behavior, whether just or iniquitous. It positively defies belief to suppose that it could of its own free will have had an inclination to the life of the body, if it had foreseen that in some people it was going to sin so grievously that it would justly receive the punishment of perpetual torment. The creator, surely, is rightly to be praised in all things, seeing that he made all things *very good* (Gn 1:31). I mean, he is not just to be praised for those to whom he has given foreknowledge, since we are right to praise him too for making the cattle, and human nature is of more value than they are, even in sinners. It is the nature of the man, surely, that derives from God, not the iniquity in which he involved himself by misusing his free will, while if he were not endowed with this, he would lack his pre-eminence in the order of nature. The man can be thought of, surely, as living justly even without foreknowledge of what the future would hold, and on that supposition one should note how his pre-eminence in enjoying free will would not stop him living rightly and pleasing God, because being ignorant of the future *he lives by faith* (Rom 1:17). So then, if you are unwilling to allow for this kind of creature among God's works, you are going against God's goodness, while if you are unwilling for it to pay the penalty for its sins, you are the enemy of his equitable justice.

The problem provisionally solved

27, 38. But if the soul is made precisely to be sent into the body, one can ask whether it may be forced to go even if it is unwilling. But it is better to suppose that it wills this by nature, that is to say that it is created with a nature to will this just as we have a natural will to live, while to live badly does not come from nature, but from perversity of will, which is justly followed by punishment.

39. So then it is futile to ask from what sort of material the soul might have been made, if one can rightly understand it to have been made in those first works of creation, when the day was made. Just as those things, after all, were made out of nothing, so too this soul among them.[26] But if there was also some

---

26. A rather free paraphrase of what he puts more enigmatically: "Just as those things, which were not, were made, so too this among them."

formable material, both bodily and spiritual, this too, however, set up by none other but God. which indeed came before its formation, not in time but in origin, as the voice does with the song, what can be a more fitting assumption than that the soul was made from spiritual material?[27]

To maintain that the soul was created only when it was breathed into
the man already formed will not square with these texts of scripture

28, 40. If, however, you wish to maintain that the soul was only created when it was breathed into the body already formed, you must consider what answer you will give when you are asked what it was made from. I mean, you are either going to say that God made, or still makes, something out of nothing after he finished all his works, and then you must look hard for an explanation of the man being made to the image of God, and this can only be rightly understood with reference to the soul, on the sixth day—that is, in what nature the causal formula was made of a thing which did not yet exist in itself; or else you will say that the soul was made from something already in existence. And then you will have the trouble of inquiring what the nature of that something might be, whether bodily or spiritual, going over the questions which we have been thrashing out above. Added to this, you will still be bothered with the problem of which substance it was, among the creatures originally set in place in the six days, in which he made that causal formula of the soul which he had as yet made neither from nothing nor from something.

41. If you wish to avoid this problem by saying that the man was also made from mud on the sixth day, but that this was mentioned later on by way of recapitulation, then you must consider what you are to say about the woman, because *male and female*, it said, *he made them and blessed them* (Gn 1:27-28). If you answer that she too was made on that day from the bone of her man, then ask yourself how you can assert that the *flying things which were brought to Adam* (Gn 2:19) were made on the sixth day, when scripture insists that every kind of flying thing was created on the fifth day out of the waters; and how about the trees too on the sixth day, which were planted in Paradise, when the same scripture has attributed this kind of creature to the third day?

You must also consider what these words mean: *He still cast up from the earth every tree that had a beautiful look about it and was good for eating* (Gn 2:9), as if the ones which the earth had cast up on the third day were not beautiful to look at and good for eating, although they were among the works which God made *all very good* (Gn 1:31). And what about this: *God still fashioned from the earth all the beasts of the field and all the flying things of heaven* (Gn 2:19), as

---

27. He is here harking back to his extended commentary on Gn 1:2 in Book I.

though they were not all things that had been produced first—or rather as though they had none of them been produced before. It does not say, after all, "And God still fashioned from the earth the other beasts of the field and the other flying things of heaven" as though the earth had produced less on the sixth day or the water less on the fifth; but *all the beasts*, he says, and *all the flying things*.

And think about this too: how on the one hand God made all things in the six days; on the first the day itself, on the second the solid structure, on the third the appearance of sea and earth and from the earth grass and trees, on the fourth the lamps and constellations, on the fifth aquatic animals, on the sixth terrestrial ones; and how on the other it says later on: *When the day was made, God made heaven and earth and all the greenery of the field* (Gn 2:4-5), seeing that when the day was made[28] he made nothing but the day itself. How too did he make *all the greenery of the field before it was upon the earth, and all the hay of the field before it sprang up* (Gn 2:5)? Would we not all say, I mean, that the time it was made was when it sprang up, not before it sprang up, unless we called the words of scripture to mind? You must also remember that it is written: *The one who lives for ever created all things simultaneously at once* (Sir 18:1), and then ask yourself how things can be said to have been created simultaneously when their creation was spread over intervals of time, not just of hours but of days.

You must undertake as well to show how each of these apparently contradictory statements can be true: both that *God rested on the seventh day from all his works* (Gn 2:2), which the book of Genesis says, and that *he is working until now* (Jn 5:17), which is what the Lord says. You should take another look too at the things that were said to have been finished, and how in almost the same breath they were said to have been begun.[29]

42. It was by all these evidences, you see, of the divine scripture, of which none doubt the veracity but unbelievers or the ungodly, that we were led to the necessity of saying that God from the start of the ages first created all things simultaneously together, some already in their established natures, some in their pre-established causes. Thus the Almighty made not only things actually present but also things that were to come in the future, and rested from them as made, so that from then on as he administered and regulated them he would also create the series of times and of time-bound things. And so he had both finished them because of the limit set to all the different kinds of things, and begun them because of the extension of the ages into the future. Thus he could rest because they were finished, and could be working until now because they were begun. But if there is a better way in which this can all be understood, not only shall I make no objection, I shall also be positively in its favor.

---

28. Back in Gn 1:3-5.
29. Gn 2:1 and 3, in Augustine's version. See Book IV,1,1 above for his text; 12,22 for his explanation.

Conclusion: he hopes readers will at least have learned how to discuss hard questions without making rash assertions

43. Now, at any rate, I will affirm nothing as certain about the soul, which God breathed into the man by blowing into his face, except that it comes from God in such a way as not to be the substance of God and yet to be incorporeal; that is, not a body, but a spirit, not begotten of the substance of God nor proceeding from the substance of God,[30] but made by God; and not made in such a way that the nature of any kind of body or of non-rational soul can be turned into its nature; and consequently made from nothing. Also that it is immortal as regards life in the ordinary sense, life which it cannot lose in any way at all; but that as regards a kind of mutability by which it can change for better or for worse, it cannot improperly also be seen as mortal, since he alone has true immortality about whom it is strictly and exclusively said, *who alone has immortality* (1 Tm 6:16).

I trust that everything else I have said in this volume by way of discussion will at least have this value for readers, that they will either have learned how matters on which scripture does not speak plainly are to be investigated without making rash assertions; or else, if they are not satisfied with this manner of investigation, that they will let me know how they would set about it. Then if they have something to teach me, I hope I will not reject it, while if they have not, let them join me in seeking the one from whom we all have lessons to learn.

---

30. That is, neither like the Son nor like the Holy Spirit.

Book VIII

Genesis 2:8-17: The planting of Paradise

Three ways of taking the account of Paradise: literally, figuratively, or both

1, 1. *And God planted a paradise in Eden to the East, and put there the man whom he had fashioned* (Gn 2:8). I am well aware that many people have said many things about Paradise. There are, however, three generally held opinions about this topic; one held by those who think Paradise should only be understood in the literal material sense,[1] another by those for whom only the spiritual sense is true, the third by those who take Paradise in each way, differently though in the material, differently in the spiritual sense. So then, in a word, I admit that it is the third opinion which I favor. This is the line on which I have here and now undertaken to talk about Paradise (to the extent that the Lord sees fit to help me); that the man made out of mud—which of course is a human body—is to be understood as having been placed in a bodily paradise; and so Adam himself, even if he stands for something else in the way the apostle said he is the form of the one to come,[2] is still to be taken as a human being set before us in his own proper nature, who lived a definite number of years and after producing a numerous progeny died just as other human beings die, though he was not born of parents like others but was made from the earth, as was required at the beginning of the line; and so the paradise too, in which God placed him, is to be understood as quite simply a particular place on earth, where the man of earth would live.

2. The narrative indeed in these books is not cast in the figurative kind of language you find in the Song of Songs, but quite simply tells of things that happened, as in the books of the Kingdoms[3] and others like them. But there

---

1. His word is *corporaliter*, and he is certainly thinking about the bodily objects mentioned in the story, especially trees and the bodies of the man and the animals. But here it will not quite go literally into English as "bodily" or "corporeal."
2. See Rom 5:14. The Latin *forma* here renders the Greek *typos*, which is perhaps more usually translated *figura*; Adam figuratively represents Christ; he is the "type" of Christ, in the technical sense of the word, taken straight from the Greek, as used by theologians.
3. The name given in the Greek Septuagint to what we call, following the Hebrew Massoretic style, the books of Samuel and Kings.

things are being said with which ordinary human life has made us quite familiar, and so it is not difficult, indeed it is the obvious thing to do, to take them first in their literal sense, and then to chisel out from them what future realities the actual events described may figuratively stand for. Here on the other hand, because things are being said which do not meet the gaze of eyes fixed on the ordinary course of nature, some people think they should not be understood in their proper sense, but just figuratively, and they suggest that history, that is, the account of events that actually happened, begins from the moment when Adam and Eve, turned out of Paradise, came together and had children[4]—as though forsooth we are quite familiar with people living as many years as they did, or with things like Enoch being taken, or a very old and barren woman giving birth, and other things of that sort![5]

3. "But the telling of marvelous deeds," they say, "is one thing, quite another the telling of the establishment of creation; in the first case, after all, the unusual events themselves make it clear that natural occurrences are one thing, miracles another—these are also called *mighty works* (Acts 2:11; Ps 71:19; Ps 106:21, etc.). But here we are being told about the actual institution of created natures."

To which the answer is: "But this too is unusual, precisely because it comes first. What, I ask you, is so unique and without parallel in the set-up of things of this world as the world itself? So must we assume that God did not make the world just because he is not still making worlds, or that he did not make the sun because he is not still making suns?"

This in fact is the answer one should give to those who are bothered about the man himself, not about Paradise. But now, while these people believe that the man was made by God in a way no other has been made, why are they not prepared to believe that the paradise was made in the the same way as they now see woods being made?

4. I am addressing, of course, those who accept the authority of these writings; some of them, you see, are not prepared to have Paradise understood literally and properly, but only figuratively. As for those who are altogether opposed to these writings, I have dealt with them elsewhere and in another way,[6] although here in this work of ours too we are defending their literal meaning to the best of our ability in such a way that those who, prompted by an obstinate or just stupid turn of mind, unreasonably refuse to believe these things may still find no grounds at all on which to convict them of being false.

But as for these people of ours, who have faith in these divine books and are not prepared to have Paradise understood according to the proper literal sense—as a most delightful place, that is, shady with groves of fruit trees and

---

4. See Gn 4:1.
5. See Gn 5, passim; especially 5:24; and the story of Sarah, Gn 18:9-15 and 21:1-7.
6. *On Genesis: A Refutation of the Manichees*, II, which he will shortly be quoting.

extensive too and rendered fertile by a huge spring—when they can see so many large tracts of grassland turn into woods without any human labor, just by the hidden work of God, I only wonder how they can believe that the man himself was made in a way they have never seen. Or if he too is to be understood figuratively, who was it who begot Cain and Abel and Seth? Or did they also only exist in figure, not also as real human beings born of human beings?

So then they should pay very close attention to where this assumption of theirs is leading them, and try hard with us to take all these primordial events of the narrative as actually having happened in the way described. Is there anyone, after all, who would not support them as they turned their minds next to working out what lessons these things have for us in their figurative meaning, whether about spiritual natures and experiences or even about events to come in the future?

Certainly, if the bodily things mentioned here could not in any way at all be taken in a bodily sense that accorded with truth, what other course would we have but to understand them as spoken figuratively, rather than impiously to find fault with holy scripture? On the other hand, if these things understood in a bodily sense, far from being an embarrassment to the divine narrative, actually lend it more solid support, nobody I imagine will be so disloyally obstinate as to insist on remaining wedded to his old opinion that they can only be taken figuratively, when he sees them, on being expounded in their proper sense, to be in accordance with the rule of faith.[7]

What he said on this point in his two volumes on Genesis against the Manichees

2, 5. I too, you see, shortly after my conversion wrote two volumes against the Manichees,[8] who do not just go wrong by taking these books of the Old Testament in a way that is not correct, but who blaspheme by rejecting them outright with detestation. So my aim was to confute their ravings as quickly as possible, and also to prod them into looking for the Christian and evangelical faith in the writings which they hate. Now at that time it had not yet dawned on me how everything in them could be taken in its proper literal sense; it seemed to me rather that this was scarcely possible, if at all, and anyhow extremely difficult. So in order not to be held back, I explained with what brevity and clarity I could muster what those things, for which I was not able to find a suitable literal

---

7. I here omit a phrase, *si forte illi visa fuerant*, "if perchance they had seemed/appeared to him," as totally impossible to fit meaningfully into this sentence. I suspect some scribble in a margin which crept into the text.

8. *On Genesis: A Refutation of the Manichees, I and II*; written about 389, after his return to Africa from Milan, when he was settled on his own property in Thagaste with a few like-minded friends.

meaning, stood for in a figurative sense; I did not want them to be put off by
being faced with reams of obscure discussion, and so be reluctant to take these
volumes in their hands. Bearing in mind, however, what I really wanted but
could not manage, that everything should first of all be understood in its proper,
not its figurative sense, and not altogether despairing of the possibility that it
could so be understood, this is what I put near the beginning of the second
volume:[9]

> Certainly (I say) whoever wishes to take everything that is said quite liter-
> ally, that is, to understand it not otherwise than the text actually reads, and
> in so doing can avoid any blasphemy, and can set it all out in accordance
> with the Catholic faith, not only should one not begrudge him this, one
> should hold him to be a remarkable and most praiseworthy understander.[10]
> If however there is no way out available, in order that what is written may
> be understood in a manner that is pious and worthy of God, except for us to
> believe that these things have been set forth figuratively and in enigmas,
> we have the authority for this of the apostles, by whom so many of the
> enigmas in the books of the Old Testament are solved. But in this case let
> us hold to the standard which we are proposing—with the help of the one
> who urges us *to ask, to seek and to knock* (Lk 11:9)—and explain all these
> figures of things, whether they belong to history or to prophecy, in accor-
> dance with the Catholic faith, but without prejudice to any better or more
> careful exegesis, whether by us or by others to whom the Lord may see fit
> to reveal it.

That is what I said at that time. Now, however, it has pleased the Lord that
after taking a more thorough and considered look at these matters, I should
reckon (and not, I think, idly) that I am able to demonstrate how all these things
were written straightforwardly in the proper, not the allegorical mode. So then
let us now examine what follows about Paradise in the same way as we decided
to explain what came earlier.

---

9. See 2, 3.
10. *Intellector* in the Latin; a word I suspect Augustine invented, as he is the only authority quoted
for it in Lewis & Short's *Latin Dictionary*. They refer to *Teaching Christianity* II,13,20,
without mentioning this use of the word here. In my translation of that work I was able to render
the passage a little more freely; here I think I am obliged to follow Augustine's example and
invent "understander." But no, I find I do not have that distinction; the word is given in the
Oxford English Dictionary, as first used in the fifteenth century, its last use quoted being by Dr.
Pusey in 1853, *Doctrine of the Real Presence, Note S 527*. So perhaps all I can claim is to have
revived it.

What is said about Paradise is reconciled with what is written about the third and sixth days

3, 6. So then, *God planted Paradise in delights*—that, you see, is the meaning of "in Eden"—*and put the man there whom he had fashioned* (Gn 2:8). That, you see, is how it was written, because that is how it was done. Next he recapitulates, to show how what he has stated briefly actually was done; that is, just how God planted the paradise and there established the man he had fashioned; this after all is how it goes on: *And God still cast up from the earth every tree that had a beautiful look about it, and was good for eating* (Gn 2:9). He did not say: "And God cast up from the earth another kind of tree" or "the rest of the trees," but *he still cast up*, it says, *from the earth every tree that had a beautiful look about it and was good for eating.* So then the earth had already produced every tree that was both beautiful to look at and good for eating, that is, on the third day; because on the sixth day he had said: *Behold, I have given you every seed-bearing fodder seeding seed which is over all the earth, and every fruit tree which has in it fruit of seed-bearing seed, which shall be for you as food* (Gn 1:29). So did he give them one thing then, and now decide to give them something else? I hardly think so. But since these trees laid out in Paradise are of the same varieties as the ones the earth had already produced on the third day, it still went on producing them in their proper time, because what is written about the earth having produced them earlier on refers to what was done causally in the earth; that is, that it had then received the latent power of producing them, the power by which it happens that even now the earth continues to bring forth such things openly and in their own time.

7. So then, the words of God saying on the sixth day, *Behold I have given you every seed-bearing fodder seeding seed which is over all the earth*, etc., are not words that were uttered audibly in time, but just as in his Word there is the power of creating[11]—but what God said without any time-measured sounds could only be conveyed to human beings through such sounds in time. It was, after all, still in the future that the man now formed from mud and animated by God's puff[12] would use for food all the things that were going to spring up over the earth from that generative power which the earth had already received. In setting up the causal formulae of this future in creation, God was speaking as if it had already

---

11. This clause could be rendered, "but in the way that there is in his Word the power of creating." But I do not think he meant that; I think he was starting to give an explanatory comparison, and then interrupted himself, feeling that it would not really fit his theory of the *causales rationes*, the causal formulae written into the original creation in the works of the six days. So he abruptly changes tack.

12. Here I omit a phrase which is syntactically incoherent, and has to me every appearance of some marginal scribble that subsequently found its way into the text: *et quidquid ex illo humani generis extitisset*—"and whatever of humankind had come into existence from him."

come into existence, speaking with an inward and intimate truth which *eye has not seen nor ear heard* (1 Cor 2:9), but which his Spirit surely revealed to the writer.

How to explain the tree of life and the tree of knowledge of good and evil in an historical as well as an allegorical sense

4, 8. What comes next, certainly, *and the tree of life in the middle of Paradise and the tree of knowledge of discerning good and evil* (Gn 2:9), calls for more careful consideration, to avoid its forcing us into allegory and having to say that these were not real trees, but that they signify something else under the name of tree. It is said about Wisdom, after all, that *she is the tree of life to all who embrace her* (Prv 3:18). However, while there is an eternal Jerusalem in the heavens, there is also the city founded on earth by which that one is signified; and although Sarah and Hagar signified the two covenants, they were also none-theless two women;[13] and while Christ waters us with a spiritual stream through his suffering on the tree, he was also nonetheless the rock which poured out water to a thirsty people when struck with a wooden rod, and about which it is said, *now the rock was Christ* (1 Cor 10:4). All these things stood for something other than what they were, but all the same they were themselves bodily realities. And when the narrator mentioned them he was not employing figurative language, but giving an explicit account of things which had a forward reference[14] that was figurative.

So then the tree of life also was Christ, like the rock; and indeed God did not wish the man to live in Paradise without the mysteries of spiritual things being presented to him in bodily form. So then in the other trees he was provided with nourishment, in this one with a sacrament—a sign of what else but of the Wisdom of whom it is said, *She is the tree of life to those who embrace her*, just as it would be said of Christ that he was the rock pouring out water to those who thirsted for him? He is rightly called whatever came before him in order to signify him. He himself is the sheep which is sacrificed at the Passover;[15] and yet that represented him not just by the telling, but also by actually happening. It is

---

13. See Gal 4:26.24; also Heb 12:22.
14. His word is *praecessio*, a word not given in Lewis & Short or the Oxford Latin Dictionary. But it is to be found in the Vienna *Thesaurus Linguae Latinae*, which also refers us to Sermon 239 I,1 and 265,I,2 (volume III/7 of this series); in those places its translation presented no problem, while here it is rather more unusual. It is first attested in Chalcidius' commentary on Plato's *Timaeus*, 85 and 151. I owe this information to Mr. Duncan Cloud, Professor Emeritus of Classics at Leicester University. The word, of course, gives us the English word "precession," which we seldom use except in connection with the equinox. The Oxford English Dictionary derives it from late Latin, but only gives a general reference to Boethius. The word does not figure in Du Cange's Glossary of Late Latin.
15. See Ex 12:3-11.

not, after all, the case that that sheep was not a sheep; clearly it was a sheep, and it was killed and eaten; and yet by that very fact something else was also being signified. It was not like that fatted calf, which was killed to make a feast on the younger son's return;[16] here the whole story is figurative, not a story of things actually done with a figurative significance.

I mean, it was not the evangelist but the Lord himself who told it, while the evangelist told the story of the Lord telling it. Thus it is then that the story told by the evangelist was of what also actually happened, namely that the Lord really said all that, while the story told by the Lord himself was a parable, about which it is never required that what it tells of should be shown to have happened literally. Christ is also the stone anointed by Jacob, and *the stone rejected by the builders which became the cornerstone;*[17] but the first was something actually done in the course of events, while the second was only foretold in figurative terms. In the first instance the narrator was writing of events in the past, in the second the foreteller was pointing only to things yet to come in the future.

The same continued, with a discussion of certain complicating factors

5, 9. Thus Wisdom—which is the same as Christ himself—is also the tree of life in the spiritual paradise, where he sent the thief on from the cross;[18] but the tree of life was also created in the bodily paradise (to signify Wisdom, indeed) because the passage of scripture said so which was telling of things that happened in their own time, and which told of the man both made in bodily form and set up there living in the body.

Or if anyone thinks that when souls depart from the body they are contained in places that are visible to bodily eyes though bodiless themselves,[19] let him defend his opinion; people will not be lacking to support it, and so to argue for that rich man in his thirst having certainly been in a bodily place. They thus have no hesitation in declaring that the soul itself is quite simply bodily, on account of his burning tongue and his longing for a drop of water from the finger of Lazarus.[20] I for my part will not be in a hurry to take them on over such an important question. It is better, surely, to remain in doubt over obscure matters, than to quarrel over uncertain ones. I have no doubts, to be sure, about having to take

---

16. See Lk 15:23.
17. See Gn 28:18; Ps 118:22.
18. See Lk 23:43.
19. He appears to have in mind people who assumed that the text of Gn 2:7 refers only to the making of the human soul (using figurative language, of course). The Alexandrian theologian, Origen (d. 253) held such a view, and considered that human souls were fitted out with bodies as a punishment for sin, interpreting in this figurative sense Gn 3:21, God clothing Adam and Eve with garments of skin.
20. See Lk 16:19-26.

that rich man as enduring searing, punishing pains and that poor man as enjoying a cool, refreshing rest. But in what way we are to understand that flame of hell, that bosom of Abraham, that tongue of the rich man, that finger of the poor man, that torture of thirst, that cool, refreshing drop, well it can hardly be ascertained even by those who look into it quietly and gently, never by those who go in for obstinate, quarrelsome arguments over it.

But certainly the following quick answer is called for, or else this deep question which requires lengthy discussion will hold us up; if souls, even when stripped of their bodies, are contained in bodily places, then that thief could have been brought into the selfsame paradise where the first man's body had been. About this I hope to show at some more suitable place in the scriptures, if the need really arises, either what questions I ask, or even what conclusions I manage to reach.[21]

10. For the moment, however, I do not doubt, and I do not suppose anybody else does, that Wisdom is not a body, and therefore not a tree either. But you will only reckon that Wisdom cannot be thought of as being signified through a tree, that is, through a bodily creature as if by a kind of sacrament or sacred sign, if you fail to notice how many bodily sacraments of spiritual realities there are in the scriptures, or if you maintain that the first man did not need to live with any such sacrament, in spite of what the apostle says about what scripture said of the woman, who all agree was made for the man from his side: *For this reason a man shall leave father and mother and shall stick to his wife; and they shall be two in one flesh* (Gn 2:24); that *this is a great sacrament in Christ and in the Church* (Eph 5:32).

It is indeed astonishing, and scarcely to be borne, how people will have Paradise to be a figurative story, and will not have it to be a figurative fact. But if they do allow that as in the case of Hagar and Sarah, of Ishmael and Isaac, these things too were both facts that happened and yet were also figurative, I simply cannot see why they should not admit that the tree of life was both some kind of real tree and yet was also a figure of Wisdom.

11. I would also add this: that while that tree did indeed provide bodily food, it was of such a sort that the man's body would be fortified by it with enduring health, not as with other food, but by some hidden infusion of vigorous well-being. That scone, after all, with which God warded off a man's hunger for forty days,[22] though made of ordinary flour, clearly had something a little extra about it. Or will we perhaps hesitate to believe that for the sake of some deeper signification God was providing the man through the fruit of a particular tree

---

21. He briefly mentions the matter again in volume XII of this work, 34,66; and also in his *Questions on the Gospels* II,38,5, when he is again discussing the story of the rich man and Lazarus.

22. See 1 Kgs 19:4-8, Elijah's flight from Jezebel, and his journey to Horeb.

with the means of ensuring that his body would not change for the worse through ill-health or old age, or even succumb to some accident, when he provided ordinary human food with such a wonderful staying power, that flour and oil in earthen vessels would restore human strength that was running out and not run out themselves?[23] Here too let one of that disputatious crew stand up and say that it was proper for God to perform such miracles in our present world, but not proper for him to do so in Paradise—as though he had not there made the man from dust or the woman from her husband's side, greater miracles than his here having raised the dead.

On the tree of knowledge of good and evil

6, 12. It remains for us to see about *the tree of knowledge of discerning good and evil* (Gn 2:9). Naturally this too was a visible and bodily tree like all the others. So then, that it was a tree is not to be doubted; but why it was given this name is something that has to be looked into. Now as I consider the question again and again, words cannot express how delighted I am with the opinion that it was not a matter of that tree having poisonous fruit—the one who had made all things *very good* (Gn 1:31) would not have planted something bad in Paradise—but of the man's transgression of the commandment having been bad for him.[24] Now it was necessary that the man, placed under God as his Lord and master, should be prohibited from doing something, so that obedience might itself be his virtue by which to deserve well of his master. This, I can indeed say with absolute truth, is the one and only virtue for every creature that is a rational agent under the authority of God, while the first and greatest vice, puffing it up to its own downfall, is the wish to assert its own authority, the name of this vice being disobedience.

So the man then would have had no reason to reflect that he had a Lord and master, and to feel it in his bones, unless he had been given some order. And so that tree was not evil, but it was given the name of the knowledge of discerning good and evil, because if the man should eat of it after being forbidden to do so, there was in it the future transgression of the commandment, as a result of which the man would learn through his experience of the penalty what a difference there was between the good of obedience and the evil of disobedience. Accordingly this too is to be taken not just as a metaphor but as a real tree, which was not given its name from the fruit or apple which would grow on it, but from the

---

23. See 1 Kgs 17:8-16, the story of Elijah and the widow of Zarephath.
24. He speaks as though this was not an original idea of his own, but one he had heard from others. I have not found Ambrose saying anything quite like this in his little work on Paradise; so it seems to me that it was probably an opinion put forward by one of Augustine's circle of friends in discussion on the point.

painful reality that was going to follow on its being touched in spite of the prohibition.

On the rivers of Paradise

7, 13. *Now a river came out from Eden, which was watering Paradise, and from there it was divided into four parts. Of these the name of one is Pishon; this is what goes round the whole land of Havilah, where there is gold. Now the gold of that land is good, and there is carbuncle there and leek-green stone. And the name of the second river Gihon; this is what goes round the whole Ethiopian land. The third river, though, Tigris; this is what flows over against the Assyrians. The fourth river, though, Euphrates* (Gn 2:10-14). About these rivers, why should I bother any more to establish that they are real rivers, not just metaphors, as though they did not exist but only the names signified something, seeing that they are obviously known in the regions they flow through, and indeed their fame has spread abroad to practically all peoples? On the contrary, since it is agreed that they certainly exist, two of them, though, have had their names changed since antiquity, just as the river now called the Tiber was earlier known as the Albula.[25] Gihon, that is to say, is the one now called the Nile, while the one that used to be called Pishon is the one they now call the Ganges. The two others, the Tigris and Euphrates, have kept their ancient names; we should let ourselves be advised to take all the rest to begin with according to the strict literal sense and not to assume that it is being talked about figuratively, but that the things and events which are being related both exist and also stand figuratively for something else.

This is not because the parable mode of speech could not take something from real life which without question is not being mentioned in any proper historical sense; take the way the Lord speaks, for instance, about the man who was going down from Jerusalem to Jericho and fell among thieves.[26] Is there anybody who would not perceive straightaway that this is obviously a parable, and that the whole story has a figurative meaning? And yet there are two cities named in it, which can be shown you to this very day in their own place. But that is the way in which we would take these four rivers too, if any necessity obliged us to take the other things that are told about Paradise only in a figurative and not a proper sense. Now however, since there is no reason preventing us from taking these things first of all in a proper, literal sense, why should we not simply follow the authority of scripture in its narrative of things done, and first accept that the things really were done, and then only after that investigate what else they signify?

---

25. See Virgil's *Aeneid*, VIII,332.
26. See Lk 10:30-35.

14. Or shall we be disconcerted by people saying about these rivers that while the sources of some of them are well known, those of others are utterly unknown, and for that reason we cannot take it literally that they are divided from the one river of Paradise? Surely we should rather believe that since the actual site of Paradise totally escapes human ken, the waters from it are indeed divided into four parts, as the utterly trustworthy testimony of scripture assures us, but that those rivers whose sources are said to be known have gone underground somewhere, and after wending their way through extensive regions have gushed out in other places, where their sources are held to be known. Is anybody unaware, I mean, that there are streams which regularly do this? But it only comes to our attention where they do not flow underground for any great distance. So then, a river was going out from Eden, that is from the place of delights, and was watering Paradise, that is to say all the beautiful and fruit-bearing trees which provided shade for all the grounds of that region.

Question about the man being put in Paradise to work

8, 15. *And the Lord God took the man whom he made, and put him in Paradise for working and guarding. And the Lord God commanded Adam saying: From every tree that is in Paradise for food you shall eat; but from the tree of getting to know good and evil you all*[27] shall not take a bite from it; but on the day you all eat from it, you all shall die the death (Gn 2:15-17). When he had briefly said above that God had planted Paradise and established the man there whom he had fashioned, he went on to recapitulate and to tell us in what way Paradise had been established. So now too he mentions by way of recapitulation in what manner God had placed the man there whom he had made. And so let us see what is meant by its saying *for working and guarding*; what's the force of *for working* and what of *for guarding*?

The Lord, surely, did not wish the first man to work at agriculture, did he? Is it not simply incredible that he should have condemned him to hard labor before sin? Certainly we would judge it to be so, had we never seen how some people till the fields with such pleasure, such uplift of spirit, that it is a severe punishment for them to be called away from that to anything else. So then whatever delights there are to be found in agriculture, they were of course far and away more complete at that time when neither earth nor sky was putting any difficulty in the way. You see, there was no stress of wearisome toil but pure exhilaration of spirit, when things which God had created flourished in more luxuriant abundance with the help of human work. As a result the creator himself would be

---

27. I employ this piece of what I believe is Southern dialect to indicate that the text has changed from the second person singular to the second person plural—a distinction which that dialect is very properly concerned to maintain in spoken English.

praised more copiously for having given a soul set in an animal body the rational facility of working as much as would satisfy its willing spirit, not as much as it would be reluctantly forced to do by the wants of the body.

16. What greater or more wonderful spectacle can there be, after all, or when is human reason more able after a fashion to converse with "The Nature of Things,"[28] than when after seeds have been sown, cuttings potted, shrubs planted out, graftings made, each root and seed is questioned, so to say, on what its inner vital force can or cannot do, what helps and what hinders it, what is the range of the inner, invisible power of its own numerical formula,[29] what that of the care bestowed on it from outside? And then to perceive by these very considerations that *neither the one who plants is anything nor the one who waters, but the one who gives the growth, God* (1 Cor 3:7), because the work and skill applied from the outside is applied by one who also was nonetheless created and is being governed and directed invisibly by God?

The same continued, on a cosmic scale

9, 17. From this the eye of the mind can now be raised up to the universe itself as if it were all some huge tree, and in this too will be discovered the same twin functioning of providence, partly through natural, partly through voluntary activity; through natural activity indeed is working the hidden management of God, by which he also gives growth to trees and herbs, while voluntary activity comes through the works of angels and human beings. As regards the first mode celestial things are arrayed up above, terrestrial ones down below, the great lights and constellations shine, day and night are moved around in turn, the earth with its foundations in the waters has them washing round it and in amongst it, the air is poured over it at a higher level, shrubs and animals are conceived and born, grow up, grow old and perish, and whatever else happens in things through the inner impulses of nature; while in this other mode signs are given, taught and learned,[30] fields cultivated, communities administered, arts and skills practiced, and whatever else is done, whether in the higher company of the angels or in this earthly and mortal society, in such a way as to be in the interests of the good even through the unwitting actions of the bad. And in the human individual we see the same twin power of providence at work; first with respect to the body, nature

---

28. *Cum rerum natura*, an allusion, surely, to the strange epic poem, *De Rerum Natura* of the great Latin poet Lucretius, older contemporary of Cicero, and enthusiastic advocate of the Epicurean philosophy. Were it not for this allusion, I would more happily render the phrase, "converse with Nature herself."

29. Of its "numbers"; see Wis 11:20.

30. See *Teaching Christianity* I,2 for his distinction between "things" and "signs," which then governs the rest of that work. Chief among signs is language and words; but then some things signified by words can also be used as signs, and these he will often call sacraments.

provides for its coming to be, its growth, its aging, while the provision of food, clothing, shelter, health care is left to voluntary activity; likewise with respect to the soul, nature ensures that it is alive, sentient and conscious, while to learn and give its consent is left to the will.

18. Now just as in the case of a tree agriculture acts from the outside to ensure the effectiveness of what nature is busy with on the inside, so in the case of a human being; as regards the body, what nature is doing for it inwardly is being preserved outwardly by medicine; and again as regards the soul, in order that nature may be blessed within, education offers its services from without. On the other hand, what neglect of cultivation is to the tree, that is what failure to take proper medical care is to the body, is what slackness over studies is to the soul; and what harmful spraying does for a tree, that is what poisonous food does for the body, what inducement to wickedness does for the soul.

And so God, then, Most High above all things, who established all things and governs all things, creates all natures out of his goodness, disposes all wills according to his justice. How therefore can it be abhorrent to the truth, if we believe that the man was set up in Paradise to work at agriculture, not in servile toil, but with genuine pleasure and uplift of spirit? What, after all, is more innocent than such work for our moments of leisure, and what can provide more material for our serious reflection?

Question about the man being put in Paradise to guard it

10, 19. What, though, about *for guarding*? For guarding Paradise itself? Against whom? Certainly there was no invasion from a neighbor to fear, no trouble on the borders, no thief, no aggressor. How therefore are we going to understand that the material paradise could have been guarded by the man in a material way? But then scripture did not actually say, "for working and guarding Paradise," but just *for working and guarding*—though if it were expressed more carefully word for word from the Greek, this is how it is written: *And the Lord God took the man whom he made, and put him in Paradise to work it and guard* (Gn 2:15). But whether he just put the man there to work—that, you see, is what the person thought who translated *for working*—or whether it was to work, or operate, the same paradise,[31] that is that the man should work Paradise, well it sounds ambiguous, and the expression called for seems rather to be, not "to work Paradise," but "in Paradise."

---

31. As one talks about working or operating a machine? The obvious meaning (which Augustine too, never a slave of the obvious, has until now been taking for granted) is "to till it." But because of the fastidiousness over words he is indulging in here in this whole passage, I have had to translate as literally as possible—and avoid the obvious meaning.

20. However, in case it may have said "to work Paradise" in the same way as it said above *and there was no man to work the land* (Gn 2:5)—it is the same grammatical construction, of course: "to work the land" and "to work Paradise"—let us discuss the ambiguous sentence according to either possible meaning. If, you see, we do not have to take it as meaning "to guard Paradise," but only "in Paradise," then to guard what in Paradise? We have just discussed what we thought working in Paradise could mean; could it be that what he worked on the land he should also guard and keep in himself through discipline; that is, that just as the field submits to the man tilling it, in the same way the man himself should submit to his Lord and master commanding him, so that having grasped the commandment he might yield the harvest of obedience, not the thorns of disobedience? Eventually, since he refused to guard in himself by his submission the likeness of Paradise tilled by himself, he was condemned to receive in the field the likeness of himself: *Thorns*, it says, *and thistles shall it bring forth for you* (Gn 3:18).

21. If on the other hand we are to understand that he should work Paradise and guard Paradise, he could indeed work Paradise, as we said above, by tillage, while he could guard it, not against shameless or hostile men, but possibly against wild beasts. But how or why even to that extent? Were wild beasts, after all, already raging against the man, which would not happen unless he sinned?[32] When all the beasts were brought to him, in fact, as will be mentioned later, he himself put names to them; he himself, also on the sixth day, by the law of God's word received food to be shared in common with them all.[33] Or if there was already some threat to be feared from wild beasts, by what conceivable stretch of the imagination could one man fortify that paradise against it? It was not, after all, a little plot of land, which was watered by such a huge spring. Yes indeed, he should have guarded it, had it been possible to secure Paradise with such an enormous fence, in such a way that the serpent could not enter it; but it would have been astonishing if before he had fenced it, he could have kept all serpents out of it.

22. Accordingly, why should we overlook the meaning that is staring us in the face? The man of course was put in Paradise to work this same paradise, as we argued above, by cultivating it in a way that was not painfully laborious but simply delightful, furnishing the sensible and observant mind with the most important reminders and useful advice, while he was to guard and keep this same paradise for himself, and not allow anything there which would earn him expul-

---

32. *Quod nisi peccato non fieret.* Literally, this can only be translated, it seems to me, as "which would not happen except to him having sinned"; in other words, the past participle *peccato* is being used as an active participle; quite a liberty to take with Latin grammar—but if one may say so, a genuinely "liberating" liberty!

33. See Gn 2:20; 1:29-30.

sion from it. Finally he also received a command, in order for there to be something by which he might guard Paradise for himself, that is, by observing which he might avoid being thrown out of it. You are rightly said, after all, to have guarded or kept your property when you have acted in such a way as not to lose it, even if it is preserved undamaged for someone else, who may have found it or have been considered to receive it in turn.[34]

23. There is another meaning in these words, which I consider is not improperly to be preferred, that God should work and guard the man himself. Just as a man works the land, you see, not in order to make it be land, but to be neatly cultivated and fruitful, so much the more does God, who created the man to be a man, work him to be a just man, if he does not part company with God through pride; that, you see, is *to apostatize from God*, which scripture says *is the beginning of pride* (Sir 10:12). So then, God is the unchangeable good, while the man is a changeable thing both in soul and in body; unless therefore he remains turned and directed towards the unchangeable good which God is, he cannot be formed into being just and blessed. And thus the same God who creates the man to be a man, is himself the one who works and guards him into also being good and blessed. For this reason the turn of phrase by which the man is said to work the land, which is already land, into also being landscaped and fertile, is the same as the one by which God is said to work the man, who was already a man, into also being godfearing and wise; and to guard him, because the man could not safely be left to delight in his own power and authority rather than that of the one above him and to ignore his rights as Lord and master.

Why God is only called "the Lord God" from this point on[35]

11, 24. Accordingly I do not regard it as in any way void of significance, but as drawing our attention to something, to something very important too, that from the start of this divine book, from where it began, *In the beginning God made heaven and earth* (Gn 1:1), up to this point, it has never put "the Lord God," but simply "God." Now however, where it has come to the point of God setting up the man in Paradise and working and guarding him by means of a command-

---

34. This rather curious afterthought, assuming that you do lose your property because you have not guarded it well, may be seen as carrying a profound and important implication. What did Adam, after all, lose by not guarding his property well, what was this property? It was grace, the grace of what is termed original justice. Now when he lost it, this grace was preserved undamaged—what after all can damage grace?—for the one who "found it," who was considered worthy to receive it, namely the last Adam, Jesus Christ, and through him all who have put off the old Adam and put on the new.
35. This is the case in the Greek Septuagint, which the Latin Augustine is commenting on follows. English versions start using the phrase from 2:4, following the Hebrew, in which it is in fact "YHWH God"; "Lord," Hebrew *Adonai*, being the word actually pronounced instead of the sacred proper name.

ment, this is how scripture has spoken: *And the Lord God took the man whom he made and put him in Paradise to work him*[36] *and guard* (Gn 2:15). Not that God was not the Lord of the creatures mentioned earlier; but this was not being written on account either of the angels or of the other things that were created, but on man's account, to remind him how expedient it was for him to have God as his Lord, that is, to live obediently under his dominion as lord and master, rather than without any restraint to misuse his own personal power and authority. So scripture did not wish to use this expression anywhere earlier on, until it came to the placing of the man in Paradise and to working and guarding him. Here it would not say, as with everything else above, "And God took the man whom he made," but rather, *And the Lord God took the man whom he made, and put him in Paradise to work him*, so that he might be just, *and to guard*, so that he might be safe, under God's dominion and authority of course, which is of use to us, not to himself.

He, that is to say, has no need of us as his servants or slaves, but we do need him as our lord and master, to work us and guard us. And that is the reason why he alone is truly Lord, because we are his servants and slaves for our benefit and welfare, not for his; I mean, if he needed us, by that very fact he would not be a true lord, since we would be helping him in his neediness, to which he would himself be the slave. Rightly did the man say in the psalm, *My God are you, since you have no need of my good things* (Ps16:2). Nor should what I have said, that we are his slaves for our benefit and welfare, be taken in the sense that we should look for anything else from him but himself, seeing that he is himself our supreme benefit and welfare. In this way, you see, we love him freely and for nothing, according to the words, *But for me to stick to God is good* (Ps 73:28).

More about how God works and guards man

12, 25. Human beings, after all, are not the sort of things that, once made and left to themselves by the one who made them, could do anything well all by themselves. No, the sum total of their good activity is to turn to him by whom they were made, and by him always to be made just, godfearing, wise and blessed; not to be made so and then leave, like being cured of some bodily ailment by a physician and going away, because the physician has been working outwardly on the body, at the service of nature working inwardly under God, who works health of all kinds with that twin activity of providence of which we

36. He is now following the "correct" text of the Greek Septuagint, and his Latin rendering of it is *operari eum*. The pronoun is masculine, and so can agree in Latin either with Paradise or with the man. So earlier, when he was still thinking of the man working, I had to translate by "to work it and guard"; but as he is now assuming that God is the subject of "to work," it has to be "to work him and guard."

spoke above. So human beings ought not to turn to God in such a way that when they have been made just by him they take their departure, but in such a way that they may always be made so by him. In the very fact of their not taking their leave of him they are being justified and enlightened and blessed by his presence with them, by God "working and guarding" them as the lord and master of obedient subordinates.

26. Nor, as we were saying, is it exactly like the man working the land to make it neatly cultivated and fertile, and going away once he has finished his work, leaving the land ploughed or sown or irrigated or whatever else; the work that has been done remains when the worker has departed. That is not how God works human beings to make them just, not how he justifies them, that is to say, so that if they withdraw, what he has done remains in them.[37] Rather, just as we have to say that the sky is being made bright by the presence of light, not that it has been; because if it had been made so without still having to be made so, it would remain bright even when the light was withdrawn; in the same way human beings are being enlightened by the presence of God with them, but immediately relapse into darkness with the absence of him from whom one distances oneself not by local movement but by a turning away of the will.

27. And so may he who is himself unchangeably good "work" human beings into being good and "guard" them. We ought always to go on being made by him, always being perfected by him, sticking to him and persevering in that way of life which is directed towards him, about whom it is said, *But for me to stick to God is good* (Ps 73:28), and to whom it is said, *I will guard my strength for you* (Ps 59:9). "For we are his fashioning, created" not only just to be human, but in addition for this, to be good. The apostle too, you see, when he was commending the grace by which we have been saved to the faithful who had been converted from ungodliness, had this to say: *For by grace you have been saved; and this not from yourselves, but it is the gift of God, not from works, lest anyone should exalt himself. For we are his fashioning, created in Christ Jesus in good works, which God has prepared that we may walk in them* (Eph 2:8-10). And elsewhere, after saying, *With fear and trembling work at your own salvation*, in case they should think this should be attributed to themselves, as though they would make themselves just and good, he immediately added: *for it is God who is working in you* (Phil 2:12-13). So then, *the Lord God took the man whom he made, and put him in Paradise to work him*, that is to work in him, *and guard him.*

---

37. Here he has rather carelessly returned to the comparison with the human physician, and the patient going away from him, rather than the one with the ploughman's work remaining after he has gone home.

On the command given to Adam

13, 28. *And the Lord God commanded Adam, saying: From every tree that is in Paradise you shall eat for food; but from the tree of getting to know good and evil you all shall not take a bite from it; but on the day you all eat from it, you all shall die the death* (Gn 2:16-17). If that tree had been something evil which God was putting out of bounds to the man, then it would appear that his death was due to poison by the nature of that evil. But because the one who had made all things *very good* (Gn 1:31) had planted nothing but good trees in Paradise, nor was there anything there that was evil by nature, because there is nothing evil by nature anywhere (we shall discuss this more thoroughly, if the Lord so wishes, when we come to talk about that serpent), that tree, which was not evil, was put out of bounds to him, so that the very keeping of the commandment might be what was good for him, and its transgression what was bad.

29. Nor could there have been a better and more effective demonstration of how great an evil disobedience is in itself, than that the man became guilty of wickedness for the simple reason that he touched the thing he had been forbidden to, when if it had not been forbidden and he had touched it, that would certainly not have been a sin. I mean, if someone says, for example, "Don't touch this plant," he is warning you of death if you do touch it, because it happens to be poisonous; so death indeed will follow if you ignore the command; but you would also die of course if you touched it without anyone having told you not to. The thing would in itself, after all, be a danger to health and life, whether you were warned off it or not.

Again, take someone forbidding something to be touched, because it would be against his interests, not those of anyone who did touch it; so if anybody laid hands on another person's property after being forbidden by that person to do so, this would indeed be a sin on his part, because it would harm the one who told him not to. But when something is touched which would harm neither the one touching it if it were not forbidden, nor anybody else whenever it might be touched, for what other reason can it have been forbidden, but to demonstrate that obedience in itself is a good thing and disobedience is in itself an evil?

30. Finally, the sinner was aiming at nothing else but not to be under God as his Lord and master, when he committed an act where the only reason to be attended to for not committing it was the command of his Lord and master. If this were all that was attended to, what else would he be attending to but God's will? What else but God's will would he be loving? What else but God's will would he be preferring to a human will? The Lord indeed will have seen why he gave the order; what he ordered is to be done by the servant, and then perhaps he too may deserve to see why the order was given. But still, to avoid spending any more time looking for the reason for this order, if serving God is in itself of great benefit to humanity, simply by giving an order God makes whatever he wishes

to order beneficial; with him, surely, we never have to fear that he could order anything injurious.

Further reflections on the nature of good and evil; why Emmanuel did not have to experience the difference between them

14, 31. Nor can it be that his own will does not drop on a man like a ton of bricks,[38] if he exalts himself by preferring it to the will of the one above him. This is what the man experienced by ignoring God's command, and this is what he learned by the experience—what the difference is between good and evil, the good of obedience, that is to say, and the evil of disobedience, of pride, that is, and insubordination, of a perverse imitation of God,[39] and of claiming a harmful freedom. Now the tree by which it was possible for this to happen took its name, as we have already said above, from this very event. We would have no awareness of evil, after all, except by experience, because there would not be any unless we had committed it. Evil, you see, is not a nature of any kind, but the loss of the good has been given this name.

The unchangeable good, of course, is God, whereas human beings, as far as the nature is concerned in which God made them, are indeed a good, but not an unchangeable one like God. Now the changeable good, which comes after the unchangeable good, becomes a better good, when it clings to the unchangeable good by loving and serving it with its own rational will. This is indeed the nature of a great good, that it also received the ability to cling to the nature of the highest good. If it refuses to do this, it deprives itself of a good, and this is bad for it, the consequence of which by the justice of God is also torment. What, after all, could be so inequitable as that it should go well with a deserter of the good? Nor indeed is there any way in which this could really happen; but sometimes the loss of the higher good is not perceived as evil, when the lower good, loved in preference to it, is possessed. But the divine justice ensures that those who have been willing to lose what they ought to have loved will be grieved by the loss of what they have in fact loved, while praise in every case continues to redound to the creator of all natures. The good, you see, whose loss brings grief is still good, because unless it were still something good by nature, there would be no grief over its loss by way of penalty.

32. That person, however, should have his praises sung above all other human beings, who takes pleasure in the good without any experience of evil, so that

---

38. Literally, "with a great weight of ruin," *grandi ruinae pondere*.
39. This applies more immediately to the sin of Lucifer; see Is 14:13-14, where he is understood by the tradition as being presented to us under the figure of the king of Babylon, and Ez 28:2, where it is under the figure of the prince of Tyre. But he involved Adam and Eve in this pretension, when he tempted them by saying, *Your eyes will be opened, and you will be like God, knowing good and evil* (Gn 3:5).

before ever being conscious of the loss of the good, he chooses to hold on to it in order not to lose it. In fact if this were not a quite unique theme of praise, it would not have been attributed to that child who from the nation of Israel became Emmanuel, God-with-us, and reconciled us to God, the man who was mediator between men and God,[40] the Word at home with God, flesh at home with us,[41] Word-flesh between God and us. It is about him, of course, that the prophet says: *Before the child knows good or evil, let him shun malice in order to choose good* (Is 7:16).

How can he either shun or choose what he does not know, if not because these two are known in one way by the common sense of good people, in another by the experience of bad ones? Evil is known by the common sense of good people, even without their feeling it; they hold on to the good, you see, to avoid by losing it the experience of evil. Again, the good is known through the experience of evil, since those with whom things go badly on the loss of the good feel what it is that they have lost. So then, before the child knew by experience either the good which he would be deprived of or the evil which he would feel on loss of the good, he shunned evil in order to choose good; that is, he refused to lose what he had, lest he should feel by its loss what he ought not to lose. A unique example indeed of obedience! That, certainly, of the one who did not come to do his own will but the will of the one by whom he had been sent,[42] not like that other one who chose to do his own will, not that of the one by whom he had been made. How right it is that *just as through the disobedience of one man many have been constituted sinners, so by the obedience of one man shall many be constituted as just* (Rom 5:19); because *just as in Adam all die, so in Christ shall all be made alive* (1 Cor 15:22)!

More problems about the naming of the tree of knowledge of good and evil

15, 33. It is quite groundless, however, for some people to be brightly dull-witted[43] by asking how it could be called the tree of discerning good and evil, before the man had transgressed the commandment attached to it, and had discerned by experience what the difference was between the good which he lost and the evil he committed. Well, the tree received that name, you see, to put him on his guard, while it remained untouched in accordance with the prohibition, against what he would undergo if he touched it in spite of its being prohibited. It was not, after all, because they took a bite from it in spite of the commandment,

---

40. See 1 Tm 2:5.
41. See Jn 1:1.14.
42. See Jn 6:38.
43. He says, literally, "to be sharply blunted," *acute obtunsi*. The important thing is to reproduce the oxymoron, even if it means changing the metaphor.

that it became the tree of discerning good and evil; but of course, even if they had been obedient and not grabbed anything from it in spite of the commandment, it would still properly be called what would happen to them there if they did do the grabbing. It is as if there were something called a filling-and-stuffing tree, because people could stuff themselves full from it; that surely would not mean, would it, that if nobody came near it, such a name would be unsuitable for it, seeing that when they did come up to it and stuff themselves full, they would prove how appropriately this tree was so named?

16, 34. And how, they say, could the man understand what was meant when he was told it was the tree of discerning good and evil, when he was altogether ignorant of what evil itself was? People who think like this pay insufficient attention to the way in which all sorts of things unknown may be understood through their contraries which are known, so that no hearer is flummoxed when the names of things that do not exist are introduced into the conversation. What does not exist at all, I mean, is called "nothing"; and nobody fails to understand these two syllables who hears and speaks English.[44] How so, if not because their common sense has a grasp of what does exist, and so recognizes what does not by subtracting it? In the same way too, when the word "empty" is uttered, by considering the fullness of a body we understand "empty" as meaning its contrary lack or subtraction, just as with our sense of hearing we make judgments not only about sounds and utterances, but also about silence.

In the same way the man would also be able, from the life that was in him, to beware of its contrary, that is, the elimination of life which is called death. And as for what would cause him to lose what he loved, that is, any action of his by which it would come about that he would lose life, whatever syllables were used to name it (as when in English it is called sin or evil), he would understand them as being the sign of what he discerned with his mind. How do we, after all, understand what is meant by "resurrection," which is something we have never experienced? Is it not because we are aware of what it is to be alive, and the deprivation of that we call death, and the return from this to what we are aware of we call resurrection? And in whatever language it is called by any other name, this is a sign, of course, by which the mind, on hearing it from the speaker, recognizes what it could think about even without any sign.

Is it not indeed wonderful how nature avoids the loss of things it has, even when it has not experienced it? Who, after all, has taught cattle about shunning death, if not their sense of being alive? Or who taught the small child to cling to the person carrying him if he has threatened to throw him down from the roof? While such a reaction only occurs, indeed, at a certain age, it is still before the child has experienced anything of the sort.

---

44. Latin, of course; the two-syllable word he mentions is *nihil*.

35. In the same way, then, life was sweet to the first human beings, and accordingly they shrank from losing it, and were able to understand God, by whatever means or sounds he signified these things. Nor could they otherwise have been persuaded to sin, if they had not first been persuaded that they were not going to die as a result of that deed; that is, that they were not going to lose what they had and what they enjoyed having—about which we will have to speak at the proper place.

So if you are bothered by this question, how they could understand God naming and warning them of things they had not experienced, you should notice how, without in any way being torn by doubt or hesitation, we recognize the names of all things we have not experienced simply from their contraries which we already know, if they are the names of deprivations, or from things like them if they are the names of specific natures. Unless of course you are worried by the question of how they could talk, or understand someone talking, when they had not learned all this by growing up among talkers or from some teacher—as though it would be a big problem for God to teach them how to talk, having made them such that they would be able to learn this even from other other people, if there had been any around!

Whether God gave the command to the man alone, or to the woman as well

17, 36. The question is properly asked, whether God gave this command only to the man, or to the woman as well. But the story has not yet been told how the woman was made. Or perhaps she had been made, is that it, but the story of how this, though carried out earlier, was in fact carried out is told later by way of recapitulation? You see, this is how the words of scripture run: *And the Lord God commanded Adam, saying*—it did not say "commanded them"; then it continues: *From every tree that is in Paradise you shall eat for food*—it did not say "you all shall eat"; then it adds: *but from the tree of getting to know good and evil you all shall not take a bite from it.* Here at last it is speaking in the plural as though to both of them, and he concludes the command in the plural, saying: *but on the day you all eat from it, you all shall die the death* (Gn 2:16-17). Or was it that knowing he was going to make the woman for the man, he gave the command most appropriately in this way, so that the Lord's command would reach the woman through the man? This is a discipline that the apostle maintains in the Church, when he says: *But if they wish to learn anything, let them question their husbands at home* (1 Cor 13:35).

In what way did God speak to Adam?

18, 37. Again one may ask, in what way God now spoke to the man he made, who was already for sure endowed with sensation and intelligence, so that he would be capable of hearing and understanding. In no other way, after all, could he be a transgressor of the command received, unless he understood it when he received it. So in what way, then, did God speak to him? Was it inwardly in the mind, directly to his intelligence, that is so that he would clearly be aware of the command and understand God's will without any bodily sounds or likenesses of bodily things? But I do not somehow think that that is how God spoke to the first man. Scripture, I mean, is telling the sort of story which should lead us to suppose, rather, that God spoke to the man in Paradise just as he also spoke later on to the fathers, as he did to Abraham, as he did to Moses, that is, in some kind of bodily appearance. That, you see, is how they heard his voice as he took a stroll in Paradise towards evening and they then hid themselves.[45]

More about the twofold operation of divine providence

19, 38. And thus a great topic is being proposed to us, one certainly not to be passed over, that we should look more deeply, as best we may, to the extent that he is graciously prepared to grant us his assistance, into that twofold operation of divine providence which we glanced at in passing earlier on when we were talking about agriculture.[46] This will begin to get the mind of the reader into the habit of observing something that is of the greatest help against our forming any unworthy ideas about the very substance of God.

So then, we say that this supreme, true, one and only God, Father and Son and Holy Spirit, God, that is, and his Word and the Spirit of both, the Trinity itself, neither confused nor separated, the God *who alone has immortality and dwells in light inaccessible, whom no human being has ever seen or can see* (1 Tm 6:16), is not contained in any place whether of finite or infinite space, nor altered by the passage of times, whether finite or infinite. For there is nothing in the substance by which he is God that is smaller in the part than in the whole, as must be the case with things that are in place; nor was there in his substance anything that is not there now or that will be and is not yet, as is the case with natures which can experience the changes and chances of time.

20, 39. So this God, then, living in unchanging eternity, *created all things simultaneously* (Sir 18:1), from which point times would run their course and places would be filled, and the ages would unroll with movement in time and space. Some of these things he created were spiritual, some corporeal, and he set

---

45. See Gn 3:8.
46. See above, chapters 8 and 9, sections 15-18.

them up by forming or shaping a basic material which none other but he himself had put in place as shapeless, and capable of being formed or shaped in such a way that it did not precede its formation in time, but simply as its source.[47] But he put the spiritual before the corporeal or bodily creation, because the spiritual could only be changed through moments of time, while the corporeal was changeable both through the succession of times and the change of places. For example, spirit undergoes motion in time, whether by remembering what it had forgotten, or learning what it had been ignorant of, or willing what it had not wanted, while body is moved through places, whether from earth to sky or from sky to earth, or from east to west, or in any other similar fashion. Everything, though, that is moved in place cannot but also be moved simultaneously through time, while not everything, on the other hand, that is moved through time is necessarily also moved through space or place.

So then just as the substance which is only subject to movement in time has precedence over the substance which is subject to movement in time and place, in the same way it yields precedence in its turn to the substance which is not subject to movement either in place or in time. And thus, just as the created spirit, being moved itself only through moments of time, itself moves the body through time and place, so the creator Spirit, not subject itself to movement either in time or in space, moves the created spirit through moments of time. But the created spirit moves itself through time and the body through both time and place, while the creator Spirit moves itself without either time or place, moves the created spirit through time without place, moves the body through both time and place.

The point illustrated by a closer look at the way the soul moves the body

21, 40. For this reason, if you are striving to understand how the Eternal One, the truly eternal and truly immortal and unchangeable God, not being moved himself either through place or through time, yet moves his creation in terms both of time and of place, I think you will not succeed unless you first understand how the soul, that is to say a created spirit, itself subject to movement only through time and not through place, moves the body through both time and place. I mean, if you cannot yet grasp what is going on in yourself, how much less what is above you!

41. Now the soul, being infected by its familiarity with the senses of the flesh, thinks that while it is moving the body through place, it is itself also being moved through place together with it. But let it only take a thorough look at the pivots, as it were, of the parts of its own body and how they are disposed through the

---

47. See Book I,15,29 for his introduction of this distinction, when he was discussing the formlessness or shapelessness of the earth in Gn 1:2. The terms he uses are that the basic material, *materia*, is prior to that which is formed out of it not *tempore* but *origine*.

sockets of the joints to provide the thrust without which movement cannot begin; and it will discover that those parts that are being moved through local space are only moved by those which are stationary in place. A finger, you see, is not moved unless the hand is stationary, so that from its joint the finger may be moved as from a motionless pivot. In the same way when the whole hand is moved from the elbow joint, the elbow from the shoulder joint, the shoulder from the shoulder blade, the pivots of course remaining stationary to give thrust to the movement, the part being moved goes through a certain local space.

Likewise the foot has its joint in the ankle, which stays still for the foot to be moved; so too the shank's pivot is in the knee, the whole leg's in the hip. And there is no movement of any part of the body at all which the will can move that does not start from some pivot in a joint which a nod from the will first holds steady, so that the part to be moved can be started off with a thrust from the one that is not moving through local space. Finally, when you are walking, you cannot lift a foot unless the other one is firmly on the ground, carrying the whole weight of the body, until the one which is moving from the place it is being lifted from comes to rest in the place it is being lifted to, its pivotal joint remaining motionless throughout.

42. So now then, the will does not move any part of the body by local movement without starting it from that part's pivotal joint which it does not move; and yet both parts of the body, the one that is being moved and the one that remains stationary for the other to be moved, have their bodily quantities, occupying local space. How much more, then, does the soul, at whose beck and call, as it pleases, one of these parts will remain stationary to provide the necessary thrust for another to be moved—since the soul is not of a bodily nature, nor does it fill the body as its local space, like water filling a bottle or a sponge, but in wonderful ways it is mixed into the body it animates, and with its incorporeal nod, so to say, it powers or steers the body with a kind of concentration, not with any material engine[48]—how much less, I am saying, is this "nod" of its will the subject of local movement itself, in order to move the body locally, when it moves the whole body through its parts, and only moves some parts locally through others which it does not move locally!

---

48. He clearly lacks words to say how the incorporeal soul moves the body, that is, how it initiates movements, the mechanics of which he has been rather curiously setting forth. The phrase he uses which I have translated "with a kind of concentration, not with any material engine" is *quadam intentione, non mole.*

*If this cannot be understood it must be believed, as also the truth about God's
immovability which this about the soul is meant to illustrate*

22, 43. But if this is hard to understand, let both these things be believed, both
that the spiritual creature moves the body locally without being locally moved
itself, and that God without being moved through time moves the spiritual creature through time. But if you do not wish to believe this about the soul—which in
fact you would not only believe but also undoubtedly understand if you could
think about its being incorporeal, which it is; anyone could easily see, surely,
that something which is not extended through local space can scarcely be moved
through space. But whatever is extended through local space is a body; and
therefore it follows that the soul cannot be thought of as being moved through
space if it is not a body. But, as I was on the point of saying, if you are unwilling
to believe this about the soul, there is no need to press you unduly; unless,
however, you believe that the substance of God is not subject to movement
through either time or space, then you are not yet believing that he is completely
and perfectly unchangeable.[49]

*Returning to the twofold operation of God's providence, and the order
established thereby*

23, 44. But the nature of the Trinity is altogether unchangeable; and thus God
is eternal in such a way that nothing can be co-eternal with him, and while he
remains with and in himself without any time or place, he nonetheless moves the
creation subject to him through time and place. He creates natures by his goodness, regulates wills by his authority, so that among natures there is none that
does not come from him, while among wills none is good which does not benefit
from him, none bad which he cannot put to good use. But he did not give all
natures free will, while those he did give it to are the higher, more powerful ones;
so the natures which do not have free will are necessarily subordinate to those
which do, and this by the creator's design, who never punishes a bad will in such
a way as to eliminate the nature's rank or worth. Since therefore no mere body
and no non-rational soul has free will, these things are subordinate to the natures
which are in fact endowed with free will—not every one of them to all of them,
but according to the just distribution of the creator.

So then, God's providence rules and administers the whole of creation, both
natures and wills; natures so that they may simply be, wills on the other hand so
that neither the good ones may be unfruitful nor the bad ones go unpunished.

---

49. In Augustine's theology God's unchangeability was almost the basic divine attribute, what in
   the more refined and accurate terminology of Aquinas and his fellow scholastics would be
   called God's absolute simplicity.

First of all he subjects all things to himself, and then the bodily creation to the spiritual, the non-rational to the rational, the earthly to the heavenly, the feminine to the masculine, the weaker to the stronger, the needier to the better endowed; while with wills he subjects the good ones to himself, the rest on the other hand to those who are at his service, so that the bad will may suffer what the good one does on God's orders, whether directly or through another bad will, by means of things at least which are by nature subject even to bad wills, which is to say by means of bodies. For bad wills have within themselves as their interior punishment their very own iniquity.

24, 45. And thus to the sublime angels, who enjoy God in obedience and serve him in bliss, are subjected every bodily nature, every non-rational form of life, every will whether weak or bent. This is so that they may act upon or together with the things subjected to them, whatever the order of nature requires in all of them, on the orders of him to whom all things are subject. Accordingly they see in him unchangeable Truth, and in accordance with this they direct the wills subordinate to them. They therefore are made participants in the eternity, truth, and will of the one who is always without time and place. But at his direction, while he remains motionless in terms of time, they are moved in terms of time; not, however, in such a way that they pull or drift away from contemplating him, but simultaneously they contemplate him without place or time, and carry out his orders in the lower spheres, moving themselves in time, bodies in both time and place as their activity requires. And thus it is that God presides over his universal creation by the twofold operation of his providence; over specific natures that they may come to be, over wills on the other hand that they may do nothing without either his orders or his permission.

More on the interaction of creatures, especially of angels on lower orders of creation

25, 46. The nature, therefore, of the total bodily or material universe does not receive any external assistance in material or bodily form; after all there is no material body outside it—if there were it would not be the universe. But internally it is assisted in a non-material, non-bodily way by God so acting that it should simply be, *since from him and through him and in him are all things* (Rom 11:36). The parts, however, of the same universe are assisted both inwardly in a non-bodily manner—or rather they are made to be the natures they are; and also outwardly in a bodily manner to help them be in better shape, as with nourishment, agriculture, medicine and all the things that are done by way of adornment, so that they may not only be healthy and more fruitful, but also more presentable.

47. The created spiritual nature, however, if it is perfect and blessed as in the holy angels, insofar as in itself it is just and is wise, is only assisted inwardly and

in non-bodily fashion. Inwardly, that is to say, God speaks to it in a wonderful and inexpressible way: neither through writing imposed on bodily materials, nor through words sounding in bodily ears, nor through the likenesses of bodies such as are formed in the imagination, as happens in dreams or in a kind of ecstatic state.[50] Visions of this kind, after all, though occurring more inwardly than the things that are brought to the spirit's attention through the senses of the body, are still like them, so that when they happen they cannot be distinguished from them at all (or at least very rarely and with difficulty). So because they are more external than what the rational and intellectual mind gazes upon in the unchangeable Truth itself, which is the light by which it passes judgment on all these other things, I consider that they are to be classed among things which happen externally.

So then the spiritual and intellectual creation, when perfect and blessed as in the holy angels, insofar as in itself it is just and is wise and blessed, is only assisted inwardly, as I was saying, by the eternity, the verity, the charity of the creator; outwardly though, if it can be said to be assisted at all, it is perhaps only in the fact that they see each other and enjoy their mutual company in God, and that with all creatures spread out on all sides to their gaze too, they give thanks and praise to the creator. As regards the activity, though, of the angelic creation, through which care is taken by the providence of God for all the different kinds of things, above all for humankind, this gives them external assistance, both through those visions which resemble bodily things, and through bodies themselves, which are under the power and authority of the angels.

A summing up of what has been said about God in relation to time and space, and about the twofold operation of his providence

26, 48. All this being so, God the almighty, holding all things under his sway, always the same in his unchangeable eternity, truth and will, while unmoved himself either through time or space, moves the spiritual creation through time, the bodily creation also through time and space. By such movement he administers outwardly the natures which he set in place inwardly, doing this both through the wills subject to him, which he moves through time, and through the bodies which are subject both to him and to these wills, and which he moves through time and space, the time and local space whose idea or formula is life in God himself [51] without either time or place.

---

50. His phrase is *in aliquo excessu spiritus*; and he goes on to explain that this is called *ekstasis* in Greek, "a word we now also make use of in Latin." As we make even more common use of it in English, without having a parallel home-grown word like his *excessus*, it seemed best to put it all in this footnote, and not in the text.

51. See Jn 1:3-4, which Augustine always read as: "All things were made through him, and without him was made nothing. *What was made in him was life.*"

So then, when God does anything of this sort, we should not conclude that his substance, by which he is God, is changeable in time and place, or moveable through times and places; but we should realize that in the operation of divine providence these things do not happen in the operation by which he creates natures, but in the one by which he also administers externally the natures he has created internally. This is because by his immutable and surpassing power, not in any local or spatial sense, he is both interior to every single thing, because *in him are all things* (Rom 11:36), and exterior to every single thing because he is above all things. Again, by his immutable eternity, and not in any temporal, time-connected sense, he is both older than all things because he is before all things, and newer than all things because again he is himself after all things.[52]

Returning to the question of how God spoke to Adam

27, 49. Accordingly, when we hear scripture saying: *And the Lord God commanded Adam, saying: From every tree that is in Paradise you shall eat for food; but from the tree of getting to know good and evil you all shall not take a bite from it; but on the day you all eat from it, you all shall die the death* (Gn 2:16-17), if we inquire about the way in which God spoke these words, it is a way indeed that cannot directly be grasped by us. We most certainly have to maintain, however, that God spoke either through his own substance or through some creature subject to him. But then he does not speak through his own substance except for creating all natures,[53] though as regards spiritual and intellectual ones he speaks not only for creating but also for enlightening them, since they are now able to grasp his speech as it is in his Word, which *was in the beginning with God, and God is what the Word was through whom all things were made* (Jn 1:1.3). But to those who are not able to grasp this, when God speaks he only does so through a creature, either through a spiritual one alone whether in dreams or in ecstasy in the likeness of bodily things, or also through a bodily one, when some specific appearance is presented to the senses of the body, or some sounds and words are heard.

50. So if Adam, then, were such that he was able to grasp the speech with which God addresses the minds of the angels through his own substance, then there can be no doubt that God, without being moved himself through time, moved Adam's mind through time in a wonderful and inexpressible way and impressed upon it the beneficial and wholesome command of the Truth, and also showed it in the same inexpressible Truth what punishment would be owed to its transgressor. This would happen in the same way as all good commands are

---

52. See, for example, Rv 1:8; God the Alpha and the Omega, the first and the last, the one who is and who was and who is to come.
53. See Gn 1:3, etc.; Ps 148:5.

heard or seen in unchangeable Wisdom herself, who *conveys herself into holy souls* (Wis 7:27) at this or that time, while in her there is no movement in time.

If however Adam was a just man in such a way that he still needed the intervention of another holier and wiser creature through which he could come to know God's will and his orders, as we needed the prophets, they the angels, why should we have any doubts that God spoke to him through some creature of that sort, with such vocal signs as he would be able to understand? When it comes, you see, to what is written a bit further on, that after they had sinned *they heard the voice of the Lord God taking a stroll in Paradise* (Gn 3:8), nobody who has the least sense of the Catholic faith will have any doubt at all that this was done through some creature subject to God, and not through his own substance.

The reason, I may say, why I have wanted to range somewhat more widely in discussing this point is that there are some heretics who think that the substance of the Son of God, even without his taking to himself a body, is in itself visible,[54] and that is why, they consider, he appeared to the fathers even before he received a body from the Virgin, as though it were of the Father alone that it says, *whom no human being has seen or can see* (1 Tm 6:16), because the Son was seen also through his own substance before *receiving the form of a slave* (Phil 2:7). Such an impious idea is to be utterly rejected by Catholic minds.

But let us discuss this matter more fully elsewhere, if the Lord so pleases.[55] This volume ends here, and it is in the next one that you must await what follows, that is, how the woman was created from the side of her man.

---

54. Here the editors of the CSEL text follow the Maurists in saying that the Arians were the heretics he had in mind here. But I doubt if this is the case. While the Arians did indeed hold that the Son was a creature, and so "less than the Father," because "there was a time when he was not," they were far too sophisticated to hold such an idea as his being "substantially visible," and Augustine knew them well enough to be aware of this. The idea of the Son being "the visible member of the divine triad" goes back long before their time. We find both Justin and Irenaeus in the second century maintaining that it was the Son who appeared to the fathers under the old covenant, an idea which Augustine demolished ruthlessly in *The Trinity* II. Here is what Irenaeus has to say: "By the Word made visible and palpable (in Old Testament theophanies) the Father was being shown. . . . For the Father is the invisibility of the Son, and the Son is the visibility of the Father" (*Against Heresies* IV,6,6). But he later qualifies this statement to avoid the crass misunderstanding which is the heresy Augustine has in mind here, and he says (ibid. 20,5): "It is not, as some people say, that the Father of all things being invisible there is another who could be seen by the prophets." We are not concerned here with how Irenaeus goes on to explain what he did mean by calling the Son the visibility of the Father. But the crass misunderstanding he disclaims does seem to have been held both by Tertullian at the beginning of the third century and by Novatian in the middle of it; and there were still a few Tertullianists and Novatianists around when Augustine was writing this. They, surely, are the heretics he has in mind here.

55. Possibly he has *The Trinity* II, in mind.

Book IX

Genesis 2:18-24: The making of the woman from the man's side

Recapitulation about the making of the animals

1, 1. *And the Lord God said: It is not good for the man to be alone; let us make him a help suited to him. And God still fashioned from the earth all the beasts of the field and all the flying things of heaven, and he brought them to Adam to see what he would call them; and everything that Adam called a live soul, that is its name. And Adam called out names for all cattle and for all the flying things of heaven and for all the beasts of the field. For Adam, however, there was not found a helper like him. And God cast an ecstasy upon Adam, and he fell asleep. And he took one of his ribs and filled up its place with flesh. And the Lord God built the rib which he had taken from Adam into a woman, and brought her to Adam. And Adam said: This now, bone out of my bones and flesh from my flesh, this shall be called woman since she was taken out of her man; and for this reason a man shall leave father and mother and be glued to his wife; and they shall be two in one flesh* (Gn 2:19-24).

If the reader found what has been discussed and written down in the earlier volumes to be of any help, we ought not to delay any longer over the point raised by the words *God still fashioned from the earth all the beasts of the field and all the flying things of heaven*, the reason it said "still," which is because of the first setting up of creatures, finished in the six days, in which all things together were simultaneously completed and begun causally, so that from then on these causes might be brought to a head in their effects—all this, to the best of my ability, I have already stated earlier on.[1] And should you think that this knotty problem ought to be disentangled in a different way, you must pay as careful attention as I paid to all those details in order to reach my conclusion; and then if you can winkle out from them all a more likely solution, not only must I not oppose you, I will also be obliged to congratulate you.

---

1. See Book VI,5,7 above.

2. Should you be bothered, though, because he did not say, "God still fashioned from the earth all the beasts of the field, and from the waters all the flying things of heaven"; but as though he had fashioned each kind from the earth, *And God still fashioned*, it goes, *from the earth all the beasts of the field and all the flying things of heaven*; try and see that it can be understood in two ways. According to the first way, it kept quiet about what he fashioned the flying things of heaven from, because even though it is not mentioned, it could occur to the reader that God is not to be taken as fashioning each kind from the earth, but only the beasts of the field, and that even with scripture keeping quiet on the point, we should understand what it was he fashioned the flying things of heaven from, being people who know that in the first establishment of causal formulae they were produced out of the waters. Or else, according to the second way, the word "earth" is used in a general sense to include the waters, as it is in that psalm, where once the praises of heavenly beings is concluded, the psalmist turns to the earth, and says: *Praise the Lord from the earth, dragons and all abysses,* etc. (Ps 148:7), and does not go on to say, "Praise the Lord from the waters." Where, in any case, are all the abysses, which praise the Lord from the earth all the same? Where too the reptiles and winged fowl, which nonetheless praise the Lord from the earth? It is according to this general meaning of "earth," which we also have where it says about the whole universe: *God, who made heaven and earth* (Ps 124:8), that whatever was created either from the earth or from the waters is truly to be understood as having been created from the earth.

Various ways in which God could have spoken

2, 3. Now at last, then, let us see how we are to take it that God said, *It is not good for the man to be alone; let us make him a help suited to him* (Gn 2:18); whether God said this with words and syllables uttered in time, or whether the actual idea or formula was being recalled, which was originally in the Word of God, that the woman should be so made,[2] the kind of idea which scripture was also alluding to and taking up every time it said "And God said, Let this or that be made," when all things were being established to begin with. Or did God say this perhaps in the mind of the man himself, just as he speaks to some of his servants in his servants themselves? Such a servant was the one who said in the psalm: *I will hear what the Lord God will speak in me* (Ps 85:8). Or was an actual voice

---

2. The words he has just quoted introduce the making of the animals, not immediately of the woman, who only comes in when Adam has named all the animals, and "no helper like him" was found among them. The slight change of word in his text is significant; in the verse here quoted God says, "Let us make him a help," an impersonal noun, *adjutorium*; but then in 5,20 the personal noun, *adjutor*, helper is used.

produced through some bodily creature, like the one from the cloud, *This is my Son* (Mk 9:7)?

So which precisely of these it was that actually happened we may not be capable of grasping clearly; but at least let us hold as absolutely certain both that God did say this, and that even if he said it with a bodily voice uttered in time in some bodily likeness, it was not through his own very substance that he said it, but through some creature subject to his command, as we discussed the matter in the previous book.[3]

4. God, you see, also appeared later on to holy men, at one time with a head of hair white as wool, at another with the lower part of his body like gilt brass,[4] at others like this or like that. But for all that, he did not grant those visions to men in the substance which he is in himself, but showed what he wished and spoke by means of things subject to him which he created, and in the likenesses of bodily forms and voices. About this there is complete certainty for those who either faithfully believe, or exceptionally understand, that the substance of the Trinity being unchangeably eternal, it is not moved through successive times and places, and yet causes movement through times and through places. So then, let us not still go on asking how God said this, but rather let us try to understand what it is he said. That a help indeed for the man that was suited to him was to be made is there in eternal Truth herself, through whom all things were created. And it is in her that those hear this who are able to perceive in her why anything was created.

It was only for the procreation of children that the man needed the woman's help

3, 5. If the question is asked, though, for what purpose it was necessary for this help to be made, no more likely answer suggests itself than that it was for the sake of procreating children—in the same sort of way as the earth is a help to the seed, so that the plant may be born of each of them. This, after all, is what was said at the first establishment of things: *Male and female he made them, and God blessed them, saying: Increase and multiply and fill the earth and lord it over it* (Gn 1:27-28). This reason for the setting up and joining together of male and female and this blessing did not fall away after the man's sin and punishment; it is in terms of it, after all, that the earth is now full of men and women and being lorded over by them.

6. Although, you see, it was when they had been turned out of Paradise that they are reported to have come together and brought forth, I still cannot see what could have prevented their also being wedded with honor and bedded *without*

---

3. See Book VIII,27,49-50. He is not in fact going to rehash the whole subject again, as he will say himself at the end of this chapter and section 4.
4. See Rv 1:14-15, which is quoting respectively Dn 7:9 and Ez 1:27, somewhat modified.

spot or wrinkle (Eph 5:27) in Paradise, God granting this right to them if they lived faithfully in justice and served him obediently in holiness, so that without any restless fever of lust, without any labor and pain in childbirth, offspring would be brought forth from their sowing. This would not be in order that children might take the place of their parents when they died; the parents, rather, would remain in their prime[5] and receive bodily vigor from the tree of life which had been planted there, while their offspring would be brought up to the same perfect adult state until some definite number of human beings had been reached. Then, if they all lived lives of justice and obedience, the change would be brought about by which their merely "ensouled" animal bodies would be converted without dying into something of a different kind, and be entirely at the beck and call of the spirit governing them, and with only the spirit quickening them would live without having to be sustained by any bodily nourishment; their bodies would in fact be called spiritual.[6] This could have happened, if the transgression of the commandment had not earned the punishment of death.

7. Those, I mean, who do not believe that this could have happened are only paying attention to the usual way in which nature runs its course after sin and the human penalty; we though should not be in the class of those who only believe what they have usually seen. Can you doubt, after all, that what I have said could have been granted the man had he lived an obedient and religious life, if you have no doubts about the garments of the Israelites having a certain "stay of execution" of their own kind bestowed on them, so that for forty years they did not wear out through age?[7]

---

5. The meaning, I take it, of a rather odd phrase: *in aliquo formae statu*, literally, "in some stay of form/shape/beauty"; there would be no aging for Adam and Eve, nor for their offspring once they had reached perfect manhood or womanhood.
6. The background text to what he is saying here is 1 Cor 15:42-49, where Paul is answering the question, "How will the dead rise; what sort of bodies will they have?" The point of what Paul says there, and hence of what Augustine is saying here, is missed in nearly all translations, because Paul uses two words which have no real equivalents in modern English. In verse 44 he writes (literally): "It is sown a *psychic* body, it is raised a *pneumatic* body;" which translates (literally) into Latin: "It is sown an *animal* body, it is raised a *spiritual* body." He is, in fact, contrasting body as quickened or animated (ensouled) by soul, and body, in the resurrection, as quickened by spirit. If I may give here my translation of the passage, which I did for the English Jerusalem Bible, and which was modified in the second edition, but was still there in the first edition, and survives in the current Breviary in the first alternative reading for the Office of the Dead: "When it is sown it embodies the soul, when it is raised it embodies the spirit. If the soul has its own embodiment, so does the spirit have its own embodiment. The first man, Adam, as scripture says, became a living soul (Gn 2:7); but the last Adam has become a life-giving spirit. That is, first the one with the soul, not the spirit, and after that the one with the spirit." For further notes on this crucial linguistic point see Book VI,xix,30, notes 23 and 25 above; and Books X,12,20, notes 15 and 17; and XI,18,24, note 21 below.
7. See Dt 29:5. "Stay of execution" is the translator's slight elaboration of the single word *status*, "stay," which we have had before.

Why they did not in fact couple in Paradise

4, 8. So then, why did they not in fact couple until they had departed from Paradise? The quick answer can be given: because no sooner was the woman made than before they came together the transgression occurred, which earned them their sentence of death and their departure from that place of felicity. Scripture, you see, does not state how much time elapsed between their being made and Cain being born of them. It could also be said that it was because God had not yet ordered them to couple. Why, after all, should they not have waited for divine authority for this business, when no lust, like a spur of the disobedient flesh,[8] was driving them on? The reason however that God had not given this order was because he was disposing all things according to his foreknowledge, by which he undoubtedly foresaw their fall, from which time onward it would be a mortal human race that had to be propagated.

Except for the purpose of procreation, another man would have been a more suitable companion for Adam

5, 9. Or if it was not for help in producing children that a wife was made for the man, then what other help was she made for? If it was to till the earth together with him, there was as yet no hard toil to need such assistance; and if there had been the need, a male would have made a better help. The same can be said about companionship, should he grow tired of solitude. How much more agreeably, after all, for conviviality and conversation would two male friends live together on equal terms than man and wife? While if it was expedient that one should be in charge and the other should comply, to avoid a clash of wills disturbing the peace of the household, such an arrangement would have been ensured by one being made first, the other later, especially if the latter were created from the former, as the female was in fact created. Or would anyone say that God was only able to make a female from the man's rib, and not also a male if he so wished? For these reasons I cannot work out what help a wife could have been made to provide the man with, if you take away the purpose of childbearing.[9]

How one generation could have given way to the next had there been no sin

6, 10. But now, if it was right and proper for parents to give way to their children by departing this life, so that in this way the whole human race could mount up to a definite predetermined number through a succession of generations, it

---

8. See 2 Cor 12:7 for the phrase; not that Augustine would have supposed that it was this kind of spur or sting that Paul was given, to stop him getting swollen-headed.
9. Augustine in this little chapter does seem to have put himself in the class "of those who can only believe what they have usually seen" (above, 3,7).

would also have been possible for human beings, after breeding children and justly carrying out their duties, to be transferred to better things by some kind of change other than death. This could either be that supreme change by which on getting back their bodies[10] they will become *like the angels in heaven* (Mt 22:30); or else, if this may only be properly granted to all mankind together at the end of the world, it would be by some kind of lesser change, which for all that would still bring about a better condition than either this body has, or even the bodies of the two who were created at the beginning, the man's from the mud of the earth, the woman's from the man's flesh.

11. Elijah, you see, is not to be reckoned as already being like what the saints will be when, the work of the day being done, they will all equally receive the wage of a tenner,[11] nor on the other hand like people who have not yet departed this life, from which he did still depart, not by death but by special conveyance.[12] And so he already enjoys something better than he could have done in this life, although he does not yet enjoy what he is going to do at the end in consequence of a life well lived here. For they were looking forward to better things for us, lest they should be perfected without us being perfected too.[13]

Or if you suppose that Elijah could not have earned such a blessing if he had married a wife and begotten children—he is believed not to have had one because scripture did not say he did, although for that matter it did not say anything about his being celibate either—what reply will you give about Enoch, who pleased God after having had children, and did not die, but was conveyed away?[14] So then, if Adam and Eve had lived justly and had chastely begotten children, why could they not have made room for these to succeed them, not by dying but by being conveyed away?

---

10. In the case he has in mind they would not have lost their bodies, because they would not have died; but he is of course thinking of the resurrection of the dead, to which we now look forward, achieving the effect which would have been granted to them, without their having to die first.
11. See Mt 20:1-16, the parable of the workers in the vineyard, in which all received a *denarius*; a penny in the old translations, because that is what a *denarius* became. But it was a coin which was worth ten even smaller coins, and much is often made by Augustine of its derivation from the number 10; so "tenner," even though colloquial, seems to be the best modern equivalent.
12. See 2 Kgs 2:11.
13. "They" are the saints of the Old Testament of whose faith we are reminded in Heb 11. Augustine is here alluding, very freely from a slightly inaccurate memory, to verses 39 and 40 of that chapter. His final clause reads *ne sine nobis perfecti perficerentur*—"lest being perfected they should be perfected without us." I have presumed to emend *perfecti* to *perfectis*, to agree with *nobis*. Neither form is in the actual text of Hebrews.
14. See Gn 5:21-24.

Why set aside the reason of having children? A comparison of the values of marriage and virginity

7, 12. And so I do not see what other help a wife was made to provide the man with, if you set aside the reason of having children; why in any case you should set it aside I cannot imagine. It is true that faithful and religious virginity now earns the great reward of being greatly honored by God; but that is only because in this present *time to refrain from embracing* (Eccl 3:5), when the abundant supply of people from all nations is amply sufficient for filling up the number of the saints, the lust for indulging sordid pleasure cannot claim for itself what the necessity of supplying offspring no longer requires. And then the weakness of either sex tilting them towards collapse into shameful behavior is shored up by the honorable state of marriage, so that what could be just a duty for the healthy can be a remedy for the sick.

I mean, just because immoderate sexual activity is an evil, it does not follow that marriage, even between over-sexed persons, is not a good. Quite the contrary; not only does that evil not make this good blameworthy, this good makes that evil pardonable, since what is good in marriage can never be a sin. This good, in fact, is threefold: fidelity, offspring, sacrament.[15] What fidelity means is that neither partner should sleep with another person outside the marriage bond; offspring means that children should be welcomed with love, brought up with kindness, given a religious education; sacrament means that the union should not be broken up, and that if either husband or wife is sent away, neither should marry another even for the sake of having children. This is, so to say, the set-square of marriage, good either for embellishing the fertility of nature, or putting straight the crookedness of lust.

But I have discussed all this sufficiently in the book which I recently published on *The Good of Marriage*, where I also compared with it the self-denial of widowhood and the pre-eminence of virginity; so there is no need to keep my pen busy with it any further here.

---

15. The famous trio of the goods, or ends of marriage: *fides, proles, sacramentum.* That is the order he puts them in here; but in the little work he goes on to mention, *The Excellence of Marriage* 32, he puts them in the order that comes to dominate the tradition, *proles, fides, sacramentum,* offspring being seen as the primary end of marriage, and of sexual activity within marriage. It is only since Vatican II that in official teaching the goods or ends of marriage have been given parity of value.

A bad reason for supposing that they would not have been allowed to mate in Paradise

8, 13. Now, you see, we must ask what help the woman would have been made to provide the man with, if they had not been allowed to mate in Paradise. People who hold this opinion may perhaps assume that all sexual intercourse is sinful. It is indeed difficult for people who shun one set of vices for the wrong reasons not to fall promptly into the contrary set. Thus someone horrified by miserliness becomes a spendthrift, horrified by extravagance becomes a miser; you reprove him for indolence, he becomes restless; for restlessness he becomes indolent; on being reproved for daredevilry he begins to hate it, and takes refuge in timidity, or in his effort not to be timid he so to say bursts his chains and abruptly behaves rashly. This happens when people assess wrongdoing by opinion, not by reason. In the same sort of way, when they are ignorant of what it is in adultery and fornication that is condemned by divine law, they execrate conjugal intercourse even for the sake of procreation.

Another misapprehension on the point

9, 14. There are others who do not make this mistake, but who still feel that God bestowed fertility on the flesh just to provide mortal creatures with successors; and they too think that those first human beings could not have mated if they had not been going to die on account of the sin they had committed, and had not thus needed to provide themselves with successors by begetting them. But they fail to observe that if successors could properly be sought for those who were going to die, with much more propriety could companions and community have been sought for those who were going to go on living. Once the earth was filled, you see, by the human race, it would be quite right for offspring only to be sought in order to take the place of those who were going to die; but for the earth to be filled through just two human beings—how could they possibly fulfill this social duty except by having children?

Or can anyone be so intellectually blind as not to perceive what an ornament to all lands the human race is, even when only a few of its members live straight and laudable lives, and what value public order has in restraining even sinners with the bonds of a kind of earthly peace? Even the most crooked and depraved human beings, after all, still rank in value above cattle and birds. And yet can anybody fail to take pleasure in considering how this lower part of the universe is embellished with all the various species of fauna allotted to each region? Could anyone on the other hand be so crass as to suppose that the world would have been less beautifully furnished if it were filled with just and upright men and women who did not die?

15. You see, it is because the heavenly city of the angels is populated by such countless millions that it would not be right for them to be coupled in marriage if they were not going to die.[16] It was with foreknowledge of the completion of this vast multitude in the resurrection of the saints joining the company of the angels that the Lord said: *In the resurrection they are neither married nor do they take wives; for they will not be going to die, but will be equal to the angels of God* (Lk 20:36). Here, however, the earth still had to be filled with human beings; and since for the sake of a close family relationship, and above all for giving the highest commendation to the bond of unity, it was essential to start its being filled from one man, for what other reason was a helper like him sought in the female sex, than that a wife by her very nature should assist him, like fertile soil, in sowing and planting out the human race?

In Paradise they were not the slaves of carnal concupiscence

10, 16. However it would be better, more becoming to believe that the "ensouled" bodies[17] of those two established in Paradise, not yet having been condemned by the law of death, were such that they did not have the same lust for carnal pleasure as these bodies of ours do now, derived as they are from the propagation of death. It was something, you see, not just nothing, that happened in them when they had eaten of the forbidden tree, seeing that God had not said, "If you eat, you shall die the death," but: *on the day that you all eat, you shall die the death* (Gn 2:17). This means that this day produced in them the very result which the apostle describes with groans when he says: *I take delight in the law of God according to the inner man; but I see another law in my members fighting back against the law of my mind, and taking me prisoner under the law of sin, which is in my members. Unhappy man that I am, who will deliver me from the body of this death? The grace of God through Jesus Christ our Lord* (Rom 7:22-25). Would it not have been enough, I mean, for him to say, "Who will deliver me from this mortal body? But *from the body*, he said, *of this death*. Like that other place too: *The body indeed*, he said, *is dead because of sin* (Rom 8:10); he did not say "mortal" there either, but "dead"—though of course it was also mortal, because it was going to die.

---

16. We nowadays assume that angels do not marry simply because of their angelic nature; that they are not marrying or marriageable beings; and we assume that that is what our Lord meant in his answer to the Sadducees, Lk 20:36 (Augustine is clearly quoting Luke, not the parallel Mt 22:30 which his editors always refer to in this connection), when he said that in the resurrection human beings will not marry but will be equal to the angels. However, he and the Sadducees, and Augustine, would have been aware of the passage in Gn 6:1-4, which talks of the sons of God seeing the daughters of men, that they were fair, and taking to wife such of them as they chose, and would have known that the phrase "sons of God" in the Old Testament usually means the angels. So here Augustine at least has in mind a case of angels being coupled in marriage in a way that was by no means right and proper.

17. *Corpus animale* in the Latin. See note 6 above.

It is not to be supposed that the bodies of those two were like that; but though they were only embodiments of soul, not yet of spirit, they were not for all that dead, that is, under the necessity of dying; this only happened to them, that they became dead, on the day when they touched the tree in spite of the prohibition.

17. Take our bodies here and now; we talk about a kind of health they have in some measure, and if this is ruined to the extent that a lethal disease is already gnawing at our vitals, and the doctors after examining us declare that death is imminent, then of course the body is also said in that case to be mortal, but rather differently from when it was in good health, although undoubtedly due to die some time or other. In somewhat the same way, those first human beings did indeed have merely "ensouled" bodies, but ones that were not going to die unless they sinned, being due instead to receive an angelic form and a heavenly quality; but as soon as they transgressed the commandment, they contracted death itself in their members, like some lethal illness which altered that quality by which they so dominated their bodies that they would not have to say, *I see another law in my members fighting back against the law of my mind*. Even if their bodies, you see, were not yet "enspirited," only "ensouled," they were for all that not yet "the body of this death" from which and with which we have been born.

What else, after all, did we start on—I won't say when we were born, but quite simply when we were conceived—but a kind of illness of which we are of necessity going to die? I mean, a person suffering from dropsy or tuberculosis or elephantiasis is not as certainly and necessarily going to die of that disease, as any person is certainly going to die who begins to have this body by which all human beings are *by nature children of wrath* (Eph 2:3), because what has brought this about is nothing but the penalty of sin.

18. This being so, why should we not suppose that before sin those two human beings were able to control and command their genital organs for the procreation of children in the same way as their other limbs, which the soul moves for all kinds of action without any trouble or any sort of prurient itch for pleasure? Look at how the almighty creator, after all, who is to be praised more than words can express, and who is great even in the smallest of his works, allows bees to go about the producing of children in the same way as they do the making of elegant wax combs and the honey dripping from them.[18] So why should it seem incredible that he made bodies for the first human beings of such a kind, that if they had not sinned and straightaway contracted a sort of disease of which they would die, just as they commanded the feet when they went walking, so they could have commanded at will the organs that bring the fetus into being, so that it would have been neither sown in palpitating heat nor brought forth in piteous pain?

---

18. I take it his chief "authority" for this was Virgil; see his *Georgics* IV, which is devoted entirely to bees—and a little to bee-keeping. On the particular point of their freedom from both sordid lust and the pangs of childbirth, see lines 197-202.

Now however, as the just deserts of their transgressing the commandment, they found the movement of that law fighting back against the law of the mind in the members of the body of that death they had contracted, a movement which marriage regulates, continence subdues and curbs, in order that just as the sin was turned into punishment, so the punishment might be turned into merit.

To doubt that the woman was made for the man to effect the peopling of the earth, is to call in question everything we believe

11, 19. And so the woman, being made for the man, from the man, in that sex and shape and distinction of parts by which females are known, gave birth to Cain and Abel and all their brothers and sisters, from whom all human beings would be born. Among them she also gave birth to Seth, through whom we come to Abraham and the people of Israel and the nation now so widely known among all the nations, and to all nations through the sons of Noah. To doubt this is to undermine the foundations of everything we believe, something therefore the faithful should put entirely out of their minds. So then, when you ask what help that sex was made to provide the man with, the only thing that occurs to me after carefully considering everything to the best of my ability is that it was for the sake of having children, so that the earth might be filled from their stock; and a stock not engendered, what is more, in the way human beings are engendered nowadays, when the law of sin is in their members fighting back against the law of the mind, even when by God's grace they virtuously overcome it. We have to believe, after all, that this could not have been the case except in "the body of this death," the body that "is dead because of sin."

And what juster penalty could there be than that the body, the soul's henchman, should fail to serve it at its every beck and call, just as the soul itself declined to serve its own Lord and master? But whether God creates each from the parents, body from body, soul from soul, or whether he makes souls in some other way, it is certainly not for a task that is impossible or for a paltry reward; it is in order that the soul, religiously subjecting itself to God, may itself conquer through grace this law of sin which is in the members of the body of this death, and so receive a heavenly reward with all the greater glory, thus demonstrating what praise is due to the obedience of one who has been able virtuously to over-come the penalty of another's disobedience.[19]

---

19. The second half of this section is very loosely written. Not only is the syntax somewhat incoherent, the question of how God makes souls (a question Augustine never succeeded in answering to his own satisfaction) is not immediately relevant to what he is concerned with here. It is, to be sure, very relevant to the question of how original sin is transmitted, and that question, no doubt, was at the back of his mind.

It was for a prophetic or symbolic reason that the animals were brought to
Adam to be named, and that thus the need arose to make him a helper like him

12, 20. But we have now investigated sufficiently, in my opinion, what kind of help it was that the woman was made to provide for the man. What we should now see is why it was done after all the beasts of the field and all the flying things of heaven had been brought to Adam for him to put names to them, and that it was in this way that the necessity, as it were, arose for creating him a woman from his side, when among those animals a help like him had not been found. Well, it seems to me that it was done on account of some prophetic significance—but still it was actually done, so that once the historical fact has been established, the field is left free for its figurative interpretation.

What then is the meaning of this, that Adam put names to flying things and terrestrial living things, but not to fishes and all swimming things? After all, if one consults human languages, one finds that all these things are called by names which people have given them by speech: not only these things to be found in the waters and on land, but also the land or earth itself and the water and the sky or heaven, and things which can be seen in the sky and things which cannot be seen but which are believed to exist; they are all called by a diversity of names according to the diversity of national languages.

21. We have been taught, to be sure, that there was but one language originally, before the pride that constructed that tower after the flood divided human society with sounds of diverging significance;[20] whatever that language may have been, is there any point in trying to find out? It was certainly the language Adam used to speak, and it is in that language, if it continues to this day, that the words were articulated with which the first man put names to the land animals and the flying things. Is it in the least credible, therefore, that in the same language the names for fishes were fixed by God, not by the man, and that later on the man learned them at God's dictation? Well, even if it had happened like that, there would undoubtedly be a mystical significance to be found in why it had happened like that. But no, we must assume that names were put to the different species of fish as little by little they came to be known.

Then, however, when the cattle and the wild beasts and the flying things were in fact brought to the man, for him to put names to them, assembled before him in their distinct species (and he could also have given them names little by little, if this had not been done, and much sooner than the fishes), what could the reason for this have been, if not to signify something that would serve to foretell future events? It is above all the very order and style of this narrative that points to this conclusion.

---

20. See Gn 11:1-8, the story of the tower of Babel.

And then, was God really unaware that he had not created anything among the animal species of a sort that could be a help for the man by being like him? Or perhaps there was a need for the man himself also to realize this, and for him to value his wife all the more, because in all flesh created under heaven and breathing the same air as himself nothing could be found that was like him; is that it? It would be very surprising, though, if he could only have known this after the animals had all been brought to be reviewed by him. I mean, if he believed and trusted God, God could have told him this in the same way as he gave him the commandment, in the same way as he questioned and passed judgment on him when he sinned; while if he did not believe or trust him, then it follows he could not have known whether the one he did not trust had in fact brought all of them to him, or whether perhaps he had hidden away in some of the remoter parts of the earth a few that were like him, which he had not shown him. And so I reckon there can be no doubt at all that this was done for the sake of signifying something prophetically—but that it was done all the same.

22. In this work I have not undertaken to investigate the meaning of prophetic riddles, but to emphasize the proper or historical sense as a trustworthy account of what actually happened. This means that to the best of my ability and as far as God gives me help, I must try to demonstrate by my arguments that what seems to shallow and unbelieving minds to be impossible is not in fact impossible; and what seems on the evidence of a contrary text to go against the very authority of holy scripture is not in fact contrary to it.

Where, however, something is apparently possible and carries no hint or suggestion of any contradiction, but can still, nonetheless, strike some people as what you could call superfluous, or even plain silly, here I would demonstrate in my discussion of it that the reason it was not done according to what might be considered the natural or usual course of events was so that it might be entrusted to our hearts, given the supremely trustworthy authority of the holy scriptures, as something mystical (because plain silly it cannot be)—though as a matter of fact, I have either already presented this kind of interpretation or inquiry elsewhere, or else must put it off to some other time.[21]

---

21. In his youthful work, *On Genesis: A Refutation of the Manichees* II,16, he has a very brief comment on why the animals were brought to Adam to be named, before the story goes on to the making of the woman. He says it was to show Adam his superiority over the animals, in virtue of his possessing reason; not, surely, a very obviously allegorical interpretation of the text. As for any further "mystical" or "prophetic" interpretation, I doubt if he ever bothered later on to attempt it. So the field remains wide open to the imaginative skills of modern typological exegetes.

The account of the making of the woman also clearly calls for a mystical or prophetic interpretation

13, 23. So what then is the meaning of a wife being made for the man from his side? Granted it is true we should believe that it was fitting for this to be done in that way in order to emphasize the force of the union effected by wedlock; does the same reason or necessity also demand that it should be done to him while he was fast asleep, and by the extraction of a bone, the place it left being filled up with flesh? After all, could not flesh itself have been extracted, for a wife to be more suitably formed from that, being of the weaker, or inferior sex? Or perhaps with so many things to be added to it God was able to build a rib into a woman, but could not manage it with flesh and fat, though he had made the man himself from dust—is that it? Or if it had to be a rib that was extracted, why was it not replaced with another rib? Why too did it not say "fashioned" or "made," as in all the previous works, but *The Lord God built*, it says, *the rib* (Gn 2:22), as if it was a question of a house, not a human body?

So accordingly there cannot be any doubt, since these things were done and cannot be plain silly, that they were done to signify something, with God in his foreknowledge already mercifully foretelling in his actual works the fruit to be derived in the age to come from the very origins of the human race, so that in due course they would be revealed to his servants, whether by tradition through successive generations, or by his Spirit or by the ministry of angels, and then written down to provide evidence both of promises for the future being made and of their fulfillment being acknowledged. This will all become more and more apparent in the events that follow.[22]

Back to the "literal" explanation of Adam's encounter with the beasts and the birds

14, 24. So let us see then—what we have undertaken in this work—how all this can be taken, not as prefiguring things to come, but according to the proper or historical sense, not the allegorical one, of things that actually happened. *And God still fashioned*, it says, *from the earth all the beasts of the field and all the flying things of heaven* (I have already sufficiently stated my ideas on that) *and he brought them all to Adam to see what he would call them* (Gn 2:19). To save us from being crassly literal-minded about how God brought them to Adam, we

---

22. *In consequentibus*; in God's unfolding revelation, through the events of the sacred history recorded in scripture, reflected on and successively interpreted by the prophets, reinterpreted and partly fulfilled, partly projected once more into the future by Christ and the Church in the New Testament. *In consequentibus* could also mean in what follows in this work on the literal meaning of Genesis; but I rather think that the disproof of that pudding will be in the eating! We can but wait and see.

should find some help in what we discussed in the previous book about the twofold working of divine providence.[23] It is not to be supposed, I mean, that this was done in the way hunters and fowlers track down and drive into the nets whatever animals they catch. Nor did some commanding voice issue from a cloud in words which rational souls are used to understanding and obeying when they hear them; neither beasts nor birds, after all, received this capacity.

But all the same they do in their own fashion submit to God, though not by any rational decision of the will, but in the way that he moves all things around at the appropriate times, without being moved through periods of time himself, by the ministry of angels. These grasp in his Word what has to be done and at what time, and without his being moved through time, they are themselves so moved, in order to carry out his instructions in things that have been made subject to them.

25. Every live soul, you see, not only the rational kind as in human beings, but also the non-rational as in cattle and flying things and fish, is moved by the sight of things. But the rational soul, by a free voluntary decision, either consents or does not consent to such sights, whereas the non-rational does not have this power of judgment, but is all the same stimulated, according to the nature of its kind, when in contact with something seen. Nor does any soul have control over what sights may strike either its bodily senses or its innermost spirit;[24] and it is by these sights that the appetite of any sort of animate being at all is moved.

And thus it is that when these sights are presented from above through the obedience of the angels, God's instructions reach not only human beings, not only birds and cattle, but also things that lurk under the waters, like the whale which swallowed Jonah; and not only these bigger ones, but also a little worm—because we read that this too was instructed by God to gnaw the root of the gourd under whose shade the prophet had gone to have a rest.[25]

Think of how God, in setting man in his place, has bestowed on him the ability, even when he is carrying "the flesh of sin,"[26] not only to subdue cattle and beasts of burden and domestic fowls to his uses, but also to catch and tame birds that fly around free, all sorts of savage beasts too, and in a wonderful way to rule them with the power of reason, not by brute force; and then how trainers do this by working on the appetites and pains of the animals, softening them up gradually by enticements, by applying pressure and relaxing it, until they have, as it were, stripped them of their wild habits and clothed them with human manners.

---

23. See Book VIII,9,17-18; 21-26,40-48.
24. That is, the sense memory and imagination, both elements, in varying degrees, of every kind of animal's sensory equipment.
25. See Jn 1:17; 4:6-7.
26. I think he must have had in mind here a text like Rom 6:6, which in fact, however, talks of "the body of sin"; but it mentions its being destroyed by our baptism into Christ's death.

How much more are angels able to do this, who register his orders in that unchangeable Truth of his which they gaze upon everlastingly! Then moving themselves through time and the bodies subject to them through both time and place with a wonderful agility, they can effectively produce for every living soul the sights by which it will be moved and the appetite to satisfy some fleshly need, so that it may be brought all unconsciously to wherever its presence is needed.

How the formation of the woman was actually done

15, 26. So now let us see how the formation of the wife, which was mystically also called a work of building, was actually done. The nature of the woman was of course created, although out of the man's which was already there; it was not made by any moving around or changing of existing natures. Now angels are not able to create any nature whatsoever; the one and only creator of any nature you like, great or small, is God, that is to say the Trinity itself, Father and Son and Holy Spirit. So it is a different kind of question, how Adam was put to sleep, and his rib extracted from the structure of the body[27] without his feeling any pain. We may perhaps say that these things could have been done through angels; but to form or build the rib into being a woman was something that only God, who maintains nature as a whole in being, was able to do—so much so that I cannot even believe the supplying of the man's body with flesh to take the place of his rib was done by angels, any more than the making of the man himself from the dust of the earth. Not that the angels contribute no work at all to the creation of something, but that does not make them creators, just as we do not call farmers the creators of crops and trees, since *neither the one who plants is anything, nor the one who irrigates, but the one who gives the growth, God* (1 Cor 3:7). An instance of such growth is also to be found in a human body, when the place left by the removal of a bone has been filled up with flesh—by God doing the same sort of work, that is, as he did when he set up all natures in being, as he also did when he created the angels themselves.

27. And so it is the farmer's work to conduct the water through the right channels when he irrigates;[28] but it is not his work to ensure that water flows downhill; that is the work of the one who *has disposed all things in measure and number and weight* (Wis 11:20). Again, it is by the farmer's work that the sucker is pulled off from the tree, and committed to the earth; but it is not by his work that it drinks in moisture and puts out shoots, so that it fixes one part of itself in

27. A Ciceronian echo; *a corporis compage*. See the master's *De Senectute* 21.77.
28. Watering gardens and fields in the Mediterranean world of Paul and Augustine, especially in summer when it was most needed, was of course not a matter of hose-pipes and sprinklers, but of leading water from a tank or dam down channels to the plots to be watered, the farmer or gardener doing this by closing off one channel and opening another with a hoe.

the soil by stabilizing its roots, pushes another upwards into the open air by toughening its trunk and spreading out its branches, but by the work of "the one who gives the growth."

Again, the doctor prescribes a diet for the ailing body, and a dressing for the wounded one. In the first place, however, he does not do this with things he has created but with ones which he finds already created by the work of the creator; in the second, he has been able to prepare the food or drink and to administer it, to fashion the plaster, smear it with the ointment and apply it to the wound; but is he also able to work with the things he uses and actually create strength or flesh? Nature does that with some inner impulse that is totally obscure to us. But if God withdraws from nature the innermost activity of all, by which he makes her and sets her in place, she will at once, so to say, be extinguished and "leave not a rack behind."[29]

28. No angel, accordingly, can create a nature any more than it can create itself. But since God administers the whole of his creation, as we explained in the previous book, by the operation of his providence divided somehow into two parts,[30] doing this in both natural and voluntary activities or movements, the angelic will is able, in obedient submission to God and in execution of his orders, to provide from things subject to it the material, so to say, for the movements of nature, so that something may be created in time in accordance with either the primary uncreated ideas in the Word of God, or with those ideas or formulae causally created in the works of the first six days; this in the kind of way farmers and doctors assist the functioning of nature.

So as to what kind of service the angels helped God with in the formation of the woman, who would be rash enough to make any definite assertion? What I will say with complete certainty, nonetheless, is that the flesh which filled up the place left by the rib, and the woman's body and soul and the shape and arrangement of her limbs, with all the entrails, all the senses and everything else which marked her as both creature and human and female, all this was made by none but God, not acting through angels but directly himself; not working and then leaving the thing made, but continuing to work in such a way that no nature of any other things, not even of the angels themselves, would remain in being if he were not so working.

Continuing the comparison between God's work and that of the angels

16, 29. But as far as our limited human experience goes of the nature of things, we do not know of any way in which animate and sentient flesh comes to birth,

---

29. It is astonishing how Augustine keeps on quoting Shakespeare's *Tempest*!
30. Book VIII,9,17-18; 21-26. 40-48.

except that it is either from these basic material elements—water and earth, that is—or from shrubs or the fruits of trees, or even from the flesh of animals like innumerable kinds of worms or reptiles, and of course from the mating of parents; we certainly have no knowledge of any flesh being born of the flesh of any kind of animate being, which would be so like it as to be only distinguishable by its sex. We look for something to compare in the things of this creation with the wife being made from the side of her man, and we cannot find anything. And the only reason for this is that while we know how human beings work the land on this earth, we certainly have no knowledge of how angels do their farm work, so to say, in this world.

I mean it is clear that if the intervention of human skills were set aside and it was only the course of nature that was at work in shrubs, all we would know is that trees and herbs are born from the earth and from their seeds—and from these, what is more, simply as falling from them to the ground. Would anything come to our knowledge about the efficacy of grafting, so that a tree of one species can support from its own roots the apples or plums of another, which as the union is sealed have already become its own? We have learned this from the works of farmers, though they themselves are in no way at all the creators of the trees, but lend their services as a kind of favor to God who is indeed the creator of the course of nature. Nothing at all, surely, would come from their labors, unless nature as a result of God's work were inherently sympathetic to them. So why be surprised if we do not know how a human being was made from the bone of a human being, when we are ignorant of how the angels serve God in his act of creation—we who could not know about a tree being made from the shoot of a tree in the trunk of another one, if we were likewise ignorant of how farmers serve God in his act of creating these things?

30. But for all that, we have not the slightest doubt that the only creator both of human beings and of trees is God, and we faithfully believe that the woman was made from the man independently of any sexual intercourse, even if the man's rib may have been served up for the creator's work by angels:[31] in the same way we faithfully believe that a man was also made from a woman independently of any sexual intercourse, when *the seed* of Abraham *was disposed by angels in the hand of the mediator* (Gal 3:19).[32] Both things are incredible to unbelievers; but why should believers find what happened in the case of Christ quite credible when taken in the literal, historical sense, and what is written about Eve only acceptable in its figurative signification?

31. A splendid picture this conjures up, of angels, suitably clad in aprons, and with napkins over their arms, serving Adam's rib up to God on a dish, for him to carve it into being Eve!
32. See his correction of what he says here in his *Revisions*, II,24, in the extract from that work printed at the beginning of Book I in this work. He refers there to the first occasion on which he misapplied this text, in Book V,19,38. See note 25 in that book for further comment.

Is it that a man could be made from a woman without anyone coupling with her, but a woman could not so be made from a man; and that a virgin's womb had in it the material for making a man, while a man's side did not have in it the means for making a woman, though there it was a case of the Lord and master being born from a maidservant, here of a maidservant being formed from a field hand? Well, the Lord too could have created his flesh from a rib or any other part of the virgin; but while he would in this way have been able to show that he had repeated in his own body what had been done already, it was more to the point for him to show in his mother's body that nothing which is chaste is to be treated as something to be ashamed of.

The different levels from which the causal ideas or formulae function

17, 31. But you may ask where, in this connection, that setting up of causes comes in, by which God first of all made man to his image and likeness—it says there too, of course: *male and female he made them* (Gn 1:27); whether that formula, which God "concreated" with the first works of the world and set fermenting[33] in them, was programmed to mean that it was now necessary for the woman to be made from the man's side, or whether it was only programmed to mean that she could be made; but that she had to be made like that had not already been prescribed there but was hidden away in God. So then, if you do ask this, I will say what I think without rashly asserting anything; still, when I have said it, it may be that those who are already imbued with Christian faith will judge, on giving the matter serious consideration, that there can be little doubt about it, even if now is the first time they have taken cognizance of these things.

32. The whole course of nature that we are so familiar with has certain natural laws of its own, according to which both the spirit of life which is a creature[34] has drives and urges that are somehow predetermined and which even a bad will cannot bypass, and also the elements of this material world have their distinct energies and qualities, which determine what each is or is not capable of, what can or cannot be made from which. It is from these base-lines of things, so to say, that whatever comes to be takes in its own particular time span, its risings and continued progress, its ends and its settings, according to the kind of thing it is. Hence the fact that beans are not produced from grains of wheat or wheat from beans, nor human beings from cattle or cattle from human beings.

---

33. *Concrevit*, from *concresco*, properly speaking an intransitive verb meaning to grow together, and so condense, curdle, stiffen, congeal, etc.; I am simply quoting Lewis & Short. That dictionary gives no instance of the verb's being used in a transitive sense with an object, as it clearly is being used here. So I am taking it as meaning "making to grow together," hence to ferment, like yeast, because that does seem to be the way Augustine envisaged these *rationes causales* as functioning.
34. As distinct from the uncreated Spirit of life.

But over and above this natural course and operation of things, the power of the creator has in itself the capacity to make from all these things something other than what their seminal formulae, so to say, prescribe—not however anything with which he did not so program them that it could be made from them at least by him. He is almighty, for sure, but with the strength of wisdom, not unprincipled might; and he makes from each thing in his own time what he first inscribed in it that he could make from it.

So then there is one standard for things according to which this plant germinates in this way, that one in that, this age gives birth, that one does not, a human being can speak, an animal cannot. The formulae for these and suchlike standards are not only in God, but have also been inserted by him in created things and set fermenting in them.[35] But that a wooden rod cut out of the ground, quite dead and polished smooth, entirely without roots, without earth and water, should suddenly flower and bear fruit; that a woman barren throughout her youth should give birth in old age; that a donkey should talk,[36] and anything else there may be of that sort—all this he did indeed give to the natures he created so that these things too could be made from them. After all, even he would not make from them what he himself had predetermined could not be made from them, since not even he is more powerful than himself. But still he gave it to them in a different way, so that they would not have these possibilities in them according to their natural operation, but in virtue of their being so created that their natures would be more thoroughly subject to his mightier will.

The same, continued, extending the point to the working of grace

18, 33. So then, God has in himself the hidden causes of certain deeds and events, which he did not insert in things he had made; and he does not activate them by that work of providence by which he set up natures in order for them to be, but by that other one by which he administers as he may wish the natures he established as he wished. Among these causes too is the grace by which sinners are saved. I mean, as far as a nature distorted by its own wicked will is concerned, it has no recourse in itself, but only in the grace of God, by which it is helped and restored. People should not be despaired of, you see, because of that judgment where it is written: *All who walk in it shall not return* (Prv 2:19); this was said with regard to the pull of their wickedness, so that the fact that those who will return do return is not something they should attribute to themselves but to God's grace—*not from works, lest any should exalt themselves* (Eph 2:9).

---

35. See note 33 above.
36. See Nm 17:8, Aaron's rod blossoming; Gn 18:11, 21:2, Sarah's conceiving and giving birth to Isaac; Nm 22:28, Balaam's donkey reproving him.

34. That is why the apostle said that the mystery of this grace was not hidden in the world, as are the causal formulae of all things that are going to take their rise in a natural way, as Levi was hidden in the loins of Abraham, *when he too was tithed* (Heb 7:9-10), but in God, who created them all.[37]

Accordingly all the things too which were done miraculously, not by natural processes, to signify this grace, had their causes also hidden in God. If one of these was the woman being made like that from the side of the man, and of him fast asleep what's more, and her being made strong through him, as though strengthened by his bone, while he was weakened on her account, because the place of his rib was not filled up with another rib but with flesh,[38] none of this was prescribed in the first establishment of things, when it was said on the sixth day "male and female he made them," in such a way that the woman quite simply would be made like that. All that was prescribed there was that she could be made like that, and that God would not make anything by a vacillating change of mind, against causes which he had deliberately instituted. What precisely would be done, however, such that there would be nothing different taking place at all, all that was *hidden in God, who created all things* (Eph 3:9).

35. But since he said that it was hidden in God precisely *in order that the manifold wisdom of God might be made known to the princes and the powers in the heavenly places* (Eph 3:10), the most likely supposition is that just as "the seed for which the promise was made was disposed by angels in the hand of the mediator,"[39] so all the things that were done miraculously in the realm of nature, but against the usual course of nature, to predict or to proclaim the advent of that seed, were done through the ministry of angels, provided it is understood that in every instance the one and only creator and repairer of creatures, whoever planter or irrigator may be, is *the one who gives the growth, God* (1 Cor 3:7).

Adam's prophetic utterance on waking from his ecstasy

19, 36. So by the same token that ecstasy, which God cast on Adam, to put him into a deep sleep, may rightly be understood as cast upon him precisely in order that he too in his mind might through ecstasy become as it were a member of the angelic court, and so *enter into the sanctuary of God and understand the last*

---

37. Nowhere does the apostle talk in so many words about the mystery of grace being hidden in God; but it will become clear at the end of this section that Augustine has in mind Eph 3:9: *to enlighten them all about the dispensation of the sacrament* (that is the word in the Vulgate, but it is possible that Augustine's versions had "mystery" here) *hidden from ages ago in God, who created all things.* For he will go on later to quote v.10. But other related texts are Col 1:26, 2:3 and 3:3.
38. The "grace" here being prophetically or mystically signified is clearly the relationship of Christ with his Church: Christ weakened and "asleep" on the cross, and the Church, in the form of its sacraments, issuing from his side as blood (the eucharist) and water (baptism).
39. See note 32 above.

things (Ps 73:17). Finally, on waking up, full of prophecy so to say, when he saw his wife brought to him he immediately burst out with what the apostle holds up to us as a great sacrament:[40] *This now bone out of my bones and flesh from my flesh, this shall be called woman, since she was taken out of her man; and for this reason a man shall leave his father and mother and shall stick to his wife; and they shall be two in one flesh* (Gn 2:23-24).

While scripture itself testifies that these were the words of the first man, the Lord all the same declared in the gospel that God spoke to them; he said, you see: *Have you not read that the one who made man from the beginning made them male and female? And he said: For this reason a man shall leave father and mother and stick to his wife, and they shall be two in one flesh?* (Mt 19:4-5). From this we may conclude that through the ecstasy which Adam had just experienced he could be treated by God as a prophet. But I now have the pleasure of bringing this book to an end, so that by starting off from a new base-line readers may come with freshly revived attention to what comes next.

---

40. See Eph 5:32.

Book X

On the origin of human souls

The idea that the woman's soul was made out of the man's

1, 1. Now, to be sure, the unfolding of the story seems to require that we should discuss the sin of the first man; but because scripture related how the flesh of the woman was made, while saying nothing about her soul, this has made us much more intent on looking into this matter with greater thoroughness, to see how, if at all, we may be able to refute those who believe that a person's soul, like flesh from flesh, is made by the parents, with a transfusion of the seeds of each thing into the children. What induces them, you see, to take up such a position is this: they say that God made one soul, which he blew into the face of the man whom he had fashioned from the dust, so that from that one soul might be created the souls of all other human beings, just as the flesh of every human being derives from that man's flesh, since Adam was first formed, and then Eve. And about him, indeed, we are told where he got his body from and where his soul—his body, that is to say, from the dust of the earth, his soul from the puff of God; whereas when we are told of her being made from his side, it does not say that God likewise animated or "ensouled" her with a puff. So it looks as if each part of her, flesh and soul, was derived from the one who had already been "ensouled."

It should either have kept quiet, you see—so their argument runs—about the man's soul too, so that as best we could we should understand, or at the very least believe, that it was given him by God; or else, if the reason scripture did not keep quiet about this was to stop us assuming that the man's soul like his flesh was made from the earth, it should also not have kept quiet about the woman's soul, to stop its being thought to be derived by transmission from his, if that is not true. Accordingly, they say, it is precisely because it *is* true that her soul as well was propagated from the man, that there is no mention of God puffing it into her face.

2. This line of argument is easily countered. If the reason, you see, they think that the woman's soul was made from the soul of the man, is that the text does not say that God puffed into the woman's face, why do they believe that the woman

398

was "ensouled" from the man, when the text does not say that either? Hence if God makes all the souls of human beings when they are born as he made that first soul, then scripture kept quiet about the others because it could reasonably be understood that what is recorded as being done with the first one also applies to the rest.

So granting, for the sake of argument, that we had to be given some guidance in this matter through this passage of scripture: if something different was done in the woman's case which had not been done in the man's, namely that her soul should be derived from his "ensouled" flesh and not as with her husband, body from one source, soul from another, scripture should definitely not have kept quiet about the fact that it was now being done in a different way, or we would naturally assume that it was being done exactly as we had already learned it was done in his case.

Accordingly, because the author did not say that the woman's soul was made from the soul of the man, it is more appropriate to believe that he thereby wished to advise us not to assume anything different in this case from what we knew about the man's soul; that is, that the woman was given hers in the same manner. What particularly supports this conclusion is that the most obviously suitable occasion for saying that her soul derived from his, apart from the moment when she was formed, would have been when Adam said, *This now bone out of my bones and flesh from my flesh* (Gn 2:23). With how much greater love and appreciation would he have added, "and soul from my soul"! None of this, however, is enough for us to say that such a great problem as this has already been solved, so that we may hold any particular one of these answers to be clearly and definitely the right one.

Recapitulation of what has been said in the previous books on the origin of the soul

2, 3. What therefore we first have to see is whether this book of holy scripture, carefully gone through from its starting point, allows us to have any doubts on the matter; then maybe we will have the right to inquire, either which opinion is the more to be preferred, or else what method we ought to follow if this turns out to be altogether uncertain. It is quite certain, you see, that on the sixth day *God made man to his image*, where it also says, *male and female he made them* (Gn 1:27). We took the first of these two points, where the image of God is mentioned, to refer to the soul, the second about the distinction of sex to refer to the flesh.[1]

---

1. The editors here simply refer us back to Books VI and VII. I think I can be a little more precise, and helpful, than that. The whole topic, for one thing, was first broached in Book III,22,33-34; for another, very little indeed is said about it in Book VI, apart from the introductory chapter, 1,1-2. The whole of Book VII, certainly, is devoted to the question, and airs a great many possibilities; for what may be called his final solution, see there 24,35—28,42.

On the other hand there was a great amount of weighty evidence, which was there considered and discussed, that would not allow us to hold that on the same sixth day the man was also formed from mud and the woman from his side. No, we came to the conclusion that this was done after those primary works of God, in which he created all things simultaneously together. And so we asked ourselves what we should believe about the man's soul; and after discussing all the possibilities presented in the debate, we decided it would be more credible and tolerable to say that the man's soul was made among those works, while it was just the formula or idea of his body that was made, or so to say seeded, in the corporeal world. This was to get out of having to say against the words of scripture, either that the whole was made on the sixth day, the man from mud, that is, and the woman from his side; or else that in those works of the six days man was not made in any way at all; or else that it was only the human body's causal formula that was made then, not any such formula of the soul, though it was primarily with reference to the soul that man was made to God's image.

Or else again we would have to say something that would be very hard to tolerate, even if it did not go openly against the words of scripture; that is that the formula of the human soul was made in some spiritual material[2] which had been created for this sole purpose, though the creation of such a thing is not mentioned among the works of God; or alternatively that the formula of the soul was made in one of the creatures that is mentioned among those works, in the same sort of way as the formula of children yet to be born has been made in human beings who already exist, but is only latent in them, and hence we would have to think of the soul as the daughter either of angels or even more unacceptably of some bodily material element.

A choice to be made between three possibilities: a) that the formula of the soul was made in some primary creature; b) that only the first man's soul was made among those primary works, and from it all other human souls derive; c) that new souls are made subsequently, without any formula of them being made in the works of the first six days

3, 4. But now then, if the reason for the assertion that the woman did not receive her soul from the man but like him had it made for her by God is that God makes individual souls for all individuals, it follows that the woman's soul was not made among those primary works; or else if a general formula for all souls had been made then, like the formula for breeding children inherent in human beings, we find ourselves back with that hard stumbling block of having to say that human souls are the daughters of angels, or—what is totally abhorrent—of the material heaven or even of one of the lower elements.

---

2. See Book VII,6,9—9,13.

And so it is that we have to see which of three possibilities can at least be said to be the more acceptable, even if it continues to elude us which is actually the true one: whether the one I have just stated; or that the single soul of the first man was made in those first works of God, for all other human souls to be created from its "slips"; or that new souls are being made from then on, of which no formula would have been made to precede them in those works of God in the first six days. Now of these three the first two do not clash with those primordial works where all things were created simultaneously together. For whether the formula of the soul was made in some creature, as in a kind of parent, so that all souls might derive from that but be created by God when they are given to individual human beings, like their bodies from human parents, or whether it was not the formula of soul, like the formula of offspring in parents, but quite simply the soul itself that was made when the day was made, as the day itself was made, as heaven and earth and the lights in the sky,[3] it fits in well with the words, *God made man to his own image* (Gn 1:27).

5. But as for this third one, it is not so easy to see how it can avoid clashing with the opinion according to which the man is taken both to have been made to the image of God on the sixth day and to have been visibly created after the seventh day.[4] The point is that if we say new souls are being made, which were not made either in themselves or in their formula, like that of offspring in parents, on that sixth day among the works from which God rested on the seventh after finishing and starting them, then there is the risk that scripture's painstaking insistence that God finished in six days all his works, which he made very good, was all quite futile, if he was still going to create some natures which he had not made then either in themselves or in their causal formulae.

But on the other hand God could be understood to have kept in himself the formula of souls to be made one by one and given to people when they were born, and not to have inserted it into some part of his creation; or else, because these souls are not creatures of a different kind from the one with which the man was made on the sixth day to the image of God, it is not correct to say that God is making now things that he did not finish then. He had, after all, already made a soul then of the same kind as he is making now. And thus it is that he is not making some new kind of creature now which he did not create then in his finished works. Nor is this activity of his going against those causal formulae of things to come in the future which he inserted then in the total creation, but rather going along with them, seeing that it accords with them that human bodies, of which the propagation in continuous succession stretches on from those primary works, should have souls inserted into them of the same kind as he is now making and inserting.

---

3. See in particular Book I,19,38 and III,20,30-31.
4. The opinion espoused by Augustine himself, and defended in detail in Book VI.

6. Accordingly, whichever of these three opinions may win the prize of being declared the most likely, we need have no fear of seeming to take a line against the words of this book which were written on that primordial six-day establishment of creation. So with God's help let us undertake the more thorough examination of this question; and even if we do not end with a limpid judgment which leaves no room at all for any further doubt, let us see if we cannot perhaps come to a conclusion of such general acceptability that it would not be absurd for us to hold it until something more certain emerges. But if we cannot even manage this, with the weight of the evidence wobbling equally now on this side of the scales, now on that, it will at least be clear that our doubts and hesitations are the result not of our shirking the labor of investigation, but of our shunning the rashness of dogmatic assertion. Then, if any others are sure about having the right solution, I hope they will be good enough to instruct me in it; while if it is not the authority either of the divine word or of clear reasoning, but just their own assumptions that make them so certain, I trust they will not disdain to share my doubts.

Some things that definitely cannot be said about the nature of the soul

4, 7. But let us begin by holding with the firmest possible conviction that it is not in the nature of the soul to be turned into the nature of body, so that what has once been soul becomes body; nor into the nature of non-rational soul, so that what was once a human being's soul becomes an animal's; nor into the nature of God, so that what began as soul becomes what God is; and thus, the other way round, that neither body nor non-rational soul nor the substance by which God is himself can be changed and become a human soul. This too should be no less certain, that the soul is the creation of none but God.

Accordingly, if God has made the soul of a human being neither from body nor from non-rational soul nor from himself, it remains that he either makes it from nothing, or else from some spiritual, but still rational created material. But to say anything is still being made from nothing is to wish to do violence to the finished works in which he created all things together simultaneously, and I do not know of any clear evidence to support this view. Nor is something to be required of us which no mortal is capable of grasping, or which, if anyone is capable of this, it will be astonishing if he can persuade anyone of its truth except the kind of person who can also already understand such a thing without any human being trying to teach him.[5] It is safer therefore in matters of this sort not to rely on human guesswork, but to search and scrutinize the evidence given by the divine witness.

---

5. Augustine merely repeating, surely at his most tortuously intricate worst, what he has just said quite clearly in the previous sentence!

*The idea of souls being created from some spiritual, angelic, matter aired
and dismissed*

5, 8. So then, the idea that God creates souls from the angels as their parents,
so to say, has no authority in the canonical books that I can think of; much less,
therefore, that it is from the corporeal elements of the world—unless maybe
what inclines you to this is the passage from the prophet Ezekiel in which the
resurrection of the dead is being indicated, and once the corpses have been reas-
sembled the spirit is summoned from the four winds of heaven, so that when it
blows upon them they are brought to life and rise up. This, you see, is how the
passage goes: *And the Lord said to me: Prophesy over the spirit, son of man,
prophesy and say: Thus says the Lord: Come from the four quarters of the winds
of heaven and breathe into these dead, and let them live. And I prophesied as the
Lord commanded me, and the spirit of life entered them, and they came to life
again and stood upon their feet, a very great gathering* (Ez 37:9-10). Here it
seems to me that what was being prophetically signified is that human beings
were going to rise again not just from that plain, where the event was being
demonstrated, but from the entire globe, and that this was represented by the
breath coming from the four quarters of the world.

I mean to say, not even that breath from the Lord's body was the very
substance of the Holy Spirit, that time when he breathed and said, *Receive the
Holy Spirit* (Jn 20:22); but it was certainly signified in this way that the Holy
Spirit proceeds also from him, just as the breath proceeded from his body. But
the world, after all, is not attached to God to make one person with him in the
same way as that flesh was to his only-begotten Son; so we cannot say that the
soul comes from the substance of God in the same way as that breath from the
four winds was made from the nature of the world. But still I reckon that what it
was is one thing, what it signified another, which can be rightly understood from
the example of the breath proceeding from the Lord's body. And this I maintain
is so, even if what the prophet Ezekiel foresaw there by that symbolic revelation
was not the resurrection of the flesh as it is really going to take place, but the
totally unexpected restoration of a despairing people through the Spirit of the
Lord, which has filled the entire globe.[6]

---

6. See Wis 1:7.

The three positions to be tested against the evidence scattered through the scriptures

6, 9. So then, what we must now look at is which opinion wins the most support from the multiple evidence of the divine witness; is it the one which says that God made one soul and gave it to the first man, to make the others from it as he makes the bodies of the rest of mankind from that man's body, or the one which says that he makes each individual soul for each individual person as he made that one for that man, and does not make the rest from that one? You see, what he says through Isaiah: *I made every breath* (Is 57:16), the verses that follow show clearly enough that he is saying it about the soul, can be taken either way, because whether it is from the one soul of the first man, or from some secret store of his own, there is no doubt at all that he makes all souls himself.

10. Then there is the text: *Who fashioned their hearts one by one* (Ps 33:15); if by "hearts" we wish to understand souls, this too does not run counter to either of the two opinions we are now arguing about. After all, it is he himself of course who is fashioning them one by one, just as he does with bodies, whether it is from that single one which he puffed into the face of the first man; or whether he is fashioning and dispatching them one by one, or fashioning them actually in the persons to whom he dispatches them. This latter, however, does not seem to me actually to be said anywhere, except with reference to our souls being renewed through grace and formed to the image of God; about this the apostle says: *For by grace you have been saved through faith, and this not from yourselves, but it is the gift of God; not from works, lest perhaps any should exalt themselves. For we are his fashioning, created in Christ Jesus in good works* (Eph 2:8-10). We cannot, after all, understand it as meaning that our bodies have been created or fashioned through this grace of faith, but as it says in the psalm: *A clean heart create in me, O God* (Ps 51:10).

11. This is also, I presume, where that other text comes in: *who fashioned the spirit of man in him* (Zec 12:1); as though it were one thing to dispatch a soul already made, another to make it in an actual human being, that is, to remake and renew it. But even if we are to understand this to be about the nature with which we are born, not about the grace with which we are renewed, it can still fit either opinion; either God fashions in a person something like the seed of a soul drawn from that single one of the first man, to give life to the body, or else he likewise fashions the spirit of life through the mortal senses of the flesh, not from that kind of "slip," but poured into the body from somewhere else, so that the person may be made into a living soul.

7, 12. Certainly a more thorough examination is called for of that text from the book of Wisdom, where he says: *I obtained a good soul by lot, and since I was good rather more, I came into an undefiled body* (Wis 8:19-20). It does seem, after all, to give more support to the view according to which souls are believed to come into bodies from above, and not to be propagated from a single one. But all the same, what is the meaning of "I obtained a good soul by lot"? As if in that reservoir of souls (if there is such a thing) there are some good souls, some not so good, and they emerge from it by a kind of lottery which decides which should be allotted to which person; or else as if at the moment when people are being conceived or born God makes some good souls, some not so good, from which each individual draws whatever falls to him or her by the turn of the wheel.

It would be surprising anyhow if this did help the case of those who believe that souls are made elsewhere and dispatched singly by God into every single human body, and not rather those people who say that souls are sent into bodies according to what they have deserved by actions committed before the body. How, after all, can some be supposed to be already good, some not good, when they come into bodies, except according to their works? It cannot, I mean, be according to their natures, in which they are being made by the one who makes all natures good. But perish the thought that we should contradict the apostle, who says that those not yet born *have done nothing either good or bad* (Rom 9:11). He says this by way of confirming that it was not as a result of works but of God's calling that the answer was given to Rebecca's question about the twins still confined in her womb: *The elder shall be slave to the younger* (Gn 25:23). So then, let us put aside for the moment this testimony from the book of Wisdom. Those people, you see, are not to be ignored, whether they are wrong or whether they have hit upon the truth, who think that this was said specially and uniquely about the soul of the *mediator between God and men, the man Christ Jesus* (1 Tm 2:5). If necessary, we shall consider this later on,[7] so that if the text cannot in fact fit Christ, we may go on to ask how we ought to take it, without challenging the apostle's faith and assuming that souls deserve anything for works done before they begin to live in bodies.

8, 13. Now let us see what the bearing on our subject is of the text: *You will take away their spirit, and they will fail and turn back into their dust. You will send forth your spirit and they will be created; and you will renovate the face of the earth* (Ps 104:29-30). Well, this does seem to chime in with the idea of those who reckon that souls are created, like bodies, from parents, when it is understood as follows: that the reason he called it "their spirit" was because human beings had received it from human beings; and when they died, it could not be given back to them by human beings for them to rise again, because it is not then derived once more from parents as it was when they were born, but from God, who will give it back when he raises the dead. And thus he called one and the same spirit theirs when they die, God's when they rise again.

---

7. See below, 17, 30, 31.

Those however, who assert that souls come, not from parents, but from God sending them, can claim the text for their opinion by understanding it like this: he called it their spirit when they die because it was in them and departs from them, but God's when they rise again, because what is sent by him is given back by him. Accordingly this testimony too is not opposed to either view.

14. I however reckon that this is best understood as said about the grace of God by which we are inwardly renovated. In a certain manner, you see, their own spirit is taken away from proud people living according to *the man of earth* (1 Cor 15:48), when they *strip off the old man* (Col 3:9) and become weak, in order to be made whole when pride has been driven out, and they say to the Lord in humble confession: *Remember that we are dust* (Ps 103:14), having been told themselves: *What does earth and ashes have to be proud of?* (Sir 10:9). Thus gazing with the eyes of faith upon the justice of God, to avoid wanting to establish their own,[8] they despise themselves and fade away, and count themselves but *earth and ashes* (Job 30:19), as Job says.[9] That, you see, is the meaning in the psalm of "they will turn back to dust." But when they have received the Spirit of God they say: *I am alive though, now not I, but it is Christ alive in me* (Gal 2:20). In this way the face of the earth is being renovated through the grace of the New Testament with a multitude of saints.

9, 15. As for what is written in Ecclesiastes: *. . . and the dust is turned into the earth as it was, and the spirit returns to God who gave it* (Sir 12:7); it does not give its vote to either opinion against the other, but stays firmly in the middle between them. When these, you see, on this side say that this proves the soul is given by God, not derived from parents, because once the dust is turned into its earth (that means the flesh, which was made from dust), "the spirit returns to God who gave it"; the others on that side answer: "Certainly, that is so; the spirit, you see, returns to God who gave it to the first man when he puffed into his face, once the dust, that is the human body, has been turned into the earth it was originally made from. There is no question, after all, of the spirit returning to the parents, although it is created from there, out of that one spirit given to the first man, just as the flesh itself after death does not return to the parents, from whom we all agree it was certainly propagated. So then, in the same way as the flesh does not return to the human beings from whom it was created, but to the earth from which it was formed for the first man, the spirit also does not return to the human beings from whom it was transfused, but to God by whom it was given to that first flesh."

---

8. See Rom 10:3.
9. I have transferred "as Job says" from just after "despise themselves," where it is fairly clearly out of place; an easy mistake for a copyist to make if he was lagging a little behind the reader dictating the text; or even for a corrector to insert the phrase, omitted by a slow copyist, in the line above where he meant to put it.

16. This evidence, for sure, is a sufficient reminder to us that it was out of nothing that God made the soul which he gave to the first man, not out of some creature already made, like the body out of earth; and that is why when it goes back it has nowhere to go back to except the author who gave it, not to any creature it was made out of, like the body to earth. There is, after all, no creature it was made out of, because it was made out of nothing. And thus the one that goes back goes back to its maker, by whom it was made out of nothing. They do not all go back, you see, since there are those of whom it is written: *a spirit walking about and not returning* (Ps 78:39).

Testing these various opinions by the evidence of scriptural texts proves inconclusive

10, 17. So we are finding how difficult it is to tie up together[10] all the testimonies of the holy scriptures on this matter. Even if this can be done, and they are not only listed but also studied and discussed, they will stretch our discourse out to quite inordinate lengths. But still I do not know how this question can be solved by the testimony of the divine literature unless it can offer something as certain as the definitive proofs by which it shows that God made the soul or that he gave it to the first man. Had it been written, you see, that God puffed in the same way into the woman's face when she was formed and that she was made into a living soul, that would indeed have given us the green light for believing that the soul is not given from the parents to any human flesh when it is formed—though we would still be left in two minds over what we should hold in the case of offspring born of woman,[11] which is the manner of one human being coming from another that we are used to. The first woman, though, was made in a different way, and that is why it could still be said that the reason God did not give Eve her soul out of Adam was that she did not derive from him as offspring. But if scripture had related that the first one to be born of them had been given his

---

10. I here make bold to emend the text's *colligere*, meaning "to collect," and read instead *colligare*. There is not the slightest manuscript support for this emendation; but it seems clear to me that from 6,9 onwards he has been collecting all the relevant texts, and trying to tie them together or harmonize them, to establish on the authority of scripture what the right theory about the origin of the soul might be. The change for a copyist from one word to the other is of course minimal; the reading in the text does make immediate sense; and copies containing the word I think Augustine wrote or dictated may simply have disappeared.

11. Here again I find it necessary to add a phrase to the text, from which it does seem that something has dropped out, because as it stands it is impossible Latin. It reads: *quid proprie teneretur in prole, qui nobis modus usitatus est hominis ex homine.* Now *proles* is feminine, and Augustine cannot have thought of it as the antecedent of the masculine relative *qui,* which is anyway clearly agreeing with *modus;* and offspring just by itself can hardly be "the manner familiar to us of human being from human being." So what I am suggesting has dropped out after *prole* is a phrase like *nata ex femina;* then the antecedent of the relative clause would just be the whole verbal phrase, "offspring born of woman."

soul from above, without deriving it from his parents, then that would certainly have to be understood to apply to all the rest, even with scripture remaining silent about them.

The bearing on the matter of a text to do with original sin, Romans 5:12 etc.

11, 18. So now let us also consider another text, and see if it can be accommodated to each of these opinions, without confirming either of them: the text where it is written: *Through one man sin entered into this world and through sin death, and thus it passed into all men, in whom all sinned* (Rom 5:12); and a little later: *just as through the offense of one to all men unto condemnation, so too through the justification of one to all men unto the justification of life. For just as through the disobedience of one man many have been constituted sinners, so too through the obedience of one shall many be constituted as just* (Rom 5:18-19).

Those, you see, who maintain that souls are propagated, strive to support their opinion from these words of the apostle like this: "If sin and sinner can be understood as referring solely to the flesh," they say, "we are not obliged by these words to believe that the soul comes from one's parents. But if, while granting it is through the allurements of the flesh, it is still nonetheless only the soul that does the sinning, how are we to take what it says here: *in whom all sinned*, if the soul also has not been propagated, like the flesh, from Adam? Or how are people constituted sinners through his disobedience, if they were only in him as regards the flesh and not also as regards the soul?"

19. What we have to beware of, you see, is either making God appear to be the author of sin, if he gives a soul to flesh in which it must necessarily sin, or suggesting that there can be any soul besides that of Christ himself which is not in need of Christian grace to set it free, because it did not sin in Adam, if it is said that all sinned in him only as regards the flesh which has been created from him, not also as regards the soul. This is in fact directly opposed to the Church's faith, to the extent that it would mean parents hasten in vain[12] even with tiny tots and infants to receive the grace of baptism; if it is from the bonds of a sin only affecting the flesh, not also the soul, that they are being absolved, the question naturally arises what harm it would do them if they departed from the body at that age without baptism.

After all, if by this sacrament care was being taken for their bodies, not also for their souls, they ought to be baptized even when they have died. But we see in fact that the Church everywhere holds that parents should hasten with their

---

12. Yet again, I emend a syntactically chaotic text, this time by assuming the addition of a single word, *frustra*. Without it, he would seem to be suggesting that it is contrary to the Church's faith for parents to hasten to get their small children and babies baptized. Of course, if there is one thing Augustine would never be suggesting, this is it.

babies while they are still alive and help them while still alive,[13] because when they have died nothing can be done that will do them any good. So we do not see what else can be understood in this passage but that every single tiny tot is nothing but Adam in both body and soul, and for that reason in need of the grace of Christ. That age, of course, has in itself done nothing either good or bad; accordingly the soul there is totally innocent, if it has not been propagated from Adam. So anyone holding this opinion about the soul, who can demonstrate how it can with any justice go unto condemnation if it departs from the body without baptism, is indeed to be greatly admired.[14]

What is meant by flesh and spirit lusting against each other

12, 20. It is certainly as true and trustworthy as can be, the text that runs: *The flesh lusts against the spirit and the spirit against the flesh* (Gal 5:17); but still everyone, I think, would agree, educated and uneducated, that the flesh cannot lust after anything without the soul. And thus the cause of fleshly lust is not to be found in the soul alone. but much less in the flesh alone.[15] It arises, after all, from both; from the soul, that is, because without it no enjoyment can be felt, and from the flesh because without it there cannot be felt any specifically fleshly enjoyment. And so what the apostle is calling flesh lusting against spirit is undoubtedly fleshly enjoyment, which the spirit has from the flesh and with the flesh, lusting against the enjoyment which the spirit has alone. The sort it has alone, if I am not mistaken, is that kind of desire, unmixed with the pleasure of the flesh or with a passion for fleshly things, with which *the soul is longing and fainting for the courts of the Lord* (Ps 84:2). Alone it also has that about which it is told: *You have lusted after Wisdom; keep the commandments, and the Lord will grant her to you* (Sir 1:26).

After all, when the spirit orders the body's limbs to serve this kind of desire which it is stirred by on its own, when a book is picked up, for example, when something is being written, being read, being discussed, being listened to, when finally bread is being broken for the hungry and the other works of mercy and humanity are being performed, the flesh is rendering obedience, not stirring up lust. When it is with these and similar good desires, with which the soul alone can be said to lust, that it confronts something in which the selfsame soul takes

---

13. Much neater in the Latin: *ut cum viventibus curratur et viventibus succurratur.*
14. Anyone, that is, rejecting as erroneous the doctrine of traducianism, as in fact the Catholic Church does. Augustine was certainly inclined to favor it; but in 14,24 below he will at least try out some arguments against it.
15. It is worth noting here that he is treating "spirit" and "soul" as synonymous, which of course he has been doing throughout in his references to scriptural texts. But here in particular, as in similar Pauline contexts, it will involve him in misinterpreting the apostle in a neo-Platonist direction; because what Paul in fact treats as synonymous are "soul" and "flesh."

delight in the wake of the flesh, that is when the flesh is said to lust against the spirit and the spirit against the flesh.

21. The phrase *the flesh is lusting*, you see, means that the soul is doing that in its wake, and here the word "flesh" is being used in much the same way as one talks about the ears hearing and the eyes seeing; can anybody, I mean to say, be unaware that it is rather the soul which hears with the ears and sees with the eyes? That is how we also talk when we say, "Your hand has relieved the man," when something to relieve his distress has been given with an outstretched hand. Why, it is even said about the eye of faith, of which the function is to believe precisely what cannot be seen by the flesh: *All flesh shall see the salvation of God* (Is 40:5; Lk 3:6). This is really being said, of course, about the soul by which the flesh lives, since even devoutly to look on Christ, that is, on the form with which he clothed himself for our sakes, by means of this flesh of ours,[16] is not a matter of the lust of the flesh but of the service it provides, in case anyone should wish to take *all flesh shall see the salvation of God* in that crude sense. How much more suitably, then, is the flesh said to lust when the soul, as well as animating the flesh with "soulish"[17] life, also covets or lusts after things in its wake. It is not in its power not to lust or covet like this as long as sin is there in the members, that is to say, a certain violent allurement of the flesh *in the body of this death* (Rom 7:24), which arises from the punishment of that sin we trace our roots back to, in the wake of which we are all, before grace, *children of wrath* (Eph 2:3).

It is against this sin that those who "are constituted under grace" do battle, not in order to eliminate it from their bodies, as long as they are mortal in such a way as by rights to be called dead,[18] but to prevent it reigning in them. Now it does not reign as long as obedience is not rendered to its desires, those, that is, which lust against the spirit in the wake of the flesh. Did the apostle say, after all, "Do not let sin be there in your mortal bodies"? He knew well enough that the attraction of sin, which he calls sin, is there as the result of our nature being distorted by that first transgression. No, but *Do not let sin reign*, he said, *in your mortal bodies for you to obey its desires, and do not offer your members to sin as weapons of iniquity* (Rom 6:12-13).

Question of the involvement of infants in original sin

13, 22. In accordance with this opinion we are guilty neither of the absurdity of saying that the flesh can lust without the soul, nor of agreeing with the

---

16. This does rather suggest that icons or statues of Christ were already a common feature of Christian piety in the African Church.

17. "Soulish"; *animalis* from *anima*. For more detailed notes on this important linguistic point see Books VI,19,30, notes 23 and 25; and IX,3,5, note 6, above; and XI,18,24, note 21 below.

18. See Rom 8:10.

Manichees who, on observing that flesh cannot lust without soul, assumed that the flesh has some kind of soul of its own, derived from another nature in opposition to God, with which to lust against the spirit. Nor are we obliged to say that there is any soul which is not in need of the grace of Christ, when people say to us: "How has the soul of an infant deserved that leaving the body without having received the sacrament of Christian baptism should mean its final ruin, if it has not committed any sin of its own, and does not come from the soul which first sinned in Adam?"

23. We are not, you see, dealing here with bigger children, whom some people are unwilling to hold responsible for their own personal sins until the age of fourteen, when puberty begins. We would certainly agree with that if there were no sins except those committed with the sexual organs. But would anybody have the nerve to say that stealing, lying, perjury are not sins, unless they wanted to commit such sins with impunity? Well, the age of childhood is full of these sins, though they are not thought to deserve such punishment as they do in adults. That is because one hopes that as they come to the years of discretion in which their powers of reason gain in strength, they will be able to appreciate the commandments of salvation better and to obey them more cheerfully. But now we are not dealing with boys and girls who, if truth and fairness launch an attack on their sensual and puerile appetites of body or spirit,[19] will fight back with all the verbal and muscular powers at their command. And for what, exactly, if not for the falsehood and unfairness that will support them in getting hold of what attracts them, or getting out of what irks them?

No, we are talking about infants, and not because they are frequently born of adulterous *liaisons*. The gifts of nature are not to be blamed for depraved behavior, nor will seed fail to produce a crop merely because it has been sown by the hand of a thief. Or would even their parents find their own wickedness standing against them, if they put themselves right by turning back to God? How much less would it stand against their children, if they lived upright lives!

14. No, the urgent problem this age of infancy raises is how the soul which has no sin of its own deliberate choice may be justified through that one man's obedience, if it is not liable or guilty through that other one's disobedience. That is the tune sung by those who would maintain that human souls are created out of human parents—by none other, indeed, than God the creator, but in the same sort of way as bodies are. With these too, after all, it is not the case that parents create them, and not the one who said: *Before I formed you in the womb, I knew you* (Jer 1:5).

---

19. *Animi*, a word impossible to find a regular English equivalent for; what it should never, or hardly ever, be rendered by is "soul," as if it were just a synonym for *anima*. The kind of gratifications, and their opposites, to be sought or avoided by the *animus*, would be things like fame, praise, "the best seats in the synagogues," as against humiliations, mockery, never being noticed.

A possible response to this opinion

24. To this the reply can be made that God does indeed give souls to the bodies of human beings one by one; but to this end, that in the *sinful flesh* (Rom 8:3) coming from the original sin[20] they may live uprightly and subdue the lusts of the flesh under the grace of God, and in this way merit the reward of being transferred together with the body to a better state at the time of the resurrection, and live for ever in Christ with the angels. But this means it is necessary for them to be overcome by a kind of oblivion when they are fitted in a marvelous fashion into bodies that are earth-bound and mortal, and above all propagated from sinful flesh, in order first of all to make them alive, and next at the appropriate age to govern them.

If this oblivion were somehow or other insuperable,[21] it could be attributed to the creator; but in fact the soul is able little by little to shake itself out of the torpor of this oblivion and be converted to its God, and then to earn his mercy and faithfulness,[22] first of all by the filial act of conversion and then by persevering in keeping his commandments. So what disadvantage can it be for it to be sunk, as it were, in that sleep for a little while, from which as it wakes up little by little into the light of understanding (which is why it was made a rational soul), if it is able by a good will to choose to live a good life? This it could not do, indeed, unless helped by the grace of God through the mediator. Any who neglect all this will be Adam not only as regards the flesh but also as regards the spirit; while if they take it seriously, they will be Adam as regards the flesh alone, and by living upright lives in accordance with the spirit they will deserve to receive back the culpable element derived from Adam, now cleansed of the blemish of sin by that transformation which the resurrection holds out for the saints.

---

20. *De originali peccato.* What this expression usually means for Augustine, as in all the theology derived from him, is the flaw or "vice of nature" which we are all born with, as we are born with human nature; what it does *not* usually mean is the first sin, the one committed by Adam, from which this flawed nature of ours derives. But here I think he must mean the sin of Adam, the first sin, seeing that "sinful flesh," or "the flesh of sin" is the manifestation of our flawed nature, and can hardly be said to come from it.

21. He uses the rather more graphic word *indigestibilis*. What he means by this oblivion is the soul's total unconsciousness in infancy—and of course in the womb. Such lack of consciousness is a kind of oblivion on the supposition which is being made here that the soul already existed by itself in some kind of divine storeroom, before being fitted into a body, and in that state the presumption is that it was fully, rationally conscious. Totally to obliterate this pre-embodiment consciousness is something only God could do, as it would be a kind of annihilation; and that is why the oblivion would have to be attributed to the creator if the soul never snapped out of it. But as it does, as a rule, do so, this infantile oblivion is simply a phase, the first one, in the process of human living.

22. His *misericordia et veritas*, the regular Latin translation, through the Greek Septuagint, of that wonderful Hebrew pair, *hesed* and *emeth*; essentially family virtues, the parents' love for their children and their reliability in looking after them, and the corresponding love of the children for their parents and their loyalty to them. So it is in that sense that we need God's truth as well as his mercy in our lives—in a word, his grace.

25. But before they reach the age at which they can live in accordance with the spirit, they need to receive the sacrament of the Mediator, so that what they are not yet able to do through their own faith can be done through that of those who love them. It is by his sacrament, you see, that even in the age of infancy they are absolved from the punishment of original sin, and without its help they will not even succeed as young men and women in taming fleshly lust, and in winning, after bringing it to heel, the reward of eternal life—except by the gift of the one whose favor they are eager to win. That is why it is right and proper for an infant to be baptized while still alive, so that the soul's association with "the flesh of sin" may not be to its disadvantage, seeing that by sharing in the flesh the infant soul is rendered incapable of savoring anything in accordance with the spirit. Its being affected, not to say infected, like this weighs upon the soul even when it has stripped off the body, unless it is purged while still in the body through the unique sacrifice of the true high priest.[23]

Wrestling with the problem of infants dying unbaptized

15, 26. "So then," someone will say, "what if their people do not bother about this, being either unbelievers, or simply careless?"

Well, the same could be said about adults; they too, after all, can die suddenly, or be taken ill among people where nobody will come to their assistance by seeing they are baptized.

"Yes, but these," he says, "have their own personal sins which they need to be absolved from; and if they have not been forgiven them, nobody would dream of saying that they are being struck off undeservedly for wrongs they have deliberately committed during their lives. But the soul which has contracted a kind of contagion from 'the flesh of sin' cannot in any way have this put down to its account, if it has not been created from that first soul that sinned; so why will it be forbidden entry to eternal life if (it is not, after all through any sin, but by nature that it has been made in this way, and given to the flesh by God as the giver) nobody has come to its assistance by baptizing an infant? Or perhaps this will not in fact do it any harm? Then what good does it do a soul to be assisted in this way, if not being so assisted does it no harm?"

---

23. This section puts in a nutshell almost the complete doctrine of the sacrament of baptism. It is the sacrament of the Mediator, because through it Christ imparts to the soul the grace of God, standing as mediator between God and humanity (1 Tm 2:5); it is the sacrament of faith, because it presupposes that those being baptized believe in God and Christ and trust them, and with what we now call confirmation (in those days regarded as part of the baptismal rite) it sets the seal of the Holy Spirit on their faith; this faith can if necessary be professed vicariously by others on behalf of the one to be baptized, being seen as indeed the faith of the Church, which is in the sacrament giving birth to the new Christian; finally, what is effective in the sacrament is the sacrifice of Christ on the cross, purging or atoning for all sin, including original sin (see Rom 6:3-11).

27. Here I must confess that I have not yet heard, or even read anywhere up till now, what case in answer to this the others can make for their own point of view, those, that is, who are trying to maintain in accordance with the holy scriptures, as either the doctrine which is to be found in them, or at least does not go against them, that new souls, not derived from parents, are given to bodies. That, surely, is no reason for abandoning the cause of absent parties, if anything should occur to me by which it could be assisted. They can still answer, you see, that God knows in advance what kind of life each soul would live if it lived longer in the body, and that he makes sure *the bath of salvation* (Ti 3:5) is administered to the soul which he foresees would lead such a loving and loyal life were it to come to the years capable of faith, if it did not now, for some hidden cause, have to be overtaken by death.

A hidden secret it is then, and utterly beyond human ingenuity—well certainly beyond mine—to unravel, why an infant should be born which is immediately or very soon going to die. But it is so hidden as to assist neither of the parties between which we are now trying to decide. We have already, you see, hooted off the stage the opinion that souls are thrust down into bodies according to the deserts of a life lived previously, so that the one which did not commit many sins would seem to deserve an earlier release. (This, in order not to contradict the apostle's statement that those not yet born have done nothing either good or bad.[24]) That being so, neither those who affirm that the soul is transmitted from parents, nor the ones who would have new souls being given singly, one by one, to every single individual, are able to show in support of their view why some people should be hurried on to death, others endlessly delayed. So then the cause of this is indeed a hidden secret, and in my judgment fails either to support or undermine the case of either party.

16, 28. First let us take those who on this matter of infant mortality were being pressed to explain why the sacrament of baptism should be necessary for everyone, though souls have not been derived (in their opinion) from that one *by whose disobedience many have been constituted sinners* (Rom 5:19). They answer that all have indeed been constituted sinners as regards the flesh, but as regards the soul only those who have lived bad lives in the time they could have been living good ones; that the reason all souls, however, including those of infants, need to have the sacrament of baptism is that it is a bad thing to depart this life without it even at that age, because the contagion of sin, which is picked up from "the flesh of sin" and overwhelms the soul when it is inserted into this body, will stand in its way after death unless it is purged while still in the flesh by the sacrament of the Mediator. So God, they continue, has to ensure that this assistance is accorded to the soul which he has foreknown would have lived here lovingly and loyally, had it come to years suited to faith, but which for some

---

24. See Rom 9:11.

reason known only to himself he has wished to be born in the body and has then a short while later withdrawn from the body.

So when they give this kind of answer, how else can they be rebutted, except by saying that this also makes us unsure about the salvation of those who, after living a good life, have died in the peace of the Church, if people are to be judged not only on the kind of lives they have lived but also on the kind they would live if they had been able to live longer? I mean, if God takes account of what we deserve for future as well as past crimes and misdemeanors, then death will not deliver us from liability for them if it overtakes us before we have committed them, nor has any benefit been conferred on the one who *was snatched away lest viciousness should change his understanding* (Wis 4:11). God, after all, has foreknowledge of his future viciousness; so why will he not be judging him rather with reference to this, if it is because he foreknew the soul of a dying infant, were it to live, would live a life of loyal faith and love, that he has judged it should be assisted through baptism, lest it be disqualified by the filthy backwash of sin from the body?

29. Or is it because this little loophole is my invention that it can be so easily blocked? But perhaps those who insist on the rightness of this view[25] can produce either scriptural evidence or arguments of reason to dispel this uncertainty, or definitely to show how their idea does not go against what the apostle says to commend with all possible earnestness the grace by which we are saved: *Just as all die in Adam, so shall all be brought to life in Christ* (1 Cor 15:22); and: *Just as through one man's disobedience many were constituted sinners, so through one man's obedience many shall be constituted as just* (Rom 5:19). And by these "many being sinners" he clearly wishes us to understand "all," with no exceptions, since he says about Adam a verse or two earlier on: *in whom all sinned* (Rom 5:12). So that other party, which favors souls being derived from the stock of one man, has every right to think that that "all" proves that the souls of infants cannot be excepted, as does the practice of coming to their aid with baptism, unless it can be rebutted either by some sound, clear argument of reason which is not repugnant to the holy scriptures, or by the equally clear authority of the scriptures themselves.

---

25. The view—just to remind the reader—that souls are inserted by God into bodies without being derived through parents from the soul of the first man, Adam.

Back to a difficult text from the book of Wisdom

17, 30. And so now let us take a look, as far as the needs of this work we have undertaken permit us,[26] at the meaning of a text which we deferred consideration of a few pages ago. It is written, you see, in the book of Wisdom: *But I was a talented boy and I obtained a good soul by lot, and since I was good rather more, I came to an undefiled body* (Wis 8:19-20). While this testimony, you see, may seem to help those who say that souls are not created from parents, but come or descend to the body as God dispatches them, this in particular, on the other hand, stands in their way: his saying, *I obtained a good soul by lot.* What they undoubtedly believe, I mean, is that the souls which God dispatches into bodies either trickle somehow from one source or spring like little rivulets, or else are all made equal in nature, but not that some are good or good rather more and others not good or good rather less.

What after all could make souls good or more good, or not good or less good, but either their morals freely and deliberately chosen, or the differing temperaments or constitutions of bodies, while some are more, some less weighed down by *the body which is perishing and weighs down the soul* (Wis 9:15)? But in the first place no souls did anything before coming to bodies by which their respective morals could be distinguished; and in the second place this man could not say that his soul was good as a result of his body being less of a weight to it, seeing that he says, *I obtained a good soul by lot, and since I was good rather more, I came to an undefiled body.* He says, you see, that his also coming to an undefiled body was a bonus added to the goodness he was good with, having obtained, that is to say, a good soul by lot. He was good therefore from some other cause before he came to the body. But this was certainly not in virtue of distinctive morals, because there was no merit from conduct in some previous life; nor was it the result of some distinct quality of the body, because he was good before he came to the body. So where then did his goodness come from?

31. As for those, though, who assert that souls are created as slips or cuttings transmitted from that soul that transgressed, his saying indeed, *I came to a body*, may not seem to chime in with their opinion; this nonetheless fits in with the rest without any incongruity. Thus after saying *But I was a talented boy*, he adds straightaway, to explain where he got his talents from, "and I obtained a good soul by lot," namely from his father's talents or bodily constitution. Next, *since I was good rather more*, he goes on, *I came to an undefiled body.* If this is understood as being his mother's, not even his saying *I came to a body* will clash with this opinion, when it is accepted that it was from his father's soul and body that

---

26. "This work we have undertaken" means here, I presume, the work of investigating the origin of the human soul—specifically the work of this Book X. He first raised the problem of the *Wisdom* text back in 7,12.

he came to his mother's body, which was undefiled by menstrual blood. It is commonly said, you see, that natural talents are "weighed down" by this, that is to say, or by contamination from adulterous intercourse. And thus these words of this book tend rather to favor those who talk of the transmission of souls, or else, if the other party too can interpret them in its own behalf, they swing between the two sides.

Seeing if the text can be applied to Christ

18, 32. Should we wish to take all this as said about the Lord, with reference to the human creature assumed by the Word, there are indeed in the whole context of the passage some things which are not appropriate to that unique excellence. Above all there is what the very person who is talking in this book said a little earlier on, when he started the speech containing the words we are now dealing with; he stated that he *was curdled in blood from the seed of a man* (Wis 7:2), a manner of coming to birth, of course, wholly alien to the child-bearing of the Virgin, who did not conceive the flesh of Christ from the seed of a man, as no Christian will doubt for a moment. But then in the Psalms, where it certainly says, *They dug my hands and feet, they counted all my bones; they, however, gazed at me and inspected me, they divided my garments among them and over my vesture they cast lots,* words that properly fit him alone; it also says there, *God, my God, attend to me; why have you forsaken me? Far from my salvation are the words of my misdeeds* (Ps 21:17-19.1), words which on the contrary do not fit him, except insofar as he is transposing to himself *the body of our lowliness* (Phil 3:21), since we are members of his body.

Then again, in the gospel itself *the boy was advancing in age and wisdom* (Lk 2:40); if even those things we read on this question in the book of Wisdom can be applied to the Lord himself because of the lowly *form of a slave* (Phil 2:7) and the unity of the body of the Church with its head, what could be more talented than that boy whose wisdom at the age of twelve had the elders marveling? And again, could anything be better than this soul? But even if those who insist that souls are transmitted through parents win their case by proof, not just by debating power, will the result not be that this soul too must be supposed to have been transmitted from that one of the first transgressor; and so through the disobedience of that man will not this one also be constituted a sinner, the single one by whose obedience alone many are delivered from that guilt and constituted as being just?

And what could be more undefiled than that womb of the Virgin, whose flesh, even if it derived from the propagation of sin,[27] still did not conceive from the

---

27. The doctrine of the Immaculate Conception of Mary had not even begun to be formulated in Augustine's time.

propagation of sin? So not even the body itself of Christ was sown in Mary's womb under that law which has been planted in the members of the body of death and fights back against the law of the mind.[28] The holy patriarchs who were married kept a tight rein on this law, only relaxing it to the extent allowed for marital intercourse; it was not however only to the extent allowed that they endured its assaults.[29] Accordingly the body of Christ was indeed assumed from the flesh of a woman which had been conceived from that propagation of *the flesh of sin*; but because it was not itself conceived there in the same way as that flesh had been conceived, it was not in its turn the flesh of sin, but *the likeness of the flesh of sin* (Rom 8:3).

Thus he did not receive from that source the liability to death which is made manifest in the involuntary motions of the flesh, not willed, indeed, but to be mastered by the will, against which *the spirit lusts* (Gal 5:17), but he received from there what would suffice, not indeed for cleaning up the contagion of that primal transgression, but for discharging the debt of a death he did not owe and for demonstrating the resurrection that had been promised. Of these one would avail to overcome our fear, the other to strengthen our hope.

33. Finally, if I were to be asked where Jesus Christ received his soul from, I would much rather hear about it from those better qualified and more learned than myself; but still for my part, for what it's worth, I would be happier answering, "from where Adam did," than "from Adam." After all, if dust taken from earth in which no man had worked was fit to be animated, or "ensouled," from on high, how much more would a body, taken from flesh in which again no man had worked, have obtained a good soul by lot! There, I mean to say, a man was being set on his feet who was going to fall, while here another was coming down who was going to lift him up. And perhaps the reason he said, *I obtained a good soul by lot* (provided, of course, that this can be rightly understood of that other man) is that things given by lot are usually given from on high by God.[30] Or else, and this must be said with every confidence, it was lest that soul should be thought to have been borne aloft to such a peak as a result of some previous good works. So when the Word eventually became that flesh and dwelt among us, this idea of its being a lottery presented itself, to dispel any suspicion of preceding merits.

---

28. See Rom 7:23-24.
29. That is, that in their legitimate and restrained use of sex in marriage they could not avoid or eliminate that *concupiscentia*, that lust forbidden by the law which says "You shall not covet (or lust)." It is this bad concupiscence, inseparable in fallen humanity from even legitimate intercourse, that in Augustine's theology transmits original sin. Among the holy patriarchs he mentions he doubtless has in mind the Blessed Virgin's parents.
30. He doubtless had in mind the procedure by which Matthias was chosen to take the place among the apostles vacated by Judas, Acts 1:21-26.

The bearing of Hebrews 7:4-10 on the question

19, 34 In the letter which is entitled "To the Hebrews"[31] there is a passage that deserves the most careful attention. The person of Melchizedek had just been introduced as a type of this reality that was to come, and through him the author goes on to distinguish the priesthood of Christ from that of Levi: *See therefore, he says, what sort of man this is, to whom even Abraham the patriarch gave a tenth part from the first-fruits. And these indeed who are of the sons of Levi, on receiving the priesthood have a mandate from the tithes of the people according to the law,[32] that is from their brothers, although they too came out from the loins of Abraham. One however who is not of their kin tithed Abraham and blessed the one who had the promise. But without any contradiction the one who is less is blessed by the one who is greater. And here indeed dying men receive tithes, but there one who testifies that he lives. And, as it is right to say, because of Abraham Levi too, the receiver of a tithe, was tithed; for he was still in the loins of Abraham* (Heb 7:4-10).

So if the fact that Christ as high priest was prefigured by the one who tithed Abraham also serves to underline by how great a margin the priesthood of Christ surpasses the Levitical priesthood, then assuredly Christ was not tithed by him.

"But if the reason Levi was tithed is that he was in the loins of Abraham, then the reason Christ was not tithed is that he was not in the loins of Abraham."

But now, if we accept that it was not according to the soul but only according to the flesh that Levi was in Abraham, then Christ too was there, because Christ

---

31. In *The City of God* Book 16,22, Augustine simply states his awareness of the question of the authorship of Hebrews without expressing his views on the subject. As there was no doubt in any quarters of the Catholic Church about the letter's canonicity, he doubtless thought that the question of whether Saint Paul was its author or not did not claim his serious attention. But earlier on in his career he does seem to have oscillated between the two positions. Thus here he seems to align himself with those, mainly in the Churches of the East, who denied Pauline authorship. He uses the same kind of expression as we have here in Sermon 7,6 (III,l in this series). There (note 15) I refer the reader to an article by O. Rottmanner in *Revue Bénédictine*, 18 (1901); *"S. Augustín sur l'auteur de l'Epître aux Hebreux."* I have not been able to consult this volume, but thanks to the researches of my friend Dr. Robert Markus, professor emeritus of Medieval History at Nottingham University, I can now inform the reader of what Rottmanner has to say. In one of his earliest works, his *Unfinished Commentary on the Letter to the Romans*, written before he became bishop, Augustine again states his awareness of the issue, and his basic lack of interest in it, but all the same he includes the letter among those of "the apostle." In works written shortly after he became bishop, 397 to 400, he simply refers to it as being by the apostle. Then in mid-career, so to say, he changed to the kind of language we have here, where the Pauline authorship is at least doubted. But in Sermon 159,l (date about 417), we are back again with the letter being attributed to the apostle. Clearly the issue did not belong to the kind of biblical "criticism" that Augustine went in for, or was bothered about.

32. I am giving a literal translation of Augustine's text, which is a very bad, ill-educated rendering of the Greek of what was probably a very inferior Greek manuscript, in which the verb *apodekatoun*, to tithe, may have appeared, or been read, as *apo dekatois*, from tithes.

too according to the flesh is from the seed of Abraham;[33] and thus he too was tithed.

"So why bring in, as indicating the great difference between Christ's priesthood and Levi's, the fact that Levi was tithed by Melchizedek since he was in the loins of Abraham, where Christ also was, so they were both equally tithed—unless it is because we have to understand that there is a certain way in which Christ was not there?"

But who would deny that he was there according to the flesh? Therefore he was not there according to the soul. Hence the soul of Christ is not derived from the transmission of Adam's transgression, otherwise it too would have been there in the loins of Abraham.

The difference in the ways in which Levi and Christ were in the loins of Abraham and its bearing on the transmission of original sin

20, 35. Here the defenders of the transmission of souls step forward, and say their opinion is confirmed, if it is agreed that Levi was in the loins of Abraham, in whom Melchizedek tithed him, according to the soul as well, so that Christ may be distinguished from him in this tithing. For since he was not tithed and yet was in the loins of Abraham according to the flesh, it remains that he was not there according to the soul; and that is why it follows that Levi was there according to the soul.

This does not concern me greatly, since I am readier still to go on listening to the discussion between the parties than to uphold the opinion of one or other of them. Meanwhile what I have wished to do by this text is to exclude the soul of Christ from the origin of this transmission. For the rest, the others will perhaps find how to answer them by saying something which does indeed interest me no little.

"Although nobody's soul," they affirm, "is in the loins of his father, still Levi was in the loins of Abraham according to the flesh and was tithed, and Christ was there according to the flesh and was not tithed. This is because Levi was there according to that seminal formula by which he was going to come into his mother through sexual intercourse, a formula by which the flesh of Christ was not there, though Mary's flesh was there in that way."

So then, neither Levi nor Christ was in the loins of Abraham as regards the soul, while both Levi and Christ were there as regards the flesh: Levi, however, in accordance with fleshly concupiscence, Christ by contrast only in the substance of his body.

Since, you see, there is in the seed both visible bodiliness and an invisible formula, each of these ran from Abraham, or even from Adam himself, as far as

33. See Mt 1:1; Gal 3;15.

the body of Mary, because this too was conceived and born in that way. Christ, however, indeed took the substance of his flesh from the flesh of the Virgin; but the formula for his conception did not come from male seed, but in a very different way and from above. Accordingly, following this line of argument, what he received from his mother was also in the loins of Abraham.

36. So that one then was tithed in Abraham who, though only there as regards the flesh, was still in his loins in the same way as Abraham had been in his father's, that is, who was born of his father Abraham in the same way as Abraham was born of his father, through *the law,* to wit, *in the members fighting back against the law of the mind* (Rom 7:23) and through invisible concupiscence, although the chaste and good rights of marriage do not allow it to prevail except insofar as by means of it they can provide for replacements to continue the human race.

Not also tithed there, however, was that other one, whose flesh drew from there not the inflammation of the wound but the material for healing it. That tithing, after all, was about prefiguring the healing,[34] so while that which was to be cured was tithed in the flesh of Abraham, that by which it was to be cured was not. The very flesh indeed, not just of Abraham but of that first and earth-made man, had in it simultaneously the wound caused by the transgression and the medicine to heal the wound; the wound from the transgression in the law of the members fighting back against the law of the mind, which through all the flesh propagated from there is, so to say, encoded in the seminal formula; and the medicine for the wound in what, without any lustful activity, was taken from there of the Virgin in its bodily material alone by means of a divine formula for its conception and formation—this for the sake of sharing in death without iniquity, and of providing an instance of resurrection without falsity.

Accordingly, that the soul of Christ does not come by transmission from that soul which was the first to transgress is something, I think, that even those who support the transmission of souls will agree, because their idea is that the seed of the soul is also transfused with the father's seed in the sexual act, a kind of conception quite foreign to Christ. Again they will agree that if he had been in Abraham as regards the soul, he too would have been tithed; but scripture testifies to his not having been tithed, distinguishing his priesthood from the Levitical priesthood as it does by this very fact.

21, 37.Or perhaps they will say: "Just as he could be there as regards the flesh and not be tithed, why not also as regards the soul without any tithing?" Here is the answer: Because not even those who reckon the soul to be a body—that means most of the people who are of the opinion that it is created from the parents—have thought that its simple substance can be increased by bodily

---

34. He is here referring to Melchizedek tithing Abraham, not to the consequent tithing of Levi in Abraham's loins.

growth. Now in the body's seed[35] there can be an invisible energy which regulates the numbers[36] and is to be distinguished by the intelligence, not the eyes, from the bodily mass that is perceived by sight and touch. And the very size of the human body, so incomparably bigger, to be sure, than the tiny quantity of the seed, makes it abundantly clear that something can be taken from the seed which does not have that seminal energy, but only the bodily substance which was taken and formed into the flesh of Christ from above by God and not by sexual reproduction. Is there anyone, though, who would be capable of affirming about the soul that it has each of these things, both the manifest material of seed and the hidden formula of seed?

But why should I slave away at a matter which cannot be put across to anybody in words, except to someone so stupendously clever that he can fly ahead of the speaker's efforts and not have to wait till the end of the talk to grasp the whole thing? And so let me put it all in a nutshell. If this could happen with the soul too (what was possibly understood when we were saying it about the flesh), then the soul of Christ comes from such transmission in such a way that it has not dragged along with it the blemish of the original transgression; but if it could not come from that source without this liability, then it did not come from that source.

As for the way all other souls arrive, whether out of their parents or from above, let those win the argument who can. I am still hesitating between the two parties, and inclining sometimes this way, sometimes that—with this firm proviso at least, that I do not believe the soul to be either a body or any bodily quality or interlock,[37] if that is the right way to put what the Greeks call *harmonia*; and I trust that God will help me to stay in my right mind and never believe anyone who babbles such rubbish.

A text from the gospel: John 3:6

22, 38 There is another text that should not be overlooked, which those who think souls come from above can present as evidence in their favor; something the Lord himself says: *What is born of the flesh is flesh, and what is born of the spirit is spirit* (Jn 3:6). "What," they say, "could be more definite than this state-

---

35. As distinct from the soul's. In the traducianist view, at least as Augustine is presenting it, there is a soul seed by which parents reproduce souls as well as the body seed by which they generate bodies—presumably the two act in tandem.
36. See that verse, Wis 11:20: *You have disposed all things in measure and number and weight.*
37. *Coaptatio*, a word which, according to Lewis & Short, Augustine invents to render the Greek *harmonia*, applied to the construction of the human body. So I feel at liberty, indeed constrained, to invent a word too—the same word, however, as I invented in the translation of *The Trinity* IV,2,4; see note 12 there. See also *The City of God* XXII,24,4.

ment that the soul cannot be born of the flesh? What else, after all, is the soul but the spirit of life, the created one of course, not the creator spirit?"

Against them: "Well, what else," those others reply, "do we on our side think, saying as we do that flesh comes from flesh, soul from soul? Because man consists of each, and each we consider comes from him, flesh from the flesh that acts, spirit from the spirit that lusts—to leave aside for the moment the fact that the Lord was not talking there about carnal bodily birth but about spiritual rebirth."

Summing up the debate

23, 39 So then, having run through all these texts and arguments as thoroughly as the time allowed us, I would pronounce judgment that the weights of rational argument and scriptural evidence balance each other equally or almost equally on either side, were it not that the opinion of those who think souls are created from parents outweighs the opposition over the baptism of babies. What answer could be given them on this point has not so far occurred to me. If God by any chance should suggest something later on, if he should even endow those who devote themselves to studying such things with a facility in writing about them, I will not take it amiss. For the moment, nonetheless, I officially declare that the testimony of babies is not to be disdained, so that nobody bothers to refute it, as it were, if the truth happens to go against it.

For either, you see, there is nothing further to be asked on this matter, and it should be enough for our faith that we should know where we are going to arrive by living devout and loyal lives, even if we are ignorant of where we have come from; or else, if it is not a piece of impudence on the part of the rational soul to be in a fever to know this too about itself, at least let there be no obstinate wrangling, but rather diligent seeking, humble asking, persistent knocking, so that if it is expedient for us to know this, the one who certainly knows better than we do what is expedient for us may also give us this, the one who gives good gifts to his children.[38] The custom, all the same, of mother Church in baptizing babies is never on any account to be spurned nor in any way to be set aside as superfluous; nor should one believe at all that it is anything but an apostolic tradition.[39] That infant age too, after all, bears testimony of great weight, seeing that it was the first to have the privilege of shedding its blood for Christ.[40]

---

38. See Lk 11:9-13.
39. I think this is what it must mean; but it is a very odd phrase in the Latin: *nec omnino credenda nisi apostolica esset traditio*; at first sight this means, "nor should it be believed at all (that is, one should not believe in baptizing infants), unless it were an apostolic tradition." Perhaps that is what Augustine did mean; take your choice.
40. See Mt 2:16-18.

An admonition never to think of the soul as being a material body

24, 40. Certainly I have an admonition, which I would make as forceful as I can, for those who rather fancy this opinion, and believe that souls are propagated from parents, that they should take a good look at themselves to the best of their ability and should in the meantime be fully aware that their souls are not bodies. There is no nature, you see, closer to God than the one that was made to his image, one therefore of which a thorough examination will make it possible for God also to be thought of in a non-bodily way, God who remains unchanged and unchangeable above all his creation; and there is nothing you are nearer to, once you believe that the soul is a body, or nothing which will more inevitably follow, than your believing that God too is a body.

You see, there are people who have gotten into the habit of limiting their conscious awareness to what they perceive with the senses of the body; and the reason they give for refusing to believe that the soul is anything different from a body is that if it were not a body it would be nothing. And thus they shrink even more fearfully from believing that God is not a body, because they are terrified of having to believe that God is nothing. Their attention, you see, is so concentrated on the fancies and pictures in the imagination which are turned out by thought about bodies that they are terrified, if these are set aside, of perishing in a vacuum. Thus they are under the necessity of painting both justice and wisdom in their minds with shapes and colors, which cannot be thought of as incorporeal; and yet they do not say, when prompted by justice or wisdom either to praise them or to do something in line with them, what color, what stature, what features[41] they have been contemplating.

But we have already had much to say about these people,[42] and God willing, if the subject ever seems to require it, we shall say more. For the nonce, as I had started off saying, if some people have no doubts about the transmission of souls from parents that that is how it is, while others do doubt whether that is in fact how it is; still, let them at least never presume to believe or say that the soul is a body—especially for the reason I gave, that they might then be drawn to opine that God himself is also nothing but a body, even if the most excellent one there is, even if of a special nature far surpassing all the rest—but still a body nonetheless.

---

41. Here the Maurists add: "or what sort of shapes."
42. For example in Book VII,15,21—21,31 above, especially 27-31. See also *The Trinity* X,6,8—10,16.

Tertullian's belief that the soul is a body

25, 41. Finally, Tertullian[43] believed the soul is a body simply because he was unable to conceive its being incorporeal, and therefore feared it would be nothing, if it were not a body; and so he was also incapable of having any different idea about God. But he was certainly clear-sighted enough to be overcome by the truth from time to time against his own opinion. What after all could be truer that what he says in one place: *Every bodily thing is possible?*[44] So he ought to have changed the statement in which he had said a little earlier on that God too is a body. I cannot, I mean to say, imagine that he was so out of his senses as to believe God also to be passible by nature, so that one would have to believe that Christ is subject to suffering and change not only in the flesh, and not only in flesh and soul, but also as the Word through which all things were made—far be such a thought from any Christian heart!

Again, when he would also give the soul an airy, luminous color, he came to the senses with which he attempted to equip it organ by organ like a body, and he said: "Here there will be an inner, and also an outer man, one man doubled, that inner man too having his eyes and ears, with which the people ought to have seen and heard the Lord, having other organs too which he makes use of in his thoughts and performs with in dreams."[45]

42. There you have the kind of ears and the kind of eyes with which the people ought to have heard and seen God—the kind the soul performs with in dreams—when if anybody had seen Tertullian in a dream, he himself would never say that he had been seen by that person and had a talk with him, not having seen him in his turn himself! Lastly, if the soul sees itself in dreams, while it wanders about through the various images that it sees, and while its body and its organs, of course, are all lying in one place, has anyone ever seen it in dreams having an airy, luminous color? Well yes, it is possible to see this too; but God forbid that when you wake up you should believe it is really like that; otherwise, when you see yourself differently, which happens rather more frequently, either your soul will have been altered, or else not even then is the substance of the soul being seen, but an incorporeal image of the body, which as in waking thought is formed in a wonderful manner. Did any Ethiopian, for example, ever see himself in dreams as anything but black? Or if he did ever see himself as of another color,

---

43. The first African theologian, and the first significant Christian author to write in Latin; born in Carthage, the son of a Roman centurion, about 155, died in Rome shortly after 220.

44. *On the Soul* 7.

45. *On the Soul* 9. As regards the eyes and ears which the inner man has, and with which the people ought to have seen the Lord, he is no doubt thinking of texts like Mk 8:18: *Having eyes, do you not see, and having ears, do you not hear?*, and Mk 4:23; *If anyone has ears to hear, let him hear*. As for the other organs the inner man or soul is equipped with, he specifically mentions the tongue of the rich man in hell, the finger of Lazarus and the bosom of Abraham, Lk 16:19-31.

it cannot have surprised him much, if it coincided with some memory.[46] As being of an airy and luminous color, on the other hand—well, I do not know if he would ever have seen himself like that if he had never read or heard of such a thing.

43. And what if people let themselves be led by the nose by such dreams and visions, and wish to prescribe to us from the scriptures that, not the soul, but God himself is actually something of the kind in which he shows himself figuratively to the spirits of the saints, in which he is also presented in allegorical passages? Those dream visions are assuredly very similar to such forms of expression. And that in fact is how they go astray, setting up the idols of their deluded ideas in their hearts, and not understanding that the saints made the same sort of judgment about their own visions of this kind as they made on reading or hearing about such things said by God in figures; as for example that the seven ears of corn and the seven cows are seven years, that the sheet tied up by four lines like a dish full of various animals is the whole wide world with all its peoples.[47] And so with all the rest, and much more so when incorporeal realities are signified not by actual bodily things but by bodily figments of the imagination.

26, 44. For all that. however, Tertullian would not have the soul grow in substance like the body, and he also states why he shrinks from allowing this: "in case its substance should also be said to decrease," he says, "and thus should be thought liable to fade away altogether as well." And yet. because he stretches the soul locally throughout the body, he cannot find a way out of admitting its growth, as he would have it remain commensurate from a tiny seed with the size of the body, and he says: "But its energy, in which its natural properties are embedded and retained, is gradually extended with the flesh, while its substance keeps to the modest measurements in which it was breathed into the body from the start." We would perhaps be unable to understand this unless he made it plain with a comparison, which he went on to state.

"Take," he says, "a certain weight of gold or silver, still an unworked mass; it is heaped up together in a pile, and while the mass is occupying less space for the moment than it will do, it is still within the outlines of the model all pure gold or silver. From then on, when the mass is laminated into gold or silver leaf, it is made bigger than it was to begin with by the spreading out of that certain weight, not by addition to it, while it is being stretched out, not while it is being

---

46. Here I have altered the punctuation of both Maurists and CSEL editors, who make this passage about the Ethiopian all one sentence, and put the question mark here. That gives the sense: ". . . or if he did ever see himself in another color, did it not surprise him all the more if it coincided with some memory?" But that is a sense that seems to me to be lacking in sense, because if he could link this dream with some memory, it would not surprise him very much at all, while if he couldn't, it certainly would.

47. See Gn 41:26 and Acts 10:11-12. The "saints" who made the right judgment about these visions are first and foremost Joseph in the first instance and Saint Peter in the second.

increased—even if it is also increased while it is being stretched out; for increasing it by working it is permissible, while doing so by adding to it as it stands is not.[48] At that point too the actual brilliance of the gold or silver is heightened, which was indeed there before in the mass, but darker—not totally lacking though. At that point too it acquires various other qualities, depending on the skill with the material which the goldsmith has who is fashioning it, and who brings nothing more to the model than the engraved design. Accordingly the soul's increments too are not to be reckoned as substantive but as elicited."[49]

45. Who would believe that this man could have been so eloquent with ideas like that? But they are ideas to be feared, not to be laughed at. Would he ever have been driven to this, after all, if he had been able to envisage anything that is both real, and not a body? What, though, could be more absurd than to think that a mass of any kind of metal can expand in one direction while it is being hammered, unless it contracts in another, or that its breadth can increase unless its thickness diminishes? Or that there is any material body which grows all round while keeping its natural quantity, unless its density is thinned out?

How therefore will the soul from that droplet of seed fill the whole extent of the body it animates, if it too is a body the substance of which grows without any addition to it? How, I ask you, will it fill the flesh which it animates, unless it becomes thinner and thinner as the body it has animated grows stouter and stouter? He was afraid, remember, that if it could grow it would also fade away altogether by diminishing—and he was not afraid of its fading away by thinning out when it grew!

But why should I dwell on the point any longer when on the one hand my discourse is verging on that more copious style which the necessity of bringing it to a conclusion demands, and on the other it is already well enough known what my opinions are, both what I hold as certain and what I am still doubtful about and why? Accordingly this book too must now be concluded, so that we may go on to take a look at what comes next.[50]

---

48. Tertullian's Latin is much more idiosyncratic than Augustine's, and I suspect that in this comparison with gold or silver he is using some technical goldsmith's language. In particular at the end of this passage he contrasts increasing the mass of metal *habitu*, which is permissible, with doing so *statu*, which is not. I have just had to guess what that means; the dictionaries give me no clue. The beginning of the passage is also very obscure; the Latin for what I have translated as "it is heaped together in a pile" being *collectus habitus est illi*. I think the picture he has in mind is of a certain weight of precious metal given to a goldsmith for working into gold leaf, and consisting of perhaps some gold dust, some coins, and other such odds and ends that the owners do not want. Possibly he also had in mind Exodus 32, Aaron collecting all the gold rings from the people to make them the golden calf. Another word I have difficulty with in the passage is *modulus*; I eventually decided that "model" was the best rendering of it.

49. *On the Soul* 37.

50. At what comes next in Genesis, which is the story of the fall.

Book XI

Genesis 2:25—3:24: The temptation and the fall
of Adam and Eve

The text of the chapter: the nakedness of the man and the woman

1, 1. *And they were both naked, Adam and his wife, and they were not ashamed. Now the serpent was the cleverest of all the wild beasts that are upon the earth, which the Lord God had made. And the serpent said to the woman: Why is it that God said, You all shall not eat from the whole wood of Paradise? And the woman said to the serpent: From the fruit of the wood that is in Paradise we shall eat; but about the fruit of the tree that is in the middle of Paradise God said, You all shall not eat of it, nor shall you touch it, lest you die. And the serpent said to the woman: You shall not die the death; for God knew that on the day you take a bite of it your eyes will be opened, and you all will be like gods, knowing good and evil.*

And the woman saw that the tree was good for eating and that it was a pleasure for the eyes to see and was fine for gaining knowledge. And taking of its fruit she ate and gave also to her man with her, and they ate. And the eyes of both of them were opened, and they noticed that they were naked; and they sewed fig-leaves together and made themselves aprons. And they heard the voice of the Lord God strolling in Paradise in the evening, and they hid themselves, Adam and his wife, from the face of the Lord God in the middle of the wood of Paradise.

And the Lord God called Adam and said to him: Adam, where are you? And he said to him: I heard your voice as you were strolling in Paradise, and I was afraid because I am naked, and I hid myself. And he said to him: Who told you that you are naked—unless you have eaten from the tree of which I commanded you, from it alone you shall not take a bite? And Adam said: The wife whom you gave with me, she gave me of the tree and I ate. And the Lord God said to the woman: Why did you do this? And the woman said: The serpent led me astray, and I took a bite.

And the Lord God said to the serpent: Because you have done this, accursed are you from all cattle and from all wild beasts which are upon the earth. Upon your bosom and your belly shall you walk, and earth shall you eat all the days of your life. And I will set hostilities between you and between the woman and between your seed and between her seed. She will look out for your head, and you will look out for her heel.

And to the woman he said: Multiplying I will multiply your sorrows and your groaning. In sorrows shall you bring forth children, and your turning round shall be towards your husband, and he shall lord it over you. But to Adam he said: Because you have hearkened to the voice of your wife and have eaten of the tree about which I commanded you from it alone not to eat, accursed is the earth in your works. In sorrows shall you eat it all the days of your life. Thorns and thistles shall it bring forth for you, and you shall eat the hay of the field. In the sweat of your face shall you eat your bread, until you are turned into the earth from which you were taken, because earth you are and into earth shall you go.

And Adam called the name of his wife "Life," since she it is who is the mother of all the living. And the Lord God made Adam and his wife tunics of skin and clothed them. And the Lord God said: Behold, Adam has become like one of us in gaining knowledge of good and evil. And now, lest he should stretch out his hand and take of the tree of life and should live for ever—and the Lord God sent him away from the paradise of pleasure to work the earth from which he had been taken. And he threw Adam out and set him down over against the paradise of pleasure; and he ordered the Cherubim and the flaming sword which twists and turns to guard the way to the tree of life[1] (Gn 2:25—3:24).

2. Before we deal in due order with the text of this passage of scripture that we have before us, I consider it advisable to repeat the reminder which I remember having already given elsewhere in this work,[2] that what is being demanded of us is that anything the author who wrote it relates as historical event should be upheld as such in its proper literal meaning. If, however, in the words of God or of any person performing the prophetic office something is said which taken literally is simply absurd, then undoubtedly it should be understood as being said

---

1. The oddities of this version—for example, Adam being told that he will eat earth and the hay of the field—derive from the Greek Septuagint of which it is an over-literal translation. But there is one exception—the serpent being told about the woman and her seed that *she*, not he or it, will be looking out for its head, and it for *her* heel. Though "seed" is neuter in Greek, the Septuagint has the masculine here, thus enabling a messianic prophecy to be read into the text by the earliest Christian tradition. Putting it in the feminine seems therefore to be the responsibility of the old Latin translators alone, possibly prompted to this by the scene in Rv 12:1-6 of the Woman and the Dragon. This Marian implication of the passage was presumably so well entrenched in the Latin-speaking Churches, that when Jerome came to make his new Vulgate translation of the Old Testament, he did not dare to change the gender of the pronouns here.

2. In Book VIII,1,1—7,14; and not infrequently elsewhere almost from the beginning of the whole work.

figuratively in order to signify something more profound. That it was said, though, it is in no way lawful to doubt. This, after all, is required of us by the trustworthiness of the author and the commitment of the expositor.

3. So then, *they were both naked.* It is true, the bodies of the two human beings living together in Paradise were stark naked. *And they were not ashamed* (Gn 2:25). What should they be ashamed of after all, when they were aware of no law in their members fighting back *against the law of their minds* (Rom 7:23)? This punishment of the sin dogged their steps after their deviation from the due direction,[3] with disobedience daring to do what had been forbidden, and justice punishing what had been committed. Before this happened they were naked, as has been said, and were not embarrassed; there was no movement in their bodies of which to be shy; they did not think anything needed to be covered up, because they had not experienced anything needing to be held in check. How they were going to breed children has already been discussed earlier on;[4] but in any case it is not to be supposed that it would have been in the same manner as they did after the retribution just mentioned had followed the commission of the offense; from that moment on, though, before they died, death already conceived would whip up the disorderly behavior of disobedient members in the bodies of disobedient human beings as an eminently just tit for tat. Adam and Eve were not yet persons of that sort, when they were both naked and not embarrassed.

The serpent's cleverness; the relation of the serpent to the devil

2, 4. *Now the serpent was the cleverest*—there, yes indeed; but—*of all the wild beasts that were upon the earth which the Lord God had made* (Gn 3:1). It was called "the cleverest," you see, by straining the word's meaning a little; several Latin manuscripts have "the wisest," not in its proper meaning, in which wisdom is usually taken as being something good whether in God or angels or in the rational soul; it's as though we were also to call bees and ants wise because of their constructions which seem to reflect wisdom. Though this serpent could be called the wisest of all wild beasts not in its own non-rational soul, but with an alien spirit, the devil's, that is. However much, after all, the rebellious angels deserved to be cast down from their heavenly thrones for their forwardness and pride, they are still by nature superior to all wild beasts in virtue of their supreme intelligence. So what is so surprising about the devil now filling the serpent with his own inspiration, joining his own spirit to it in the way the oracles of demons

---

3. An attempt, a little forced, perhaps, to convey the rather startling, and I think deliberate, alliteration in the Latin: *Quae illos poena peccati post perpetrationem praevaricationis secuta est.* The word *perpetrationem* seems entirely superfluous to the sense, and so looks as if it were introduced simply to hammer the alliteration home.
4. Book IX,3,5—11,19.

are usually inspired, and rendering it indeed the wisest of all wild beasts in its living non-rational soul?

"Wisdom" is here being used improperly in a bad sense, like "cunning" in a good sense, when properly and more usually, in Latin at least, people are called wise by way of praise, while the cunning are understood to be clever in a bad way. Hence some translators, as we find in several manuscripts, have rendered not the word but rather the meaning to fit the Latin idiom, preferring to call this serpent not wiser but more cunning[5] than all the wild beasts. What the usage is in Hebrew, whether people there can properly, and not improperly, be called wise in a bad sense, let us leave to those who have a thorough knowledge of that language. We do, however, read in another place of the holy scriptures of people being wise for evil not for good purposes;[6] and the Lord says that *the sons of this world are wiser than the sons of light* (Lk 16:8) in making provision for their future, though they do it by fraud, not by legal means.

Only with God's permission could the devil use the serpent in this way

3, 5. We certainly should not suppose that the choice of the serpent as the means by which to tempt them and persuade them to sin was just the devil's own; but while his eagerness to deceive was all his own because of his twisted and jealous will, the only animal he was able to use for the purpose was the one he was permitted to be able to use. Any spirit, you see, can of itself have the crooked will to do harm; but the power to do so only comes from God, and this in accordance with some hidden and lofty justice, since there is no iniquity with God.[7]

Why God permitted the man to be tempted

4, 6. So then, if you ask why God allowed the man to be tempted, knowing beforehand that he was going to consent to the temptation, I have to confess that I

---

5. *Astutiorem* in the Latin. This is closer, in fact, to the Hebrew word, *arum*, which is more often used in an uncomplimentary sense, though occasionally more positively, like the English "cunning," or "wily." But the word Augustine is referring to as the original they are translating is the Greek word of the Septuagint, *phronimotatos*.

6. Jer 4:22, reading in the Authorized Version "they are wise to do evil," in the Latin Vulgate, *sapientes sunt ut faciant mala*. Here the Hebrew and the Greek have the more usual words for "wise," *hakam* and *sophos* respectively.

7. This, of course, is a general principle of moral theology, that an evil will is entirely the sinner's responsibility, but that the actual exercise of it is only possible as and if permitted by God. Why he allowed the devil to choose the serpent as his instrument will emerge clearly in 36,49 below, where Augustine follows up a suggestion he had made in 12,16 that the curse of the serpent must be interpreted figuratively, even though God's addressing the serpent is to be treated as an actual historical event; that is to say, the serpent is seen as a much more convincing symbol of evil and representative of the devil than, say, a lion or a bird of prey or a rat, or any other creature generally regarded as "nasty."

am quite unable to plumb the depths of his purpose and plan, and that it is far and away beyond my powers. So then, there is very possibly some more secret cause, reserved for better and holier people to discover, by his grace rather than by their own merits. But all the same, insofar as he grants me the capacity to form some idea or allows me to say what I think, it does not seem to me that it would have been greatly to the man's credit in the future, if the reason he was able to lead a good life was that nobody was prompting him to lead a bad one, since he had in his nature the power, and in his power the will not to consent to such promptings, with the help, however, of the one *who opposes the proud but gives grace to the humble* (Jas 4:6).

And so why should he not allow him to be tempted, even while knowing beforehand that he was going to consent? After all, he was going to do this of his own free will, and was due to be set to rights through an equitable penalty imposed by God. So God in this way would also demonstrate to the proud soul, for the instruction of the saints of future generations, how fairly and squarely he himself makes use of even the bad wills of souls, when they make perverse and crooked use of natures that are good.

The first sin, before the act of disobedience, was pride

5, 7. Nor is it to be supposed that this tempter was going to succeed in throwing the man, unless there was first in the man's soul a certain self-aggrandizement that needed to be stamped on, so that, humiliated by sin, he might learn how false and unjustified was his presumptuous opinion of himself. True indeed is the saying: *The heart is exalted before ruin and humbled before glory* (Prv 18:12); and perhaps it is this man whose voice is heard in the psalm: *I myself said in my abundance: I shall not be shaken for ever*; and who after experiencing what evil follows on proud self-reliance on his own powers, and what good on the assistance of God's grace, *Lord,* he says, *by your will you have bestowed power on my comeliness; but you turned away your face and I became troubled* (Ps 30:6-7). But whether that was said about this man or about another, the soul at any rate that exalted itself and was excessively over-confident, for instance, in its own powers, had to be given a demonstration by experiencing punishment of precisely how not well a nature fares that has been made, if it draws away from the one that made it.

This also brings home to us most effectively what sort of good it is that God must be, when nobody fares well who draws away from him. Those, you see, who wallow in the enjoyment of death-dealing pleasures, cannot escape the fear of the contrary pains; while as for those whose pride renders them even more insensitive, so that they fail totally to perceive what is so evil about their desertion of God, they do strike others, who have the discernment to note these things, as being indeed more wretched still. And so, even if they refuse to take the medicine of shunning such things, they are of use as an example of why such things should be shunned.

This, after all, is like what the apostle James has to say: *Each one is tempted on being dragged along and inveigled by his own concupiscence. Next, when concupiscence conceives she gives birth to sin; while sin, when he has matured, begets death* (Jas 1:14-15). From this one can rise again when the tumor of pride has been healed if, where before the experience the will was lacking to remain with God, at least after the experience the will is there to go back to God.

More reflections on why God allows us to be tempted

6, 8. Some people, though, are bothered about God's permitting the first man to be tempted in this way, without apparently noticing that the whole human race is incessantly being tempted by the devil's snares. Why does God permit this too? Is it because it is an effective test and exercise of virtue, and because the palm for not having given in when tempted is more glorious than for having been beyond the possibility of temptation? Even those, you see, who forsake the creator and go off behind the tempter, also put more and more temptations in the way of those who abide by the word of God, and present them with a good reason against any hankering after going astray, and hammer into them a godly fear of pride. It is in this connection that the apostle says: *looking to yourself lest you also be tempted* (Gal 6:1).

It is, in fact, astonishing with what continuous care all the divine scriptures commend to us the humility of subjecting ourselves to the creator, in order to stop us from relying on our own spiritual resources, as though we had no need of his help. So then, considering that it is by means of the unjust that the just make progress, and the godly by means of the ungodly, it is pointless to say, "God should not have created people he knew beforehand were going to be bad." Why indeed should he not create people he knew were going to profit the good, so that they would first be born to act as useful warnings to the good and to be the means of training their wills in virtue, and then be punished for their own bad will?

7, 9. "He should have made man," they say, "such that he would have had no will to sin at all." Look, we for our part happily concede that a nature which cannot sin at all is the better one; let them concede in turn that a nature is not bad which has been so made that it would be able not to sin if it did not wish to, and that the sentence of punishment on it is a just one when it has sinned deliberately, not by any necessity. So then, just as true reason teaches that the creature which finds absolutely no joy in anything unlawful is the better one, so too nonetheless does true reason teach that that creature is also good which has it in its power to check unlawful enjoyment, and in such a way that it not only rejoices in other lawful ones and in things rightly done, but also in the checks it imposes on crooked, perverse joys.

So then, since this nature is good, that one better, why should God only make that one, and not rather make them both?

And accordingly those who were all set to praise God for that one alone ought to praise him all the more exuberantly for each of them: that one as it is found in the holy angels, this one in holy human beings while as for those who have chosen to join forces with iniquity and have distorted an admirable nature by means of a reprehensible will, the fact that God had foreknowledge of them is no reason at all why he should not have created them. They too, you see, have their place to fill in the scheme of things for the benefit of the saints. God, I mean to say, stands in no need even of the justice of any upright person; how much less of any person's iniquity!

The same, with the emphasis on the way in which bad people can be of service to the good

8, 10. Is there anybody, though, who would say on sober second thoughts: "He would have done better not to create one he foreknew could be reformed by means of another's wickedness, than also to create one he foreknew would earn damnation for his wickedness"? This after all amounts to saying: "It would have been better for one person not to exist who would have been mercifully granted a heavenly crown for making good use of another's evil behavior, than for the evil person also to exist who would be justly punished for his deserts." When reason clearly presents us with two unequal goods, one superior, the other inferior, the dull-witted do not understand that when they say, "Each should have been like the better one," what they are really saying is, "There should only have been the better one." When they want to give equal value to different kinds of good, they just cut down the number, and by inordinately rating one of them too high, they merely eliminate the other. Who, though, would listen to them, if they said, "Since the sense of sight is better than that of hearing, it would have been better to have four eyes and no ears"?

Thus the rational creature is indeed the more excellent which without any punishment to make comparisons with, without any pride, submits itself to God; but still there is also one that has been created among human beings which could not appreciate God's goodness to itself without observing the punishment inflicted on another, warning it *not to be high-minded, but to fear* (Rom 11:20), that is, not to be overconfidently reliant on self, but to rely on God. Could anybody with a proper understanding say, "This one should have been like that one," and fail to see that this amounts to saying, "This one should not have existed, but only that one"?

But if this is in fact said by the illiterate and the foolish, the answer is: So why then should God not have created those he foreknew were going to be bad, *wishing to display his wrath and demonstrate his power*, and for this reason *bearing in much patience with the vessels of wrath, which have been completed for perdition, in order to make known the riches of his glory upon the vessels of mercy, which he prepared beforehand for glory* (Rom 9:22-23)? This, you see, is why *the one who glories should glory only in the Lord* (1 Cor 1:31), when he comes to know that it is not from himself but from God that he gets his very being; and what is more, that his well-being also comes only from the one from whom is derived his mere being.

11. And so it is altogether too thoughtlessly crude to say, "They should not exist," about those to whom God would give such a great demonstration of his mercy, if the only way for them to exist was for these others also to exist in whom he would vindicate and demonstrate his justice.

9. Why, after all, should not both sorts exist, when in each of them is justly displayed both God's goodness and fairness?

12. But then: "If God wished, these too would be good." How much better is what God actually did wish, that they should be what they wished; fruitlessly good, however, while their being bad would not go unpunished and would thereby be profitable for others! "But he knew beforehand that their will was going to be bad." He certainly did, and because he cannot be mistaken in his foreknowledge, that is why their will, not his, is bad. "So why then did he create them, foreknowing that they were going to be like that?" Because, just as he foreknew what bad things they were going to do, so he also foreknew what good he himself was going to do with their bad deeds. He made them, you see, in such a way as to leave to them the means of doing something by which they would discover that however reprehensible their choice, he would make admirable use of them. It is from themselves of course that they have a will that is bad, from him that they have both a nature that is good and a punishment that is just, the place that is their due, providing others with an aid to training in virtue and a salutary example to fear.

10, 13. "But he could have changed even their will," he persists, "for the better, since he is all-powerful." He could have done, certainly. "So why didn't he, then?" Because he didn't want to.

Why he didn't want to is his secret. We ought not, after all, *to be more wise than we have to be* (Rom 12:3). All the same, I think I showed sufficiently a short while ago[8] that even that rational creature is of no small value which shuns evil by a comparison of evils; and this kind of good creature would not exist if God Almighty had changed the bad wills of all people for the better, and did not inflict due punishment on any wickedness; and in this way there would only be the one kind of good rational creature, which makes progress without noting

---

8. See 8,10 above.

comparisons either with the sins of the wicked or the penalties they pay for them. This looks like increasing the number included in the more excellent kind by simply reducing the number of good kinds of creature.

That the good can benefit from the punishment of the wicked is a matter of common experience

11, 14. "And so," they say, "there is something in the works of God, is there, which needs the evil of another to help it make progress to the good?" Have people grown so deaf and blind through heaven knows what dedication to controversy, that they can neither hear nor see how many are the people whose behavior improves on some being punished? I mean to say, is there a pagan, is there a Jew, is there a heretic who cannot prove the point daily in his own household? But when it comes to discussion and inquiry into the truth, people refuse to attend to their own senses, and to ask themselves what work of divine providence it is that winds them up to imposing discipline, so that even if those who are punished show no improvement, their example may nonetheless strike fear into the hearts of the others, and their justly deserved calamity may ensure the welfare of the rest. God, after all, is not the author, is he, of the ill-will or wickedness of those whose just punishment he uses in the interests of others, whose interests he has decided are to be served in this way? Of course not.

But while he foreknew that they were going to be bad by their own vices, he did not for all that desist from creating them. Instead he assigned them to the benefit of those others whom he created in this group of people that would be unable to make progress towards the good without bad people to compare themselves with; after all, if they did not exist, they could of course not be of any use to any other thing. Was it a trifling good to ensure the existence of those who would assuredly benefit that kind of person? Anyone who does not want this kind to exist is only ensuring that he does not belong to it himself.

15. *Great are the works of the Lord, precisely wrought for all his wishes* (Ps 111:2). He foresees those who are going to be good and creates them; he foresees those who are going to be bad and creates them, bestowing himself on the good to be enjoyed by them, lavishing much of his bounty also on the bad, pardoning with mercy, taking vengeance with justice—and again taking vengeance with mercy, pardoning with justice; having nothing to fear from anyone's malice, nothing he needs from anyone's justice; not serving his own interests even with the works of the good, and serving the interests of the good even with the works of the bad.

So then, why should he not allow the man to be tempted, and by that temptation to be duly shown up, convicted, punished, when the proud concupiscence or lust for his own independent power and authority brought forth what it had conceived, and he was put to confusion by that progeny?[9] In this way his descendants, for whom the writing and publishing of this story was being prepared, would have the deterrent of the distress so justly inflicted on him, to keep them from pride and the evil of disobedience.

Why a serpent, particularly?

12, 16. If however you ask why it was a serpent, particularly, that the devil was permitted to employ for the temptation, the answer is that this was done for the sake of some deeper meaning. Who could fail to see that this is a lesson which has all the authority of scripture behind it, conveying by prophecy as many and as great proofs of divinity as already fill the world with its effects? Not that the devil wished to signify something for our instruction; but seeing that he could not proceed to the business of temptation unless permitted, he surely could not use any other instrument, could he, than the one permitted? So whatever meaning it is that was signified by that serpent, it is to be credited to the same providence as that under which the devil himself has indeed his own longing to do harm, but only the actual ability to do so which is given him, either for the perdition of *the vessels of wrath,* or for the humbling or testing of *the vessels of mercy* (Rom 9:22.23).

As for the serpent's nature, then, we know where it came from; the earth, you see, produced at God's word all cattle and serpents and wild beasts;[10] and the whole section of creation that has in it a living, non-rational soul is subject by the law of God's plan to the rational creation, whether that is of a good or a bad disposition. So why be surprised if the devil should be permitted to do something by means of a serpent, when Christ himself allowed demons to enter pigs?[11]

Of the nature of the devil himself, and of his sin

13, 17. It is the general practice to inquire more minutely into the devil's own nature, which some heretics,[12] put off by the vexing problem of his evil will, strive to remove entirely from the creation of the supreme and true God, and to provide with another source, which is God's opposite. They are incapable, you

---

9. That is, by the uncontrolled turbulence of his genitals; we are back here now with the first man, and why God allowed him to be tempted, after our long digression through the temptations that befall the rest of us and so on. But there is clearly an allusion here to Jas 1:14-15, quoted above in verse 7, where concupiscence gives birth to sin, who in turn begets death. The sign, the first inkling of death, however, is for Augustine the uncontrolled, involuntary erections of the genital organs.
10. See Gn 1:24-25.
11. See Mk 5:12-13.
12. He has the Manichees in mind.

see, of understanding that everything that is, insofar as it is a substance, is not only good but also unable to exist at all, unless it comes from that true God from whom every good comes, while a bad will is one that is inordinately disposed to prefer lower goods to higher ones; and that thus it came to pass that a spirit of the rational creation, delighting in its own power as surpassing that of all other creatures, became swollen with pride and thereby fell from the bliss of the spiritual paradise, and was eaten up by jealousy.

All the same, there is in such a spirit this goodness that it has life and gives life to a body, whether an airy one, like the spirits of the devil himself and the demons, or an earthy one like the soul of any human being, even an evil and crooked one. Thus it is, that while these heretics will not have anything that God made sinning by its own will, they say that the substance of God himself was first of necessity and then of its own will irremediably corrupted and distorted. But of these people's raving lunacy and their error I have already had much to say elsewhere.[13]

14, 18. In this work, however, our task is to inquire, in the light of holy scripture, what has to be said about the devil. In the first place, whether it was from the very beginning of creation that delighting in his own power he withdrew from that fellowship and charity which is bliss for the angels who enjoy God, or whether he himself too was for some time in the holy company of angels, equally just and enjoying equal bliss. Several authors say, you see, that what brought about his fall from the supernal regions was his jealous grudging of the man being made to the image of God. But against that is the fact that jealousy or envy[14] comes after pride, not before it; jealousy after all does not cause pride, but pride does cause jealousy.

Since pride, then, is the love of one's own superiority, while jealousy is the hatred of another's good fortune, it is easy to see which comes from which. I mean, anyone in love with his own superiority will be jealous of his peers because they are treated as his equals, and of his inferiors in case they should become his equals, and of his superiors because he is not treated as their equal. Thus it is pride that makes people jealous, not jealousy that makes them proud.

---

13. In tracts all written before he became a bishop. They were replies to the teaching of Manichee leaders, Fortunatus, Adimantus, Secundinus, and especially their leading evangelist in Africa, Faustus. There are also the "Acts" of a public debate he held with a Manichee called Felix, and a book, perhaps the earliest of them, which he wrote against a letter of Manes, the founder of the sect, called the *Epistola Fundamenti*, "The Letter of Foundation."

14. *Invidia*. "Envy" is the obvious translation; but it has a much narrower range of meaning than the Latin; so from now on I will render it only by "jealousy," though this does not have quite such a bad press in English as the vice—the capital vice—signified by *invidia*.

Intermezzo on pride and avarice

15, 19. Rightly has scripture designated pride as the beginning of all sin, saying, *The beginning of all sin is pride* (Sir 10:13). Into this text can be slotted rather neatly that other one also from the apostle: *The root of all evils is avarice* (1 Tm 6:10), if we understand avarice in a general sense as what goads people to go for anything more greedily than is right because of their superiority and a kind of love for their very own property. The Latin—and English—languages have given such property a very shrewd name by calling it "private," a word clearly suggesting loss rather than gain in value; every privation, after all, spells diminution. And so the very means by which pride aims at pre-eminence serve to thrust it down into sore straits and want, when its ruinous self-love removes it from what is common to what is its own property.[15]

There is a particular sort of avarice, though, which is more usually called love of money,[16] and it was by this name, signifying the general by the particular, that the apostle wished universal avarice to be understood, when he said, *The root of all evil is avarice.* It was through this also that the devil fell—not of course that he loved money, but his own personal power. Accordingly his twisted love of self deprives that swollen, puffed-up spirit of holy companions, and confines him, so eager to sate himself through wickedness, in an ever hungry wretchedness.

Thus it is that the apostle, after saying in another place, *For there will be people who love themselves*, added straightaway, *lovers of money*, coming down from that general avarice, of which pride is the source, to this particular kind which is proper to humanity. Not even human beings, after all, would be lovers of money, unless they thought that the richer they were, the more superior they would be too. In contrast with this disease *charity does not seek her own*, that is, does not rejoice in private pre-eminence and superiority; and rightly therefore is also *not puffed up* (1 Cor 13:5.4).

20. These two loves—of which one is holy, the other unclean, one social, the other private, one taking thought for the common good because of the companionship in the upper regions, the other putting even what is common at its own personal disposal because of its lordly arrogance; one of them God's subject, the other his rival, one of them calm, the other turbulent, one peaceable, the other rebellious; one of them setting more store by the truth than by the praises of those

---

15. For further reflection on this point, see *The Trinity* (I/5 in this series) XII,9,14, and note 42 there, where I remark that any notion of the sacred rights of private property would have been abhorrent to Augustine, and that he would regard the desire for private possession as "a kind of mark of Cain, the stigma of man alienated from God."
16. The Greek word rendered by *avaritia* in the Latin is in fact *philargyria*, "money-love." Hence the Authorized Version's "The love of money is the root of all evil," almost invariably misquoted as "Money is the root of all evil."

who stray from it, the other greedy for praise by whatever means, one friendly, the other jealous, one of them wanting for its neighbor what it wants for itself, the other wanting to subject its neighbor to itself; one of them exercising authority over its neighbor for its neighbor's good, the other for its own—these two loves were first manifested in the angels, one in the good, the other in the bad, and then distinguished the two cities, one of the just, the other of the wicked, founded in the human race under the wonderful and inexpressible providence of God as he administers and directs everything he has created. These two cities are mixed up together in the world while time runs its course, until they are sorted out by the last judgment, and one of them, joined to the good angels, attains eternal life in its king, while the other, joined to the bad angels, is dispatched with its king into the eternal fire. About these two cities we shall perhaps have more to say, ranging more widely over the subject, if the Lord so wishes, in another place.[17]

Back to the devil and his sin

16, 21. So then scripture does not say when it was that pride cast the devil down so that he distorted the goodness of his natural being by a twisted will; reason nonetheless declares unambiguously that this happened first and that as a result of this pride he became jealous of the man. It is easy, I mean, for all to see who look into these things that pride is not born of jealousy, but rather jealousy of pride. Nor can it be said that it is idle to think that the devil fell by pride from the beginning of time, and that there was no time before that in which he lived at peace and in bliss with the holy angels. On the contrary, from the very starting point of creation he apostatized from his creator;[18] so turning to what the Lord said: *He was a murderer from the beginning, and has not stood in the truth* (Jn 8:44), we should understand both parts to be "from the beginning"; not only that he was a murderer, but also that he has not stood in the truth. A murderer indeed from the beginning of the time when the man could be murdered, and of course he could not be murdered before he existed to be murdered. So then, the devil is a murderer from the beginning, because he murdered the first man, before whom there was no human being. But his not standing in the truth dates from the beginning of the time when he was himself created, able to stand in it, if to stand in it had been his wish.

---

17. This he does, of course, in *The City of God*. This was begun, at the request of his friend the Proconsul Marcellinus, a year or so after the sack of Rome by the Visigoths under Alaric in 410. I think we may infer accordingly that this part of *The Literal Meaning of Genesis* was written about the time he promised Marcellinus to set out the workings of divine providence which he has referred to here, and so to answer the attacks of the pagans who blamed the fall of the city on the supercession of its ancestral tutelary deities by the upstart Christian religion.

18. Here he is alluding to the first part of that text of Ecclesiasticus, quoted above in 15,19, "The beginning of all sin is pride," where it says in the previous verse, *The beginning of pride is to apostatize from God* (Sir 10:12).

17, 22. How can he be supposed, after all, to have led a blessed life among the blessed angels, having no foreknowledge of his future sin and punishment, that is of his desertion and of eternal fire? If he had no foreknowledge of it, we have the right to ask why not. The holy angels, after all, are left in no doubt about their eternal life and blessedness; how can they be blessed, I mean, if they are in doubt? Or are we to say that God did not wish to reveal to the devil, while he was still a good angel, either what he was going to do or what he was going to suffer, while he did reveal to the rest that they were going to abide forever in his truth? If that is the case, it means he was already not equally blessed, or rather that he was already not fully blessed at all, seeing that those who are fully blessed are in no doubt of their blessedness, and so have no nagging fears. And how would he have deserved to be so distinguished from the rest that God would not even reveal to him the future that was his very own? God surely would not be an avenger, would he, before the other was a sinner? Perish the thought! God simply does not condemn the innocent.

Or perhaps he belonged to a different class of angels, to whom God did not grant foreknowledge even of their own futures? How these could be blessed I simply cannot see, if they were in doubt about their very blessedness. Some people, you see, have entertained this idea that the devil was not of that most sublime angelic nature which is supercelestial, but one of those who were made somewhat lower down in the universe and assigned to various duties. Perhaps, you see, it might be possible for this sort to take delight in something unlawful, a delight, however that they could curb by their free choice if they refused to sin. In this they would be like human beings, especially that first one, who did not yet experience the punishment of sin in his members, seeing that holy men who submit themselves to God succeed through his grace in overcoming this temptation by their dutiful love.[19]

About the blessed life, and its various degrees

18, 23. Next,this problem about the blessed life, whether anyone can really be said to possess it who is uncertain whether it is going to remain with him or whether misfortune will at some time or other displace it, can also crop up with the first man, because if he was aware of his future sin and the divine punishment of it, in what way could he be blessed? Therefore he was in Paradise without enjoying bliss. But in fact, on the contrary, he had no foreknowledge of his future sin. Therefore, as a result of this ignorance he was either unsure about this self-same blessedness—and how then was he already truly blessed? Or else he was sure of it with a false hope, not genuine knowledge—and then how was he not just fooling himself?

24. Yes, but nonetheless the man was still only equipped with an "ensouled" body, and was still to be admitted, if he lived obediently, to the company of the

---

19. Their *pietas*, that wonderful, untranslatable word!

angels, with his body changed from being "ensouled" to being "enspirited";[20] so we can understand him to have enjoyed a blessed life to a certain degree, even without any foreknowledge of his future sin. After all, those people had no such foreknowledge either, to whom the apostle says: *You who are spiritual, instruct such a person in a spirit of mildness, looking to yourself lest you too should be tempted* (Gal 6:1); yet we are not being absurd or outrageous when we say that they were already blessed by the very fact of being spiritual, not yet indeed as "enspirited" in body, but in the justice of faith, *rejoicing in hope, patient in tribulation* (Rom 12:12).

So how much more then, and in ampler measure was the man blessed in Paradise before his sin, who while uncertain about his coming fall was rejoicing in hope because of the reward of his transformation to come, and to the extent that there would be no tribulation for him to strive patiently to bear with! He would not, you see, like a fool be vainly and presumptuously certain about something uncertain, but would be hoping in trust and faith, before he laid hold of that life where he would be absolutely certain about his eternal life to come.[21] And so he would be able to *exult*, as it is written, *with trembling* (Ps 2:11). And in this exultation he would be much more abundantly blessed in Paradise than the saints are now in these earthly regions; to a lesser degree indeed[22] than in that eternal life of the holy and supercelestial angels, but still not to no degree at all.

Taking up the point of there being, perhaps, two kinds or categories of angels

19, 25. But to say about some angels that in their category or whatever it is they could be blessed while being unsure of their wickedness and damnation to come, or of their assuredly perpetual salvation, though they would not even be supported by the hope that they too by some transformation for the better would later achieve certainty about this—well, it is a scarcely tolerable assumption; unless, maybe, it were also to be said that these angels were created to be assigned to services in the world under other more exalted and more blessed

---

20. From being *animale* to being *spiritale*. See Book IX,3,6 above and note 6 there, and 10,16, note 17; also Book VI,19,30, notes 23 and 25; and on a similar point of language, with reference to "flesh" and "spirit," see Book X,12,20 and notes 15 and 17.

21. If Adam and Eve had not sinned, as Augustine sees it, they would not have died, but at some time predetermined by God they and their progeny would have been transformed by being given the kind of terrestrial immortality that the fruit of the tree of life was designed to confer. It would be in that state that they would be absolutely certain of the eternal life to be enjoyed in due course in the company of the angels, when there would be another transformation, the kind we hope to undergo at the resurrection, and their terrestrially immortal, but still merely "ensouled" bodies, would be "enspirited"—by none other than the Spirit of God.

22. I here take the liberty, without manuscript support, of emending the text's *modo quodam inferiore*, "to a certain lesser degree," to *modo quidem inferiore*, which suits the whole structure of the sentence better.

ones, and that so for rightly carrying out their duties as officers they could hope to receive that blessed and more exalted life, about which they could have the most perfect assurance. Rejoicing then in this hope, they might already not incongruously be called blessed.

If it was from their number that the devil fell with his comrades in wickedness, then this is like human beings also falling from the justice of faith by plowing a furrow made crooked by a similar pride.

26. But let those maintain these two kinds of good angels who think they can: one of supercelestials, among whom the one that became the devil by falling was never included, and another of angels of the world among whom he was. For my part, I confess I have not so far discovered any support from the scriptures for this position. But I have been constrained by the question whether he had any foreknowledge of his fall before he fell, to insist that not even for a moment were the angels uncertain of their blessedness. So I have said that one can have good reason to think that it was from the beginning of creation, from the very beginning of time, that is, or from the moment he was himself created that he fell, and that he never stood in the truth.

The view that the devil was created in wickedness; a text of Job misapplied

20, 27. So it is that some people think that it was not by a free choice of his will that he turned aside to this wickedness, but that he was quite simply created in it, though by the supreme Lord and true God and creator of all substantive natures; and they bring forward evidence from the book of Job, since it is written there, when there is talk of him:[23] *This is the beginning of the Lord's fashioning, which he made for his angels to make fun of* (Job 40:19). This is matched by the sentence in the psalm: *This dragon which you fashioned to make fun of him* (Ps 104:26); but the difference is that here he said "which you fashioned," not as it is there, "This is the beginning of the Lord's fashioning," as though he fashioned him at the very beginning as evil, as jealous, as a seducer, so that the devil would quite simply not have turned crooked of his own free will, but would have been created like that.

---

23. In fact of Behemoth; it is more usually Leviathan, about whom God goes on to speak next, that is traditionally identified with the devil. Modern commentators usually identify these two monsters with the hippopotamus and the crocodile respectively. But an excellent article by J.V. Kinnier Wilson in *Vetus Testamentum*, January 1975, "A return to the problems of Behemoth and Leviathan," gives a much more profound and fascinating explanation. In brief, first God challenges Job to do God's own work for him and create something—and the result is the absurd monstrosity of Behemoth. Next he invites him to tame Leviathan, who is a traditional mythical sea monster; see Job 3:8, Is 27:1, and Ps 104:26, which is quoted next, and where "this dragon" translates "this Leviathan." Job, of course fails both tests, and repents in sackcloth and ashes. The Septuagint reading Augustine follows here, that the Lord made this monster for the angels to make fun of, suits Kinnier Wilson's reconstruction much better than the one in all modern translations.

21, 28. They do strive indeed to demonstrate how this opinion, that the devil did not turn crooked of his own accord but was made bad by the Lord God himself, does not go counter to where it is written, *God made all things, and behold they were very good* (Gn1:31). They assert, you see, and not without some show of wit and learning, that not only at the first establishment of the universe but even now, when there are so many crooked wills around, all things that have been created, that is, quite simply, the whole created universe, are nonetheless at the final count "very good." Not that the bad are in fact good in it, but that under the command, the power, the wisdom of God its administrator they do not succeed with their badness in disfiguring or upsetting at any point the beauty and order of the whole. Definite and suitable limits on what they have the power to do, you see, are set to the wills, even the bad ones, of each and every person, and their deserts are all weighed up, so that with them being fairly and squarely set in order the whole may remain beautiful.

That is the case they make;[24] nonetheless, it would be manifestly contrary to justice—a truth surely obvious to anybody—for God to condemn in anyone, without any previous deserts, what he had himself created in them; and in any case the definite and evident sentence on the devil and his angels is passed in the gospel where the Lord announced beforehand what he would be going to say to those on his left: *Go into the eternal fire, which has been prepared for the devil and his angels* (Mt 25:41). On these grounds, therefore, it is to be firmly believed that in no way was it the nature in which God created him, but his own evil will that was to be visited with the punishment of eternal fire.

22, 29. Nor is it his nature that is signified by the words, *This is the beginning of the Lord's fashioning, which he made for his angels to make fun of*, but either the airy body which God suitably adapted to such a will, or his own plan of making him useful to the good even against his will. Or else it may mean that while foreknowing he was going to turn out bad of his own free will, God still made him, not holding back his goodness in providing what was even going to be a noxious will with life and substantive being, at the same time foreseeing how much good use he was going to make of him by his own wonderful goodness and power.

However, he was not called *the beginning of the Lord's fashioning, which he made for his angels to make fun of* because God made him before anything else, or made him bad at the beginning. But rather, while God knew he was going to turn out bad of his own free will and so do much harm to the good, he still created him to this end, that through the devil he himself might benefit the good. That,

---

24. I have added this short sentence, to make it quite clear where the argument for the defense ends, and where Augustine begins to state the prosecution's case. His opponents are not here the Manichees, but people who agreed with him that there was never a moment in which the devil "stood in the truth," when he was not the devil; but from this they concluded, too simply, that he was created as the devil. It is probable that they had little patience with Augustine's crucial distinction between God permitting and God causing evil, that is the evil of sin, of a bad will.

you see, is the meaning of *for his angels to make fun of*; the way he is made fun of is by his temptations being of benefit to the saints when he strives to debauch them by these means, so that the malice, which he himself deliberately chose to be in the grip of, might prove useful against his will to the servants of the God who fashioned him with this in mind.

The reason he is "the beginning for making fun of" is that bad human beings too, the instruments of the devil and so to say the body of which he is the head, are made fun of in the same way. God foreknew, of course that they were going to be evil, but he nevertheless created them for the benefit of the saints. This is when their wishing to do harm bestows on the saints a salutary warning from comparison with them, and a lovingly respectful humility under God, and an appreciative understanding of grace, and good practice in putting up with bad people, and a good test of how much they really *love their enemies* (Mt 5:44). He, though, is "the beginning of the fashioning," which is made fun of like that, because he precedes these others both by a very long time and by his pre-eminent malice.

God however does this to him through the holy angels according to that working of providence by which he administers created things, namely by subjecting bad angels to good angels, so that their shameless villainy may be able to achieve only as much as it is allowed to, not as much as it aims at. This applies not only to the bad angels but also to human beings, until this *justice*, with which one lives by faith,[25] which is now being patiently practiced among such people by the saints, *is turned into judgment* (Ps 94:15), so that they too may judge not only the twelve tribes of Israel but angels as well.[26]

23, 30. So then the idea that the devil never stood in the truth, never led a blessed life with the angels, but fell from the very beginning of his creation, is not to be taken as meaning that he was created evil by the good God, not perverted by his own free choice. Otherwise he would not be said to have fallen from the beginning—he did not fall, after all, if he was made like that. But the very moment he was made, he turned away from the light of truth, swollen with pride, and corrupted by delight in his own personal power. Thus he never tasted the sweetness of the blessed life of the angels. It is not that on receiving it he turned up his nose at it, but that by refusing to receive it he turned his back on it and let it slip through his fingers.

Accordingly he could not have had foreknowledge of his fall either, since wisdom is the fruit of piety.[27] He, however, immediately proved impious, and consequently also mentally blind. So he did not fall from something he had

---

25. See Rom 1:17.
26. See Mt 19:28; 1 Cor 6:3.
27. This is said as though it had some scriptural authority behind it; all that occurs to me, however, is Is 11:2, the list of the gifts of the Holy Spirit, in which wisdom is the first and piety the last. The inference may have been that the first and greatest derives from the last and least.

received, but from something he would have received had he been willing to submit to God; and because he assuredly refused to do this, he both fell from what he was about to receive and also failed to escape from the power and authority of the one beneath whom he refused to be. Thus the result for him of the weight of his deserts was that he could neither be delighted by the light of justice nor delivered from its sentence.

Texts from Isaiah and Ezekiel, usually applied to the devil, more readily fit his "body"

24, 31. So then we come to what is said against him through the mouth of the prophet Isaiah: *How he has fallen from heaven, Lucifer rising in the morning! He has been crushed into the ground, who used to send to all the nations. You, though, said in your thoughts: I will climb up to heaven, upon the stars of heaven I will set my throne, I will take my seat on a lofty mountain above the lofty mountains to the north, I will climb up above the clouds, I will be like the Most High. Now, however, you shall climb down to the netherworld*, etc. (Is 14:12-15). This is all generally understood as being said against the devil under the figure of a king, supposedly of Babylon. But most of it is better suited to his "body," which he also gathers together from the human race, and chiefly to those members of it who stick to him through pride, by apostatizing from the commandments of God. Just as the one who was really the devil, you see, has also been called a man, as in the gospel: *An enemy man has done this* (Mt 13:28), so too one who was really a man has been called the[28] devil, as again in the gospel: *Have I myself not chosen you twelve, and one of you is the devil?* (Jn 6:70).

And just as the body of Christ, which is the Church, is called Christ, as in that text: *You all are the seed of Abraham*, when he had just said a little earlier on: *It was to Abraham that the promises were made and to his seed. It does not say "and to seeds," as though for many, but as though for one, "and to your seed," which is Christ* (Gal 3:29.16); and again: *For just as the body is one and has many members, but all the members of the body, though they are many, is[29] one body, so also Christ* (1 Cor 12:12). In the same way the devil's body too, of which the devil is the head, that is to say, the multitude of the godless, and supremely of those who fall away from Christ or from the Church as from heaven, is called the devil, and many things are said figuratively against him

---

28. Of course it should be "a" devil; but in this passage Augustine is clearly talking about "the" devil. We have the benefit in English of definite and indefinite articles which were not at his disposal in Latin. But he usually confines *diabolus* to "the devil," Satan, and for lesser members of the diabolic confraternity will almost always use the words *demones*, or *demonia*.

29. Yes, it should be "are"; but Augustine's Latin text is slavishly reproducing the Greek idiom of singular verb for neuter plural subject; so I follow suit, on the principle of translating scriptural quotations as literally as possible.

which do not suit the head so much as the body and members. And so Lucifer, who was rising early in the morning and fell, can be understood as being the whole tribe of apostates from Christ or from the Church, who are converted to the darkness on letting go of the light they were carrying, in the same sort of way as those who are converted to God pass from darkness to light, that is, those who were darkness become light.[30]

25, 32. Again under the figure of the prince of Tyre the following words are generally understood to be directed against the devil through the mouth of the prophet Ezekiel: *You are a seal of likeness and a crown of beauty; you were in the delights of the paradise of God. You were adorned with every precious stone* etc. (Ez 28:12.13); but they can more suitably be taken as directed against his body than against the prince of *the spirits*[31] of wickedness (Eph 6:12). The Church, you see, is called a paradise, as we read in the Song of Songs: *A garden enclosed, a fountain sealed, a well of living water, a paradise with the fruit of apples* (Song 4:12.15.13). From that place there fell either all heretics by an open, bodily rupture, or all who *returned to their vomit*, when they had walked for a while in the way of justice[32] after the remission of all their sins, whose *last condition has become worse than the first, and for whom it would have been better not to know the way of justice, than knowing it to turn their backs on the holy commandment entrusted to them* (2 Pt 2:22.20.21).

This most evil generation is described by the Lord when he says that the wicked spirit goes out of a man, and comes back with seven others and enters the house which he has now found tidied up, so that the last state of the man is worse than the first.[33] To people of that sort, you see, who have already become the devil's body, the following words can suitably be applied: *From the day on which you were created with the cherub*, that is, with God's seat, which means "manifold knowledge,"[34] *and I set you in the holy mountain of God*, that is, in the Church, as in the text: *And he heard me from his holy mountain* (Ps 3:4), *you*

---

30. See Eph 5:8.
31. I emend the text's *principem spiritum nequitiae*, "the prince spirit of wickedness," to . . . *spirituum nequitiae*, seeing it as an allusion to Eph 6:12, where Paul talks of our wrestling being against the *spiritualia nequitiae*, which the old Douai/Rheims bible translates as "the spirits of wickedness."
32. See Sir 4:12; Mt 21:32.
33. See Lk 11:24-26.
34. That the cherub is the same as God's seat is an Old Testament commonplace; see 2 Kgs 19:15, Ps 80:1, Is 37:16. As for God's seat or throne being interpreted as meaning *multiplicata scientia*, we have this passage from Sermon 53,14 (Vol III/3 of this series), probably preached about the same time, or a year or two later than this Book XI of *The Literal Meaning of Genesis*; it is on the two texts, Is 66:1, *Heaven is my throne*, and Is 40:12, *Who measured the heaven with the palm of his hand*: "So—God is seated in heaven, and he is measuring heaven with the palm of his hand. Does the same heaven become wide when he is sitting in it, and narrow when he is measuring it? Or is God himself the same size in his seat as he is in his palm?. . . So then, take

were in the midst of flaming stones, that is, of the saints *fervent in spirit* (Rom 12:11), *living stones* (1 Pt 2:5); *you walked without fault, yes you in your days, from the day on which you, yes you, were created, until your crimes were found in you* (Ez 28:13-15). All this could be discussed in more detail, to show perhaps that not only can these words be understood in this way, but also that no other way at all is possible.

Summing up what has been said about the devil's fall

25, 33. That, however, would require another long discourse devoted to this problem alone. So for the time being it must suffice to state the various possibilities about the devil's fall. It was either, then, that from the first moment of his creation he fell, out of impious pride, from the bliss which he would have received had he wished to, or else that there are other angels assigned to lower duties in this world, among whom he had lived in their degree of bliss that lacks foreknowledge, and from whose company he fell through proud impiety as a sort of archangel over angels subject to him, if this idea can really be maintained, and it would be most surprising if it can.

Alternatively, an explanation certainly has to be sought how all the holy angels (if the devil with his angels lived among them for a time, sharing their bliss) also lacked definite foreknowledge of their perpetual felicity,[35] but only received this after his fall; or else we have to ask how the devil with his companions deserved before his sin to be distinguished from the rest, so that he remained ignorant of his coming fall, while they were quite sure about their remaining where they were.

What, in any case, we must have not the least doubt about is that according to the faith of the apostles[36] the angels that sinned were thrust down into this foggy atmosphere round the earth as into a prison, where they are being kept in order to be punished at the judgment; while in that heavenly bliss of the holy angels there is no uncertainty at all about eternal life, nor about our future share in it by God's mercy and grace and most faithful promise, when we join them after the resurrection and transformation of these bodies of ours. It is towards this hope, after

---

"heaven" as standing for all the saints, since earth too stands for all who are on the earth: *Let all the earth worship you* (Ps 66:4). If we are right in meaning all those who live on earth when we say "Let all the earth worship you," then we are right in meaning those who live in heaven when we say "Let all the heaven be occupied by you." The saints who are still living on earth . . . they too are heaven because they are God's throne; and when they proclaim the words of God, it's the heavens that are declaring the glory of God (Ps 19:1).

35. As Saints Perpetua and Felicity were two of the most venerated African martyrs, on the meaning of whose names he happily expatiates in Sermons 280 to 282 (again Vol. III/8), I feel it incumbent on me just to transliterate his *perpetuae felicitatis* here.

36. See 2 Pt 2:4.

all, that we direct our lives, being created anew by the grace he has given us as promised. As for anything that can be said about why God created the devil when he foreknew what he was going to be like, and why being almighty he did not divert his will to good ends, possible answers may be found in what we said when asking similar questions about evil human beings[37]—whether you understand these answers, or just believe them, or can find better ones.

The devil and the serpent

27, 34. So then, the one who wields supreme authority over all the things he has created only gave the devil permission to tempt the woman through the serpent and the man through the woman. But it was the devil himself who spoke in the serpent, using it like an organ, and moving its nature[38] to give expression to the verbal sounds and bodily gestures by which the woman would be made to understand what he wished to persuade her to do. In the woman herself though, because she was a rational creature and could use her vocal chords to make words, he did not speak himself, but he was acting on her inwardly by a hidden, persuasive impulse, as he had done outwardly by means of the serpent.

He could have produced the same result, indeed, in a soul already wrapped in a proud love of its own power, had he acted by such hidden impulse alone, as he did in Judas, prompting him to betray Christ.[39] But as I have said already, the devil has the will to tempt, but does not have it independently in his power either to do so or to decide how to do so. It was because he was permitted to, therefore, that he tempted the woman, and he did so in the way he was permitted to. What kind of human beings, though, would profit from what he was doing he did not know, and would not have wished it if he had; and that is how he was being made fun of by the angels.

28, 35. And so the serpent did not understand the sounds of the words which were being uttered from it to the woman. Nor is it to be supposed that its soul was turned into one of a rational nature, seeing that not even human beings, who are rational by nature, know what they are saying when a demon is speaking in them in that condition for which an exorcist is required. How much less would that creature have understood the sounds of the words which the devil was producing through it and out of it! After all, it would not understand a human being

---

37. See above, vi,8—xi,15.
38. Here I omit a phrase which is hard to fit into the run of the sentence, and could easily have been a marginal comment of some reader or copyist which later crept into the text: "moving its nature *eo modo quo movere ille et moveri illa potuit,* in that way in which it (or he) could move and she could be moved." When he says the devil used the serpent like an organ, I think he has a musical organ in mind, not an organ of the body. What I am treating as a marginal gloss may be seen as a comment on such serpentine organ music.
39. See Jn 13:2.

speaking, if it heard him while not possessed by the devil. As for snakes being thought to hear and understand the words of the Marsi,[40] so that they frequently jump out of their holes when they are being charmed by them, here too diabolical power is operating, to help us acknowledge providence at work everywhere and to observe what thing it subjects to which in the natural order, and what it permits even to evil wills by the wonderfully wise exercise of authority, so that it is far more common for snakes and serpents to be swayed by human incantations and charms than any other kind of animal.

All this too, you see, lends no little support to the truth of human nature at the beginning having been seduced by the conversation of a serpent. Demons, I mean to say, rejoice at having been given the power to get snakes dancing at the incantations of human beings, always eager to deceive in any way at all those whom they are able to. They are permitted to do this, however, to keep the memory alive in us of that first deed, which showed on what familiar terms they are with that species. What is more, that first deed was permitted in order to give the human race, for whose education this narrative would duly have to be written down, a significant symbol in snakes of all diabolic temptation. This will become clearer, when we come in due course to the first words of the divine sentence passed on the serpent.

29, 36. So then, *the cleverest*—that is the most cunning—*of all the wild beasts* (Gn 3:1); the serpent was said to be this on account of the devil's cunning, which was displaying his trickery in and through the serpent. It is like the way we talk about a clever or cunning tongue, which is moved by a clever or cunning person to make a clever or cunning point. This, I mean to say, is not a power or capacity of the bodily organ which is called a tongue, but of course of the mind which is making use of it. In the same way the typewriters of journalists[41] can be said to lie; while lying, you see, only falls in the province of living and sentient beings, the typewriter is said to lie because a liar spreads his lies by means of it. Indeed this serpent could be called a liar, because the devil used it like a typewriter to spread his lies.

37. The reason I have thought it worthwhile dwelling on this is in case anyone should reckon that animals innocent of reason have a human understanding of things, or can suddenly be changed into rational animals; this would be the first erring step to holding that ridiculous and noxious opinion about the changing round either of human souls into animals, or those of animals into human beings.

---

40. "A people in Latium, on the Lacus Fucinus, celebrated as wizards and snake-charmers; in the Social War the most zealous enemies of the Romans"; so Lewis & Short. It is disappointing to see Augustine, usually so interested in exotic natural phenomena, jumping to the conclusion that snake-charming is something only to be done with diabolical cooperation.

41. *Scribarum*; I cannot resist calling them journalists, though Augustine's times were innocent of that nowadays all-pervasive—and indeed invaluable—tribe of scribblers. What I have turned into their typewriters is the rather more archaic *stilus*.

So then the serpent spoke to a human being in the same way as the donkey Balaam was riding spoke to a human being,[42] the only difference being that the first instance was the work of the devil, the second of an angel.

There are some works, you see, that both good and bad angels can do equally, like Moses and Pharaoh's magicians.[43] But even in these works good angels are the more effective, and bad angels cannot even do anything of this sort, unless God's permission is passed on to them through good angels. This ensures that each person is paid back in accordance either with their own attitude or with the grace of God, each of them justly and benevolently, thanks to *the depths of the riches of the wisdom and knowledge of God* (Rom 11:33).

Back to the story of Genesis 3

30, 38. So then *the serpent said to the woman: Why is it that God said, You all shall not eat from every tree of Paradise? And the woman said to the serpent: From the fruit of the wood that is in Paradise we shall eat; but about the fruit of the tree that is in the middle of Paradise God said, You shall not eat of it, nor shall you touch it, lest you die* (Gn 3:1-3). The reason we have the serpent first asking this question and the woman giving this answer is to show that there was no excuse at all for the breach of duty, and that in no way could it be said that the woman had forgotten what God had commanded, although forgetting a commandment, especially when there was only one and that one so basic, would also incur the maximum penalty for gross negligence. Nonetheless her transgression is all the more evident when the commandment is retained in the memory, and in the commandment God is so to say present in attendance himself, and being defied. That is why it was necessary in the psalm, after saying *and retaining his commandments in the memory*, to add *in order to do them* (Ps 103:18). Many people, you see, retain them in memory in order to ignore them with the greater sin of breach of duty, where there is no excuse of forgetfulness.

39. So then, *the serpent said to the woman: You shall not die the death; for God knew that on the day you take a bite of it your eyes will be opened, and you will be like gods, gaining knowledge of good and evil* (Gn 3:4-5). When would the woman have believed this assertion, telling them they had been held back by God from something good and beneficial, if there had not already been in her mind that love of her own independent authority and a certain proud over-confidence in herself, of which she had to be convicted and then humbled by that very temptation? Finally, not content with the serpent's words she inspected the tree herself, and *saw that it was good for eating and fine to look at*

---

42. See Nm 22:27-30. The ridiculous and noxious opinion he has in mind is not now Manichee doctrine, but the transmigration of souls.
43. See Ex 7:10-11.22; 8:7.18-19.

(Gn 3:6), and not believing that she could die from it, she assumed, in my opinion, that God's words, *if you take a bite of it you shall die the death*, were not to be taken literally, but had some other meaning. And that is why she took some of its fruit and had a bite, and also gave it to her husband with her, maybe with a word of encouragement which scripture does not mention, leaving it to be understood; or did the man perhaps not need any encouragement now, when he observed that she had not died of that food?

Their eyes were opened, and they realized they were naked

31, 40. And so *they ate, and the eyes of them both were opened* (Gn 3:7)—for what, if not for lusting after each other, as a punishment for the sin, a punishment conceived by the death of the flesh itself? So now the body would no longer be simply "ensouled" or animal, capable in due course of being changed, if they had remained obedient, into a better and more "enspirited" condition[44] without death intervening; but from now on it would be a *body of death, in which the law in the members fights back against the law of the mind* (Rom 7:24.23).

After all, they had not been made with closed eyes, and left to wander about blind in the paradise of delights, feeling their way, and so to reach and touch all unawares the forbidden tree too, and on feeling the prohibited fruits to pick some without knowing it. Again, how were the animals and birds brought to Adam to see what he would call them, if he could not see them? And how was the woman herself brought to her husband when she was made, for him to say about her, though unable to see her, "This now bone out of my bones and flesh from my flesh," etc.? Lastly, how did the woman see "that the tree was good for eating and a pleasure for the eyes to see and fine for gaining knowledge," if their eyes were closed?

41. All the same, just because one word is employed metaphorically, it does not mean that the whole passage is to be taken in a figurative sense. She will have seen, after all, in what sense the serpent said, *Your eyes shall be opened.* This I mean is what the writer of the book tells us it said; but what precisely it meant to signify he allowed readers to decide for themselves. The sentence, though, *And their eyes were opened, and they realized that they were naked*, is written just like all the rest of the narrative of actual events, nor is that any reason why the expression should lead us to treat the whole story as allegorical.

The evangelist, after all, in telling his story, was not introducing someone else's figurative words, instead of telling the story of what actually happened in his own words, when he said about those two, one of them Cleopas, that when the Lord had broken bread for them, *their eyes were opened, and they recognized*

---

44. See 18,24, note 19, above.

him (Lk 24:13-31), though they had not recognized him along the road, not of course because they were walking along with their eyes shut, but because they were not yet capable of recognizing him. So then, the narrative in this place is no more figurative than it is there, even though scripture uses a word metaphorically, and talks of eyes being opened which were wide open already; but opened of course for looking at something and giving it thought which they had never previously noticed.

Bold, shameless curiosity, you see, was moved to transgress the commandment, being greedy for fresh experiences, such as seeing what precisely would follow on touching the forbidden object, and thoroughly enjoying the guilty liberty of snapping the reins of the prohibition; so they reckoned it was highly unlikely that the death they feared would be the result, we must assume, I imagine, that the apple on that tree was the same kind as the apples they had already found to be harmless on other trees,[45] and preferred to believe that God could easily forgive sinners, rather than to put up patiently with never finding out what precisely the result would be, or why he had forbidden them to take food from that source. No sooner then had they transgressed the commandment, than they were inwardly stripped stark naked, bereft of the grace which they had offended against by a kind of feverish delusion, and by the proud love of their own independent authority; then they turned their eyes on their own genitals, and lusted after them with that stirring movement they had not previously known. So that is what their eyes were opened to, something to which they had previously been closed, though wide open to everything else.

32, 42. This death happened on the very day that the deed God had forbidden was committed. By this deed, in fact, they forfeited the wonderful condition, which was to be bestowed upon them through the mystical virtue in the tree of life. In this condition it would have been impossible for them to be tried by disease or altered by age; thus in their flesh, though it was still just "ensouled" and due only later to be transformed for the better, their eating from the tree of life (which is the sacrament or symbol of Wisdom[46]) would already represent and point to what feeding spiritually on Wisdom does for the angels, by making them partakers of eternity, and thus immune from any change for the worse. When they forfeited this condition, then, their bodies contracted that liability to disease and death which is present in the flesh of animals—and thus also that motion of the genitals which stirs in animals the desire to mate, and so ensures the birth of young to take the place of those which die.

---

45. So there is no special, death-dealing quality about the fruit of the tree of knowledge, parallel to the mystical virtue Augustine thinks must lie hidden in the fruit of the tree of life. It is purely and simply the act of disobedience that makes eating of the tree of knowledge fatal.

46. See Prv 3:18.

But for all that, in this very punishment the rational soul gave an indication of its natural nobility by feeling embarrassment at this animal motion in these organs of its flesh, and covering it with shame. This was not only because it was experiencing something there it had never felt before, but also because this shame-producing motion came from the transgression of the commandment. It perceived it, you see, in that part of the body which had previously been clothed with grace, when in its nakedness it had experienced nothing unbecoming. There the psalm verse was fulfilled: *By your will you have bestowed power on my comeliness; but you turned away your face, and I became troubled* (Ps 30:7).

Next in that troubled state they had recourse to fig-leaves, they sewed them together into aprons, and because they had disowned these organs as something to be proud of, they covered them up as something to be ashamed of. I do not suppose for a moment that they thought those leaves were in any special way suited to covering up organs already aroused; but their troubled state drove them to this by some hidden impulse, so that such an appropriate sign of their punishment might be unwittingly enacted by them, to convict the sinner by being performed, and teach the reader by being written down.[47]

About the "voice of the Lord"

33, 43. *And they heard the voice of the Lord God walking in Paradise in the evening* (Gn 3:8). That was certainly a suitable hour for defectors from the light of truth such as they were to be visited. Now it is possible that previously God used to talk to them in other interior ways, whether expressible in words or not, as he also talks to the angels, enlightening their minds with the unchangeable Truth itself; there understanding means knowing simultaneously whatever things are also happening, not simultaneously, in time. It is possible, I repeat, that that is how he used to talk to them, even if he did not give them such a full participation in the divine Wisdom as the angels can take, but still visiting and speaking to them in the same way, however much toned down and adjusted to their human capacity. Perhaps, on the other hand, it was by means of some created manifestation, as happens when bodily images, through which God is to

---

47. For the symbolic significance of fig leaves see Sermons 98,3 and 122,1 (vol.III/4 in this series). In the second of these, on our Lord seeing Nathanael under the fig tree (Jn 1:48), Augustine just states that the fig tree stands for sin, for no other reason, it seems, than that Adam and Eve had sewed its leaves together to cover their private parts, that were now *pudenda* because of sin. But in the first, where he is talking about the tree Jesus cursed because it had no fruit on it, though it was not the season for fruit (Mk 11:13-14), he says it stands for people who are unwilling to bear fruit, people like the Jews, "who had the words of the law and didn't have its deeds—full of leaves and bearing no fruit." So fig leaves, in general, stand for the plausible words and excuses with which we so readily cover up our moral nakedness, our failure to produce fruit; and of that we are profitably reminded when we read Gn 3:7.

be seen or heard, are presented either to the spirit in a state of ecstasy, or to the senses of the body. This is how God is in the habit of being seen among his angels, or of thundering from a cloud.[48]

Now, however, their hearing the voice of God walking in Paradise in the evening can only have been effected visibly[49] through some creature, lest that invisible substance of the Father and the Son and the Holy Spirit, which is everywhere whole, should be supposed to have appeared to their bodily senses by movement in space and time.

44. *And they hid themselves, Adam and his wife, from the face of the Lord in the middle of the wood which is in Paradise* (Gn 3:8). When God turns his face away inwardly and the man becomes troubled, we should not be surprised at these things being done which give every indication of his being out of his mind; done out of extreme shame and fear, that hidden impulse again being at work to do all unwittingly things that had a further significant meaning, which would be picked up at some later time by their posterity, on whose account this story has been committed to writing.

The conversation between Adam and God

34, 45. *And the Lord God called Adam and said to him: Adam, where are you?* (Gn 3:9). Words of reproof, not of ignorance. And this too is surely not without significance, that just as the commandment had been given to the man, by whom it was to be passed on to the woman, so it is the man who is first questioned. The commandment, you see, went from the Lord through the man as far as the woman, while the sin went from the devil through the woman as far as the man. All this is full of mystical significance, not put there by the characters between whom it took place, but by the supremely potent Wisdom of God directing them to that end. However, we are not now engaged in unlocking the treasures signified, but in defending the reality of the things actually done.

46. So then, Adam replied: *I heard your voice in Paradise and I was afraid, because I am naked, and I hid myself* (Gn 3:10). It is probable enough that God was in the habit of showing himself to those first human beings in human form by means of something created to suit such activity. However, as he was then

---

48. Being seen among his angels, as by Isaiah (6:1-13); or by the less distinguished prophet Micah, who was sent for by Ahab to prophesy before the battle of Ramoth-gilead, and said: *Hear the word of the Lord; I saw the Lord sitting on his throne, and all the host of heaven standing beside him on his right hand and on his left, etc.* (1 Kgs 22:19); or by John the Evangelist (Revelation, passim); thundering from a cloud, as on Mount Sinai, or the Mount of the Transfiguration.
49. Augustine knew as well as we do that it was an audible effect that needed to be produced for them to hear God's voice; but he is making the contrast with what he is just going on to call God's invisible substance; and it was simply not part of the common theological language to talk of God's inaudible substance.

drawing their attention up to heavenly matters, he never allowed them to take any notice of their nakedness, until after they sinned and then felt the shameful motion in their members under the penal *law in the members* (Rom 7:23). So then, they were embarrassed as men and women usually are embarrassed under the eyes of men and women; and such was his embarrassment at the punishment of the sin, that he wanted to escape the notice of one whom nothing escapes, and to conceal his flesh from one who is the inspector of the heart.

But why should we be surprised, if after wanting proudly to be like gods *they gave way to futile thoughts, and their silly heart was darkened* (Rom 1:21)? What it amounts to in fact is that *they said they were wise in their abundance, and when he turned his face away they became fools* (Rom 1:22; Ps 30:6-7). What they were ashamed of, you see, in each other's presence—which is why they made themselves aprons—they were much more terrified of being seen, even covered up like that, by the one who through some visible creature used to come and see them like a friendly relative, with seemingly human eyes. If the reason, after all, that he used to appear to them like that was so that human beings might be able to talk to him as to one of themselves, as with Abraham at the oak of Mamre.[50] Then this very friendliness, which used to put them at ease before their sin, began after they committed it to burden them with shame; nor would they any longer have the nerve to display to such eyes the nakedness which was now an embarrassment to their own.

Excusing self, blaming others

35, 47. So then the Lord, after interrogating the sinners in the manner prescribed by justice, wished now to inflict a severer punishment than this one they were forced to be ashamed of; so *Who told you*, he said, *that you are naked—unless you have eaten from the tree which I commanded you, from it alone you shall not take a bite?* (Gn 3:11). It was the death, you see, conceived by this act, according to the sentence which God had threatened to pass, that made them lustfully notice their members when their eyes were said to be opened, and what they were ashamed of followed. *And Adam said: The wife whom you gave with me, she gave me of the tree, and I ate* (Gn 3:11). Oh, pride! Did he say, "I have sinned"? He is awkward enough to be confused, not humble enough to confess.

The reason all this was committed to writing because this questioning was assuredly conducted in order that it might all be truthfully and profitably written down—if it was false it would obviously not be profitable—was so that we might mark what a diseased pride people today are infected by, who attempt to

---

50. See Gn 18:1-15.

put the blame solely on the creator for whatever evil they do, while for anything good they do they wish to take all the credit for themselves. *The woman*, he said, *whom you gave with me*, that is, whom you gave to be with me, *she gave me of the tree and I ate*; as though she was given him to ensure that she would not obey her husband, and neither of them God!

48. *And the Lord God said to the woman: Why did you do this? And the woman said: The serpent led me astray, and I took a bite* (Gn 3:13). Nor does this one confess the sin, but puts the blame on another, the man's equal in impudence, if not in sex. Nonetheless from these two there traced who is "his" descent without following their example, though certainly plagued by many more evils than they, one who said—and will go on saying till the end of the world: *I said: Lord have mercy on me; heal my soul since I have sinned against you* (Ps 41:4). How much better if these two had done the same!

But the Lord had not yet broken sinners in; still to come were toil and trouble, pain and grief, death and all the wear and tear of the world—and the grace of God with which at the appropriate time he would come to the aid of a humanity, which he had taught by affliction not to be presumptuously self-confident and self-reliant. *The serpent*, she said, *led me astray, and I took a bite*, as if anybody's persuasive suggestion should be given preference over God's commandment!

The punishment of the serpent

36, 49. *And the Lord God said to the serpent: Because you have done this, accursed are you from all cattle and from all wild beasts which are upon the earth. Upon your bosom and your belly shall you walk, and earth shall you eat all the days of your life. And I will set enmities between you and between the woman and between your seed and between her seed. She will look out for your head, and you will look out for her heel* (Gn 3:14-15). The whole of this sentence is figurative in meaning, and all that the writer's credibility and the truth of the story guarantees is that we need have no doubt that it was actually uttered. The words *And the Lord God said to the serpent* are the writer's, to be taken in their proper literal sense; so it is true, therefore, that this was said to the serpent. All the other words are now God's, and it is left to the reader's free judgment whether they should be taken literally or figuratively, as we said earlier on at the beginning of this volume.[51]

Accordingly, the reason the serpent was not interrogated about why it had done this would seem to be that it had not done it in its own nature and by its own

---

51. Book XI,1,2 above.

will, but that it had been the devil operating from it and by it and in it, and he had already been assigned to eternal fire for the sin of his own disloyalty and pride. So now then, what is said to the serpent and really of course being addressed to the one who had operated through the serpent is undoubtedly figurative. These words, you see, are giving a description of that tempter which fits what he was going to be like for the human race in the future, the human race that began to be propagated precisely when this sentence was passed on the devil as if on the serpent. So these words are to be treated in the way figurative language is explained, and I discussed them as best I could in those two volumes on Genesis which I published against the Manichees;[52] and if on another occasion I can do it again more thoroughly and suitably, I am sure God will be at hand to help me carry out the task. Now however, I am intending to do something else, and I must not be distracted from it at anybody's insistence.

The punishment of the woman

37, 50. *And to the woman he said: Multiplying I will multiply your griefs and your groaning; in griefs shall you bring forth children, and your turning round shall be towards your man, and he shall lord it over you* (Gn 3:16). These words too, addressed to the woman, can be much more aptly understood in a figurative and prophetic sense. Nonetheless, the woman had not yet given birth, and the pains and groans of childbirth come from *the body of this death* (Rom 7:24), the death that was conceived by that transgression of the commandment, in members[53] which even then were just animal or "ensouled," but if the man had not sinned were certainly not going to die, and were going to live in some more favorable condition, until they earned after a life well lived the reward of being changed for the better, as I have suggested above in several places. So this punishment can be taken in the proper literal sense—though we will have to see how the last part, *and your turning round shall be towards your man, and he will lord it over you*, can in fact be taken in the proper sense. It is not fitting, after all, to suppose that even before sin the woman was made otherwise than to have the man lording it over her and to be herself turning towards him in service.

But we can rightly take it that the service indicated here is one of social status rather than of affection; so this kind of service, by which human beings later on began to be the slaves of other human beings, turns out to have arisen from the punishment of sin. The apostle indeed says, *Serving one another through love* (Gal 5:13); but he would never have dreamed of saying, "Lord it over one

---

52. See above, Book VIII,1,5, note 8.
53. The background of his thought here is all the time Romans 7, which accounts for this rather odd use of the word "members" to mean in fact the whole body.

another." And so married couples can indeed serve each other through love; but the apostle does not allow a wife to lord it over her husband.[54] It was God's sentence, you see, that gave this position to the man, and it was by her own fault that the woman deserved to have her husband as her lord, not by nature. Unless this is accepted and observed, however, nature will become even more distorted, and the fault will be aggravated.

The man's punishment

38, 51. So then he also said to her husband: *Because you have listened to the voice of your wife and have eaten of the tree about which I commanded you from it alone not to eat, accursed is the earth in your works. In grief shall you eat it all the days of your life. Thorns and thistles shall it bring forth for you, and you shall eat the hay of the field. In the sweat of your face shall you eat your bread, until you are turned into the earth from which you were taken, because earth you are and into earth shall you go* (Gn 3:17-19). Who does not know that these are the toils and troubles of the human race on earth? And that they would not have been so had the felicity to be found in Paradise been held onto is certainly beyond question; thus there should be no reluctance to take these words first and foremost in their proper historical sense. All the same a prophetic signification is to be looked for and expected, and it is this that the divine speaker here has chiefly in mind.

Nor was it for nothing, after all, that Adam himself was also wonderfully inspired at that point to give his wife the name of "Life," even adding, *since she it is who is the mother of all the living* (Gn 3:20), because these are not the words of the writer telling the story and making this statement, but are rather to be understood as the words of the first man himself, saying *since she it is who is the mother of all the living* in order to explain why he called her Life.

The tunics of skin; God's anxiety

39, 52. *And the Lord God made Adam and his wife tunics of skin and clothed them* (Gn 3:21). This too was done in order to signify something, but still it was done, like those things that were said in order to signify something, but were still said. What is required of the story teller giving an account of actual events, as I have said often enough and will not grow tired of saying more often yet, is that he should tell us that what was actually done was done, and what was actually said was said. But just as about things done one inquires both what it is that was done and what it may signify, so one does about words, both what it is that was said,

---

54. See 1 Tm 2:12.

and what it may signify. What we are told was said may have been meant to be taken metaphorically or literally, but its actually being said ought not to be treated as a metaphor.

53. *And God said: Behold, Adam has become like one of us in gaining knowledge of good and evil* (Gn 3:22). Since it was God who said this, by whatever means or in whatever way, but still God, his saying *one of us* is not to be understood in any other sense but as referring with the use of the plural to the Trinity, just as it was said earlier on, *Let us make man* (Gn 1:26), just as the Lord too said about himself and the Father: *We shall come to him and make our abode with him* (Jn 14:23). So in this way the result the proud man had longed for from the serpent's suggestion, *and you will be like gods*, was turned back on his own head. *Behold*, he says, *Adam has become like one of us.*

These are God's words, you see, spoken not so much in ironic mockery of this man, as with the intention of deterring the rest of us, on whose account these things were written down, from indulging in the same kind of pride. *He has become*, he said, *like one of us in gaining knowledge of good and evil*; how else are we to understand this but as an example given to strike fear into our hearts, because not only had he not become such as he had wanted to become, but he did not even keep hold of what he had become?[55]

Adam cast out of Paradise

40, 54. And now, God says, *what if he should ever stretch out his hand and take of the tree of life and eat, and should live for ever. And the Lord God sent him away from the paradise of pleasure to work the earth from which he had been taken* (Gn 3:22-23). First we have God's words, then the action that followed on the words. Adam, you see, had not only estranged himself from the life he was going to have received with the angels had he kept the commandment, but also from the one he had been living in Paradise in a privileged kind of bodily condition. So he naturally had to be barred from the tree of life, whether because it would enable him to continue in that privileged bodily condition through some invisible virtue in a visible thing, or because it was also a visible sign or sacrament of invisible Wisdom.[56] In any case he certainly had to be cut off from it, whether because he was now going to die, or because he was also being in a way excommunicated, as nowadays in this paradise which is the

---

55. And what was that? I think Augustine must be referring back to man's creation in God's image and likeness, Gn 1:26, to which he has just alluded a few sentences earlier. We have to remember that the Latin for "to become" is the same as for "to be made." So—but it would not really be English—we could have translated God's words as "Behold, Adam has been made like one of us," and then gone on to say that not only was he not made such as he wanted to be made (like gods), but did not keep what he had been made (God's image and likeness).

56. See Prv 3:18.

Church people are commonly barred from the visible sacraments[57] of the altar by Church discipline.

55. *And he threw Adam out and set him down over against the paradise of pleasure* (Gn 3:24). This too was done in order to signify something, but still it was done, so that the sinner might pitch up living, wretchedly of course, over against the paradise, by which the blessed life was also signified, *And he ordered the cherubim and the flaming sword which turns to guard the way to the tree of life* (Gn 3:24). We are of course to believe that this was done by heavenly powers even in the visible paradise, in order to mount a fiery guard there of angelic sentinels. It is not to be doubted however that it was not done pointlessly, even if it did not also signify something about the spiritual paradise.

Some other opinions about the story

41, 56. I am not unaware, however, that some people have thought those first human beings were in too much of a hurry in their desire for the knowledge of good and evil, and so wanted to grab before the time was ripe what was being kept back for them at a more opportune moment; and so the tempter induced them to offend God by picking too soon what they were not yet ready for. In this way they deprived themselves of the benefit of a thing which they would have been able to enjoy with profit to their health if they had approached it at the right time, as God wished; and so they were expelled and condemned as being now at variance with what God had intended. If by any chance these people mean to take that tree in a figurative sense, and not as a real one with real apples, this opinion may possibly lead to ideas that are agreeable to right faith and the truth.

57. There are also others who think that those two first human beings pre-empted their marriage and slept together before the one who had created them joined them together; this, they maintain, is what was signified by the name of the tree, and what was forbidden them before they should be joined together in holy matrimony at the appropriate time. As if, forsooth, we are to believe they were made at the age in which mature puberty is still to come, or as if that were not then lawful when it could first be done—which obviously would not be done before it could be; or perhaps the bride still had to be given away by her father and the vows officially pronounced and the wedding breakfast celebrated, and the dowry agreed upon and the register of marriages duly filled in and signed! The whole idea is ridiculous; besides which, it departs from the actual account of

---

57. Not that Augustine thought of the eucharist as two sacraments in the strict modern sense of "sacrament"; but since by "sacrament" he meant any sacred sign, or sign of the sacred (like the tree of life being a sacrament of divine Wisdom), and the bread and wine of the eucharist are both such signs, he often talked in this way of the "sacraments of the altar."

events, which is what we have undertaken to affirm, and have been affirming as far as God has wished.

Why Adam was led into sin by Eve, not also by the serpent; the dreadful example of Solomon

42, 58. A much more serious and difficult question is this: if Adam was already spiritual, "enspirited" in mind that is, though not yet in body, how could he have believed what was said by means of the serpent, that the reason God forbade them to feed on the fruit of that tree was that he knew that if they did they would be like gods on account of distinguishing between good and evil—as though the creator begrudged his creature such a great good as this? It would be astonishing if a man endowed with an "enspirited" mind could have believed such a thing. Or is it precisely because he could not possibly believe this that the woman was approached,[58] as being of little intelligence and perhaps still living according to the sense perception of the flesh, not according to *the spirit of the mind* (Eph 4:23)? And is that why the apostle did not accord her the image of God? That is what he says, you see: *Man indeed ought not to cover his head, since he is the image and glory of God; but woman is the glory of man* (1 Cor 11:7).

Not indeed that the mind of the woman cannot receive this image, since he says that in that grace we are neither male nor female,[59] but that perhaps she had not yet received what she was going to receive gradually as she came to recognize God under the guidance and management of the man. It is not for nothing, after all, that the apostle also says: *For Adam was the first to be formed, next Eve. And Adam was not led astray, but the woman being led astray became in transgression* (1 Tm 2:13-14), that is, so that the man also transgressed through her—because he also calls him a transgressor, where he says: *in the likeness of the transgression of Adam, who is the model of the one to come* (Rom 5:14); but all the same he denies that Adam was led astray. I mean when he was questioned himself, he did not say, "The woman whom you gave me led me astray, and I took a bite," but, "She," he said, "gave me of the tree, and I took a bite"; while as for her, "The serpent," she said, "led me astray."

59. Take Solomon, for instance, a man of such outstanding wisdom; are we really to believe that he believed there is anything to be gained by worshiping idols? But he was unable to resist the love of women dragging him into this evil,

---

58. Reading with two manuscripts *adita est* instead of the text's, both of the Maurists and CSEL, *addita est*, "the woman was joined on, was brought in." Treating *adita est* as a straightforward perfect passive of *adeo* may seem at first sight not to be accordance with the best classical Latin; but treating *adeo* as a transitive verb is good classical usage, so Dr. Duncan Cloud, professor emeritus of classics at Leicester University, assures me.

59. See Gal 3:28; also 2 Cor 3:18; Col 3:10.

and into doing what he knew ought not to be done, to avoid crossing his death-dealing darlings, on whom he was wasting and draining away his life.[60] In the same way Adam too was unwilling to cross the woman who had taken a bite from the forbidden tree after being led astray, and had given some to him so that they might eat together; he believed she might easily pine away without him to comfort her, if she found herself estranged from his way of thinking, and might quite simply perish from that conflict. So what led to his downfall was not any lust of the flesh, which he had not yet felt in *the law in the members fighting back against the law of the mind* (Rom 7:23), but a kind of loving concern for their mutual friendship, which often leads to God being offended, in case friends should turn unfriendly. That Adam should not have done this he was shown clearly by the result—the just sentence passed on him by God.

60. So then he also was deceived, but in a different kind of way; but I am convinced that in no way at all could he have been led astray by that serpentine trickery which took in the woman. This was given the proper name of seduction by the apostle,[61] where the persuasive argument, though false, was believed to be true; that is, that the reason God forbade them to touch that tree was because he knew they would become like gods if they did do so, as though having made them human beings he begrudged them any share in the godhead.

But even if the man's mind, in its proud self-assurance which could not escape God's scrutiny of his inmost being, was allured by a kind of greed for fresh experience, when he saw that the woman had not died after taking that food, as I suggested earlier on,[62] I still cannot imagine how, if he was already endowed with an "enspirited" mind, he could possibly have believed that God forbade them to eat of that tree out of envy or jealousy. But why go on about it? They were persuaded to commit that sin in whatever way such as they were could be persuaded. But the account of it was written down in the way in which it should be read by all, even if it would only be understood in the way in which it should be by a few.

---

60. See 1 Kgs 11:1-13.
61. See 2 Cor 11:3.
62. See above, 30,39.

Book XII

On the Heavenly Paradise: different kinds of vision

On Paul being snatched up to the third heaven, and to Paradise

1, 1. From the starting point of holy scripture, which is entitled Genesis, until the first man was sent away from Paradise, I have discussed the text and written down as best I could in eleven books what seemed certain to me, and have affirmed and defended it; and about its many uncertainties I have inquired, hesitated, balanced different opinions, not to prescribe to anyone what they should think about obscure points, but rather to show how we have to be willing to be instructed wherever we have been in doubt about the meaning, and to discourage the reader from the making of rash assertions where we have been unable to establish solid grounds for a definite decision.[1]

In this twelfth book, however, no longer engaged in the business of interpreting the sacred text which has claimed our attention hitherto, we will be freer to tackle in more detail the question of Paradise, because we do not wish to give the impression that we have shirked the problem raised by the apostle's apparently locating Paradise in the third heaven. He does this where he says: *I know a man in Christ fourteen years ago, whether in the body I do not know, or out of the body I do not know, God knows, such a one snatched up to the third heaven. And I know such a man, whether in the body or out of the body I do not know, God knows, that he was snatched up into Paradise and heard inexpressible words, which it is not permissible for a man to speak* (2 Cor 12:2-4).

2. The first question usually asked here is: what is it he calls the third heaven; next, whether he meant us to understand Paradise as being there, or whether after being snatched up to the third heaven he was also snatched up to Paradise, wherever Paradise might be; so being snatched up to the third heaven and into Paradise would not be the same thing, but first into the third heaven, and later on from

---

1. Reading *sententiae* with the Maurists and one manuscript instead of *scientiae* with CSEL and the other manuscripts. My translation really covers either reading; the second, more literally, would be rendered "any solid basis of knowledge."

there into Paradise. His words are in fact so ambiguous that it does not seem to me the question can be solved, unless somebody finds something, not in this passage from the apostle, but possibly in other passages of scripture or else in a convincing rational argument, which would show us that Paradise either is or is not in the third heaven. It is not, in any case, entirely clear what the third heaven is, whether it is to be understood as existing in the material or the spiritual sphere.

It could indeed be said that a person could only be snatched with the body into some bodily place. But as he stated the matter in such a way as to say that he did not know whether he was snatched up in the body or out of the body, would any have the nerve to say that they in fact know what the apostle says he did not know? However, if spirit cannot be snatched up to bodily places without body, and body cannot be snatched up to spiritual places at all, this very hesitation of his practically compels us to conclude that it is impossible to discern whether what he was snatched up to was something bodily or spiritual. No one, of course has the slightest doubt that he said this about himself.

On various ways of dreaming and different kinds of ecstasy

2, 3. You see, when bodily images are exhibited in dreams or in ecstasy, they are not distinguished at all from real bodies, except when we return to consciousness and realize that we were in a world of images which we had not imbibed through the senses of the body. Do any of us, after all, on waking up from sleep, fail immediately to realize that the things we were seeing were simply imaginary, though when we were seeing them while asleep we were unable to distinguish them from bodily sights seen by us when awake?

Though as a matter of fact there is something which I know has happened to me, and which consequently I have no doubt can also have happened or still happen to others; that is that when I have been seeing things in a dream I have been aware that I was seeing them in a dream, and even while still asleep have been aware and absolutely sure that those images, which have habitually gained my consent by false pretenses, were not real bodies but were being put before me in a dream.

However, I was once duped and tied up in knots in this kind of dream; I was trying hard to persuade a friend of mine, whom I was also seeing in the dream, that the things we were seeing were not bodies but the fantasies of dreamers, while he of course was also appearing to me in the same way as they were. But still I was also telling him that it was not really true that we were talking together, but that he too was also seeing something quite different in his sleep and was totally unaware that I in my sleep was seeing these things. Yet while I was exerting myself to persuade this very same man that he was not really there, I was also being driven to suppose that he really was, because naturally I would not be talking to him if I were absolutely sure without a shadow of doubt that he was not. Thus the soul of a sleeper, though somehow marvelously awake, could not but be led a pretty dance by the images of bodies, as if they really were the bodies themselves.[2]

4. As for ecstasy, I have been able to listen to one man, and him a rustic scarcely able to express what he perceived;[3] he knew both that he was awake and that he was seeing something, and not with the eyes in his head. So, to use his own words as far as I can recall them: "My soul," he said, "was seeing him, not my eyes; still I did not know whether he was a body or the image of a body." The man was not, you see, the sort of person naturally to make such a distinction; nonetheless he was a believer of such simplicity that as I listened to him it was as if I myself had seen what he was telling me that he had.

5. The question then is: how did Paul see Paradise? Was it in the same way as that dish let down from heaven appeared to Peter, or as everything that John recorded he had seen in the Apocalypse did to him, or as that field with the bones of the dead in it and their resurrection did to Ezekiel, or as God seated on his throne and the Seraphim in his presence and the altar from which a coal was taken to purify the prophet's lips did to Isaiah?[4] If so, then he obviously could have been left in ignorance about whether he was seeing it in the body or out of the body.

A closer look at the apostle's words, to learn what he may have seen, if it was when he was "out of the body"

3, 6. But if they were seen out of the body and were not bodies, we can still ask whether they were images of bodies, or the kind of substance which carries no bodily likeness, like God, like the human mind or intelligence or reason, like the virtues, prudence, justice, chastity, charity, loyalty and any others there are. These we count, distinguish, define by understanding them and thinking about them, not of course by observing their features or colors or what they sound like or smell like or taste like in the mouth, or what they inform those who feel and handle them about how hot or cold they are, how soft or hard, how smooth or rough. No, we observe them by a quite different kind of vision, a different light, a different manifestation of reality, and one that altogether outclasses the rest in its reliability.

7. Let us again, therefore, go back to the apostle's very words and investigate them more carefully, and make this our indisputable starting point, that the

---

2. I cannot help feeling that only someone of Augustine's uniquely tortuous—and nimble—mind could have had such an involuted, "Chinese boxes," "self-cataloguing library catalogue" kind of dream as this!

3. In all probability because his mother tongue was not Latin but Punic, the Phoenician language of the old Carthaginians.

4. See Acts 10:10-16; Rv 1:10-20; Ez 37:1-10; Is 6:1-13.

apostle had a much better and incomparably more thorough knowledge than we do, of what we lesser mortals try in whatever way we can to know about the bodily and non-bodily spheres. So then, if he knew that it is quite impossible to see spiritual things through the body and bodily things when out of the body, why did he not also discern by the very things he saw the manner in which he was able to see them? If, after all, he was certain that they were spiritual, why was he no less certain in consequence that he was out of the body when he saw them? If however he knew that they were bodily, why did he not also know that they could only be seen through the body? So then what makes him uncertain whether he saw them in the body or out of the body, unless perhaps he is also uncertain whether they were bodies or just the likenesses of bodies?

And so let us first see in the context of these words what he has no doubts about, and thus with the things he does have doubts about left over as a remainder, it will become clear, maybe, from what he is sure about how he can still be uncertain about these.

8. *I know*, he says, *a man in Christ fourteen years ago, whether in the body I do not know or out of the body I do not know, God knows, such a one snatched up to the third heaven* (2 Cor 12:2). So then he knows that fourteen years ago in Christ a man was snatched up to the third heaven. This he is not in the least unsure about, so neither should we be. But whether in the body or out of the body he is unsure about; so with him being unsure about it, which of us will have the audacity to know for certain? Surely it does not also follow from this, does it, that we should have doubts about there being a third heaven to which he says a man was snatched up? If, you see, the real thing itself was shown him, then the third heaven was shown him; while if some image in the likeness of bodily things was produced, then it was not the actual third heaven, but the showing was so arranged that he seemed to himself to climb up to the first heaven, above which he saw another, and on again climbing up to that he once more saw another one higher up still, so that when he had reached that he could say he was snatched up to the third heaven. But that what he was snatched up to was the third heaven he neither had any doubts about himself nor wished us to have any. That, I mean to say, is why he began with "I know," putting it first, so that the only ones who do not believe there is any truth in what the apostle says he knows are those who do not believe the apostle.

4, 9. So then, he knows that a man was snatched up to the third heaven; hence what he was snatched up to really and truly is the third heaven, not some bodily sign, like the one that was shown to Moses.[5] He for his part was so conscious of the difference between the very substance of God and the visible creature in

---

5. He means the pillar of cloud, the cloud of God's glory which came down to stand at the door of the tabernacle, when Moses went in there to speak with the Lord *face to face, as a man speaks to his friend*, Ex 33:7-11.

which God used to make himself present to people and their bodily senses, that he said: *Show yourself to me* (Ex 33:13.18). Nor was it some image of a bodily reality, like what John saw in the spirit and then asked what it was, and was given the answer, "It is a city," or "They are peoples" or something else, when he saw a beast or a woman or waters or something of that sort.[6] No, but *I know*, Paul said, *a man snatched up to the third heaven.*

10. But if he had wanted to give the name of a heaven to some spiritual image similar to a bodily one, then it would have also been in an image of his own body that he was snatched up and ascended there. So in this way he would also be calling it his own body though it was just an image of his body, as he called that a heaven though it was just an image of a heaven. In that case he would not be bothering to distinguish between what he knew and what he did not, saying, that is, that he knew a man snatched up to the third heaven, but did not know whether it was in the body or out of the body, but would simply be giving an account of his vision of those things, and calling them by the name of the things of which they were the likenesses. We too, after all, when giving an account of our dreams or of some revelation in them, say, "I saw a mountain, I saw a river, I saw three men"[7] and so on, giving the images the names of the things they represent. The apostle, though, "This," he said, "I know, that I do not know."

11. But if each was an appearance to him in the imagination, then each is equally known and equally unknown; while if the heaven's was a proper appearance—and is therefore known—how could the appearance of that man's body just be in the imagination?

12. I mean, if a bodily, material heaven was being seen, why did it elude him whether it was being seen with bodily eyes? While if it was uncertain whether it was being seen with the eyes of the body or with the spirit—and that is why it says, *whether in the body or out of the body I do not know*—how was it not also uncertain whether the bodily, material heaven was really being seen, or was being shown him in his imagination?

Again, if it was an incorporeal substance that was being seen, not in some bodily image, but in the way that justice, wisdom and anything of that sort is seen, and this is what that heaven was, then this too is evident enough, that anything of that sort cannot be seen with the eyes of this body. And accordingly, if he knew that it was something of that sort which he saw, he could have had no doubts that he did not see it by means of the body. *I know*, he says, *a man in Christ fourteen years ago.* Let nobody who believes me have any doubt that I know this; but whether *in the body or out of the body I do not know, God knows.*

---

6. See Rv 17:1-18.

7. Allusions, I suggest, to Nebuchadnezzar's dream, told him by Daniel, Dn 2:34-35; to Ezekiel's vision of the river issuing from the east gate of the temple in the new Jerusalem, Ez 47:1-14; and to the Lord appearing to Abraham in the guise of three men, Gn 18:1-15.

The apostle questioned a little more closely

13. So then, what do you know in fact, which you distinguish from what you do not know, so that believers may not be misled? *The same man*, he says, *was snatched up to the third heaven.* But that heaven was either material body or spirit. If it was body, and seen by bodily eyes, why is it known that that heaven exists and not known that it was also seen in the body? If however it was spirit, then it either presented the image of a body, and so it is as uncertain whether it was a body as it is uncertain whether it was seen in the body; or else it was seen in the way that wisdom is seen by the mind without any bodily images, and so it is no less certain that it could not have been seen through the body. So either then each thing is certain or each is uncertain; or else how is it certain that it was seen, and uncertain by what means it was seen?

After all, it is obvious that a thing of a non-bodily nature could not have been seen by him through the body. As for bodies though, even if they can be seen[8] without the body, they are certainly not thus seen by means of the body but in a manner that is very very dissimilar—if indeed there is such a manner. So it would be surprising indeed if this manner of seeing could mislead the apostle or force him to have doubts, as if it were completely similar; force him to say, if he did see a material heaven with eyes that were not material, that it was uncertain to him whether he saw it in the body or out of the body.

14. So then, one other possibility remains, since the apostle, who took such pains to distinguish between what he knew and what he did not, could not possibly be lying. This is that which we should understand him to be ignorant of, whether he was in the body when he was snatched up to the third heaven in the way that the soul is in the living body, either of someone who is awake or asleep or alienated from the senses of the body in ecstasy; or whether he departed totally from the body so that it lay there dead, a corpse, until on the completion of that revelation the soul returned to the dead limbs, and he did not just wake up like a sleeper or return to ordinary consciousness like someone alienated in ecstasy, but quite simply being dead came back to life.

In that case what he saw when snatched right up to the third heaven (which he also assures us that he knew), he saw in its own proper reality, and not by means of images. But because he was uncertain about the nature of this alienation from the body, whether it left his body totally and simply dead, or whether while the

---

8. This is the reading of the Maurists and most of the manuscripts: *etiam si possunt videri.* The CSEL editors, however, without quoting their manuscript support (presumably one manuscript at least), read: *etiam si non possent videri,* "even if they could not be seen without the body." This entirely fails to make the contrast, or to make sense of what he goes on to say. It looks like the correction of an earnest but singularly dim copyist, or else like a marginal scribble, "but they couldn't be," *non possent,* which an equally dim copyist then put in place of the text's *possunt.*

soul was in some way still there animating his living body, his mind was torn away to see or rather hear the *inexpressible words* (2 Cor 12:4) of that vision; that, perhaps, is why he said, *whether in the body or out of the body, I do not know, God knows.*

A scale of different kinds of vision

6, 15. Now anything that is seen not in images but as it properly is in itself, and is not seen through the body, is seen with a kind of vision that surpasses all the other kinds. I will carefully explain the differences between them, so far as the Lord may assist me. Here is an example in a single commandment. When you read, *You shall love your neighbor as yourself* (Mk 12:31), three kinds of vision take place; one with the eyes, when you see the actual letters; another with the human spirit,[9] by which you think of your neighbor even though he is not there; a third with the attention of the mind, by which you understand and look at love itself. Of these three the first is evident to everyone; it is the vision, after all, with which we see heaven and earth and everything in them that is visible to our eyes. Nor is it difficult to indicate the second one, by which absent bodies are thought about in a bodily fashion.[10] After all, even when we are standing in the dark, we can think about the sky and the earth and all the things we can see in them; we are not seeing anything with the eyes in our heads, but we are looking all the same at bodily images with the spirit,[11] whether they be true ones like the bodies we have seen and retained the memory of, or fictitious ones the imagination may have constructed. After all, we think about Carthage, which we know well, in one way, in another about Alexandria, which we do not know.[12]

But the third kind, by which love is understood and looked at, touches on things which do not have any images that are like them without actually being

---

9. *Per spiritum hominis*; here "spirit" is being used in its least spiritual meaning, for what are also called the inner senses, memory and imagination. No, not quite its least spiritual meaning; it is sometimes used for the vapor or fluid or whatever it was that the ancients thought filled the nervous system. But he will go on shortly himself to list the different applications of the word.

10. A slight textual problem here; the CSEL text reads, without offering any manuscript support: *quo absentia corpora corporalia cogitantur*, "by which absent bodily bodies are thought about." Such a pointless tautology surely cannot be what Augustine dictated. The Maurists, supported in CSEL's own apparatus by three manuscripts, omit *corpora*, and so give us, "by which absent bodily things are thought about." I break all the rules of textual criticism and combine both readings, only emending *corporalia* to *corporaliter*, which could have been misheard by stenographer or copyist as *corporalia*.

11. This time, *animo*.

12. See *The Trinity* VIII,6,9, where the same comparison is made between these two cities; there however it is used to illustrate the difference between knowing something and believing something on someone else's authority. But in the latter case one's picture of what one accepts on authority, one's picture of what Alexandria looks like, will still be the work of imagination, and not memory.

what they are. I mean, a man or a tree or the sun or any other bodies, celestial or terrestrial, can both be seen when present in their own shapes, and be thought about when absent in their images impressed upon the spirit, and so they give rise to the first two sorts of vision: one through the senses of the body, the other through the spirit in which those images are held. But is love seen in one way, in its proper appearance, when present, and in another way when absent, in some image that is like it? Of course not. Insofar, though, as it can be discerned by the mind, it is being discerned as it is in itself, more by one person, less by another; if however some kind of bodily image is being thought about, it is not love itself that is being discerned.

7, 16. These are the three kinds of vision, about which we have said something in earlier books as the subject matter seemed to require, though we did not mention their number.[13] But now that we have done this, and having raised the question are constrained to give it more copious consideration, we ought to label them with definite and suitable names, or repeated description will hold us up in our discussion of them. So let us call the first kind of vision "bodily," because it is perceived through the body, and presented to the senses of the body. The second one "spiritual"; anything, you see, that is not body and for all that is still something can now correctly be called spirit, and the image of an absent body, though like a body, is of course not itself a body, and neither is the glance or gaze by which it is perceived. The third one, finally, "intellectual" from the intellect, because if we call it mental from *mens*, mind, the very novelty of the word will render it disagreeable to the ear.[14]

17. Were I to give a more detailed explanation of these words, it would mean a more long-drawn-out and complicated treatment, for which there is really no need—certainly no urgent need. So then it is enough to know that something is called bodily either properly, when one is dealing with bodies, or in a transferred sense, as when it says: *because in him dwells the fullness of divinity in a bodily way*. Divinity, after all, is not something bodily; but because he also calls the sacraments of the Old Testament *shadows of what is to come* (Col 2:9.17), it was in comparison with shadows that he said the fullness of divinity dwells in Christ in a bodily way, because in him are fulfilled all those things that were represented by those shadows; and thus Christ is himself somehow the body of those shadows, that is to say he is the truth represented by those figures. So just as those figures are called shadows in a significantly transferred sense, and not properly, so too in saying that the fullness of divinity dwells in him in a bodily way, the apostle is using the word in a transferred sense.

---

13. The only place I have managed to locate is Book IX,2,3-4.
14. It is intriguing that Messrs Lewis & Short do list the word *mentalis*, as late Latin, giving as their reference Pseudo-Augustine, "Sermon 19, to the Brethren in the Desert," but not referring to this passage of ours here.

18. The word "spiritual," however, is used in several ways. I mean even the body, as it is going to be in the resurrection of the saints, is called spiritual by the apostle, where he says: *It is sown an ensouled body, it is raised a spiritual body*[15] (1 Cor 15:44), because in marvelous ways it will be subject to the spirit and thereby rendered both capable of doing anything and imperishable, so that without any need of bodily nourishment it will be kept alive solely by spirit; not because it is going to have an incorporeal, immaterial nature. After all, this body such as we now have does not have the same nature as the soul, is not what the soul is, just because it is called "ensouled."

Again, this air, or at least its movement or blowing, is called spirit, as where it says: *Fire, hail, snow, ice, spirit of the storm* (Ps 148:8). The soul too, whether of cattle or of human beings, is called spirit, as where it is written: *And who knows if the spirit of the sons of man ascends upwards, and if the spirit of cattle descends downward into the earth?* (Sir 3:21). The rational mind also is called spirit, where there is a sort of eye of the soul, where the image and recognition of God is to be found. In this sense the apostle says: *Be renewed in the spirit of your minds and put on the new man, who has been created in accordance with God* (Eph 4:23-24), while elsewhere he also says about the interior man: *Who is being renewed in recognition of God in accordance with the image of him who created him* (Col 3:10). Again, after saying: *I myself therefore serve the law of God in the mind but the law of sin in the flesh* (Rom 7:25), he refers to the same idea in another place where he says: *The flesh lusts against the spirit, and the spirit against the flesh, so that you do not do what you wish* (Gal 5:17). Thus what he called "mind" he also named "spirit." God too is called spirit, as the Lord said in the gospel: *God is spirit, and those who worship him ought to worship in spirit and truth* (Jn 4:24).

8, 19. It is not on any of these ways we have listed of using the word "spirit" that we have drawn in order to call this kind of vision we are now dealing with "spiritual," but on this one way which we find in the first letter to the Corinthians, in which "spirit" is distinguished from "mind" in the clearest possible terms. *For if I pray*, he says, *in a tongue my spirit is praying, but my mind is without fruit* (1 Cor 14:14). The tongue in this place is to be understood as talking in mysterious utterances of obscure significance; take away from these the mind's understanding, and nobody is built up or edified by hearing what they do not understand. This is why he also says: *For the one who talks in a tongue is not speaking to human beings but to God; for nobody hears, but the spirit is uttering*

15. See Book XI,18,24 above, and note 21 there for these difficult words, *animalis* and *spiritalis*. The way I have myself translated this text is: "When it is sown it embodies the soul, when it is raised it embodies the spirit," and have gone on to render the next sentence: "If the soul has its own embodiment, so does the spirit have its own embodiment." But here I have to keep the word "spiritual," because that is what he is explaining.

mysteries (1 Cor 14:2). This is sufficient indication that what he calls a tongue in this place is an utterance whose significance is wrapped up in images and likenesses of things, which need the penetrating glance of the mind in order to be understood. But when they are not understood, he says they are in the spirit, not in the mind. Thus he says more plainly: *If you bless in the spirit, how will the one who occupies the place of the outsider say "Amen" to your blessing, seeing that he does not know what you are saying?*(1 Cor 14:16).

So then, it is because when we speak with the tongue, that is, with the bit of the body we move around in the mouth, we are of course presenting signs or signals of things, not the things themselves, that by a transferred application of the word he called any presentation of signs before they are understood a tongue. When understanding dawns, which is the speciality of the mind, revelation is achieved, or recognition or prophecy or teaching. Accordingly he says: *If I come to you speaking in tongues, what do I profit you, unless I speak to you with some revelation or with some recognition, or with some prophecy or with some teaching?* (1 Cor 14:6); which means, when understanding is added to the signs, that is to the tongue, so that what is going on may go on not only in the spirit but also in the mind.

The point illustrated by the stories of Joseph and Pharaoh, and Daniel and Nebuchadnezzar

9, 20. Accordingly, for those people to whom signs were shown in spirit through the likenesses of bodily things, it was not yet prophecy, unless the mind lent its services for these signs to be understood; the one who could interpret what the other had seen was more of a prophet than the one who had seen it. From this it is evident that prophecy belongs more to the mind than to this spirit, which is called spirit in a special sense of its own, being a power of the soul lower than the mind in which likenesses of bodily things are imprinted. And so Joseph, who understood what the seven ears of corn and the seven oxen signified, was more of a prophet than Pharaoh, who saw them in dreams.[16] While his spirit indeed was molded for him to see, the other's mind was enlightened for him to understand. And thus Pharaoh had "a tongue," Joseph prophecy, because Pharaoh imagined the things, Joseph interpreted what he had imagined.

So then the one who sees in spirit only the signs of the things being signified through the images of bodily things is less of a prophet, and the one who is favored only with the understanding of them is more of a prophet; but most completely a prophet is the one who excels in both respects, so that he both sees in spirit the significant likenesses of bodily things and also understands them by the liveliness of his mind. This is how Daniel's pre-eminence was both tested and proved, when he not only told the king the dream he had seen but also

---

16. See Gn 41:1-32.

opened up to him what it signified.[17] The bodily images were evidently imprinted on his spirit, while their meaning was revealed to his mind.

So it is on this way of distinguishing spirit from mind, as when the apostle said: *I will pray in spirit, but I will also pray with the mind* (1 Cor 14:15), so that the signs of things might be molded in his spirit, and the understanding of them blaze in his mind; it is in accordance with this distinction, I repeat, that we are now labeling as "spiritual" that kind of vision in which we think upon the images of absent bodies.

The difference, if any, between intellectual and intelligible

10, 21. The intellectual vision, however, which is proper to the mind, is the more excellent kind. And it has never occurred to me at all that "intellect" can be said in several ways, as we have seen that "spirit" can be; whether we say "intellectual" though, or "intelligible," we mean the same thing. It is true that quite a few people do make a distinction, whereby it is the thing itself which can be perceived only by the intellect that is intelligible, while the mind or intelligence which understands is intellectual. But whether there is some real thing that can be discerned by the intellect alone, and that does not itself have intelligence and understanding, that is a big and difficult question.

On the other hand I do not suppose there is anyone who will either think or say that there is a real thing which enjoys intellectual perception and cannot also be intellectually perceived; mind, of course, cannot be seen except by mind. So because it can be seen it is intelligible, while it is intellectual because it can also see, according to this distinction. For this reason we shall put to one side that extremely difficult question, whether there is anything that is only intelligible and lacks intelligence, and from now on treat "intellectual" and "intelligible" as meaning the same thing.

The three kinds of vision to be considered one by one

11, 22. These three kinds of vision, therefore, bodily, spiritual, intellectual, must now be considered one by one, to enable the reason to climb up from the lower to the higher. We have already in fact put forward an example above, where all three can be seen together in one sentence;[18] when one reads, you see, *You shall love your neighbor as yourself* (Mk 12:31), the letters are seen with bodily vision, the neighbor thought about spiritually, love observed intellectually. But when the letters are not there in front of you they can also be thought about spiritually, and when your neighbor is present he can be seen with bodily vision, while love in its proper nature can neither be discerned with the eyes of

---

17. See Dn 2:1-45, where Daniel both tells King Nebuchadnezzar his dream of the great statue with a head of gold and feet of clay, and then interprets it.
18. See 6,15 above.

the body, nor thought about in spirit by means of an image resembling a body, but only known and perceived by the mind, that is, the intellect.

Clearly, bodily vision does not preside over either of the other kinds, but what is observed by it is brought to the notice of the spiritual vision as its presiding officer, because when anything is noted with the eyes its image is straightaway produced in the spirit. But its production is not discerned unless we lift our eyes from what we were seeing with them, and then find its image still in the spirit.[19] And if indeed the spirit is non-rational, like an animal's, that is as far as the eyes pass on their message; while if the soul is rational, the message is also passed on to the intellect which also presides over the spirit. Thus if what the eyes have drunk in and passed on to the spirit, for its image to be produced there, is also the sign of something; what it signifies will either be understood straightaway or be investigated, since meaning can neither be understood nor inquired about except by the functioning of the mind.

23. King Belshazzar saw the fingers of a hand writing on a wall,[20] and straightaway through a sense of the body the image of the thing done in a bodily way was imprinted on his spirit, and when the thing seen was done and finished with, the image remained in his thoughts. It was being seen in spirit and not being understood—nor was this sign understood earlier on when it was being produced in a bodily way and being manifested to his bodily eyes; but still he already understood it to be a sign, it being the mind's task to tell him so. And because he was inquiring what it signified, it was of course his mind that was engaged in the inquiry. With its meaning still undisclosed, Daniel came forward, and as his mind was enlightened by the spirit of prophecy he revealed to the anxious king what that sign portended. Thus it was he who was really the prophet by this kind of vision, proper to the mind, rather than the man who both saw with bodily vision the sign produced in a bodily way, and when it was finished still perceived its image in his spirit by thinking about it, and yet was able to do nothing with his intellect except know that it was a sign and inquire what it signified.

24. Peter in a state of mental alienation saw a container tied up by four strings[21] being lowered from heaven, full of a variety of animals, when he also

---

19. Here, once more, *in animo*.
20. See Dan 5:1-30.
21. See Acts 10:10-11. Since Peter was in Joppa (Jaffa) on the roof of a house overlooking the harbor, what he saw was most likely a sail; the text goes on to describe it just as being like a great cloth, using the same word in the Greek and Latin as the one employed for the grave clothes in which the body of Jesus was wrapped and laid in the tomb, Jn 19:40, 20:5. In Acts 27:40, where the crew of the ship taking Paul to Rome are about to beach it on the coast of Malta, Luke has them hoisting the foresail, *artemon*; but presumably what Peter saw was much bigger than that, the mainsail of a sea-going vessel; so perhaps "cloth" or "sheet" was the only appropriate word here. Sails are mentioned, in a rather unusual context, in Is 33:23; but the word used there in the Greek LXX would not have been suitable here, as in the singular it means "mast" or "weaver's beam," and only in the plural can it be used for what hangs from a weaver's beam, or is attached to a mast.

heard a voice: *Kill and eat*. As he was wondering about the vision on coming to himself, lo and behold the Spirit informed him of the messengers sent by Cornelius, saying: *Behold, men are asking for you; but arise, go down and go with them, because I have sent them*. When he came to Cornelius, he himself indicated what he had understood by that vision on hearing: *What God has cleansed do not you call common*; he said: *And God has shown me not to call any human being common or unclean* (Acts 10:13.19.15.28).

So then, when he saw that dish in a state of alienation from the body's senses, he also heard in spirit those words, *Kill and eat*, and *What God has cleansed do not you call common*. But on his being restored to normal consciousness, it was also in spirit that he thought about and took note of what he remembered having seen and heard. None of this was any kind of bodily reality; it was all images of bodily realities, whether when first seen in that state of alienation, or when remembered later on and thought about. When, however, he was wondering about it and asking himself how he was to understand those signs, it was the act of his mind striving to do this, but without success until the men who had come from Cornelius were announced. Now we have bodily vision also coming into play, and the Holy Spirit too saying to him, again in spiritual vision, *Go with them*, here both showing the signs and imprinting the words on his spirit; and so finally, assisted by God, his mind came to an intellectual understanding of what was afoot with all those signs.

Thus painstaking examination of these and similar events is enough to make it plain that bodily vision reports back to spiritual and spiritual in its turn reports back to intellectual.

12, 25. But when we are awake, and our minds not alienated from the senses of the body, we are then in a state of bodily vision, and able to distinguish from it the spiritual kind, in which we think about absent bodies in images. We think like this either by recalling in the memory bodies we know, or by picturing ones which we do not know but which all the same are somehow or other there in the working of the spirit, or by fashioning *ad lib* and by guesswork the images of bodies that simply do not exist anywhere. From all of these we easily distinguish the bodily realities we do see with our bodily sense of sight fixed on them there in front of us, so that we have no doubts about which are bodies and which the images of bodies.

But sometimes excessive concentration, or some disorder such as affects people who are delirious, or some interference by another spirit, whether a bad or a good one, will impress the images of bodily realities on the spirit as strongly as if the bodies themselves were being presented to the senses of the body, full consciousness still remaining in these same senses; and then the images of bodies being produced in the spirit are being seen just like the bodies themselves seen through the body. In this case one person present can be perceived with the eyes at the same time as another who is absent is being perceived in spirit as vividly as if it were with the eyes. We have in fact encountered people affected in this way, who were speaking both to actual bystanders, and also to others not there as if they were there too. But on coming to themselves again, some of them can relate what they have seen, others cannot—some people, after all, forget their dreams, others remember them.

When, however, the attention of the mind is totally turned aside and snatched away from the senses of the body, then you have what is more usually called ecstasy. Then whatever bodies may be there in front of the subject, even with his eyes wide open he simply does not see them at all, or of course hear any words spoken aloud. His attention is wholly taken up in gazing either at the images of bodies with the spiritual kind of vision, or with the intellectual kind at incorporeal realities that no bodily image can represent.

26. But when the soul[22] is alienated through and through from the senses of the body, and the spiritual vision is engaged with the images of bodily realities, whether in dreams or in ecstasy, the things being seen may have no significance, and then they are simply the imaginings of the soul itself. Even when we are awake, after all, and in full possession of our wits, unaffected by any alienation from the senses, we still turn over in our thoughts the images of many bodies that are not present to the body's senses; the only difference is that then we are always in a fit state to distinguish these from the real bodies in front of our eyes.

Sometimes however they do have a significant meaning, whether they are being presented to people in their sleep, or to people who are awake and seeing bodies in front of them with their eyes at the same time as they perceive the images of absent bodies with the spirit, or when the soul is totally alienated from the senses of the body by what is called ecstasy. This is a strange and wonderful way indeed; but[23] it can happen by the interaction of another spirit that the things this spirit knows are shown through images of this sort to the person it is interacting with, whether they are being unfolded to his understanding, or just as things understood by another. If these things, you see, are being demonstrated, and yet are naturally such as cannot be demonstrated by a body, what else can we say but that they are being demonstrated by some spirit?

---

22. Here *animus*, which I have also been translating "spirit" and "mind."
23. Reading with the Maurists, *sed commixtione alterius spiritus fieri potest*, with the support of one manuscript; the CSEL follows the others, and even earlier editors, in reading *si commixtione . . .*: "This is a strange and wonderful way indeed, if it can happen. . . ."

The question of divination

13, 27. Some people indeed would have it that the human soul has a certain power of divination in itself; but if that is the case, why can it not always make use of it, since it would always like to? Or is it that it does not always get help to enable it to do so? So when it does get help, this can scarcely come from nobody, can it, or from this body? Thus it remains that it gets help from a spirit. Next the question is, what kind of help? Is it that something is done in the body to loosen the soul from it, so to say, and thus to let its attention scout around until it comes to where it can see in itself significant likenesses that were already there but were not being seen, just as we also have many things in the memory which we are not always looking at? Or are such likenesses produced there which were not there before, or are they in some spirit to which the soul can break out, and see them there on emerging from the body?

But if they were already in the soul as properly belonging to it, why does it not consequently also understand them? Sometimes, after all, most times indeed, it does not understand. Or is it that just as its spirit has had help to see these likenesses in itself, so the mind also cannot understand the things the spirit contains unless it is given help? Or is the case, perhaps, not that bodily hindrances are removed, or their grip as it were loosened, so that the soul is thrust out by its own impetus at the things that are to be seen, but that it is taken directly up to these things itself, whether they are to be perceived by spiritual vision or also to be comprehended by the intellectual kind? Or finally, does it sometimes see these things in itself, sometimes through the interaction of another spirit? Whichever of these it is, there should be no hasty assertion of it.

About one point nonetheless there should be no doubt, that the bodily images which are perceived by the spirit are not always signs of other things, whether in people who are awake or asleep or delirious. It would be most surprising however, if there could be a case of ecstasy in which such likenesses of bodily things did not signify anything.

28. It is not in the least surprising, on the other hand, if those who have a demon sometimes say true things which are not apparent to the senses of bystanders. This must certainly happen by heaven knows what hidden mingling of spirits, so that it is as if there is just one spirit of sufferer and tormentor. But when it is a good spirit taking or snatching up a human spirit to see these things, there cannot be any doubt whatsoever that these images are signs of other things, of things which it is profitable to know about; this after all is a gift of God's. Discernment is certainly extremely difficult when the evil spirit acts is it were in a quieter manner, and without any harassment of the body says what it can through the human spirit it has taken over, or when it even says things that are

true and makes useful announcements, *transforming itself*, as it is written, *like an angel of light* (2 Cor 11:14), with the intention of first winning people's confidence in manifestly good matters and then seducing them to its own ends.

This sort, I consider, can only be discerned by the gift of which the apostle said, when talking about the variety of God's graces. *to another the distinguishing of spirits* (1 Cor 12:10).

14. It is no great thing, after all, to tell such a spirit apart when it does things or leads people to do them that are against good morals or the rule of faith; then it can be discerned by many people. But by this gift it is distinguished from the outset, while it is still striking many people as being good.

29. Nonetheless while good spirits instruct and evil ones deceive by means both of bodily vision and of the images of bodily realities which are exhibited in the spirit, the intellectual kind of vision on the other hand cannot be deceived; for either the one who supposes it means something different from what it actually does fails to understand,[24] or else if he does understand then it is *ipso facto* true. The eyes, you see, have nothing they can do when they see something like a body which they cannot distinguish from another, and the spiritual vision has nothing it can do when the likeness of a body is produced in the spirit which it is not capable of distinguishing from a real body. But then the intellect is applied, asking what those things signify or what useful lesson they are teaching, and it either finds the answer and attains its object, or it does not find it and holds itself in suspense, in order not to lapse by some perniciously rash judgment into a fatal error.

30. The sober intellect, assisted by God, makes a judgment about which and how many are the matters where it does the soul no harm to treat them as other than they really are. Thus good people may think a bad person is good, his badness being concealed; this is disastrous for him but does no damage to their integrity, if they are not mistaken about what the real goodness is that makes anyone good. Again, when people are asleep it does them no harm if they reckon that those things are real bodies which they see the likenesses of in their dreams. Nor did it do Peter any harm, when he was released from his shackles and led out by an angel, that he happened to think in this unexpected miracle that he was seeing a vision,[25] or when he answered in that ecstasy: *Certainly not, Lord, because I have never eaten anything common or unclean* (Acts 10:10-14), thinking that the things being shown him in the dish were real animals.

When we find such things to be other than we thought they were as we were seeing them, we do not think we have to repent of their having seemed like that to us, if some obstinate infidelity is not being brought to light, or a vain, a sacrile-

---

24. And hence there is no intellectual vision. Not, I think, a very convincing line of argument.
25. See Acts 12:6-9.

gious opinion.[26] Accordingly, even when the devil deceives people with bodily visions, it does them no harm that he is playing tricks on their eyes, if they do not go astray over the truth of faith and sound understanding, which[27] God teaches to those who submit themselves to him. Or if he plays tricks on the soul by the images of bodies in spiritual vision, so that it takes something to be a real body that in fact is not, this does no harm to the soul, provided it does not yield to his pernicious persuasiveness.

The question of wet dreams

15, 31. In this connection the question is sometimes raised about the consent given by people in a dream, when they seem to themselves to be copulating, either against their own resolution or even against lawful morals. This only happens when things which we also think about while awake, not with pleasurable consent, but as required in order to talk about such matters for some reason or other, when these things are brought to our notice in dreams and expressed in such a way that the flesh is of its nature moved by them, and emits through the genital channels what by nature it has stored up. Thus I would of course be unable to say this unless I was also thinking about it. Then if the images of the bodily realities, which I have been thinking about in order to say all this, were displayed to me as vividly in a dream as the actual bodies are displayed to people when awake, I would find myself doing that which could not be done without sin if I were awake.

Could anybody, after all, not think about what he is saying when some necessity of a sermon or conversation requires him to talk about his sexual activity? Well, when the mental pictures that occur in his thoughts while he is speaking are also imprinted on his vision while he is dreaming in such a way that he cannot distinguish between them and the real coupling of bodies, the flesh is at once stirred into movement, and the result is what usually follows upon this movement; and this happens without sin, just as when he was awake he said without sin what he undoubtedly thought about in order to say it.

However, a well-disposed soul, purified by better desires, slays many cravings which have nothing to do with this natural movement of the flesh; which chaste people keep on a tight rein while awake, but cannot do so while asleep,

---

26. This qualification seems to be somewhat out of place here; presumably if these faults are being brought to light by whatever we have been seeing in dreams and other forms of "spiritual vision," then what we have been seeing has been "true"; or at least our "intellectual vision" of its meaning is true. In any case, what we would now be repenting of is the infidelity and false opinions our dreams etc. are convicting us of, not the unreality of the dreams themselves.

27. Reading *quam* with one manuscript, instead of the *quae* of the CSEL text (which is non-construable), or the *qua* of the Maurists, which would yield the sense, "by which God teaches. . ."

because they have no control over the formation of bodily images which cannot be distinguished from actual bodies in their dreams, and because of its good disposition. Some of its merits shine out even in dreams. Thus Solomon preferred wisdom to everything else even while he was asleep, and scorning all other things asked the Lord for her; and as scripture assures us, this found favor with the Lord, who was not slow to give him a good reward for a good desire.[28]

Grading the senses and kinds of vision

16, 32. All that being said, bodily visions are the concern of the body's sensitivity, which distributes itself through five streams, as it were, capable of covering long distances, especially the one that is the finest and keenest one in the body and thus more akin to the soul than the others. This one, that is to say the light that is first poured out through the eyes, flashes out in rays from the eyes to gaze upon visible objects. Next this light is joined in a kind of mixture, first with pure air, secondly with foggy, cloudy air, thirdly with a denser humidity, fourthly with the grossness of earth, to make up the five senses together with the sense of the eyes in which this light reigns supreme by functioning all by itself. I recall having discussed all this in the fourth book and again in the seventh.[29]

Now this heaven, visible to the eyes, from which shine the great lights and the stars, is of course more excellent than all the bodily elements, just as the sense of the eyes is the most excellent in the body. But because every spirit without a doubt outclasses every kind of body, it follows that the spiritual nature, even the sort that has the images of bodily things imprinted on it, outclasses that bodily heaven, the sky, not by its location in space but by its worth in nature.

33. Here a very curious fact emerges, that while spirit comes before body, and the image of a body comes after the body, still nevertheless, because that which is last in time comes to be in that which is first in nature, the image of a body in the spirit outclasses the actual body as it is in itself. And we are certainly not to assume that a body makes anything in the spirit, as though the spirit were subjected to the body making something out of it as out of some material. The one that makes, after all, outclasses in every possible way the thing out of which it makes something, while in no way whatsoever does body outclass spirit, as spirit most evidently does body.

So then, although we first see a body which we had not seen before, and from that moment its image begins to be in our spirit, by which we can remember it when it is no longer there in front of us, still it is not the body that makes its own image in the spirit, but the spirit itself which makes it in itself with a wonderful

---

28. See 1 Kgs 3:5-15.
29. See Book IV,34,54, and note 48 there; VII,13,14,20, and notes 13, 14 and 15; 17-19,23-25, and note 17, about the ventricles of the brain and the inner senses.

swiftness that is infinitely removed from the sluggishness of the body; so no sooner is the body seen by the eyes than its image is formed without the slightest interval of time in the spirit of the person seeing. Again with hearing; unless the spirit immediately formed in itself the image of a voice heard by the ears, and stored it in the memory, you would not know whether the second syllable was the second, since the first would now no longer exist, having vanished after striking the ear.

And thus all the value of speech, all the sweetness of singing, finally every single movement of the body in all our activity, would collapse and fall away and achieve no progress at all, if the spirit did not retain in the memory the body's movements as they were performed, to join the following ones onto them in any activity; and of course it only retains them by constructing their images in itself. Again, the images of future movements precede the conclusions of our actions. Is there anything, after all, that we do with the body, which the spirit has not anticipated by thinking about it, and by looking in itself at the likenesses of all the visible operations involved, and after a fashion arranging them in due order?

Some instances of paranormal or demonic communication

17, 34. It is difficult to find out and explain how these spiritual likenesses of bodily realities in our spirits[30] become known even to unclean spirits, or what kind of obstacle our souls experience from these earthly bodies,[31] so that we are unable in our turn to see them in our own spirits. There have, all the same, been the most definite and certain indications to establish that what people have been thinking has been made public by demons; and yet if these could observe in people the inner beauty of their virtues, they would not even try to tempt them. Thus if the devil had been able to observe in Job that wonderful, noble patience of his, he would undoubtedly have been most unwilling to be defeated in his effort to tempt him.[32]

For the rest it should cause no surprise that they make public things already done somewhere a long way away, which are confirmed as being true a few days later. They are enabled to bring this off, you see, both by the acuteness of their perception even of bodies, which incomparably outclasses ours, and also by the remarkable swiftness of their bodies, which are of course of a far and away finer material than ours.[33]

---

30. Again, *in animo nostro*.
31. An allusion to Wis:9:15; "For the perishable body weighs down the soul, and the earthly dwelling oppresses the mind thinking many things."
32. See Job 1:20-22; 2:9-10.
33. As has been noted several times before, demons (and angels) were commonly thought to have airy bodies. This and the other paranormal phenomena he is talking about here are also discussed in *Answer to the Academics*, I,6,16—7,21.

35. We have also heard of someone suffering from an unclean spirit, who while confined to his house used to announce when a priest from twelve miles away was setting out to visit him, and then say where he had got to through all the stages of his journey, and how near he was getting, and when he entered the estate, and the house, and the bedroom, until he stood there in front of him. The patient observed none of this with his eyes, but if he was not observing it in some way or other, he would not be stating it all so accurately. But the man was in the grip of a fever, and used to say all this as if he were delirious. And perhaps he really was delirious, but because of all this he was thought to be suffering from a demon.

He would not take any food from his own family, but only from that priest. He used to put up a violent resistance against his family, as much as his strength allowed him to, and only when that priest arrived would he quiet down, and submit only to him and answer him submissively. His loss of wits however, or demonic possession, did not give way even to the priest, except when he was cured of his fever, as delirious people usually are cured, and after that he did not experience the same sort of thing again.

36. We also know beyond a shadow of doubt of a person in a delirium foretelling that a certain woman would shortly die. But this certainly did not look like divination; rather he was recalling it as an event that had already happened, because when her name was mentioned in his presence, "She's dead; I've seen her carried out," he said; "They passed by here with her body," and this while she was still living, hale and hearty. But a few days later she died suddenly, and was carried out past the place that he had foretold.

37. Again there was a boy at our place who at the onset of puberty used to suffer the most acute pain in the genitals, and the doctors were quite unable to diagnose it, except that they could see that the penis itself was withdrawn so far inwards that not even when they had cut off the foreskin, which was hanging down at quite inordinate length, could it appear, but later on it was pulled out with some difficulty. Meanwhile a sticky, stinging fluid would be burning the testicles and groin. But he did not suffer the acute pain continuously; and when he did suffer it, he would wail and scream at the top of his voice and toss and turn, as people usually do when suffering excruciating bodily pain, but would still remain in full possession of his wits.

Then between his cries he would be snatched away from all his senses and lie there with his eyes open, seeing none of the people standing round, not moving at all or responding to any amount of pinching. After a while he would seem to wake up, and no longer being in any pain would give an account of what he had seen. Then after the interval of a few days he would go through the same thing all over again. In all or nearly all of his visions he said he saw two people, one of advanced age the other a boy, by whom the things were told or shown him, which he declared he had heard and seen.

38. One day he saw the joy and happiness of the godly playing their harps in a marvelous light, and the various and atrocious pains of the ungodly in outer darkness, with these two persons leading him round and showing it all to him and suggesting how each sort earned their respective good and bad lot. Now he saw this on Easter Sunday, when he had suffered no pain through the whole of Lent, having been spared it scarcely three days before.

But at the actual start of Lent he had seen these two promising him that for forty days he would feel no pain; later on they gave him what you could call medical advice, to have the length of his foreskin cut off, and when that was done he had no pain for a long time. When however he once more felt the same sort of pain and began to see the same sort of things, he again received advice from them, this time that he should walk into the sea up to his groin, and come out again after a certain length of time; and they promised him definitely that from then on he was not going to suffer that extreme pain, but only the inconvenience of that sticky fluid; and so it turned out. Nor after that did he ever experience such a withdrawal of his mind from his senses, or see any such things as he had done previously when in the middle of his pain and horrifying screams he had been suddenly snatched away and fallen silent. Afterwards, though, when the doctors had cured the rest of his ills and restored him to health, he did not keep to his resolution of holiness.

A tentative assessment of these phenomena

18, 39. Should anyone be able to trace the causes of these visions and divinations and of the forms they took, and definitely establish them, I would much rather listen to him than have people expect me to analyze them myself. Nonetheless I shall not hide what I think, stating it though in such a way that the learned do not laugh at me as positively asserting it, and the unlearned do not lap it up as if I were teaching it; instead I would have them both take me as inquiring and debating possible answers rather than knowing the right ones.

I compare all these visions with the things people see in dreams. These too, after all, are sometimes false sometimes true, sometimes troubled sometimes tranquil; while the true ones are sometimes entirely like events to come, clearly described, sometimes foretelling them under obscurely significant signs and in a kind of figurative language. Well, it is exactly the same with these extraordinary cases. But people love to marvel at things outside their experience and to look for the causes of unaccustomed events, while for the most part they are not interested in knowing about similar things of daily occurrence which often spring from even more hidden origins.

Take words: that is to say the signs we employ in speaking; on hearing an unusual word they first ask what it is, that is what it means, and on learning that, they then go on to ask what it comes from, while about so many words they use all the time when talking they have not the slightest idea what they come from and could not care less. So too when something unusual happens whether in the realm of bodily or spiritual vision, they anxiously ask about its causes and meaning, and pester the pundits for an explanation.

40. Now it has been my practice, when someone asks me, for example, what "skere" means, and I reply "steep or sheer,"[34] and that does not satisfy him, but he goes on to ask what the word "skere" comes from, my practice has been to toss the ball back to him and ask him what "sheer" comes from. Of course he has no idea, but because it is quite a common word, he happily puts up with not knowing its origin, while whenever a new word has come to his ears, he thinks it is not enough to learn what it means unless he also inquires what it comes from.

So then, whenever anyone inquires of me how it is that visions similar to bodily realities are seen in ecstasies, which rarely happen to the soul, I toss the ball back and inquire how they are seen by people in their sleep, which is part of the soul's everyday experience; and nobody is concerned, or not very much, to look into that point, as though, forsooth, the nature and source of such visions is less wonderful simply because they happen every day, and a matter of less concern simply because everybody has them. Or else, if they are acting rightly in not inquiring about these things, they would be acting even more rightly if they were not so curious about the other sort as well.

I myself, however, am filled with much greater wonder, not to say total stupefaction, at the swiftness and ease with which the soul manufactures in itself the images of bodies which it has seen through the eyes of the body, than at the visions seen in dreams or even in ecstasies. But in any case, whatever the nature of such visions may be, it is certainly not something bodily. If you are not satisfied with knowing this, go and inquire of others what also gives rise to them; I myself, I readily admit, just do not know.

The causes of such visions are to be found either in the body or the spirit, or in the action of good or evil spirits

19, 41. Many physical conditions, of course, like extreme pallor, blushing, trembling, or even diseases, sometimes have their causes in the body, sometimes in the soul; in the body when it gets soaking wet, or when food or some other substance is inserted into the body from outside; in the soul on the other hand when it is troubled with fear or embarrassed with shame, or is angry or in love or anything of that sort. It is indeed entirely natural if the animating and controlling

---

34. The Latin words are *catus* and *prudens vel acutus*. Finding an unusual English word very like an ordinary one necessarily took me away from words meaning the same as the Latin. It would have been wonderful if "cute" had been an unusual word, being related to "acute" in much the same way as *catus* to *acutus*, with a more or less similar range of meanings. But alas, it isn't.

element causes more acute agitation, the more acutely it is affected itself. Well, there is plenty of evidence to show that the soul in its turn is sometimes acted on by the body, sometimes by the spirit, to rouse it to seeing things that it is not being informed about by the body's senses but by some incorporeal reality, and to wake it up to noticing them in such a way that it cannot make out whether they are actual bodies or the likenesses of bodies.

The body acts on it to this effect either by its natural interaction, as in the case of dreams—it is our bodies, after all, that need sleep; or by disturbing the senses with some kind of ill health, as when delirious patients simultaneously see actual bodies and visions like bodies as if they were there in front of their very eyes; or when the senses are totally blocked off, as when people have been seriously injured, and as their condition grows worse they are often absent from the body for a long time,[35] and then on being restored to their fellows they say they have seen many things.

The spirit[36] is the agent, on the other hand, when souls are snatched away into a state of alienation while the body is in good health and uninjured, whether this happens to them in such a way that they both see bodies with the senses of the body and also some similar things in the spirit which they cannot distinguish from bodies, or whether they are totally removed from the senses of the flesh, and while perceiving through them nothing whatsoever are dwelling by that spiritual vision among the likenesses of bodies. But when it is an evil spirit that snatches souls away like this, it makes them into demoniacs or fanatical enthusiasts or false prophets, while when a good spirit does so, it makes them faithful speakers of mysteries or true prophets if their understanding is also enlightened, or ensures that they see and make public what it was opportune for them to be shown at that time.

Strict limits to the influence of the body

20, 42. But when the cause of such visions being observed comes from the body, it is not the body that displays them; it does not, after all have the power to form anything spiritual. But sometimes the route of the brain's attention, which governs the mode of sense perception, is either stilled or disturbed, or even blocked off. Thus the soul, which cannot of its own accord cease from functioning in this way, finds itself not allowed by the body (or not fully and freely allowed) to sense bodily realities or direct the force of its attention to bodily things. So it throws up the likenesses of bodily things in its spirit or else gazes at

---

35. Just to remind ourselves that for Augustine, in the Platonic tradition of thought, the soul is the human person, the body is the person's dwelling, its senses the windows through which the person looks out onto the bodily world.
36. That part or factor of the soul responsible for what he has been calling spiritual vision, not to be confused of course with the good and evil spirits he is shortly going to mention.

ones that are held up to it; and if it throws them up itself, they are imaginative fancies, while if it is gazing at ones held up to it they are showings.

Finally, when the eyes are sightless or have been put out, visions of this sort do not occur, because the cause is not in the base of the brain which governs attention to sense perceptions, although in this case too an obstacle to the observation of bodily realities is put there by the body. The blind, in fact, see things more when asleep than when awake; when they are asleep, after all, the sensory channel in the brain which leads the attention to the eyes is stilled, and for that reason the attention is turned away to something else and observes the things seen in dreams as if specific kinds of bodies were actually present, so that the sleeper seems to himself to be awake, and thinks that he is seeing actual bodies, not just bodily likenesses. But when the blind are awake, the intention of seeing is led along those routes, and on coming to the place of the eyes is unable to reach out to the world outside, but has to stop there; so while knowing they are awake they feel they are in greater darkness by staying awake even in the daytime, than by going to sleep whether in the day or at night.

I mean, even those of us who are not blind frequently sleep with our eyes open, seeing nothing through them—but not thereby simply seeing nothing, since we are observing the stuff of dreams in the spirit. If on the other hand we have our eyes closed while awake, we are not receiving the visions of either the sleeping or the waking state. However, the fact that the sensory channel from the brain, being neither stilled nor disturbed nor blocked off, reaches our eyes and conducts the soul's intention as far as these doors of the body, closed though they be, means that we can indeed think about the images of bodies without in any way mistaking them for real bodies that are perceived through the eyes.

43. The only thing that makes a difference is where the hindrance to the perception of bodily realities is set up, when it occurs in the body. If, you see, it is set up in the actual outlets and so to say doorways of the senses, like the eyes, the ears and the other senses of the body, only the perception of bodily realities is hindered, while the soul's attention is not diverted elsewhere in such a way that it will take the images of bodies for the bodies themselves.

But if the cause is inside, in the brain, from which the channels are directed to the perception of things outside, then this means the stilling or disturbing or blocking off of the very agencies with which the soul is striving to observe or perceive things in the world outside. But since it does not just abandon its yearning for them, it proceeds to fashion their likenesses with such accuracy and vividness that it is incapable of telling the difference between them and these images of them, and so does not know whether it is among these or those; and when it does know, it is in a way quite other than when it is mulling over the likenesses of bodies that occur in its thoughts, a way that can only be grasped by those who have experienced it. Thus it was, you see, that once in my sleep I knew I was seeing things in a dream, and yet did not distinguish those likenesses of bodily realities I was seeing from real bodies, in the way we habitually do when thinking about them even with our eyes closed or when we are standing in the dark.

If it is in the brain, through which the mind tries to direct its attention to things in the outer world, that something occurs to divert it elsewhere, then it does indeed know that it is perceiving the likenesses of bodies, not bodies themselves; or if it is less sophisticated and does regard them as being actual bodies, it at least senses that it is seeing them with the spirit, not the body. But this is very different from the awareness with which it is present to its own body, as when it comes to the sense outlets and finds them closed. Thus the blind in their turn know that they are awake when they distinguish with full knowledge and certitude the likenesses of bodies they are thinking about from the bodies they are unable to see.

Whatever their cause, the nature of spiritual visions is always the same

21, 44. But sometimes, though the body is in good health and the senses are not stilled in sleep, the soul is snatched away by some hidden spiritual operation to the vision of things which are like bodies; but this does not mean, just because the manner is different, that the nature of the vision is different, since there are of course differences even in the causes that stem from the body. Thus it is not by being asleep that those who are delirious have the sensory channels disturbed in the head, so that they see the same as dreamers see, when their attention is diverted by sleep from their waking senses to seeing these other things. So while it happens through sleep in one instance and in another not, still in each case the things seen are of no other kind but of the nature of spirit, from which or in which the likenesses of bodies are constructed.

Thus while the attention is being alienated by a different cause when the soul is snatched away by some hidden spiritual power from someone who is awake and in good health, so that instead of bodies it sees in spirit the express likenesses of bodily realities, the nature of the visions is still the same. Nor can it be said that when the cause is in the body, then the soul is just churning out of itself the images of bodies, as it is also in the habit of doing when just thinking, without any presentiment of future events, while when it is snatched away in the spirit to see them, it is then being shown things by God. Scripture quite openly says, after all: *I will pour out from my spirit upon all flesh, and young men shall see visions, and old men shall dream dreams* (Jl 2:28), attributing each to the divine activity; and: *The angel of the Lord appeared to the man*[37] in dreams, saying: Do not be

---

37. The Maurist editors very naturally put "to Joseph" instead of *homini*; but this latter is in all the manuscripts, and is almost certainly what Augustine actually dictated, or wrote, while no doubt meaning to say or write *Joseph*.

afraid to take Mary as your wife, and again: *Take the child and go into Egypt* (Mt 1:20; 2:13).

Some unusual cases of divination

22, 45. And so I do not believe that a human being's spirit is ever taken up by a good spirit to see images of this kind unless they signify something. When however the cause of the human spirit fixing its attention upon them more expressly is in the body, it is not to be supposed that they always signify something; but the times they are significant are when they are breathed by a spirit by way of demonstration into someone who is asleep or suffering something else in the body which alienates from the senses of the flesh.

We also know that thoughts can be inserted by some hidden prompter into people's minds when they are awake and not afflicted with any disease or mentally disturbed, thoughts that will prove prophetic when uttered; and this not only when the person has something else in mind, like Caiaphas the high priest, who prophesied when he did not have the slightest intention of so doing,[38] but also when they deliberately undertake to say something by way of divination.

46. There were, for example, some young men who for a joke, to pull people's legs, pretended while in a staging post for travelers that they were astrologers, though they scarcely knew one of the twelve signs of the zodiac from another. When they noticed the innkeeper's astonishment at the things they were saying, and heard him swear they were absolutely true, they boldly proceeded to say more; and he vouched for it all, his astonishment knowing no bounds. Finally he asked them about the welfare of his son, whom he was eager to see after a long absence, and he was anxious about what might have happened to him to delay his return home so much beyond the expected time of his arrival.

Now they did not care if the truth would out after their departure, provided at least that they could make the man happy there and then; so they answered, since they would soon be on their way, that he was safe and sound and drawing near, and was going to arrive that very day on which they were saying this. They had no fear, you see, that when the day passed without this happening the man would follow them the next day to complain. Why say more? While they were still getting ready to depart, lo and behold the lad suddenly came in as they were still standing around.

47. Again, there was another youth dancing before a concert, in a place where there were many idols set up throughout some festival of the pagans; he was not possessed by any spirit, but was parodying the possessed in a mock imitation, with the full knowledge of those standing around and watching. It was the custom, you see, when the sacrifices were finished and the dervishes had done

---

38. See Jn 11:49-51.

dancing[39] before dinner, that if any youngsters wanted to play about in that way after dinner, none of them would be forbidden.

So then this fellow, having called for silence in an interval between dances and surrounded by a laughing crowd, jokingly foretold that during the very night which was coming on, in that very wood nearby, a man was going to be slain by a lion, and that with the dawning of the day the crowd was going to pour out to gape at the corpse, leaving the place of that festival quite deserted. And so it happened, though to everyone present it was evident enough from all his gestures that he said this as a joke and part of the game, his mind being in no way disturbed or alienated. He himself was more astonished than anybody, since he knew better than anybody else in what spirit and tone of voice he had spoken.

48. How, we ask, do these visions come to a person's spirit? Are they formed there to begin with, or are they introduced already formed and then perceived by a kind of joint action, with angels showing human beings their own thoughts in this way, and the likenesses of bodily things which they preform in their own spirit through their knowledge of future events? They indeed can also see our thoughts, not of course with eyes, because it is not with the body but with the spirit that they see them. This though is the difference, that they know our thoughts even if we do not want them to, while we cannot know theirs unless they are shown to us. This in my opinion is because they have it in their power to conceal their thoughts by spiritual means, just as we, by putting things in the way, can hide our bodies from being seen by other people's eyes.

And then, what is it that happens in our spirit, so that sometimes we observe only significant images, but do not know whether they signify anything? Sometimes they are perceived to signify something but we are left in ignorance of what it is, while at yet other times the human soul is vouchsafed something like a full demonstration and both sees them in spirit and sees with the mind what they signify. To know the answers to these questions is extremely difficult, and if we should already happen to know them, to analyze and explain them would be a task unimaginably laborious.

Summing up about the spiritual element in us, the locus of spiritual vision

23, 49. The one thing certain, which I think it is enough to insist on for the time being, is that there is a kind of spiritual element in us where the likenesses of bodily things are formed. This can be when we make contact with a body through a sense of the body, and its likeness is straightaway formed in the spirit and stored away in the memory. Or it can be when we think about absent bodies already known to us, so that a kind of actual spiritual seeing is formed out of

---

39. A rather free rendering of *agitatisque fanaticis*, "and the fanatics having been agitated"—which would not, I think, be a more acceptable translation.

them, as they were already there in the spirit even before we started thinking about them. Or it can be when we look at likenesses of bodies which we do not know but still do not doubt their existence; so we picture them not as they really are but as it happens to occur to us. Or it can be when we think *ad lib* or by guess-work about other things that either do not exist or are not known to do so by us. Or it can be when, coming from heaven knows where, various forms of bodily likenesses churn around in our thoughts without our wanting them to in the least.

Or else it is when we are about to engage in some bodily activity, and we arrange in our thoughts the things that will be involved in it, and in fact run over everything first in our thoughts. Again in the action itself, when we are either saying or doing something, for us to be able to perform all the bodily movements involved, their likenesses have to precede them inwardly in the spirit—not even the shortest syllable, after all, could be uttered in its proper place, unless it had been foreseen and provided for.

Again it happens when sleepers see dreams that signify either something or nothing or when the inner sensory channels are disturbed by bodily ill health, and in consequence the spirit so mixes up the images of bodies with real bodies that they can scarcely be told apart, or indeed not at all, and they either signify something or spring up without any significance in them whatsoever. It happens when some disease or bodily pain gets so much worse that it quite blocks off the internal routes through which the soul's attention was striving to reach out and sense things through the flesh; and so with the spirit being whisked away much more deeply than in sleep, the images of bodily things spring up in it or are shown to it, whether they signify anything or appear without any signification.

It happens, without any cause arising from the body, when the soul is lifted up to see such bodily likenesses by some spirit picking it up and snatching it away, and it mixes them up with the bodily realities seen by its simultaneous use of the senses. It happens when the soul is so caught up by some spirit that it is alienated from every sense of the body and is turned away from there to have its attention gripped by the spiritual vision of likenesses of bodies, in which case I do not know whether any can be seen that have no significance at all.

The hierarchical order of the three kinds of vision

24, 50. So then, this spiritual nature, on which it is not bodies but the like-nesses of bodies that are impressed, has visions of a kind inferior to that enjoyed by the light of the mind and the understanding. This is what both assesses these inferior ones and perceives things which as well as not being bodies have no forms or shapes similar to bodies, such as the mind itself and every good disposi-tion of the soul, as well as their opposites, its vices, which are very properly blamed and condemned in human beings. In what other way, after all, is the understanding observed but by understanding? So too *charity, joy, peace, long-suffering, kindness, goodness, faithfulness, gentleness, restraint* (Gal 5:22-23) and the rest, by which one draws near to God, and God himself, *from whom are all things, through whom all things, in whom all things* (Rom 11:36).

51. Accordingly, it is indeed in one and the same soul that visions are brought about; ones perceived through the body, like this bodily heaven and earth and whatever in them can be known, to the extent that they can be; ones like bodies that are seen by the spirit, about which we have already said so much; and ones that are understood by the mind, which are neither bodies nor the likenesses of bodies. But they have, of course, their proper order, and one kind ranks higher than another. Thus spiritual vision outclasses the bodily kind, and in turn the intellectual outclasses the spiritual.

There can, after all, be no bodily vision without the spiritual, seeing that the moment contact is made with a body by a sense of the body, some such thing is also produced in the spirit, not to be exactly what the body is, but to be like it; and if this were not produced, neither would there be that sensation by which extraneous things present are sensed. It is not the body, you see, that senses, but the soul through the body, using it as a kind of messenger in order to form in itself the message being brought in from outside. And so no bodily vision can occur unless spiritual vision also occurs simultaneously; but they are not told apart except when the sense is withdrawn from the bodily object, and what was being seen through the body is now still to be found in the spirit. Spiritual vision, on the other hand, can occur without the bodily kind, when the likenesses of absent bodies appear in the spirit, and when many pictures are fabricated in it as it chooses, or shown to it quite apart from its choice.

Again, spiritual vision is in need of the intellectual kind in order to have a judgment or assessment made of it, while the intellectual is in no need of this inferior spiritual kind.[40] And thus bodily vision is subordinate to spiritual, while each of them is subordinate to the intellectual kind. When therefore we read, *Spiritual people judge all things, while they themselves are judged by nobody* (1 Cor 2:15), it is not referring to the spirit which is distinguished from the mind as where it says, *I will pray with the spirit, I will pray also with the mind* (1 Cor 14:15); but we should rather take its meaning from where it says, *But be renewed in the spirit of your minds* (Eph 4:23). We have already explained above,[41] you will remember, that the mind too is also in another context called "spirit," and it is in accordance with this that spiritual people judge all things. Accordingly I do not consider it either absurd or inconsistent to treat spiritual vision as a kind of

---

40. It is here that Saint Augustine's Platonic epistemology, to give it a rather grand name, differs most radically from that of Saint Thomas's and Aristotle's; for they insisted that the intellect (the *human* intellect, that is) requires the phantasms or images in what Augustine is calling the spirit as the material for it to work on, and so come to an understanding of the world.
41. 7,18 in this volume.

halfway house between the intellectual and bodily kinds. I think in fact that it is not incongruous to call what is not body but still like body the halfway house between what is really body and what is neither body nor like body.

How the soul can be deceived in these visions through its own mistaken judgments, not by the objects seen

25, 52. The likenesses of things, however, can cause illusions in the soul, not through any fault of theirs but through the soul's own mistaken assumptions, when it accepts the likenesses for the things they resemble, failing to use its intelligence. So then it is deceived in bodily vision when it thinks something is happening in the bodies themselves which is in fact happening in the senses of the body. Thus things on land which are stationary seem to people sailing by to be moving, and to those gazing at the sky the stars which are moving seem to be stationary, and when you stretch the rays from the eyes apart you see the lamp double,[42] and an oar in the water looks as if it is broken—and many other instances of this sort.

Or it may mistake one thing for another because it has a similar color or sound, or smells or tastes or feels very like it. In this way, you see, some wax plaster being sterilized in a cooking pot may be thought to be a vegetable, and the sound of a passing cart be mistaken for thunder; and if it is left to the nose alone and not explored by any of the other senses, a citron will be mistaken for the plant called bee balm,[43] and food treated with some sweetish juice or other will be assumed to have been flavored with honey, and an unfamiliar ring handled in the dark will be assumed to be of gold while in fact it is brass or silver.

Or when the soul is amazed by sudden and totally unexpected bodily sights it may think it is seeing them in a dream or being affected by some spiritual vision of that sort. Thus it is that in all bodily visions both the evidence of the other

---

42. See *The Trinity* XI,2,4 for a little picture of Augustine experimenting together with his secretaries on this phenomenon.
43. A citron, *citrium*, can be taken for *herba quae vocatur apiaria*. Through a leading bee-keeper of the Cambridge area, Mrs. Eleanor Witter, I was put in touch with the top authority on bees in England, Dr. Eva Crane. She told me there is a kind of balm known as bee balm, whose Latin name is *melissa officinalis*. Its interest to the beekeeper, according to F.N.Howes, another authority whom Dr. Crane quotes, "is in the aromatic lemon-scented leaves." Dr. Crane also very kindly sent me references to a learned book published in 1958, *The Roman Cookery Book*, a critical translation of *The Art of Cooking* by Apicius, made by Barbara Flower and Elisabeth Rosenbaum, which enabled me to improve on what Lewis & Short have to say about *citrium*, which is simply that it is "a kind of gourd." But Flower and Rosenbaum, in note 1 on page 53 of their book, say: *Citrium, citreum, citrum, citrus,* means here the fruit of the citron tree (*Citrus medica*, Linn.); this appears to be the only variety of citrus fruit known in ancient Italy. They agree elsewhere (note 3, page 113) that in another place of Apicius' cookery book *citrium* must have the meaning of *citrullus*, pumpkin. But the citron fruit is almost certainly what Augustine had in mind here.

senses and supremely of the mind and reason is to be applied, so that what is really true in this area of reality may be ascertained, as far as this is possible.[44]

With spiritual vision on the other hand, that is, with the likenesses of bodies which are seen by the spirit, the soul is deceived when it judges the things it sees in this way to be the bodies themselves, or assumes that what it has itself made up on suspicion or false guesswork is also there in bodies, which it has not seen but which it guesses are real. In its intellectual visions, by contrast, it is not deceived; for either it understands the matter, and then it is true; or if it is not true, the soul does not understand. From this we conclude that it is one thing for the soul to go wrong over things which it sees, another to go wrong precisely because it does not see.

Two stages or degrees of rapture

26, 53. For this reason, when the soul is rapt away to sights perceived by the spirit as being like bodies, so that it is altogether cut off from the senses of the body much more completely than is the case in sleep, but less than in death, this is a helpful warning to it from God that it should realize it is not perceiving bodies, but visions of things like bodies—not unlike the case of those who know even before they wake up that they are seeing things in a dream. It may be that future events are also seen then, in such a way that they are definitely known to be in the future, while their images are seen as being in the present, and this can be by the person's mind being aided by God, or by someone among the things seen explaining what they signify, as John had things explained to him in the Apocalypse. If so, it is a great revelation, even if the person these things are being shown to does not know whether he has gone out of the body, or is still in the body, but seeing it all with the spirit alienated from the senses of the body. Someone thus rapt away, you see, may be left in ignorance on the point if this too has not been shown him.

54. Next, however, just as he has been rapt away from the senses of the body to find himself among these bodily likenesses which are seen in spirit, so too he may be rapt away from these to be carried up to that region, so to say, of things intellectual or intelligible. There, without any bodily likeness the pure transparent truth is perceived, overcast by no clouds of false opinions. There the virtues of the soul are not a matter of hard labor or toil; no lust, after all, has there to be braked by the work of self-restraint, no hardships to be borne with the work of fortitude, no iniquities to be punished by the work of justice, no evils to be avoided by the work of prudence.

---

44. A Platonic reserve about how far the material world, the world of appearances, of "seeming," is in fact knowable.

There the one and only and all-embracing virtue is to love what you may see, the ultimate bliss to possess what you love. There, after all, the blessed life is to be drunk from its own fountain, from which something splashes over to this human life of ours, so that in the trials and temptations of this age we may live temperately, bravely, justly and prudently. In order to attain that state of undisturbed rest and that vision of inexpressible truth, we undertake here the labor of restraining ourselves from pleasure and enduring adversity and assisting the needy and resisting the fraudulent. There the glory of the Lord is to be seen, not through some significant vision, whether of the bodily kind such as was seen on Mount Sinai, or the spiritual such as Isaiah saw or John in the Apocalypse, not in code but clearly, to the extent that the human mind can grasp it, depending on God's grace as he takes it up, so that God may speak mouth to mouth with any whom he has made worthy of such conversation—the mouth of the mind not the body, which is how I consider we have to understand what is written about Moses.[45]

To what extent did Moses see God?

27, 55. He had longed, I mean, to see God, as we read in Exodus, not just as had seen him on the mountain nor as he used to see him in the tabernacle,[46] but in his very substance as God, without any bodily creature being assumed which could be presented to the senses of mortal flesh, and not either in spirit in figurative bodily likenesses, but clearly in his very self, insofar as a rational and intellectual creature can grasp that, withdrawn from every sense of the body, from every coded symbol of the spirit.

This, you see, is what is written: *If therefore I have found favor in your sight, show yourself to me, let me see you plainly,* while a few verses above you can read: *And the Lord spoke to Moses face to face, as a person speaks to his friend* (Ex 33:13.11). So then he was aware of what he was seeing and he desired what he was not seeing. In fact a little later on, after God had said to him, *For you have found favor in my sight, and I know you better than all,* he replied, *Show me your glory* (Ex 33:17.18). And then indeed he received an answer from the Lord in figurative terms (which it would take too long to discuss now), when he said to him: *You will not be able to see my face and live; for man shall not see me and live.* Then he went on to say to him: *Behold there is a place by me, and you shall stand upon the rock; the moment my greatness passes by, and I will put you in a lookout of the rock and I will cover over you with my hand, until I pass by; and I will take away my hand and then you shall see my back; for my face shall not appear to you* (Ex 33:20-23).

Scripture, however, does not go on to describe this as actually happening in a bodily fashion, and this is sufficient indication that it was said figuratively to

---

45. See Nm 12:8; compare also 1 Cor 13:12.
46. See Ex 19:18; 33:9.

signify the Church. That you see, is the place by the Lord, because the Church is his temple, and is itself built on the rock,[47] and the other things said in the passage fit in with this understanding of it. All the same, unless Moses had earned the right to see the glory of God he so desired and longed for, God would not have said to Aaron and Miriam, his brother and sister, in the book of Numbers: *Listen to my words; if there is your prophet, in a vision as the Lord I will make myself known to him and in a dream I will speak to him. Not so in the way my servant Moses is faithful in all my house; I will speak to him mouth to mouth in person and not through coded symbols, and he has seen the glory of the Lord*[48] (Num 12:6-8).

Nor is this, after all, to be understood in terms of a substantive body presented as their object to the senses of the flesh, because God certainly used to speak to Moses like this in person, "face to face," one to one; while when, on the other hand, Moses said to him, "Show yourself to me," and now on this occasion when he was scolding these two and rating the merits of Moses higher than theirs, he was speaking by means of a bodily creature presented to the senses of the flesh as their object.

So then, in that other way, in the form by which he is God, he speaks in an ineffably more secret and intimate way, in inexpressible words, where nobody, living this life which is lived in these bodily senses, can see him. But this can only happen if a person somehow dies from this life, whether by completely departing from the body, or by being so turned away and alienated from the senses of the flesh that he quite rightly does not know, as the apostle says, whether it is in the body or out of the body when he is rapt and carried up to that vision.

Suggestion that the third kind of vision may be what was signified by the third heaven and paradise to which Paul was rapt

28, 56. Accordingly, if this third kind of vision, which is superior not only to every bodily vision by which bodies are perceived through the senses of the body, but also to every sort of that spiritual vision by which the likenesses of bodies are perceived with the spirit not the mind, if this is what the apostle called the third heaven, it is in this that the glory of God can be seen. It is for a sight of this that hearts are purified, as it says: *Blessed the heart-pure, because they shall see God* (Mt 5:8), not through any figure signified in either bodily or spiritual vision, as *through a mirror in a code,* but *face to face* (1 Cor 13:12), or as was

---

47. See 1 Cor 3:16.17; 6:19; 2 Cor 6:16; Mt 16:18.
48. Augustine's text is a garbled, as well as a rather bad translation of the Greek Septuagint; thus, "your prophet" translates two words which could indeed mean that in the right context, but in this context mean "a prophet of yours." But I am sticking to my principle of being very literal in my renderings of his biblical quotations, precisely because of their over-literal character.

said about Moses, "mouth to mouth." That is to say, it will be through the very form by which God is whatever he is, however limited the extent to which he can so be grasped by the mind (which is not what he is), even when it has been cleansed of all earthly grime and alienated and rapt away from every sort of body and bodily likeness. But being weighed down by this mortal and perishable burden,[49] we are strangers to this vision as long as *we are walking by faith and not by sight* (2 Cor 5:6.7), even when we are living just lives here.

Why then should we not believe that God wished to demonstrate to such a great apostle, *the teacher of the nations* (1 Tm 2:7), by snatching him up to this all-surpassing vision, the life in which we are to live forever after this life? And why should this not be called paradise, in addition to the one in which Adam lived in the body among shady groves of fruit-trees, seeing that the Church too, which gathers us all together into her loving lap, is called *a paradise with the fruits of apples* (Sg 4:13). But this is said in a figurative sense, as if the Church had been signified, through the form of the future Adam,[50] by that very paradise where Adam was to be found in the literal sense, though in fact more thorough reflection may suggest that the bodily paradise in which Adam was to be found in the body signified both this life of the saints which is now being lived in the Church and that eternal life that is coming after this one. In the same way Jerusalem, which means "vision of peace,"[51] and is demonstrably nonetheless a particular earthly city, signifies the Jerusalem which is our eternal mother in heaven, whether realized in those who have been saved by hope, and while hoping for what they do not see wait for it in patience, whose numbers mean that the children of the deserted wife are many more than those of the one who has a husband; or realized in the holy angels themselves through the Church of the manifold wisdom of God,[52] with whom after this exile we look forward to living without toil and without end.

---

49. See Wis 9:15.
50. *Per formam futuri*; literally, I suppose (though it is a distinctly odd phrase), "through the shape of the future," that is, presumably, with reference to the future. But almost all figurative or "spiritual" meanings of Old Testament figures had reference to the future. So I take the oddness of the expression as hinting that *futuri* refers to the future Adam, the last Adam; especially as *forma* is the key word in that crucial christological text, Phil 2:6-11, "Who being in the *form* of God . . . emptied himself, taking the *form* of a slave." Furthermore, it is the bridegroom in the Song of Songs who is the speaker of our text, and he of course was universally taken to be Christ, singing these love song duets with his bride, the Church.
51. See Heb 7:2 for the second part of this interpretation, Salem meaning peace (*shalom*), Melchizedek being king of Salem. The first part of the name Jerusalem, however, has no connection with the Hebrew verb meaning "to see"; so this etymology, though clearly very old in the Christian tradition, has no roots either in biblical or rabbinic sources.
52. Here he is running together texts from Rom 8:24-25 and Gal 4:26-27, to have what seems to be the heavenly Jerusalem realized on earth in the Church, and turning Eph 3:10 on its head for the Church of the angels in heaven.

29, 57. If however we suppose that beyond the third heaven to which the apostle was carried there was also a fourth and a few more heavens higher up, beneath which is this third heaven, as in fact some people maintain that there are seven of them, others eight, others nine or even ten, and they affirm that in this one which is called the firmament there are many grades, and thus they reckon that they are bodily heavens—but it would take too long now to discuss their calculations and opinions.[53] Now it could well be that someone will wish to argue, or even demonstrate if he can, that in the spiritual or intellectual spheres too there are many grades, and that they are distinguished in accordance with the more or the less illuminating revelations they convey.

But however that may be, and however these opinions may be accepted, one by this person, one by that as they please, I for my part have not so far been able to discern or teach that there are any other kinds of visions or things seen besides these three, in body or spirit or mind. But how many differences in each kind, or how important, so that in each kind there is a hierarchy of these differences—of that I happily confess my ignorance.

Gradations in bodily and spiritual vision

30, 58. However, just as in this bodily light there is the sky which we look up at above the earth, from which shine the great lights and the constellations, bodies far and away better than terrestrial ones, so too in that spiritual kind, in which the likenesses of bodies are seen by its own kind of incorporeal light, there are some superlative, not to say divine, images which angels show us in marvelous ways. Whether they do this by a sort of easy and potent conjunction or mingling with our spirit so that their visions also become ours, or whether they have the knowledge, I know not how, to shape and inform our vision in our spirit, is a matter difficult to sort out and even more difficult to state.

There are, though, other ordinary, merely human visions, some of which arise in many ways from the spiritual element in us itself, others with which the spirit is somehow or other furnished from the body, depending on whether we have been affected by flesh or by spirit. It is not only when awake, you see, that people mull over their preoccupations by thinking about them in bodily likenesses, but also when asleep that they often dream about what they are badly in need of; this is because they carry their daily business with them as a result of their souls' desires, and so if they have happened to go to bed hungry and thirsty, in their dreams they greedily apply themselves to guzzling and carousing. I think we can compare all these visions to angelic showings in the same way as in the realm of bodily vision we compare the terrestrial and the celestial.

---

53. A long, unfinished sentence in the Latin, which the translator cannot presume to finish in correct form.

Gradations in things seen by intellectual vision

31, 59. So too in that third category of things seen by intellectual vision, there are some that are seen in the soul itself, like the virtues, all with their contrary vices; either virtues that are going to abide, like loving kindness,[54] or ones that are useful for this life and will not be needed hereafter, like faith by which we believe what we cannot yet see, or hope by which we look forward with patience to things to come, or patience itself by which we put up with all adversity until we reach the destination we desire. These and similar virtues, to be sure, are now very necessary for carrying on with our earthly pilgrimage, but will not be needed in that life for the attainment of which they are so necessary. Yet it is only intellectually that they can be seen; they are not, after all, bodies nor do they have bodily images.

But the light itself is something else, the light by which the soul is enlightened in order truly to understand and observe all things either in itself or in this light. For this light is now God himself, while the soul is a creature, even though a rational and intelligent one made to his image. So when it strives to gaze upon that light, it blinks and shivers in its weakness, and quite simply lacks the power to do so. Yet that light is what enables it to understand whatever is within the range of its power. When therefore it is snatched up there, and being withdrawn from the senses of the flesh is set more firmly in the presence of that vision, not spatially but in its own kind of way, it also sees above itself the one by whose aid it also is enabled to see whatever it can see in itself by intellectual understanding.

Where does the soul go when it leaves the body? The reality of hell —and heaven

32, 60. You may ask, though, what happens to the soul when it quits the body: is it carried away to some bodily places, or to non-bodily ones like bodily places, or on the contrary not even to these but to that which surpasses both bodies and bodily likenesses? Then I reply at once that to bodily places it is either not carried at all unless together with a body of some sort, or at any rate is not carried by local motion. So now let him demonstrate who can that it has some sort of body when it quits this body; I for my part think not.

To spiritual places on the other hand it is carried away according to its merits, or else to places of punishment resembling bodies, such as have often been exhibited to people who have been carried away from the body's senses and have lain there as if they were dead. They have seen the pains of hell since they

---

54. *Pietas*; here fairly clearly meaning the same as *caritas*; both coming ultimately, through the Greek *eleos*, from the Hebrew *hesed*, which like the Latin *pietas* is the essential family virtue, together with *emeth*, faithfulness or trustworthiness. 1 Cor 13 is clearly at the back of Augustine's mind in this passage.

have borne in themselves some sort of likeness of their own bodies, by means of which it was possible for them to be carried away to those places and to experience such things with something like their senses.[55] And I cannot see in any case why the soul should have a likeness of its body when, with its body lying there senseless but still not totally dead, it sees such things as many people have told of on being restored to the living after they had been hauled up onto the beach like that,[56] and not have it when death overtakes it and it quits the body for good. So either it is carried away to those places of punishment, or to those others which likewise resemble bodily places, not however this time of punishments but of tranquil rest and enjoyments.

61. Nor, you see, can it rightly be said that those are deceptive pains or that that is deceptive rest and joy, because visions are only deceptive when by a mistake of judgment one kind is taken for another. Thus Peter was deceived when he saw that dish and thought that there were real bodies in it, not just likenesses of bodies; and again on the other hand, the time when he was released by an angel from his bonds and went along walking in the body and in the presence of real bodily shapes, and thought he was seeing a vision, he was still nonetheless being deceived. Those things in the dish, you see, were spiritual shapes like real bodies, and this real physical release from bonds by a miracle was like something spiritual. The soul was being deceived both times, but only because it mistook one kind of vision for another.

So then, although it is not bodily sights but sights resembling bodily ones that souls divested of their bodies are affected with, for better or worse, since they appear to themselves as being like their own bodies, what they see is both real joy and real affliction, made from spiritual substance. After all, even in dreams it makes a great difference whether we find ourselves in joyful or sorrowful circumstances. Thus sometimes we have regretted waking up from dreams in which we were set among things we had always longed to have, while at other times, on waking up after being terrified out of our wits and subjected to frightful

---

55. Reading *similitudinibus sensuum* with the Maurists, who adopt this reading from earlier editors to bring order and sense into a whole variety of defective manuscript readings. The CSEL text reads just *similibus* without mentioning its manuscript support; this would give the meaning (?) "to experience such things with similars."

56. An admittedly elaborate rendering of *ex illa subductione*; but the only meaning given by Lewis & Short and other dictionaries for this extremely rare word is "a hauling ashore of a ship," with references to Caesar's *Gallic War* 5,1 and to Vitruvius, 10,2,10, both authors with whom Augustine would have been familiar. No doubt he had had to plod his weary way through Caesar as a schoolboy. Now the hauling ashore of a vessel which would, I am sure, have occurred to him here in this context, is the one of which we are told in John 21, when the risen Christ appears on the shore of the sea of Galilee to the disciples who are fishing in the sea; and in his sermons on the passage Augustine invariably explains the shore, the dry land, as representing heaven, the sea this life. Admittedly here in our passage the travelers had been restored to the living after being taken on a tour of hell; but they could be thought of as viewing hell from the other side of the abyss, like Lazarus in Abraham's bosom.

tortures, we have been afraid to go to sleep again in case we should be fetched back into the same horrors. And it is of course not to be doubted that the things said about hell are much more vivid than such dreams, and so are experienced much more forcibly. I mean, those who have been detached from the senses of the body, less totally indeed than if they had actually died, but still more profoundly than if they were just asleep, have described much more vivid sights and experiences than if they had been describing dreams. So there is then most certainly a substantial reality to hell, but I consider it to be of a spiritual, not a bodily nature.

33, 62. Nor should we listen to those who maintain that hell unfolds in this life, and does not exist after death; they will have noticed, I suppose, how the fictions of the poets are interpreted.[57] We though ought not to depart from the authority of the divine scriptures, which alone are to be trusted in this matter—though we could show that their wise men too had no doubt at all about the reality of the netherworld,[58] which collects the souls of the dead after this life. One may, however, rightly inquire how hell or the underworld can be said to be under the earth, if it is not a bodily place, or how it comes to be called the netherworld if it is not under the earth.[59]

I make bold to declare, on the other hand, that I do not think, I well and truly know, that the soul is not corporeal; nonetheless, if you deny that it can have a resemblance to the body with all its parts, you can also deny that it is the soul which in dreams sees itself walking or sitting or being carried hither and thither on foot or even in flight, none of which could happen without some likeness of the body. Accordingly, if it bears this likeness, which is not bodily but like a body, even in the nether world, so too it would seem to be in places that are not

---

57. The *Iliad* and *Odyssey* of Homer and the *Aeneid* of Virgil had long been subjected to figurative or "spiritual" exegesis, mainly by Alexandrian scholars; it was from them that Philo and later on Christian scholars borrowed the technique to apply it to the great biblical epic.

58. We have to remember that the Latin *inferi* means first and foremost the netherworld, the "lower regions," where all the dead go, and then later takes on the meaning of our English hell, as a place of torment. The word "hell" in fact originally meant only the lower regions, where all the dead go. And indeed in scripture it is from below that for instance the ghost of Samuel is conjured by the witch of Endor (1 Sm 28:8-19); and in the gospels, apart from this story of the rich man and Lazarus, the usual word for what we mean by hell is Gehenna, literally the valley of the sons of Hinnom, where the citizens of Jerusalem burnt their rubbish, it having once been the place, Tophet, where they sacrificed infants by fire to Moloch. On my one and only visit to Jerusalem I was being shown around the city by a delightful French Dominican of the priory of Saint Stephen, the *Ecole Biblique*, and we came to the high point of the city, Herod's palace, from which we looked down to this valley, now a suburb on the south of the city, very popular with artists; and my guide stretched out his hand and said: "Voilá la Géhenne; aujourd'hui la Géhenne est devenu un faubourg tres chic."

59. See *Revisions* II,24 on this passage and indeed this whole chapter: "In the twelfth volume I think I ought simply to have taught about hell that it is under the earth, rather than giving reasons why it should be believed or said to be under the earth, as if it were not so in fact."

bodily but like bodily places, whether places of ease and rest or of punishment and pain.

63. However I have to admit that I have not yet found the name of netherworld given to the place where the souls of the just are at rest. We do indeed not improperly believe that even Christ's soul came to the places in which sinners are being racked, in order to release from their torments those whom he judged, by a justice hidden from us, to be due for release. I do not see how else we are to take the text: *Whom God raised up, having loosed the pangs of death, because he could not be held by them* (Acts 2:24), unless we take it that he loosed the pangs of some of those in hell by the power which is his as Lord, *to whom every knee must bow, in heaven, on earth and under the earth* (Phil 2:10), the power by which he was also unable to be held by the very pangs he loosed.

But then neither Abraham nor the poor man in his bosom, that is in the secluded place of his rest, were in pain, and between their place of rest and those torments of the netherworld we read of a great chasm being fixed; and of course they are not said to have been in hell. *For it happened*, it says, *that the destitute man died and was taken away by angels into the bosom of Abraham; now the rich man also died and was buried. And when in the netherworld he was in torment* etc.(Lk 16:19-26). Thus we see that no mention of the netherworld is made as regards the poor man's rest, but only as regards the rich man's punishment.

64. Then there is what Jacob says to his sons: *You will bring down my old age with sorrow to the netherworld* (Gn 44:29); what he really seems to have been afraid of is that he would be so overwhelmed with excessive grief that he would go to the hell of sinners and not to the resting place of the blessed.[60] Sorrow, you see, is no trifling evil of the soul, seeing that the apostle was so anxious about a certain man, lest he should be swallowed up by greater sorrow.[61]

So it is, as I said above, that I have not yet found—and I am still looking, so far without any luck—I have not found anywhere in the scriptures, at least the canonical ones, where the netherworld occurs in a good sense, while I cannot imagine anyone allowing that the bosom of Abraham and the restful ease to which the poor man was carried by angels could be understood in any but a good sense. And therefore I do not see how we could possibly believe that it is in the netherworld.

---

60. But no; what he was really afraid of was that his sons would cause him to die prematurely of grief, of being brought down to Sheol, the Hebrew equivalent of the Greek Hades and the Latin *inferi*—all of them the place of the dead. See note 59 above.

61. See 2 Cor 2:7.

Back to the question of the third heaven and Paradise once more

34, 65. But now, while we are looking for this scriptural text and either finding it or not, the length of this book is urging us to bring it at some time or other to a close. Now we set out at the beginning of it to talk about Paradise, because of what the apostle said, that he knew a man snatched up as far as the third heaven, but did not know whether it was in the body or out of the body, and that he was snatched up into Paradise, and heard inexpressible words, which it is not lawful for a man to speak.[62] But we are not going rashly to assert either that Paradise is in the third heaven, or that he was snatched up first to the third heaven and then again from there into Paradise. Paradise,[63] you see, is properly the name for a place of shady groves, but by a stretching of terms every spiritual region, as it were, where it is good for the soul to be, may also rightly be called Paradise.

So it is not only the third heaven, whatever that is, assuredly something great and superbly glorious, but also the joy of a good conscience in a person that is a paradise.[64] Thus the Church too is rightly called a paradise for holy people living sober, just and godly lives, being endowed with an abundance of graces and chaste delights, seeing that she glories in tribulations, rejoicing exceedingly in her very patience, because God's consolations cheer her soul according to the multitude of sorrows in her heart.[65] How much more therefore after this life can the bosom of Abraham also be called a paradise, where there are now no trials or temptations, where there is such perfect rest after all the pains and sorrows of this life! There is light too there, properly so called of its own kind, and assuredly of immense brilliance, considering that the rich man could still see it from the torments and darkness of hell, so far away, with the huge chasm in between, and could there recognize the poor man he had once held in such contempt.

66. All this being so, we can see why hell is said or believed to be under the earth; the souls of the dead, after all, deserve hell by having sinned out of love of the flesh, and it is customary for this flesh when it is dead to be buried under the earth. So souls are very suitably shown hell in spirit as being under the earth in an exhibition of such likenesses of bodies. Finally, hell is called the netherworld because it is underneath the world, *inferi* in Latin because it is *infra*, below. Now just as in the sphere of material bodies all the heavier things, if they keep to the natural order of their weight, are at the lower, inferior level, so in the sphere of spirit all the sadder things are at the lower, inferior level. Thus it is that in the Greek language the origin of their name for hell or the netherworld sounds, so we are told, as if it means "What has nothing pleasant or sweet about it."[66]

---

62. See 2 Cor 12:2-4.
63. It is just the Persian word for a park, after all.
64. See Sir 40:27.
65. See Rom 5:5; Ps 94:19.
66. A charming etymology for Hades: as if it came from *a* + *hedys*, "un-sweet."

Nonetheless our Savior, having died for us, did not disdain to visit that part of creation, in order to release from there all who were due to be released, as he could not but be aware, in accordance with a mysterious divine justice. Accordingly, it was not the netherworld where sins are punished that he presented to the soul of the robber to whom he said, *Today you shall be with me in Paradise* (Lk 23:43), but either repose in the bosom of Abraham—there is nowhere, after all, where Christ is not present, since he is himself the Wisdom of God, *reaching everywhere because of her purity* (Wis 7:24) or this Paradise, whether it is in the third heaven or anywhere else, where the apostle was snatched up to after the third heaven—if, that is to say, the souls of the blessed are not all in one place, which is called by various names.

67. So then, suppose we are right in taking the first heaven to be all this bodily sky and in general whatever is above the waters and the earth,[67] while the second consists in the bodily likeness which is perceived in spirit, like the one from which that dish full of animals was lowered down to Peter in his ecstasy;[68] then finally the third is the one that is observed by the mind, when it has been so secluded and removed and totally snatched away from the senses of the flesh and purified, that it is inexpressibly enabled by the charity of the Holy Spirit to see and hear the things that are in that heaven, and the very substance of God and God the Word *through whom all things were made* (Jn 1:3).

We consider then that that is where the apostle was not unsuitably snatched away to, and where the paradise is, that is better than all others, the paradise of paradises, if we may so call it. If the good soul, after all, finds joy in the good things in the whole of creation, what could outdo the joy which is to be found in the Word of God, through whom all things were made?

Question of the resurrection of the body

35, 68. But if anyone has a problem about what need there is for the spirits of the departed to get their bodies back in the resurrection, if that supreme blessedness can be offered them even without their bodies, it is indeed too difficult a question to be completely tied up in this work. Nonetheless it is not to be doubted in the least that the human mind, when snatched away from the senses of the flesh, and when after death it has laid the flesh aside and also soared above all likenesses of bodily things, still cannot see the unchangeable divine substance in the way that the holy angels see it. This may be due to some more hidden cause, or the reason may be that there is ingrained in the soul a kind of natural appetite for administering the body, and that as long as it does not have a body at its

---

67. See Gn 1:6-8,
68. See Acts 10:10-12.

disposal, it is somehow or other held back by this unsatisfied appetite from pressing on with undivided attention to that highest heaven.

Now clearly, if the body is such that the administration of it is difficult and burdensome, like this flesh of ours *which mars and weighs down the soul* (Wis 9:15), deriving as it does from the handing on of the first transgression, the mind will be even more completely distracted from that vision of the highest heaven. So that is why it had necessarily to be snatched away from the senses of this flesh, for that vision to be shown it in whatever measure it could grasp it. Accordingly, when it receives back this body, now no longer just "ensouled" but thanks to the transfiguration to come "enspirited,"[69] it will have the measure of its proper nature complete, it will be both obeying and commanding, both quickened and quickening with such inexpressible ease, that what was once its burden is now its glory.

36, 69. Undoubtedly even then there will be these three kinds of vision, but there will be no false impressions with one thing being taken for another either in bodily or spiritual visions, let alone in intellectual ones. These will be enjoyed in such vivid and immediate clarity that it will make our sight of these bodily things we have all round us seem positively blurred. Our contact with these of course is through the senses of the flesh, and many people are so attached to them that they reckon they are the only things that really are, and assume that anything not of that nature simply does not exist. The wise, however, while agreeing that bodily sights seem more immediately and certainly present to us, are themselves much more certain all the same about those things they have some kind of advance intellectual sight of, independently of bodily sights, independently too of bodily likenesses—this, even though they are not able to observe them with the mind as clearly as they can look at these other things with the senses of the body.

The holy angels however also preside over the judging and administering of these bodily things, without of course being more inclined to them as things with which they are more immediately familiar; and they are so good at discerning their significant likenesses in the spirit, and somehow manage them with such authority, that they can mix them into the spirits of human beings by way of revelation. And they gaze so raptly upon that unchangeable substance of the creator, that they not only put the sight and love of it before everything else, but also make judgments about everything in accordance with it, and align themselves on it in order to make themselves useful, and from it draw the lines on which to make use of other things.

Finally, though the apostle was snatched away from the senses of the flesh to the third heaven and to Paradise, he certainly lacked that full and perfect knowledge of things which the angels have, in that he did not know whether he was in the body or out of the body. This certainly will not be lacking when bodies have

---

69. See Book XI,18,24 above and note 19 there.

been received back in the resurrection of the dead, and *this perishable thing puts on imperishability, and this mortal thing puts on immortality* (1 Cor 15:53). Then, you see, all things will be crystal clear and out in the open without any false impressions, distributed without any ignorance in their respective orders, the bodily, the spiritual and the intellectual, in perfect bliss with their natures entire and undiminished.

Conclusion to the whole work

37, 70. I know indeed that some of those, who have expounded the sacred scriptures before me in a way that is much admired,[70] have also explained what the apostle calls the third heaven like this; they wish to distinguish here between the "body-bound" person, the "soulish" person, and the spiritual person, and to have the apostle snatched up to the contemplation with surpassing clarity of that kind of incorporeal reality, the kind which even in this life spiritual people love above the rest and long to enjoy. Why I myself, on the other hand, have preferred to call spiritual and intellectual what they perhaps have called "soulish" and spiritual, thus simply giving other names to the same realities, I have already explained at sufficient length in the first pages of this book. If within the limits of my abilities I have duly discussed these matters, then spiritual readers will either give me their approval, or else in order to grow more spiritual will derive some profit from their reading, with the help of the Holy Spirit.

But now at long last, with this conclusion we bring this whole work to an end, contained in twelve volumes.

---

70. The CSEL editors refer to the *Questions about Genesis* of Ambrose and Jerome, but without giving precise references.

Index of Scripture

(prepared by Michael Dolan)

(The numbers after the scriptural reference refer to the section of the work)

On Genesis: A Refutation of the Manichees

Index

(prepared by Kathleen Strattan)

The Roman numerals in the Indexes are the chapter numbers.
The Arabic numbers are the paragraph numbers.

On Genesis: A Refutation of the Manichees

Unfinished Literal Commentary on Genesis

The Literal Meaning of Genesis